MW01095123

THE JEWISH DIALOGUE WITH GREECE AND ROME

THE JEWISH DIALOGUE WITH GREECE AND ROME

Studies in Cultural and Social Interaction

BY

TESSA RAJAK

BRILL ACADEMIC PUBLISHERS, INC.
BOSTON • LEIDEN
2002

Library of Congress Cataloging-in-Publication Data

Rajak, Tessa, 1946–
    The Jewish dialogue with Greece and Rome : studies in cultural and social
    interaction / by Tessa Rajak.
        p. cm.
    Includes bibliographical references and index.
    ISBN 0–391–04133–9
        1. Judaism—Relations—Greek. 2. Hellenism. 3. Jews—History—586
    B.C.–70 A.D. 4. Jews—History—168 B.C.–135 A.D. 5. Jews—Historiography.
    6. Josephus, Flavius. 7. Jews—Civilization—Greek influences. 8. Jewish diaspo-
    ra. I. Title.

    BM536.G7 R35 2002
    296.3'9—dc21

                                                                    2002066274

ISBN 0–391–04133–9

© Copyright 2001 by Koninklijke Brill NV, Leiden, The Netherlands

All rights reserved. No part of this publication may be reproduced, translated, stored in
a retrieval system, or transmitted in any form or by any means, electronic,
mechanical, photocopying, recording or otherwise, without prior written
permission from the publisher.

Authorization to photocopy items for internal or personal
use is granted by Brill provided that
the appropriate fees are paid directly to The Copyright
Clearance Center, 222 Rosewood Drive, Suite 910
Danvers MA 01923, USA.
Fees are subject to change.

PRINTED IN THE UNITED STATES OF AMERICA

CONTENTS

PREFACE

Twenty-seven studies have been collected in this volume; twenty-four were previously published, and three of them (chapters 1, 7 and 22) are new. The former have been corrected where necessary and very lightly updated, but they remain essentially the same, reflecting the different dates of their writing. The immediate cause of the making of the collection is an invitation from Martin Hengel, to whose warm support and sound advice I am profoundly grateful. In addition, Fergus Millar's continuing interest and encouragement, has, as so often, been indispensable. That the volume has finally seen the light of day is due also to the enthusiasm of three others: Jim Aitken of Cambridge University, who brought to it both his meticulous scholarship and his technical skills, Theo Joppe, formerly of Brill (and now of Van Gorcum, Assen), and Harry Rajak.

Yet for a collection of this kind a fuller justification is required than the prompting of others, by a convention which is by no means empty; and here there are a number of purposes which will, I hope, be served. First, the material is gathered from a range of journals and volumes, a range which is perhaps wider than usual in academic writing. This is no accident, but a consequence of the interdisciplinary nature of the enterprise and of the varied learned audiences addressed. This means that not all of those publications are equally familiar or accessible to all, as has become clear to me from the eclectic use made of the papers included here over the years by different groups of scholars. Especially, my hope is that the collection will make it easy for Classicists and Ancient Historians to be drawn into a world which they are manifestly now keen to explore but into which, it is fair to say, they have, with a few notable exceptions, so far dipped only one foot.

The pieces span more than two decades, though the majority were written towards the end of the period, and ten of them in fact belong to the last five years. During this time scholarship in the fields which they exemplify has flourished as never before and has been transformed almost beyond recognition. Unsurprisingly, methodologies have become more sophisticated. A particularly important development is the growing awareness of the pluralism of many ancient milieux, an awareness which probably flows from current, more receptive attitudes to the pluralisms of the world around us, and which has yielded many new angles of approach. Such indeed is the rapidity of development and the intensity of publication that those doing research today do not always have the leisure to look very far back. Yet not all is new, and it can go unnoticed when an old argument is re-invented, appearing perhaps in up-to-the-minute dress, but essentially similar. The earlier items in the book may therefore serve as a reminder of debts to the past. At the same time, and inevitably, the new developments are reflected here, above all in the posing of fresh questions in the later of the articles.

Further justifications for the collection arise from what might seem to be contradictory claims. On the one hand, the book, while falling into four parts, has an overall coherence, derived from the author's continuing interests and persistent pursuit of a number of basic questions: how to interpret texts as expressions of ethnic, religious or cultural identity; how to describe the coming together in these texts of diverse traditions; how far it is ever possible or desirable to disentangle Hellenism as a cultural force from Judaism; how Jewish groups meshed with the wider society; how best, in brief, to understand group interaction and cultural change. The 'dialogue' of the volume's title is a metaphor for that interaction. On the other hand, there is a thematic progression which may have its own interest, from historiographical and cultural concerns to more sociologically-based questions about group behaviour, and from a preoccupation with the impact on the Jews of Greek, or rather of Greco-Roman, thought to a questioning of the actual mechanisms of integration and separation at the level of religious communities and of individuals. Finally, the last three essays open up wider perspectives.

It may be worth adding that the volume perhaps derives further unity from the presence of a consistent stylistic goal in the various papers—the search for that elusive blend of detailed, original scholarship with readability and vigour from which even the most technical of academic writing can benefit. Whether any of those goals have been at any point achieved is for others to judge.

The papers have not been organized chronologically. The reason for starting with a fresh reconsideration of the debate about the relationship between Judaism and Hellenism is to show both the centrality of that debate to the scholarship of this period and the progress which has been made in the terms in which the discussion is conducted, to which this author may have contributed in a modest way. It is now quite widely understood that the Jews absorbed and internalized many aspects of Greek culture, including even religious ideas, so that it becomes for many purposes impossible coherently to talk about Hellenism as something separate, outside or antithetical to Judaism. The studies in Part I draw directly on this insight in different ways. It also comes to inform the approach to Josephus in Part II, where the earliest piece, on Justus of Tiberias, was written not so long after Hengel's pathbreaking *Judentum und Hellenismus* (1968) launched the modern phase of the debate. At the same time, there is an attempt in Part II to come to grips with at least a fraction of the range of Josephus' multifarious source material and of the individuality of the historian's versions of his sources. That individuality of approach cannot be explained crudely as dictated by Roman demands, by Greek stylistic requirements, or by apologetic imperatives.

Part III by contrast, concerns life in Greek cities in the Roman period, seen often, though by no means exclusively, through the mirror of inscriptions. The 'Diaspora' of the title should not be taken as implying that there were rigid boundaries, a lack of connection, or sharp differences between Palestine and the rest of the Jewish world, or that it is always useful to study them as two separate milieux. Indeed one paper, on the Beth She'arim necropolis, explores how Jews from Palestine and those from the Diaspora were involved in a common burial enterprise. Still, it is undeniable that life for a minority within a pagan city brought with it particular political and social pressures and special needs. The aim is to explore some of those, by looking at a number of important locations, extending from Sardis in Asia Minor to Rome. Here it should become clearer why there are three parties to the dialogue of the title, for the impact of Roman power, especially as expressed in systems of patronage at local as well as central levels, was as much a determining factor in Jewish life as the influence of the Greek language and Greek thought. The final part of the volume represents some of the author's recent attempts to go beyond the Classical perspective to more complex, and again tripartite, relationships. Some account is taken, by way of an extended book review, of the supposedly Semitic cultures which surrounded and interpenetrated the life of the Jews of Palestine, then of the appropriation by a Christian writer, Justin Martyr, of both Hellenic and Jewish modes of discourse, their juxtaposition, and their exploitation in the formation of his Christian identity; and lastly of modern uses and abuses of the Greek-Jewish polarity as exemplified by three nineteenth-century writers in three different languages, Heinrich Heine, Ernest Renan and Matthew Arnold. That seems an appropriate place to close, since, with this look at the history of that cultural construction which was examined in the opening essay, the wheel has come full circle. If the reader remains with the sense that the surface has only been scratched and that there is much more work to be done before we can grasp the meaning of the Greek-Jewish polarity in its different contexts, this is to the good. The way we understand the terms of the dialogue may have changed, but the dialogue itself is far from closed.

ACKNOWLEDGEMENTS

The material reprinted with minor alterations in this volume first appeared in the following forms and locations. The editors and publishers are thanked for permission to reproduce them here:

I.2 'The Sense of History in Jewish Intertestamental Writing', in *Crises and Perspectives*. Oudtestamentische studiën 24; Leiden: Brill, 1986, 124–145.

I.3 'Hasmonean Kingship and the Invention of Tradition', in P. Bilde *et al.* (eds). 1996. *Aspects of Hellenistic Kingship*. Studies in Hellenistic Civilisation 7; Aarhus: Aarhus University Press, 96–116.

I.4 'The Hasmoneans and the Uses of Hellenism', in P.R. Davies & R.T. White (eds). 1990. *A Tribute to Geza Vermes*. Journal for the Study of the Old Testament Suppl. 100; Sheffield: Sheffield Academic Press, 261–280.

I.5 'Roman Intervention in a Seleucid Siege of Jerusalem?', in *Greek, Roman and Byzantine Studies* 22 (1981), 65–81.

I.6 'Dying for the Law: The Martyr's Portrait in Jewish-Greek Literature', in M.J. Edwards & S. Swain (eds). 1997. *Portraits: Biographical Representation in the Greek and Latin Literature of the Roman Empire*. Oxford: Clarendon Press, 39–67.

II.8 'Friends, Romans, Subjects: Agrippa II's Speech in Josephus' Jewish War', in L. Alexander (ed.). 1991. *Images of Empire*. Journal for the Study of the Old Testament Suppl. 122; Sheffield: Sheffield Academic Press, 122–134.

II.9 'Justus of Tiberias as a Jewish Historian', reproduced in part from 'Justus of Tiberias', *Classical Quarterly* 23 (1973), 246–268.

II.10 'Josephus and Justus of Tiberias', in L.H. Feldman & G. Hata (eds). 1987. *Josephus, Judaism, and Christianity*. Leiden: Brill, 81–94.

II.11 'The Against Apion and the Continuities in Josephus' Political Thought', in S. Mason (ed.). 1998. *Understanding Josephus. Seven Perspectives*. Journal for the Study of the Pseudepigrapha Suppl. 32. Sheffield: Sheffield Academic Press, 222–246.

II.12 'Ciò che Flavio Giuseppe Vide: Josephus and the Essenes', in F. Parente & J. Sievers (eds). 1994. *Josephus and the History of* *the Greco-Roman Period. Essays in Memory of Morton Smith.* Studia post-biblica 41. Leiden: Brill, 141–160.

II.13 'Josephus and the "Archaeology" of the Jews', in G. Vermes & J. Neusner (eds). 1983. *Essays in Honour of Yigael Yadin. Journal of Jewish Studies* 33. Totowa, New Jersey: Allanheld, Osmun, 465–477.

II.14 'Moses in Ethiopia: Legend and Literature', in *Journal of Jewish Studies* 29 (1978), 111–122.

II.15 'The Parthians in Josephus', in J. Wiesehöfer (ed.). 1998. *Das Partherreich und seine Zeugnisse. Beiträge des internationalen Colloquiums, Eutin (27.–30. Juni 1996).* Historia. *Einzelschriften* 122. Stuttgart: Franz Steiner, 309–324.

III.16 'Was there a Roman Charter for the Jews?', in *Journal of Roman Studies* 74 (1984), 107–123.

III.17 'The Jewish Community and its Boundaries', in J. Lieu, J. North & T. Rajak (eds). 1992. *The Jews among the Pagans and Christians. In the Roman Empire.* London: Routledge, 9–28.

III.18 'Jews and Christians as Groups in a Pagan World', In J. Neusner & E.S. Frerichs (eds). 1985. *"To See Ourselves as Others See Us": Christians, Jews, "Others" in Late Antiquity.* Scholars Press Studies in the Humanities Series; Chico, California: Scholars Press, 247–262.

III.19 'Benefactors in the Greco-Jewish Diaspora', in H. Cancik, H. Lichtenberger, & P. Schäfer (eds). 1996. *Geschichte Tradition— Reflexion. Festschrift für Martin Hengel zum 70. Geburtstag.* Band I: Judentum. Tübingen: Mohr (Siebeck), 305–319.

III.20 '*Archisynagogoi*: Office, Title and Social Status in the Greco-Jewish Synagogue', with David Noy in *Journal of Roman Studies* 83 (1993), 75–93.

III.21 'Inscription and Context: Reading the Jewish Catacombs of Rome', in W. van Henten & P.W. van der Horst (eds). 1994. *Studies in Early Jewish Epigraphy.* Arbeiten zur Geschichte des antiken Judentums und des Urchristentums 21; Leiden: Brill, 226–241.

III.23 'The Synagogue in the Greco-Roman City', in S. Fine (ed.). 1999. *Jews, Christians and Polytheists: Cultural Interaction during the Greco-Roman Period.* Baltimore Studies in the History of Judaism. London/New York: Routledge, 161–173.

III.24 'The Rabbinic Dead and the Diaspora Dead at Beth She'arim', in P. Schäfer (ed.). 1998. *The Talmud Yerushalmi* *and Graeco-Roman Culture*, I. Texte und Studien zum antiken Judentum 71; Tübingen: Mohr (Siebeck), 349–366.

IV.26 'Talking at Trypho: Christian Aplogetic as Anti-Judaism in Justin's *Dialogue with Trypho the Jew*', in M. Edwards, M. Goodman & S. Price, in association with C. Rowland (eds). 1999. *Apologetics in the Roman Empire: Pagans, Jews and Christians*. Oxford: Oxford University Press, 59–80.

IV.25 'Jews, Semites and their Cultures in Fergus Millar's 'Roman Near East', in *Journal of Jewish Studies* 51 (2000), 63–68.

IV.27 'Jews and Greeks: The Invention and Exploitation of Polarities in the Nineteenth Century, in M. Bidiss & M. Wyke (eds). 1999. *The Uses and Abuses of Antiquity*. Bern: Peter Lang, 57–77.

The following chapters have not been previously published:

I.1   'Judaism and Hellenism Revisited'.
II.7   'Ethnic Identities in Josephus'.
III.22 'Jews, Pagans and Christians in Late Antique Sardis: Models of Interaction'.

LIST OF ABBREVIATIONS

Publications Frequently Cited

Broughton, MRR	Broughton, T.R.S. 1951–86. *The Magistrates of the Roman Republic*, 4 vols. New York.
BS	*Beth She'arim: Report on the Excavations During 1936–1940.* New Brunswick, N.J., 1973–76. Vol. I by B. Mazar; vol. II M. Schwabe & B. Lifshitz; vol. III. N. Avigad.
CIJ	Frey, J-B. 1939, 1951, 1956. *Corpus Inscriptionum Iudaicarum* I–II. Rome, 1939–1951; reprint of vol. I with prolegomena by B. Lifshitz. 1956. New York.
CIG	Boeckh, A. (ed.). 1828–77. *Corpus Inscriptionum Graecarum*, 4 vols. Berlin.
CIL	*Corpus Inscriptionum Latinarum: consilio et auctoritate Academiae Litterarum Regiae Borussicae editum*, vol. 1–Berlin, 1863–.
CIRB	*Corpus Inscriptionum Regni Bosporani.* 1965. Moscow.
CJZC	Lüderitz, G. (ed.). 1983, with Joyce Reynolds, *Corpus jüdischer Zeugnisse aus der Cyrenaika.* Wiesbaden.
CPJ	Tcherikover, V., Fuks, A. & Stern, M. 1957–64. *Corpus Papyrorum Judaicarum*, I–III. Cambridge, MA.
CRINT	Safrai, S. & Stern, M. (eds). 1974–76. *The Jewish People in the First Century: Compendia Rerum Iudaicarum ad Novum Testamentum*, Section 1, 2 vols. Assen.
Enc. Jud.	*Encyclopaedia Judaica.* 1972. Jerusalem.
FGrH	Jacoby, F. 1940. *Die Fragmente der griechischen Historiker.* Leiden.
IG	*Inscriptiones Graecae.* 1873–. Berlin.
Hengel, *Judaism*	Hengel, M. 1974. *Judaism and Hellenism*, Eng. transl. London.
Hengel, *Hellenization*	Hengel, M. 1989. *The Hellenization of Judaea in the First Century after Christ*, Eng. transl. London.

Holladay, *Fragments*	Holladay, C.R. 1983. *Fragments from Hellenistic Jewish Authors, vol. 1: Historians.* Pseudepigrapha series 10. Atlanta, GA.
IGLS	Dessau, H. 1892–. *Inscriptiones Graecae et Latinae Selectae.* Berlin.
JIGRE	Horbury, W. & Noy, D. 1992. *Jewish Inscriptions of Graeco-Roman Egypt.* Cambridge.
JIWE	Noy, D. 1993–95. *Jewish Inscriptions of Western Europe* vols. I and II, Cambridge.
MAMA	Buckler, W.H. & Calder, W.M. 1939. *Monumenta Asiae Minoris Antiqua*, vol. 6. *Monuments and Documents from Phrygia and Caria.* Publications of the American Society for Archaeological Research in Asia Minor 6. Manchester.
OGIS	Dittenberger, W. 1903–15. *Orientis Graeci Inscriptiones Selectae* I–II. Leipzig.
PG	Migne, J.-P. (ed.). 1857–66. *Patrologia Graeca.* Paris.
PIR	E. Groag *et al.* 1933–. *Prosopographia Imperii Romani.* 2nd ed. Berlin/Leipzig.
PL	Migne, J.-P. (ed.). 1841–64. *Patrologia Latina.* Paris.
Rajak, *Josephus*	Rajak, T. 1983. *Josephus: the Historian and his Society.* Classical Life and Letters. London.
RE	Pauly, A. & Wissowa, G. (eds). 1894–1980. *Realencyclopädie der classischen Altertumswissenschaft.* Stuttgart/München.
RPC	Burnett, A., Amandry, M. & Ripollès, P.P. 1992. *Roman Provincial Coinage.* Vol. 1. *From the Death of Caesar to the Death of Vitellius (44 BC–AD 69).* London/Paris.
Schürer Revised	Schürer, E. 1973–1987. *The History of the Jewish People in the Age of Jesus Christ. A New English Edition.* Revised and edited by G. Vermes, F. Millar & M. Goodman. Edinburgh.
SEG	*Supplementum Epigraphicum Graecum.* 1923–. Leiden/Amsterdam.
Wacholder, *Eupolemus*	Wacholder, B.Z. 1974. *Eupolemus: A Study of Judaeo-Greek Literature.* Monographs of the Hebrew Union College No. 3. Cincinnati.

Names of Ancient Authors and Works

1 Macc.	1 Maccabees
2 Macc.	2 Maccabees
4 Macc.	4 Maccabees
AJ	*Antiquitates Judaicae*
Ann.	*Annals*
Apophth. Reg	*Regum et imperatorum apophthegmata*
Av. Zar.	*Avodah Zarah*
b.	Babylonian Talmud
BJ	*Bellum Judaicum*
CA	*Contra Apionem*
Chron.	*Chronici canones*
Cic.	Cicero
Contra Cels.	*Contra Celsum*
C. Th.	*Codex Theodosianus*
de Die Nat.	*de Die Natali*
Deiot.	*pro Rege Deiotaro*
Dem. Evang.	*Demonstratio Evangelica*
de Vir. Ill.	*de Viris Illustribus*
Diod.	Diodorus
Dion. Hal.	Dionysius of Halicarnassus
Ep.	*Epistles*
Eus.	Eusebius
Flac.	*pro Flacco*
HA	*Historia Augusta*
Haer.	*adversus Haereses*
HE	*Historia Ecclesiastica*
Her.	Herodotus
Hypothet.	*Hypothetica*
j.	Jerusalem Talmud
Just.	Justinian
Leg.	*Legatio ad Gaium*
Meg.	Megillah
Mor.	*Moralia*
Nov.	*Novellae*
Or.	*Orationes*
Pan.	*Panarion*
Per.	*Periochae*
Praep. Ev.	*Praeparatio Evangelica*

QOP	*Quod omnis probus liber sit*
Steph. Byz.	Stephanus of Byzantium
t.	Tosefta
V	*Vita*

Periodicals and Serials

AJA	American Journal of Archaeology
AJP	American Journal of Philology
ANRW	Aufstieg und Niedergang der römischen Welt
ASTI	Annual of the Swedish Theological Institute
BASOR	Bulletin of the American Schools of Oriental Research
BCH	Bulletin de Correspondance Hellénique
BE	Bulletin Epigraphique
BZ	Biblische Zeitschrift
CBQ	Catholic Biblical Quarterly
CP	Classical Philology
CQ	Classical Quarterly
DJD	Discoveries in the Judaean Desert
EPRO	Études préliminaires aux religions orientales dans l'Empire romain
ExpT	Expository Times
GRBS	Greek, Rome and Byzantine Studies
HSCPh	Harvard Studies in Classical Philology
HTR	Harvard Theological Review
HUCA	Hebrew Union College Annual
IEJ	Israel Exploration Journal
IsrNumJ	Israel Numismatic Journal
JAC	Jahrbuch für Antike und Christentum
JAOS	Journal of the American Oriental Society
JBL	Journal of Biblical Literature
JEA	Journal of Egyptian Archaeology
JJS	Journal of Jewish Studies
JQR	Jewish Quarterly Review
JRS	Journal of Roman Studies
JSHRZ	Jüdische Schriften aus hellenistisch-römischer Zeit
JSJ	Journal for the Study of Judaism in the Persian, Greek and Roman Period
JSNT	Journal for the Study of the New Testament
JSOT	Journal for the Study of the Old Testament

JTS	Journal of Theological Studies
MonGeschWissJud	Monatsschrift für Geschichte und Wissenschaft des Judenthums
MusHelv	Museum Helveticum
NT	Novum Testamentum
NTS	New Testament Studies
NYRB	New York Review of Books
PAAJR	Proceedings of the American Academy for Jewish Research
Proc.Camb.Phil.Soc.	Proceedings of the Cambridge Philological Society
REG	Revue des études grecques
REJ	Revue des études juives
RhM	Rheinisches Museum für Philologie
SCI	Scripta Classica Israelica
TAPA	Transactions and Proceedings of the American Philological Association
TSAJ	Texte und Studien zum antiken Judentum
VT	Vetus Testamentum
ZNTW	Zeitschrift für die neutestamentliche Wissenschaft

PART ONE

GREEKS AND JEWS

CHAPTER ONE

JUDAISM AND HELLENISM REVISITED

The Jews in the Greco-Roman period, at least as much as previously in their history, were exposed to a range of highly intrusive influences from other cultures. It is striking, however, that scholarship in the modern era has focussed on the relationship with Greek culture far more than any other. And indeed a good part of this volume, inevitably a reflection of the overriding concerns of the period in which its individual studies were written, embodies that prioritization visibly and perhaps, for the taste of some, excessively. It is appropriate at this point, therefore, to cast a critical eye over the assumptions behind the agenda. In doing so, we should not forget the vantage point of the observer: there is an evident link with that privileged role which, until very recently, was occupied in European culture by an idealized vision of Greek civilization. One would not wish to deny this. The relevance of this Hellenocentrism to the external image and self-understanding of the Jew since the period of emancipation is explored in the concluding essay of the book.

At the same time, the evidence itself offers some compelling justifications for an emphasis on Hellenism, even if perhaps in a nuanced and moderated form. Above all, perhaps, the cause lies in the strong reaction evoked by the force which we call Hellenism. It is fair, after all, to describe the Greek way of life as the most dynamic 'package' with which the Jews engaged. This was the language, these the social forms, which encroached on others. How far this reality should be seen as springing from qualities inherent in Greek civilization is a matter for debate. Whatever its merits, the Jews knew perfectly well that the Greek culture of the day was the culture of the ruling power. It turned out, indeed, that for them, this culture was an instrument of three successive empires to which they fell, the Ptolemaic, the Seleucid and, lastly the Roman. For Roman rule in the east drew on the Greek language, incorporated Greek political ideas and fostered Greek literature. Furthermore Roman rule was mediated through Greekness in a particularly noticeable way in that small corner which was Palestine owing to the power of Herod and the Herodian dynasty who flaunted themselves as benefactors and Philhellenes around cities of the Roman east and even as far as the Roman emperor.[1] It is of great assistance in running an empire to have a culture to 'sell'. And having an empire to run is a stimulus to evolving an impressive cultural 'product'. At least as long as foreign rule was not stabilized in Palestine, the symbols of the culture which was its tool would be inescapable. At times they would be perceived as a threat and a provocation.

But this is far from the sum total of the Jewish account with Greece. There was also a different reality. Greek culture was deeply intertwined with Jewish life from the early Hellenistic period to an extent where contemporaries were not themselves wholly aware of the strands.[2] By 63 B.C., when Pompeius marched into Judaea, many aspects of Greek culture had been an intrinsic part of Judaism for some centuries. The Jews of Palestine, arguably themselves somewhat less exposed, were well aware that around the Roman empire lived Jews who knew no Hebrew, spoke no Aramaic, lived their lives, heard their Bible in a special form of Greek—the language of their Septuagint, did their reading (if they did it) in high Greek. Indeed it is commonly held that by the first century B.C. the majority of the Mediterranean world's Jews lived in this Diaspora. Those Jewish communities were far from invisible, and they contributed, we should not forget, to the evolving Hellenism of their environments as well as taking from it. Moreover, even if in Palestine the balance was different, already in the Second Temple period Greek was widely spoken by Jews who were often (as Jews have been through the ages) actively multilingual. That there was Hellenization there as well as in the Diaspora is no longer in doubt: it is the great achievement of Martin Hengel to have demonstrated this, above all, as far as the early Hellenistic period goes, in his classic first work on the subject.[3]

And yet fundamental disagreements continue about the depth of Hellenization in Jewish Palestine during the Second Temple period. Paradoxical though it may seem, I would suggest that those who have taken Hengel on, choosing to highlight Jewish exceptionalism,

---

[1] On the novelty of Herod's pathbreaking benefactions, see now Millar 1993: 353–356. Cf. Kokkinos 1998.
[2] Bickerman 1988. And for a more recent, powerful statement of the inseparable connections, see Gruen 1998.
[3] Hengel *Judaism* (1974); Hengel *Hellenization* (1989). Critique in Feldman 1977.

are no less justified than he.[4] They too can bring telling evidence
to bear on the question. Thus, it can scarcely be denied that, in
Palestine at least, Jewry had its own rooted social and cultic organization. The Temple and priesthood governed the shape of Jewish
life, rural as much as urban.[5] These were *sui generis*. The vigorous
evolution of flourishing and long-lasting sectarian groupings displays
another facet of this powerful individuality: for all attempts to clas-
sify the Qumran sect as a Greco-Roman association, it remains irre-
ducibly different. Furthermore, the Jews' reaction to foreign rule was
politically, through a succession of resistance movements, to accen-
tuate their uniqueness and, in the realm of the spirit, in due course
to systematize their own religious tradition through the work of the
rabbinic class.

And so, if the debate about the Hellenization of the Jews has
seemed inconclusive, this, I would further suggest, is because both
sides are right in their own terms. The quest for resolution may then
be superfluous, since the agendas are simply disparate. For Hengel
speaks of specific phenomena—language, tangible ideas, material culture. He reminds us of the literary productivity of Jerusalem: 'between
the Maccabaean period and its destruction, the extent of its literary
production was greater than that of the Jews in Alexandria.'[6] Particular
attributions of Greek influence, will always be open to dispute. How,
in the end, do we measure the impact of the Greek conception of
paideia (in itself highly elusive) on the pessimistic wisdom of Qohelet?
Or, again, is there a true parallel between Pythagorean purity regulations (which themselves can only be extrapolated from much later
evidence) and those of the Essene community? Nevertheless, the
cumulative impact of the data on the pre-Maccabaean period presented in *Judaism and Hellenism* is incontrovertible; and equally so is
Hengel's brilliantly-focussed analysis, in his short later book, of the
Greek culture of Jewish Palestine in the era leading up to 70. For
the latter, new archaeological evidence continues to fill out the picture. The alternative viewpoint, that of Hengel's opponents, makes
its case by highlighting those aspects of Judaism which stand apart.
They can justify their choice by recalling that the sense of difference
between the Jews and their conquerors, or even their neighbours,

---

[4] Especially Millar 1978. And see ch. 25 in this volume.
[5] This is the underlying theme of E.P. Sanders' magisterial work of 1992.
[6] *Hellenization*: 29.

had the more powerful impact on lives, sparking off both small conflicts in Greek cities and large-scale revolts. At the same time, historical hindsight lends significance to the uniquely Jewish, since Judaism triumphantly survived through its distinctive form, rabbinism, rather than its more obviously Hellenized manifestations, which were for the most part subsumed by Christianity.

Yet it will be clear that neither of these considerations remove from under Hengel's feet the ground on which he rests his empirically-based argument for extensive Greek influence in Palestine. A shift of emphasis may, however, make it easier to see how reconciliation is possible. Insights yielded by recent sociological work on questions of cultural, and ethnic identity—and of these there has been a torrent—offers a route to making sense of the mismatch between the two kinds of argument. The understanding which has resulted, already now a commonplace, grasps that identities are social constructions, dependent upon subjective criteria as well as, or even more than objective ones. The perceptions of participants should therefore play a central role in analysis. In an elaboration of this basic assertion cultures are read as expressions of symbolic identity, relational and shifting with context.[7] For such interpretations, ethnic boundaries become attitudinal, and significant symbols crucial objects of study.[8] Attitudes to others can be exposed not only by the obvious means of verbal or visual interpretation but by action, gesture and countless minor choices.[9] These, too, are the means by which boundaries with others are drawn. Tension between groups may, but does not have to be involved in such boundary-drawing.

Our attention may usefully turn therefore to symbolic aspects of the engagement between Judaism and Hellenism and to the subjective meaning of this engagement. We might ask just how far a Jewish-Greek dichotomy will actually have mattered to contemporaries in their day-to-day interactions, outside those rare historic episodes when a sharp polarization became visible, episodes which might not occur even once in a lifetime. At the same time, while there is good reason to view the distinctions as activated only intermittently, we may suspect that, in the group memory, the rare occasions of tension

---

[7] Östergard 1992: 32; Anderson 1983: 15.
[8] On the interaction of subjective ethnicity with social reality, see now Jones 1998.
[9] Barth 1969: 9.

may have loomed as large as the links; for those moments when Jews saw themselves as diametrically opposed to what Greeks stood for, in the broadest sense, were indeed defining moments.[10] At such moments physical violence often accompanied ideological conflict and this will have left a lasting mark which justifies their prominent place in the historian's reckoning.

Not only the most important but also the most formative of such experiences was the revolt of the Maccabees, in the 160's B.C., which in retrospect was seen as having been provoked specifically by the promotion of a Greek life-style in Jerusalem by a Jewish high priest Jason, followed by his supplanter, Menelaus, and backed by the Seleucid-Greek imperial government. It is worth pointing out, however, that this division does not justify the modern tendency to describe as 'Hellenizers' those unreconciled members of the Jewish establishment who held out against the Maccabees in Jerusalem's Akra fortress after the rededication of the altar. The Maccabaean literature does not specify their identity, and we may blame subsequent interpretation for making too much of the Jewish-Greek Kulturkampf within the political conflict.

To put it simply, by the late Second Temple period, symbolic opposition to Hellenism, associated with remembered times of crisis, was an obvious part of the way in which the Jews of Palestine constructed their own identity. It was helpful, and ultimately indeed creative, to see the Greeks as different from themselves in particular respects. We naturally find in literature reflections of the symbols of those contrasting identities, revealing to us that to distinguish between Jews and Greeks was a commonplace in Second Temple Jewish society. To Paul this was a primary division in society: salvation is for 'the Jew first, but the Greek also' (Rom. 1:16). It is also worth noting that in this same passage, speaking to the Christian community of Rome about his message to the world, Paul draws on the formula which was also to come to Josephus' lips, when he points to both Greeks and barbarians as its recipients (Rom. 1:14) and qualifies that dichotomy with the designations 'wise' on the one hand and 'simple' on the other, suggesting that the contrast is mainly a matter of education. However, the Greek-Jewish distinction is the central one for Paul's thought, and it is precisely because this distinction

---

[10] See Rajak 1990 = Ch. 4.

comes so naturally that he can claim that faith abolishes, along with other differences between person and person, the gap between Greek and Jew.[11] The implication is that this pair of opposites, whether taken as ethnic, linguistic, religious, social, or all of these, represented familiar identity markers in Paul's world. And it is of course from the Jerusalem scenes in Acts that comes the unique evidence for a split between the group known as 'Hellenists' and the group known as 'Hebraists' in the earliest church (6:1), mirroring, we are told, a division in Judaism itself. This evidence is supplemented by a later statement that Saul in Jerusalem debates exclusively with the Hellenists (9:9).

It is worth recalling that in the post-70 era the emphasis was to change quite dramatically. Many of the later Palestinian rabbis would be overtly relaxed about 'Greek wisdom', while 'idol-worshipper' was to become the main identity-forming label, the obvious antithesis to 'Jewish'. Other components of Hellenism, such as use of the Greek language and of Greek visual iconography, became less of a threat, as, perhaps, did the Roman government itself.[12]

At that stage the idolatry which, after all, was always a crucial part of what Jews did not like in the Greek cultural 'package', stood out more sharply than earlier from the rest of the distinctive features of the Greek way of life.

For the Second Temple period, the challenge is now no longer to measure Hellenism on an artificially-constructed unitary scale, but to keep the focus of our observation on the experience of the participants and its ramifications. The task is to assess with greater sophistication what made up that consciousness which the Jews of Palestine, and to a lesser extent those of the Diaspora with whom they remained linked, of standing apart both from Greeks and from many things Greek, at the same time as they had happily, or indeed unconsciously assimilated many of the other side's habits of thought and life. Martin Hengel has enabled us to understand the extent and depth of that assimilation in the Jewish heartland. His critics have enabled us to realize that this is not the whole story. The new perspectives show us how to build the two, seemingly contradictory,

---

[11] Rom. 10:11–12; Gal. 3:28; cf. Col. 3:11, where barbarians and Scythians also figure by way of contrast with Greeks.

[12] For the spectrum of rabbinic attitudes. see now the assessment by Levine 1998: ch. 3. There are important new investigations in Schäfer 1998.

arguments into a single picture, a picture which gives the subjective element its due place and is sensitive to the constraints and instabilities of the relationships between groups or even individuals.

It is reasonable to predict that the concepts of 'Hellenism' and 'Hellenization' will continue to play a major role in the study of Jewry in the Second Temple period (and beyond too). They may be toppled from their pinnacle by ideological shifts. They may have to compete against a stronger sense of other pressures on the Jews of Palestine, be they the hitherto largely neglected Roman influences or local 'Semitic' elements or even, from the inside, the symbolic power of the Hebrew language which has recently had renewed and welcome attention. But Hellenism is a long way from being written out of the story. What we may hope is that future research will at any rate be guided by greater conceptual clarity between objective and subjective definitions of ethnicity and of culture. The reader may notice in the remaining papers in this collection a growing sense of the importance of this distinction and of questions that arise to be done in the exploration of the subjective dimension. In this sense too this book, I believe, speaks clearly for the period—the last decades of the twentieth century—when almost all of it was written.

BIBLIOGRAPHY

Anderson, B. 1983. *Imagined Communities: Reflections on the Origins and Spread of Nationalism.* London.

Barth, F. (ed.). 1969. *Ethnic Groups and Boundaries: the Social Organization of Cultural Difference.* London.

Bickerman, E.J. 1988. *The Jews in the Greek Age.* Cambridge, Mass./London.

Feldman, L.H. 1977. 'Hengel's "Judaism and Hellenism" in Retrospect', *JBL* 96: 371–382.

Gruen, E.S. 1998. *Heritage and Hellenism: The Reinvention of Jewish Tradition.* Berkeley/Los Angeles/London.

Jones, S. 1998. 'Identities in Practice: towards an Archaeological Perspective on Jewish Identity in Antiquity', in S. Jones & S. Pearce (eds), *Jewish Local Patriotism and Self-Identification in the Greco-Roman Period.* Sheffield, 29–49.

Kokkinos, N. 1998. *The Herodian Dynasty: Origins, Role in Society and Eclipse.* Journal for the Study of the Pseudepigrapha Supplement Series 30. Sheffield.

Levine, L.I. 1998. *Judaism and Hellenism: Conflict or Confluence.* Seattle/London.

Millar, F. 1978. 'The Background to the Maccabean Revolution: Reflections on Martin Hengel's *Judaism and Hellenism*', *JJS* 29: 1–21.

—— 1993. *The Roman Near East 31 B.C.–A.D. 337.* Cambridge Mass./London.

Östergard, U. 1992. 'What is National and Ethnic Identity?', in P. Bilde, T. Engberg-Pedersen, L. Hannestad & J. Zahle (eds), *Ethnicity in Hellenistic Egypt.* Aarhus, 18–38.

Rajak, T. 1990. 'The Hasmoneans and the Uses of Hellenism', in P.R. Davies &

R.T. White (eds), *A Tribute to Geza Vermes: Essays on Jewish and Christian History and Literature.* JSOT Supplement Series 100. Sheffield, 261–80 = Ch. 4 in this volume.

Sanders, E.P. 1992. *Judaism: Practice and Belief: 63 B.C.E. to 66 C.E.* London/ Philadelphia.

Schäfer, P. (ed.). 1998. *The Talmud Yerushalmi and Graeco-Roman Culture* I. Texte und Studien zum Antiken Judentum 71. Tübingen.

CHAPTER TWO

THE SENSE OF HISTORY IN JEWISH
INTERTESTAMENTAL WRITING

In post-Biblical and pre-Rabbinic Judaism, forms of historical thought are ubiquitous but also elusive. They are present in such diverse literary types and contexts that even a summary survey would be a lengthy affair. I shall take up two lines of approach, relatively narrow in themselves, but for that reason perhaps a little less familiar, and through them seek to make some general observations. The first is a matter of theory, the second of practice.

The historian Josephus is at his most original and interesting (all his readers will know how laboured and derivative he can be at other times), in his remarks on Jewish history at the opening of the polemic against Apion. There he has to confront the claim, which he says has sprung up in response to his published *Jewish Antiquities*, that the Jewish race is proved of recent origin by the silence of Greek historians and other writers.[1] Antiquity, in the Classical world, meant distinction—as the early Christians were to discover to their cost. So the argument is an important one. And Josephus' demonstration of Jewish antiquity has attracted a good deal of attention, not least because of its direct exploitation (often, be it said, with due acknowledgement) by Christian writers such as Tatian, Theophilus of Antioch, and Origen.[2] But what is less familiar is the first stage of that discussion in *Against Apion*. Because the issue is one of proof through written sources, the age and reliability of such Greek literature as deals with prehistory has first to be evaluated, in contrast with oriental traditions, and above all with the internal Jewish evidence, which naturally tells quite a different story about the earliest peoples. This whole evaluation deserves notice because in fact, going beyond the immediate case, it adds up to a brief but wide-ranging exploration of what constitutes a historical tradition and especially—

---

[1] We may presume the claim to be not a new one: in both books of *Against Apion*, Josephus' named opponents are all of earlier generations than himself.

[2] Tatian, *Cohortatio ad Graecos*, 37–38; Theophilus, *ad Autol* III 21–22; Origen, *Contra Celsum* I 16; IV 11.

once the Greeks have been got out of the way—of the meaning and uses of history among the Jews.

There is no reason to suspect that Josephus has borrowed these arguments from some literary source, and, to the best of my knowledge, for once no such claim has been made about him. While some of the exposition of the Jewish Law in book II (145–219) has uncomfortably close affinities with surviving fragments of a work by Philo referred to as the *Hypothetica*,[3] the historically-orientated book I would have had no place in the *oeuvre* of the philosopher. On the other hand, it is directly connected with many of Josephus' own preoccupations. Some of the claims made by the Hellenistic Graeco-Oriental chroniclers, like Manetho of Egypt and Berossus of Babylon, may come the closest to some of Josephus conceptions, but there is nothing to suggest that those writers stopped to expatiate separately upon the meaning of what they were doing—they seem to have been writers of an extremely matter-of-fact kind.[4] The same applies to Josephus' Hellenistic-Jewish predecessors, as we shall see.

The argument shapes itself around the contrast with Greek culture—a contrast which is never far, implicitly or explicitly, from this writer's mind. It is in the course of criticizing the Greeks that he establishes the leading themes, as is natural enough, since this is the immediately point of attachment to the polemic—'my first thought is one of intense astonishment at the current opinion that in the study of the earliest events the Greeks alone deserve serious attention, that the truth should be sought only from them, and that neither we nor any others in the world are to be believed' (I 6). Such cultural arrogance was incidentally quite regular in Greek literature; it has been succinctly summarized in A. Momigliano's *Alien Wisdom*.[5]

Josephus counters with a sharp picture of the poverty of the evidence for early Greek history—a point which, if obvious, is none the less true for that, and one which has indeed been made in recent times in strikingly similar terms; take, for example Sir Moses Finley, who writes (not in any way recalling Josephus): 'we, too, cannot write a history of early Greece. The reason is very simple: there are no

---

[3] See Colson 1941: 409 n. *a* and nn. passim, pp. 422 ff.; and Vermes 1982: 301–302, n. 50, citing other discussions.

[4] On this type of writer, see Rajak 1982: 472–473 = Ch. 13: 249–250 in this volume. The importance of Josephus' discussion of historiography is noted by Momigliano 1977: 195; also in id. 1966.

[5] Momigliano 1975.

documents. Before the year 700 B.C. such documents never existed'.[6] Josephus analyses this poverty as springing both from inadequacy in the record, determined in the first place by the late arrival of the alphabet to Greece, and then by the loss of the archives through climate and natural disaster, as well as, more generally, by an absence of the recording habit. In a passage much adduced in quite other contexts, he stops momentarily to consider the status of the Homeric poems as history; a status much diminished, he says, by the work's oral formation. Here Josephus is no doubt dependent upon Alexandrian scholarship, but it is remarkable that it is his perceptive formulation which has survived alone, to serve eventually as (in Theodore Reinach's words) one of the 'pierres angulaires' of Wolf's famous *Prolegomena* to the Homeric poems. There Josephus is brought in to underpin the argument that Homer consists of separate traditional 'lays' joined together.[7]

However, my interest lies not in what Josephus has to say about Greek history and historiography *per se*, but about the way he perceives the essential difference between the Greek and the Hebrew approach. He puts up the paradoxical and in some ways even absurd argument that the Greek historical tradition exposes its weakness through the contradictions between its various authors. The charge sheet reaches its climax with the statement that 'on many points even Thucydides is accused of error by some critics, notwithstanding his reputation for writing the most accurate history of his time' (I 18). Today, we would be inclined to think that the spirit of debate and criticism, if serious, is just what stimulates and strengthens a historical enquiry and that it is just as well that no reputation should be immune; specious and ostentatious controversies, like some of the ones to which Josephus refers, are, of course, another matter. In this outlook, our idea of history-writing is closer, I suppose, to that of the Greeks. Josephus, however, expresses the plain view (we cannot help feeling that there is a touch of the Greek rhetoric schools about his neat presentation of it!) that contradiction must mean unreliability, a case which could only hold, in fact, in a situation where true knowledge was demonstrably visible and did not have to be proved. And Josephus asserts that that is exactly how it is for the Jews: their records contain no discrepancies. The tradition is the soundest and the most reliable.

---

[6] Finley 1975: 20.
[7] Reinach 1930: n. *ad* I 12.

He claims, in effect, that the Jews as a nation are distinguished
for being historically-minded, that their historical documents are qualitatively different from others'—though nearer to those of Orientals
than those of Greeks—and that their entire attitude to the past,
above all the distant past, is unique. The formulation is one which
suits his calling, as a Greek historian, and his purpose, to vindicate
his *Antiquities* by taking on his critics. Without that challenge, and
without the Greek orientation of the debate, he perhaps would not
or even could not have formulated the matter thus. Yet, at the same
time, he is positioning himself outside the framework of Greek thought
and he will satisfy us that he is drawing directly on Jewish practices
and conceptions. In other words, there is a genuine fusion here of
the two cultures: in the context of Josephus' writing career, this is
hardly surprising, and is no different in principle from the blend
which, for example, H.A. Attridge has pinpointed in the Biblical
parts of the *Antiquities*.[8]

Against Apion I then, offers an explicit, perhaps the only explicit
statement there is, of a first century Jew's ideas about Scripture as
history. Josephus deserves acknowledgement in this sphere, as much
as for another (in a sense parallel) contribution made by his *Against
Apion*, that of offering us a 'theological précis compiled by a contemporary of the New Testament writers which is probably the earliest Jewish theological system' (to take words from G. Vermes).[9] In
many ways, indeed, this short tract has hit the mark. The work was
issued in the 90's A.D., and cannot have been put together before
the publication of the *Antiquities*, which came in 93/4 at the earliest. In this Josephus confronts us with another paradox, for his eulogy
of history emerges from well into that post-70 era when the central
tradition of the Jewish people is commonly said to have become profoundly ahistorical, following upon the loss of nationhood and Temple.
That diagnosis may indeed apply to the inner core of the Rabbinic
tradition—and Jacob Neusner some years ago suggested an explanation, in the disillusion which made it unattractive in those circles
to think too much about a Messianic future and therefore pointless
any longer to contemplate the sweep of the past. The Rabbis, it is

---

[8] Attridge 1976; Attridge emphasizes the 'apologetic' character of this fusion.

[9] 1982: 301–302 with n. 50. In conclusion, Vermes proposes that Josephus' 'inter-
nalization' of the Torah, with its bias towards the religious and ethical, may even be
Palestinian Jewish, rather than Hellenized or for the benefit of a foreign readership.

said, felt that interest had to be removed from the ultimate direction of history and the uncertainties of redemption; the question (it is asserted) became not when but how this might come.[10] Now, at this time in his life, if not before, Josephus adheres manifestly to the mainstream, incipiently Rabbinic, erstwhile Pharisaic element in Judaism.[11] None the less, perhaps due to his being now a Diaspora resident; perhaps because of his surface Hellenization as a writer (the two are not the same thing, as Hengel's work has shown us),[12] and perhaps because of his essentially personal orientation as a relic of a lost generation and, through circumstance, an essentially backward-looking individual; for whatever reason, Josephus' historical view constitutes a powerful exception to the alleged post-70 dismissal of history (not only in *Against Apion*, but, it could be said, in his whole career). All in all, it is probably most correct to analyse the situation by seeing him as the *conclusion* of a period of great activity and variety in Jewish historical thinking.

We have looked at Josephus claim that the Jews had accurate archives. What is even more interesting is his view of what constitutes the authoritative tradition and of the people's relation to it; the underlying assumptions are in some ways as revealing as what is stated. He claims that among the Jews the records are so good because they are valued and that one reason why they are valued is that they are in active use. The memory of the past is protected by its use in the present and this guarantees, rather than, as we might think, diminishes it.[13] The intimate link between history and practice is in Josephus view and in Jewish tradition itself provided by the Law, since this is at the heart of the Scriptural record and inseparable from the narrative. Divine injunction is the source, and

[10] Neusner 1966: 153–171.
[11] I have argued that this was always his basic affiliation: see Rajak *Josephus*: 32–34. In any event, there is little room for doubt, when it comes to the 90's A.D.; see Cohen 1979: 236–239, where self-interest is described as the main explanation for this choice; Attridge 1976 concludes that 'many of the interpretative elements in the *Antiquities* are not inconsistent with Rabbinic Judaism, and thus perhaps with Pharisaism. These agreements, however, are not so specific that we are compelled to call Josephus a Pharisee because of them' (p. 178). Josephus' lack of interest in the food laws and such aspects of ritual purity, not only in *Against Apion*, but even in the *Antiquities* (III 258 ff.) would have been remedied by his projected work *On Customs and Causes*: see Vermes 1982: 292.
[12] Hengel *Judaism*.
[13] Cf. Josephus, *Vita* 6, on Josephus' own priestly genealogy as recorded in the public archive.

does not go unmentioned by Josephus; but it has in fact been shifted from its key position, evidently because such an emphasis would have been unpersuasive to outsiders and weakened the argument. At the same time, there is no concealment of the divine contribution, as we shall see; and it is always implicitly there.

I have defined what I think is the essence of Josephus' understanding, but his own presentation is, of course, concrete and specific. A personal slant guarantees that this is the author's own voice, a point which does not detract from its broader interest. For he says that the keeping of records was assigned by 'our ancestors' to high priests and prophets (29). He will have some more to say about prophecy, but first he spells out an aspect of the special role of the priesthood, in an unashamedly anachronistic fashion: it is because of the obligation to keep priestly genealogies pure and thus to supervise priestly marriages (see Lev. 21:7) that the archives have been cherished, the names of remote ancestors preserved, and two thousand years' worth of high priests' names recorded (30–36). Josephus' pride in his own priestly and also Hasmonean (therefore high priestly) descent comes out in the curious focus of this statement: he had not so long ago boasted about those origins in the opening sentences of his autobiography, earlier, the prophecy to Vespasian which had secured his survival had been explained as a priestly gift; and at various times he had presented Judaea as a theocracy under priestly rule; his consciousness of his priesthood is an enduring trait.[14] He perhaps does not mean here literally to bring the whole of Scriptural tradition under the priestly umbrella; and he may in part be influenced by thought of the priests' role in maintaining the Temple archives of Egypt and Babylon, phenomena about which Herodotus had already had much to say, and which Josephus himself does like to bring up as a parallel. But the deeper and more serious point in what he writes is that the Jewish tradition is something alive to each observing generation, and each generation has a vested interest in it correctness.

He continues with a careful explanation of what Scripture is, showing us unequivocally that a canon was taken for granted in his day and informing us of the way it was divided in the circles in which he moved: five books of Moses—of laws and traditional history—

---

[14] Rajak *Josephus*: 14–22; Vermes 1982: 295.

(παράδοσις), prophets in thirteen books, and four for hymns and precepts, giving a total of twenty-two, and, in fact, corresponding closely
to what has become the accepted Jewish tripartite classification.[15] In
this classification the historical books are, it should be noted, not
separated off from the rest; and *all* the history is attributed by Josephus
to prophetic inspiration, starting with that of Moses. The prophets,
according to Josephus, received their insight from God; but this succession ceased in the time of Artaxerxes (to which time Josephus
ascribed the book of Esther).[16] So subsequent writing has been without the same authority. What is more, the Bible itself really records
events over the whole of time (37–38). This implies, as Hengel has
pointed out, that authority has constantly to be sought in the past.
Such a view of the prophetic succession again corresponds to Rabbinic
ideas, as expressed, for example in *m.Avoth*'s statement on the chain
of tradition travelling from Moses to the prophets and then to the
men of the Great Synagogue, or perhaps in the utterance of 4 Ezra,
where the prophet is told that after his day 'truth shall go far away
and falsehood shall come near).[17] Documents were preserved through
the agency of priestly care. The formula of Deuteronomy (6:2 and
13:1), invoked also in Rabbinic literature and previously by Josephus
himself in explaining the procedure of his *Antiquities* (I 5) is re-echoed
here in the statement that nothing has been added to the original
texts nor taken away from them.[18]

The links between history and Law and between history and life
are most forcibly asserted in the statement that Jews adhere to their
writings because they take them as God's decrees and would endure
martyrdom, as did indeed occur in the theatres, rather than deny
the Laws or the other writings (the reference is probably to quite
recent events, in 66 or 70, or possibly even later, and not just to

---

[15] Even if Josephus' total of twenty-two, instead of twenty-four, raises problems,
as does his division by which only four books are assigned to the third section. The
Septuagint's general grouping is markedly different. See Anderson 1970: 114–117,
124–125, 136–139.

[16] *AJ* XI 184 ff.; Ezra and Nehemiah are transferred by Josephus to Xerxes'
reign, in a correction of Scripture—see *AJ* XI 120 ff.

[17] At *Aboth* I i; 4 Ezra 14:18. Talmudic texts generally put the beginnings of the
Great Synagogue in the generation of Ezra; but the chronological implications are
sometimes confused; on this see Sperber 1971: 629–631.

[18] *CA* I 42; Rajak 1982: 471–472 = Ch. 13: 248; Vermes: 290, n. 4, who prefers,
however, the interpretation of van Unnik: 26–40, that Josephus seeks to make no
substantive point with this formula, beyond reassuring his readers of his trustwor-
thiness. My reading is closer to that of Feldman 1968: 338.

the long-gone martyrdoms of the Maccabean era.[19] The people was
always ready to carry the 'burden of history', however heavy.[20] Far
from there being a separate sphere for history, for Josephus, and for
the Jews of his time, the dependence of precept and of faith upon
the written report of the past is self-evident. It is all quite different
for the Greeks, whose writings are composed, as Josephus would
have it, to suit the tastes of the authors—something on which he
puts, for the purposes of his argument, the most derogatory implication; still, his concentration on the role of Greek historians as
entertainers or rhetoricians is, we may feel, not entirely unjustified.

Though it is mainly the remote past which is in question, the line
of tradition is drawn as continuous and as continuing to be in some
sense authoritative; thus Josephus does not shrink from extending his
theory to cover contemporary history and then, more particularly
(this need not surprise us, knowing his personality) to defend his own
eye-witness account of the Jewish War by contrast with others 'published by persons who never visited the sites nor were anywhere near
the action' (46). The descent from the sublime to the ridiculous calls
for no further comment. And Josephus' defence leads into a digression about his own first book which replaces the expected conclusion to the whole first section of the *Against Apion*, winding up the
discussion about the two kinds of history and leading on to the criticisms of his critics.

Some excesses in Josephus' observations can easily make us lose
sight of their value. In general terms, he is right to insist that having the Scriptures caused the Jews to be continually recalling their
past, that in many respects they had as a people a peculiar interest
in such matters, and that that interest was part and parcel of the
business of their daily lives. Having analysed the theory, we now
must examine contemporary practice. In what ways, beyond mere

---

[19] In addition to *CA* I 42–43, see also II 232–234, 272. There were massacres
in 66 A.D. at Gaza, Askalon, Ptolemais, Tyre, Philadelphia, Gerasa, Pella, Gadara,
Hippos, Scythopolis, Damascus and Alexandria, as well as Caesarea; in 67 at Antioch;
'*sicarii*' were suppressed in 72/3 in Alexandria and Cyrenaica; under Domitian, the
harsh exactions of the Jewish tax and the emphasis laid upon the imperial cult
appear to have led to local persecutions, though the evidence is weak. On all these
events, see Smallwood 1976: ch. XIV. Hengel 1961: 267, cites this passage of
Josephus in connection with Essene martyrdoms.
[20] On this conception of history as expressed in the twentieth century, see White
1960: 111–132. The Jewish people might be conceived of as in a special way subject to this burden.

possession of a sacred text, did the Bible create a special relationship with the past among the Jews of Josephus' day? It would be
foolish to spend much time seeking appearances of pure 'history' in
our accepted meaning of the word in intertestamental literature: perhaps even not in those works, and they are not so very numerous,
which are formally designated 'histories' (both the books of the
Maccabees embody major distortions and fictions). Moreover, we
must be aware that the boundaries between the categories in Jewish
literature correspond neither to those of the Greeks nor to our own.[21]
But in what respects was there a developed historical consciousness
in this literature? And of what kind was it?

What we should not look for is proof of straight, disinterested,
scholarly enquiry. Indeed, it is probably a mistake to seek such manifestations in any consistent form, even in the admired historiography of the Greeks and Romans, as Classical scholars are now beginning
to note (some of them, perhaps, with a degree of overreaction).[22]
Our own academic aspirations in this field—even supposing them
to be attainable—may be themselves no more than a temporary
aberration, some kind of 'historical accident', as Hayden White has
called it.[23]

On any broader conception of history, intertestamental Judaism
is a culture that is historically-minded and notably prolific in historical thought. A sense of history is, after all, no more than an
interest in the past, seen as some sort of continuity, within a context (even if a false one) of time. Furthermore, whatever uses this
past be put to—understanding the ways of God, describing one's
own identity or relating to others, interpreting current events or pre-
dicting future ones, defending one's nation or justifying one's party,
producing social cohesion, controlling the younger generation or
understanding the older one (and there may be many more)—it is

---

[21] It is worth noticing in this connection the implications of the chapter division
in the volume edited by Stone (1984): 'The Stories', 'the Bible Rewritten', 'Historiography', 'Testments' etc.
[22] I refer to the approach of, e.g., Wiseman 1979 (on the early Roman tradition) or Woodman 1983. What must be avoided, in this new realism, is reducing
all historiography to the same level; judged as mere rhetoric or romance; for a
reaction, see the words of Momigliano 1982: 225: 'There is a widespread tendency
both inside and outside the historical profession to treat historiography as another
genre of fiction'.
[23] 1960. On the roots of the modern approach in Greek evaluations of reliability, see Momigliano 1977: 190–192.

a prerequisite for something of an attitude of enquiry and curiosity
to be present among creators and consumers. For one thing, without
such a shared attitude, the past simply could not be a potent force.

So, even if it is true that, as Finley has reported, drawing on the
anthropologists, 'wherever tradition can be studied among living people, the evidence is that it does not exist apart from the connection
with a practice or belief',[24] it must also be the case that the same
practices and beliefs depend upon an independent momentum of
remembering and asking, within the tradition. Visions of the past,
if they are allowed to, will exert their own spell. Intertestamental
Judaism—as Josephus perceived—was a paradigm case of movement
in both directions.

The most characteristic modern way of doing history is distinguishing truth from fiction. Josephus, following the Greeks, talks a
great deal about historical truth, but since he believes himself to
adhere to a tradition which is all true, his prime concern will be
different. Certainly, the truth/fiction distinction is not a central one
in the Hebrew tradition; and, by all accounts, the application of this
distinction to memories of the past has been, everywhere a rare activity.[25] It will be apparent that when this distinction is left out of
account, there is still ample scope for historical enquiry: it can ask
questions about how or why things happened, or about what things
were like in the past; it can try to fill disturbing gaps in the record
(even though this may require imaginary incidents) and it can make
links between events. These tasks, surprising as it may seem at first
sight, become not less but more pressing the more a tradition is
respected and the more it is felt that the content, however problematic, has to be saved. Even before the Biblical books had become
canonical, their importance to the Jews was such that continuing
interpretative and expansionist labour of this nature was called for.
Thus, in the intertestamental period just as the legendary is not
sharply divided from the historical, so there is no clearly-marked distinction between literature which is described as exegetical and that
normally categorized as historical.[26] The fusion of history with Aggadic
Midrash is displayed in clear and extended form in the Biblical parts
of Josephus' own *Antiquities*, especially the first six books, where the

---

[24] 1975: 27.
[25] Finley 1975.
[26] See the introductory remarks to the chapters by Nickelsburg in Stone 1984.

amplifications and interpretations of scripture are at their most abundant. S. Rappaport, G. Vermes and T. Franxman have demonstrated the intimate connection of this material with contemporary and later traditions of exegesis, and the strength of the cumulative case they have built up cannot be resisted.[27]

Now, however, we cannot dwell on the strange amalgam that is the *Jewish Antiquities*. We shall look at earlier texts to see how Biblical writings prompted post-Biblical historical questioning and how history was conceived within a Biblical framework. I think that this viewpoint and the perspective of Josephus' idea of Biblical history, offer a fresh approach to literature that is not unfamiliar. Here I shall concentrate on a limited area, on historical or quasi-historical works which are Biblical in subject matter. This seems appropriate to the present occasion; and the major historians whose subject matter was contemporary, both in Hebrew and in Greek—that is to say, the author of 1 Maccabees on the one hand, and on the other Jason of Cyrene and his Epitomator (who is the author of 2 Maccabees), must be left for another time.[28] It would be possible, too, to pursue the theme further in a different direction, and to explore the presentation of the historical process, past, present and, above all, future, embodied in some of the Testaments and in the Apocalypses, which are perhaps the era's most distinctive literary form.

Most of the present subject matter will consist of works surviving (insofar as they do survive) in the Greek language. Yet it would be wrong to assign Judaeo-Greek historiography particularly to the Diaspora: the Epitomator of Jason of Cyrene appears to have written in Palestine, as Jason himself may well have done, in view of his likely first-hand acquaintance with the Maccabean revolution;[29] again, not all of those normally regarded as Alexandrian Jewish writers can, from their fragments, be assigned even as a probability to that milieu.

---

[27] Rappaport 1930; Vermes 1961; Franxman 1979. The depth and seriousness of Josephus' concurrent Hellenization of the narrative still awaits a definitive description: for Attridge 1976 this is one essential component of the author's apologetic theology, while for Feldman in various studies, they lie at its very heart: see especially his review of Franxman (1981: 121–123, with nn. 23 and 31 referring to his other papers on the subject).

[28] But see some preliminary comments below.

[29] On the long-standing debate about Jason's date and sources, see Hengel *Judaism*: 95–98 and nn., with the cautious conclusion that 'the suggestion of Niese, that Jason spent at least some time in Palestine in those decisive years after 175 B.C. . . . . still has a certain degree of probability'.

The identification of Eupolemus, whom I shall be discussing shortly, with the Palestinian ambassador of that name is strongly favoured by some scholars. We shall also find that there are points of similarity between this literature and *Jubilees* or the Genesis Apocryphon. Samaritan writing, too, fits in an interesting way into this group. It is, indeed, particularly important to note that no sharp differentiation can be made from the point of view of either language or provenance between Palestinian and non-Palestinian material.[30]

The now fragmentary Hellenistic-Jewish writers who precede Philo have never been fully restored to the place in Judaism from which they were displaced by the closing in of the religious tradition after the disaster of 70, by the subsequent destruction of the Alexandrian community under Trajan, by the interest shown in them on the part of early Christian writers, and by their own severe limitations as authors and thinkers. The fragments are too few to build very much on (while, by contrast, Philo's works are perhaps too copious for comfort); but they are part of a culture which is in its own way a remarkable phenomenon. Recent editions and commentaries (sometimes, it must be admitted, inflated to disproportionate size) stimulate a fresh look, and Freudenthal's book of 1874–75 provides a solid, if to our taste over-speculative foundation.[31]

The retelling of Biblical history, with expansions, contractions and even modifications was everywhere, as I have said, a major branch of literary activity in the period, notwithstanding the special status held by the canonical books and the obligation not to add or subtract emphasized by Josephus. We may take it that this was regarded as permissible activity, in that it could be viewed as another way of expressing what was already there in the text.[32] Now this is a kind of activity that leaves little room for concerns about distinguishing truth from fiction: rather the opposite: it adds further accretions of fiction to a tradition where invention is already inextricably intertwined with true recording, in a mixture hallowed by respect for the text. With such an ever-expanding tradition, it is never really possible to get anywhere with distinguishing the well-founded from the

[30] The remarks of Vermes with Goodman 1984; and Hengel *Judaism*: I, 104–105.
[31] Freudenthal 1874–75; Walter 1976; id. 1975; Holladay *Fragments*; of the latter two series, only Holladay's gives the Greek texts; the fragments are also in Denis 1970: 175–228.
[32] Cf. above, n. 18. On Midrash as part of the text, see Vermes 1961: 176–177.

invented (even were that desired) except, to a very limited extent, using the tools of modern scholarship. Once a version is accepted, there is no longer room for disbelief. Morton Smith's formulation catches the point, when he talks, in relation to the role of the ancient 'editors', of an old-established historical interest in Israel, 'extending itself to organize what was apparently a body of non-historical texts'.[33] This is not to say that writings will not contain visibly differing proportions of pure romance; nor to deny that they will be different valued, within specific circles or more generally; and some authors may begin and end their careers in an altogether fringe role. To take one case, it may be that no group of readers set much store as literal truth by the flights of fancy of that dubious Jew Artapanus on the subject of Moses/Mousaios, the teacher of Orpheus, who founded Heliopolis and buried his wife Merris at Meroe.[34] But for us it is usually difficult if not impossible to judge their impact; the ancient criteria for setting a value will have been complicated ones, with factual accuracy playing at most a minor role.

In his authoritative book on literary falsification,[35] W. Speyer classes the remains of the so-called Hellenistic-Jewish historians as 'geschichtliche Verfalschungen'. Such a description (which is accommodated, of course, to the theme of the book) rests on positivistic premises which seem inappropriate to this literary context; its logical consequence is to present, as he does, these figures as pure propagandists, *Tendenzschriftsteller*; but this, even on the very limited evidence we have, seems unjustifiably narrow. Such they may have been; but not only that, and perhaps not mainly that.

Without making excessive claims for what these writings could ever have contained, I would suggest that we should not hesitate to treat them as a species of historical narration genuinely stimulated by Scripture, and to regard them as works with an internal role within the Hellenized-Jewish culture. This is not an altogether new view—a fact from which I take some comfort. For one scholarly approach has been precisely to hold that the psychological needs of the Alexandrian community are the primary explanation of its own curious literature. Most important, V. Tcherikover in two justifiably well-known articles, one of a general nature and one dealing with

---

[33] 1972: 191–227.
[34] Holladay *Fragments*: 209–213 (Artapanus, frag. 3).
[35] 1971: 150–160.

the letter of Aristeas, set out to establish this position.[36] Martin Hengel, N. Walter, Salo Baron (in brief) and B.Z. Wacholder in his monograph on Eupolemus[37] have all by and large supported him. The influential voice on the other side, asserting the extra-mural and competitive character of the writing, was E. Bickerman, in a classic paper on Demetrius the chronographer. Bickerman makes apologetics seem dominant, and the author's principal objective is defined as countering 'Hellenocentric' history; J.J. Collins has taken up a similar line.[38] Much of Tcherikover's case rested upon the social and political realities of the Alexandrian milieu, but, in relation to Aristeas (itself, incidentally, a legend written up as a historical document, and incorporated by Josephus into the *Antiquities* as history), Tcherikover puts forward a very interesting argument which draws on the text itself. In the account of the Jewish way of life (128–171) offered by the high priest Eleazar, the choice of material is quite unexpected: specialized dietary rules like those about animals with the 'parting hoof' and the 'cloven foot', and esoteric habits like the use of *tefilin* and *mesusot* are scarcely of a kind to make sense to pagans; they tended to be entirely ignored and indeed there is no hard evidence in pagan literature that these customs ever caught the attention of outsiders (for all that Eleazar has opened his exposition with the earnest declaration that the question of unclean animals is one that arises great interest in 'most men', 128–129).

Such detailed observation of content is the right way forward and there is room to exploit it in the case of other authors. I shall look, therefore, more at the texts themselves than at any hypothetical setting for them. While Tcherikover's instance is of a halakhic nature, the concern of this paper is with what falls under the heading of *aggadah*. The earliest so-called historian of the tradition is the writer Demetrius, probably of the third century B.C.[39] Some have called him the 'father of Hellenistic-Jewish history', while others have claimed him as an exegete: but the disagreement is an empty one.[40] What is visible in his work is the exploitation of Midrashic-type questions and answers, which aim mainly at disposing of historical difficulties

---

[36] 1956: 169–93; 1958: 59–85.
[37] 1974.
[38] Bickerman 1975: 72–84; Collins 1983: ch. I.
[39] Holladay *Fragments*: 51–92, with bibliography on pp. 57–61; Jacoby, *FGrH* no. 722.
[40] Collins 1983: 28.

in the text. Primarily, these difficulties are matters of chronology and
it is, after all, any historian's first job to make his chronology work
out. Peter Fraser has offered a surprisingly simplistic judgement: 'the
Jews of Alexandria did not need a chronological study of the book
of Genesis'.[41] Such a statement is only possible when an author like
Demetrius is taken entirely out of the context of Jewish culture.

The hazards of transmission make it difficult to grasp the overall
purpose of Demetrius' original work, for with this author as with
the other fragmentary writers in the group, there has been a double process of selection: we now have only the Christian authors by
whom the fragments were cited—principally Eusebius in book IX
(mainly) of the *Praeparatio Evangelica*, but also, to a lesser extent,
Clement of Alexandria, in *Stromata*, book I; but they took them all
from a volume on the Jews by a first century B.C. Roman freedman called Alexander Polyhistor, who made excerpts about different
peoples.[42] Two sets of specialist but obscure criteria therefore governed the selection. Of Demetrius we have only six fragments altogether (not that the other authors are better represented) and only
one of them (fragment two) is even as much as several pages in
length. Fragment 1, moreover, is technically unattributed. But the
reader does not get the impression that the chronological investigations are there for polemical purposes at all; that is to say, the surviving fragments do not reveal a Demetrius busy impressing pagans
by slotting Biblical history into Greek or, still less, into universal history; nor does he seem preoccupied with establishing priority for the
Hebrews (in the fashion of the *Against Apion*). What he offers is an
artless, though not entirely charmless, retelling of the Biblical narratives—in his case, it would appear, exclusively drawn from the
Greek version; and the retelling has a distinct numerical focus reminiscent of *Jubilees*. The flavour of his writing is best conveyed directly.
This is part of fragment 2: 'Jacob set out for Haran in Mesopotamia,
leaving behind his father Isaac who was 137 years old, whereas he
himself was 77 years old. Thus, after he had spent seven years there,
he married Leah and Rachel, the two daughters of his maternal
uncle. At that time he was 84 years old. Now in the next seven
years twelve children were born to him: in the eighth year and tenth
month Simeon; and in the tenth year and sixth month Levi . . . Now

---

[41] Quoted by Collins 1983: 29, from Fraser 1973: I, 693.
[42] See Stern 1974: I, no. 30, pp. 157–164.

because Rachel was not bearing children, she became jealous of her sister and made her own handmaid Zilpah lie with Jacob. (There is an error here). This was at the time that Bilhah also became pregnant with Naphtali, that is, in the eleventh year and fifth month . . .'.[43] The interest in ages and dates here comes across as almost domestic, suggesting perhaps a sort of affection for the text and its characters. However, in the end, we remain at a loss to know quite why it should be a matter of importance to the author or his clientele that when Dinah was raped by Shechem, son of Hamor, she was 16 and four months, while Simeon and Levi were 21 and four months and 20 and six months respectively when they avenged her. The Biblical dates are such that, as will be obvious, a figure like Jacob's seventy-seven years requires careful extrapolation: he died at age 147 (Gen. 47:28), he was 14 years in Laban's service (Gen. 31:41), and at the end of this period Joseph was born; 30 years later Joseph entered Pharaoh's service (Gen. 41:46) and spent 7 years of plenty and two years of famine there before his brothers came (Gen. 45:6); 17 years later Jacob died (Gen. 47:28). So this total (14 + 30 + 9 + 17 = 70) has to be subtracted from 147 to give Jacob's age when he left for Haran to enter Laban's service.

The text as we have it contains some simple mistakes vis-à-vis Biblical narrative, such as the just-noticed case of Zilpah, who was in fact Rachel's handmaid. Editors have been ready to emend the text (they always are) but it is not impossible that Demetrius was capable of crude mispressions arising from his own need to make simple personal sense of the characters' interaction and to turn them into flesh and blood individuals.

That the author did not have the outside world in view as audience emerges from his readiness to ascribe social inferiority and also dishonesty to the patriarchs (contrast Josephus who tends to remove all such elements from the *Antiquities* and certainly never multiplies them). This is an indicator that appears not to have been noticed. Demetrius is happy to say, of Joseph in Egypt, that 'though Joseph had good fortune for nine years, he did not send for his father because he was a shepherd as were his brothers too, and Egyptians consider it a disgrace to be a shepherd. That this was the reason he did not send for him, Joseph himself declared. For when his kin

---

[43] Holladay *Fragments*: frag. 2, 2–3 (pp. 64–65).

did come, he told them that if they should be summoned by the
king and were asked what they did for a living, they were to say
they were cowherds'. The text, at Gen. 46:31–34, conveys a different
impression in several respects: attention is *not* drawn to Joseph's
unfilial delay in sending for his father; the embarrassment about
being shepherds in juxtaposed but not linked by way of motive with
the delay (and it can hardly be said to be a worthy one), and lastly
there is no question of real dishonesty in the brothers calling themselves herdsmen, as they are said to have had both flocks *and* herds;
still less was there any contrived deception. It is instructive, by way
of contrast, to see how Josephus (*AJ* II 184–186) turns the motif in
yet another direction. Like Demetrius, he regards the Jews as in
principle *exclusively* shepherds, but says that they were advised by
Joseph to show goodwill towards the Egyptians by putting aside this
forbidden occupation (presumably he would now provide for them!).
Thus in Josephus' version the thrust of the story is acutely apologetic; the Jews are shown to be positively eager to accommodate
themselves to the customs of others, thereby evincing the opposite
of the misanthropy and peculiarity of behaviours commonly ascribed
to them.[44]

Here our concern is with Demetrius, and it would be absurd to
suggest that his interpretation is designed to *discredit* the patriarchs:
rather he seems to be struggling simply to make everyday sense of
the events in terms of the data provided in the original version: the
text is processed to provide an explanation for what happened, and
this is standard Midrashic procedure of a primitive kind.[45] It is also
primitive history-writing—especially as the explanation offered is one
which catches up and builds upon a specific datum of social history
about the gap between shepherd peoples and others supplied by the
book of Genesis (whether there is any foundation in that, I leave
open here). One might recall the term 'historiated Bible' which
M. Gaster used to describe such writings. It is worth noting, however,
that fragment 2 as we have it does engage in one telling apologetic

---

[44] See Stern 1976: 1101–1159; Sevenster 1975.

[45] Cf. Wacholder *Eupolemus*: 280 ff. On Midrash in Graeco-Jewish literature, cf.
Jacobson 1983: 20–23. The question-answer procedure implicit here has been likened
by Freudenthal and by Gutman 1969: 138–144 to that of early Greek literature
and of the Homeric scholia. But there is little or no real similarity in form or content between these very different types of literature; Gutman, in any case, accepts
that any influence would be superficial.

device, by way of what looks like deliberate omission; for Genesis
says of the dinner given to greet Jacob that 'They served him (Joseph)
by himself, and the brothers by themselves, and the Egyptians who
were at dinner were also served separately; for Egyptians hold it an
abomination to eat with Hebrews' (Gen. 43:32). That last, unhappy
statement, so close to the heart of many difficulties between Jews
and their neighbours, is not to be found in Demetrius: instead, he
fills the story out at this point by his favourite game of numerology,
building on the information that Benjamin's portion was five times
as large as any of the others' (43:34) with the observation that seven
sons had been born to his father by Leah and only two by Rachel,
so that Benjamin had five portions and Joseph himself two[46] making a total of seven, as many as all the sons of Leah received.

   With the next historian, Eupolemus,[47] we have an author who is
likely to be some three generations later in date (from the second
half of the second century, it would seem) and has, perhaps for this
reason, a little more sophistication in the five surviving fragments
(one could hardly have less). Another reason might be that he is
closer to the mainstream of the scholarly traditions of his time, since
his affinities are Palestinian, his orientation is towards the Temple,
his style and syntax are Hebraic, and his Bible may sometimes be
the Hebrew one; furthermore, according to a now-favoured identification (which still, it should be said, falls short of proof), he wrote
in Jerusalem, was of priestly family and is the same man as Eupolemus,
son of John, son of Accos, who served as aide to Judas Maccabeus
and is named as one of his envoys to Rome in 161 B.C. at 1 Macc.
8:17–20 and 2 Macc. 4:11.[48] B.Z. Wacholder has sought to position
this author within Jewish literature, comparing his re-writings, additions and contractions to those of the Chronicler operating upon
Kings, describing as Biblical his way with architectural minutiae and
measurements, and tentatively reviving Ewald's comparison between
the Solomonic correspondence in Eupolemus and Apocryphal material. In spite of some dubious evidence of the subsidiary use of a

---

   [46] The MS texts read 'one', but a correction is necessary: see Holladay *Fragments*:
n. *ad loc.*
   [47] Holladay *Fragments*: 93–156, with bibliography on 105–111; Jacoby, *FGrH* No.
723; note also Wacholder *Eupolemus*.
   [48] Wacholder *Eupolemus*: 1–21.

pagan historian (or romancer), in the shape of Ctesias,[49] there is no unequivocal sign of the outside world being addressed.

It is true, however, that in presenting Moses as a *Protos Euretes* (like the Moses of Artapanus[50] and like Abraham in pseudo-Eupolemus), who invents the alphabet and teaches it to the Phoenicians (fragment 1) and in incorporating Solomon's correspondence with Vaphres king of Egypt and Souron king of Tyre, Eupolemus does betray a concern with placing the Hebrews on the map of general history, at least for his and their own self-satisfaction. None the less, if we are to judge from the fragments, a principal objective seems to have been the same as that of Demetrius, simply to illuminate the historical sections of Scripture. The inclusion of correspondence between monarchs—like the Solomonic one here—is an accepted mode in Jewish history-writing, with direct precedents in Solomon's letters from Kings and Chronicles;[51] and in this mode fictional elaboration takes its place beside possibly authentic documentation rather in the way that speeches are treated in the classical writers. (Here the fiction is compounded by the fact that Vaphres, the Egyptian correspondent chosen is extra-Biblical, while the properly attested Hiram king of Tyre is turned into Souron—Josephus was to claim that the Tyrian monarch's correspondence with Solomon was in his own day extant in the Tyre archives: *CA* I 111). Eupolemus, however, may have believed all the letters he cited to be authentic, as suggested by Wacholder.[52] The hypothesis of an *apocryphon* from which Eupolemus actually derived his material can neither be proved nor refuted; nor can the case for direct dependence upon the *Letter of Aristeas* (which need not even be prior in date). What can be clearly seen is the business of the forger: he seeks, at this point, to stress Solomon's

[49] The dependence is supposedly shown by Eupolemus' introduction of Astibares, a king in Qtesias, as a Median collaborator with Babylon in the attack on Jerusalem: Holladay *Fragments*: 153, n. 110. But Wacholder *Eupolemus*: 255, was wrong to take this as proof of a direct literary debt.

[50] This is undeniably a Greek motif: see, for the classical precedents, Kleingunther 1933; Thraede 1962: esp. 1242–1246 on the Jewish adaptations.

[51] 1 Kings 5:2–6; 2 Chron. 2:3–10: The letters in Chronicles are generally longer and more elaborate than those in Kings: Holladay *Fragments*: 114, n. 47.

[52] On Eupolemus' own stance, Wacholder *Eupolemus*: 157–158. The letter of Vaphres (Holladay *Fragments*: 118, frag. 2) is headed ἀντίγραφος (copy). The name Vaphres appears to be connected with the name of the Pharaoh Hophra in Jeremiah (44:30), Οὐαφρης in the Egyptian king lists and Ἀπρίης in Herodotus (II 161; IV 159); see Holladay *Fragments*: 141, n. 23.

piety, to visualize how the king collected and how he fed his enormous labour force, and to conjure up in graphic form the respect
paid to the pious king and his God by foreign powers: 'when I read
your letter I rejoiced greatly. I and my entire administration set aside
a feast day upon the occasion of your succeeding to the kingdom
of such a kind man and one approved of by so mighty a God'.[53] It
is interesting that the basically Palestinian Eupolemus is, on the showing of the fragments, more interested than Demetrius, the supposedly
Diaspora writer, in clarifying the Jewish people's place in a wider
world.

When it comes to the (undated) fragments of Artapanus' *On the
Jews*,[54] we are, as I have indicated, in a different realm, that of historical extravaganza or romance, with links with the text that seem
often slighter than its associations with Egyptian animal cult and
other unexpected matter. There are, however, touches of the flesh
and blood realism that we have seen in the other two authors, and
there may be some affinities with Jewish tradition, for example, in
the description of Moses' appearance—'tall, ruddy complexioned,
with long flowing gray hair and dignified' (frag. 3).

Artapanus' subject matter (as it survives) is Moses; Demetrius had
retold the book of Genesis; Eupolemus harmonized Kings and Chronicles. An author who is scarcely more than a name to us, another
Aristeas,[55] gives early testimony to traditions about Job, whom he
makes the son of Esau (perhaps in the sense of 'descendant').
Cleodemus Malchus,[56] cited by Josephus, attaches Abraham's descendants to Libyan legend. The scholarly theory that the latter was a
Samaritan sprang principally from his name; but yet another identifiable author, generally and unattractively termed pseudo-Eupolemus[57]
(though described by Eusebius in one case as 'Eupolemus' in another
as 'some anonymous writings') may well more properly (though still
not certainly) be designated Samaritan, because he recounts that
Abraham was received by the city at the temple Argarizin, which is
interpreted Mountain of the Most High, where the patriarch met

---

[53] Holladay *Fragments*: 119, frag. 2.
[54] Holladay *Fragments*: 189–243, with bibliography on 199–203; Jacoby, *FGrH*
726. In this, as in most cases, reliance cannot be placed upon the ascribed title.
[55] Holladay *Fragments*: 261–276; Jacoby, *FGrH* 725.
[56] Holladay *Fragments*: 245–260; Jacoby, *FGrH* 727.
[57] Holladay *Fragments*: 157–188, with bibliography on 166–168; Jacoby, *FGrH* 724.
See especially Wacholder 1963: 83–113 and Wacholder *Eupolemus*: 287–293.

Melchizedek the priest. This author also embodies themes found in the Samaritan book *Asatir*.[58] The fragments again are quite slight and only two in number, but the procedure is in principle similar to what we have already seen in Jewish authors, as is evident from Eusebius' erroneous conflation of this figure with Eupolemus.

Hengel has given us a brilliant portrait of this anonymous writer,[59] whom he dates to before the Maccabean revolt; he emphasizes the way that pagan deities are demythologized, for example Bel and Kronos through the identification of both with Noah/Nimrod; this reduces them to being not only mortals, albeit of giant frame, but markedly evil ones, whose descendants had to be punished. The universalizing traits and the cultural interests of the author emerge in the extraordinary idealization of a Biblical figure, Abraham, who is here the discoverer of astrology and divination (as also, later in Josephus). But I should like to draw attention to the significance of other aspects, not overlooked by Hengel but easily overshadowed: the probability that the author knew Hebrew;[60] and the connections with what might be called Jewish apocryphal traditions (Genesis Apocryphon, *Jubilees* and 1 Enoch), above all in the notion that Enoch learnt astrology from the angels.[61] Another such case are the details of what happened to the Pharaoh who tried to have intercourse with Sarah: her chastity was providentially protected, and his household began to perish until diviners came and revealed to him the lady's identity; similar aggadic elaborations, again, are in Genesis Apocryphon and *Jubilees*, as well as in Josephus, Philo and even, on the other side, Genesis Rabbah.[62] But the closest parallel here is the Samaritan *Asatir*.

We must accept that the Samaritans of this period (before the great rift) shared in the Jewish world of Bible interpretation and

---

[58] Though none of these traditions appear to be unique to Samaritan sources; however, the Samaritan parallels are the closest when it comes to matters of detail: e.g. Armenians as the antagonists of Israel; Enoch's astrological revelations (see Gaster 1927: 9–41). The reading of the association Salem/Shechem as a Samaritan version may be thought to require reexamination in the light of the LXX version of Gen. 33:18, 'Jacob went to Salem, city of the Shechemites', where Salem is not present in the MT; this suggests the Salem-Shechem link to be an interpretation with wide currency. See Holladay *Fragments*: 183 (n. 21); Hengel *Judaism*: II, 59, n. 239.

[59] Judaism I, 88–92.

[60] Judaism II, 60, n. 242.

[61] See Hengel *Judaism*: 89 and n. 243.

[62] Holladay *Fragments*: 184, n. 24.

allowed it to feed their historical consciousness in the same way. Here we have a phenomenon of the first importance, and it reveals a community whose culture and self-awareness may have had different overtones from that of the Jews, yet which ran parallel to theirs. We need not take too seriously, however, the information derived from Eusebius (*PE* IX 17–1–9) that Alexander Polyhistor reported the title of this work by 'Eupolemus' as 'Concerning the Jews of Assyria'. In general the titles ascribed to the various works cited by Polyhistor in his Jewish collection seem either arbitrary or obvious, and in this case, where even the author's name has had to be rejected, there is even more room for doubt.[63] If this historian is Samaritan, he constitutes a literary correlative of newer archaeological evidence: I refer here to the discovery made on the island of Delos of two steles, found near the προσευχή erected by οἱ ἐν Δήλῳ Ἰσραελεῖται οἱ ἀπαρχόμενοι εἰς ἱερὸν Ἀργαριζείν. The steles are dated palaeographically to 250–175 to 150–50 B.C., respectively. This Diaspora community of Samaritans was located, it seems, near the Jewish place of assembly, and, it has been suggested, the two Bible-based groups may have drawn together in conditions of exile and remained close even after the schism of 129.[64]

Most of the Hellenistic Biblical historians, whether Jewish or Samaritan, were not named by Josephus in his *Antiquities* (hence our dependence on the pagan-Christian line of transmission for our limited knowledge of them).[65] We might be tempted on this basis to form the view that they had little importance or at any rate no influence. But that view would be ill-founded. The reasons why Josephus referred little to them are discernible and specific. He had direct access to the Hebrew Bible and also to richer veins of tradition and interpretation (oral and perhaps even written) in Hebrew and Aramaic Midrash; where he drew from Greek originals, it was always where the style and Hellenized form as well as the substance had something to contribute to his history, and could ease the labour of composition in Greek (the letter of Aristeas and the additions to

---

[63] See Holladay *Fragments*: 159, for disputes on the subject; there is no use in pursuing them.

[64] See Bruneau 1982: 465–504.

[65] Josephus refers to Alexander Polyhistor only once; he cites Cleodemus Malchus once; and he regards Eupolemus as pagan (*AJ* I 239–241; *CA* I 218). See Attridge 1976: 34–35.

Esther, both utilized by Josephus, are obvious examples). None of the historians considered here could be so described, even if Eupolemus may have been too harshly judged by some of his critics.[66] In any event, Josephus, in keeping with other Classical historians, is not given to naming his sources except for special purposes, and we should remember that even Philo lacks proper mention, though was demonstrably used by the historian.

Though the Hellenistic Jewish and Samaritan writers rose beyond Septuagint Greek, they seem to have written like the antiquarians which, much of the time, they were. For it remains an open question, on the evidence of the fragments, how far their authors were concerned with the larger processes of history: the indications of a broader vision are, it might be said, just sufficient for us to call their thinking historical, if we take into account a phenomenon like Eupolemus' overarching, chronological and outward-looking geographical frameworks. It is certainly hard to imagine that any of them could have achieved a grand opening like that of *Jubilees* (a book which, of course, is deeply concerned with the future as well as the past and especially with the working-out of covenantal history): 'this is the history of the division of the days of the Law and of the testimony, of the events of the years, of their (years') weeks, of their *Jubilees* throughout all the years of the world, as the Lord spake to Moses on Mount Sinai when he went to receive the tables of the Law and of the commandment, according to the voice of God as he said unto him, "Go to the top of the Mount"', or that any of them could have aspired to the supreme theme tackled by *Jubilees*' author: 'and Moses was on the Mount forty days and forty nights, and God taught him the earlier and the later history of the vision of all the days of the Law and of the testimony' (1:5). This education is followed in *Jubilees* by a directive from the angel of God to Moses to 'write a complete history of the creation'.

In the face of that blinding prospect, it is difficult to know how to proceed. *Jubilees* is, in its overall conception, more historical than our author, in its minor features perhaps less. In date it is quite likely to be contemporary with the Maccabean revolt since there is a fairly explicit hostile reference to the Hellenizers at one point, and thus it

---

[66] See Freudenthal 1874–75: 109; Wacholder *Eupolemus*: 256–257.

may be contemporary with Eupolemus on one side, with the non-extant Jason of Cyrene on the other.[67] The Epitome and 1 Maccabees come a generation or more later. It was undoubtedly the great events of the persecution, the revolt and the ensuing wars of liberation that enabled Jewish history-writing to grow, in what was already fertile soil (just as the great revolt produced Josephus).

These events were to call forth, in 1 and 2 Maccabees both a Biblical and a contemporary historiography, written in the shadow of the Bible. In the first book we find not only an imitation of Biblical form but even a modelling of narrated incidents upon Biblical prototypes; the model of David for example in the narrative of the wars of Judas, where echoes extend even to the battle numbers, to the nature of the fighting for the sanctuary and to the description of the victory (1 Macc. 3–4); and also the model of Joshua (chap. 11 ff.).[68] In 2 Maccabees, we are struck first and forcibly by the Hellenistic format of the original (whether we call it pathetic historiography or temple propaganda or epiphanic history or whatever) and with the avowedly secular, pleasure-giving aims of the Epitomator, extending even to the comparisons he draws from dinner parties, architecture, and the mixing of wine. But we soon discover that the Old Testament theory of punishment and forgiveness is at least as prominent:[69] punishment, it is said, always comes to the people of Israel even before their sins have reached their height (6:14), and falls upon the *whole* people, even innocent children; yet anger turns to mercy when Maccabeus organizes his band (8:5). All understand that God's rebuke is to be shortlived (7:33). The pattern is a familiar one, with occasionally a special twist. Here, then, in yet another way, new life has been breathed into the old mould and an Old Testament schema has engendered something new.

That single crisis should produce two major histories, each with its own strengths and weaknesses, its own accuracies and inaccuracies and, above all, its own very distinctive character, as well as historical reflections of itself in other works (*Jubilees*, Daniel), is testimony to the power of the Bible-based tradition from which those works spring. It is not, I think, fanciful to include the Graeco-Jewish his-

---

[67] For the dating of *Jubilees*, see Nickelsburg 1981: 78–79 (a date between 175 and 100 B.C.).

[68] See Goldstein 1976, in which the 'typology' is fully annotated.

[69] See Habicht 1976: intr., 185–191; Doran 1981.

torical fragments in that tradition, and thus to challenge Martin Goodman's sceptical assertion that there exists no such thing as a school of Judaeo-Hellenistic historiography.[70] I hope that I have managed to cast a little new light on that tradition and on the forms of its historical awareness. Although it is not possible to disentangle the historical ideas of the Jews, whether Biblical or post-Biblical, from either theology or Law, I believe it to be worth the effort occasionally to adopt a change of perspective and to give history, even if not true history, pride of place.

BIBLIOGRAPHY

Anderson, G.W. 1970. 'Canonical and Non-Canonical', in P.R. Ackroyd & C.F. Evans (eds), *The Cambridge History of the Bible: Vol I. from the beginnings to Jerome.* Cambridge, 113–159.

Attridge, Harold W. 1976. *The Interpretation of Biblical History in the* Antiquitates Judaicae *of Flavius Josephus.* Harvard Dissertations in Religion 7. Missoula, Mont.

Bickerman, E.J. 1975. 'The Jewish Historian Demetrius', in J. Neusner (ed.), *Christianity, Judaism and other Greco-Roman Cults. Studies for Morton Smith at Sixty,* III. Studies in Judaism in late antiquity 12 iii. Leiden, 72–84; reprinted in Bickerman, *Studies in Jewish and Christian History,* II. Arbeiten zur Geschichte des antiken Judentums und des Urchristentums Bd. 9, pt. 2. Leiden, 1980, 347–358.

Bruneau, P. 1982. 'Les Israélites de Délos et la Juiverie délienne', *BCH* 106: 465–504.

Cohen, Shaye J.D. 1979. *Josephus in Galilee and Rome: his Vita and Development as a Historian.* Columbia studies in the classical tradition 8. Leiden.

Collins, J.J. 1983. *Between Athens and Jerusalem: Jewish Identity in the Hellenistic Diaspora.* New York.

Colson, F.H. 1941. *Philo,* IX. Loeb Classical Library. London.

Denis, A.M. 1970. *Fragmenta Pseudepigraphorum quae supersunt Graeca.* Leiden.

Doran, Robert. 1981. *Temple Propaganda: the Purpose and Character of II Maccabees.* [CBQ Monograph 12. Washington, D.C.

Feldman, L.H. 1968. 'Hellenizations in Josephus' Portrayal of Man's Decline', in J. Neusner (ed.), *Religions in Antiquity: Essays in memory of E.R. Goodenough.* Studies in the history of religions; Numen suppl. 14. Leiden, 336–353.

——— 1981. 'Josephus' Commentary on Genesis', *JQR* 72: 121–123.

Finley, M.I. 1975. 'Myth, Memory and History', in *The Use and Abuse of History.* London, 11–33.

Franxman, T.W. 1979. *Genesis and the 'Jewish Antiquities' of Flavius Josephus.* Biblica et Orientalia 35. Rome.

Fraser, P.M. 1973. *Ptolemaic Alexandria.* Oxford.

Freudenthal, J. 1874–75. *Hellenistische Studien. Alexander Polyhistor und die von ihm erhaltenen Reste jüdaischer und samaritanischer Geschichteswerke,* 2 vols. Breslau.

Gaster, M. 1927. *The Asatir: the Samaritan book of the 'Secrets of Moses'.* London.

Goldstein, Jonathan A. 1976. *I Maccabees: a new translation with introduction and commentary.* Anchor Bible 41A. Garden City, NY.

---

[70] Vermese Goodman 1984.

Gutman, Y. 1969. *The Beginnings of Jewish Hellenistic Literature*, I [Hebrew]. Jerusalem.
Habicht, Christian. 1976. *II Makkabäerbuch*. Jüdische Schriften aus hellenistisch-römischer Zeit I, 3. Gütersloh.
Hengel, Martin. 1961. *Die Zeloten: Untersuchungen zur Jüdischen Freiheitsbewegung in der Zeit von Herodes I. bis 70 N.Chr.* Arbeiten zur Geschichte des Spätjudentums und Urchristentums 1. Leiden.
Jacobson, H. 1983. *The Exagoge of Ezekiel*. Cambridge.
Kleingunther, A. 1933. *Protoi eyretai: Untersuchungen zur Geschichte einer Fragestellung*. Philologus Suppl. 26, 1. Leipzig.
Momigliano, A. 1966. 'Time in Ancient Historiography'. *History and Theory*, Beiheft 6.
—— 1975. *Alien Wisdom: The Limits of Hellenization*. Cambridge.
—— 1977. 'Time in Ancient Historiography', in *Essays in Ancient and Modern Historiography*. Blackwell's classical studies. Oxford, 195–210.
—— 1982. 'Biblical Studies and Classical Studies: Simple Reflections about Historical Method', *Biblical Archaeologist* 45, 4: 224–228.
Neusner, J. 1966. 'The Religious Uses of History', *History and Theory* 5: 153–171.
Nickelsburg, G.W. 1981. *Jewish Literature between the Bible and the Mishnah: A historical and literary introduction*. Philadelphia.
Rajak, T. 1982. 'Josephus and the "Archaeology" of the Jews', *Essays in Honour of Yigael Yadin: JJS* 33: 465–477 = Ch. 13 in this volume.
Rappaport, Salo. 1930. *Agada und Exegese bei Flavius Josephus*. Frankfurt.
Reinach, Th. (ed.). 1930. *Contre Apion/Flavius Josephus: texte établi et annoté*. Paris.
Sevenster, J.N. 1975. *The Roots of Pagan Anti-Semitism in the Ancient World*. Novum Testamentum Suppl. 41. Leiden.
Smallwood, E.M. 1976. *The Jews under Roman Rule: from Pompey to Diocletian: a study in political relations*. Studies in Judaism in late antiquity 20. Leiden.
Smith, M. 1972. 'Pseudepigraphy in the Israelite Literary Tradition', Fondation Hardt. *Entretiens sur l'Antiquité Classique* 18: 191–227.
Sperber, D. 1971. 'Synagogue the Great', in *Encyclopedia Judaica* XV. Jerusalem, 629–631.
Speyer, W. 1971. *Die literarische Fälschung im heidnischen und christlichen Altertum: ein Versuch ihrer Deutung*. Handbuch der Altertumswissenschaft I, 2. München.
Stern, M. 1974. *Greek and Latin Authors on Jews and Judaism*, I. Jerusalem.
—— 1976. 'The Jews in Greek and Latin Literature', in S. Safrai & M. Stern, (eds), *The Jewish People in the First Century: Historical Geography, Political History, Social, Cultural and Religious Life and Institutions*, 2. Compendia Rerum Iudicarum ad Novum Testamentum, Section 1, Volume 2. Assen, 1101–1159.
Stone, M. (ed.). 1984. *Writings of the Second Temple Period: Apocrypha, Pseudepigrapha, Qumran, sectarian writings, Philo, Josephus*. Compendia Rerum Iudaicarum ad Novum Testamentum II. Assen, Netherlands/Philadelphia.
Tcherikover, V. 1956. 'Jewish Apologetic Literature Reconsidered', *Eos* 48.3: 169–193 = *Symbolae R. Taubenschlag Dedicatae* (1957).
—— 1958. 'The Ideology of the Letter of Aristeas', *HTR* 51: 59–85.
Thraede, K. 1962. 'Erfinder II', in T. Klauser (ed.), *Reallexikon für Antike und Christentum: Sachwörterbuch zur Auseinandersetzung des Christentums mit der antiken Welt*. Stuttgart, 1191–1278.
van Unnik, W.C. 1978. *Flavius Josephus als historischer Schriftsteller*. Franz-Delitzsch-Vorlesungen, n.F. 1972. Heidelberg.
Vermes, G. 1961. *Scripture and Tradition in Judaism: Haggadic Studies*. Studia Post Biblica 4. Leiden.
—— 1982. 'A Summary of the Law by Flavius Josephus', *NT* 24.4: 301–302.
Vermes, G. with M. Goodman. 1984. 'La littérature juive intertestamentaire à la lumiere d'un sècle de recherches et de découvertes', in R. Kuntzmann & J. Schlosser (eds), *Études sur le Judaïsme hellénistique*. Association catholique française pour l'étude de la Bible. Congrès de Strasbourg 1983. Paris, 19–39.

Wacholder, B.Z. 1963. 'Pseudo-Eupolemus' Two Greek Fragments on the life of Abraham', *HUCA* 34: 83–113.

Walter, N. 1975. *Fragmente jüdisch-hellenistischer Exegeten.* Jüdische Schriften aus hellenistisch-römischer. Unterweisung in lehrhafter Form. III, 2. Gütersloh.

—— 1976. *Fragmente jüdisch-hellenistischer Historiker.* Jüdische Schriften aus hellenistisch-römischer Zeit. Historische und legendarische Erzdhlungen I, 2. Gütersloh.

White, Hayden V. 1960. 'The Burden of History', *History and Theory* 5: 111–132.

Wiseman, T.P. 1979. *Clio's Cosmetics: Three studies in Greco-Roman literature.* Leicester.

Woodman, A.J. 1983. 'From Hannibal to Hitler: The Literature of War'. Repr. from the University of Leeds Review, 1983.

CHAPTER THREE

HASMONEAN KINGSHIP AND THE INVENTION OF TRADITION[1]

Models of Jewish kingship

Biblical ideas of kingship were alive and well in third century Palestine. The desiderata for a Jewish king had been set out in uncompromising terms by the author of Deuteronomy. These rules were strongly prescriptive: rather than being derived from palace life at the height of the monarchy, they might even have been intended as implicit criticism of some of the practices of David and Solomon. Their thrust was the undesirability of concentrating status and wealth in the hands of one pre-eminent individual. Ultimately, monarchy was a concession and must not derogate from God's kingly supremacy, from that perfect system for which Josephus later coined the term 'theocracy' (*CA* II 165). The introduction to the Deuteronomic rules makes the point perfectly clear:

> ... when you come into the land which the Lord your God is giving you, and occupy it and settle in it, and you then say, 'Let us appoint over us a king, as all the surrounding nations do', you shall appoint as king the man whom the Lord your God will choose.

This also emerges clearly from the narrative about Samuel's agreement to let the Israelites make Saul king (1 Sam. 8:5).

The king, an Israelite, was to accumulate neither horses nor wives nor riches. The interests of the Almighty would be powerfully represented by the priests and Levites, who, at every ascension, were entitled to dictate a book of statutes. A symbolic physical adherence to this code was demanded of every king: 'he shall keep it by him and read from it all his life.' The function of God's endorsement was not to elevate the king but to cut him down to size—'in this way he shall not become prouder than his fellow countrymen.' The

---

[1] I am grateful to Lester Grabbe and Daniel Schwartz for his improvements to this paper.

contract was with God, and it was two-way: 'then he and his sons will reign long over his kingdom in Israel' (Deut. 17:14–20).

These were the provisos. In spite of the preliminary reservation, kingship came to be fully accepted and normal in Judah and Israel, and doubts were usually in abeyance.[2] The monarchies were terminated only by the exile. Then, somewhere in the middle of the Second Temple period, we find the Deuteronomic statutes of the king given fresh prominence as relevant Torah, at least in certain circles. In the Qumran Temple scroll (cols 56:12–59), the statutes are restated, expanded and apparently updated in the manner typical of contemporary handling of the Bible.

Subtle reworkings include the claim that the priests themselves were to copy the law (whatever is meant by that), rather than, as in Deuteronomy, the king on the advice of the Levitical priests (which might have been thought quite limiting enough); and also the total omission at that point in the scroll of the Levitical element. Polygamy is explicitly excluded for the king, in keeping with the sect's abhorrence of it. But most noticeable are the major expansions, devising, in the council of thirty six priests, Levites and laymen a wholly new institution; stipulating a standing army of twelve thousand (derived from Numbers 31:4); and specifying the level of mobilization appropriate to different levels of emergency, as well as the correct division of spoil. Here patterns from 1 Samuel are interwoven.

The scroll's editor, Yigael Yadin,[3] and others in his wake, have read this updated version as a critical comment on Hasmonean rule, and, indeed, on a specific Hasmonean ruler. While Yadin saw allusions to John Hyrcanus (thus dating the scroll to the late second century B.C.),[4] Hengel, Charlesworth & Mendels[5] argued for Alexander Jannaeus (early first century). By contrast, Johann Maier rightly insisted that there was nothing which *compelled* a specific contemporary application.[6]

The problem of interpreting possible reference to contemporary events is, of course, a general one in understanding material from Qumran. In the case of the Temple scroll especially, an alternative,

---

[2] Liver 1962: 1086.
[3] 1983; 1985: 192–217.
[4] 1983; 1985: 192–204.
[5] Hengel, Charlesworth & Mendels 1986.
[6] 1985: 125.

non-specific reading is readily available, because the author is, after all, describing the rebuilt Jerusalem; and the restored, correct monarchy may be merely a part of that new order, an anticipation of the end of days. The new Jerusalem naturally required a Jewish ruler, even if not yet the final ruler of all, the expected king Messiah, son of David. Clearly, then, the terms in which the good ruler was described at Qumran could, but certainly need not, be intended as criticism of known figures.

Nor can chronology help in assessing the Hasmonean reading, since, as with other Qumran texts, there are scarcely any grounds for choosing between a third or early second century B.C. date, and a Hasmonean date, unless we have recourse to perceived allusions in the text itself, producing a wholly circular argument.

Despite these uncertainties, some firm ground remains. Even if the monarch of the Temple scroll is just an ideal figure for an ideal world (or after-world), there are still conclusions to be drawn from the degree of interest displayed by the author or authors, and, we may suppose, by the sect, in the detailed requirements for Jewish kingship. Utopias are not conjured up for wholly academic reasons; and their concern for correct interpretation of the Bible was their way of commenting on reality. For our purposes, what is important is that the model was being reworked in Hellenistic Palestine. The biblical conception of kingship was seen as relevant.[7] A tentative Hasmonean dating makes good sense, but we cannot put it more strongly than that.

There is further evidence from Qumran. In the collection of legal precepts designated MMT,[8] a letter concerned with holiness and purity concludes with references both forward and backward in time. The judgement expected in the last days is invoked; and, at the climax, the kings of Israel are recalled (23–26):

> ... think of the Kings of Israel and contemplate their deeds, that whoever among them feared the Torah [?] was delivered from troubles ... Think of David who was a righteous man and he was delivered from many troubles and he was forgiven.

The subordination of ruler to Torah is unequivocal here; and the contractual element is, once again, emphasized.

---

[7] Cf. Mendels 1979.

[8] *Miqsat Ma'asei Torah*, which might be translated 'Some Torah Teachings': Qimron & Strugnell 1994.

Ben Sira (the author of the book known in English as Ecclesiasticus) certainly remembered David and the other kings of Israel. This book of lively teaching and preaching belongs to the earlier part of the second century B.C., probably pre-dating the Hasmonean era; but the Greek translation, made by the author's idealistic grandson, is a product of the Hasmonean period, dated in the translator's prologue to soon after the year 132 B.C., when he says he went to Egypt. The accepted description of the book, as a tradition-based response to the threatening encroachment of incipient Hellenism in the period, rests on questionable assumptions.[9] Hengel does more justice to the complexity of the issues,[10] but still observes an underlying 'controversy with Hellenistic liberalism'. I shall have more to say about such conceptions of Hellenism shortly. For the moment, a helpful perspective is provided in Bickerman's brilliant, posthumously published volume.[11] Ben Sira is central to Bickerman's study, emerging as an interweaving of older and newer thinking, in which ancient near eastern patterns combine with what is specifically biblical, and occasionally also with a thread of classical Greek thought. The focus here is on the social and cultural currents of a transitional Judaism, rather than on the specific engagement of Judaism with Hellenism. One would be hard put to it, indeed, to say that the amalgam reflected in Ben Sira is either hellenized or not hellenized.

Ben Sira puts considerable emphasis on political leadership. His review of the history of Israel spells out how Saul established the monarchy, and then expatiates on David and Solomon. The features of David's rule are especially interesting. God empowered him to win great victories, and by virtue of these military achievements, he was offered a diadem of glory.[12] In thanking and praising God, 'he gave splendour to the festivals', and organized their yearly round in the Temple. His kingship (and, it would seem, those of his successors) was given by way of covenant, διαθήκην βασιλέων (47:13 [11]). We shall find echoes of these conceptions in the ideology of Hasmonean rule.

Solomon is said to have been given peace within secure borders by God; and yet, for all his Temple-building and his wisdom, he

---

[9] Momigliano 1975: 94–96; Revised Schürer: III.1, 200–201.
[10] 1974: 138–154.
[11] 1988.
[12] 47:6 [7] διάδημα δόξης; perhaps to be translated, with NEB, 'the royal diadem'.

erred in taking women. Ben Sira reveals an interesting ambiguity of attitude to kingly wealth, when he addresses this king with the words 'in the name of the Lord God, who is known as the God of Israel, you amassed gold and silver as though they were tin and lead' (47:18). Ben Sira hovers between defending and attacking the king's greed. At any rate, all the kings of Judah except David, Hezekiah and Josiah were sinners (we were earlier told, as in MMT, that David was forgiven his sins), and as a consequence they lost their power to a foreign conqueror and to the burning of the streets of Jerusalem (47:4–7).

The high priesthood

It is not clear whether Bickerman was justified in taking Ben Sira to mean that he rated the priesthood above the kingship.[13] But there can in any case be no doubt of Ben Sira's readiness to see a high priest as pre-eminent political and religious leader of the nation in his own day, at least if that high priest should follow in the footsteps of the great Simon son of Onias. This was the system of government known to Ben Sira. His precise political motives in endorsing the Temple, the Aaronite priesthood and the Oniad family in his eulogy of Simon II (50:1–21), are perhaps less interesting than the terms in which he chooses to depict the high priest and the high priestly office. There was as yet no monarchy, but the role of the high priest as here described has a political as well as a cultic dimension, and it therefore falls within the ambit of contemporary visions of rulers.

Simon's first achievement was the fortification of the Temple, his second, the preparation of the city against siege. There was no conquest, of course, for this ruler, but a very passable substitute: 'he applied his mind to protecting his people from ruin.' Only then, and with a suddenness which is quite literally dramatic, comes the famous succession of similes, as the high priest flashes forth from behind the curtain 'like the morning star appearing through the clouds'. The emphasis is on the dazzling magnificence of the Aaronite priests standing round the altar and participating in the sacrifice; but, above all, on that of Simon himself, as the sacrificial portions are handed

---

[13] 1988: 143.

to him by the other priests. The appeal is directly to the senses: the
splendour of the vestments, the fragrance of the libation wine, the
shouts of the priests, the fanfare of the silver trumpets, the sweet
singing of the choir. However, the impact is more than sensory: the
word δόξα figures repeatedly in the Greek version, and it is crucial
that δόξα is seen as passing from the high priest to the sacred place,
rather than the reverse (50:12). Again, the essential participation of
the people is expressed both in their prayers and in their acceptance
of the priestly blessing, and this motif is given a prominent concluding position.

The Hasmoneans became high priests long before they could
become kings. The high priesthood was an old office, re-invented
and enhanced in the post-exilic period, when, Bickerman maintains,
the high priest became for the first time the only member of the
priesthood to be anointed with the sacred oil. The novelty in this
arrangement is perceived by Bickerman, who associated the new
practice with the Seleucid handling of subject aristocracies. It is at
any rate hard to better Bickerman's observation that:

> ... although it appears that the 'Great Priest' of Jerusalem was not
> held in awe as a living symbol before . . . Ben Sira needed eleven poet-
> ical figures to describe the effects of the High Priest's appearance at
> sacred ceremonies and compared him with the shining sun . . . Although
> the Torah confers on any priest the authority to interpret the Law
> (Deut. 33:10) . . . Ben Sira reserved this role for the High Priest alone.[14]

The new supremacy of the high priesthood was expressed, then, in
the emergence of an appropriate ceremonial. And so the Hasmoneans,
when they sought to define their power, would find a ready language of display, designed to elevate one unique figure in and through
the powerful context of divine worship. This imaging, as we can see
from Ben Sira, had been generated out of memories of the first
Temple, to suit the requirements of the second. Equally, Ben Sira
shows us that literary patterns for describing that ceremonial had
already evolved. Such restated 'native' traditions would be more powerful than any external influences in shaping the way in which
Hasmonean rulers could present themselves.

---

[14] 1988: 142.

External influence

To say this is not to deny the force of external political influence on the accumulation of Hasmonean power. Arguably, it is precisely when a native ruler is legitimized by a suzerain power, that it becomes particularly desirable for him to make his own authority palatable by stating it in supposedly authentic local terms. This may already have been the case under the high priest Simon II. For even if the Seleucid 'charter' for Jerusalem which survives in Josephus mentions only the Jewish *gerousia*, Simon will have been a key figure in the negotiations with Antiochus III, after the victory at Panion in 200 B.C. and the Seleucid acquisition of Palestine.[15] Yet Simon's image in Ben Sira was that of a figure enveloped in sanctity, a supreme minister of the cult.

It is customary to identify the prominent individual of this depiction with Simon the Just, the first sage in the traditional chain of teachers which begins with Moses and the exponent of a pithy résumé of Judaism (*m.Avoth* 1.2). Thus Bickerman can conclude that Rabbinic tradition likewise remembered Ben Sira's high priest as a religious mentor rather than a mediator. It is worth noting, however, that Josephus ascribes the epithet 'Just' unequivocally and exclusively to Simon I, grandfather of Simon II (*AJ* XII 43), and therefore the identification has had its critics.[16]

When it comes to the first phase of Hasmonean rule, based on the high priesthood but not yet kingship, the picture clarifies and it becomes possible to see how external authorization came together with internal validation; this is both because public activity intensifies greatly as Judaea grows, and (not unconnected) because there is now detailed evidence. Although Hasmonean power in Judaea emerged out of revolt, the authority of successive members of the family had as much to do with grants and privileges from rival Seleucids as it did with any popular mandate. New definitions of the leader's position were constantly generated. Although these were external—in two senses—it would be a mistake to belittle their internal political consequences.

---

[15] Hengel *Judaism*: 271.
[16] Herford 1925: 20.

Our ability to reconstruct at least a part of this story is due in the first instance to the interest in diplomatic dealings and their outcome of the author of 1 Maccabees: not only does he detail titles and honours, but he even notices accoutrements, such as Antiochus VI's gift of gold plate and his permission to Jonathan to drink from a gold cup and to wear purple with a gold clasp (11:58). This anonymous author supplies us, in fact, with some of the best information we have anywhere on Seleucid court titulature;[17] and the blend between such interests and his militantly religious outlook is an important key to Hasmonean ideology, as we shall shortly see. By contrast, the account in Josephus on which we depend for the period after the accession of John Hyrcanus in 134 is more concerned with military matters or court crises, and constitutional information is scanty.

As early as c. 155 B.C., Jonathan, the youngest brother of Judas Maccabaeus, is found 'judging the people' at Michmash[18] was allowed to raise an army by Demetrius I. After Jonathan had managed to occupy most of Jerusalem, Demetrius' rival, Alexander Balas made the non-Aaronite Maccabee high priest, as it were outbidding Demetrius. After Demetrius' death, the title meridarch and the status of a First Friend to the king were added. The young Antiochus VI had in his turn to buy support, and he, as well as renewing Jonathan's high priesthood, made his brother Simon στρατηγός of the coast and, similarly, First Friend.

Jonathan died by the treachery of the pretender Tryphon, and with Simon's high priesthood and rule, comes a display of Judaean autonomy. Though the Seleucid claims did not disappear for more than another decade, Simon's symbolic statements of 142 B.C. are heavily stressed in 1 Maccabees—a history which will have been written, it should be noted, under John Hyrcanus, Simon's son, and which probably drew on the memoirs of Hyrcanus, fulsomely advertised in the text (1 Macc. 16:23–24). Demetrius II, in the aftermath of his conflict with Tryphon, apparently held out to Simon remission from tribute and some tax relief, together with the offer of peace. While it is not clear whether a grant from above lay behind each of Simon's subsequent advancements, we may presume that permission was required for them, and their character is visibly influenced by the prevalent Hellenistic formulae. Moreover, we find

---

[17] Bickerman 1938: 32–44.
[18] Bickerman 1933 = 1980: 136–137.

the freedom of Jerusalem and the various remissions endorsed in a letter written by Antiochus VII after the imprisonment of Demetrius, in 140 B.C. or thereabouts.

The right to coin is certainly a specific award, granted by Antiochus in the same letter. No coins of Simon are known, so it is improbable that the right was ever exercised.[19] A new chronological era was established by Simon, and this time we are simply told that 'the people began to write on their records and contracts, in the first year of Simon, the great high priest, στρατηγός and leader of the Jews' (1 Macc. 13:41–42). This era, it should be said, has left no more trace in the record than the right to coin. Also in 140, the assembled people declared Simon high priest, commander and ethnarch in perpetuity. The title of ethnarch sounds like one conferred by a suzerain and the author may well have chosen here not to mention that fact, so as not to detract from the aura of a great historic moment. Instead, a portentous note is struck with the significant phrase, 'for ever, until a trustworthy prophet shall arise', which would be an odd way of expressing a limitation on Simon's rule,[20] and may even be meant to hint at the establishment of a dynasty. In any case, following the international style, the declaration was set in bronze, and displayed in the Temple precinct, as well, it seems, as on Mount Zion,[21] with copies in the Temple treasury (1 Macc. 14:48–49). The text made explicit mention of Simon's purple robe and gold clasp.

With Hyrcanus, the high priestly title remained the basis of power, having been transmitted by an apparently automatic dynastic succession. Antiochus VII's withdrawal from his siege of Jerusalem in 134 B.C. had finally left the Jewish ruler in control.[22] Under Hyrcanus, a bronze coinage almost certainly went into production.[23]

It is nevertheless unclear whether internal caution alone prevented Hyrcanus from calling himself king: it may well be that so big a step still required Seleucid approval. Josephus certainly regards it as

---

[19] Tcherikover 1959: 250.

[20] As argued by Sievers 1990: 127.

[21] Unless the words of 1 Macc. 14:26 are to be taken as metaphor rather than as referring to a separate stele.

[22] See Rajak 1981 = Ch. 5 in this volume.

[23] The dating of the Johanan coinage to Hyrcanus II becomes less attractive as new material comes to light: Rappaport 1976; Barag & Qedar 1980; Grabbe 1992: 242–245.

a major landmark in post-exilic history when finally, in 104 B.C., the diadem is adopted by Aristobulus, Hyrcanus' son and short-lived successor (*AJ* XIII 301). Interestingly, the technical phrase, διάδημα πρῶτος περιτίθεται is used here by the historian.

Alexander Jannaeus, one of the less prominent of Aristobulus' brothers, is said to have had his succession arranged by Aristobulus' widow Salome (Salina) Alexandra (*AJ* XII 320), whom he later married. He continued as both king and high priest, to be succeeded in his turn by the redoubtable Salome, again a widow, now ruling in her own right. This female involvement in the transmission of power is generally viewed as yet another instance of Hellenistic influence, but close precedents are lacking. Ptolemaic example may perhaps be invoked, and such an explanation gains support from the repeated appearance of Ptolemaic troops in Palestine at this time, accompanied by Jewish contingents, and led by a queen, Cleopatra III.[24]

Hellenism?

Thus, both in its early days, as a Seleucid creation, and in its more or less independent phase, Hasmonean government adopted current forms. Moreover, the rulers operated with increasing adroitness (though with a high level of risk) on the near eastern political stage and beyond—in the senate at Rome;[25] they clearly had close relations with some of their peers abroad; one might reasonably call them cosmopolitan.

Whether such growing sophistication should be understood as representing an increasing hellenization is quite another matter. It is true that the Seleucid monarchy could be perceived as Greek from the vantage point of Judaea. This is presumably what lies behind Aristobulus' self-styling as *philhellenos* (*AJ* XIII 318—if that is the correct understanding of Josephus' words).

And this is what had made it possible for 'hellenism', a concept whose very first appearance on the stage of history is, notoriously, in 2 Maccabees (4:13; Hyldahl 1990: 193), to become the great political catchword of the crisis of the late 160's and to imply that they were compromised by involvement with the ruling power. To den-

[24] Sievers 1989: 134–135.
[25] Giovannini & Müller 1971.

igrate the opposition in the civil troubles, you accused them of un-Jewish practices, of which intermarriage was the nadir. And you used their Greek names. A construct of the Greek way of life was encapsulated in the well-known caricature which has the young men of Jerusalem dashing off to the gymnasium of their new polis if that is what it was), fresh from successful plastic surgery, sporting nothing but the πέτασος (2 Macc. 4:12; cf. 1 Macc. 1:15). My version is scarcely an exaggeration. Certain practices, then, were symbolic of alien ways[26] and were convenient propaganda: the term ἀλλοφυλισμός is deployed alongside ἑλληνισμός, and perhaps scholars would have been spared a lot of trouble if the former had been the term to survive, rather than the latter. It has been aptly pointed out that we never hear what the 'hellenizers' had to say for themselves and we do not know how Jason or Menelaus would have criticized their opponents.[27]

It is reasonable to assume that the polarity dates from the period of crisis itself. Then, by the time of 1 Maccabees, somewhere in the late second century, the opposition were no longer 'hellenists', but were termed, for the author's purposes, the ἄνομοι, the impious, a term which appears already in the poem of praise for Judas the warrior (1 Macc. 3:3–9). The development may well be more than a question of style: hellenism was probably no longer an issue with political capital. And there is no reason for us to suppose that developments in Hasmonean rule were constantly measured, by friend or foe, in terms of Greekness. On the contrary, with a better understanding of Seleucid history, we now see that a reassertion of what can be called native tradition was a regular part of government. This was the Seleucids' own technique, and probably that of the Achaemenids before them.[28]

Archaism

A recent discussion by Seth Schwartz[29] relies, in effect, on the old dichotomy, to suggest that the militant and indiscriminately anti-Gentile spirit of 1 Maccabees fits ill with the worldly way in which

---

[26] Rajak 1990: 261–266 = Ch. 4: 61–67; Grabbe 1992: 163–164.
[27] Grabbe 1992: 256–258.
[28] Briant 1990; Sherwin-White & Kuhrt 1993.
[29] 1991.

the Hasmoneans dealt with other peoples, and that the Hasmonean wars were a far cry from the Deuteronomic values on which 1 Maccabees is predicated. He therefore calls into question the commonly accepted view of that narrative as reflecting a Hasmonean voice. Schwartz's solutions are an early date and a 'conservative', non-Hasmonean provenance for 1 Maccabees.

The dichotomy is, however, a false one. Schwartz delineates well the traditionalist themes in 1 Maccabees. He pinpoints successfully, if with some overstatement, the transformation whereby Judaea came to be 'governed by a priest-king whose entourage consisted of a coalition of wealthy Palestinians from all sorts of ethnic and religious backgrounds' (p. 17). He rightly concludes that 'Judaism itself must have changed in comparably radical ways.' But that is precisely why the ideology of 1 Maccabees fits the pragmatic Hasmoneans. Reinvented tradition was exactly what they needed and what they purveyed. Precisely in this way, approval could be sought for 'a dynasty which relied for its existence on the support of a troop of foreign mercenaries and of a variety of barely judaized Palestinian pagans', as Schwartz describes the Hasmoneans (p. 36). The rhetoric of 1 Maccabees is by no means mere literary 'classicism' and the political purpose sought by Schwartz shines through.

Rediscovered tradition, as we know so well from the age of Augustus at Rome, is generally a patchwork: sometimes the old and important is resuscitated, but equally some minor antique observance may grow into a major new practice or ceremony, or else an outmoded one may be given a wholly new look. At the same time, practice which is wholly out of keeping with the spirit of the age, perhaps embarrassing or incriminating, can perfectly well be consigned to oblivion.

The Hasmonean case might seem different: the Bible was there as precedent; it was certainly not forgotten. Indeed, the composition of the latest books was not a remote event: for Josephus, the biblical period ended with the rise of Alexander.[30] And we know that all the books were read in the Second Temple period, because fragments of every one except Esther have been found at Qumran. Yet, at the same time, the multifarious recollections of the first Temple both biblical and probably from oral tradition were employed selectively

---

[30] Leiman 1989: 54.

and creatively, in varied religious and political contexts. Adaptation was unavoidable. We have seen that, on the role of the king, at Qumran the texts were read in a particular way; the Hasmoneans, we may divine, had a different reading, yet still a Bible-based one.

We are now in a position to define more closely the Hasmonean process of creative rediscovery. A positive evaluation of the institution of a Jewish kingship was the background, and to this I can find only one possible exception. In the preamble to Judas' treaty with the Roman senate in 1 Maccabees, comes the famous account of the Romans as seen from Judaea—their military achievements and their formidable alliances. They appoint kings and they depose kings; 'yet for all this, not one of them made any claim to greatness, by wearing the crown or donning the purple' (1 Macc. 8:16). The collective decisions of the senate are here depicted as an alternative to monarchy; and the annual appointment of a supreme magistrate whose power excites no envy evidently inspires the author's admiration. An easy, but not very persuasive, explanation of these unexpected opinions would be to associate the passage with a crisis in the history of the Hasmonean regime: Goldstein, relying on the literary evidence, mainly from Josephus, for opposition to Jannaeus, as well as on a literal interpretation of overstruck coin issues of Alexander Jannaeus, argues that this monarch for a time abandoned the title of king.[31] To make sense of the 1 Maccabees passage, however, it is perhaps more constructive to consider its internal nuances. The Romans are depicted as unique, and their peculiar traits are not held out as a possible pattern for others. Kingship is implied to be the norm in the known world. The Romans avoid the trappings of monarchy and their senate meets daily; but even they depend on the acceptance of an absolute, if temporary, consular authority. The risks inherent in kingship, in visibly and permanently elevating a single individual, are what they avoid with notable success. Readers would be aware that a proper Jewish ruler was restricted in rather different ways, but to the same end.

By contrast, 2 Maccabees, which is generally less enthusiastic for the Hasmonean family, though more for the Temple,[32] yields an unqualified accolade for kingship. This is mentioned among the gifts for which Israel must be grateful, in the curious letter concerning

---

[31] 1976: 355–356.
[32] Doran 1981; van Henten 1989.

the purification of the Temple supposedly sent by Judas to the Jews in Egypt, and cited as the second of the two 'festal letters' with which 2 Maccabees opens (2 Macc. 2:16–17). The obvious falsity of the attribution to Judas[33] does not diminish from the interest of the demand, composed under his successors, that the festival of 25 Kislev be celebrated because:

> God has saved his whole people and granted to all of us the holy land, the kingship, the priesthood, and the consecration [or—the holy temple: τὴν κληρονομίαν ... πᾶσιν καὶ τὸ βασίλειον καὶ τὸ ἱεράτευμα καὶ τὸν ἁγιασμόν], as he promised by law; and in him we have confidence that he will soon be merciful to us and gather us from every part of the world to the holy temple.

The statement is direct and unequivocal, scarcely necessitating a reading such as that of Habicht,[34] who takes the passage to refer not to a king, but to Israel as God's kings, priests and holy people, echoing Exodus 19:6, 'for the whole earth is mine, and you will be a kingdom of priests [in the Septuagint, 'a kingly priesthood'] and a holy people'. In fact, in spite of verbal reminiscences,[35] the two passages are different in substance: Maccabees speaks not about the consecration of the people of Israel but about their rewards, not about γῆ (ha-aretz) in the sense of 'the whole world', but, patently, about the Holy Land. In any case, the more closely we relate the Maccabees passage to Exodus, the more visible becomes the new emphasis placed on the kingship as a distinct phenomenon in Maccabees. The conclusion is inescapable that we have here a clear expression of divine sanction for a monarchic figure in Israel. This and other divine signs were re-asserted, according to the letter of 2 Maccabees, by God's miraculous protection of the Temple, and especially through the mysterious preservation of Jeremiah's concealed altar fire.

In retrospect, the later Hasmoneans were honoured as both kings and high priests, as the historian Josephus tells us in expatiating upon his own ancestry (Josephus, *Vita* 2). A little earlier, Philo ascribed to the Herodian Agrippa I the sentiment that the high priesthood was far superior 'for the office of one was to worship God, of the other to have charge of men' and the claim that his Hasmonean

---

[33] Bickerman 1933 = 1980: 136–137.
[34] Habicht 1976: n. *ad loc.*
[35] So Goldstein 1983: 188.

forebears had valued their high priesthood above their monarchic title (*Embassy to Gaius* 278); but this is part of a passionate defence of the Temple, and even here the kingship receives ample attention.

Ceremonial

Ben Sira's King David was, as we saw, praised for instituting the celebration of the festivals, while Simon the high priest was flatteringly depicted in the act of ministering at the sacred altar. The Temple cult and the pilgrim festivals would naturally be highlighted by the Hasmoneans, at least as much as ceremonies centred on their own persons. Having occupied the high priesthood, they had precluded themselves from the central ritual of the Jewish kings, the anointment by the high priest with sacred oil.

No sustained account of a Hasmonean public event survives, but a number of highly suggestive passages in our sources make it possible to imagine something of what the rulers made of their great occasions. Ceremonies were designed not only to enhance the high priestly or royal dignity, but, strikingly, also to express the all-important connection with the Judaean past and, in effect, to touch the wellspring of religious consciousness.

We have observed that two important public displays in Jerusalem were associated with the confirmation of Simon's powers, around the year 140. The expulsion of the enemy garrison from the Akra fort (either west or south-east of the Temple Mount) was marked by a ceremony of reoccupation and cleansing reminiscent of the rededication of the altar by Judas, complete with the chanting of praise and with song, with the music of lutes, cymbals and zithers, and also, it would appear, with the waving of palm branches (1 Macc. 13:51–52). The latter are rendered by the obscure Greek word βάϊον, and, if this refers to palm branches, there may be a reference here to the all-important festival of Tabernacles, of which more below. In very similar fashion, the conquest and purification of Gezer (Gazara) had involved a formal entry 'with songs of thanksgiving and praise' (1 Macc. 13:48).

The procedure for the official appointment of Simon to his full powers, in the third year of his high priesthood, is given as quotation from the text inscribed on the bronze tablets (1 Macc. 14:27–28), and is omitted in Josephus' version of 1 Maccabees. The focus might be called constitutional, and it seems that this was a ceremony of a more political character. This time the role of the assembled people is stressed, in keeping with biblical patterns for appointing a king, and at the end of the document (14:46) their unanimity is paraded. Also involved are the priests and the Jerusalem γερουσία.

The ideology of popular participation was clearly a consistent theme of Hasmonean government, publicized in the featuring on coinage, from John Hyrcanus onwards, of the *hever* of the Jews. This troublesome term may refer to a political council, or else it may signify, simply, the Jewish δῆμος. Either way, participation in rule is implied. Some Yehohanan coins are inscribed 'Yehohanan the high priest and the council of the Jews', while another group, closer in spirit to the investiture decree of Hyrcanus' father Simon, has 'Yehohanan the high priest, head of the *hever* of the Jews'.[36]

It is scarcely surprising that there is no reflection on the coinage of Hyrcanus of a further attribute sometimes associated with him, and which may at times have been the basis of his appeal to the people, the gift of prophecy. Josephus describes him as unique in uniting in his person the three attributes of secular command, high priesthood and prophecy (*AJ* XIII 300). Both Josephus and Talmudic tradition record him as hearing God's voice directly at the moment of his sons' victory in Samaria, and while he was burning incense alone in the Temple.[37]

In the letter ascribed to Judas (1:18) and similarly in the preceding letter which opens 2 Maccabees (1:9), the feast of the dedication (Hanukkah) was called a feast of Tabernacles. We can only speculate as to exactly what that meant,[38] but there is no reason to take the name as anti-Hasmonean.[39] On the contrary, I would suggest that the Hasmoneans annexed Tabernacles, taking care to associate it with their personal rule. This pilgrim feast had already under the monarchy been known as '*the* festival' *tout court*; and it was the season of Solomon's dedication of the Temple (1 Kings 8; 2 Chron. 5:3). The reforms of Ezra had enhanced its symbolic value (Nehemiah 8:13–18). Thus, for Zechariah (14:16), a great Tabernacles celebra-

---

[36] Meshorer 1982: 47–48; Rajak 1994: 287.

[37] On these traditions, see Thoma 1994, who suggests that the possession of three attributes made Hyrcanus a Messiah figure. In any event, the prophetic role puts him, as a prophet after the age when prophecy was deemed to have ceased, strikingly in direct line with biblical tradition.

[38] Doran 1981: 4–6.

[39] So Goldstein 1976: 282.

tion would mark the end of time. At Tabernacles, God's kingship was glorified.

The Tabernacles motif runs through the dynasty's history, in both good times and bad, and the ruler's appearance in Jerusalem on this occasion was a moment of great political sensitivity. Four years after the death of Judas, Jonathan donned the high priest's vestments at Tabernacles; this scene is apparently intended as his installation ceremony (1 Macc 10:21; *AJ* XIII 46). A turning point in the reign of Jannaeus occurred when he was pelted with the ritual citrons by hostile bystanders, while performing the festival sacrifice at the altar (*AJ* XIII 372). Numerous executions ensued, after the crowd declared that his descent from a slavewoman made his high priesthood illegitimate. In a less well-known episode which took place some twenty years earlier, Antigonus, the brother of King Aristobulus, was denounced and killed on account of suspicions incurred at the same season: the ostentatious self-assertion with which he and his hoplites went up to the Temple for the sacrifice, bloody from battle, laid Antigonus open to destruction by his opponents. We may surmise that he had sought to transform the ritual of the pilgrim festival into a personal victory celebration.

Militarism and judaization

The fatal display of power mounted by Antigonus, while readily criticized, was probably not unfamiliar. An emphasis on military achievement was the hallmark of the Hasmonean dynasty from its earliest days; and the strong biblical antecedents to this ideology meant that its cultivation was always more than just the making of a virtue out of necessity. Justification lay in the doctrine that a king's victories were the victories of the Lord of hosts,[40] both won by divine might and a mark of divine approval. The clearest statement is in Psalm 21:

> The king rejoices in thy might, O Lord
> well may he exult in thy victory,
> for thou hast given him his heart's desire
> and hast not refused him what he has asked (Ps. 21:1–2).

The earlier Hasmoneans had a family tomb at Modi'in, their ancestral village, in the Judaean hills west of Jerusalem. This was reconstructed

---

[40] Brettler 1989: 57–68.

by Simon and is described in association with Jonathan's prolonged obsequies (1 Macc. 13:25–30). A tall monument of polished stone bore seven pyramids, apparently for the four dead brothers and their parents. On the pyramids were panoplies, and, beside these, carved ships. The symbolism could not have been plainer. Sadly, no funeral is described.

Simon's *raison d'être* as successor to his brother Jonathan was, quite simply, to continue the fight: 'fight our war and we will do whatever you tell us' (1 Macc. 13:9–10). His official position as high priest would scarcely in the past have entailed such a commitment. But a remarkable new conception of a warrior high priesthood seems to have emerged, of which traces have been spotted in two Pseudepigrapha of this period, *Jubilees* and the *Testament of Levi*.[41]

Peace and prosperity won by the sword were the finest of possessions, portrayed with biblical resonance in the evocation of Simon's age of plenty, when 'each man sat under his own vine and under his own fig tree. The enemies left the land and the enemy kings were crushed in those days' (1 Macc. 14:12–13). Though not a king, Simon had equalled David and Solomon combined. There is no sense of strain in the juxtaposition of this image with lavish praise for Simon's protection of the poor, echoing, this time, the sentiment of Psalm 72, where the ruler who is able to 'deal out justice to the poor and suffering' is one in front of whom 'all kings shall pay . . . homage and all nations shall serve'. Simon's devotion to the law, and his glorification of the Temple (ἐδόξασεν) are also singled out, as we might expect.

The annals of Simon's son and successor, John, are summarized at the conclusion of 1 Maccabees in decidedly martial terms, without even the variety of accomplishment credited to Simon: 'the rest of the story of John, his wars and the deeds of valour he performed, the walls he built, and his exploits, are written in the book of the days of his high priesthood' (16:23–24).

The typology inherent in such characterizations is, I would argue, more than a literary matter. In relation to the Hasmonean wars of conquest, image was certainly not far removed from reality. The defensive campaigns of Judas and Jonathan soon shaded into wars of expansion. The net result would be a Jewish state rivalled in its

---

[41] Arenhoevel 1967: 46–47.

dimensions only by that of David.[42] How far considerations beyond
the immediate ones of strategy and tactics went into the design of
those campaigns is a subject which would repay separate study.[43]

One prominent and intriguing aspect of the Hasmonean conquests,
however, has attracted interest recently and is relevant here. This is
the judaization by circumcision of the Ituraeans and Idumaeans,
neighbouring Semitic peoples; the conversions are normally associated
with and discussed alongside the resettlement by Alexander Jannaeus
of conquered 'Greek' cities, notably Gazara and Pella, with Jewish
inhabitants.[44] Ample disgust at idolatry, and intense hostility to 'the
peoples round about' is voiced in 1 Maccabees; but the precise motivation of these acts of judaization is still hard to discern. Shaye
Cohen acutely observed that real biblical precedent was lacking;[45]
the closest is the story of the rape of Dinah and its aftermath, but
there the conclusion is distinctly different. Cohen therefore diagnosed
a radical innovation in policy.

Our new understanding of Hasmonean traditionalism suggests
that this otherwise attractive analysis requires refinement. Like many
Hasmonean innovations, this one is pervaded by archaism. The
absence of exact biblical precedent was no bar to a claim of biblical
authority. These measures were, it may be suggested, a new way of
re-invigorating an old and fundamental conception, that of the sanctity of the Land.

W.D. Davies noticed that there was no direct appeal to the conception of the Land of Israel in Maccabean propaganda.[46] I would
concur with his judgement that a lack of explicit statement does not
mean a lack of belief: 'they do not refer to the Land: they silently
assume its importance and their right to it.' Threats to Torah or to
Temple were understood as threats to their true location in Zion.
It is precisely this missing articulation which, it might be suggested,
was supplied in the later Hasmonean generations, under Hyrcanus,
Aristobulus and Jannaeus, by the notion of expelling the carriers of
idolatrous contamination from newly acquired territory and by the

---

[42] Schwartz 1991: 16–18; Rajak 1994.
[43] For the military aspect, see Shatzman 1991.
[44] The degree of destruction involved remains a matter of debate: Kasher 1988;
1990; Cohen 1990; Rajak 1990 = Ch. 4; Schwartz 1991: 19–21; Feldman 1993:
324–326.
[45] 1990: 217–218.
[46] 1982: 61–68.

circumcision of indigenous peoples. Here indeed was the embodiment
of the theology of purifying the Land, evolving precisely at the stage
where mere defence was scarcely any longer an adequate ideological basis: another old idea in a new guise. Close analysis of the evidence suggests that in practice the implementation of the idea was
far from systematic or thorough.[47]

Unfortunately, Josephus' narrative for the crucial years reveals far
less than do the books of the Maccabees about the language of the
regime and the internal dynamics of events; Josephus simply fails to
offer the kind of information which could confirm or refute our interpretation. This has to rest on putting together earlier ideology with
later action. A recent reading of Judith, *Jubilees* and the *Testaments
of the Twelve Patriarchs*, together with fragments of Jewish chroniclers
in Greek,[48] has also detected a growing preoccupation in the rewritten Bible with territorial expansion as a political goal; but even these
allusive texts cannot place before us the rationale of the judaizers.

Conclusion

The recovery of Hasmonean ideology, possible only to a limited
extent, depends principally on the interpretation of complex literary
material. Of the evidence yielded by archaeology, coinage has the
most to contribute. But even 1 Maccabees, on which we are greatly
dependent, is not an official history, even if, as we have seen, the
old view of the author as a supporter of the dynasty still has much
to recommend it.

But we do know enough to say that the rediscovery, or invention
of native tradition is, at any rate, a central preoccupation, pervad-
ing the Hasmonean high priesthood and kingship. This process is a
key to interpreting the mentality and the image of these rulers. Some
light might also be shed on the activities of other native rulers, where
the evidence is considerably poorer still, and where the native culture is less tangible. Thus the prominence of this aspect of Hasmonean
activity renders the study of their government a fruitful and important one, not just in a conventional narrative of events, but in any
modern, post-colonial Seleucid history. Finally, it is worth observing

---

[47] Rajak 1990: 271–277 = Ch. 4 in this volume.
[48] Mendels 1990.

that such a line of approach brings with it the great advantage of setting an agenda which does not derive from the over-discussed problematic of Hellenization.

BIBLIOGRAPHY

Arenhoevel, D. 1967. *Die Theokratie nach dem 1. und 2. Makkabäerbuch.* Walberger Studien, Theologische Reihe 3. Mainz.

Barag, D. & Qedar, Sh. 1980. 'The Beginning of Hasmonean Coinage', *IsrNumJ* 4:8–21.

Bi(c)kerman, E.J. 1938. *Institutions des Séleucides.* Paris.

—— 1988. *The Jews in the Greek Age.* Cambridge, Mass.

—— 1933. 'Ein jüdische Festbrief vom Jahre 124 v. Chr. (II Macc. 1,1–9)', *ZNW* 32:233–254 = *Studies in Jewish and Christian History* II. Leiden 1980, 136–158.

Brettler, M.Z. 1989. *God is King. Understanding the Israelite Metaphor.* JSOT Suppl. 79. Sheffield.

Briant, P. 1990. 'The Seleucid Kingdom, the Achaemenid Empire and the History of the Near East in the First Millennium B.C.', in P. Bilde, T. Engberg-Pedersen, L. Hannestad & J. Zahle (eds), *Religion and Religious Practice in the Seleucid Kingdom.* Studies in Hellenistic Civilization 1. Aarhus, 40–65.

Cohen, S. 1990. 'Religion, Ethnicity and "Hellenism" in the Emergence of Jewish Identity in Maccabaean Palestine, in P. Bilde et al. (eds), *Religion and Religious Practice in the Seleucid Kingdom.* Studies in Hellenistic Civilization 1. Aarhus, 204–223.

Davies, W.D. 1982. *The Territorial Dimension of Judaism,* 2nd edn. Berkeley.

Doran, R. 1981. *Temple Propaganda: the Purpose and Character of II Maccabees.* CBQ Monograph Series 12. Washington, D.C.

Feldman, L.H. 1993. *Jew and Gentile in the Ancient World.* Princeton, N.J.

Giovannini, A. & Müller, H. 1971. 'Die Beziehungen zwischen Rom und die Juden im 2. Jh. v. Chr.', *MusHelv* 28:156–171.

Goldstein, J.A. 1976. *I Maccabees. A New Translation with Introduction and Commentary.* Anchor Bible 41. Garden City, New York.

—— 1983. *II Maccabees. A New Translation with Introduction and Commentary.* Anchor Bible 41A. Garden City, New York.

Grabbe, L.L. 1992. *Judaism from Cyrus to Hadrian.* Minneapolis.

Habicht, C. 1976. *2 Makkabäerbuch.* Jüdische Schriften aus hellenistisch-römischer Zeit 1.3. Gütersloh.

Hengel, M., Charlesworth, J.H. & Mendels, D. 1986. 'The Polemical Character of "On Kingship" in the Temple Scroll: An Attempt at Dating 11QTemple', *JJS* 37: 18–38.

Herford, R.T. 1925. *The Ethics of the Talmud. Sayings of the Fathers. Pirke Aboth.* London = New York 1962.

Hyldahl, N. 1990. 'The Maccabaean rebellion and the question of "Hellenization"', in P. Bilde, T. Engberg-Pedersen, L. Hannestad & J. Zahle (eds), *Religion and Religious Practice in the Seleucid Kingdom.* Studies in Hellenistic Civilization 1. Aarhus, 188–203.

Kasher, A. 1988. *Jews, Idumaeans and Ancient Arabs.* Texte und Studien zum antiken Judentum 18. Tübingen.

—— 1990. *Jews and Hellenistic Cities in Eretz-Israel. C.E.* Texte und Studien zum antiken Judentum 21. Tübingen.

Leiman, S.Z. 1989. 'Josephus and the Canon of the Bible', in L.H. Feldman & G. Hata (eds), *Josephus, the Bible and History.* Detroit, 50–58.

Liver, J. 1962. 'King, Kingship', in *Encyclopedia Miqrait (Encyclopedia Biblica)* [Hebrew], IV. Jerusalem, 1085–1111.

Maier, J. 1985. *The Temple Scroll: An Introduction, Translation and Commentary.* JSOT Supplement 34. Sheffield.

Mendels, D. 1979. '"On Kingship" in the "Temple Scroll" and the Ideological *Vorlage* of the Seven Banquets in the "Letter of Aristeas to Philocrates"', *Aegyptus* 56:127–136.

—— 1990. *The Land of Israel as a Political Concept in Hasmonean Literature.* Texte und Studien zum antiken Judentum 15. Tübingen.

Meshorer, Y. 1982. *Ancient Jewish Coinage* I–II. New York.

Momigliano, A. 1975. *Alien Wisdom: The Limits of Hellenization.* Cambridge.

Qimron, E. & Strugnell, J. 1994. *Miqsat Ma'asé Ha-Torah. DJD X. Qumran Cave 4, V.* Oxford.

Rajak, T. 1981. 'Roman Intervention in a Seleucid Siege?', *GRBS* 22:65–81 = Ch. 5 in this volume.

—— 1990. 'The Hasmoneans and the Uses of Hellenism', in P.R. Davies (ed.), *A tribute to Geza Vermes.* JSOT Supplement 100. Sheffield, 261–280 = Ch. 4 in this volume.

—— 1994. 'Judaea under Hasmonean Rule', in *Cambridge Ancient History*, IX, 2nd edn. Cambridge, 274–309.

Rappaport, U. 1976. 'The Emergence of the Hasmonean Coinage', *Association of Jewish Studies Review* 1:171–186.

Schwartz, S. 1991. 'Israel and the Nations Roundabout: I Maccabees and the Hasmonean Expansion', *JJS* 42.16–38.

Shatzman, I. 1991. *The Armies of the Hasmoneans and Herod.* Tübingen.

Sherwin-White, S. & Kuhrt, A. 1993. *From Samarkhand to Sardis: A New Approach to the Seleucid Empire.* Hellenistic Culture and Society 13. London.

Sievers, J. 1990. *The Hasmoneans and their Supporters. From Mattathias to the Death of John Hyrcanus.* South Florida Studies in the History of Judaism 6. Atlanta, Georgia.

Tcherikover, V. *Hellenistic Civilization and the Jews.* Philadelphia/Jerusalem.

Thoma, C. 1994. 'John Hyrcanus as Seen by Josephus', in F. Parente & J. Sievers (eds), *Josephus and the History of the Greco-Roman Period. Essays in memory of Morton Smith.* Studia Post-Biblica 41. Leiden, 127–140.

van Henten, J.W. 1989. 'Das jüdisch Selbstverständis in den ältesten Martyrien', in Henten, J.W. van (ed.), *Die Entstehung der jüdischen Martyrologie.* Leiden.

Yadin, Y. 1983. *The Temple Scroll*, I–III. Jerusalem.

—— 1985. *The Temple Scroll: The Hidden Law of the Dead Sea Sect.* London.

CHAPTER FOUR

THE HASMONEANS AND THE USES OF HELLENISM

1. *Concepts*

The meeting between Judaism and Hellenism is one of the most dis-cussed relationships in cultural history. From the later nineteenth century on this has been a polarity which has assumed a special importance for scholars, both Jewish and non-Jewish, and for obvi-ous reasons.[1] It has served both as a heuristic tool and as a target of enquiry in itself. On the one hand, certain Jewish interpreters applauded Jewish responsiveness to the forces of supposed Hellenic enlightenment, order and rationality, and perhaps even chose to emphasize areas of integration, if not assimilation, between the two cultures. On the other hand, for any historian whose education was influenced by the European classical tradition, there was an incli-nation to see the spread of Greek culture as the central historical phenomenon of the era of Alexander and his successors and to give it, in the recent words of Kuhrt and Sherwin-White,[2] 'overriding significance'. A Christian perspective could lend its own concern with the kinds of Judaism which were penetrated with Hellenism.

Christianity, after, all *was* in some sense a cross between the two cultures. Furthermore, the dichotomy was transferred at an early stage to analyses of Christianity itself with a contrast between a 'primitive' Palestinian Christianity and a 'Hellenistic' variety serving, at times, as a favourite tool of research for critics of the stature of Bultmann.

For all that, the Judaism-Hellenism distinction is not a modern invention. It is important to appreciate that there were moments when it loomed large in the consciousness of the actors in the ancient period itself. The very concept of Hellenism, and the related one of Hellenization are, in fact, first and best attested in the eastern Mediterranean precisely in the context of Jewish thought; and it may

---

[1] For some significant works centering on this dichotomy, see Heinemann 1932; Liebermann 1962; Hengel *Judaism*; Will & Orrieux 1986; and the many studies by Louis Feldman of Biblical figures in Josephus' *Antiquities*.
[2] Kuhrt & Sherwin-White 1988.

even be the case that the Jews of the time were responsible for forming and transmitting the perception that the Greek culture with which they met was a force capable of encroaching upon their own values, that there was a major influence there, to be either embraced or rejected. Historically, this seems probable; and it is also what the surviving verbal evidence suggests.

For the very word ἑλληνισμός first appears in the second book of Maccabees (4:13). There, in the expression ἀκμὴ τοῦ ἑλληνισμοῦ, 'a climax of Hellenism', it refers to the 'package' of Greek customs allegedly introduced into Jerusalem by the high priest Jason after he had bribed his way into the high priesthood. A Greek political entity, if not an actual *polis*, had been set up within Jerusalem. The symbols of the Greek life style that belong with it are, in this highly rhetorical chapter, made to centre upon athletic pursuits: the gymnasium with its associated institution for young men, the sports stadium, the wrestling school and the athlete's hat are all singled out for mention. Nudity as such is not alluded to here. We may wonder, in fact, whether any more than one single despised institution need lie behind the entire tirade, rather than a truly comprehensive Hellenization of Jerusalem life on the part of Jason.[3] We may also point out that the Maccabaean cultural crisis developed out of *political* quarrels concerning, in effect, conflicting relationships with the ruling power. These are points worth pondering. But the fact remains, that whatever exactly it was that was brought to Jerusalem, this was immediately seen as standing for a whole culture, and one whose pursuit contravened Jewish Law (2 Macc. 4:12). The expressions τὸν Ἑλλενικὸν χαρακτῆρα (which might be rendered 'the Greek way of life') and τὰς Ἑλληνικὰς δόξας ('the Greek scale of values', perhaps) also figure. 2 Maccabees is a summary, composed before 124 B.C., of a history written close in time to the Maccabaean crisis itself.[4] Its author will be reflecting an ideology not entirely remote from those who participated or from those who observed; and there must therefore have been some who interpreted the events not just as the defence of the Temple, but as a struggle against Jewish Hellenism and against Antiochus IV or his successors as agents of Hellenization.

---

[3] On the 'Hellenistic reform in Jerusalem, see Bickerman 1937; id. 1962: 93–111; Tcherikover 1966: 152–174; Millar 1978; Bringmann 1983.

[4] For a convenient discussion see Collins 2000: 77 ff. and the literature there referred to.

The original history had been written in Greek, by a man known as Jason of Cyrene. Perhaps Jason's origins in the Greek-speaking Diaspora had sharpened his awareness of the boundaries between Jews and Greeks.

At the same time, the rest of Jason's history as reflected in the 2 Maccabees summary, and certainly the first book of Maccabees, with its consciously Biblical idiom, operate with quite other categories. The wars of Judas are against pollution or against the Gentiles. The pro-Seleucid Jews, to be identified with the former Hellenizers, are the 'lawless', ἄνομοι (1 Macc. 9:23, etc.); when they occupy the Akra fortress, they are 'the men in the citadel'. Elsewhere, we do not hear of Greeks or Greek sympathizers. We may guess that the issue of Hellenism as such ceased for the time being to be in the forefront, overshadowed by the military struggle between the Maccabees and their opponents. In later Jewish writings, it surfaces again, as we shall see.

The key text in 2 Maccabees indicates two separate kinds of development. The one which is the most visible on the surface is that upper-class Jews in the period leading up to 165, including (or perhaps especially) members of the high-priestly circles, were attracted by practices typical of Greek cities: they were becoming *Hellenized*. The other, which is probably at the heart of the matter, is that the deliberate adoption of certain such practices were a highly contentious public issue, linked with politics as much as with religion, and able itself to divide society. The latter, conscious process, in which certain features of Greek culture possessed a kind of symbolic significance and carried political implications, will here be called *Hellenism*. This is a narrowing of the familiar usage, originated by J.G. Droysen, where 'Hellenism' refers generally to Greek civilization after Alexander the Great, as a distinctive culture, in all its aspects.[5]

2. *Hellenization*

The coming together of ancient statement with modern prejudice has highlighted Hellenization, so that it has loomed large in interpretations of post-Biblical Judaism. One major debate has focussed, on the one hand, on the assertion that Palestinian Judaism was heavily

---

[5] Droysen 1836. See Momigliano 1970 = 1975; also in 1977: 307–324.

penetrated with Greek culture from an early date (as in Martin Hengel's great work), on the other, on the denial that the totality of apparent influence has any deep significance, given the continuing separation and distinctiveness of Judaism. In this debate, and equally in analyses of other periods, situations or authors, the Jewish-Greek polarity has been taken for granted.[6]

It is hard to see how such debates can ever be concluded. No one would wish to deny the steady Hellenization of the material culture of Palestine, both Jewish and non-Jewish, during the whole of the period. Most would agree that even a sealed-off environment like Qumran was not immune. Such Hellenization is visible in architecture and art, in everyday uses of the Greek language and in some aspects of political behaviour. When it comes to the higher realms of thought and belief, we have to face far greater uncertainty about the meaning of apparently parallel developments. But I think that putting the question itself in perspective may be of some assistance. There are immense logical and empirical difficulties in seeking to measure Jewish Hellenization. They can be summed up, perhaps, by saying that there is a task which is logically prior, one whose complications historians are only just beginning to grasp. We need to get some picture of the Greek culture with which we are dealing, that is to say, of the kind of Hellenization that was embraced, or in other cases avoided, by the peoples who lived around and among the Jews. We ought not to rely on rather general and long-unexamined notions about the norms and forms of Greek city life, and to doctrines about the way in which that specially Greek institution, the *polis*, was carried to the far corners of the backward east. Only this enquiry can give any real historical sense to the specific problem of the Hellenization of the Jews, and to the possibility of Jewish impermeability.

The need for a new logic becomes clear when we remember that what we are thinking about, in thinking about Hellenization, was, after all, a two-way process, not just a matter of native cultures being imbued with the Greek one. Admittedly, a leading dynamic in the

---

[6] The deep penetration of Greek culture into Judaism was also stressed by Bickerman. Its imperviousness was stressed, among others, by Wolfson, in his great work on Philo (1947), by F. Millar, by Feldman (see especially 1977), and, for a later period, by M. Goodman and M. Stone. By questioning the dichotomy itself, we alter the terms of at least some of the questions involved.

Mediterranean world (and even beyond), if we are to concentrate on major trends, was the politico-cultural imperialism, first of Alexander and of the Ptolemies and Seleucids, and then of the Romans—for the Romans were also major (probably indeed *the* major) carriers of Greek culture in the east. It is true, too, that the net effect of several centuries of change would eventually be to create, during the high Roman empire, an amazingly uniform elite culture based upon Greek rhetorical and philosophical education and on a revival of the Attic past. It would be foolish to ignore this force for movement towards ever greater Hellenization. It would also be foolish to deny that the high Greek culture had patent charms and attractions (without of course ignoring those of the late oriental civilizations, Judaism included). Nonetheless, in spite of all its pretensions, Greek culture too was constantly changing under the impact of those peoples towards whom it came. Where small groups of true Greek colonists lived in a small unit in an alien world, as they often did in the years after Alexander, there was possibly some chance of their preserving their way of life intact for several generations. But when the *ephebes* in a gymnasium or the citizens of a *polis* were native born, it would be absurd to expect them simply to conform to standard patterns, without modifying those patterns and causing something new to be transmitted.

Therefore, Hellenization can mean several different things: in its full sense, it would be the suppression of a native culture and language and its replacement with a fully or mainly Greek style—something which, I suspect, is rather rare, except over a long period; or it might be the creation of a truly mixed, hybrid form, the much-discussed *Verschmelzung*; or, again, we might see the addition of Greek elements to a persisting culture whose leading features remained visible and relatively constant. The distinctions are most easily grasped in the sphere of architecture. Thus, the well-known tombs in Jerusalem's Kedron Valley, known as the tomb of Zechariah and the tomb of Absalom but in fact belonging probably to priestly families of the first century B.C., are excellent examples of a hybrid style, with their Greek columned porticoes, their prominent pointed roofs, their separate outbuildings or *nefashim*.[7] Their mixed style is related to that of some of the Petra rock-cut tombs, which in itself is a suggestive fact about the evolution of a regional idiom embracing Nabateans as well

---

[7] For a brief study, see Avigad 1975: 17–20.

as Jews. But, of course, the adoption of a hybrid architecture need
not be associated with a comparable fusion in other departments of
life. To judge whether a society at a particular time should overall
be deemed Hellenized in the first, the second or the third sense will
rarely be a simple matter. There is room for argument as to whether
the Jews were closest to the second or the third class, but most scholars would probably hold that their Hellenization was a relatively
superficial matter and that a hybrid culture was not created, thus
putting them in category three.

3. *Hasmonean Hellenism*

My purpose has been to expose the complex conceptual problems
that underlie any discussion of processes of Hellenization, whether
Jewish or otherwise. In various departments of life, a steady influx
of Greek modes and manners will have occurred without much notice
being given to the matter: it need not have been apparent to the
agents that what they were doing or making was, or had once been,
characteristically Greek. By the time customs are taken over, they
may well be emptied of their associations, or even have acquired
new ones. Archaeological material alone can tell us nothing about
such overtones. For these reasons, it may well be more advantageous
for historians, whose concern will, after all, be with the *mechanism* of
cultural interaction, not just with labelling, to fix their attention less
on Hellenization, than on Hellenism, in the sense which I gave to
that term; that is to say, on the *conscious* adoption of Greek ways,
or else its reverse, where there is at least some indication that the
agents see a real significance (one that might be, say, political or
religious) in the Greekness of those customs. The questions that the
historian will then want to ask will be about the factors which promoted Hellenism or anti-Hellenism in particular circumstances, involving explicit pressure from above, commercial requirements, international
contact, intellectual links, or other matters; and about the consequences of different choices.

   The study of ancient history rarely provides us with convenient
answers even to such more narrowly delimited questions. The sources
tend to be lacking just where we most want them. Nonetheless, for
the Hasmonean period, we do have the unusual advantage of Josephus'
detailed narrative, following on from the books of the Maccabees,

or rather, to be precise, overlapping with them. We are doubly fortunate where we can combine this with archaeological, numismatic
or other types of evidence, as we can do to some extent for the later
Hasmonean period, covering the years after the revolutionary wars
of Judas, and extending from 161 to 63 B.C. They are important
years for the expression of Hellenism in Palestine and also of antagonism to Hellenism. It will be helpful first to give some impression
of the period.

The central fact is the rise and fall in Palestine of an independent state, comparable in Jewish history only with the kingdom of
David. This national experience marked the people, through the classical period and far beyond. From the military leadership of Judas
Maccabaeus had emerged, in due course, permanent authority, a
dynastic succession and, eventually, a monarchy. Defensive wars led
to territorial expansion: to the west to occupy most of the cities of
the coast, to the east to the Jordan and even beyond, south into the
whole of Idumaea and north into Samaria and the Galilee. However,
neither internal nor external stability of an enduring kind were
achieved. Geographical factors alone would tend, of course, to make
Palestine vulnerable. And elements from within declared the domination of the Hasmoneans to be unacceptable. The ruling family fell
prey to a war of succession at the time of Pompey the Great's annexation of Syria, and the door was open to Roman intervention. One
of the rival Hasmoneans then remained in control of a reduced
Jewish entity, but one that was not as small as it had been before
this period; and he was made subject to Roman taxation and Roman
administrative arrangements: this was what remained, together with
a divided population and substantial discontents. It would be left to
the Idumaean Herod, in an inventive exploitation of the roles of
eastern client king and Hellenic patron under Augustus, to reconstruct what the Hasmoneans had built, in the spirit of his own day
and age.

These developments did not occur in isolation. Internal forces
combined with external circumstances to make the growth of the
Jewish state possible. The decline in Seleucid power, and then the
collapse of that extended kingdom into continuous dynastic wars,
presented the Hasmoneans first with overlords who were increasingly
distracted and afterwards with opportunities for profitable meddling.
Alliances with Rome, which at this stage may have helped, and certainly did not hinder the Hasmonean expansion were another part

of the external contribution. Judaea was by no means the only small
state in the east to achieve freedom under her own rulers in the late
Hellenistic period, though her growth, with all its consequences, was
particularly spectacular. What needs to be underlined was that the
new state was one whose destiny depended upon the complex and
sometimes chaotic interplay of eastern power-politics, and her rulers
had to be able to deal confidently with a variety of other rulers or
aspirants. In other words, she had become a Hellenistic kingdom. I
need hardly say that no assumptions may be made as to the degree
and type of Hellenization in such a kingdom.[8]

But we can at any rate see that some Greek trappings were appropriate. And the Hasmoneans did not hang back, when it came to
adopting these. They appear to have stepped readily into their parts.
Indeed, one may wonder whether Judas himself had been as stoutly
opposed to all things Hellenized as he is painted. Since he had nailed
his flag to the mast of anti-Hellenism and allied himself with the
rigorous *hasidim*, the other elements in the picture could hardly be
allowed to emerge in the tradition. It is noteworthy that, of our two
accounts of the Maccabaean crisis (not counting Josephus' version
of 1 Maccabees), the one which makes the most of Judas, to the
exclusion not only of his brothers but even of his father Mattathias,
is 2 Maccabees. Unlike 1 Maccabees, the epitome of Jason of Cyrene
which makes up the bulk of the second book (to that epitome are
added two letters), was originally written in Greek, and exploits various dramatic devices characteristic of the so-called 'pathetic' Greek
historiography fashionable at the time. The more 'Hellenized' writer,
therefore, is the one whose hero is Judas.[9] To this perhaps rather
indirect argument might be added the general observation that the
Maccabaean revolt, quite contrary to its image in later popular
mythology, was never a peasant uprising, although it may well, as
Josephus claims, have attracted many ordinary people at an early
stage. Mattathias was addressed by the Syrian representative Apelles
as an important man in his region, and a number of pointers in our
narratives suggest that the family was propertied from the beginning.

---

[8] For types of conscious Hellenism, and also of Hellenization, in differing contexts, see Millar 1983; Hornblower 1982; and, for reflections on Rome, Wallace-
Hadrill 1988.

[9] On the thrust of 1 and 2 Maccabees, see Arenhoevel 1967; Doran 1981.

Almost twenty years after the death of Judas, in 143/2 B.C., his brother Jonathan was killed by the treachery of Tryphon, a claimant to the Seleucid throne. The death seems in a sad way an appropriate one, for Jonathan's leadership of his people had moved away from the military patterns which he had inherited from Judas, to the paths of diplomacy. Jonathan had been accepted the high priesthood from one of the Seleucid rivals, Alexander Balas. Later, in a desperate attempt to outbid another claimant, Demetrius I, that same Alexander had made Jonathan *meridarch* (governor) and one of his First Friends; the latter title had given Jonathan official status at court. Jonathan's body was released and taken by his younger brother Simon for burial in the ancestral town of Modi'in. There Simon built a new family tomb, which served also for his father and mother. That 1 Maccabees stops to describe this monument in detail shows what significance was attributed to it. The grandeur, the power symbolism and the hybrid Greco-Oriental style of the tomb, so reminiscent of those in the Kedron valley mentioned earlier, shows something of the distance the family had already travelled: 'Simon had the body of his brother Jonathan brought to Modi'in, and buried in the town of their fathers [note that 1 Maccabees describes Modi'in as a *polis*!]; and all Israel made a great lamentation and mourned him for many days. Simon built a high monument over the tomb of his father and his brothers, visible at a great distance, faced back and front with polished stone. He erected seven pyramids, those for his father and mother and four brothers arranged in pairs. For the pyramids he contrived an elaborate setting: he surrounded them with great columns surmounted with trophies of armour for a perpetual memorial, and between the trophies carved ships, plainly visible to all at sea [Modi'in is at least ten miles from the sea]. This tomb which he made at Modi'in stands to this day' (1 Macc. 13:25–30).

Simon began as he meant to go on. There are several features of public life under his regime which must be described as overtly Greek. And they are acts of political importance surrounded by ceremony and display, such that they can only be seen as consciously chosen and contrived. To bring out these features of Hasmonean conduct is not to say anything new. They were emphasized, and occasionally overemphasized, by Bickerman, and well understood even by Tcherikover.[10] Schürer, I suppose, approved them, since he

---

[10] See n. 4.

could not find it in himself to accept the Maccabees' earlier exploits: his words still ring out from the pages of the revised version of his first volume: 'the earliest incidents reported represent Jonathan's companions more as bandits than as members of a religious party'.[11] It is not wholly clear whether the later course of Jonathan's career make him and his followers look more, or less, like members of a religious party. What is necessary is to pursue their implications, especially because the picture as usually painted contains a large and puzzling contradiction.

Our sources give us a fair impression of some aspects of the later Maccabees' Hellenism. In the year 142 B.C., and soon, no doubt, after Jonathan's burial (the great tomb may not yet even have been completed), 'the yoke of the Gentiles was taken away from Israel', as 1 Maccabees has it (13:41–42). The autonomy here referred to, and arising in fact in the form of a grant of freedom from tribute and taxes by Demetrius II, was expressed in classic form, by the establishment of a new chronological era: 'and the people began writing on their records and their contracts, "in the first year of Simon, great high priest, commander and leader of the Jews"'. (So far as we know, this era did not endure as a lasting base of reckoning.) Simon was granted the right to issue a coinage, but he did not do so. Of course, the powers granted to Simon were defined in the manner established at Jerusalem during the Persian period, with the high priesthood as the principal political position. Traditionally Jewish, too, was the ceremonial of 141, when the liberation of the Akra from his Jewish opponents, the so-called Hellenists, was celebrated with the waving of palm branches, and with psalms and instruments. Yet in 140, when the assembled people declared Simon high priest, commander and ethnarch for ever, 'until a trustworthy prophet shall arise', the decree was inscribed in bronze and set up in the Temple precinct and in its treasury, just as was supposed to happen in a Greek city (1 Macc. 14:41 ff.).

The first Hasmonean to mint his own coins was in all probability John Hyrcanus, the son and successor of Simon. That both John and all his successors confined their output to bronze *perutot*, and never produced silver, the regular sign of autonomy, is probably to be explained in purely economic terms. The familiar and very hand-

---

[11] Revised Schürer: I, 174.

some Tyrian silver shekels continued to be the common large currency in the whole area, and were even acceptable for payments of
the Temple tax; Judaea did not, of course, have its own source of
silver. What is more telling in terms of ideology is that Hasmonean
coins remained, to the end, aniconic, replacing the customary ruler's
portrait with a second symbol. This might suggest that constraints
were placed on the ruler by the susceptibilities of the pious, or of
certain religious leaders. We have a clear indication that the symbolism of the coins was thought to matter—and can therefore be
taken by the modern interpreter as a genuine reflection of the dynasty's
self-image—in that it displays a manifest respect for the people's will.
Hyrcanus' coins carry two types of formula, reading either 'Yehohanan
the high priest and the council (or community, *hever*) of the Jews',
or else, 'Yehohanan, the high priest, head of the *hever* of the Jews'.
Alexander Jannaeus, more than a generation later, was unambigu-
ously titled king; none the less, at a certain point in his reign, and
perhaps in response to a major crisis with the Pharisees about which
we read in Josephus, some of his coins were overstruck on the obverse
with 'Jonathan, the high priest and the *hever* of the Jews'.[12]

Coinage is thus an area in which we can observe how a political
exploitation of Hellenism can well be juxtaposed with a resonant
assertion of native values. It is not, at all times, a matter of incom-
patibilities or even necessarily of oppositions. From Hyrcanus' coins,
which in Jewish terms would be described as extremely conservative, we conclude that Judaea did not care to see itself as just another
Hellenistic state and that religious tradition still had an important
place. The script is a deliberately archaic palaeo-Hebrew evoking
the days of the first Temple; it was used also in some Qumran texts.
Yet a generation later, Alexander Jannaeus was issuing coins inscribed
in Hebrew, Aramaic and Greek with his Greek name, 'Alexandros'
replacing 'Jonathan' in the Greek versions. As far as the symbols
went, to the small repertoire depicted on Hyrcanus' coins, which
was neutral or vaguely Jewish—a wreath around the name, ears of
corn and double cornucopias with a pomegranate between them—
Jannaeus added a more 'international' set of symbols: a star and diadem (overtly announcing his kingship), the anchor known in the
region from the coins of Antiochus VII and Antiochus VIII (though,

---

[12] Meshorer 1982: 77.

also, of course evoking his family's tomb), and lilies also associated with coins of the same Seleucids. The development is a striking one.[13]

4. *The Hasmonean conquests and the Greek cities of Palestine*

Yet, if the style of the rulers was increasingly involved with Hellenism (in the active sense which I have given to that term), their military policies, as commonly understood, reflect a very different image. The motive force is held to be an implacable enmity with the Greek cities in and around Palestine; not merely with their inhabitants, as neighbours with whom one might not agree, but with the settlements themselves and what they stood for, as representatives of a pagan, and especially (given the Hellenocentric tendencies present even in the Jewish scholarship) of a *Greek* culture which was, on this account, anathema to Judaism.[14] The picture derives from the way in which successive Hasmoneans treated alien peoples in the course of their conquering careers. From Judas Maccabaeus onwards, we find several patterns which it is possible to connect: imposed segregation of Jews from others, possibly accompanied by an act of purification; brutal reprisals against enemies, in the course of which their cities were destroyed and their citizens expelled, if not eliminated; or forced Judaization, such as was carried out in specific cases by Aristobulus in his short reign and by John Hyrcanus. Alexander Jannaeus, the most expansionist of all the rulers, emerges as the climax of these manifestations. No reconciliation has been sought between this stark picture of their actions and the other types of evidence, which indicate a fair degree of Hellenism among the Hasmoneans.

The facts that we have are these. In the books of the Maccabees, the wars of Judas Maccabaeus are conceived of as directed in an overall way against 'the Gentiles'. The origins of this hostility cannot be traced, but it evidently has some connection with the Jewish civil conflicts, for we hear how the aged Mattathias had renegade Jews chased up and circumcised and that he found them (not surprisingly) sheltering among the Gentiles (1 Macc. 2:45–48). The war between Jew and heathen is visualized in total terms: we are told

---

[13] Meshorer 1982: 60–68.

[14] See, notably, Revised Schürer: I, esp. 228; and Tcherikover 1966: 243 ff., whose assessment is just as extreme.

that the non-Jewish inhabitants of the region flocked to the Syrian general Nicanor to escape Judas, 'thinking that defeat and misfortune for the Jews would mean prosperity for them' (2 Macc. 14:14). After Jonathan was kidnapped, the surrounding peoples are said to have been enchanted with the possibility of destroying Judaism root and branch (1 Macc. 12:53). In fact, however, we can be sure that not all the local peoples were unfriendly during this period, for the Nabataean Arabs across the Jordan gave the Maccabees useful information more than once, and, at Scythopolis, the native Gentile populace (no doubt a mixed one) offered expressions of friendship and goodwill to their own Jewish inhabitants and to Judas when he passed (2 Macc. 12:29–31). There is no reason to think that a distinction between 'Greeks' and 'Orientals' was made by the Jewish fighters: Gentiles seem to be all as one. But the basic problem is that the Biblical archaism of our narratives does not allow us to discern the real ideology of the war against the heathen: we cannot tell how far the spirit reflects the agents' own attitudes and how far it is a literary overlay.[15]

Both the separation of Jew from Gentile and the destruction of Gentile settlements seem to have been justified by Judas on the grounds either of security or of revenge; and, at the same time, the aura of a holy and cleansing war was never far away. Already in 164 B.C., the Jews were rescued from parts of the Galilee and from Gilead after fierce fighting, and transported to Jerusalem in a triumphal procession. The harbour at Joppa, where the people led their Jewish neighbours into a trap and drowned them, was burned together with its ships, but Judas left when he found the city gates closed. Very similar action is said to have been taken at Jamnia, to forestall violence against the Jews there (2 Macc. 12:3–9). In a different situation, operating among the 'Philistines', Judas burned the cult images of the deities of Azotus and pulled down their altars (1 Macc. 5:67–68). The venerable city of Hebron, in the hands of the Idumaean 'sons of Esau', appears to have been treated more leniently, with just the destruction of its fortifications and of the strongholds in the villages around it (1 Macc. 15:65).

Judas was succeeded as leader by his more politically-minded brother, Jonathan (161–143/2 B.C.), who played a major role in shaping a new order. He is not, in fact, associated in 1 Maccabees with

---

[15] Cf. Rappaport 1980.

a religious militancy of the intensity of that of Judas. However, as part of an intensive consolidation of his power through Judaea, Jonathan did evict the population of Beth-Zur in southern Judaea, after besieging the town; and he put a garrison inside it. Another brother, Simon, followed Jonathan to power (143/2–135/4 B.C.), and he returned to the port of Joppa, an outlet to the sea for his nascent state (1 Macc. 13:11; 14:34). There too he installed a garrison, and his expulsion of the natives was perhaps a reprisal for the atrocity they were said to have committed on Judas' day. How total the expulsion was we cannot tell, though we should observe that Philo, nearly two centuries later, could describe Joppa as a Jewish town— whatever that meant (*Leg.* 200). Simon's other major conquest, after a siege which seems to have been a highly professional affair, was Gezer (Gazara), an important defensive position lying on the west side of Judaea. In this case, there are interesting details of a cleansing operation: 'he threw them out of the town and he purified the houses in which the idols were, and so he made his entry with singing and praise, and he expelled all impurity from the town and settled in it men who practised the Law' (1 Macc. 13:47–48).[16]

From such roots came the actions of the later leaders. But, again, there are hazards in ascribing policy to action, and it is all too easy to foist an ideology onto a scattering of recorded incidents. What has happened is that the militant Judaism depicted in the Maccabees has been attached by extension to the entire history of the dynasty. The removal of Gentile pollution in conquered territory is understood as a prime aim of expansion. Judaization of the inhabitants was one possible route; their removal or even their elimination, another. The policy would thus have been expressed in a stark choice put before a defeated people, either to convert, or to face dispossession or worse. This reconstruction takes account of a distinction between, on the one hand, a small minority of peoples that did accept circumcision and all that followed—a part of the Ituraeans of upper Galilee and the Hernion area during the short reign of Aristobulus, styled 'Philhellene' (104–103 B.C.; *AJ* XIII 318–319), together with the Idumaeans of southern Judaea under the expansionist John Hyrcanus (*AJ* XIII 252; XV 255)—and, on the other,

---

[16] For possible archaeological traces of the operation, see Reich & Geva 1981.

the so-called Greek cities, where such a course would be out of the question. The Greek cities then emerge as the victims of the greatest hostility and the worst brutality. A view of Palestine as deeply polarized between Greek and Jew need be only a step away.

There is no doubt that, from the outside, the Jewish kingdom (as it became) was, in its own day, seen as aggressively expansionist. A valuable sentence in Strabo's *Geography* calls the Hasmoneans 'tyrants', which is a technically correct application of Greek political terminology, since their power was acquired and not inherited, and it describes them, with only a little exaggeration, as subduing much of Syria and Phoenicia. Yet we should notice that, in Strabo, there is no imputation of noteworthy enmity towards defeated aliens on the part of these rulers. Another Augustan writer, Timagenes (a man known for his obstreperousness) is cited by Josephus in a tantalizing fragment as expressing admiration for the way Aristobulus had served his country when he added the Ituraeans to it by their circumcision (*AJ* XIII 319). It is, of course, just possible that Timagenes had gone on to draw an *unfavourable* contrast with the harsher way in which Greeks had been treated by the Jews, but the apparent tone of the remark (if it be correctly quoted) does not suggest that. There are no other statements made by, or attributed to, outsiders.[17]

We depend for the most part, then, upon material found in Jewish writing, and, after the death of Simon, that means Josephus alone. However, his story is not to be taken at face value, least of all where it concerns Alexander Jannaeus. The existence of two separate Josephus versions, an early one in the introduction to his *Jewish War* and the main one in the *Antiquities*, does make it somewhat easier to stand back critically from what he says. We see that it is with Jannaeus that the image of an implacable Jewish hatred for Greek cities gets crystallized, on the basis of rhetoric incorporated in Josephus' text. The focal point lies in the connection made between Jannaeus' acts and the subsequent reversal of his dispensation brought about by Pompeius in 63 B.C., when he swept through Palestine. The Roman general, who divested Judaea of most of its Hasmonean acquisitions, came as the liberator of established Greek cities and the founder of

---

[17] For the Timagenes fragment, see Stern 1974: no. 81; Josephus says he has it from Strabo's *Histories*. On the Idumaeans and the Ituraeans, cf. Kasher 1988a: 44–86.

new ones. He was presented as a latter-day Alexander and was a proponent of Hellenism in the active, political sense.[18] It would evidently have been to his purpose to have the Jewish monarchy, which he effectively terminated, depicted as an arch-enemy of Hellenism, the barbarous destroyer of the *polis*. Moreover, for Pompeius, it was better to be able to say that he had rebuilt a city from its foundations than that he had merely given one a new name. We know that extensive propaganda in both Latin and Greek accompanied and followed Pompeius' conquests and that historians especially were (not untypically) harnessed to the cause. Both of Josephus' known principal sources, Strabo's *Histories* (not the *Geography*) and Nicolaus of Damascus' *Universal History*, will unavoidably have drawn on material tainted by this propaganda, and we can see that the Jewish writer did not escape its influence, even though in so doing he came into conflict with the loyalties that sprang from his own Hasmonean descent and from his Jewish patriotism. Such a passive approach to his task as historian is also to be found elsewhere in his work.

The link between Jannaeus' depredations and Pompeius' restorations stands out particularly sharply in the *Jewish War* version, where we are told that the Roman conqueror liberated and returned to their rightful citizens all those cities of the interior which the Jews had not earlier 'razed to the ground'—Hippos, Scythopolis, Pella, Samaria, Jamnia, Marisa, Azotus and Arethusa (*BJ* I 156). There is also talk of the reduction of the coastal cities of Gaza, Raphia and Anthedon to servitude. The *Antiquities* make no such claim in connection with the seizure of Raphia and Anthedon. Nor is any unusual devastation associated here with the siege of Gadara (in Transjordan), by contrast with the claim in the *War* that Gadara lay in ruins until its instant rebuilding was ordered by Pompeius to gratify a favourite freedman, Demetrius. At Gaza, brutalities are, in fact, acknowledged by the *Antiquities*, and there is a vivid description of Jannaeus' army, admitted into the city by treachery, running riot and massacring the council, while the king turned a blind eye (*AJ* XIII 262). But such uncontrolled behaviour is far from unknown in ancient warfare, and it reflects nothing more than the savagery and greed of the soldiery. The reputation of his antagonist, Ptolemy Lathyrus, easily outdid that of Jannaeus, for, according to Josephus, Strabo reported Lathyrus

---

[18] On this imitation of Alexander, see Bosworth 1988: 181.

as ordering his troops to chop up women and children in the villages of Judaea, boil them in cauldrons and then taste the flesh (*AJ* XII 345–347). It is also worth remembering in this context that both John Hyrcanus and Alexander Jannaeus employed mercenaries, and especially that Jannaeus, unable to rely on local people because of their intense hostility, had drawn on Pisidians and Cilicians, who are labelled 'Greeks' by Josephus (*AJ* XIII 374; 378). Another case of destruction in the *Antiquities* is that of Amathus, dealt with during a campaign against the Arabs and Moabites, and scarcely, therefore, a Greek centre. Its demolition is put down to the simple reason that its ruler, Theodorus, flatly refused to come out and fight.[19]

In the *Antiquities* (XIII 395–397), we are also given a list, avowedly partial but none the less interesting, of towns and cities 'of Idumaea, Syria and Phoenicia' which were 'held by the Jews' at the end of Jannaeus' life. Eight of these figure in the *War* among the places ruined by the Jews, but the later version bears no comment about their treatment, except in one case alone, that of Transjordanian Pella, where it is announced that the demolition was due to the particular reason that 'the inhabitants would not agree to adopt the customs of the Jews'. In spite of the marked absence of any indication that such a procedure had been applied anywhere else, the explanation would perhaps seem to imply a general practice, and to invite the conjecture that the other places listed in the *War* had suffered for a similar refusal, even if it is, to say the least, peculiar that such dramatic events should have been passed over in silence. Equally, successful conversions anywhere at all are not likely have passed unnoticed and should have remained in the record. If we are, then, disposed to envisage a widespread phenomenon behind the events at Pella, it is necessary to be clear about what that phenomenon can possibly have been. What Jannaeus may realistically have sought, and in some places achieved, was not so much the creation of thousands of new Jews, but rather a new structure that recognized the supremacy of a Jewish element in the towns and of the norms of that element. This would be an entirely intelligible move, when, in many cases, Hasmonean campaigns had been justified precisely by the ostensible need to protect Jewish communities. Such a reading of the words used by Josephus, τὰ πάτρια ἔθη, 'the ancestral customs', would undoubtedly be valid, since, after all, Hellenized

---

[19] On all these episodes, see Stern 1981: 22–46.

Jews perceived the Mosaic Law as a national constitution, at any rate when they were expressing themselves in Greek. That control of the political organs of a city could be a matter of desperate contention between Greek and Jewish co-residents, we learn from Caesarea's appeal to Nero on that very matter in the years immediately before the revolt of 66 A.D. (*War* II 266). This is what Pella will have scorned, to its cost, and this is the constitutional arrangement which Pompeius will have undone on arrival in a town, the cornerstone of his much-vaunted reconstruction.

That the feature of Jewish barbarism in the stories has been played up in the historical record, and that it is simply not credible that numerous major conurbations were reduced to rubble at this time (as claimed, especially, in the *Jewish War*), when we know them to have been flourishing a generation later, are contentions recently made in an exhaustive and vigorous fashion by Aryeh Kasher. He also correctly concludes that the distortion should be traced back to Josephus' Greek sources.[20] But it is less easy to follow him in ascribing the trouble to the antisemitic impulses of those sources; not so much hostility to Judaism as enthusiasm for Hellenism would appear to be the issue, and our knowledge of the specific concerns of Pompeius offers us a precise context. Apart from that, we must remember the rhetoric which time and again led Greek historians to exaggerate the catastrophes of war; A.H.M. Jones noted comparable treatment of Alexander's operations at Gaza and at Tyre (interestingly enough, in the same part of the world).[21]

Hellenism, then, was Pompeius' instrument. It had also been Jannaeus'. Neither man could afford to go too far, because the home market would only buy so much 'Greek wisdom' (in the case of Rome, we have only to remember what Octavian was to be able to make of the Alexandrian interests of Marcus Antonius). But, in his conflict with Hasmonean Judaea, Pompeius was able to win the war of words as easily as he was able to hold the field of battle. Indeed, he was able to divest the Hasmoneans of all the credit they had laboriously built up as masters of a Hellenistic state. And, by his powerful impact on a historical record controlled by Greeks, he even brought the Hasmonean-born historian, Josephus, unwittingly into his camp.

---

[20] See Kasher 1988b: 113 ff.
[21] Jones 1971: 237.

It will be clear enough from our review that, during a century of Hasmonean activity, the leaders' relation to Hellenism did not remain constant; nor, of course, did the forms of Greek culture around them. But for our purposes, the development matters less than the pattern, and that is present already in the careers of the early leaders. Already, an understanding of the uses of Hellenism is visible. This could become a contentious matter and be seen as an assault on the Law, but often enough it was acceptable: there was no automatic contradiction between what was Jewish and what was Greek. Such a policy naturally brought in its wake an undercurrent of diffused cultural change, of Hellenization, in my sense of that term. In this, the Jews developed along lines similar to the peoples around them, in spite of the modifications wrought by the complexity of their inherited religious culture. Hellenization passed for the most part unnoticed, though it would be wrong to deny that there were moments of revulsion. Generally, it is the conscious reactions, with all their political resonances, which are most amenable to purposeful study.

Bibliography

Arenhoevel, D. 1967. *Die Theokratie nach dem I und II Makkabäerbuch.* Mainz.
Avigad, N. 1975. *Jerusalem Revealed: Archaeology in the Holy City 1968–1974.* Jerusalem.
Bickerman, E. 1937. *Der Gott der Makkabäer.* Berlin.
—— 1962. *From Ezra to the Last of the Maccabees.* New York.
Bosworth, A.B. 1988. *Conquest and Empire: the Reign of Alexander the Great.* Cambridge.
Bringmann, K. 1983. *Hellenistische Reform und Religionsverfolgung in Judaa,* Göttingen.
Collins, J.J. 2000. *Between Athens and Jerusalem: Jewish Identity in the Hellenistic Diaspora,* 2nd edn. Grand Rapids, MI.
Doran, R. 1981. *Temple Propaganda: the Purpose and Character of II* Maccabees. CBQ Monograph series, 12. Washington, D.C.
Droysen, J.G. 1836. *Geschichte des Hellenismus,* vol. 1, Hamburg, 1836; vols. 1–3, ed. Bayer, Tübingen, 1952–53.
Feldman, L. 1977. 'Hengel's *Judaism and Hellenism* in Retrospect', *JBL* 96: 371–382.
Heinemann, I. 1932. *Philons griechische und jüdische Bildung,* Breslau.
—— 1989. *The Hellenization of Judaea in the First Century after Christ,* London/ Philadelphia.
Hornblower, S. 1982. *Mausolus.* Oxford.
Jones, A.H.M. 1971. *The Cities of the Eastern Roman Provinces,* 2nd edn. Oxford.
Kasher, A. 1988a. *Jews, Idumaeans and Ancient Arabs.* Texte und Studien zum Antiken Judentum 18. Tübingen.
—— 1988b. *Canaan, Philistia, Greece and Israel: Relations of the Jews in Eretz-Israel with the Hellenistic Cities (332 B.C.E.–70 C.E.)* (Hebrew). Jerusalem.
Kuhrt, A. & Sherwin-White, S. (eds). 1988. *Hellenism in the East.* London.
Lieberman, S. 1962. *Hellenism in Jewish Palestine.* Texts and Studies of the Jewish Theological Seminary 18. New York.
Meshorer, Y. 1982. *Ancient Jewish Coinage,* vol. 2. New York.

Millar, F. 1978. 'The Background to the Maccabean Revolution: Reflections on Martin Hengel's *Judaism and Hellenism*' *JJS* 29: 1–21.
—— 1983. 'The Phoenician Cities: a Case-Study of Hellenization', *Proc. Camb. Phil. Soc.*, 55–68.
Momigliano, A.D. 1970. 'J.G. Droysen between Greeks and Jews', *History and Theory* 9: 139–153
—— 1975. *Quinto contributo alla storia degli studi classici e del mondo antico*, I. Rome.
—— 1977. *Essays in Ancient and Modern Historiography*. Oxford.
Rappaport, U. 1980. 'The Hellenistic Cities and the Jews of Eretz Israel in the Hasmonean Period', in B. Bar-Kochva (ed.), *The Seleucid Period in Eretz Israel* (Hebrew). Jerusalem, 263–275.
Reich R. & Geva, H. 1981. 'Archaeological Evidence of the Jewish Population of Hasmonean Gezer', *IEJ* 31: 48–52.
Stern, M. 1974. *Greek and Latin Authors on Jews and Judaism*, vol. 1. Jerusalem.
—— 1981. 'Judaea and her Neighbours in the Days of Alexander Jannaeus', *The Jerusalem Cathedra*, 22–46.
Tcherikover, V. 1966. *Hellenistic Civilization and the Jews*. Philadelphia.
Wallace-Hadrill, A. 1988. 'Greek Knowledge, Roman Power', *Class.Phil.* 83: 224–233.
Will, E. & Orrieux, C. 1986. *Ioudaïsmos-Hellénismos: essai sur le judaïsme judéen à l'époque hellénistique*. Nancy.
Wolfson, H.A. 1947. *Philo: Foundations of Religious Philosophy in Judaism, Christianity and Islam*. Cambridge, Mass.

CHAPTER FIVE

ROMAN INTERVENTION IN A SELEUCID
SIEGE OF JERUSALEM?

In the Annals of the decline of the Seleucid dynasty, the reign of
Antiochus VII Sidetes (139–129 B.C.) is seen as a period of partial,
if abortive, revival. Bevan wrote of 'one more man capable of rule
and of great action, one more luminous figure, whom the house
which had borne the empire of Asia had to show the world before
it went out into darkness.'[1] In Jewish history, Sidetes' contemporary
John Hyrcanus (135/4–104) marks the political high point of Maccabean power, and in Emil Schürer's view he 'created a Jewish state
such as had not existed since the dispersal of the ten tribes, and
perhaps not since the partition of the kingdom after the death of
Solomon.'[2] It is not my purpose to assess these judgements, but simply to suggest that, in a strange and dramatic episode, when these
two luminaries came into collision, it was neither the one nor the
other, but the Roman senate, far removed and operating through
diplomacy alone, which controlled the situation.

In 135–134, the fourth year of his reign and the first year of John
Hyrcanus, the third Maccabee to rule in Judaea,[3] the Seleucid
Antiochus VII Sidetes invaded Palestine. He was attempting to revive
the fortunes of his declining dynasty, and specifically to avenge an
earlier defeat at the hands of John's predecessor Simon the Hasmonean
and restore the country to its former status as a Seleucid dependency. Simon had been murdered by his son-in-law at a drunken
banquet and was succeeded as ruler and high priest by John, Simon's
third son.

---

[1] Bevan 1902: 236.
[2] Revised Schürer: I, 215.
[3] The text of Josephus also puts the events in the 162nd Olympiad, 132–128
B.C. His two datings might just be reconciled if the siege be supposed to have
dragged on for two years or more; but in any case Porphyry's year 3 of Olympiad
162 (Eus. *Chron.* I 255 Schoene) cannot be saved, and so some sort of error must
exist in the tradition. Josephus' first dating makes better historical sense. For a clear
and complete discussion see Revised Schürer: I, 202–203, n. 5.

Antiochus had at first made peaceful overtures to John Hyrcanus, then changed his policy. After devastating the country, he besieged Hyrcanus in Jerusalem, and the Jewish king soon surrendered. Josephus in his narrative history of the period gives a detailed account of the siege and of the conduct of Antiochus, which he strikingly praises (*AJ* XIII 236–246). When the attack from the north was making little headway, but at the same time the Jewish provisions were beginning to run out and Hyrcanus had had to expel the useless part of the population, leaving them to roam desperately between the walls and the Greek army, a seven-day truce for the feast of Tabernacles was requested and granted. Antiochus himself acted in strong contrast, Josephus points out, to the notorious Antiochus IV Epiphanes, who had flagrantly desecrated the temple and founded his own cult there. Sidetes contributed sacrifices which were handed over at the temple gates to the priests; and so men called him 'Eusebes', Pious. When Hyrcanus, impressed by the behaviour of Antiochus, sent a message pleading for the restoration of Jewish autonomy, the Seleucid for his part ignored the advice of those who urged him to liquidate the Jews, and promptly proposed terms, limiting himself to imposing tribute for some cities, taking hostages, and pulling down some part of the walls of Jerusalem. The Jews would not accept a garrison, owing to their dislike of outsiders, and were spared one.

Sidetes' rather sudden withdrawal and the respect he showed for the temple are the central features of this account. When we stop to consider the sequence of events, it emerges as somewhat puzzling. Contributions to the sacrifices at subject temples are characteristic acts of Hellenistic monarchs. But what could have brought Antiochus to send a sacrifice to an enemy temple before the cessation of hostilities? The timing makes the action an unusual one, and raises questions about the Seleucid king's motives in showing respect for a hostile god. A contribution would be intelligible as a gesture with which to mark a peace treaty; but Josephus does not treat the truce as intended to be a first step towards peace, rather saying that it was Antiochus' piety which first persuaded Hyrcanus that he *could* make peace with him.

The explanation of piety has other drawbacks. Some years earlier, Josephus himself in his *Jewish War* had written a different account; in a brief paragraph on this incident he said that Hyrcanus, having rifled the tomb of David, *bribed* Sidetes to end the siege (*BJ* I 61); here Josephus was offering the traditional ancient explanation of an unexpected political move. The rifling of the tomb is in fact not ignored in *Antiquities* XIII; it is mentioned a little after our passage; but there Josephus has, of course, to ascribe to it a different purpose, asserting that the money was used to pay mercenaries (XIII 249). Finally, we should not forget that Josephus mentions our incident also apropos of David's burial (*AJ* VII 393), where he tells the same bribery story as in the *War*:

Ὑρκανὸς ὁ ἀρχιερεὺς πολιορκούμενος ὑπ᾽ Ἀντιόχου τοῦ εὐσεβοῦς ἐπικληθέντος, υἱοῦ δὲ Δημητρίου, βουλόμενος χρήματ᾽ αὐτῷ δοῦναι ὑπὲρ τοῦ λῦσαι τὴν πολιορκίαν καὶ τήν στρατιὰν ἀπαγαγεῖν, καὶ ἀλλαχόθεν οὐκ εὐπορῶν, ἀνοίξας ἕνα οἶκον τῶν ἐν τῷ Δαυίδου μνήματι καὶ βαστάσας τρισχίλια τάλαντα μέρος ἔδωκεν Ἀντιόχῳ καὶ διέλυσεν οὕτω τὴν πολιορκίαν.

This passage is a digression inserted by the historian into the biblical narrative, and so it is evident that this is the version that he himself remembered and believed at the time of writing. Two points emerge. First, there was a sudden and mysterious end to the war, which required explanation. And second, the early Josephus knew nothing of the theme of the pious Antiochus, and not only when he wrote the *War* (c. A.D. 75) but also in the early stages of the composition of the *Antiquities* (any time between 75 and 93/4) he believed that bribery had been the principal factor. New information obtained during the composition of *AJ* XIII must have led him to think differently; at that stage, Greek historiography, rather than Jewish oral tradition, will have been responsible for the change.

On grounds of probability, too, the version of the incident found at *AJ* XIII is not likely to be Jewish propaganda. Patriotic Jewish sentiment, in contrast to the later and cosmopolitan Josephus, could hardly regard with very great favour a man who had had the temerity to lay siege to Jerusalem. What is more, there are signs that he was not so regarded. Apart from the notion that it was bribery that made him withdraw, there are the accusations of greed and corruption (πλεονεξία, φαυλότης, παρανομία, XIII 225–226) levelled at him by Josephus in connection with his reneging on his agreement with Simon, John Hyrcanus' predecessor, and the same implication in the 1 Maccabees version of the incident (15:25 ff.).

Thus, Josephus' assessment of Antiochus' character apropos of the siege is an unexpected one. And we do, in fact, have solid evidence that its source was a Greek historian. For a narrative which contains features unmistakably related to Josephus' account is to be

found among the fragments of Diodorus (**XXXIV**). The presentation
of the incident there is very similar to Josephus'. The advice offered
to Antiochus, that he should exterminate the Jews after their capit-
ulation, appears in Diodorus in an extended form. Diodorus' source
for this part of his history is generally thought to be Posidonius,[4]
and, in spite of recent reserve, this is quite possible;[5] but it does not
matter to our argument what the name of the Greek historian was.
It must simply be noted that Josephus' immediate source was probably one of the two Greek works which he names in connection
with the period of John Hyrcanus' high priesthood—the *Universal
History* of Nicolaus of Damascus (XIII 249) and the *Histories* of Strabo
(XIII 286).

It is true that as they stand the two narratives, of Josephus and
Diodorus, have very different effects—at any rate if we are to judge
by the excerpted passage of Diodorus that survives; and it is reasonable to do so, for it is not likely that Photius, its preserver, significantly
compressed it. For Photius was interested in what Diodorus had to
say about Jews, and sought out relevant passages (Cod. 244, 379a–
381a). In any case it would make no material difference to our argument if, in what follows, Photius' name were substituted for that of
Diodorus. Most of the space in the passage cited by Photius is taken
up with the speech of the malevolent advisers, which recalls and
endorses Antiochus Epiphanes' treatment of the Jews. It includes an
outrageous account of an ass-cult which Epiphanes had found in the
temple, as well as a description of the Jewish religion; and it approves
his sacrifice of a sow on the altar. The rest is told in a few words:

---

[4] It is widely believed that Posidonius is the source of Diodorus from book 32
onwards. See the literature listed in Strasburger 1965: 42, n. 28. Busolt: 321 ff., is
fundamental. See also Jacoby *ad FGrH* 87 (p. 157). The Diodorus fragments are
omitted from the edition of Posidonius by Edelstein and Kidd (1972), on the grounds
that Posidonius is nowhere there mentioned by name.

[5] One of the main arguments against the attribution is that the attitude to the
Jews of the Diodorus passage is so different from that found in Strabo 16.2.34–40,
which is also often attributed to Posidonius. But this falls away with the demonstration (see *infra*) that in Diodorus we have only half the original presentation.
Josephus' ascription of anti-Jewish statements to Posidonius at *CA* II 79 ff. is no
guide, for apparently all that Josephus knew of what Posidonius had said came
through Apion's invocation of him as an ally: there are no signs elsewhere in
Josephus of independent knowledge of Posidonius. Furthermore, Josephus' wording,
in the surviving Latin translation of this section, does not even allow us to judge
precisely with what statements Posidonius is supposed to be associated. Cf. Stern
1974: 141–144.

Sidetes dismissed the charges against the Jews, exacted the tribute due, and dismantled the walls of Jerusalem. In spite of Sidetes' rejection of the advice, the negative picture of Judaism is not really cancelled. Sidetes' sacrifice is not even mentioned.

In Josephus the story looks different. The contrast with Antiochus Epiphanes is brought in earlier, and is used to cast additional credit on Sidetes, not to indicate a possible course of action for him: while Epiphanes had bespattered everything with pig-fat, Sidetes had sent bulls with gilded horns to sacrifice. Then we get Hyrcanus' submission, and Antiochus' rejection of his anti-Jewish advisers, on the grounds that he believed the Jews to be truly pious. Here the negative judgement of the advisers becomes insignificant.

The comparison suggests that some material from the source has been omitted by Diodorus; and, particularly, that Sidetes' sacrifice in the temple, which does not appear in Diodorus, was to be found in the source. The structure of the Diodorus passage, as it stands, is defective. It has a very abrupt end—the long anti-Jewish exposition of his advisers being simply ignored by the king. The latter's reasons for acting seem to be missing; there is only the very weak explanation in terms of the king's virtue—ὁ δὲ βασιλεὺς μεγαλόψυχος ὢν καὶ τὸ ἦθος ἥμερος—which might well be contributed by Diodorus himself. If this is so, Diodorus was more antagonistic to Judaism than his source: the latter will have presented the case *for* the Jews as well as that *against* them, probably in two parallel speeches, and perhaps even showing the former as the stronger. As for the sacrifice of the golden-horned bulls, we find the incident which Josephus describes mentioned in a work ascribed to Plutarch (*Apophth. Reg.*, *Mor.* 184F) in words that are almost identical:

Τῶν δὲ Ἰουδαίων, πολιορκοῦντος αὐτοῦ τὰ Ἱεροσόλυμα, πρὸς τὴν μεγίστην ἑορτὴν αἰτησαμένων ἑπτὰ ἡμερῶν ἀνοχάς, οὐ μόνον ἔδωκε ταύτας, ἀλλὰ καὶ ταύρους χρυσόκερως παρασκευασάμενος καὶ θυμιαμάτων καὶ ἀρωμάτων πλῆθος ἄχρι τῶν πυλῶν ἐπόμπευσε· καὶ παραδοὺς τοῖς ἐκείνων ἱερεῦσι τὴν θυσίαν αὐτὸς ἐπανῆλθεν εἰς τὸ στρατόπεδον. οἱ δὲ Ἰουδαῖοι θαυμάσαντες εὐθὺς ἑαυτοὺς μετὰ τὴν ἑορτὴν ἐνεχείρισαν.

It is improbable that Plutarch (or his imitator) quarried this story from Josephus,[6] and much more likely that he learnt it from the common source of Josephus and Diodorus (or a derivative of that

[6] Cf. Stern 1974: 564. There is no evidence that Josephus was noticed by contemporary pagan Greek authors.

source). Thus we can with a fair degree of confidence clear the story
of the suspicion of being an invention of Josephus, or an importation from some Jewish apologist.

We can now easily disentangle the personal contribution of Josephus.
In what he writes, Sidetes' sacrifice is, as we have seen, linked by
a contrast made by the author with that of Epiphanes, to the discredit of the latter; while in Diodorus, Epiphanes figures as a glorious
exemplar adduced by the advisers. It is this latter arrangement which
more likely occurred in the source, since Diodorus had less need to
think of a change here than Josephus. Josephus, then, by making
the simple transfer, has effected a great modification in the tone of
the whole narrative, in exactly the opposite direction to that of
Diodorus—excluding most of the anti-Jewish argument, to which the
source gave a hearing. It was probably Josephus, too, who added
the name of the Jewish festival, Tabernacles, for which Antiochus is
said to have granted this truce and sent the sacrifices. This was the
seven-day festival which fell at a suitable time of year, the end of
the campaigning season.

A feature found only in Josephus is the ascription to Antiochus
VII of the title 'Eusebes', and it is not a title associated with that
monarch elsewhere.[7] But that is no puzzle. Bikerman[8] explored the
mechanics of the attribution of such titles, showing that ancient
authors combined indiscriminately many different kinds of names for
kings—official appellations, popular epithets, cultic titles, and so
forth—and also that different names were used concurrently in different places. It occasions little surprise, therefore, that the title 'Eusebes'
does not recur. It should not then be regarded as Josephus' invention, nor as having necessarily come to him through Jewish tradition.

The title given the king, and the story as a whole, shed credit

---

[7] Except again by Josephus, at *AJ* VII 393 (the passage about David's burial),
and also at *CA* II 82, according to an excellent emendation by Niese of MSS' *dius*
to *pius*.

[8] 1938: 136 ff.; Will 1967: 346–347, has no reason to say that Josephus ascribes
this title to Antiochus 'faussement.' In a partially erased inscription from Acre
(Landau 1961: 118–126) which records a dedication to Zeus in the name of an
Antiochus who is most likely the VIIth, the king is styled 'Soter', 'Euergetes', and
'Kallinikos'. 'Euergetes' is attested also on coins; 'Soter' would support the testimony of Josephus (*AJ* XIII 222 and 271) to that title; and 'Kallinikos' is given
nowhere else. Fischer 1970: 102–109, argues that the Cleopatra also mentioned
must be invoked as the monarch's mother, and that therefore Antiochus VII cannot be in question. It is interesting that Antiochus X, grandson of VII, was regularly styled 'Eusebes'.

upon Antiochus. This element of justification is prominent, and we naturally ask why. An answer readily suggests itself, for we can formulate a reasonably strong hypothesis about the realities underlying the incident, and hence see that the tradition found in Diodorus, Josephus, and pseudo-Plutarch serves to conceal something.

The end of the war was unexpected. Hyrcanus' provisions had not yet run out, and he was apparently making successful sallies against the enemy shortly before the feast of Tabernacles (XIII 239–240). He would have required some inducement to yield when he did. The terms of the treaty (245 ff.) may be regarded as having offered him this, for his power remained effectively unimpaired and his kingdom was not actually diminished. Tribute was owed to Sidetes only on those cities, such as the coastal town of Joppa, which had been outside Judaea but had been conquered by John's predecessor. Yet, according to the message which the latter had once received from Sidetes (1 Macc. 15:28), not only Joppa and Gazara and other towns in the same category but even the citadel in Jerusalem were claimed by the Seleucids. And indeed we may wonder why Antiochus had gone on to besiege Jerusalem at all, if he was only interested in the disputed border towns; he could have withdrawn after retaking them. So he must have wished to inflict a total defeat on John. He achieved considerably less than this. Josephus reports the curious fact that owing to their ἀμιξία, their dislike of foreigners, the Jews refused to accept a garrison in Jerusalem, and Antiochus acceded to their request. Again, his alleged respect for the Jewish way of life is used as the explanation of a concession. The Jews offered hostages, including Hyrcanus' brother, and an indemnity of 500 talents instead. τὴν στεφάνην τῆς πόλεως was, Josephus says, to be pulled down: this strange expression may well have meant not the whole walls but the battlements alone, and in that case the gesture would have been a symbolic one.[9]

It is therefore surprising that, with the notable exception of Schürer in the early editions of his work, the prevailing opinion has been that the terms were very harsh.[10] Subsequent events speak against

---

[9] See Revised Schurer: I, 204, n. 6 on the interpretation of this expression. But the precise statement of Josephus is in my view to be preferred to the vaguer Diodorus and Porphyry. And cf. *BJ* IV 117: part of the walls of Giscala removed νόμῳ καταλήψεως.

[10] See for example de Sanctis 1960: 204–206; Ginsburg 1928: 65 ff. Though Schürer in his early editions stressed their mildness (see the English translation of

this view; for Hyrcanus retained sufficient resources to allow him to mount major expeditions into Syria and Samaria as soon as he heard of the death of Antiochus in 129 B.C. (XIII 254). And his person-ally accompanying Antiochus on the elaborate and luxurious Parthian expedition (where the Seleucid met his death) is the gesture of an equal and an ally, not of a humble subject. On this campaign Antiochus expressed his regard for Hyrcanus by honouring his request for a two day halt in Assyria at the Lycus (Zabatus) river, so that the Jewish contingent might not have to march during a festival (or the Pentecost and the Sabbath preceding it, according to Josephus' interpretation).[11] This, then, is the position in which the treaty must have left him.

Some factor must have intervened to break the impasse, and induce Antiochus to sacrifice, and then offer generous terms. Klausner sug-gested that he had become anxious to go off to Parthia. But we know of no recent change in the situation there; Parthian power had been expanding, under Mithridates I, for over a quarter of a century; and Antiochus' brother Demetrius had been a Parthian prisoner since 140. The hypothesis that the crucial change in the situation was a statement from Rome is here explored.

One of the more remarkable of the public documents preserved by Josephus is a decree of the Roman senate ascribed by him to the time of John Hyrcanus and inserted in his narrative just after the death of Antiochus VII, but not dated to any precise moment in John's period of rule (XIII 259 ff.). Clearly, Josephus, or the his-torian who was his source, took it from a collection of documents, and did not himself know where it fitted into the historical picture; though he seems (without basis) to describe it as a confirmation treaty made at John's accession. The decree, after the formal preamble, contains first some of the requests transmitted to the senate by three named Jewish envoys; these centre on the barring of Antiochus' troops from Jewish territory and the return of places captured in war. Then there is the senate's brief resolution; the rest of the sen-ate's response, which is to defer further discussion, follows as indi-

---

the third edition, I.1 276 ff.), later he appears to have somewhat moderated this opinion. No clear comment either way is made by Bouche-Leclerq 1913: 375.

[11] *AJ* XIII 249–253; the other main sources on this campaign are Diod. XXXIV 15–17; Just. XXXVIII 10; App. Syr. 359; Porphyry, *FGrH* 260F32.19. The cam-paign is fully discussed by Fischer 1970. Its chronology is uncertain, but it seems to have begun in 131 B.C.; Fischer tentatively proposes two campaigns.

rect statement, and Josephus' excerpt concludes with the senate's arrangements for the envoys' return home (to be assisted by a further *senatus consultum*). The short resolution is the most important part of the document; it simply asserts the renewal of the Roman alliance and friendship with the Jewish people—presumably the one that had first been made in 161 B.C. under Judas Maccabaeus, and repeated under Simon.[12] It is most reasonable to identify as Antiochus VII the Antiochus mentioned in the Jewish request which precedes the decree. This request includes a demand for the reversal of a situation in which Antiochus possessed cities—Gazara, Joppa, Pegae—taken from the Jews in war, and we know from Josephus' narrative that they had been at issue, and had probably fallen, in the war conducted by Sidetes which ended with the siege of Jerusalem (while in his earlier war against Simon they had not fallen). The other possible identification, adopted by a small number of scholars, is with the troubled son of our Antiochus, Antiochus IX Cyzicenus. But the (albeit few) known facts of his reign include no campaign of the relevant kind, only an unsuccessful attack on Samaria; and the only reason for assigning this document to him is the existence, in another context in Josephus, of an even more problematic document which seems to refer to a similar situation, and to Antiochus IX.[13]

If we prefer Sidetes, the negotiations must be put either during or after his second war in Palestine, and it has not been found easy to decide between the two. The name of the presiding praetor,

---

[12] And perhaps already under Judas' successor Jonathan. These famous treaties have been repeatedly discussed, especially in the late nineteenth century, and are now generally regarded as largely genuine. For the texts see 1 Macc. 8 and *AJ* XII 414–419; 1 Macc. 12:1–4 and 16 and *AJ* XIII 163–170; 1 Macc. 14:24; 15:15–24 and *AJ* XIV 145–148. On the problems they raise, and for bibliography, see first Revised Schürer: I, 171–172, 184, and 195–196; more fully, Timpe 1974: 133–152. The *senatus consultum* at *AJ* XIV 145–148, referred by Josephus to Hyrcanus II, which has itself spawned a vast literature, has sometimes, alongside our document, been put under Hyrcanus I; an L. Valerius presided over its signing, and an L. Valerius was praetor c. 134. But the argument that we have here some of the same ambassadors, the same gift of a shield, and substantially the same treaty as is associated with Simon in 1 Macc. is telling; see now Giovannini & Müller 1971: 160–166.

[13] See the Revised Schürer's excellent discussion of this point: I, 205–206, n. 7. For the case in favour of Antiochus IX, of whom very little is known but who fought over the remains of the Seleucid kingdom with his half-brother Antiochus VIII Grypus between c. 116 and 95, see Giovannini and Müller 1971: 156–160, whose interpretation is a modification of that of Reinach 1899: 161–171; but it is not explicitly argued from the historical circumstances. The decree that suggests, by its similar contents, the later date for our decree, is the one from the Pergamene archive discussed *infra*.

Fannius son of Marcus, does not offer a date, since neither the identification of the Fannius in question nor the careers of the Fannii of the period are secure.[14] The post-war period involves, as Schürer saw, the problem that according to the peace treaty the disputed cities remained in Jewish hands (albeit subject to tribute); it is thus hard to see how the Jews could request their return. If Antiochus had broken the treaty and failed to return the cities, John would hardly have accompanied him to Parthia. Various dates shortly following Antiochus' death have, more recently and somewhat arbitrarily, been proposed; but the document implies that aggression against the Jews is still taking place, and the disastrous familial wars of the Seleucids at the time make this impossible. It is scarcely credible even that the king's arrangement; should have remained in force. Only one serious argument has been offered against fitting the negotiations into the war period; it alone has persuaded most scholars, although it rests upon one of the Jewish proposals whose text is uncertain. I suggest a reading of that text which will eliminate the difficulty as well as clarify the diplomatic situation.

The crucial words are: καὶ ὅπως τὰ κατὰ τὸν πόλεμον ἐκεῖνον ψηφισθέντα ὑπὸ Ἀντιόχου παρὰ τὸ τῆς συγλήτου δόγμα ἄκυρα γένηται. These words, it has been argued, imply that the war is already over.[15] And it is true that if we are to make *any* sense of the clause as it stands it must be taken as referring to the king's arrangements, as decreed in a final settlement.

The difficulty would be reduced by adopting the alternative MS reading (of **F**, **V**, and **L**) ψηλαφηθέντα, which would mean 'handled', 'touched', and so 'attempted'.[16] For the 'attempts' referred to, unlike the decrees, could have occurred well before the war was finished. This way out, however, is barred. The association of the

---

[14] See Revised Schürer: I, 205–206, n. 7. On the problem, which Cicero already could not resolve, whether there were one or two C. Fannii in the Gracchan period, see now Sumner 1973: 53–55 and 173, Broughton 1984: 509, thinks in terms of only one C. Fannius, and is anxious to downdate his praetorship in order to bring it closer to his consulship. Fischer 1970: 67 follows the same line or reasoning.

[15] See for example Fischer 1970: 72–73 (with the additional argument that only after the mighty Antiochus' death would a reversal of his settlement be conceivable); Stern 1961: 9, who also selects a date in the years following Antiochus' death; Bevan 1902: 303.

[16] This reading is preferred in the Revised Schürer: I, 205, n. 7, presumably as the *lectio difficilior*. Stern 1961 would seem to be mistaken in maintaining that which word appears in the text makes no difference to the chronological implications of the whole.

passive participle with the adjective ἄκυρα, which has the precise technical meaning 'invalid', 'unratified', and is applicable to decrees, laws, and the like, guarantees the correctness of ψηφισθέντα. Things which have been merely attempted could hardly become ἄκυρα.

But is the sense of the whole sentence with the reading ψηφισθέντα really satisfactory? It is not usual for a monarch victorious in war to make his dispensations by way of proposing decrees or casting votes. Where would this be done, and what would constitute invalidation of it? Nor can the language be metaphorical, given the constitutional precision of the context. For the ordinances of a monarch there were a number of words available in Greek as equivalents to the Latin *decreta*. διάγραμμα and ἐντολή are used in Hellenistic royal documents. διάταγμα came into use during the Roman principate. δόγμα is used of the emperor's census decree in Luke 2:1. A cognate of ψηφίζω is found once in apparent reference to an individual ruler's decision, and that is in the edict of Tiberius Julius Alexander, where it may refer to the emperor's policies; but a quite different interpretation is preferred by Dittenberger. In Sophocles, *Antigone* 60, ψῆφος is simply a metaphor for the verdict of the tyrant, who is envisaged as casting a solitary and decisive vote against Antigone. For the verb ψηφίζω there seem to be no comparable instances. The Jewish requests in our document are clearly part of the official senatorial record; it is indisputable that accurate Greek versions of *senatus consulta* were produced at Rome; and even if some changes have been made in texts transmitted by historians, we should hardly expect ψηφισθέντα to have been altered.[17] Dissatisfaction with this word on the part of a learned scribe was perhaps what gave rise, through a correction, to the more *recherché* ψηλαφηθέντα in some MSS. Naber's emendation λεηλατηθέντα, 'plundered', fulfills the same function, but it gives poor sense, and it too fails to satisfy the requirement suiting the predicate.

---

[17] See Bradford Welles 1934; Mason 1974: 126–131. For Tiberius Julius Alexander, *OGIS* 669.1; the prefect claims that his fiscal leniency συμφέρειν . . . καὶ ταῖς κυριακαῖς ψήφοις; the emperor's wishes may be meant, but Dittenberger comments on the inappropriateness of συμφέρειν (instead of συμφέρεσθαι) if that interpretation be adopted, and suggests the sense 'rationes' for ψήφοις. On Greek *senatus consulta* see Viereck 1888; Sherk 1969: 13 ff. Moehring 1975: 142, shows that *AJ* XIII, 260–264 is a formally correct *SC*, lacking only the mark of approval. His further argument, however, for the spuriousness of this and other documents, on the basis of the latter omission alone, does not command support.

The remedy is simpler. The ψηφισθέντα may be not Seleucid but Roman, passed in behalf of Antiochus. For I would argue that ὑπό is a corruption of ὑπέρ, and the passage should read: καὶ ὅπως τὰ κατὰ τὸν πόλεμον ἐκεῖνον ψηφισθέντα ὑπὲρ 'Αντιόχου παρὰ τὸ τῆς συγλήτου δόγμα ἄκυρα γένηται. The word ὑπό is suspect because this unexpected form appears, with good MS attestation, in place of the more usual ὑπ'. Josephus is an author who is generally to be found observing elision in prepositions, even when reproducing documents. In fact, later in the same sentence all the texts (save only the Peirescian excerpts) read ὑπ' 'Αντιόχου (263). It is true that some MSS (AMVW) offer the same in our passage; but not the Palatine codex, which Niese valued most highly and which led him to retain an unusual ὑπό in his text. We may follow what must have been his line of reasoning, and suppose that a scribal correction produced ὑπ' in those MSS that have it. The original ὑπό then requires explanation, and it could have arisen, at some stage in the transmission either of the document or of the text of Josephus, through an error for ὑπέρ; such an error would be easy to make, especially with ὑπ' 'Αντιόχου appearing two lines below.

This emendation gives a better reading than any previously offered. And we can now fit the document into an intelligible historical situation. Decrees in Antiochus' favour will recently have been voted in the senate, and the Jews wanted them annulled. Perhaps Antiochus' magnificent gifts of 134 B.C. to Scipio Aemilianus at Numantia[18] were not unconnected with them. And there are two significant earlier occurrences: in the late 140s the pretender Tryphon had sent a golden victory statue to the senate in an attempt to persuade them to recognize him as king, but they inscribed it instead with the name of the murdered boy Antiochus VI; while it is probable that, shortly afterwards, when Scipio Aemilianus and his colleagues went on the famous embassy that settled various matters in the East, and renewed Rome's ties with many kings and peoples, they endorsed the claim of Antiochus VII to the Seleucid throne.[19] Antiochus, then, will have seen that his best chance of rebuilding his kingdom was under Roman

[18] Livy, *Per.* 57. According to Cicero (*Deiot.* XIX 7), gifts from Attalus III arrived at that time; but there is no need to suspect a doublet.

[19] On Antiochus VI see Diod. XXXIII 28a. On the embassy, and the sources for it, see Astin 1967: 127 (esp. n. 3) and 138–139; and also Astin 1959: 221–227. For arguments supporting the view that Scipio's embassy backed Antiochus VII, see Liebmann-Frankfort 1969: 121–122.

patronage. The senatorial decrees in his favour must have come during the early stages of the war, before the siege of Jerusalem. But now Simon, Apollonius, and Diodorus, the emissaries from Judaea, were arguing for the reversal of the pro-Antiochus decrees and maintaining that they were contrary to a previous senatorial decree. That was presumably the one issued in favour of Simon, which they had just described Antiochus as contravening by holding Joppa, Gazara, and Pegae. On this later occasion, the Jews elicited a new expression from the senate of the Romans' friendship for and alliance with the Jewish people; it need not even have taken the form of a proper *senatus consultum*, although the Greek ἔδοξεν suggests that it probably did. Their other proposals were shelved for subsequent discussion (XIII 265, where τῶν πραγμάτων, the better reading, will be the affairs discussed in the Jewish request), and the text does not indicate what happened to the resolutions in support of Antiochus.

These appeals to Rome have far more point during than after the war.[20] τὰ κατὰ τὸν πόλεμον ἐκεῖνον ψηφισθέντα ὑπὲρ 'Αντιόχου are all those pro-Antiochus statements made since the beginning of the war or in connection with it. The senate did not respond to all the Jewish requests, but as on previous occasions confined itself to the vague treaty of friendship, together with a promise of future discussion, an assertion that there should be no further injustice, and an offer to pay for the envoys' return journey. The Jews hoped that Roman representatives would go out and supervise the return of the disputed cities, and these were probably never sent (XIII 263). Yet Rome's statement was obviously to be taken seriously. A reassertion of her alliance with the Jews was an adequate condemnation of Antiochus' attack on them. No more had to be said; and it is clear why she did not want to commit herself to a full acceptance of the Jewish requests, for this would have meant taking the Jewish view on a future settlement, and being obliged to send out representatives to evaluate the damage done by Antiochus and to supervise the return of the disputed cities. Moreover, the timing of her response

---

[20] That Jerusalem is not explicitly mentioned in the document is not grounds for ascribing it to a phase of the war before the city was under siege, as does Smallwood 1976: 10. We should not expect the Jews to have made a naked request that Rome arrange for the siege to be lifted; the senatorial record gives a list of some of their formal demands, and these are such as are relevant to a future settlement of the area. The envoys would, however, first have apprised the senate of the current situation, in a 'briefing' which would not have entered the record.

may have worked out felicitously. It presumably reached Jerusalem, both through the Jewish envoys and by other channels of information, at a time when the siege seemed to be dragging on. In terms of Roman interests, the intervention made good sense: to have given Antiochus Rome's blessing for an operation on the periphery of Jewish territory was one thing; to allow the status quo to be substantially altered by a renewed Seleucid grip on Jerusalem was quite another. And for Rome to weaken her support of the Seleucid king, and to hint disapproval of his action by expressing friendship for his enemy, was enough to make him step back. In the generation after a Roman legation's instructions had made Antiochus IV withdraw from Egypt, there is no difficulty in understanding how Rome could impose her will on the East by words alone.[21] To judge from Livy's account (XLIV 19), this episode is indeed a close parallel, for Antiochus is said to have been besieging Alexandria and within sight of success when told to withdraw by Popilius Laenas and his colleagues. Certainly, through the mid-second century, Rome's authority is unquestionable, however erratic the exercise of it was and however indeterminate her general objectives.[22]

There is in fact evidence of her issuing positive orders in the very area with which we are concerned, in another *senatus consultum* from Josephus, embedded in a decree of Pergamum.[23] This orders that no injury be done to the Jews, who are Roman allies, that Antiochus restore all places taken from them, that they may tax goods exported from Jewish harbours (except by Ptolemy king of the Alexandrians, also a Roman ally), and that the garrison be expelled from Joppa, in accordance with the Jews' request. Instructions about the safe

---

[21] See Badian 1958, esp. 111; Stern 1961: 1 ff. Cf. the comment in Justin XXXV 3.9, *facile tunc Romanis de alieno largientibus*. The notion that Rome may be responsible for the moderation of Antiochus VII is hinted at by Will 1967; it is dismissed by Bouche-Leclerq 1913: 376–377 for the inadequate reasons that she was too busy at the time and that the document may not be genuine. Schürer offers in passing the suggestion of Roman intervention.

[22] All three features have now been admirably illustrated for the case of Anatolia by Sherwin-White 1977: 62–75; I believe that Gruen 1976: 73–95, claims too great a degree of inertia in Rome's eastern policy.

[23] *AJ* XIV 24 ff. Cf. the decree in favour of Simon, which had been sent to Demetrius, Attalus, Ariarathes, Arsaces, Sampsame, Sparta, Delos, Myndus, Sicyon, Phaselis, Cos, Side, Aradus, Gortyn, Cnidus, Cyprus, and Cyrene, as well as to Simon himself (1 Macc. 15:22–24). The existence of this document (whatever its application) in the Pergamene archive, proves that on occasion copies really were distributed.

return of the Jewish envoys are also included. In fact, our chronological case could be buttressed by placing this decree in the historical context under discussion, as Schürer, following Mendelssohn, proposed; for it could be the follow-up of the decree discussed above, a firm order from Rome to Antiochus. One of the five Jewish envoys has the same name as one of the three in the first decree, Apollonius son of Alexander. As Schürer also saw, however, the dating of this decree is even more difficult, and will remain speculative. The text has 'Antiochus son of Antiochus' (XIV 249), which is correct for Antiochus IX but not Antiochus VII (who was son of Demetrius), and emendation of the name is a last resort. We should not therefore rely on it for our argument, and there is nothing to be gained by discussing it further here.[24]

There is in any case enough to suggest an explanation of the abrupt termination of hostilities and the character of the settlement. And we now understand the genesis of the account in our sources. The king would wish at all costs to expunge his humiliation from the record. Weakness was explained as piety and magnanimity; and for this to be possible, the Jews had to be held up as worthy recipients. Antiochus Sidetes may well have been characterized by εὐσέβεια; but the historians protest too much. Hyrcanus' account, by contrast, would probably have emphasized the Roman alliance with Judaea, which Antiochus' altogether omitted (the treaty reached Josephus from elsewhere, as we have seen). Still, Hyrcanus was no doubt able to approve of the sacrifice with which Antiochus marked his withdrawal, and this approval will have led to a rapprochement, and to John's going on the Parthian expedition.

Thus, to save face, Antiochus eulogized the Jews and Judaism, and the king's propaganda entered the Greek historical tradition.[25] But for late Hellenistic writers and their readers, the showing of respect to Jews would occasion some surprise and require explanation: justification was provided in the discussion between the king and his advisers; the debate in Diodorus' source would probably have been, in effect, a consideration of the merits and demerits of the Jewish way of life. Such a debate had no place in Josephus,

---

[24] On the historical issues involved in dating this decree within the period of activity of Antiochus IX, see Fischer 1970: 73–82.

[25] Cf. Bickerman 1927: 171–187 and 255–264, who emphasizes that it was an important virtue for a Hellenistic king to show respect for foreign cults.

where the merits naturally dominate. Yet in other respects it is
Josephus who has preserved more of the original account, and has
enabled us to detect its *Tendenz* (which suited his own purposes well
enough), as well as the reasons which dictated it.

This reconstruction of the events, together with the emended text
of one of the Jewish proposals in the senatorial decree of friendship,
yields several points of significance. The Roman decree has been
shown to fit best the situation during the actual siege of Jerusalem
by Antiochus VII: that is not a new interpretation, but the case for
it is now strengthened. It has emerged that the Romans were committed to Antiochus as well as to the Jews, and had expressed (no
doubt ambiguous) support for him some time before the re-assertion
of the alliance with the Jews. Rome, in other words, had been hedg-
ing her bets, and her by now traditional protection of the Jews did
not impede her freedom of action in other directions. Most striking,
it now seems that the intervention of Rome in connection with the
war, while, as usual, only verbal, was in this case totally effective—
perhaps precisely because of her involvement with both parties.[26] For
Antiochus' *volte-face*—his behaviour to the Jews was nothing less—is
best explained as a response to outside intervention. Rome will have
ended the siege, and persuaded this far from ineffectual monarch to
put aside his ambitions of restoring Jerusalem to full Seleucid control, an obvious step towards reviving the erstwhile power of his
kingdom. It may be that the strength manifested by the Jewish state
in recent years had encouraged Rome in this policy of securing its
preservation as a counterweight to the Seleucids. Fortunately for
Rome, she would be spared an extension of her complex double
involvement, by the death in 129 of Antiochus VII, and with it the
end of the possibility of Seleucid resurgence.

If this reconstruction be correct, it must be conceded that Rome's
alliances with the Jews were not merely symbolic gestures. Not all
of them were vacuous,[27] for in this case she demonstrably had both

---

[26] Comparable situations are not hard to find. When Rome, through Popilius
Laenas, told Antiochus IV to stop fighting Ptolemy Physcon, she had alliances with
both sides: Livy XLIV 19.6–14, and see still Swain 1944: 88–92, on the problems
involved. In 156 B.C., when Prusias of Bithynia made war on Attalus II of Pergamum,
Rome was associated with both sides and tried to stop the war; see Sherwin-White
1977: 6–63.

[27] As maintained, at least in the case of the earliest alliance, by Gruen 1976:
86–87.

the will and the ability to act, without herself becoming involved in any military activity. The reassertion of the alliance was a form of response which had by now become traditional and which had a clear meaning for the parties concerned. Thus the senate, in that obscure phase of its dealings with the East, the 130s B.C., has here been seen actively wielding the authority which it undoubtedly possessed.

In conclusion, it is worth summarizing the intellectual repercussions of the incident, of which we have detected at least traces. Jerusalem came temporarily into prominence as the sphere within which Rome and the Seleucids jockeyed for position. The question of the character of the Jews and their religion became for a brief moment important. Antiochus VII, even had he wished it, could not have treated Jerusalem as Antiochus IV had done (and as, Diodorus maintained, his own advisers urged him to do), because his power was limited; and it was necessary for him to find justifications for diverging from that precedent. The expressions of unusually high respect for the Jews, which were a consequence, entered the pagan literary tradition—later to be virtually expunged by the man who produced the one-sided version we find in Diodorus; and then, again, to be picked up enthusiastically by Josephus. It was the Romans who were responsible for what happened; but it may also be said that it was the existence of Judaea as a nearly independent and growing power, there for the Romans to play off against the Seleucids, that brought about favourable reports of her and her people. So that expression of public esteem for the Jewish cult was not the outcome of religious sentiment, or learned investigation, but simply of the contemporary state of international relations.[28]

BIBLIOGRAPHY

Astin, A.E. 1959. 'Diodorus and the Date of the Embassy to the East of Scipio Aemilianus,' *CP* 54: 221 227.
——— 1967. *Scipio Aemilianus*. Oxford.
Badian, E. 1958. *Foreign Clientelae*. Oxford.
Bevan, E. 1902. *The House of Seleucus*. London.
Bi(c)kerman, E. 1938. *Institutions des Séleucides*. Paris.

---

[28] This paper has been improved at various times by suggestions from Professor F. Millar.

—— 1927. 'Ritualmord und Eselskult,' *MonGeschWissJud* 71: 171–187 and 255–264.
Bouché-Leclerq, A. 1913. *Histoire des Séleucides*. Paris.
Bradford Welles, C. 1934. *Royal Correspondence in the Hellenistic Period*. New Haven.
Broughton, T.R.S. 1984. *The Magistrates of the Roman Republic*, vol. 1. Philological Monographs 15. Chico, California.
de Sanctis, G. 1960. *Storia dei Romani* III, 2nd edn. Firenze.
Ginsburg, M.S. 1928. *Rome et la Judée*. Paris.
Giovannini, A. & Müller, M. 1971. 'Die Beziehungen zwischen Rom und den Juden im 2 Jh. v. Chr.,' *MusHelv* 28: 160–166.
Gruen, E.S. 1976. 'Rome and the Seleucids in the Aftermath of Pydna,' *Chiron* 6: 73–95.
Edelstein, L. & Kidd, I.G. 1972. *Posidonius*. Cambridge.
Fischer, T. 1972. *Untersuchungen zum Partherkrieg Antiochus' VII*. Diss. Tübingen.
Landau, Y.H. 1961. 'A Greek Inscription from Acre', *IEJ* 11: 118–126.
Liebmann-Frankfort, Th. 1969. *La frontière orientale dans la politique éxterieure de la République romaine*. Academic Royale de Belgique, Classe des Lettres, Memoires 59.5. Bruxelles.
Mason, H.J. 1974, *Greek Terms for Roman Institutions: A Lexicon and Analysis*. American Studies in Papyrology 13. Toronto.
Moehring, H.W. 1975. 'The *Acta pro Judaeis* in the 'Antiquities' of Flavius Josephus: A Study in Hellenistic and Modern Apologetic Historiography', in J. Neusner (ed.). *Christianity, Judaism and other Greco-Roman Cults. Studies for Morton Smith at Sixty*, III. Studies in Judaism in Late Antiquity 12, iii. Leiden, 124–158.
Reinach, Th. 1899. 'Antiochus Cyzicène et les Juifs', *REJ* 38: 161–171.
Sherk, R. 1969. *Roman Documents from the Greek East: Senatus Consulta and Epistulae to the Age of Augustus*. Baltimore.
Sherwin-White, A. 1977. 'Roman Involvement in Anatolia, 167–88 B.C.', *JRS* 67: 62–75.
Smallwood, E.M. 1976. *The Jews under Roman Rule: from Pompey to Diocletian: a Study in Political Relations*. Studies in Judaism in Late Antiquity 20. Leiden.
Stern, M. 1961. 'The Relations between Judaea and Rome during the Rule of John Hyrcanus' (in Hebrew), *Zion* 26: 1–22.
—— 1974. *Greek and Latin Authors on Jews and Judaism*, I. Jerusalem.
Strasburger, H. 1965. 'Posidonius on Problems of the Roman Empire,' *JRS* 55: 40–53.
Sumner, G.V. 1973. *The Orators in Cicero's Brutus: Prosopography and Chronology*. Phoenix, suppl. 11. Toronto.
Swain, J.W. 1944. 'Antiochus Epiphanes and Egypt', *CP* 39: 88–92.
Timpe, D. 1974. 'Der romische Vertrag mit den Juden von 161 v. Chr.,' *Chiron* 4: 133–152.
Viereck, P. 1888. *Sermo Graecus quo senatus populusque Romanus, magistratusque populi romani, usque ad Tiberii Caesaris aetatem in scriptis publicis usi sunt examinatur*. Göttingen.
Will, E. 1967. *Histoire politique du monde hellénistique* 11. Nancy.

CHAPTER SIX

DYING FOR THE LAW: THE MARTYR'S PORTRAIT IN JEWISH-GREEK LITERATURE

Jewish martyrs

The anonymous author of the Fourth Book of Maccabees summarizes, in one long Greek sentence, the achievements of the heroes and of the heroine whose dreadful deaths he has recounted. Good rhetorician as he is, he presents the events in a variety of perspectives. At one stage they are imagined as a picture, a visual portrayal of piety in action, which cannot fail to make any spectator shudder, he now parades the ingenious device of an imaginary epitaph.[1] Here, he says, are words apt for the heroes' tombstone,[2] fit to serve as their memorial among their people:

> 'Here lie buried an aged priest, a venerable woman and her seven sons, by the violence of a tyrant bent on destroying the Hebrew nation (πολιτεία); they vindicated their people (ἐξεδίκησαν, ἔθνος), looking towards God and enduring their torments to the death' (17:9–10).

On this lapidary text, the author expands in his own voice. The feats are encapsulated in a familiar Greek metaphor, but given a Jewish twist: 'Reverence for God (θεοσέβεια) won the victory and crowned her own athletes. Who was there who did not marvel at the athletes of the divine legislation (νομοθεσία)? Who was not amazed?' (15–16). These holy ones, we further learn, are protected and sanctified by God; they have not only defeated the tyrant, but they have rescued and purified their own fatherland. They now stand before God's throne, enjoying a life of eternal blessedness.

---

[1] The author makes no claim that this text ever served as an actual epitaph. Nevertheless, its form has sometimes been taken as proof of the existence of a Jewish cult of the martyrs of Antioch: see Hadas 1953: n. *ad loc.* and van Henten 1994, and below 111–112, 119.

[2] ἐπιτάφιος is used here as a noun and must refer to an imagined gravestone, on which something could be inscribed (ἀναγράψαι). See van Henten 1994: 48–49.

What is contained here is undoubtedly what we understand as 'martyrdom', even in the absence in the text of the term itself or of any Greek equivalent. We have before us the essential attributes of the Jewish martyr, as perceived by the author of 4 Maccabees: the defence of the Divine Law (in the author's commentary), a tyrannical oppressor, a threat to the nation, heroic endurance by the ostensibly weak (women, children, the old), harrowing torture certified by detailed description, the anonymity of the martyrs and a victory which is inherent in the death itself, secured by faith and requiring nothing further to make it complete, even if the gift of immortal life happily follows. It is worth noting that the short assessment to be found in the epitaph itself, in contrast to the elaboration which follows, makes no mention of any expectation of a sequel beyond the moment of the martyrs' deaths.

Martyrology is idealized representation and the characterization of martyrs is portraiture, to a lesser or greater extent stereotyped. It is as well to recognize from the outset that martyrdoms, while presented as fact, are not mere historical events—that is, if they are history at all. As a matter of fact, the episodes to which the epitaph refers are almost certainly unhistorical; but to those concerned, as we are here, with the representation of the would-be historical, this makes little difference. Martyrdom is description, since in its very nature it demands a public, a response and a record. In the Christian tradition, the terminology itself exposes this state of affairs, for the deaths of martyrs bear witness (μαρτυρεῖσθαι) to their faith, in front of an assumed audience immeasurably greater than the immediate one at the scene. And, already, the martyr's manner of dying may well have been influenced by literature. The event is then shaped for the future in the telling, to serve, in due course, as a model for others.[3] A heroic death transcends the significance of the individual moment, transmuting its horror. This is the meaning of the epitaph in 4 Maccabees. The author himself declares that 'the tyrant was the adversary and humanity were the spectators' (4 Macc. 17:14). The old man, the mother and her seven sons 'demonstrated the nobility of faith' (17:2). In an earlier account of the same constellation of events, to be found in the Second Book of Maccabees, the matter is put even more plainly in the author's assessment of the

---

[3] The interrelationship is discussed by Cameron 1991.

death of the aged scribe Eleazar: 'so he died, by his death leaving a noble example and a glorious memory (ὑπόδειγμα γενναιότητος, μνημόσυνον ἀρετῆς), not just for the young but for the great body of the nation' (6:31, cf. 6:28). The social value—indeed, one might say the educational value—of martyrdom could not be more clearly emphasized.

Both the phenomenon and the ideology of martyrdom were crystallized in Greek texts written by Jews, before becoming part of Christianity. This is now widely recognized, even if many questions remain, when it comes to specific Christian debts and the interpretation and transmission of particular motifs. U. Kellermann[4] offers a conspectus of no less than fifty themes shared by the two traditions. Recently, there have been further welcome developments in scholarship. A series of studies by J.W. van Henten, appearing since 1989, has brought new perspectives.[5] Robin Lane Fox's fresh discussion of martyrs[6] notably resists the blurring of the distinction between Jewish and Christian martyrdoms, perhaps, in this case, as the result of emphasizing the gap between Christian religious structures and all that preceded them, whether pagan or Jewish. To contribute to enquiry into the connections between Judaism and Christianity is not my immediate purpose here.[7] The Jewish depictions of martyrs, in which Judaism and Hellenism mingle, are interesting and important in their own right, and those features in them which have no particular prominence in the Christian material are as deserving of consideration as those which do. The concern of this study is to demonstrate the existence of a continuing Jewish-Greek literary tradition in the portraiture of politico-religious martyrs, focussing on the key work in this tradition, that is the Fourth Book of Maccabees; to explore the tradition's dominant themes and emphases, drawing attention especially to some which have gone virtually unnoticed; and to suggest a broad social context in which the tradition can be understood.

If, then, we turn our attention to Jewish martyrologies, we find a situation not without paradox. We note that W.H.C. Frend, after

---

[4] Kellermann 1979: 71–75.
[5] See van Henten 1986; 1989; 1994; 1995. Also now Droge and Tabor 1992 survey a wide field, pursuing the theme of voluntary death through Greek, Jewish and Christian texts.
[6] Lane Fox 1986.
[7] For a new approach, see van Henten 1995.

fifty-six pages in which he traces virtually all the main elements of
Christian martyrdom back to Judaism, has still to comment: 'the
term [martyrdom] was apparently not used by Jewish writers to
describe the act of those who died for the Torah.'[8] And it is undeniable that the familiar terminology of martyrdom can be traced
back to the root conception of bearing witness to the resurrection,
a conception present already in the Synoptic Gospels and also found
in the Acts;[9] a connected idea is that of suffering by way of imitation of Christ's suffering, as expressed in certain Pauline epistles. A
partial qualification might be suggested, and I would draw signal a
striking anticipation of the Christian terminology in the appearance
of a verbal formation in 4 Maccabees, which seems to have gone
unremarked: the sons are said to have been called to their ἀγών, to
be witnesses for the nation (ὑπὲρ τῆς διαμαρτυρίας τοῦ ἔθνους; 16:16).
Also telling, perhaps, is the moment where Eleazar is called ὁ πανά-
γιος, the saint (4 Maccabees 7:1).

The fact remains that the absence of a developed Jewish terminology for 'martyr' or 'martyrdom', in either Greek or Hebrew, is
a striking feature of the Jewish representation. The phenomenon is
perhaps to be related to that strong strain of depersonalization in
this kind of memorializing, which I shall consider later. The medieval
idea of *kiddush ha-shem*, the sanctification of God's name, later com-
pensates in some measure. But even then, there is no single term
to be found for the persons of the martyrs, beyond, *keddoshim* (holy
ones) as in the Hebrew records of the European victims of the First
Crusade.[10]

At the same time, it is worth reflecting on the fact that today we
experience surprisingly little difficulty in talking of 'martyrdom' in
connection with Judaism; the idea has become part of a general
understanding of the Jewish past. Historians write readily, in English,
of the 'Ten Martyrs', in reference to the Rabbis, including Akiba,
Tarfon and Ishmael, whose deaths under harrowing Roman tortures
are associated in Rabbinic tradition and legend with the period of
the revolt under Hadrian and who have achieved familiarity by
annual commemoration in the post-Rabbinic *elleh eskarah* text ('these

---

[8] Frend 1965: 87.
[9] On this theme, see Fischel 1946, Frend 1965 and Lampe 1981.
[10] Ben Sasson 1972; Chazan 1991. The term can be traced back to early Rabbinic
literature: Safrai 1979.

I shall remember'), incorporated in the liturgy.[11] Nowadays, the victims of the holocaust are described as 'martyrs', by what Louis Jacobs has called 'a kind of automatic consensus.'[12] Furthermore, in the writing of modern Jewish historiography, a central role is often assigned to the mentality of martyrdom, and that not only by practitioners of the so-called 'lachrymose view of Jewish history'. This emphasis has some justification, for even in contexts where Jewish society seemed to be scarcely concerned with preserving any detailed historical record of the past or the present, lamentation for catastrophe and commemoration of victims and of heroes were actively practised, making their mark also on the religious calendar. In this sense at least, through the value put on remembering such acts, the importance of the past to the present was recognized.[13] Undoubtedly, the Jewish ideology of *kiddush ha-shem* and the Christian ideology of martyrdom influenced one another in the Middle Ages, while retaining crucial differences, especially in the valuation of relics.[14] This is one reason why we now often find ourselves able, without discomfort, to use the terms interchangeably.

The Jewish-Greek tradition

Martyr acts do not exist as an independent genre in Jewish-Greek literature.[15] The classic narratives, accounts of suffering and death under persecution in the days of Judas Maccabaeus, are embedded in the books of the Maccabees, especially in the second and fourth books. For in 1 Maccabees, a Greek translation from a Hebrew original written to glorify the Hasmonean dynasty, we follow the persecution of Antiochus IV in graphic detail, but the book's emphasis on a military and political response marginalizes the route of martyrdom, which is mentioned with respect, but not explored.[16] By contrast, in the second book, a long epitome of a lost history by one

---

[11] Herr 1972; Reeg 1985; Stemberger 1992.

[12] Jacobs 1990: 118.

[13] On the importance of the past in Judaism, see Yerushalmi 1982; Rajak 1986 = Ch. 2 in this volume.

[14] The theory elaborated by Yuval 1993 presupposes particularly close and complex interaction between Jewish and Christian ideologies.

[15] For the contrasting situation in Christianity, see Delehaye 1921.

[16] For 1 Maccabees' account of the banning of the Law (1 Macc. 1:54–64) and of disputes around Sabbath observance (2:29–38), see below, 126–127.

Jason of Cyrene, we find two chapters (six and seven), unconnected
with the battles of the Hasmoneans, which recount the tortures and
deaths in the persecution of Antiochus IV of the aged scribe Eleazar,
who rejected the pork forced on him by the king's agents, and of
the unnamed mother and her seven sons.[17] The fourth book, as we
shall see, mixes philosophical disquisition with eulogistic homily: it
has its own intellectual agenda concerning the relation between reason and the passions, even if it devotes considerable space to the
exchange between each martyr and the persecuting king, and to
description of the tortures, narration of the dying words of each martyr and enumeration of their virtues.[18]

It is, however, a mistake to infer a lack of concern in the deaths
of martyrs from the absence of a specific martyrological genre, any
more than from the absence of the terminology. We shall discuss at
a later stage possible reasons for the lack of a genre.[19] At this stage,
it suffices to register the existence of a continuing Jewish-Greek tradition of writing on the subject. The very strength of this tradition
makes it difficult to accept without qualification Glen Bowersock's
recent judgement that 'Jewish accounts . . . do not antedate the concept of martyrdom as it was shaped by the Christians', if the implication is that such accounts are simply derivative from Christian
material.[20] 2 Maccabees, though not contemporaneous with the events
it describes, must date from the late second or early first century
B.C. While chapter 7 stands in the epitome unconnected with the
rest of the book, and involves the unexplained presence of Antiochus
at the scene of persecution, as well as an emphasis on resurrection
absent from chapter 6, there are no grounds for assigning to this
chapter a substantially later date, as now suggested by Bowersock,
even were we to take the chapter as an insertion made at an advanced
stage in the original composition. 4 Maccabees, on the other hand,
evinces the florid taste of the second sophistic, along with a vocabulary most closely paralleled, within this milieu, by that of Galen.[21]
This suggests a date between the late first and the mid-second cen-

---

[17] Text, translation and commentary: Abel 1949; Zeitlin 1954; Goldstein 1983;
Habicht 1976.
[18] Text and commentary: Dupont-Sommer 1939; Hadas 1953; Klauck 1989.
Translation and commentary: Anderson 1985.
[19] See below 118, 128–129.
[20] Bowersock 1995: 10–12, 37.
[21] Renehan 1974 for parallels with Galen. See Breitenstein 1976 for a detailed
study of the language in relation to second century A.D. 'Atticism'.

tury A.D.; and Bickerman's leading argument for a mid-first century dating, derived from a single geographical specification in the text, is now rightly questioned.[22]

We can say, therefore, that our material, spreads over a substantial time span even if it is not precisely dateable. Still more telling is the existence of striking martyrological motifs elsewhere in Jewish-Greek literature, which, as it happens, neatly fill the time gap between the two major Maccabaean texts. This time less infused with legend, we have Philo's shaping of his account of the impact of Caligula's attempted desecration of the Temple and of the Alexandrian pogrom in the context of his two passionate works of advocacy. Then there is the stance of the historian Josephus, both his descriptions of the defiance of torment by Essenes and, especially, of the deaths of zealots and *sicarii* in the course of the war against Rome; and his repeated statements, in *Against Apion*, that the value of the Jewish Law can be gauged by the consistent readiness of its followers to die for it. We shall return to these authors.

It would seem that the narrative known as the third book of Maccabees, at least in its final version, also belongs to the early Roman period. Its imaginative account of a persecution under the Ptolemies, from which the Jews of Alexandria were redeemed by divine agency, is quite close to our theme, and the work has echoes of 2 Maccabees in its descriptions of sufferings.[23]

Echoes of martyrdom, and allusions to the Maccabaean martyrs in particular, also appear in the prophetic and apocalyptic tradition, here in a Semitic rather than a Greek medium. There, portrayal through narration is replaced by encoded allusion and past merges with future. In the book of Daniel (11:33–34), the latest composition in the canonical Bible, we find an important evocation of the Maccabaean martyrs: 'they will fall victims to fire and the sword, to

---

[22] 'Syria, Phoenicia and Cilicia', is given as the name of Apollonius' area of control. The evidence suggests that a Roman province combining Syria and Cilicia existed for a part of the first century A.D., and possibly no later than A.D. 54: Bickerman 1945/1976. But the amalgamation of Cilicia into the province of Syria in the first century is ill-documented: Syme 1939. In any case, the author of 4 Maccabees works miscellaneous *realia* into his text and might wish to exaggerate the extent of Apollonius' power, so that his titulature for the province scarcely serves to date his book. Cf. Dupont-Sommer 1939; Van Henten 1986; Campbell 1992: 219–228. van Henten suggests a Cilician provenance.

[23] On this work, see Mélèze-Modrzejewski 1995: 141–153; on the date: Tcherikover 1961, re-examined by Parente 1988. On connections between 2 Maccabees and 3 Maccabees, Gardner 1988.

captivity and pillage . . . some of these leaders will themselves fall victims for a time so that they may be tested, refined and made shining white.' Daniel's early chapters, set in the Persian court, are also concerned with persecution: the faith of the three youths is tested by the King in the fiery furnace, and that of the favourite courtier, Daniel himself, in the lion's den. In one of the apocryphal Greek additions to Daniel, the prayer of Azariah, the young victim seeks meaning in the expected surrender of his life, at a moment when assistance from prophets and sacrifices exist any longer: 'like holocausts of rams and bulls, like ten thousand fat sheep, may our sacrifice be before you today'.[24] These are all passages concerned with aborted martyrdoms, with felicitous outcomes. We find another, even more specific allusion to the Maccabaean martyrdoms in a powerful prophetic passage which describes the mysteriously-named Levite Taxo and his seven sons preparing for death in a cave. This appears in chapter 9 of the Testament, or Assumption of Moses, itself part of a longer work, now surviving only in Latin.[25] After three days of fasting, the group will enter, ready to die, 'rather than transgress the commands of the Lord of Lords' never transgressed by their forefathers, and wholly confident that 'our blood shall be avenged before the Lord.'

In such texts, the *portrait* of the martyr can rarely be clearly discerned, but we may see them as alternative modes of expression through which deep-seated preoccupations are articulated and explored. More specifically, they reveal the wide reverberations of the Maccabaean persecutions on the Jewish consciousness.[26] These paradigms are thus indicative, but they are not decisive in determining the Jewish-Greek representation, which has its own momentum. A link between the two thought-worlds is offered in 4 Maccabees by the recurrent exploitation of a number of biblical antecedents for the suffering of the righteous. Most prominent is that of the courage of the three youths, Hananiah, Michael and Azariah, as told in the additions which survive in the Greek Daniel (13:9; 16:21; 18:12).[27]

---

[24] LXX Daniel 3:38–40; cf. de Jonge 1988.

[25] See Licht 1961. Doran 1980 argues for a strict typology which distinguishes the Taxo passage, where the death remains undescribed, from martyrdoms proper.

[26] Gardner 1988 finds in 3 and 4 Maccabees a Diaspora interpretation of the Maccabaean story.

[27] The Greek additions are now part of the text of the Septuagint; it is unlikely that all of them were originally composed in Greek.

Goldstein has vividly pinpointed the tormenting questions which
beset survivors of persecution: they need explanation, instruction—
what to do next—and consolation.[28] The relationship between God
and Israel required redefinition and re-assertion in the wake of persecution. There are many ways of snatching meaning out of the
deaths of martyrs, of turning physical disaster into psychic (and perhaps ultimately physical) victory. The diverse Jewish literature of the
period, which incorporated a highly diversified religious world, generated varied reactions. Our concern here is with responses manifested by way of the evocation and depiction of individual martyrs
and of their deaths and expressed in extended narratives.

As Jewish-Greek literature dwindled, the Maccabaean martyr traditions were diverted into other channels, which are not our concern here. Rabbinic stories evolved around the fates of religious
leaders under the Hadrianic persecution some half a century after
those events; the stories include an array of tortures and executions;
and some of these incorporate, with a characteristic mix of memory
and fantasy, barely recognizable versions of the deaths of the Maccabaean mother and her seven sons.[29]

Christian readings

The common terminology accentuates a very real problem in looking at the early history of martyrdom. One slips readily into Chris-
tianizing this history, to make much of anticipations of Christian
developments in the Jewish-Greek accounts, and to overlook the lat-
ters' individuality. It is surprising how few are the commentators
who have managed to react to the record on its own terms. It is
fair to say that the study of early Jewish martyrdom has been located
within the study of Christian martyrology under the Romans and
dominated by its patterns, often in justified reaction to earlier accounts
which had left the Jewish versions out of the picture altogether: thus,
in the British context, a strong corrective thrust is visible in Frend's
impressive and wide-ranging collection of Jewish texts and attitudes.[30]

[28] Goldstein 1983: 293.
[29] See above, n. 11. On Rabbinic traditions about the mother and her seven
sons, see Hadas 1953: 127–135; Cohen 1972: 1270–1272; Doran 1980; Stemberger
1992.
[30] E.g. Frend 1965: 21 (on H. Delehaye), 87 (on Campenhausen and Strathmann).

Even when Jewish scholars entered the arena, they often failed to alter the terms of reference.[31]

The themes generally drawn out are those which become key issues in the Christian theology of the sacrosanctity of martyrdom. They are themes which may indeed make a limited appearance in the early Jewish versions, yet their presence may be fleeting, their intention metaphorical or their articulation inexplicit. Focussing discussion on such themes, and on whatever biblical precedents and underlying religious doctrines may be found for them, has a seriously distorting effect. By such a process an accretion of Christian readings of the Hebrew prophets, many of them now thoroughly familiar, has accumulated through the ages. In other words, Jewish martyrdoms have been understood—where they are noticed at all—as preparations for Christian martyrdom. The existence of a direct connection between the two traditions, in the shape of the astonishingly long-lasting Christian cults of the Jewish martyrs of Antioch, probably played its part in validating this kind of interpretation.[32]

A brief indication of these themes will suffice here. First, it may be suggested that disproportionate interest has been lavished upon Jewish traditions concerned with the murder of prophets or men of God, as models of the unmerited suffering of the pious. It is not unreasonable to suggest that the treatment of the motif may be read as extended exegesis of Jesus' invocation of Jerusalem in Luke 13:34 as 'the city that murders the prophets and stones the messengers sent to her,' and of Stephen's equivalent accusations (Acts 7:5). Traditions which describe the suffering of men of God, with anticipation of a future vindication, are eagerly pulled out, going back to the evocation of the suffering servant of Deutero-Isaiah (53), who 'bore the sin of many and interceded for their transgressions', and thus 'exposed himself to face death', and to Nehemiah's reference to Israel's killing of the prophets who had tried to mend her ways (9:26). Such images do figure in a number of the pseudepigrapha, especially in the supposedly Jewish sections in the Martyrdom of Isaiah, which contain the tradition that the prophet was sawn in half in front of Manasseh, son of Hezekiah (5:1–16). There also circulated traditions on the death of a prophet named Zechariah, whose identification varied.[33] Such material may also turn the prophet into

---

[31] For example, Fischel 1946–47: 265–80; 363–86.
[32] See below, 119.
[33] Frend 1965: 586, n. 149; Lampe 1981: 123–129. See also Schwartz 1993 on

a visionary at his death. What is debatable is whether such images should be connected with the evolution of mainstream Jewish conceptions of martyrdom: certainly there is no justification for automatically assigning to them a central and seminal role.

Second, the expected resurrection of the martyrs is overemphasized. This theme makes a distinctive appearance in 2 Maccabees, although its expression is largely confined to chapter 7.[34] In 4 Maccabees, the immediate access of the martyrs to heaven at the resurrection of the dead is assumed and explored through various metaphors. The Christian reverberations of this understanding arise perhaps less from any prominence of the idea in the martyrologies of the early Church, than from its relevance to Jesus' own passion and resurrection.[35]

The third theological concept to be given exaggerated significance, closely related to the previous two, and the most important of all, is that of *redemptio vicaria*, the interpretation of the martyr's suffering as vicarious punishment for the sins of a whole people.[36] The shedding of his or her blood releases the people from further retribution, and, beyond this, may hasten national redemption, bringing nearer the end of days. In 2 Maccabees (7), the youngest brother in his dying speech explains that God is briefly punishing the people of the covenant for their sins but will soon be reconciled to them (32, 33); the hope is hinted at that his and his brothers' deaths will hasten this reconciliation (36, 37). It is not until we reach the fourth book that we find two passages where the spilling of the martyrs' blood seems to be endowed with the significance of a vicarious atonement. H. Anderson,[37] in a recent commentary, highlights these passages, assessing them as 'doctrinally, the most significant contribution of 4 Maccabees is the development of the notion that the suffering and death of the martyred righteous had redemptive efficacy for all Israel.'

But how does this 'doctrine' figure in the work? It surfaces first within the context of prayer: Eleazar's prayer on the verge of death includes the words 'be merciful to your people and let our punishment be a satisfaction on their behalf. Make my blood their purification

Jewish and Christian interpretations of the concept of 'life through the Law' (Lev. 18:5).

[34] But see also 2 Macc. 14. 46 (on the death of Razis). On resurrection in 2 Maccabees, Nickelsburg 1972; Kellermann 1979.

[35] Lampe 1981: 120–121.

[36] de Jonge 1988: 144.

[37] See his introduction in Charlesworth 1983: 539.

and take my life as a substitute for theirs' (6:27).[38] The only authorial endorsement comes in the homily at the end of the tract: where
the unknown author assesses the martyrdoms *sub specie aeternitatis*, and
declares that the martyrs rescued the nation, and, that, by concili-
ating God, they ensured that Israel's enemies could not prevail: their
deaths were a sort of substitute (again, ἀντίψυχον) for the nation's
sins. The explicit indication, through the use of ὥσπερ, that this is
a metaphor, suggests that we are dealing with a phrase of the author's
own devising. The blood of the pious was placatory, inducing Divine
Providence (θεία πρόνοια) to save Israel (17:22).

The basic idea in these utterances is simply that the martyrs were
instrumental in breaking the old sin and punishment cycle by the
outstanding piety manifested in their deaths. And the fact is that this
idea is readily located within the framework of a widespread Jewish
belief in the potency of the 'merits of the fathers' as bringers of
mercy and salvation to their descendants. A comparable problem of
interpretation is offered by an intriguing group of rabbinic references
to 'the blood of the *aqedah* of Isaac', with their accompanying notion
that one quarter of Isaac's blood was shed before Abraham's hand
was stayed. It has now been effectively demonstrated that such references are fully intelligible in terms of Rabbinic thought, rather
than as any kind of response to Christianity; the blood of Isaac does
not challenge the blood of Jesus. The conceit of the blood, like that
of the blood of the Passover, expressed God's acknowledgement of
His covenant with Abraham, Isaac and Jacob.[39] What needs stressing is that, in the Maccabaean literature, the theology of redemptive blood is never worked out. So much is any such idea overshadowed
by consideration of victories in the here-and-now, that the author
goes straight on to explain earnestly—if not wholly credibly—that
those martyrs' deaths helped the people in their struggle because
they were held up by Antiochus as a model to his troops: successes
in both battle and siege warfare automatically ensued for the Seleucid
monarch. Here the idea of a potent death is a device which happily links the ultimate success of the Hasmoneans' warfare and diplomacy in Palestine with the sufferings in the preceding persecution,
which were in practical terms unrelated (17:23). Our author had a

---

[38] ἀντίψυχον is not 'ransom' and should not be thus translated. On this word in
Ignatius of Antioch, see Perler 1979.
[39] Hayward 1990.

special problem, in that the persecution he relates seems to have taken place in Antioch and not in Jerusalem at all: while the incident is not physically located by him (nor in 2 Maccabees), later traditions are centred on Antioch.[40] So it may be suggested that a primary function of the ἀντίψυχον concept in 4 Maccabees was to establish a connection between persecution, in the Diaspora, and victory, in Palestine, and to bridge the awkward geographical disjunction between the two locations.[41]

4 Maccabees

A non-theological interpretation of chapters 6 and 7 of 2 Maccabees is essential to a modern study of Jewish martyrdom,[42] but at the centre of the study must stand the extended martyrology of 4 Maccabees which we took as our starting point. The story is the same as in the chapters of the earlier Maccabaean work, and, indeed, evidently dependent upon it; but the scale has grown greatly and new twists have emerged. Recent scholarship offers a number of specific studies;[43] yet the book is not well-known. It has scarcely come to the attention of scholars concerned with the Greek literature of the Roman empire, the milieu to which it obviously belongs.[44] Yet 4 Maccabees, while distressing, is a remarkable creation, in which the Greek philosophy current in the Roman empire, is blended with a parade of rhetoric and a serious Jewish ideology. The strong likelihood of a post-70 A.D. date adds to the interest of this product, making it a rare specimen from the Jewish diaspora of the Roman empire, in a period when that Diaspora produced virtually no identifiable literature.[45]

There is no question of disentangling Greek influences from Jewish in this text, even if prototypes from one or other cultural sphere are readily identifiable at moments. This will already be clear from the epitaph which we have analysed. The anonymous author was evidently

---

[40] Bickerman 1945; Hadas 1953. Rampolla 1899 was the excavator of the Roman *martyrium*.

[41] The murder in Antioch of the High Priest Onias III, as told in 2 Maccabees (4:33–34) perhaps forms another connection.

[42] Studied in van Henten 1989.

[43] For a chronological bibliography, see van Henten 1994: 45–46.

[44] An exception was Eduard Norden 1915, for whom 4 Maccabees was a prime example of the Asianic style.

[45] On the date, see n. 20 above.

at home in a developed diaspora Judaism which expressed itself primarily—and perhaps exclusively—in Greek. The point has been forcefully expressed by Versnel, in a the course of a critique of readings that assimilate the book's eulogies and the epitaph to remote classical models of ἐπιτάφιοι λόγοι: 'die Frage "griechisch" oder "jüdisch" könnt möglicherweise weniger simplistisch, jedoch befriedigenger beantwortet werden mit "hellenistisch".'[46] These are words well-worth remembering in many contexts.

A philosophical discourse on the subject of the sovereignty of reason opens 4 Maccabees and supplies the focus for the discussion of martyrdom and for the concluding narration. In his opening words, the author describes what is to come programmatically as a φιλοσοφώτατος λόγος. The connection between reason and martyrdom might seem tenuous in the extreme; but for the author, it is the Stoic virtue of the mastery of the passions by the agency of reason which enables a person to subordinate himself or herself to the rule of divine law, living temperately, displaying piety and, ultimately, if necessary, mastering fear and dying with fortitude before abandoning those same principles. This seemingly artificial argument contrives to become, through its paradoxical character, a vehement defence of martyrdom. This is because the inflexible and obdurate mind-set of the martyr was perceived by some logical spirits as the epitome of unreason. Antiochus, who is at this stage still the exponent of a would-be reasonable argument, calls the brothers' self-sacrifice μανία (10:13)—perhaps with a touch of irony, since Epiphanes himself was dubbed ἐπιμανής in some quarters (Polybius XXVI 1.10). Philo says that opponents might consider the Jews' readiness to die for their laws as 'barbaric', while in reality it was an expression of freedom and nobility (Leg. 215). Later, Marcus Aurelius, in expounding the Stoic way to die, was to say that this should be with considered judgement (λελογισμένως) and not, in the Christian manner, obstinately and showily (11:3):[47] his readers were evidently expected to pick up the allusion to the martyrs, and to understand that they exemplified a passionate and deeply unphilosophical rush to death. The key characteristic of martyrdom in 4 Maccabees is, precisely, λογισμός.

---

[46] Versnel 1989: 193, in a critique of the influential paper of Lebram 1974.

[47] The remark may be a gloss, a possibility which does not reduce its interest here: Brunt 1979; Rutherford 1989: 178.

Standing this argument on its head would seem to be the original, if not very profound contribution of the author of 4 Maccabees.
Behind the distinctive teaching in 4 Maccabees lurks the well-known
Stoic paradox that 'the sage is not merely free but also a king', on
which Philo had written his *Quod omnis probus liber sit*.[48] But the illus-
trative material is biblical—the temperance of Joseph (2:2), the controlled anger of Moses compared with the rage of Simeon and Levi
against the Shechemites (2:15–19), David's overwhelming thirst (3:6–18).

   The second part of the work is devoted to a highly dramatized
and moralizing version of the deaths first of Eleazar, then of the
seven courageous sons and finally of their mother. Various strategies are called in aid—direct comment, reported speech, dialogue in
which two opposing cases are presented, and even the tombstone
device discussed earlier. The interaction between the king and the
martyrs was already featured, though without quoting the king's
words, in the 2 Maccabees version of the brothers' deaths, though
not for the death of Eleazar. The supposed historical event is the
core of 4 Maccabees, and that perhaps explains how tradition came
to ascribe this small anonymous book to the historian Josephus, as
occurs in many early manuscripts.[49]

   The two homilies at the end of the work, the longer one of the
mother and the very brief one from the author's own mouth, refer
back to the central philosophical theme, but do not take up the
philosophical mode again. They remain deliberately within the framework of Judaism: 'O offspring of the seed of Abraham, children of
Israel, obey this Law of yours and be entirely true to your religion, in
the knowledge that pious reason is master over the passions' (18:1 ff.).
Piety is firmly lodged alongside reason, and exhortation concludes
a work which has been in turn disquisition, diatribe, dialogue and
panegyric.[50]

Archetypes

It does not take the reader long to see that the story is modelled
around a set of archetypes of persecution and martyrdom. A number

---

[48] See Renehan 1972, especially 225, on the philosophical background.

[49] On the history of the text, Hadas 1953: 135–138; Anderson 1985: introduction.

[50] Interpreters have tended to favour one genre over another, with particular
emphasis on the diatribe (whatever exactly that may be) and the funeral speech.

of these deserve a closer look. Some but not all are specific to the Jewish-Greek tradition. But the strategies for turning martyrs into heroes, and especially for handling the resultant complications of gender identities (nos. 4 and 5), were to have a long history in Christian rhetoric. The epitaph which served as our springboard has supplied us with signposts and a sequence:

1. *The Law*

Nomos is the standard term in Greek for the Jewish Law, ubiquitous in Greek-Jewish literature as the symbol and quintessence of Judaism. The word appears some forty times in 4 Maccabees,[51] having already figured memorably in the 2 Maccabees martyrology. Given the number of its appearances, there is little room for doubt as to what the author meant by the term. Reference is to the Torah, the five books of Moses, taken to be of divine origin, focussing sometimes on the text itself, sometimes to the ordinances or the teaching contained in it. Eleazar delivers a lecture on the subject (5:1–38); Antiochus invites him to renounce it in favour of a Ἑλληνικὸς βίος; the eldest brother is its defender (9:15); all the brothers sacrifice themselves for its sake (13:9–27); the mother is its vindicator (15:29, ἔκδικος). The Law teaches all the virtues, especially the supreme one of piety, as Eleazar demonstrates; and in the end it is treated as almost synonymous with them. The old man insists that a small transgression is as serious as a great one, a statement which perhaps contributes to Stoic debates on this tricky subject,[52] but which also has a part to play in the structure of the book, as the link between the immediate cause of the confrontation—tasting forbidden food—and the larger cause for which the martyrs stand.[53]

2. *The Tyrant*

Already in 2 Maccabees, the Seleucid monarch is categorized as a savage tyrant (7:27).[54] In 4 Maccabees, the word *tyrannos* is liberally

---

[51] Redditt 1983.

[52] See the analysis by Renehan 1972. Weber 1991 covers similar ground.

[53] See below, 126–129.

[54] And once such imagery is used of Menelaus the high priest, described as having 'the fury of a savage beast' (4:25). 1 Maccabees also contains one neutral use of the word τύραννος to describe the Arab ruler Aretas (5:8).

employed, making, like *nomos*, over forty appearances. In the martyrology itself, Antiochus, ὁ τύραννος, is, indeed, the archetypal tyrant, seated on a lofty throne, his fully-armed soldiers mustered around him. The confrontation between ruler and victim, in some kind of trial scene, is nearly always a defining moment in martyrdom. This, in fact, remains the case in the rabbinic versions of the Maccabaean martyrdoms.[55] In 2 Maccabees, Antiochus had not been involved in the death of Eleazar; in 4 Maccabees, his role is enhanced and he is there from beginning to end. We see him ordering his guards to bring every single Hebrew before him (5:1–2). Braziers are heated, dire threats are uttered but also cajoling temptations offered; tongues are cut out, the king is reduced to ranting and raving.

A persecuting tyrant ought not to go unpunished, and in Jewish-Greek literature such figures regularly come to a gruesome end.[56] Their agonizing deaths may be brought before the reader, and if immediate retribution is not forthcoming, then prediction is possible. Posthumous retribution may also be envisaged. In 2 Maccabees, the youngest son endures extra brutality because he dares to predict the downfall of the persecutor (7:31, 36, 39). 4 Maccabees asserts that 'the tyrant Antiochus was punished upon earth, and is yet chastised after death' (18:5), and again, in conclusion, that 'divine justice has pursued the accursed being (ἀλάστορα), and will pursue him' (18:22). The punishment of the oppressor not only restores a certain morality to the world, but enables the martyred ones to snatch psychic victory out of physical devastation. This theme continues into Christian theology, eventually supplying title and subject to Lactantius' well-known tract.

3. *The Nation*

The martyrs die also to save the nation. We saw that in the epitaph the survival of the Jewish *politeia* was at stake; and this key Greek concept articulates the biblical connection between the law of Moses and the people of Israel. The prominent national dimension to the martyrdom goes some way towards explaining the invocations of the patriarchs in 4 Maccabees (7:19; 13:17; 16:25), and, especially,

---

[55] Doran 1980.

[56] A tradition enthusiastically taken up in Christian historiography in the *de mortibus persecutorum* literature: see Creed 1984: xxxv–xlii.

the extraordinary, and still puzzling description of the seven youths as 'sons of Abraham', and of the mother as a 'daughter of Abraham', equipped with a soul like the patriarch's (6:22; 14:20; 15:28; 17:6; 18:1, 23). These heroes belong no longer to their own family group but to the people of the covenant as a whole. It is most appropriate, therefore, that their final resting place should be in Abraham's bosom (13:17). The high valuation placed on the heritage of Abraham in this period is well-known to us from New Testament literature, developed in the epistle to the Hebrews, but appearing already in Paul's theology (Gal. 3:6–9; 29). In relation to this family, however, and especially in the mother's case, we must consider the possibility of an additional resonance in the association. The mother's sacrifice of her children outstripped Abraham's readiness to bind Isaac; while it was in Isaac that the boys themselves found their inspiration (13:12; 16:20).

4. *Heroism*

Judas Maccabaeus died to rescue Temple, city and territory. The supposedly contemporaneous martyrs of Antioch are presented as victim-heroes. No less than the Maccabees, they are saviours of the nation through their fortitude; and the implication is, again, that, without the Law, there could be no physical survival. The terminology of male heroism therefore figures largely in 4 Maccabees, with evocations of warfare and athletic imagery (17:11–17 etc.), although they are, interestingly, sparser in the earlier work, 2 Maccabees.[57] These images are intrinsic to martyrology, as the agents which effect the transmutation of shaming passivity into the highest of masculine virtues. What we are offered is a concentrated inversion of the competitive, physical values which constructed masculinity for Greco-Roman society, a triumphant reversal of the power-structure, with the victim as the winner. The language of warfare is therefore deployed. Thus, Eleazar's resistance is said to transcend that of any besieged city (7:4); and it cannot be accidental that when the instruments of torture are brought on, the catalogue, complete with its catapults, reads astonishingly like a description of siege equipment (8:13–14). When it comes to the torture itself, the proliferation of horrific physical detail might seem self-indulgent or superfluous; but

---

[57] For instances of this imagery in Jewish and early Christian martyrology generally, see Kellermann 1989: 73.

the martyrs must be tormented to the limits of their endurance in order to validate, far from the battlefield, their claim to the title of heroes. The predicted downfall of the tyrant is, of course, their ultimate victory.

5. *Hero, Virgin, and Mother*

For all the masculinity associated with the martyrdoms in 4 Maccabees, one of the leading figures is not merely a woman, but, in a development from 2 Maccabees, a mother of advancing years (16:1). Can *andreia* be open to her too? In 2 Maccabees, we are told that she applied masculine spirit (θυμός) to her female mind (λογισμός). The author of 4 Maccabees goes further, insisting that the mother even transcends men in the sphere of male values: 'more noble than males in endurance, more manly than men in resistance' (15:30). With strength superior to that of any man, she has defeated the tyrant (16:14). She is a victorious athlete (15:29). The identity of the heroic martyr is thus preserved as a masculine one.[58] At the same time, this is a woman whose female identity is also heavily stressed, which undercuts her temporarily-assumed masculinity, and, as it were, restores her where she belongs. Indeed, we can hardly fail to notice that, as a woman, the mother possesses seriously-conflicting identities. On the one hand, she was and in spirit still is a chaste maiden who has kept her body pure—'I did not leave my father's home'; neither evil spirits nor any serpent have defiled her; she is, if the text has been correctly read and interpreted, the worthy protector of Adam's rib.[59] This remarkable anticipation, in a few sentences, of centuries of demonization of female sexuality,[60] accompanies the author's admiring presentation of the mother's voluntary death (perhaps something less than full martyrdom) as the preservation of her body from violation (18:6). On the other hand, and scarcely consistently, this mother of seven sons is the epitome of maternal affection, who has carried, and nursed seven children, only to lose them all and with them the hope of grandchildren (16:5–11). She is the mother of the nation, the ark of Noah; we see her suffering as though she

---

[58] The same strategies are visible in Christian martyrology. See Perkins 1995: 110–115.

[59] This is the most plausible interpretation of τὴν ᾠκοδομημένην πλευράν (18:7–8): Hadas 1953: n. *ad loc.*, following Grimm.

[60] Pagels 1988; Cameron 1989; 1993.

is giving birth again, when our author assimilates verbally the agony of losing children with the pains of childbirth (18:9).

In the concluding section, the mother, having protested her female modesty and subservience, steps into her late husband's shoes to give an indirect discourse rich in biblical prototypes and sentiments on the subject of sacrifice, zeal and deliverance. This is presented as a commemoration of his teaching: 'he, when he was still with you, taught you the Law and the prophets . . .' (18:10). By having a woman speak the epilogue, the author has perhaps taken himself off the philosophical hook: instead of returning, as might be expected, to his opening propositions, he is able simply to cap the maternal words with a brief prayer: 'the children of Abraham, with their prize-winning mother, are gathered into the choir of their fathers, having received souls that are pure and immortal from God, to whom be the glory for ever and ever. Amen.' A Jewish mother might just utter words of Torah, at any rate if she had learnt them from her husband and was giving instruction on his behalf. But she could scarcely have been heard doing Greek philosophy.

Ultimately, the mother is detached from her children. In 2 Maccabees, her short oration seems to deny her own involvement in their production: 'I do not know how you ever appeared in my womb.' The Creator of the World fashioned them; nothing else is important (7:22–23). The mother's lack of control is thus made visible: in having brought forth children to die for the nation, her own role has become doubly depersonalized, not only as Jewish martyr but also as woman. In 4 Maccabees, her childbearing (παιδοποιία) is summed up as being of 'father Abraham' (18.5), and, by her being made a mere vessel, her own role is minimized as much as that of the boys' wholly shadowy deceased father.

6. *Anonymity*

The heroic mother is a nameless heroine. Not one of her sons has a name or designation. Eleazar, the old teacher, would, by contrast, seem to be individuated, yet his is in effect a generic name, given in both the *Letter of Aristeas* and in 3 Maccabees to the venerable priest in the story. This preference for anonymity is significant: we may detect in Jewish martyrology a tendency to discourage any possible focus on personalities and, ultimately, to curb the cult of individuals. The martyrs must represent Israel as a whole. Rabbinic literature occasionally assigns the name Maria or Miriam to the mother,[61] while in Spanish versions of Josippon, the Mediaeval Hebrew Josephus, she is Hannah;[62] it is hard not to suspect Christian influence behind these developments. But it was left to Erasmus, re-writing 4 Maccabees in 1524, to give names to the sons (as well as the name Solomona to the mother).[63] Christian cults of the Maccabaean martyrs spread from Antioch as far afield as the church of S. Pietro in Vincoli at Rome and later, via Byzantium and Milan, even to Cologne.[64] But the evidence for a Jewish cult in the synagogue at Daphne, commonly assumed to have been the precursor of the Christian one, and to have been taken over by it, is extremely weak.[65]

The omission of names is one strategy in an enduring tradition of de-personalization in Jewish representations of the past. Chazan (1991) writes of the dominance of historical paradigms in the portrayal of the Jewish martyrs of Germany in the Hebrew chronicles, and one of his citations offers us a reflection of a curious attitude to individualization. The author feels obliged to qualify what he has written with a firm expression of reserve, reminding us that comparisons with religious heroes of old matter more than individual identities:

> All these things were done by those whom we have singled out by name . . . The rest of the community and the notables of the congregation, for whom we have not detailed their activities and their piety, they did *all the more*. The activities which they undertook in order to proclaim the unity of the Name of the King of kings, the Holy One blessed be he, [were] like those of Rabbi Akiba and his associates, and they stood the test like Hananiah, Mishael and Azariah.[66]

Again, Scholem[67] comments on the tendency of Kabbalistic sources to obscure the personalities and even to exclude the names of leading mystics. The namelessness of the mother and her seven sons in the Maccabaean tradition may seem a small point, but I suggest that it should be regarded as the primary defining characteristic of Jewish-Greek martyrology in this period.

---

[61] See e.g. Lamentations Rabbah 1:60.
[62] Hadas 1953: 134.
[63] Townshend 1913: 661. The names are Maccabeus, Aber, Machir, Judas, Achas, Areth and Jacob.
[64] Rampolla 1899; Schatkin 1974.
[65] There is no reason to take 4 Maccabees as a commemorative oration, as Obermann 1931, Hadas 1953.
[66] Chronicle L, translation in Chazan 1987: 267; cf. 1991.
[67] Scholem 1941: 16.

We have looked at six aspects of the representation of the Maccabaean martyrdoms. By way of brief summary, it might be said
that while the 4 Maccabees doctrine of reason versus the passions
is good Hellenistic philosophy of a crude and eclectic kind,[68] the
nexus between piety, self-mastery, life under the Law and a heroic
death for its sake is the Jewish-Greek theory of martyrdom, repeated
time and again in our literature, its essential elements not differing
greatly, even if their formal setting varies. The roots of that theory
are both circumstantial and literary, and it is hard to disentangle
them in any meaningful way.

The Socratic model

The impact of Greek thought, Classical or Hellenistic, on Jewish-
Greek martyrology has been sought by scholars in a number of directions, and the formative model of the ideal martyr in the Hellenistic
and Roman worlds, the philosopher Socrates, has not been wholly
ignored. But there are some surprisingly close connections between
the portrayal of Eleazar and the Platonic death of Socrates which
have so far escaped observation. These intricate links will indicate
that our texts, for all their Jewish content, should not be regarded
as falling outside the mainstream of Hellenistic thought.

The *Apology*, *Crito* and *Phaedo*, above all other interpretations,
moulded Socrates' semi-voluntary martyrdom into a powerful amalgamation of historical event and literary creation. The philosopher's
disdain for his accusers, his elevation of the pursuit of truth and of
the continuance of his mission above life itself, refusing to under-
mine Athenian law by evading the death sentence, for all his friends'
entreaties, were profoundly influential in all the philosophical and
religious schools of antiquity, and then beyond.[69] In effect, Plato's
Socrates died, in 399 B.C., *for philosophy*, the chosen way of life of
a self-appointed intellectual and spiritual elite—of a small minority,
in fact, among the residents of Athens. And the words ascribed to
him are designed to put it beyond doubt that such a way of life,
the route to the ultimate good, is a thing worth dying for; indeed,

---

[68] Renehan 1972.
[69] Droge and Tabor 1992: ch. 2. Versnel 1989: 178–181 brings this tradition
into connection with 4 Maccabees, but does not discuss the features identified here.

as Plato presents the matter, Socrates behaved in a way which was tantamount to seeking his own execution, this being the surest demonstration of his personal certainty. The core of Plato's *Apology* is, precisely, Socrates' vindication of his lifelong dedication to philosophy. His triumph over his enemies in the city, and over his three particular accusers, is also trumpeted loud and clear there: in the immediate present, he runs rings round them in verbal exchanges (often with weak arguments). Beyond that, we learn that they will suffer far more from the doing of an unjust deed than Socrates will from having to endure any amount of evil. And, in any case, as far as the philosopher is concerned, death is not an evil. It should be remembered, however, that Socrates, being an Athenian citizen, was not exposed to the risk of torture, in contrast to later Jewish and Christian martyrs.

The death of Socrates was a major, and evidently an unexpected blow to his disciples. The creation of a martyrology assisted Plato and others in coming to terms with the trauma to themselves personally and, more important, to their group and its ideals. A potentially shameful condemnation was transformed into a permanent triumph, and their grief into awe and wonderment. So, for the later followers of the philosophical schools, and, above all, for the Roman Stoics, it was easy for Socrates' death to became an exemplar of how a man (or occasionally a woman) should behave when driven to death by an unjust regime, especially, in practice, by a tyrannical ruler or a potential tyrant. The inbuilt need for publicity ensured that *exitus illustrium virorum* became a genre of sectarian literature.[70]

It is striking that, in 4 Maccabees, a distinctive Socratic twist is given to the concept of martyrdom in an utterance of Eleazar which is a perfect blend of the various ingredients: 'it would most surely be contrary to reason if, having lived our lives in accordance with the truth right up to our old age and having preserved our fair reputation for so living in conformity with the Law, we should now change and ourselves teach impiety to the young by setting them an example of eating unclean food (6:6 ff.). I would suggest that the expostulation about a change of course late in life echoes Socrates' indignant questions in the *Crito*. And the whole scenario here, with

---

[70] On Socrates' death as a model in Hellenistic and Roman philosophy and action, see Griffin 1986; Long 1988. The evidence adduced by Alexander 1994, for Luke's exploitation of the Socratic template, is particularly pertinent here.

the courtiers begging the grey-haired Eleazar not to destroy himself ('let us bring you some of the cooked food and you pretend to taste of the swine's flesh and save yourself': 2 Macc. 6:15) becomes blatantly Socratic by the introduction of the extraordinary notion that these courtiers of the king had previously been friends of Eleazar's: they thus assume the role enacted by Socrates' friends in the *Phaedo* and the *Crito*, when they tell him he must allow them to arrange for him to escape from prison. This motif is already integrated into the representation in 2 Maccabees (6:21 ff.), whence 4 Maccabees has adopted it. Some manuscripts of 4 Maccabees actually say that Eleazar was distinguished in philosophy.[71]

Philo

While 2 and 4 Maccabees, but especially the latter, are the key texts for any understanding of Jewish martyrdom as a literary construction, they belong in a wider framework of thought, narration and widespread awareness of martyrdom in the major authors of our period.[72] We are dealing with an ideology which transcends the imagination of individual authors, an ideology which became firmly lodged in circles not noted for their encouragement of zealous extremism in the defence of Judaism.

For a representation of the phenomenon of persecution and of the Jews as a persecuted people, we have to turn to Philo and to the events of 40 A.D. in Alexandria. These events were not inappropriately designated 'the first pogrom' in modern Jewish historiography, first by Klausner and then by Tcherikover. For Philo, a leading participant, they were far more than run-of-the mill riots, and it was perhaps not only his political engagement which led him to describe the events in considerable detail and in the strongest terms. There are two separate tracts on the subject, known to us as *Against Flaccus* and the *Embassy to Gaius*.

In Philo's view, there existed in this case more than one tyrannical persecutor: the emperor Caligula demanded to be worshipped as a God and gave orders for his statue to be placed in the Jerusalem Temple and, apparently, in Jewish synagogues. 'Gaius crushed irre-

---

[71] φιλοσοφίαν for ἡλικίαν, which is a dittography.
[72] van Henten et al. 1989: 2–4.

sistibly not only those who did not carry out his command but also those who did not do so at once.' (*Leg.* 209). He was 'naturally cruel and never satiated with revenge' (*Flacc.* 180). At Alexandria, the Roman prefect, Avillius Flaccus, set himself up as an enemy of the Jews, largely, it is alleged, in order to win back Caligula's lost favour, and he schemed against them with devillish cunning: 'for persons naturally tyrannical, who have not the addition of strength, achieve their malignant designs through cunning' (*Flacc.* 1). Flaccus 'fanned the flames of sedition, filling the inhabited world with conflict between races' (44). The attack is perceived as one directed first and foremost against the Jewish Law; the undermining of Jewish claims to citizenship (whatever they amounted to) was only secondary (53). Assaults on synagogues, either by arson or with sacrilegious portraits of the emperor, were soon followed by the ejection of the Jews from their homes around the city, supposedly at Flaccus' command. They were herded into the 'delta' quarter on the sea-shore, where they had been densest before, into what can only be described as a ghetto, in the modern usage of the term. This hounding was backed up by the looting of Jews shops and by lynchings. People became 'human brushwood'. Even corpses were violated.

The events were undoubtedly real enough; but Philo has shaped the episode. The distinction between these attacks and conventional warfare, the total helplessness of the trapped and (at this stage) unarmed Jews, the cruelty of the rampant mob and the gratuitous tortures inflicted on the victims are all vividly drawn. 'The final punishment kept in reserve was the cross' (72). Flaccus' end was that due to a persecutor: central to the work is an account of how he was recalled, condemned and executed by Caligula for misdemeanours in his governorship: 'it was the will of justice that the butcheries wrought on his single body should be as numerous as the number of the Jews whom he unlawfully put to death', and this was a proof that God's support had not been withdrawn from the Jews (189; 191). F.H. Colson, Philo's English translator, writes of 'a vindictiveness which I feel to be repulsive . . .', commenting that 'this is a tract which those who admire the beauty and spirituality so often shown [by Philo] might well wish to have been left unwritten'.[73] Comment is scarcely required.

---

[73] *Philo*, Loeb IX: 301.

It is in connection with the events in Palestine, in the *Embassy to Gaius*, that Philo is most explicit about his view of the other side of the coin, the martyrdoms which are the counterpart of persecution. The Jews who besought the Roman governor of Syria, Petronius, to oppose Caligula's planned desecration of the Temple had made it clear that they 'would willingly endure to die not once but a thousand times . . . rather than allow any of the prohibited actions to be committed' (*Leg.* 209). Submission—'let them slaughter, butcher, carve our flesh without a blow struck or blood drawn by us' (233), or group suicide—'then standing in the midst of our kinsfolk after bathing ourselves in their blood . . . we will mingle our blood with theirs' (235), would both be welcomed. In the event, neither was required on this occasion, as Caligula's death forestalled any action by Petronius. Here, again, the ultimate purpose is defence of the Law, in refusing either to violate it themselves or to allow it to be violated in any particular; and the unity of the people is a central part of this conception. Military brutality on behalf of an evil government is the expected scenario.

In philosophical vein, Philo does not depart from the understanding of martyrdom incorporated in his polemical works. Notably, *Quod omnis probus* (88 ff.) briefly sketches the evil rulers themselves, in praising the virtuousness of the Essene sect: many are the tyrants who assault them, 'outdoing wild beasts in their ferocity.'

Josephus

The thoughts of Josephus are similar, so much so indeed that the historian might have had Philo in mind in some of his emphatic assertions, written some half a century later. The *Against Apion*, where these matters are spelled out in a theoretical fashion, is as much a philosophical as a historical composition, calling forth general statements. Dying for the Law takes pride of place in the definition of Judaism. Obedience to that Law is something instilled into every individual from birth, and each is happy in the awareness that he might have to give up his life for it (*CA* I 42). 'Many of my countrymen', Josephus tells us, 'have died rather than utter a single word against the Law, and to them rebirth and a better existence is assured in the divine cycle' (II 218). Here a future life is mentioned because the specific context is a discussion of penalties and rewards.

Again, we read that Jews are educated in courage, not in order to fight battles but to endure for the sake of the Law (II 272; 292)—a version of the now-familiar redefinition of heroism, if a somewhat surprising statement from one who had been a Jewish general in the revolt against Rome. Or perhaps we should not, after all, find this reaction remarkable, given Josephus' views and his own war record; he will scarcely have understood his great opportunity for suicide at Jotapata as a valid occasion for a martyr's death.

What is truly unexpected is the historian's presentation, in his historical writing, of Jewish deviants and rebels as true martyrs. The excursus on the Essenes in the second book of the *Jewish War* recounts, as its climax, how,

> the war against the Romans fully revealed their souls. In the course of it, their limbs were twisted and broken, burned and shattered; they were subjected to every instrument of torture in attempts to force them either to blaspheme the lawgiver or to eat forbidden food. But they refused to do either, or even to plead with their murderers or show any distress. Smiling in the midst of pain, and mocking those who tortured them, they gave up their souls cheerfully, convinced that they would recover them again. (152–53)

Also in the *Jewish War*, we find Josephus recognizing, in Eleazar's Masada speech, the value of a religiously-motivated suicide, as an example to others (*BJ* VII 351), even if elsewhere the historian lays out counter-arguments with equal eloquence. He expatiates upon the joyful and noble endurance of the young refugee rebels (*sicarii*) who died under appalling torture in Egypt after the end of the revolt, although he also allows that their strength of mind may be madness (ἀπόνοια, VII 417–419). And in his *Antiquities*, written later (XV 288 ff.), he shows how *sicarii* who perished for conspiring against Herod had readily confessed their deeds 'for the sake of the communal customs which all men have long since regarded as a value to be preserved and one for which one is prepared to give up one's life' (Herod, it is suggested, had flouted these values). Considering how little love Josephus had for all such rebels, we can only conclude that his regard for martyrdom was indeed high, unless we follow Hengel in his surmise that: 'the source material available to Josephus was presumably already fashioned by a Jewish pattern of reporting cases of martyrdom.'[74]

[74] Hengel 1989: 259. My position is similar to that of Gafni 1988: 124 and 130,

The passages in the *Against Apion* demonstrate Josephus' general standpoint clearly enough. Apart from the briefer statements I have summarized, we find a more extended comment in the context of a comparison of the Jewish way of life with the much vaunted Spartan ethos and constitution: the merits of the Jewish Law can be demonstrated by the people's ready and total obedience to it. Their obedience is in turn proved by their fearlessness of death on its behalf: 'I do not refer', Josephus explains, referring once more to the matter of military courage, 'to that easiest of deaths which comes to those on the battlefield, but to one accompanied by physical torture, the kind which is thought to be the hardest of all' (*CA* II 232). There is also a reference to the gratuitous cruelty of rulers, who might even torture the Jews in order simply to observe the remarkable spectacle of their endurance, and here the choice of the word 'spectacle' (θέαμα) to describe martyrdom, is a telling one. The values which the Law incorporates, for which it is worth dying, are finally spelled out, and given a somewhat philosophical colouring: service and discipline, dictated by rules rather than individual fancy, and controlled moderation in diet, sex and spending.

Food, martyrdom and Jewish identity

It is may seem peculiar that Josephus puts the dietary regulations first among the pillars of the Law. But the issue of consumption is also central elsewhere: avoiding unclean foodstuffs becomes the primary observance from which oppressors will try to part the Jews, taking precedence in the later stages over and above the sabbath, circumcision or any other aspect of the purity regulations. We might well wonder how this originated.

We can at any rate observe that the tradition of martyrology revolving around the dietary issue evolves piecemeal and gradually. It is instructive to look first at the concise martyrdom story in the first book of Maccabees (1:41–64). This narrative opens with a broad portrayal of persecution, showing Antiochus' overseers setting up altars for the sacrifice of swine and forbidding circumcision in the cities of Judaea; the matter of eating the sacrificial meat is not men-

---

who justly questions Goldstein's confidence that Josephus' stance on martyrdom derives from 2 Maccabees.

tioned. What is in effect a miniature martyrdom text follows, not involving Eleazar, the mother or the seven sons: several months of intense activity by royal overseers in the towns and villages, with many compulsory sacrifices offered, death sentences passed and scrolls of the Law torn and burnt, culminate in the desecration of the Temple cult. Then we read a sweeping account of how mothers were put to death, their circumcized infants hung around their necks, alongside their entire families. Yet, when we come to the author's conclusion, we find an oddly specific assertion 'yet many in Israel found strength to resist, taking a determined stand against *eating* any unclean food. They welcomed death rather than defile themselves and profane the holy covenant; and so they died' (1:64). For all this, it must be said that eating does not loom as large in 1 Maccabees as controversies over Sabbath observance, and it is revealing that Josephus, recounting the tragedy in book 12 of the *Antiquities*, and following 1 Maccabees,[75] quite simply excludes altogether the declaration in 1 Maccabees about unclean food.

It is left to 2 Maccabees to give new and particular emphasis to the eating of sacrificial meat. Again, a general persecution in Judaea and in 'the neighbouring Greek cities' is described first (6:6–12), in comparable but different terms, with mention of the banning of Sabbath observance, the institution of Dionysiac processions and the parading and brutal execution of two women with their circumcized babies. But we soon move to the consequences of compulsory sacrifice, focussing wholly on consumption. Eleazar dies (by frying) rather than eat sacrificial meat. A textual uncertainty leaves us in doubt as to whether he tasted and then spat out the meat or refused to touch it.[76] The seven sons are tortured, some by having their tongues cut out, because they will not touch pork. It is telling that we have already learnt how, in the mountains, Judas and his band restricted themselves to a diet of herbs to avoid contamination (5:27). Most interestingly, an author (or epitomator) who lacks a word for martyrdom, is found adopting a semi-technical term σπλαγχνισμός (eating entrails) to mean, precisely, the enforced consumption of sacrificial

---

[75] He ignores or does not know 2 Maccabees. On this problem, see Gafni 1988: 128, n. 39.

[76] 6:20: προπτύσας is the generally accepted reading, and the author's claim seems to be that Eleazar took in and then spat out the meat; but the whole sentence has difficulties.

meat (6:7, 21; 7:42).[77] We also find the same root in verbal form
(6.8); And the term is even deployed in the sentence in which the
author concludes and sums up the meaning of the entire episode.
This unique vocabulary may well have been coined by Jason of
Cyrene, or at least by the epitomator who created 2 Maccabees from
Jason's work, and its function is to emphasize the decisive moment
in the confrontation between pagan oppressor and Jewish martyr.
Interestingly, the term was not taken up by 4 Maccabees, although
there is, paradoxically, much interest there in the entrails of the tortured Eleazar.

In any case, the dietary theme is developed considerably in the
later work, especially when Eleazar explains how important a part
of reverence for God and care of the soul are the self-imposed restrictions of Judaism: οὐ μιαροφαγοῦμεν (5:25), not only attaching the
martyrdoms to this one act of refusal, but exploring its meaning
through his dialogue. In this discussion, he eschews the most telling
point, that the act amounts to idolatry, the most fundamental of all
sins, leaving this observation to be made by his modern commentator.[78] Eleazar's self-justification is concerned with the overriding
importance of not violating the Law, and the forbidden foods are
symbolic of all its prohibitions. A specialized vocabulary is employed
here too. We find the striking verbs σαρκοφαγεῖν and μιαροφαγεῖν,
the former apparently referring, like the latter, to sacrificial flesh,
and not, as might be expected, to the consumption of dead meat
by forbidden birds of prey (cf. *Letter of Aristeas* 146). But for all the
discussion, it never emerges clearly from this book whether what is
at issue is a ban on the consumption of sacrificial meat or the specific
abstention from pork. The detailed food laws of Leviticus are not
referred to by Eleazar. We may contrast the *Letter of Aristeas*, a defence
of Judaism written in the Hellenistic period, which accords a large
part of the High Priest's exposition of the Law to the topic of unclean
foods of different kinds, and examines various prescriptions before
offering an allegorical interpretation (142–55).

In whatever vein, the prominence of the forbidden acts of consumption in the definition of Judaism offered by Jewish authors writing in Greek is not in doubt. This phenomenon can be explained

---

[77] In the last instance this word is used in the concluding sentence to encapsulate the foregoing events. Commentators have generally failed to notice the special
usage; but see Doran 1980.

[78] Hadas 1953: 119.

in terms of the specific functions of Jewish martyrology, in which a central purpose is to 'save the nation', to establish models for the preservation of Jewish identity under alien rule. The dietary laws are a vital symbolic distinguishing mark. As 4 Maccabees laboriously argues, they stand for the law as a whole. Even in a world where a subject people had an established *modus vivendi*, it was crucial to group survival to retain an awareness of what might happen, to specify what might be demanded of a person, just as it had been demanded in the past, and to teach such lessons simply and graphically. 4 Maccabees takes pains to indicate that Seleucus IV had been a beneficent ruler, under whom the Jews had obeyed the Law, lived in profound peace, and prospered; but in his wake came the tyrant (3:20).[79] The awareness of the double-sidedness of foreign rule is a recurrent theme in Diaspora literature, well-exemplified in the juxtapositions of Daniel.[80] And it is the special contribution of Jewish-Greek martyrology to integrate what had become an everyday identity-marker of Judaism, its dietary rules, with a picture of Jewish identity and faith stretched to abnormal limits in a crisis of persecution. Whether this representation was generated by a dimly remembered historic moment, a real and traumatic attempt by Seleucid overseers to force forbidden food on certain Jews, or whether by subsequent social developments, we do not know. Nor does it much matter much. Either way, this reconstruction of the past, with its distinctive archetypes of martyrdom, was fixed both in literature and in popular memory.

As the focus of a demonstration that the Law was worth dying for, the motif of resistance to force-feeding was a powerful one, representing the intrusion of alien control and then rejection at the most intimate level, announcing control of an individual and a people's destiny through control of their bodies. The ideology of death by fasting among the Stoic martyrs of the senatorial class at Rome perhaps makes a comparable statement about freedom.

Conclusion: the functions of Jewish martyrology

In the Judaism of the Greco-Roman period, representations of martyrs and martyrdoms served to encapsulate statements about national identity, to define the nation's relation to outsiders and to explore

---

[79] Seleucus Nicanor is mistakenly named in place of Philopator.
[80] Davies 1991.

potential political crises. Martyrs are national heroes or heroines,
scarcely individuated, even when their deaths are described in blow-
by-blow accounts. So martyrologies took shape not as an independent
form of literature, but within a range of literary genres, in which
they were one strand among others. The Christian perspective, it
may be suggested, would prove somewhat different, since martyrdom and the description of martyrdom, in addition to consoling and
confirming the faithful became also an essential instrument in prop-
agating the faith. Literature devoted to the depiction of martyrs triumphant as they went joyfully, even voluntarily, to their deaths, was
a powerful advertisement for a new and spreading faith. Such literature had to be widely circulated. Emphasis on the personality of
the individual, demonstrating his or her transition from ordinary life
to sanctity and then to posthumous immortality, contributed to their
impact. For Jewish martyrologies, by contrast, all this was distraction.
This contrast, if it has any validity, may be helpful in divorcing
Jewish martyrology from Christian perspectives, and in clarifying the
distinctive and sometimes puzzling features of the Jewish versions.

   Jewish-Greek martyrologies are located between several cultural
worlds. They are indissoluble fusions of various traditions. They are
a part of later Greek literature. They initiate what was to prove one
of the most enduring forms of Christian discourse. But ultimately,
the children of Abraham and their prize-winning mother ought to
be restored to the bosom of Abraham and to the choir of their
fathers where they belong.[81]

Bibliography

Abel, F.M. 1949. *Les livres des Maccabées*. Paris.
Alexander, L. 1993. 'Acts and Ancient Intellectual Biography', in B. Winter &
   A. Clarke (eds), *The Book of Acts in its Ancient Literary Setting*. Grand Rapids, Michigan,
   31–63.

---

[81] My early thoughts on this subject formed part, in 1991, of a Presidential
Address to the British Association for Jewish Studies. The final version of the text
was completed in the congenial environment of the Institute for Advanced Studies
of the Hebrew University in Jerusalem, and benefited greatly from the comments
of friends and colleagues there, especially those of Uriel Rappaport and Israel
Shatzman. I am particularly grateful to Daniel Schwartz for reading the entire text
with an eagle eye and for (as ever) copious information and bibliography; to Miriam
Griffin for valuable suggestions; and to Simon Swain for his editorial improvements.

Anderson, H. 1985. '4 Maccabees', in J.H. Charlesworth (ed.), *The Old Testament Pseudepigrapha*. New York, 2, 531–564.

Baumeister, T. 1980. *Die Anfänge der Theologie des Martyriums*. Münster.

Ben Sasson, H.H. 1972. 'Kiddush ha-Shem and Hillul ha-Shem' in *Encyclopedia Judaica* 10: 977–986.

Bickermann, E.J. 1945/1976. 'The Date of Fourth Maccabees' in *Louis Ginzberg Jubilee Volume* 1. New York, 105–112 = *Studies in Jewish and Christian History* 1: 276–281.

—— 1976. *Studies in Jewish and Christian History* 1. Leiden.

Blank, S.H. 1937–38. 'The Death of Zechariah in Rabbinic Literature', *HUCA* 12–13: 327–346.

Bowersock, G. 1995. *Martyrdom and Rome*. Cambridge.

Breitenstein, U. 1976. *Beobachtungen zu Sprache, Stil und Gedankengut des Vierten Makkabäerbuchs*. Basel/Stuttgart.

Brunt, P.A. 1979. 'Marcus Aurelius and the Christians' in C. Deroux (ed.), *Studies in Later Latin Literature and Roman History*. Brussels, 484–520.

Cameron, A. 1989. 'Virginity as Metaphor: Women and the Rhetoric of Early Christianity' in A. Cameron (ed.), *History as Text*. London, 184–205.

—— 1991. *Christianity and the Rhetoric of Empire: the Development of Christian Discourse*. London.

—— 1994. 'Early Christianity and the Discourse of Female Desire' in L. Archer, S. Fischler & M. Wyke (eds), *Women in Ancient Societies. 'An Illusion of the Night'*. London, 152–168.

Campbell, D.A. 1992. *The Rhetoric of Righteousness in Romans 3, 21–6*. JSNT Supplement 65. Sheffield: 219–228.

Charles, R.H. (ed.). 1913. *The Apocrypha and Pseudepigrapha of the Old Testament in English*, vol. 1. Oxford.

Chazan, I. 1987. *European Jewry and the First Crusade*. Berkeley.

—— 1991. 'Representation of Events in the Middle Ages' in A. Rapoport-Albert (ed.), *Studies in Jewish Historiography*. Atlanta, Georgia, 40–55.

Cohen, Gerson D. 1972. 'Hannah and her Seven Sons' in *Encyclopedia Judaica* 7: 1270–1272.

—— 1991. *Studies in the Variety of Rabbinic Cultures*. Jewish Publication Society. Philadelphia.

Creed, J.L. (ed.) 1984. *Lactantius. De Mortibus Persecutorum*. Oxford.

Davies, P.R. 1991. 'Daniel in the Lion's Den', in L. Alexander (ed.), *Images of Empire*. Journal for the Study of the Old Testament Supplement Series 122. Sheffield, 160–178.

Delehaye, H. 1921; 2nd ed. 1966. *Les passions des martyrs et les genres littéraires*. Brussels.

Doran, R. 1980. 'The Martyr: A Synoptic View of the Mother and her Seven Sons', in J. Collins & G. Nickelsburg (eds), *Ideal Figures in Ancient Judaism*. Chico, California, 189–221.

Döring, K. 1979. *Exemplum Socratis. Studien zur Sokrates Nachwirkung in der kynisch-stoischen Popularphilosophie der frühen Kaizerzeit und im frühen Christentum*. Hermes Einzelschriften 42. Wiesbaden.

Droge, A.J. & Tabor, J.D. 1992. *A Noble Death. Suicide and Martyrdom among Jews and Christians in Antiquity*. San Francisco.

Dupont-Sommer, A. 1939. *Le quatrième livre des Maccabées. Introduction, traduction et notes*. Bibliothèque de l'école des hautes études. Paris.

Fischel, H.A. 1946–47. 'Martyr and Prophet', *JQR* 37.

Frend, W.H.C. 1965. *Martyrdom and Persecution in the Early Church*. Oxford.

Gafni, I.M. 1989. 'Josephus and 1 Maccabees', in L.H. Feldman & G. Hata (eds), *Josephus, the Bible and History*. Detroit, 116–131.

132 CHAPTER SIX

Gardner, A.E. 1988. 'III and IV Maccabees: Reflections on the Maccabaean Crisis', *Zion* 53.3: 291–302 (Hebrew with English summary).
Goldstein, J.A. 1983. *II Maccabees. A New Translation with Introduction and Commentary.* Anchor Bible 41A. Garden City, New York.
Griffin, M.T. 1986. 'Philosophy, Cato and Roman Suicide', *Greece and Rome* 33: 64–77; 192–202.
Habicht, C. 1976. *2 Makkabäerbuch.* Jüdische Schriften aus hellenistisch-römischer Zeit 1.3. Gütersloh.
Hadas, M. 1953. *The Third and Fourth Book of Maccabees.* New York.
Hayward, C.T.R. 1990. 'The Sacrifice of Isaac and Jewish Polemic against Christianity', *CBQ* 52.2: 292–306.
Hengel, M. 1989. *The Zealots.* 1st German ed., 1961; Engl. transl. of 1976 German ed. Edinburgh.
Herr, M.D. 1972. 'Persecutions and Martyrdom in Hadrian's Days', *Scripta Hierosolymitana* 23: 85–125.
Jacobs, L. 1990. *Holy Living: Saints and Saintliness in Judaism.* Northvale, NJ/London.
Jonge, M. de 1988. 'Jesus' Death for Others and the Death of the Maccabaean Martyrs', in T. Baarda, A. Hilhorst, *et al.* (eds), *Text and Testimony. Festschrift for A.F.J. Klijn.* Kampen, 142–151.
Kellermann, U. 1989. 'Das Danielbuch und die Märtyrertheologie der Auferstehung' in J.W. van Henten, B.A.G.M. Dehandschutter & H.J.W. van der Klaauw (eds), *Die Entstehung der jüdichen Martyrologie.* Studia Postbiblica 38. Leiden, 51–75.
Klauck, H.-J. 1989. *4 Makkabäerbuch.* Jüdische Schriften aus hellenistisch-römischer Zeit 3.6. Gütersloh.
Lampe, G.W.H. 1981. 'Martyrdom and Inspiration', in W. Horbury & B. McNeil (eds), *Suffering and Martyrdom in the New Testament. Studies Presented to G.M. Styler by the Cambridge New Testament Seminar.* Cambridge, 118–135.
Lane Fox, R. 1988. *Pagans and Christians.* London.
Lebram, J.C.H. 1974. 'Die literarische Form des vierten Makkabäerbuches', *Vigiliae Christianae* 28: 89–96.
Licht, J. 1961. 'Taxo on the Apocalyptic Doctrine of Vengeance', *JJS* 12: 95–103.
Long, A.A. 1988. 'Socrates in Hellenistic Philosophy', *CQ* 38: 150–171.
Mélèze-Modrzejewski, J. 1995. *The Jews of Egypt from Rameses II to Emperor Hadrian.* Jewish Publication Society. Philadelphia/Jerusalem.
Nickelsburg, G.W.E. 1972. *Resurrection, Immortality and Eternal Life in Intertestamental Judaism.* Harvard Theological Studies 26. Cambridge, Mass.
Norden, E. 1915. *Die antike Kunstprosa. Vom 6 Jahrhundert v. Chr.bis in die Zeit der Renaissance.* 3rd edition. Leipzig/Berlin.
Obermann, J. 1931. 'The Sepulchre of the Maccabaean Martyrs', *JBL* 50: 250–265.
O'Hagan, A. 1974. 'The Martyr in the Fourth Book of Maccabees', *Studii Biblici Franciscani Liber Annuus* 24: 95–102.
Pagels, E. 1988. *Adam, Eve and the Serpent.* New York.
Parente, F. 1988. 'The third Book of Maccabees as Ideological Document and Historical Source', *Henoch* 10.2: 143–182.
Perkins, J. 1995. The Suffering Self: Pain and Narrative Representation in the Early Christian Era. London.
Perler, O. 1949. 'Das vierte Makkabäerbuch. Ignatius von Antiochien und die ältesten Martyrerberichte', *Rivista di Archeologia Cristiana* 25: 47–72.
Rajak, T. 1986. 'The Jewish Sense of History in the Intertestamental Period', *Oudtestamentische Studien* 24: 124–145 = Ch. 2 in this volume.
Rampolla, M. da T. 1899. 'Martyre et sépulture des Macchabées', *Revue de l'Art Chrétien* 48.
Redditt, P.L. 1983. 'The Concept of *Nomos* in Fourth Maccabees', *Catholic Biblical Quarterly* 45: 249–270.

Reeg, G. 1985. *Die Geschichte von den Zehn Märtyrern. Synoptische Edition mit Übersetzung und Einleitung TSAJ* 10. Tübingen.

Renehan, R. 1974. 'The Greek Philosophical Background of Fourth Maccabees', *Rheinisches Museum für Philologie* 115: 223–238.

Rutherford, R.B. 1989. *The 'Meditations' of Marcus Aurelius Antoninus and a Selection from the Letters of Marcus and Fronto*, transl. and notes. Oxford.

Safrai, S. 1979. 'Kiddush ha-Shem in the Teaching of the Tannaim', Zion 44: 28–42 (Hebrew with English Summary).

Schatkin, M. 1974. 'The Maccabaean Martyrs', *Vigiliae Christianae* 28: 98–208.

Schwartz, D.R. 1993. 'Leben durch Jesus versus leben durch die Torah. 'Zur Religionspolitik der ersten Jahrhunderte', *Franz-Delitzsch-Vorlesung* 2: 3–23.

Stemberger, G. 1992. 'The Maccabees in Rabbinic Tradition', in F. García Martínez, A. Hilhorst, & C. Labuschagne (eds), *The Scriptures and the Scrolls. Studies in Honour of A.S. van der Woude*. Leiden, 193–202.

Syme, R. 1939. 'Observations on the Province of Cilicia', in W.M. Calder & J. Keil (eds), *Studies Presented to William Hepburn Buckler*. Manchester, 299–332.

Tcherikover, V. 1961. 'The Third Book of Maccabees as a Historical Source', *Scripta Hierosolymitana* 7: 1–26.

Townshend, R.B. 1913. '4 Maccabees', in R.H. Charles (ed.), *The Apocrypha and Pseudepigrapha of the Old Testament in English*. Oxford, 2, 653–685.

van Henten, J.W. 1986. 'Datierung und Herkunft des Vierten Makkabäerbuches', in J.W. van Henten, H.J. de Jonge, *et al.* (eds), *Tradition and Re-Interpretation in Early Jewish and Christian Literature. Essays in Honour of Jürgen C.H. Lebram*. Studia Postbiblica 36. Leiden, 136–149.

—— 1994. 'A Jewish Epitaph in a Literary Text: 4 Macc 17:8–10', in J.W. van Henten & P.W. van der Horst (eds), *Studies in Early Jewish Epigraphy*. Arbeiten zur Geschichte des Antiken Judentums und des Urchristentums 21. Leiden, 44–69.

—— 1995. 'The Martyrs as Heroes of the Christian People. Some Remarks on the Continuity of Jewish and Christian Martyrology, with Pagan Analogy', in M. Lamberigts & P. van Deun (eds), *Martyrium in Multidisciplinary Perspective. Memorial Louis Reekmans*. BETL 107. Leuven, 304–322.

Versnel, H.S. 1989. '"Quid Athenis et Hierosolymis?" Bemerkungen über die Herkunft von Aspeketen des "Effective Death"', in J.W. van Henten, B.A.G.M. Dehandschutter & H.J.W. van der Klaauw (eds), *Die Entstehung der jüdichen Martyrologie*. Studia Postbiblica 38. Leiden, 162–196.

Weber, R. 1991. 'Eusebeia und Logismos. zum philosophischen Hintergrund von 4. Makkabäerbuchs', *JSJ* 22: 212–234.

Winter, B. & Clarke, A. (eds). 1993. *The Book of Acts in its Ancient Literary Setting*. Grand Rapids, Michigan.

Yerushalmi, Y.H. 1982. *Zachor: Jewish History and Jewish Memory*. Seattle/London.

Young, R.D. 1991. 'The "Woman with the Soul of Abraham": Traditions about the Mother of the Maccabean Martyrs', in A.J. Levine (ed.), *'Women Like This': New Perspectives on Jewish Women in the Greco-Roman World*. Society of Biblical Literature, Early Judaism and its Literature 1. Atlanta, 67–81.

Yuval, I. 1993. 'Vengeance and Damnation, Blood and Defamation: From Jewish Martyrdom to Blood Libel Accusations', *Zion* 58.1 (Hebrew with English summary), 33–90.

Zeitlin, S. 1954. *The Second Book of Maccabees*. New York.

PART TWO

JOSEPHUS

CHAPTER SEVEN

ETHNIC IDENTITIES IN JOSEPHUS

The writings of Josephus have special value as both voice and witness to the attitudes of others in Palestine in the later Second Temple
period. Any description of first century Palestine which does not allo-
cate a prominent place to Josephus' perceptions misses a golden
opportunity. Josephus wrote his historical works in Greek, outside
Palestine, after A.D. 70. But he was born, around 37, a member of
the Jerusalem priestly aristocracy, and educated in the city, as well
as with desert sects. In the early part of the Jewish revolt, he operated as a leader in upper and lower Galilee and in the Golan area.
Where the population of Palestine figures in his writings, we would
expect to find both knowledge and at least the elements of a Palestinian
perception, however distorted by hindsight and muffled by the cloak
of a Greek writer. A native provincial voice of this kind is a most
unusual phenomenon in ancient literature, and we should make the
most of it. Moreover, in contrast to the literature of the New Testament, where we also find valuable evidence, in Josephus we are dealing with a known author and man of action, of known background
and experience in the region (even if we come to learn of this from
his own mouth), and known dates (more or less).

In the forefront of consideration comes, naturally, the *Jewish War*.
Though this first work is already a book written in Greek, for Greeks
and Romans as well as Jews, the *War*, produced in the decade after
the fall of Jerusalem, is necessarily formed by Josephus' Palestinian
experience. The *Life*, written so much later, but covering a portion
of the same ground, has an occasional role to play.

It is worth putting a number of simple questions to Josephus'
text. How did Josephus himself choose to describe the Jews in relation to other peoples and cultures in the region. And further, how
do other relevant identity tags in Josephus operate? Who are Greeks
for Josephus? Do they differ in any way from Syrians? Are the Greeks
of Palestine anything to do with the Greeks of culture? Are these
living Greeks in any sense representatives of a superior culture? A
threatening culture? Is there a marked shift between *The Jewish War*
and later writings in their approaches to Greeks and Greek culture?

Jews and other Semites in the Jewish War

It may be useful first of all to establish in brief what in the *Jewish War* is meant by 'Jews'.[1] Josephus says that the Jews acquired the name Ἰουδαῖοι when they returned from Babylon, because Judah was the first tribe to resettle Palestine (*AJ* XI 173). For him, the Jews are an ἔθνος or γένος, to which affiliation in differing degrees is possible by conversion.[2] The criterion for Jewishness is not primarily linguistic, since for the most part the Jews spoke Aramaic in Palestine, thus sharing the language of the region. Hebrew was adopted in limited circles, for specific, ideological purposes.[3] The distinction between Jews and Samaritans is notably sharp, probably because of the brutal conquest of Samaria by the Hasmonean John Hyrcanus. The differentiation from the Idumaeans is also surprisingly clear, considering that this people underwent a relatively peaceful conversion by the Hasmoneans, and for Josephus they are at best 'half-Jews' (*AJ* XIV 403), though they identify enough with Judaism to fight tenaciously on the rebel side in the great revolt.[4] The boundaries of what may count as Jewish do thus appear relatively non-negotiable.

The other Semitic identities generally figure in the narrative in opposition to the Jews. But this is not always the case. Thus, Josephus seems to have been the first to enunciate a distinct conception of an Arab ethnic identity, developing a line of descent from Hagar, through Ishmael, and Ishmael's eldest son Nabaiotes, of the circumcized Ishmaelites, whom he identifies exclusively with the Nabataeans. A certain affinity between the Arab people in general, or perhaps the Nabataeans in particular and the Jews would seem to be implied in this reconstruction.[5]

[1] On this issue, see Spilsbury 1998: 12–14.
[2] Cohen 1990.
[3] See Schwartz 1995.
[4] On the conversion of the Idumaeans, see Kasher 1988: 44–78, Cohen 1990: 212–221, Kokkinos 1998: ch. 3. On Idumaean status in Jewish eyes, and the Idumaean part in the revolt, Goodman 1987: 222–223.
[5] Millar 1993a: 233–245. More fully on Arab identity, Millar 1993b: 387–407.

Greeks in the Jewish War

When Josephus deploys the label 'Greek', this usually forms part of a 'them' and 'us' dichotomy, at least implicitly. As a rule, Greeks are 'them', as we might expect. It is remarkable that in the *Jewish War*, as indeed elsewhere in his writings, Josephus makes ready use of a Greek literary cliché. He conjures up the whole world by means of expressions of the type 'both Greeks and barbarians' or 'neither Greeks nor barbarians'. Thus, the Temple altar was honoured 'by both Greeks and barbarians' (*BJ* V 117). The mother who consumed her own child during the famine in the besieged city of Jerusalem performed an act unrecorded before 'among Greeks or barbarians' (*BJ* VI 199). Where the Jews fit into this dichotomy is never clarified, but the implication would seem to be that, the Jews were (as the Christians were later to be) a third 'race', right outside the polarity. If pressed, this is what Josephus would have needed to say. Thus, while on the one hand, he was not averse to making use of the familiar rhetoric which he found in Greek writers, on the other hand this readiness need not have entailed any self-identification with the cultural categories of those writers. His agenda was different.

In fact, the use of the term 'Greeks' as a general description of non-Jews figure regularly in Josephus. The mercenaries of King Alexander Jannaeus, actually, we are told, Pisidians and Cilicians, are also simply called 'Greeks' (*BJ* I 94). Foreign oil is also Greek oil (*V* 94).

Furthermore, in a number of violent episodes surrounding the Jewish War, Greeks and Jews are presented as natural antagonists within a city. Perhaps the most striking instance is the quarrel between Jews and Greeks in Caesarea, which Josephus regards as the trigger of revolt. This revolved around the question of whether the city was a Greek one with a Greek constitution, or a city for Jews. Cultic divergences caused mutual suspicion too, with Greek mockery of practice in the city's synagogue inflaming the situation.

At Tiberias, Greeks make their only appearance in Josephus' *Life*, when all the Greek residents of Tiberias (they are not citizens, since the city is a Jewish one) are said to be massacred by the Jewish pro-revolt party (*V* 67).

Greeks and Syrians in Josephus

The most interesting pair of identity labels in Josephus involve assimilation rather than antithesis. It is unexpectedly hard to establish the
difference between the element in the population of Palestine described
as 'Greek' and that spoken of as 'Syrian'. Syrian identity is a relatively new and arbitrary phenomenon, probably reflecting the Roman
provincial division and thus to be regarded as a consequence of
Rome's disruption of the area. But for Jews, too, 'Syrian' was a convenient description, and it was used by our author almost interchangeably with 'Greek'.[6] So what significance lay in the difference?

A clear distinction does seem to emerge, and it is an important
one. Greeks, I would suggest, are urban, Syrians tend to be rural.
The cities and towns in and around Palestine are constantly and
automatically described as Greek by Josephus, and their inhabitants
simplistically as Greeks. There is a real distinction to be made between
proper Greek cities and towns which are not; when he needs to,
Josephus is quite capable of making it. Thus he explains that the
Romans took from the ethnarchy of Archelaus the Greek towns of
Gaza, Gadara and Hippos and added them to the province of Syria,
leaving the ruler with Strato's Tower, Sebaste, Joppa and Jerusalem
(*BJ* II 97). The difference between the two groups evidently lies in
their foundation and their organization.

It would seem that technically 'Greeks' are those who live in Greek
cities; more loosely, any non-Jewish town-dwellers can be Greek.
Syrians, by contrast, are the provincials, and essentially rural. The
villagers around Caesarea, attacked by parties of Jews after the troubles in the city, are described as Syrians (*BJ* II 458). But the neighbouring cities, listed by Josephus, are not included in the Syrian
area. Then, the massacre which follows the disaster in Caesarea is
referred to as a massacre of Jews by Syrians (*BJ* II 461 ff.): here
the perspective is that of events across an entire region, or perhaps
province, specified by Josephus as ὅλη Συρία, 'the whole of Syria'
(462). So under 'Syrians' he means to include all those who inhabited Syria. It is consonant with this that, still in the same context,
when Josephus enlarges upon the massacre of their Jewish popula-

---

[6] See Rappaport 1996.

tion perpetrated by the people of the Greek city of Scythopolis, the term 'Syrians' is not applied to them, and instead they are carefully designated 'Scythopolitans'.

Later, the inhabitants of Trachonitis, in the kingdom of Agrippa II, are a mixture of Jews and Syrians (*BJ* III 57). This was a region of villages. Elsewhere, troops fighting for the Romans, when not called simply 'Roman', can be admitted as Syrian (*BJ* 38). Deserting Jerusalemites who have swallowed gold coins before escaping the siege are ripped open by the Arabs among the Syrians on the other side (V 549 ff.).

In a formal sense, Syrians are those who live in the province of Syria, of which the cities, with their own territories, were, according to Roman arrangements, formally not a part. Perhaps for Josephus the term had few connotations beyond that. It follows that, if Greeks are simply the citizens of the cities, then there is not much to learn from the term about the ethnicity or culture of those thus described. It is clear that the cities will have had Greek-style constitutions, at least of a rudimentary kind.[7] And Greek was no doubt the public language of these cities. Yet even then, Greek need not have been the principal spoken language in the earlier stages of Roman rule. It is hard is to ascertain how sharp a distinction existed between the two types of city, those that were Greek in the official sense and those that were not.

Jews and Gentiles in Josephus

It is perhaps surprising to find this resonant polarity playing a part in Josephus' thinking, given his own continuing role as intermediary between the two and his avowed purpose of reconciling them (*AJ* XVI 175). The representation of the hostile crowd as made up of ἀλλόφυλοι, 'other peoples', figures in the historian's description of the Alexandrian troubles under the emperors Caligula and Claudius (*BJ* II 488): this may just be a shorthand way of taking both Greeks and Egyptians into account. At Scythopolis, in A.D. 66, the same line-up of the Jewish element against the foreign is envisaged, although this was the city where the Jews had lived in amity with their neighbours

---

[7] Jones 1940: 170–191.

and had supported them against the revolutionaries until this very
trust had brought about their downfall (*BJ* II 466). Olive oil not
produced by Jews, as well as being called 'Greek oil', is regularly
described as ἀλλόφυλον, indicating its unsuitability for Jewish use. If
Goodman is right, the basis of this practice was not any *halakhah*
(legal ruling) of any kind, but, in the first instance, instinctive revulsion.[8] On the other hand, when Josephus castigates the revolutionaries during the siege of Jerusalem, in a bitter speech which he puts
into his own mouth, he paradoxically contrasts foreign respect for
the Temple with the Jews' desecration of their own shrine (VI 102).
Further examples of this bitterly ironic contrast might be cited.

So non-Jews are 'the other', often, but not always hostile. Yet this
particular polarity does not come as readily to Josephus' lips as we
might expect. Nor, it may be pointed out, do we find any verbal
expression of separatism in Josephus comparable with that enunciated in 2 Maccabees, where the extraordinary term ἀλλοφυλισμός,
is conjured to describe the process of adopting foreign habits, and
put side by side with the author's more long-lived and famous coinage,
ἑλληνισμός.[9] Indeed, Josephus can even go so far as to stand his
normal use of the term ἀλλόφυλος on its head. In his preface to the
Jewish War (I 16), he happily describes himself as an ἀλλόφυλος, a
foreigner, addressing Greeks and Romans, thus demonstrating that
the concept did not in itself carry the strong negative implications
for him that the terms 'gentile' or 'goy' have done for Jews in many
situations.[10]

'Greekness' as a cultural entity

There is an unexpected and intemperate attack on Greek historians
in the preface to the *Jewish War* (I 13), where Josephus promotes
his own history by denigrating its predecessors. Latter-day Greeks
are not to be compared with the ancients. The Greek writers, described
as 'native-born' (γνήσιοι; I 16) are castigated as liars, voluble in the
law-courts but silent when expected to bring forth facts. These are
the hostile terms in which Roman stereotypes of the Greek charac-

---

[8] Goodman 1990: 227–245.
[9] On ἀλλουλισμός, see Hengel 1990: 22.
[10] On Jewish separation from Gentiles in the rewritten bible of Josephus' *Antiquities*,
see Spilsbury 1998.

ter were often expressed.[11] Yet the posture is a remarkable one for an author whose desired readership around the Roman empire (I 3) is described as consisting of Greeks along with 'those Romans who were not involved' (I 6). For all these aspirations he wholly detaches himself by his contemptuous critique from the Greek cultural scene of his day. But the classical historians, οἱ ἀρχαῖοι, are explicitly excluded from the strictures and by implication accorded respect.

Yet it seems that, on at least one occasion in the *War*, Greeks are 'us'. Thus, those writers who came before Josephus, here unnamed, who according to him translated Jewish writings into Greek, are simply called Greeks (I 17). Yet he can only be referring to the Hellenistic-Jewish authors whose work was based on the Greek bible, writers such as those whom he himself, many years later, named in a similar assertion in the *Against Apion* (I 218). Not only were these writers manifestly Jews, but it is extremely hard to believe that Josephus, even at tan early stage in his career, was so ignorant as to believe otherwise. There are, however, obvious apologetic considerations. The shift made it possible to claim that Greek writers had in the past taken an interest in Jewish tradition. Moreover, it could be advantageous in writing history designed for Greek readers to identify Jews with Greeks, just as it was the purpose of the first century Greek historian Dionysius of Halicarnassus, who wrote at Rome, to prove that the Romans were Greek by origin. And there is more. The passage shows that Josephus is able to deploy a linguistic and cultural rather than an ethnic definition of what is Greek. In terms of such a construction, Greekness, far from being alien to Judaism, can be something in which Jews shared. In any interpretation of Josephus' ability to speak in this way, the important fact of the existence of a large class of Jews, among them many of his readers, whose only language was Greek should not be overlooked.[12]

In other words, at the time of writing of the *Jewish War*, Josephus was on the way to forming a conception of a Greek culture as something distinct from the people who were contemporary Greeks, or would-be Greeks. Some of this culture's modern manifestations were

---

[11] See Wardman 1976: 1–13.

[12] My reading of these difficult passages is close to that suggested for the *Against Apion* passage by Wacholder, *Eupolemus*: 3. Other interpretations have been offered. For an awareness of the complications, I am much indebted to my extended discussion of the problems with Professor D. Schwartz (although his solution is different).

to him derisory, but its scope went well beyond its inadequate native exponents of historiography to a linguistic world which might in theory incorporate Jews.

Summary: Josephus' approach to Greeks and their culture

The following important points emerge from this discussion.

1. It appears that in relation to pre-70 Palestine, Greeks were for Josephus usually those who lived in cities with Greek constitution, the rest being Syrians.
2. At this stage his conceptualization of the Jew/Greek dichotomy overlaps with the Jew/Gentile dichotomy.
3. Greeks and the Greek lifestyle seem to have remarkably little to do with Jews in Josephus' representation of the scene in Jewish Palestine.
4. Josephus, at any rate, at time of writing of the *War*, did not have a unified conception of Greek culture. So it seems this was not something he had brought with him out of Jerusalem.
5. We can observe at this stage just the beginnings of a writer's awareness on his part of the cultural power of Hellenism.
6. What perhaps had been a latent interest could flourish in Josephus' personal circumstances after he took up residence in the diaspora. His later writing career shows an ever increasing awareness of the cultural significance of addressing a Greek audience and of the challenge posed by Greek culture. The aims of his later writings—that Greeks should respect and admire Jews and be drawn to Judaism—suggest that he was concerned not just with peaceful communal co-existence but with cultural claims. The terms in which he promotes Judaism there leave us in no doubt that he is at this stage fully conscious of the power of attraction exerted by the Greek tradition.

Explaining the evidence of Josephus

From Josephus we derive the impression that, while Greeks were often opponents, the Jewish society of Palestine in the late second Temple period was less disturbed by the lure of Greek culture than it had been at the dawn of Hellenism. One reason for this may lie precisely in the poor relations between Greeks and Jews in the surrounding cities: those so-called Greeks (some of them Hellenized only since Pompey) may have put Hellenism itself in bad odour for Jews. And yet to see that there is no simple connection between intergroup relationships and the broader process of cultural appropriation, we have only to think of Philo's Alexandria, where hostility between Jews and Greeks did not deter Jews like Philo himself from profound immersion in Greek thought.

Another, perhaps more important reason for the decline in the significance of Hellenism may be that in Jewish Judaea there was in reality little opportunity there to sense there of Greek culture as the dominant culture. Until the destruction of the Temple, Judaism, quite simply, held the stage in the immediate environment. That Greek culture was an instrument of empire under the Romans was at this stage a quite remote fact to Rome's subjects. Late second Temple Jerusalem was a cosmopolitan milieu containing a spectrum of humanity, as Martin Hengel has time and again shown: the prevailing style in the Jewish establishment appears to have been one of detachment from Greek institutions, even if use of the Greek language for external and even internal communication will have been a fact of life. In the pages of Josephus, we meet no Jewish Hellenizers after the Hasmonean period, only, it may be pointed out, the exact opposite—the Greek judaizers of the cities of Syria (*BJ* II 463). But that is to enter a new discussion.

BIBLIOGRAPHY

Cohen, S.J.D. 1990. 'Religion, Ethnicity and 'Hellenism' in the Emergence of Jewish Identity in Maccabaean Palestine', in P. Bilde, T. Engberg-Pedersen, L. Hannestad & J. Zahle (eds), *Religion and Religious Practice in the Seleucid Kingdom*. Aarhus, 204–223.

Goodman, M. 1987. *The Ruling Class of Judaea: The Origins of the Jewish Revolt against Rome A.D. 66–70*. Cambridge.

——— 1990. 'Kosher Olive Oil in Antiquity' in P.R. Davies & R.T. White (eds), *A Tribute to Geza Vermes: Essays on Jewish and Christian literature and history*. Sheffield, 227–245.

Hengel, M. 1990. *The 'Hellenization' of Judaea in the first century after Christ*. Eng. Trans. London.

Jones, A.H.M. 1940. *The Greek City from Alexander to Justinian*. Oxford.

Kasher, A. 1988. *Jews, Idumaeans and Ancient Arabs*. TSAJ 18. Tübingen.

Kokkinos, N. 1998. *The Herodian Dynasty: Origins, Role in Society and Eclipse*. Journal for the Study of the Pseudepigrapha Supplement Series 30. Sheffield.

Millar, F. 1993a. 'Hagar, Ishmael, Josephus and the Origins of Islam', *JJS* 24: 233–245.

—— 1993b. *The Roman Near East 31 B.C.–A.D. 337*. Cambridge Mass./London.

Rappaport, U. 1996 'Les juifs et leurs voisins à l'époque perse, hellénistique et romaine', *Annales: Histoire, Sciences Sociales* 5: 955–974.

Spilsbury, P. 1998, *The Image of the Jew in Flavius Josephus' Paraphrase of the Bible*. TSAJ 69. Tübingen.

Schwartz, S. 1995. 'Language, Power and Identity in Ancient Palestine', *Past and Present* 148: 1–47.

Wardman, A. 1976. *Rome's Debt to Greece*. London.

CHAPTER EIGHT

FRIENDS, ROMANS, SUBJECTS:
AGRIPPA II'S SPEECH IN JOSEPHUS' *JEWISH WAR*

Authorial choices

I have not yet found, in any illustrated version of Josephus, a portrayal of that extraordinary scene which took place in the summer of 66 A.D., when Marcus Julius Agrippa (the Great King), great-grandson of Herod, standing with his sister, Queen Berenice, addressed the people of Jerusalem from the roof of his palace and tried to persuade them to step back from the brink and not to rush into any action which could be taken as revolt against Rome.[1] But the picture is an arresting one. The exact date cannot be pinpointed—it falls between the beginning of June and the beginning of August. At any rate, while, in early June, Berenice was still appearing in public in the attire of a Nazirite with her head shaven and (perhaps as a suppliant) with her feet bare,[2] it seems likely that by now the period of her dedication had come to an end. We may rather imagine the pair, as they had appeared at Caesarea with Festus for Paul's interrogation, presenting themselves, as Acts so splendidly puts it, μετὰ πολλῆς φαντασίας (Acts 25:23). The drama, in Josephus' story, was high, and the speech ended with the royal couple in tears and the crowd, though not unmoved, we learn (*BJ* II 402), still clamouring for rebellion.

The episode, obviously not wholly invented, is given great prominence by Josephus, serving as that turning point which marked the transition from peace to war. It is preceded by the fruitless pleas to the people and their lay leaders, of the entire priesthood, their clothes ripped, their breasts exposed, their heads covered in dust (322), for an end to provocation of the Romans: all were to disregard the desecration of the Temple Treasury perpetrated by the procurator Florus when he had extracted tribute money. The episode is also preceded

---

[1] Josephus, *BJ* II 345–401.
[2] On the meaning of her attire, S. Schwartz 1990: 136.

by the second horrifying clash between Florus' cavalry and unarmed
Jews in the narrow alleys of Jerusalem; by the deliberate Jewish
destruction of the porticoes which linked the Antonia fortress (Florus'
headquarters) with the Temple; by an investigation conducted on
behalf of Cestius Gallus, the legate of Syria; and, most crucially, by
the refusal of the high priests and notables, strongly supported by
Agrippa, to send an embassy to Nero and to lodge a formal complaint against Florus. Agrippa's speech is followed by his ejection
from the city, by the killing of the Roman garrison on Masada, and
by the decision not to accept any further sacrifices by foreigners in
the Temple, which, as Josephus says, meant discontinuing the offerings
made on the emperor's behalf and was tantamount to a declaration
of war (πολέμου καταβολή: 409). The speech, a long and discursive
one, creates a break amidst crowded and precipitous events. So, as
well as the speech lending emphasis to those events, the special position of the words highlights their content.

Here, we enter the realm of choices made by the historian, Josephus.
He *chose* to put Agrippa centre stage and to make his oration central to the history. He also chose the words themselves that Agrippa
uttered: for there is no doubt, in view of their recurrent themes and
patterns, that Josephus (in common with other writers of his time)
invented his speeches for the most part and used them to communicate or to set off his own interpretation of what happened.[3] In this
major performance, content matches context, for here is the one
extended consideration, in the *Jewish War*, of the pros and cons of
revolt against Rome, and it sums up a realist position rather different
from any which the speaker is likely to have held, as we shall see.
Indeed it represents a voice which must have been heard among
Rome's subjects far from the confines of Judaea, but which is rarely
found in the literature. It is somewhat ironic that, when the speech
has been closely studied, it has usually been for what it has to say,
in its great survey of the peoples subjected to Rome, about the disposition of the legions which controlled the provinces.[4]

There is, in fact, much of Josephus throughout the composition;
which is not to say that it is anything so simple as an apologia for
his own conduct. Among recurrent Josephan ideas, we find the insis-

---

[3] See Rajak *Josephus*: 80–81; Villalba i Varneda 1986: 89 ff.
[4] The classic discussion is in *RE* 11.2, s.v. 'legio' (by Kubitschek-Ritterling), arguing that the disposition of troops in the speech reflects Vespasian's arrangements
and not Nero's.

tence that the enthusiasts for revolt were a vocal minority among the population; that misgovernment by individual bad procurators should not be allowed to reflect on the emperor at Rome or on the image of the empire as a whole; that Fortune has transferred her favours to the cause of Rome over all other peoples, or in a different formulation, that God has been behind the growth of her empire (360; 390–391); that for the Jews it is now too late to fight; and that they will be responsible for the destruction of their own Temple if they start a war:

> take pity at least on your mother city and its sacred precincts. Spare the Temple and preserve for yourself the sanctuary and its holy places. (400)

This last exhortation is linked with Josephus' controversial claim in a later part of the *Jewish War* that not Titus but the Jews had burned down the Temple.[5] Much of this complex of arguments will be reiterated, with little change, in the declamation in book V which Josephus makes from the walls of besieged Jerusalem,[6] though the heart of that utterance has a biblical orientation.

A presentation of Agrippa by Josephus cannot be a simple affair. While Josephus' general ideas about revolt may play a large part, he is also saying something about Agrippa specifically, and that has to be understood in the light of Agrippa's highly dubious role in the surrounding events. It is also relevant that Josephus and Agrippa had close connections, certainly from 69 on, when both were involved in Vespasian's accession and in the fortunes of the Flavian dynasty.[7] Agrippa was an important patron for Josephus, and apparently wrote sixty-two letters testifying to the accuracy of the *Jewish War* (V 364–367). Admittedly, we do find a quite open statement of Agrippa's unpopularity with his subjects in the mid-sixties in *Antiquities* XX, as well as one or two episodes which show the king in a fairly dubious light;[8] and it may be that, if these are to be explained by the fact that Agrippa was dead by the time that this passage was written[9] and that Josephus was, therefore, able to be open about certain

---

[5] Rajak *Josephus*: 206–11; Goodman 1987: 237–238.
[6] *BJ* V 362 ff.; see Stern 1987: 77.
[7] Crook 1951: 163, n. 9; Rajak *Josephus*: 187.
[8] Especially in relation to the high priests: S. Schwartz 1990: 131, 150–152 and n. 138.
[9] The date of death of Agrippa II remains a vexed question; on Josephus' unfavourable comments in connection with that date, see Cohen 1979: 177–180.

earlier reservations, then the relationship was not an entirely unclouded one. Still, the overall picture of mutual cordiality over the years is not much affected by such hypotheses, nor by the fact that Agrippa became the employer of Josephus' enemy and rival, Justus of Tiberias (Josephus would have us believe that the secretary was constantly in disgrace with his master!). Then there is the added twist of the notorious affair between Titus, Josephus' principal protector and first patron, and the Jewish 'mini-Cleopatra' (as Mommsen called Berenice), which lasted at least until her second dismissal from Rome, probably in 75, and therefore almost until the appearance of the *Jewish War*, normally dated between 75 and 79. I do not believe that we can make much progress by reviving the methods of earlier scholarship and seeking to locate strands in Josephus which reflect these various and sometimes contradictory interests. But it is important to be aware that he is performing a balancing act when he writes and that there is often more than one sub-text.

Apart from all this, a speech must, of course, be appropriate to its dramatic situation and not import incredible elements. In this case, addressing a volatile and hostile audience, Agrippa had to display tact and there are many sentiments in favour of Rome which he might have uttered were it not that the needs of the moment, to calm a raging mob, would have made it absurd for him to be shown doing so.

Why Agrippa? The troubles of a 'Client King'

These are very real complications, and there is no magic formula to help us categorize this, or indeed any other of Josephus' set pieces. We have to deal with the problems as they arise. But it is worth looking a little more closely at the question of why it should be Agrippa who receives the dubious benefit of making the central statements that appear in this speech. The fact that he made a memorable appearance on this occasion is clearly not sufficient explanation; nor even the consideration that what he said was sufficiently disturbing to provoke his expulsion from the city soon afterwards, and, about a month later, the burning of his palace and that of Berenice by Eleazar' s rebel group in company with the *sicarii*.

The speech, as well as some of Josephus' surrounding comments, shows Agrippa as putting everything into a last-ditch attempt to per-

suade restraint. Opening himself and his sister to derision, risking
life and limb to make a long and detailed address in that exposed
position up on the roof (security arrangements in first century Jerusalem
can hardly have been up to modern standards), there was, on this
account, just nothing more that he could have done to prevent war.
The stance at this point is an accentuated version of the one which
Josephus claims to have taken up himself, although Agrippa, unlike
Josephus, abandoned the Jewish cause as soon as a revolt was seen
to be inevitable. The king was to be found supplying Cestius Gallus
with infantry and cavalry for the abortive march on Jerusalem,
although it was only *after* Cestius' withdrawal that the first sizeable
crop of Jewish desertions to the Roman side is recorded by Josephus.

   In various ways, Agrippa needed exculpation far more desperately
even than ever Josephus did, and from both sides. It is not only a
question of the aftermath. For what Josephus manages to conceal
through focusing our attention on the speech, and, quite likely, deliberately, is that Agrippa's incompetence could well be regarded as
the single major cause of the breakdown in Jewish-Roman relations,
and therefore of the war. We need only recall that this was the man
who, at the age of seventeen, had not been considered fit to inherit
the position of his popular father, Agrippa I, as ruler of the Jews.
Four years later, the son had to be content with the kingdom of
Chalcis, an area around Damascus, together, it would seem, with
an uncertain role as what A.H.M. Jones calls 'controller of the
Temple': this had been briefly possessed by Agrippa's predecessor,
his uncle Herod of Chalcis, and it involved the right to appoint high
priests. Later, Claudius enlarged the domains, adding what can best
be described as 'bits and pieces', including towns in the Galilee. But
Judaea remained under procurators, and perhaps the limitations of
Marcus Julius Agrippa were evident to those who had known him
well in Rome. The *Antiquities* version of the dealings which followed
on the sudden death of Agrippa I in 44 A.D. seems conscious of the
need to explain away the rejection:

> Caesar, on hearing of the death of Agrippa . . . was grieved for him
> and angry at his ungrateful subjects. He had accordingly resolved to
> send the younger Agrippa at once to take over the kingdom, wishing
> at the same time to maintain the treaty he had sworn. He was, how-
> ever, dissuaded by those freedmen and friends whose influence with
> him was great, who said that it was hazardous to entrust a kingdom
> so important to a really young man, not yet out of boyhood: he would

find it impossible to carry the cares of administration, when the kingdom was a heavy burden even to a grown man. Caesar felt that what
they were saying was reasonable. He therefore despatched Cuspius
Fadus as procurator of Judaea and of the whole kingdom (XIX 362).

The text does not tell us why there was no question of waiting for
Agrippa to grow up a little. Whatever Agrippa's personal merits, the
crisis of 66 reveals that he was the first and foremost to be held
accountable by the Romans for good order among the Jews, and
only after him came the lay and sacerdotal leaders. For Agrippa had
the power to order the magistrates and the notables to collect tribute, and that is exactly what he did on the conclusion of his speech,
because the arrears had evidently been a major point of dispute with
Florus, and even more, no doubt, because non-payment of tribute
was an unequivocal signal of revolt (407).

There is valuable testimony, in Josephus' narrative, to the seriousness with which the duty of maintaining order was taken by the
Romans (332) and the merciless penalties to which the native authorities were subjected when they failed to do so. In short, at a time
of trouble, Roman rule was no blessing, even to the prosperous elite.
We may be sure the dispensation was not very different in other
parts of the empire, though we rarely have evidence of this quality.
It was under Florus that Jewish members of the equestrian order
were crucified in Jerusalem (308). This explains why it was such a
risky matter to send to Rome an embassy of protest, even supposing it were allowed to leave: such an embassy drew the emperor's
attention to the loss of control and was a declaration of failure on
the part of the local administration before ever it was a reproach
on the procurator. A case which collapsed would bring disaster. The
point is made explicitly in Agrippa's speech:

> the powers that be (τὰς ἐξουσίας) should be conciliated by flattery
> (θεραπεύειν) and not irritated; for when you indulge in exaggerated
> reproaches for minor errors, you only injure yourselves by your denun-
> ciation (350–351).

On a lesser scale, though potentially just as dangerous, was the
fraught question of forms of reception: would an official greeting
(ἀσπασμός) be taken as impertinent and provocative, a blatant εἰρωνεία
in the context of native bad behaviour, as happened when Florus
brought troops to Jerusalem after taking the 17 talents from the treasury of the Temple (298)? Or was it fatal discourtesy not to offer a

greeting, as the priests insisted, temporarily at odds with the lay notables, and desperate to protect the Temple when the second wave of
troops was due (323). The notables were at this point less compliant,
for they had been ordered earlier to hand over agitators to Florus,
something which we know to be deeply abhorrent to pious Jews,
and which they had therefore refused to do.[10] Any action, or lack
of action, could be taken as insubordination. Thus, when Cestius
sent the tribune Neopolitanus to Jerusalem as his representative, the
soldier may have politely paid his respects to the Temple from the
court of the Gentiles (341), but his task was the grim one of checking that all Jews were obedient to the Romans in their midst.

All this puts into perspective Agrippa's inability to do the one job
that the Romans were expecting him to do. His consciousness of
failure made him desperate to prevent any Jewish representatives
going to Rome and complaining about Florus, however strong the
case. It is interesting that, some fifteen years earlier, Agrippa *had*
been prepared to support the Jews against the Samaritans in a hearing before Claudius at Rome, thereby setting himself against the
procurator Cutmanus. Josephus seems at that stage to congratulate
Agrippa on not being intimidated by the freedmen at court, who
allegedly had rallied round Cumanus; and in the end the procurator had been condemned and exiled (*BJ* II 245–246; *AJ* XX 125–136).

In the crisis of 66, Berenice, who could not yet, of course, have
been Titus' mistress, had identified herself more closely with the
agonies of the Jews than had Agrippa, and, though a queen, she
had even been prepared to abase herself in front of Florus, begging
him to call off his troops (310–314). Her religious adherence was
perhaps stronger, though Agrippa too followed Jewish practices, as
we know.[11] This did not, however, detach her for long from her
brother's side or from his position. As for Agrippa, at that crucial
moment of Berenice's intervention, he had been away in Alexandria,
offering his congratulations to his relative by marriage, the renegade
Jew Tiberius Julius Alexander, erstwhile procurator of Judaea, on
being appointed to the prestigious prefecture of Egypt. Agrippa's

---

[10] See the classic discussion of Daube 1965.
[11] S. Schwartz 1990: 112. 135–137. It must be admitted, however, that the
Nazirite vow is the only firm evidence of Berenice's piety and that the Herodians
tended to placate their Jewish subjects with token gestures: see D.R. Schwartz 1990:
134 and n. 116.

conduct after his hasty return from Egypt could hardly be acceptable to any element in the population, and it made his stoning and
banishment from Jerusalem unsurprising and his position forthwith
untenable until after the revolt. It is amazing that he was allowed
even to finish his speech—if indeed he was. We have reason to be
sceptical.

The realist argument for Roman rule

Yet the speech according to Josephus is, weeping apart, a reasoned
and polished affair, improving rather than realistically depicting the
hapless Agrippa. Its content, as we have already begun to see, transcends the need to distract the mind from the monarch's mistakes.
In several obvious ways, it carries the voice of Josephus. And at a
deeper level, too, the question with which it is essentially concerned
is Josephus' own question (and that of those others, most of them
non survivors, who had followed paths similar to his, if rather less
tortuous): could the revolt have succeeded? The premises plainly set
out are, first, that freedom is unquestionably the state in which it
would be desirable to live:

> passing to your present passion for liberty, I say that it comes too late.
> The time is past when you ought to have striven never to lose it. For
> servitude is a painful experience and a struggle to avoid it once for
> all is just (356, Thackeray's translation).

There are shades of the Tacitean Calgacus here, and of the Roman
rhetoric of revolt, but this is distinctly not a rebel speech, and so
these echoes cannot be taken as just the conventional sentiments. The
second premise is that to live under Rome *is* to live in slavery, and no
bones are made about the Jews being slaves (356; 357). One might
find these admissions somewhat surprising, whether coming from
Agrippa or from Josephus. From these premises follow the stated
view that it would be natural and right for a people to revolt at the
moment of provincialization; and indeed that is when the majority
of revolts against the imposition of the *pax Romana* did occur, in the
history of the empire. The Jews had, then, simply missed their chance.

As Menahem Stern pointed out, the speech is notable for the
absence in it of any of the *laus imperii* which we might have expected
in so major a statement of support for Rome; Stern draws a contrast with the pacifying oration of the legate Cerealis in Tacitus'

Histories.[12] In Josephus, the *pax Romana* appears in an ambivalent light and not as a benefit to the subjects: 'do they not live at peace, under one Roman legion?', asks Agrippa about the Dalmatians (371). It could be argued that a more enthusiastic note would be so glaringly inappropriate in the situation, so provocative to the assembled Jews, that Agrippa simply could not be allowed it by the author. It could also be suggested that in the first century A.D. such themes did not drop as readily from the lips of Rome's subjects, even from members of their governing classes, as they did from Aelius Aristides, a century later. Thus, Plutarch's tone is less rapturous than Aristides', for all his connections with important Romans. Nonetheless, the underlying negative evaluation, embedded in a plea on behalf of Rome, remains a remarkable feature, and, in my view, it cannot wholly be explained away in terms of the requirements of text or context.

The claims of quiescence are expressed in the recitation, which is far from a eulogy, of the roster of distinguished and strong peoples who have yielded to Rome. This occupies the bulk of the oration. It is high Greek rhetoric, with the Athenians, 'the men who once consigned their city to the flames to maintain the liberty of Greece' (358), being given pride of place. It is an indirect compliment to Rome, perhaps, through its depiction of the staggering scope and the natural and human resources of the empire. Yet this emphasis, too, is double-edged, for there is an underlying critique in terms of exploitation:

> though encompassed by such formidable barriers, though swarming with a population of three hundred and five nations, possessing, so to say, in their native soil the springs of prosperity and irrigating wellnigh the whole world with the overflow of their products, the Gauls are yet content to be treated as a source of revenue to the Romans and to have their own prosperous fortune (εὐδαιμονίαν) meted out to them at their hands (372, Thackeray's translation).

It is instructive to contrast the twist given to the same idea by Aelius Aristides in his panegyric *To Rome* (11), when he declares that

> the lands around the Mediterranean provide the Romans abundantly with whatever is in them. Produce is brought from every land and every sea, depending on what the seasons bring forth.

---

[12] See Stern 1987: 76.

Here, the notions of Roman appropriation and of Roman control are missing. Still less is there any implication of submission. Agrippa, on the other hand, speaks openly of the Gauls being

> overawed at once by the fortune of Rome and by her power, which brings her more triumph even than her arms. That is why they submit to the orders of 1200 soldiers.

There is almost a modern theory here of deterrent power deriving from success, and the limited military force involved is in no sense a palliation.

But the true nourisher of Rome is Africa, subdued by a vast effort: apart from the corn which 'feeds the populace of Rome for eight months in the year', there is tribute and every kind of contribution to the empire (382–383). These may be given ungrudgingly, but the stress on the sheer size of the transaction leaves us in no doubt that it is exploitative.

Josephus' roster of the regions and provinces, while emphasizing, in almost Thucydidean fashion, the irresistible claims of sheer power, can hardly be meant to intimidate Jewish readers to submission in the 70s, as some have liked to think. So soon after the loss of Temple and city, after the destruction of the last few forlorn hopes in Palestine and abroad, who would have had the heart for new conflict? The argument looks back and not forwards. It is intended loudly and clearly to make one point: that those Jews who had been opposed to resistance had had every practical justification, as well as the logic of history on their side. The moral balance sheet was, on the other hand, a separate issue. Under the Greek bombast, lies some sharp questioning.

But what is interesting is not the author's personal position—and, indeed, others may form a different impression of our historians instance.[13] Significance lies, rather, in the voice represented in this speech, the voice of the realists, who knew exactly what living under an empire was about, but also that at most times it was necessary to knuckle under, to dig in and wait. Such realists well understood why their fellow countrymen hated Rome, however intensely they deplored their actions; and glimmerings of this understanding, too, come out in Agrippa's speech, even if it is not the author's overt purpose to convey them.

---

[13] On these issues, a useful guide is P. Bilde 1988: 173–181.

But that was not the end of the matter. The implication of the Josephan doctrine that God is siding with the Romans must surely be that the day will come when the tables will be turned, when he will change sides once more. But for the realists, that distant day was not something to dwell on. Klaus Wengst regards this motif in Josephus as 'an endorsement of the right of the stronger'.[14] In fact, however, there is what might be called an implicit, suppressed apocalypse in what has been taken as being the most shameless of Josephus' doctrines, the corruption at the heart of his writing. A close comparison has been noted[15] between Josephus' interpretation and the sentiments towards the Romans attributed in the Babylonian Talmud (b.Av.Zar. 18a) to the dying Rabbi Yose ben Kisma. These were spoken to a fellow rabbi, Hananiah ben Teradion, who is known in the tradition as one of the Ten Martyrs tortured and killed in the wake of the Hadrianic revolt, and they were words which counselled patience:

> do you not realize that it is Heaven who has ordained this nation to rule? For even though they have laid waste His home, burnt down His temple, slain his saints and persecuted His servants, still (the empire) is firmly established.

For Josephus, as for many rabbis, the conception of a cycle of sin, punishment, and salvation, with an eventual new beginning, lay beneath the doctrine of the transference of God's favour.[16] In his own tirade from the walls of Jerusalem, Josephus castigates the Romans at length for their sins; he then compares the Romans to the Assyrians, and reminds his hearers that God had known exactly how to destroy the Assyrians and to rescue the Jews, when once the Jews had deserved it (BJ V 403–406). But for Josephus, as for the rabbis, apocalyptic ideas are rarely, if ever, to be freely enunciated: other speakers will, I know, be commenting on Josephus' curious reticence over the identity and fate of the fourth beast in the visions of the seventh chapter of Daniel.

It is all the more striking that we find the historian suggesting deep reservations about the power of Rome, through a speaker whose object was precisely the opposite, to justify and recommend that

---

[14] Wengst 1987.
[15] de Lange 1978: 268.
[16] The leading discussion is Lindner 1972: ch. 2. See also Gabba 1976–77: 189–194.

power. Unless we wish to take the oration as an exercise in rhetorical ingenuity, a piece of tight rope walking, in which Agrippa is
made to put before an agitated populace just enough anti-Roman
innuendo to gain himself a hearing, we are obliged to treat Agrippa's
words as evoking the ambiguous stance of the native governing class,
superficially pre-Roman (in varying degrees), but harbouring doubts
and even deep resentments.

It thus becomes easier for us to understand how one section of
that class could be dragged into a revolt which it did not desire or
approve of, as happened to Josephus and his like: many such people later deserted. It is at the same time clear why Agrippa joined
Vespasian straight after being expelled from Jerusalem, and then supplied the Romans with manpower for the siege (Tacitus, *Histories*
V 1.2). His personal predicament, if nothing else, made it necessary
for him to seek to restore his reputation with the government—and
he was lucky to be reasonably well received. But the revolt's outcome, with the Temple destroyed, Jerusalem in ruins and Roman
coins depicting *Judaea capta* as a woman weeping, crouched beneath
a palm-tree, and overshadowed, sometimes, by a Roman soldier, will
not have been more tolerable to Agrippa than it was to Josephus.
It is usually emphasized that the 'colonial elites' of the Roman
provinces benefited from and therefore tended to approve Roman
rule. This is not untrue. But it is easy to forget that even for such
people foreign domination remained at best a dubious benefit. Local
dignitaries were often directly in the firing line, and, when times
were difficult, they could suffer first and most.

BIBLIOGRAPHY

Bilde, P. 1988. *Flavius Josephus between Jerusalem and Rome: His Life, His Works and their
Importance.* Journal for the Study of the Pseudepigrapha Suppl. 2. Sheffield.
Cohen, S.J.D. 1979. *Josephus in Galilee and Rome: His Vita and Development as a Historian.*
Leiden.
Crook, J.A. 1951. 'Titus and Berenice', *AJPh* 72: 162–175.
Daube, D. 1965. *Collaboration with Tyranny in Rabbinic Law.* Oxford.
de Lange, N.R.M. 1978. 'Jewish Attitudes to the Roman Empire', in P.D.A. Garnsey
& C.R. Whittaker (eds), *Imperialism in the Ancient World.* Cambridge.
Gabba, E. 1976–77. 'L'impero romano nel discorso di Agrippa II (Joseph., B.I. II,
345–401)', *Rivista Storica dell'Antichità* 6–7: 189–194.
Goodman, M. 1987. *The Ruling Class of Judaea.* Cambridge.
Lindner, H. 1972. *Die Geschichtsauffassung des Flavius Josephus im Bellum Judaicum.* Leiden.
Schwartz, D.R. 1990. *Agrippa I: The Last King of Judaea.* Tübingen.

Schwartz, S. 1990. *Josephus and Judaean Politics*. Leiden.
Stern, M. 1987. 'Josephus and the Roman Empire as reflected in the *Jewish War*', in L.H. Feldman & G. Hata (eds), *Josephus, Judaism and Christianity*. Detroit.
Villalba i Varneda, P. 1986. *The Historical Method of Flavius Josephus*. Leiden.
Wengst, K. 1987. *Pax Romana and the Peace of Jesus Christ*. Philadelphia.

CHAPTER NINE

JUSTUS OF TIBERIAS AS A JEWISH HISTORIAN

1. *The Jewish Kings*

Photius' *Bibliotheca* (p. 33) gives us our most extended account of the literary output of Justus of Tiebrias: a whole paragraph devoted to a production of Justus:

Ἀνεγνώσθη Ἰούστου Τιβεριέως χρονικόν, οὗ ἡ ἐπιγραφὴ Ἰούστου Τιβεριέως Ἰουδαίων βασιλέων τῶν ἐν τοῖς στέμμασιν. Οὗτος ἀπὸ πόλεως τῆς ἐν Γαλιλαίᾳ Τιβεριάδος ὡρμᾶτο. Ἄρχεται δὲ τῆς ἱστορίας ἀπὸ Μωϋσέως, καταλήγει δὲ ἕως τελευτῆς Ἀγρίππα τοῦ ἑβδόμου μὲν τῶν ἀπὸ τῆς οἰκίας Ἡρῴδου, ὑστάτου δὲ ἐν τοῖς Ἰουδαίων βασιλεῦσιν, ὃς παρέλαβε μὲν τὴν ἀρχὴν ἐπὶ Κλαυδίου, ηὐξήθη δὲ ἐπὶ Νέρωνος καὶ ἔτι μᾶλλον ὑπὸ Οὐεσπασιανοῦ, τελευτᾷ δὲ ἔτει τρίτῳ Τραϊανοῦ, οὗ καὶ ἡ ἱστορία κατέληξεν.

Ἔστι δὲ τὴν φράσιν συντομώτατός τε καὶ τὰ πλεῖστα τῶν ἀναγκαιοτάτων παρατρέχων. Ὡς δὲ τὰ Ἰουδαίων νοσῶν, Ἰουδαῖος καὶ αὐτὸς ὑπάρχων γένος, τῆς Χριστοῦ παρουσίας καὶ τῶν περὶ αὐτὸν τελεσθέντων καὶ τῶν ὑπ' αὐτοῦ τερατουργηθέντων οὐδὲν ὅλως μνήμην ἐποιήσατο.

Οὗτος παῖς μὲν ἦν Ἰουδαίου τινὸς ὄνομα Πιστοῦ, ἀνθρώπων δέ, ὡς φησιν Ἰώσηπος, κακουργότατος, χρημάτων τε καὶ ἡδονῶν ἥττων. Ἀντεπολιτεύετο δὲ Ἰωσήπῳ, καὶ πολλὰς κατ' ἐκείνου λέγεται ἐπιβουλὰς ῥάψαι. ἀλλὰ τόν γε Ἰώσηπον, καίτοι ὑπὸ χεῖρα πολλάκις λαβόντα τὸν ἐχθρόν, λόγοις μόνον ὀνειδίσαντα ἀπαθῆ κακῶν ἀφεῖναι. Καὶ τὴν ἱστορίαν δὲ, ἥν ἐκεῖνος ἔγραψε, πεπλασμένην τὰ πλεῖστα φασι τυγχάνειν καὶ μάλιστα οἷς τὸν Ῥωμαϊκὸν πρὸς Ἰουδαίους διέξεισι πόλεμον καὶ τὴν Ἱεροσολύμων ἅλωσιν.

If we are to take Photius' precise wording seriously, he is discussing *one work* of Justus throughout this notice. For he seems to take the war narrative to be a part of a wider work: καὶ τὴν ἱστορίαν δὲ ... πεπλασμένην τὰ πλεῖστα φασι τυγχάνειν καὶ μάλιστα οἷς τὸν Ῥωμαϊκὸν πρὸς Ἰουδαίους διέξεισι πόλεμον καὶ τὴν Ἱεροσολύμων ἅλωσιν. This wider work must be the same thing as the χρονικόν of the opening sentence, for that is the subject of the notice. It was referred to as ἱστορία as well as χρονικόν early on (although there ἱστορία might mean simply 'narration'). Photius at no point says, as is his custom in such cases,[1]

---

[1] See the notice on the historian Hesychius (cod. 69, where the last paragraph

that there also exists (or existed) another work by the same author.

Now it is clear that Photius' remarks on Justus' war narrative are derived entirely from Josephus, as are those on Justus' life and character: ἀνθρώπων δέ, ὥς φησιν Ἰώσηπος, κακουργότατος . . . ἀντεπολιτεύετο δὲ Ἰωσήπῳ . . . ἀλλὰ τόν γε Ἰώσηπον . . . ἀπαθῆ κακῶν ἀφεῖναι. He evidently did not even look at this part of Justus' work. Does this mean that the book he had in front of him did not contain the war narrative? If so, Photius may be wrong about the relationship between the two, in supposing that the war narrative fitted into a wider work.² Perhaps Photius' vagueness about the nature of the composite work points in this direction. For it is unexpected to find a summary described as an ἱστορία; Photius' usage is normally careful.³

There are in fact three major obstacles to our believing that Justus did write one compendious work which treated Jewish history from the beginning. First, Josephus' direction of the work he is discussing makes it sound like a war history.⁴ Second, if the *Jewish Kings* was the same work as the war history, it must have been published by the time that Josephus' *Life* and therefore his *Antiquities* came out;⁵ and if it covered with any thoroughness the Jewish 'kings' from Moses to Agrippa II, we should have expected Josephus to take some explicit notice of it. If, on the other hand, there were two separate works (and Photius was being careless), the *Kings* could have appeared after the *Antiquities*. Third, it is hard to imagine a composite work which did justice to both themes. A combination would only be feasible if there was some kind of introduction in the form of a list of kings

---

has: ἀνεγνώσθη δέ μοι καὶ ἑτέρα αὐτοῦ βίβλος, and that on the three works of Dexippus (82).

² Photius could be careless. For an assessment, see Henry's preface to the Budé edition of Photius' *Bibliotheca* (1965), xxiv–xxv. Such errors would be even more intelligible if N.G. Wilson's view, that Photius' claim to have worked from memory should be taken literally, is correct. See Wilson 1968. For the traditional view, that Photius took notes from texts, see Ziegler in *RE* 20 (1941), 690. A. Elter, *RhM* 65 (1910), 175–179, shows how Photius misunderstood the Neo-Platonc philosopher Hierocles through only glancing at a few parts of his περὶ προνοίας.

³ Under Phlegon of Tralles (cod. 97) we find his Ὀλυμπιονίκων καὶ χρονικῶν συναγωγή referred to as σύνταγμα and σύγγραμμα, but not ἱστορία. Cephalion's σύντομον is called ἱστορία (68), but that has 9 books. Eunapius (77) wrote a χρονικὴ ἱστορία, a work of 14 books.

⁴ See *V* 40: τὴν ἱστορίαν τῶν πραγμάτων τούτων ἀναγράφειν, and also 357–360: cf. Luther1910: 51.

⁵ Unless we suppose that there were two editions of the *AJ* or the *Life*, in which case Justus could have written after the *AJ* first came out. See below for a discussion.

and then a reasonably (and perhaps very) full account of the revolt. But then how could such a work ever have been given the title mentioned by Photius? It is most likely, then, either that Photius saw a different work from that discussed by Josephus; or, alternatively, that the *Jewish Kings* was just a digression in the war narrative, later extracted and produced under an independent title.

What can we learn from Photius' description of the contents of what he saw? And can we supplement the information at any point?

1. The work began with Moses: ἄρχεται δὲ τῆς ἱστορίας ἀπὸ Μωϋσέως. Now twice in Christian writings Justus is associated with a dating for Moses. In Eusebius' *Chronicon* this takes the form of a synchronization between Moses, the Egyptian Pharaoh Amosis, and the Argive king Inachus, all of whom are put 500 years before the Trojan war: τοῖς χρόνοις ἀκμάσαι [sc. Moses] κατὰ Ἴναχον εἰρήκασιν ἄνδρες ἐν παιδεύσει γνώριμοι Κλήμης, Ἀφρικανός, Τατιανὸς τοῦ καθ' ἡμᾶς λόγου, τῶν τε ἐκ περιτομῆς Ἰώσηππος καὶ Ἰοῦστος, ἰδίως ἕκαστος τὴν ἀπόδειξιν ἐκ παλαιᾶς ὑποσχὼν ἱστορίας (p. 7b, Helm = *FGrH* 734 F2). In Syncellus it is similar, but two different Argive kings are mentioned: οἵ τε γὰρ ἐκ περιτομῆς πάντες Ἰώσηππός τε καὶ Ἰοῦστος, οἵ τε ἐξ Ἑλλήνων Πολέμων φημὶ καὶ Ἀπίων, Ποσειδώνιος καὶ Ἡρόδοτος τὴν ἐξ Αἰγύπτου πορείαν τοῦ Ἰσραὴλ κατὰ Φορωνέα καὶ Ἄπιδα τοὺς Ἀργείων βασιλεῖς συνέγραψαν, Ἀμώσεως Αἰγυπτίων βασιλεύοντος (pp. 116–117, Dindorf = *FGrH* 734 F3).

An earlier form of the synchronization is to be found in Eusebius, *Praep. Ev.* X 10.15 (excerpting from Africanus), and *Praep. Ev.* X 12.1–3 (from Clement of Alexandria—Clem. *Strom.* I 101) and in Tatian (*Pr. Hell.* 38). The source is given as Apion, who took from the Egyptian history of Ptolemaeus of Mende the association between Inachus and Amosis, and added the Exodus. In Africanus (*ap.* Eus. *loc. cit.*) the precise references to Apion's works are given. This already presents a problem, for Josephus ascribes to Apion a much later dating for the Exodus, contemporaneous with the foundation of Carthage, which Apion put in the first year of the seventh Olympiad (*CA* II 17).[6] But it is clearly better founded than the elaborations in the later texts, which add Josephus and Justus as sources. For the attribution to Josephus is certainly false. Josephus did not date Moses to the time of Amosis and Inachus, but simply claimed that he lived a very long

---

[6] On this see Wacholder 1968: 475. The origin of the synchronism is probably Africanus. See Gelzer 1880–98: 20.

time ago: ὁ δ' ἡμέτερος νομοθέτης ἀρχαιότατος γεγονώς (*CA* II 156). He never mentions any synchronization with Amosis and Inachus made by anyone else. Josephus is thus an importation, and we may suspect the attribution to Justus. It is easy to understand the introduction of two Jewish historians at this point. It was desirable to give this piece of chronology as venerable an origin as possible and for that it had to go back to the Jews themselves. Thus it was fathered on to Josephus and on to Justus, the two Jewish historians whose names were best known to the early Church (Justus having been immortalized by Josephus).

By the time the theory has reached Syncellus, it has become totally garbled. In spite of the change in the names of the Argive kings, the same synchronization is clearly intended. While Africanus (*apud* Eusebius) wrote: μέμνηται δὲ καὶ Ἡρόδοτος τῆς ἀποστασίας ταύτης καὶ Ἀμώσιος ἐν τῇ δευτέρᾳ (already incorrect, since it is *Amasis* Herodotus talks of, and not the Exodus, but the Syrians in Palestine), Syncellus gives Herodotus as one of the actual sources of the full synchronization. He further gives Posidonius, and this looks suspiciously as though it derives from Ἀπίων δὲ ὁ Ποσειδωνίου in Africanus.[7] So neither Eusebius' *Chronicon* nor—still less—Syncellus can be trusted for information as to what Justus of Tiberias had written.

Therefore we have no reliable information of what Justus said about Moses. And Photius himself obviously did nothing more than glance at the work in front of him (or his notes or his mental picture) and record its starting point, as he often did.

We need not be surprised that Moses should be the beginning of a list of Jewish kings. To count him as a king would not have been unreasonable; Philo's *de Vita Mosis* makes this one of his four classifications, and in Jewish tradition Moses was often a king. Alternatively, βασιλεύς was used loosely.[8]

2. The history ended with the death of Agrippa II. Again Photius will have done nothing more than glance. Indeed, the statement could even be just an inference derived from Josephus' remark that Agrippa was dead when Justus published his history. For it is clear that Photius knew his Josephus, and had been through the *Life*.

---

[7] Jacoby refers the reader of the Syncellus text to the fragments of Posidonius on the Jews, which are taken from Josephus' *Contra Apionem* and from Strabo's *Geography* (*FGrH* 87 F 69–70). But there is no trace there of any ideas of this kind.
[8] See below.

We are given a few obvious facts about Agrippa's life: the reigns he lived through, and an actual date for his death, the third year of Trajan. But that date has caused much trouble, since we must date Josephus' *Life* accordingly (Josephus unequivocally talks of Agrippa's being dead at 359, and implies it by the tense at 367). But the *Life* was an appendix to the *Antiquities*, and the *Antiquities* were published in 93/4.[9] Many attempts have been made to save Photius' date, the longest-lived being Laqueur's analysis of the end of the *Antiquities* into two conclusions, of which one would have been written in 93/4, and the other for a second edition of the *Antiquities*, this time together with the *Life* (a revision of a very early work), after Agrippa's death.[10] But, apart from Photius, almost all the evidence for Agrippa's date of death points in the opposite direction.[11] It seems best, then, to take Photius' date as a mistake.[12] The evidence for the dating of Josephus' works can then be given its natural interpretation, and there is no need for elaborate accounts of his process of publication.

To trace the origins of a mistake amidst the manifold inaccuracies in our texts of the chronographers and in Photius is a hazardous exercise. But one possibility looks attractive. In Syncellus' chronological tables, the third year of Trajan appears to be 92 years after the birth of Christ.[13] According to this reckoning, the 'third year of Trajan' would indeed be the likely date for the publication of Justus'

---

[9] Niese 1887–95: *praef.* 5; *AJ* XX 267.

[10] Laqueur 1920: 1 ff. Laqueur is followed by Gelzer 1952, and Pelletier 1959: xiii–xiv. Against this view see Frankfort's remarks 1961: 52–8. There are passages throughout the body of the *Antiquities* which suggest that Agrippa II was dead when they were written. And the *Life* flatters Domitian, mentioning no subsequent Emperor.
Motzo 1924: 217–219, produced a simpler and better theory which was not exposed to these criticisms—that a second edition of the *Life* was produced as a reply to Justus' attacks. But I find it hard to see why Josephus should have rewritten his Autobiography, a work of a different kind produced seven years earlier, instead of simply sitting down and writing a defence.

[11] It is not necessary to recapitulate the arguments expounded by Frankfort 1961. There is no evidence that Agrippa was alive after 95, and perhaps not even after 92. The only possible (but not necessary) exception is an inscription (from the Hauran or Djebel Druze) where a man appears to have passed directly from the service of Agrippa to that of Trajan (H. Seyrig, *Syria* 42 [1965], 31–34).

[12] Tillemont 1690–1738: 2, note 41) already suspected this, without knowing the archaeological evidence. He suggested that Trajan's name was written in error for that of Titus or Domitian. Cf. also Rosenberg in *R.E.* x (1917), 149–50; Jones, *JRS* 25 (1935), 229; *PIR*, 872.

[13] Dindorf 1829: vol. 2, 285.

work (some year or two before the *Antiquities* and the *Life*), and thus
for a *terminus ad quem* for Agrippa's death. It therefore looks as though
the date derives from a chronographer whose mistake Photius inherited. A good candidate is Africanus.[14]

We remain ignorant of whether Justus' work gave a date for the
death of Agrippa II or not, and if it did, what that date was.

3. The extreme conciseness of the work: it is no puzzle what
Photius means by this, nor whence he derives it, for he goes on to
explain: ὡς δὲ τὰ Ἰουδαίων νοσῶν, Ἰουδαῖος καὶ αὐτὸς ὑπάρχων γένος,
τῆς Χριστοῦ παρουσίας καὶ τῶν περὶ αὐτὸν τελεσθέντων καὶ τῶν ὑπ'
αὐτοῦ τερατουργηθέντων οὐδὲν ὅλως μνήμην ἐποιήσατο. Thus Photius
is not, primarily, making a statement about the style of Justus' history.[15] The omission of Christ will have been evident from cursory
inspection and was of obvious interest.[16] At the same time, the work
he saw is not likely to have been very extensive, or Photius could
not have phrased his objection in the way he did. The description
χρονικόν also implies this.

4. We can now go back to the very first point made by Photius—
the purported title of the whole work: Ἰούστου Τιβεριέως Ἰουδαίων
βασιλέων τῶν ἐν τοῖς στέμμασιν. This is a peculiar title. Στέμμα is
both a garland and a family tree. Does the title mean '(a history of)
the Jewish Kings who are in the genealogies'? If so what were the
'genealogies'? Or could it be translated, in spite of the presence of

---

[14] See Gelzer 1952: *passim*, for Syncellus' debt to Africanus. It is likely that any
chronographer would fit into his scheme the date when Justus' sistory appeared
(based on the information of Josephus). Frankfort notes that there are almost as
many dates for the publication of Justus' work as there are chronographers. No
special claims are made for this explanantion of how the mistake arose. Another
curious detail (pointed out to me by Fergus Millar) is that Jerome's brief notices
on Justus (*de Vir Ill.* 14–15) is followed by a notice on Clement, the Apostolic father,
where Clement is also said to have died in the third year of Trajan. Luther (1910:
52, following Niese 1887–95) suggests that Photius confused the date of publication
of the chronicle with the last date in it.

[15] Jacoby, *RE* 10: 1345; Christ 1920: 2.1, 602.

[16] Cf. the treatment of Josephus in this respect. Origen remarked on Josephus'
disbelief in Christianity and claimed (incorrectly) that Josephus explained the fall of
the Temple as due to the execution of James brother of Jesus (*Contra Cels.* I 47);
Eusebius, who seems to have been the first surviving author to have had a text
containing the Testimonium Flavianum in its present, and at least partly interpo-
lated, form, made much of Josephus as a witness to Christ: *Dem. Evang.* III 124;
H.E. I 11, etc. Others followed Eusebius.

The tradition of remarking on Justus' omission had a long life; Voltaire made
the same point, *Oeuvres* 20.599 (Paris, 1818).

the article, '(a history of) Jewish Kings arranged in genealogies'? Or, again, perhaps only one genealogy is involved, since stevmma is generally used in the plural.[17]

The title occurs in a slightly different form in relation to an anecdote about the trial of Socrates in Diogenes Laertius' *Life* (41). This supposedly appears in Ἰοῦστος ὁ Τιβερεὺς ἐν τῷ Στέμματι and runs: Πλάτωνα ἀναβῆναι ἐπὶ τὸ βῆμα καὶ εἰπεῖν "νεώτατος ὤν, ὦ ἄνδρες Ἀθηναῖοι, τῶν ἐπὶ τὸ βῆμα ἀναβάντων". τοὺς δὲ δικαστὰς ἐκβοῆσαι, "Κατάβα, κατάβα". Here we are in a different world altogether, and far, it seems, from Jewish history.

Schürer interpreted the title in the first of the suggested senses and explained the passage in Diogenes Laertius by supposing that Justus wrote a whole series of royal family trees, of which Photius saw the part concerning the Jewish Kings, and Diogenes Laertius another part, referred to as one στέμμα. He drew the analogy of Castor of Rhodes, who, in the first century B.C. had written a work based on the histories of the kings of Assyria, the kings of Sicyon and of Argos, the kings of Alba and of Rome, and the Roman consuls.[18] It is not likely that Justus produced such a work. Whatever the exact character of Castor's lists,[19] to compile them was no easy task. Castor was evidently a scholar of some stature, remaining an authority, particularly for the 'prehistoric' period, long after his death.[20] Could Justus have achieved, unbeknown to us, a similar feat? If he had, he should have had a place in Josephus' *Against Apion*. But even if Josephus' spite refused him this, one of the chronographers of the Christian period would have quarried from his non-Jewish *Stemmata*, had such things existed.[21] Moreover, what we know of Justus makes it hard to envisage him as a sedentary antiquarian,

---

[17] See LSJ s.v. στέμμα.

[18] For the fragments of this author's Χρονικά see Jacoby *FGrH* II B 250. On the nature of the work, Schwartz 1895; Kubitschek in *RE* 10 (1919), 2350 ff.; Jacoby *FGrH* II B. Comm., pp. 814 ff.

[19] It is hard precisely to assess the character of Hellenistic and post-Hellenistic chronographical writings, as is clear from Jacoby's remarks in *FGrH* II B. Comm. Some of the difficulties are also apparent in the article of Wacholder. We cannot, for example, ascertain the lay-out and scope of the work of Menander of Ephesus, who, according to Josephus, wrote τὰς ἐφ' ἑκάστου τῶν βασιλέων πράξεις τὰς παρὰ τοῖς Ἕλλησι καὶ βαρβάροις γενομένας ἐκ τῶν παρ' ἑκάστοις ἐπιχωρίων γραμμάτων σπουδάσας τὴν ἱστορίαν μαθεῖν (*CA* I 116).

[20] Jacoby *FGrH* II B. Comm., p. 817.

[21] See Momigliano 1963, and Bultmann 1958: 56–58, on the special importance of relative chronology to Christian historians.

devoting his time to recondite researches and calculations. Trying to write history, or something related to history, was another matter.

Above all, it is an unwarranted assumption that Justus should have strayed beyond Jewish history. No evidence indicates it. Other interpreters have been even more daring. Luther, developing Schürer, invented a completely separate third work, whose name was Στέμμα in the sense of 'garland'.[22] (Schürer had tried to make them both one and two works at the same time, and thus to have the best of both worlds.) But the Στέμμα and the Στέμματα must surely be the same thing, whatever that is. Otto and Rühl[23] met this difficulty by postulating only one work, called Στέμματα, 'garlands', and taking this to have been a miscellany like the Στρωματεῖς of Clement of Alexandria and the Κεστοί of Africanus. We can agree with Jacoby[24] that this is implausible. Neither of those miscellanies included genealogy or chronography or any other kind of history. In addition, the hypothesis implies total ignorance on the part of Photius about the kind of book he was talking about.

In the Photius passage, where στέμματα is combined with βασιλεῖς, the sense of στέμματα can only be intended as 'genealogies'. While this is not known to us as a title for any published king-lists, it would make quite an acceptable one.

We still have to accommodate Diogenes Laertius. The anecdote could well fit into a preamble or an aside written in rhetorical style. Justus may have begun his work with, or inserted into it, a plea of lack of experience in this kind of activity, and used the anecdote as an illustration. It would parallel Josephus' modesty about his knowledge of Greek (*AJ* XX 264), a profession in which there is no doubt also a certain amount of affectation. It is clear of course that Justus' digression in itself betrays a desire to parade the author's Greek culture. That would be the case, whatever its immediate context; it is a significant revelation.

If we adopt the second proposal adumbrated, that the king-lists had been in the war history but were subsequently excerpted, then the Plato anecdote will fit in more easily, since the work in which it appeared will have been Justus' first known historical enterprise,

---

[22] Luther 1910: 53–54.
[23] Otto in *RE* suppl. 2 (1913), 14; Rühl 1916: 294; and following them, Christ: 2.1, 602.
[24] *FGrH* II B. Comm., 1344.

and a longer one. The title might then be read '(a list of) the Jewish
Kings in the genealogies of Justus of Tiberias', and 'genealogies' be
used to refer to a part of Justus' whole work—like Thucydides' ἀρχ-
αιολογία. A chronographer would have made the extract, at a time
when the whole work was still available. Africanus again springs to
mind, for his following immediately on Justus in Photius' *Bibliotheca*
might suggest that they were in the same manuscript, or, at any
rate, somehow related. This would seem to be the best solution.

There is nothing incongruous about a king-list introduced somewhere into the war history. It is noteworthy that in the *War* Josephus
does not plunge straight into his account of the revolt, but gives first
some earlier history. Also in Josephus, we find an example of a
genealogical digression: in the *Antiquities* (XX 224), when he has
reached Claudius' reign, and has mentioned the completion of the
Temple, he enumerates all the High Priests since Aaron, the first.
The same could be done for the kings of Israel.

There is another case where, independently, the same activities
on the part of an excerptor have been suspected; but, again, a simpler explanation is not excluded. The title is an almost identical one.
For Clement of Alexandria claims to quote from the περὶ τῶν ἐν τῇ
Ἰουδαίᾳ βασιλέων of Demetrius (the third-century-B.C. Alexandrian
chronographer) a passage about the two captivities, of Sennacherib
and of Nebuchadnezzar (Clem. *Strom.* I 141.1). The other surviving
fragments of Demetrius are in Eusebius (*Praep. Ev.* IX),[25] transmitted,
like the Clement quotation, by Alexander Polyhistor. Eusebius gives
no title. The fragments are a skeleton résumé of parts of the Bible
narrative. Their purpose seems to be to establish the precise chronological relationship between events, and the genealogical relationship
between persons. The first two, which are the major ones, link Moses
with the patriarchs. Some passages seem to be simple narrative, like
the one about the sweetening of the bitter water (Freudenthal 1874:
frag. 4). We cannot tell how far the summarizing is due to Polyhistor
and how far to Eusebius. As was observed by Freudenthal,[26] the title

---

[25] On Demetrius, see Freudenthal 1874: 6 ff.; *Jewish Encyclopedia* 4 (1903), 612;
RE 4 (1901), 2813 ff.; Gutman 1969: 132–148; Fraser 1972: 690–694, and vol. 2,
nn. 80–100. The fragments are collected by Freudenthal, and by Jacoby *FGrH* IIIc
722.
[26] Freudenthal 1874: 206. Clement (*Strom.* 1.153.4) gives the title to the work of
the second century writer Eupolemus. Eusebius once refers to a part of that as περί
τῆς Ἠλίου προφητείας (*Praep. Ev.* 9.30). See *FGrH* 723 F1b and 2b. But whatever

in Clement does not fit the fragments in Eusebius well. Only in a very loose sense indeed can their subject-matter be called 'the Judaean kings'. Yet it is most improbable that there were two works. Freudenthal, therefore, thought that the true title had been something like περί Ἰουδαίων, and that the title in Clement was that of an excerpt, dealing, perhaps, with the period of the monarchy. Our alternative would be to suppose that βασιλεῖς could be used freely as the title of a work containing genealogical and chronographical material.[27] Similarly, if we do not accept the excerptor theory for Justus, and hold that the title in Photius was the title of Justus' second work, then in his case too, as has been said, βασιλεῖς might be loosely used.

5. Other references to Justus of Tiberias: these imply only knowledge through Josephus. Thus Eusebius, in the *Church History* (3.10.8), writes of Josephus attacking Ἰοῦστον Τιβεριέα ὁμοίως αὐτῷ τὰ κατὰ τοὺς αὐτοὺς ἱστορῆσαι χρόνους πεπειραμένον, ὡς μὴ τἀληθῆ συγγεγραφότα . . . And Jerome (*de Viris Illustribus* 14) has 'Justus Tiberiensis de provincia Galilaea conatus est et ipse Judaicarum rerum historiam texere' etc. The entry of Stephanus of Byzantium (on Τιβεριάς) mentions Ἰοῦστος ὁ τὸν Ἰουδαϊκὸν πόλεμον τὸν κατὰ Οὐεσπασιανοῦ ἱστορήσας; and the *Suda* (s.v. Ἰοῦστος, Τιβερεύς) talks only about the work attacked by Josephus, saying ἐπεχείρησε μὲν καὶ αὐτὸς Ἰουδαϊκὴν ἱστορίαν συντάξαι καί τινα ὑπομνήματα περιγράφειν· ἀλλὰ τοῦτον Ἰώσηπος ἐλέγχει ψευσάμενον. In Jerome's notice a second work is also mentioned: 'quidam commentarioli de scripturis'. Jerome must have been confused;[28] and this illustrates the tendency to make false attributions to Justus.

Thus there is nothing from outside to add to Photius, except what we have learnt from Diogenes Laertius. To sum up: Photius provides evidence for a slight contribution of Justus to Jewish historiography apart from what Justus wrote about the revolt. Diogenes

---

flexibility there was in the attribution of titles, a work on the Jewish War by Justus could hardly have been called 'On the Jewish Kings'.

[27] If king-lists were the first chronologies, that would be quite plausible. Since the Jews did not have a continuous history of monarchy, their patriarchs and great me would have to do instead in a survey which went back to the period of the Pentateuch.

[28] Schürer 1907: 59.

Laertius shows that he dabbled in Greek culture. That is all that can be asserted with confidence.

2. *Justus of Tiberias and Jewish history*

Into the text of the *Suda* (*s.v.* Phlegon of Tralles) Justus' name has been imported, on the assumption that he did write an extensive Jewish history. The text reads as follows:

τούτου τοῦ Φλέγοντος ὡς φησι Φιλοστόργιος[1] ὅσον[2] τὰ κατὰ τοὺς Ἰουδαίους συμπεσόντα διὰ πλείονος ἐπεξελθεῖν τοῦ πλάτους, Φλέγοντος καὶ Δίωνος βραχέως ἐπιμνησθέντων καὶ παρενθήκην αὐτὰ τοῦ οἰκείου λόγου ποιησαμένων· ἐπεὶ τῶν γε εἰς εὐσέβειαν καὶ τὴν ἄλλην ἀρετὴν ἑλκόντων οὐδ᾽ ὁτιοῦν οὐδ᾽ οὗτος δείκνυται πεφροντικώς, ὅνπερ οὐδ᾽ ἐκεῖνοι τρόπον. τοὐναντίον μὲν οὖν ὁ Ἰώσηπος καὶ δεδοικότι ἔοικε καὶ εὐλαβουμένωι, ὡς μὴ προσκρούσειεν Ἕλλησι.

[1] ⟨περὶ⟩ τούτου τοῦ Φλέγοντος [ὡς] Φιλοστόργιός φησι Kuester [2] Ἰοῦστον vel potius Ἰώσηπον Vales.

Valesius' first emendation has won general acceptance.[29] But, quite apart from the assumptions about Justus' work which are involved, it would seem the best way of making sense of this tortuous passage to replace ὅσον not by the name of another Jewish historian, but by that of Josephus, who is mentioned shortly afterwards.[30] The train of thought in the quotation from Philostorgius (a fifth-century bishop and historian) would then be as follows:

a) Phlegon and Dio give brief versions in digression of the Jewish history which Josephus treats at length.
b) They are able to use him because all three men have basically the same attitude: neither they nor he are in any way interested in the Christian aspect of the events involved (τῶν γε εἰς εὐσέβειαν καὶ τὴν ἄλλην ἀρετὴν ἑλκόντων).
c) Indeed Josephus (from whom one might have expected otherwise) does the very opposite, and goes out of his way not to say anything which would not be pleasing to pagan Greeks.[31]

---

[29] E.g. Gutschmid 1893: 349; Wachsmuth 1889: 438; Schürer 1907: 52.
[30] Wacholder 1968: 475, n. 97, came to the same conclusion.
[31] For the use of Ἕλληνες to mean 'pagan Greeks', see Jones 1940: 298.

If we were to insert the name of a different Jewish historian, it would be hard to see what contrast was being subsequently drawn with Josephus. For if Josephus is writing to please Greeks his procedure will not be the opposite of the Greek historians mentioned above, but the same. And, indeed, why is Josephus introduced at all?[32]

It is of some importance to have established this, since there is now no reason to conclude from this passage that anyone except Josephus wrote an extensive Jewish history which was known to the early Church.

A serious attempt was made by Heinrich Gelzer to show that Jewish history from a source other than Josephus, and often in disagreement with Josephus, did reach the Christian world, and he then pointed to Justus as the only possible known candidate. He argued, in *Sextus Julius Africanus*,[33] that Syncellus' reports of the Maccabean dynasty, and of Alexander Jannaeus' character, his list of that king's conquests, and the story of the origin of Antipater, Herod's father (all of which he took to be from Africanus) derived from an early and independent historical source, and he identified this as Justus of Tiberias.

But he admits the divergence about the Maccabees to be insignificant. And with regard to Jannaeus, the differences also lie in minute details, mainly differences in wording and nomenclature. There is no difficulty in believing that the accounts are derivations from Josephus (together with the Maccabean literature in the first case.)

The story of Herod's descent is less easily dismissed.[34] It runs as follows (in Eusebius' version): Antipater, Herod's father, was the son of one Herod of Askalon, a temple slave (ἱερόδουλος) of Apollo. Antipater was kidnapped by Idumaean robbers and remained with them because his father was too poor to ransom him. Eventually, Hyrcanus, the Jewish High Priest, saw him and took a liking to him

---

[32] For an exposition of the passage with the emendation 'Justus', see Gutschmid 1893. The sense has to be: 'Neither Phlegon and Dio, nor Justus show any interest in what is conducive to piety. Josephus, on the other hand, avoids such subjects becAuse he is afraid of the pagans'. This interpretation involves the additional difficulty of assuming that Philostorgius was under the misconception that Justus was a pagan: hardly conceivable, if Philostorgius had read Josephus.

[33] 225–226.

[34] Referred to first in Justin Martyr, *Tryph.* 52, and then appearing in Africanus, *apud* Eusebius, *HE* I 6.2–3 and 7–11 (together with the story of how Herod had the Temple archives burnt in order to efface all memory of his ignable origins). Finally, see Syncellus, I 561.

(it is not explained how). This was the beginning of Antipater's progress.

The origin of this story is obscure. It was a fiction of which the Christians made use to explain their hatred of Herod.[35] But it is not likely to have been invented by them, and probably goes back to the Jews.[36] There are good reasons for believing that it was used as propaganda against Herod by his Jewish subjects. First, Justin Martyr (*Tryph.* 52) actually ascribes to the Jews the view that Herod was an Askalonite. Second, there is a parallel: the stigma of originating from a slave mother had been attached to an earlier Jewish king; in Josephus, it is John Hyrcanus (*AJ* XIII 288–298), while in the Babylonian Talmud (Kiddushin 66a) the same story is linked with Alexander Jannaeus. Third, it is clear that Herod's Idumaean, non-Jewish origin was displeasing to his Jewish subjects; it must have been because of this that he put out a story through his 'official historian', Nicolaus of Damascus, to the effect that his family came from Babylon.[37] Our story is such as could well have been produced by Jews. The conception of ἱεροδουλεία would not have been strange to them: the institution was widespread in the East.[38] Josephus even ascribes it to the Temple at Jerusalem (*AJ* XI 128). Why Askalon? Herod must have liked the city; it was one of those which he beautified, giving it baths, fountains, and colonnades (*BJ* I 432), and— more significant—there was a royal palace there (*AJ* XVII 321).

It seems right, then, to attribute the story to Jews. But we do not need to investigate its literary transmission, for the tradition is not of the kind which would originate or circulate in history books. Even at a late date, Justin Martyr could have heard it from his Jewish interlocutors; he lived at Flavia Neapolis (in Samaria). Africanus' home was in Jerusalem.[39] The preservation in the Babylonian Talmud of the slander against Jannaeus shows that such stories survive. In the Judaism of this period, historians were not an important instrument of tradition. Therefore we should not introduce Justus of

---

[35] Otto, *RE* VIII (1912): 1459 ff. rightly dismisses Gelzer's attempts to vindicate its truth.

[36] See Otto, and Schalit 1969: 677; the subject is treated in detail by Schalit 1962.

[37] See *AJ* XIV 8, where Josephus refers to Nicolaus. Schalit makes use of these arguments.

[38] *LSJ* s.v. ἱεροδουλεία; Otto, *loc. cit.*; Tarn & Griffiths 1952: 171.

[39] Vieillefond 1970, argues that Africanus was a Jew, but the evidence he cites seems insufficient.

Tiberias. And nothing disturbs our conclusion, that Justus did not produce an extensive work on the history of the Jews.

The scant attention paid to Justus by Christian writers is significant. If Justus' work was substantial, it is odd that it was not studied in the early Church in the way that Josephus' was, and preserved. He would have fulfilled the same needs for Christians as Josephus did. Except, of course, one: Josephus was thought to have noticed Christ. But then, a suitable interpolation could easily have been made in Justus too.[40]

It would seem permissible to go further: whatever Justus did write was submerged at an early stage. The account of the Jewish war totally disappeared. The conspectus of the Jewish kings (or of Jewish history) was known to some chronographers, and dug up by the erudite Photius. Wachsmuth[41] noticed that there was a gap in the line of literary references to Justus: 'Bis zum Anfang des fünften Jahrhunderts, hielt sich sein Werk im Ansehen, noch Philostorgios nennt ihn mit Auszeichnung neben und vor Josephus. *Dann verschwindet es aus, der Litteratur*, um noch einmal unter den Bücherschätzen von Photius aufzutauchen.' If we eliminate Philostorgios, the gap becomes more striking; and it is still longer when we remember that Eusebius had no accurate knowledge. And that of Photius was sketchy! Justus in effect faded out after the first half of the third century, when it is probable that Africanus knew him, and perhaps also Diogenes Laertius (although he may well have taken the extract from a source).[42]

For the early Church, Justus was on occasion a convenient figure to whom to attach a statement about Jews which required additional validation. For German scholarship, he was a convenient figure to whom to attach traditions for which *Quellenforschung* could not otherwise provide a home.

In fact, Justus' literary achievements must have been very limited. Perhaps the Hellenized Judaism of Palestine had not enough Greek education to produce a literary tradition, even if it did, in part, produce Josephus. Herod's historian was a Greek from Damascus. Of the philosophers and grammarians of Askalon, of the literatures of

---

[40] The *Testimonium Flavianum* is partly or wholly interpolation. Of a vast literature, Norden 1913, should be singled out.

[41] 1889: 438.

[42] Luther 1910: 52, takes the opposite view to mine, believing that Justus was popular among Christians.

Gadara, none, as far as we can tell, were Jews.[43] The very fact that
Josephus could comment on Justus' pride in his excellent Greek
shows that a Jew from Tiberias was not entirely at home in the
world of Greek culture.[44]

But we know very little; the late evidence about Justus' writings
is, sadly, of little value; even the notice of Photius scarcely increases
our knowledge. It is on the writings of Justus' contemporary, Josephus,
that we depend, and from him, we can understand something of
Justus' culture, his attitudes, and his conduct.

Justus is a figure whose interest lies in his being a representative
type, a product of those Hellenized, or partly Hellenized Palestinian
cities which we should like to understand better. Judaism and Hellenism
had, in these cities, a subtle relationship. In 66, their reaction to the
Jewish revolt was a complex one. This was a time when men's alle-
giances and assumptions were put to the test, and it is instructive
to observe what happened to Justus in these circumstances. The comparison with Josephus adds significance to the picture.

BIBLIOGRAPHY

Bultmann, R. 1958. *History and Eschatology*. Edinburgh.
Christ, W. von. 1920. *Geschichte der griechischen Literatur*. München.
Dindorf, W. (ed). 1829. *Georgius Syncellus et Nicephorus Cp*. Corpus scriptorum histo-
    riae byzantinae. 2 vols. Bonn.
Frankfort, H. 1961. 'La date de l'Autobiographie de Flavius Josephe et les oeuvres
    de Justus de Tiberiade', *Rev. Belge de phil. et d'hist.* 39: 52–58.
Fraser, P.M. 1972. *Ptolemaic Alexandria*. Oxford.
Freudenthal, J. 1874. *Alexander Polyhistor*. Breslau.
Gelzer, H. 1880–98. *Sextus Julius Africanus*. Leipzig.
Gelzer, M. 1952. 'die *Vita* des Josephus', *Hermes* 80: 67–90.
Gutman, Y. 1969. *Jewish Hellenistic Literature Before the Maccabean Period* (in Hebrew).
    Tel Aviv.
Gutschmid, A. von. 1893. *Kleine Schriften*, vol. 4. Leipzig.
Jones, A.H.M. 1940. *The Greek City*. Oxford.
Laqueur, R. 1920. *Der Jüdische Historiker Flavius Josephus*. Giessen.
Luther, H. 1910. *Josephus und Justus von Tiberias: Ein Beitrag zur Geschichte des jüdischen
    Aufstandes*. Halle.

---

[43] For the evidence that Nicolaus was not a Jew see Stern 1971: 375. On Askalon:
Steph. Byz., s.v. Ἀσκάλων. On Gadara, Jones 1940: 282.
[44] Compare Josephus on his own difficulties with Greek; he asserts that knowledge of foreign languages was frowned on by Jews (*AJ* XX 264). That does not
mean that Josephus did not know the language. This study of Justus may help to
put Josephus' position in perspective.

Momigliano, A. 1963. 'Pagan and Christian Historiography in the Fourth Century', in *The Conflict between Paganism and Christianity in the Fourth Century.* Oxford.
Motzo, B. 1924. *Saggi di Storia e Letteratura Giudeo—Ellenistica.* Rome.
Niese, B. 1887–95. *Flavii Josephi opera,* 7 vols. Berlin.
Norden, E. 1913. 'Josephus und Tacitus über Jesus Christus und eine messianische Prophetie', *Neue Jahrbucher* 31.
Pelletier, A. 1959. *Flavius Josèphe, Autobiographie.* Budé edition. Paris.
Rühl, F. 1916. 'Justus von Tiberias', *RhM.* 71: 289–308.
Schalit, A. 1962. 'Die frühchristliche Überlieferung über dieHerkunft der Familie des Herodes', *ASTI:* 109–160.
—— 1969. *König Herodes: Der Mann und sein Werk.* Studia Judaica Band 4. Berlin.
Schürer, E. 1907. *Geschichte des jüdischen Volkes im Zeitalter Jesu Christi,* vol. 1. Leipzig.
Schwartz, E. 1895. *Die Königslisten des Eratosthenes und Kastor.* Abh. Göttingen 40. Göttingen.
Stern, M. 1971. 'Nicolaus of Damascus as a Source of Jewish History in the Herodian and Hasmonean Age', in *Bible and Jewish History, Studies Dedicated to the Memory of Jacob Liver* (in Hebrew). Jerusalem.
Tarn, W.W. & Griffiths, G.T. 1952. *Hellenistic Civilization,* 3rd edn. London.
Tillemont, Le Nain de L.S. 1690–1738. *Histoire des Empereurs et des autres Princes,* 6 vols. Paris.
Vieillefond, J.-R. 1970. *Les 'Cestes' de Julius Africanus.* Florence.
Wacholder, B.Z. 1968. 'Biblical Chronology in the Hellenistic World Chronicles', *HTR* 61: 451–481.
Wachsmuth, K. 1889. *Einleitung in das Studium der Alten Geschichte.* Leipzig.
Wilson, N.G. 1968. 'The Composition of Photius' *Bibliotecha', GRBS* 9: 451–455.

CHAPTER TEN

JOSEPHUS AND JUSTUS OF TIBERIAS

Justus of Tiberias, a Jewish councillor in a minor Greek city, was a figure in the public eye during the early stages of the Jewish revolt in Galilee; later he became the secretary of a Roman client king, Agrippa II, as well as the author of a limited historical work or works, now lost. His interest for us lies first in his being a representative of the partly Hellenized Palestinian elite of the first century A.D., which was caught short and largely destroyed by the revolt against Rome in A.D. 66; second, in the fact that for a small part of his career a narrow beam of light is shed on his persona by Josephus in the *Life*—and in studying the ancient world, we have to make the most of what little we know; third, in that we can only understand what Josephus was doing as Galilee's commander only insofar as we can make sense of Justus' role there, even if it be solely by sifting through the dubious evidence of the antagonistic Josephus; and last, but not least important, in the various points of similarity which Justus has with his greater contemporary, a comparison which lends perspective and refinement to our portrait of Josephus.[1] It was with a novelist's eye for the possibilities inherent in the contrast that the German Jewish writer Lion Feuchtwanger, in his remarkable trilogy about the historian published during the thirties, elevated Justus into a lifelong rival and constant shadowing presence, dogging Josephus in Palestine and in Rome.

I am happy to have this opportunity to reassess Justus. Since my article of 1973,[2] the subject has been further explored;[3] and I myself have independently modified my views on some matters.[4] It is a good time to pull the threads together. With a debate which, in its

---

[1] That Josephus' works rather than Justus' have survived is unlikely to be a matter of accident—see Rajak 1973: 345.

[2] Rajak 1973 = Ch. 9 in part.

[3] Notably by Cohen 1979, especially Chapter 5; by Dan 1982: 57–78, and, so far as the writings go, in Holladay *Fragments*: 371–389.

[4] See Rajak *Josephus*: 152 and n. 19. I shall not refer further in these notes to specific arguments in Chapter VI of that book.

'modern' phase, has been going on for seventy-five years,[5] we ought now to be able to distinguish such conclusions as are, if not certain, at least probable, from that which remains and must remain mere hypothesis. What can be known about Justus?

There are, it may be said, two major and related questions, concerning the rival writers, which remain unresolved. (1) How far was Josephus' *Life* meant as a polemic against Justus? To what extent has this tainted what Josephus says? (2) How much of what Josephus tells us is it sensible to believe? How far are we able securely to reconstruct Justus' actions in Galilee? In presenting the evidence, I shall have these questions in mind.

The starting point must be the literary exchange, and, first of all, the writings of Justus, to which Josephus was, at least in part, replying. Here the testimony is not exclusively Josephan, though the caution has to be offered immediately that all other allusions are far from contemporary, dating in fact from considerably later periods; that the majority of them (which I shall not discuss here) presuppose knowledge of Justus derived only from Josephus;[6] and that it is Josephus' evidence which remains most useful for our purposes. It is best to begin by extracting whatever we can from Josephus.

According to Josephus, Justus had 'even attempted to write the history of these matters with the aim of overcoming the truth by means of this account' (*V* 40). 'These matters' might mean the detailed issues under immediate discussion: the pressure in Tiberias, in 66, to take up arms against Sepphoris, the resentment of Agrippa's control, the debates in Tiberias as to what to do about the revolt against Rome, and the armed attacks on neighboring Decapolis cities. Equally, however, 'these matter" may refer to the war in its entirety. In any event, the question of the coverage of the work (though not its level of detail) is later settled for us, when Josephus chides Justus for writing of happenings that he had not himself witnessed nor learnt about from eyewitnesses—the Roman invasion of Galilee, the siege of Jotapata—and of happenings on the subject of which he had failed to read the imperial commentaries, that is, the siege of Jerusalem (*V* 357–358). We also learn that Justus had, following the fashion of

---

[5] Taking as a starting point Luther 1910. It may be added that, as of 1999, the debate still continues.

[6] Eusebius, *Historia Ecclesiastica* III 10, 8; Jerome, *de Viris Illustribus* 14; Steph. Byz., s.v. 'Tiberias'; Suda, s.v. 'Justus' and s.v. 'Tiberias'.

classical historians, claimed his account as superior to any other, a claim which Josephus dismisses with scorn.

This contentious work of Justus, whatever exactly it consisted of, was made public in the nineties A.D., after the death of Agrippa II and, Josephus maintains, some twenty years after Justus had first written it (*V* 359).

Justus, then, wrote about the revolt either as a separate subject or as part of a wider work. He touched on a delicate area in Josephus' career, that is to say, the siege of Jotapata, perhaps merely in its place in the narrative, perhaps with extra emphasis, as a contrived attack on Josephus; Josephus certainly took exception to what Justus had written, but that fact does not tell us how deliberately or how virulently anti-Josephus Justus had really been. What is more, the literary weapons brandished by Josephus (and so much emphasized by some scholars) may give a somewhat exaggerated impression even of his own level of personal animosity. Then there is the long delay before publication: Josephus puts this down to what, for a historian, is the most disreputable of motives, saying that Justus had waited for the demise of the eyewitnesses, above all. King Agrippa, who might have discredited his account. But this polemical ascription of motive has, of course, no special claim to belief; indeed it appears to belong to a standard repertory of literary charges. Thus at Rome Pliny the Younger urged his friend Maximus to publish quickly certain pieces defending himself and criticizing the prefect of Egypt, Pompeius Planta; Pliny expressed the fear that the objectivity of the work would be discredited now that Planta had died if people imagined that Maximus had been cravenly waiting for just that event: 'You must keep up your reputation for standing by your convictions, and can do so if it is known to your friends and enemies alike that you did not pluck up courage to write as a result of your enemy's death, but that your work was already finished for publication when his death intervened' (Pliny, *Ep.* IX 1). Justus' much-maligned delay may, then, have had quite a different motive from that alleged by Josephus. I suggested before that Justus could not publish before Agrippa had gone, because Agrippa had endorsed the Josephan version.[7] But it must be admitted that extraneous factors of a more creditable kind could equally have been responsible. Cohen suggested

[7] Rajak 1973: 355.

that of local patriotism: it would have been natural for Justus' work
to have a local bias, and the death of Agrippa would have been the
right moment to claim autonomy for the city of Tiberias.[8] And we
may even wish to go in a different direction and suggest that Agrippa's
death might have been associated with the timing of the publication
only by the critical Josephus. The long delay could be explained
simply by the demands of the work, an explanation which will be
even more attractive to those who suppose that the passages on the
war were part of something bigger.

Yet here we merely touch upon another area of uncertainty. For
our picture of Justus' output as a whole has its own limitations, so
that we cannot be sure how the war story fitted into the wider framework. This is largely because the brief notice of Photius,[9] upon which
we are dependent, does not state in clear fashion the scope and content of what he saw. The patriarch reports 'a chronicle of which the
superscription was "Justus of Tiberias' [book] of the Jewish kings in
the genealogies"' (ἐν τοῖς στέμμασιν); and goes on to make a few
points about this Chronicle—its starting point (Moses), its end point
(the death of Agrippa II, with a patently mistaken dating of that
event),[10] its concision and (which may explain why the work is
described as too concise) its omission of Jesus Christ and all that
concerned him (since the author suffered from 'the Jewish disease').
Our present difficulty stems from the final short section which is of
a biographical nature. Having given us the name of Justus' father, it
cites Josephus on Justus' character ('the worst of rogues') and speaks
of the argument between the two men. Nothing in this section suggests direct knowledge of what Justus had written on the subject: the
terms used are 'it is said' (λέγεται) and 'they say' (φασί). Nor, on
the other hand, does it explicitly state that Photius was aware of the
existence of another work by Justus, a war history, which he did not
see but knew merely by repute. All we can say is that Photius had
not read any such work himself, for his practice where he really has
read more than one work by a particular individual is to say quite
clearly that there also exists a different book by the same author;[11]

---

[8] Cohen 1979: 138–139.
[9] Photius, *Bibliotheca* 33 = Jacoby, *FGrH* 34 T2.
[10] The dating is to the third year of Trajan. Yet all other evidence points to
Agrippa's being dead by the date of the composition of Josephus' *Antiquities*, A.D.
93–94. See Revised Schürer: 1, 480–483. If the wrong date were inserted by Photius,
such an error would be unsurprising. See now also Barish 1978: 61–75.
[11] As he did, for example, in the case of the historian Hesychius (cod. 69).

while it is evident that here he was relying upon his memory of Josephus' remarks on the subject. That Photius was fully acquainted with Josephus is perfectly well established.[12] Though there is one allusion to Justus' *writings* (as distinct from the actions) at this point, it takes a very vague form: 'They say that the account (ἱστορίαν) which Justus wrote is fictitious for the most part and especially where he recounts the Roman war against the Jews and the capture of Jerusalem.' The word ἱστορίαν means both a narrative or story and a written history; so its use here does not enable us to choose between the two possibilities: on the one hand, that there was a work called the 'History' separate from the 'Chronicle'; nor, on the other hand, that one and the same work had both appellations and contained the war story along with other things. The resulting ambiguity is most unfortunate. As Photius does not choose clearly to explain, and perhaps was himself ignorant, where the war history of Justus came in, it is hardly surprising that we too are unsure. There may have been a separate account of the war, which Photius did not have and which had perhaps been lost before his time.[13] Equally, Justus may have attached the war story to the chronicle, of which it could have formed the culmination and conclusion; it was possibly, then, a summary account, like the rest of the chronicle; or, again, the chronicle might have been a mere digression (like, say, Josephus' retrospective list of high priests at *Antiquities* XX 224 ff.) in a mainly contemporary history.[14] On this hypothesis, either it was Photius' decision not to bother with that part of the work, which would not be uncharacteristic of his procedures,[15] or else the matter would have been decided for him by the prior extraction and separate publication of the genealogical section of the work.[16]

The crucial question, as to the scale and balance of the war history, thus, cannot be settled. An impression does, however, emerge that Justus did not compose on a broad canvass; neither Josephus, in relation to the war narrative, nor Photius, in the so-called 'chronicle,'

---

[12] See Hägg 1973: 192. Photius claimed, in fact, to have worked from memory: see Wilson 1968: 451–455.

[13] See Cohen 1979 (referring to earlier exponents).

[14] So, notably, Rühl 1916: 289–308. Dan 1982: 60, suggests two works, put together at a date preceding Photius, who saw both bound together, but noticed mainly the chronicle.

[15] Cf. Cohen 1979: 143, n. 145, and Hägg 1973: 199.

[16] Rajak 1973: 360, 364 = Ch. 9: 163, 169.

in any way suggests that they were dealing with large-scale works. The name 'chronicle'—whether it was Justus' original title or applied to his work later—implies a summary account.[17]

It is true that a more discursive approach might be suggested by an anecdote ascribed, unexpectedly, to Ἰοῦστος ὁ Τιβερεὺς ἐν τῷ Στέμματι by Diogenes Laertius in his third-century life of Socrates (41). Plato, at Socrates' trial, is said to have ascended the rostrum and professed his inexperience at public speaking, whereupon the judges shouted at him to come down. But this anecdote could perhaps have found a place in some kind of self-justifying preface or conclusion by Justus, where it might have formed a parallel to Josephus' famous protestations about his ignorance of Greek in the closing section of the *Antiquities* (XX 263–265). This citation does not justify our enlarging our model of Justus' historical works,[18] or altering our conviction that he was no Josephus. If we regret the loss of his works, it is for the information they would have given us, not for literary reasons.

I shall have more to say later about the literary comparison with Josephus. Here we return to the controversy about the revolt. Whatever Justus' principal purpose, one effect of what he wrote was to challenge Josephus. This, in turn, casts some light on the composition and publication of the *Life*, but without explaining everything; yet it was taken more or less unquestioningly as the work's sole cause by most scholars (including, initially, by myself).[19] Now I would suggest that it is well worth remembering Josephus' other critics, even if Justus is the only one addressed by name. Such people dogged his entire career;[20] but information contrived to do him damage may have begun to circulate with renewed intensity around the time when publication of the *Antiquities* was known to be imminent. All of them

[17] On the nature of such a compressed work (for which the Latin would normally be *breviarium*) see Woodman 1975: 282–288 and especially 284, n. 4. This point refutes the view of the old source critics that Justus' lost history was the origin of various traditions about Jewish history that do not derive from Josephus: for an example see Gelzer 1880–98: 225–226. Such theories can now be happily buried. For discussion, see Rajak 1973: 365–368 = Ch. 9: 171–175.

[18] To make it into a work of general rather than Jewish culture, as Otto does (1913: 14). There is less justification in positing a third work, as in Luther 1910: 53–54.

[19] The position was, however, correctly stated by Cohen 1979: 144.

[20] See *V* 424–425, 429; *CA* I 45–46. It is unreasonable to take Justus as the specific target of the *Contra Apionem* refutation, as proposed by Gelzer 1952: 67.

would have contributed to the decision of appending the *Life*, with its detailed defense of Josephus' generalship, to the twenty books of the *Antiquities*, with their broad scope and large ambitions. Here, too, it is easy to credit Justus with too much simply because we know all too little about him. After all, in the *War* he had not even merited a single mention.

The one clear fact is that Josephus accorded Justus the dubious honour of addressing certain direct remarks to him by name, in a passage inserted prominently into the body of his narrative and aptly called by Cohen 'the great digression' (345–367). In it, Josephus rejects Justus' smear that he, Josephus (together with the 'Galilaeans'), bore responsibility for making the city of Tiberias revolt against Rome. The charge is then flung back at its author: Justus and his party had taken up arms first, in marching out against the territories of nearby cities of the Syrian Decapolis—Gadara, Hippos, and Scythopolis (*V* 340–344).

The real issue is warmongering: who had been the more anti-Roman of the two? And the focus is narrow—just the locality of Tiberias. It is understandable that in the nineties A.D., and especially in the context of a Romano-Greek literary ambiance, a revolutionary past should have been deeply disgraceful. In 66–67, things may well have been somewhat different; and even in the seventies, when Josephus wrote the *Jewish War*, he could still afford to admit that he had at first prosecuted the campaign with vigor (albeit under compulsion). Now he had to emphasize his efforts to maintain peace.

Far from being confined to the digression against Justus, this important argument is, indeed, one of the leading strands in the *Life*. It can be traced right through the work and while it is relevant to the quarrel with Justus, there may have been other targets as well, now nameless, but once to be found among Josephus' many enemies. Thus the 'peace-loving argument' (as we may name it) lies behind the early emphasis in the *Life* on the massacres of Jews in the Greek cities; for the conclusion drawn from those unhappy events is that the revolt was born of necessity not choice (27); and that, of course, implies that Josephus could not have been the man who made it take root in Galilee. Again, it is the 'peace-loving argument' which lies behind Josephus' insistence that he did nothing but obey Jerusalem's instructions once he had taken up his post (28–29). After a period of waiting and equivocation, these instructions led to the struggle to subordinate and control the revolutionaries; to obstruct aggressive acts, such as the seizure of a supply of the emperor's corn by John of Gischala (70–76), which he claims his colleagues, and not he, had been responsible for allowing; and, in general, to suppress the unhealthy influence of John, a local leader who early on became, one way or another, committed to a largely pro-war stance.

The long, drawn-out explanation of the commander's dealings with the influential John of Gischala is the lynchpin of the *Life*. It links the one main theme, the 'peace-loving argument,' with the other prop of Josephus' self-defence, which revolves around his command. It may be noticed that a large part of the *Life* is taken up with the question of Josephus' authority. His problem is to justify his hanging on to his position once the provisional government of Jerusalem had decided to replace him and to explain why he had dodged the four emissaries sent out to divest him of it. Here Josephus needed somehow to clear himself of the dishonor of being rejected by his own associates, who included, after all, such authoritative and scholarly figures as Simeon ben Gamaliel. Josephus rests his case upon the contention that John had instigated the dismissal and (according to the *Life* though not the *War*) that he had employed bribery to bring it about. Thus, John's rascality becomes in its turn a central point, and it is in fact John, rather than Justus, who is the principal villain of the piece. By the date of publication John himself was long gone, for we may presume that he was not seen again after the Judean triumph, when the Romans consigned him to perpetual imprisonment (*BJ* VI 433–434); anything could therefore be permitted as far as his reputation was concerned. This whole aspect of the *Life* is not necessarily connected with the argument with Justus.

Again, we cannot judge to what extent the moral side of Josephus' defence, that is to say, those statements which are patently designed to clear his own besmirched character, are responses to matters raised by Justus. On the one hand, vituperation is likely to have had a place in Justus' history, given the predilection of ancient writers for colourful verbal assaults on their personal enemies; on the other hand, we may notice that there is relatively little mud slung in the other direction, that is to say at Justus by Josephus, apart from the accusation of irresponsible personal ambition (36) and general villainy (344, 393). The most bitter and wild invective is reserved for the more important (and perhaps more talented) John. The defenses, based on character and ably disentangled by Drexler and later by

Schalit,[21] turn out to be, in part, refutations of the standard charges
employed by Greek and Roman writers (and, indeed, by many others
through the ages) and, in pan, specifically Jewish in their orientation.
In the first category we may put the charges of bribery and corruption, vindictiveness, aspirations to tyranny, and the fostering of *stasis*
(79–83, 100, 260–261). Josephus' counter-assertions about his own
public spirit, honesty, moderation, forbearance, clemency, and reticence are frequent (100, 102–103, 110–111, 265, 321, 329–330,
379–80, 385 ff.). In the second category come the charges surrounding
observance of the Law: the other side insisted that Josephus had
flouted it (135, 149), while he stressed his respect for the Sabbath
(159). In just the same way, he in his turn had many times over in
the *Jewish War* accused the revolutionaries of religious improprieties
of every kind—culminating in the desecration of the sanctuary itself
(*BJ* VII 260–264, etc.).

Such a mix of Greek and Jewish patterns could well have featured in Justus' writings too, but we are not in a position to attribute
these specific arguments to him, except in so far as the mild treatment of Tiberias or Tiberians is briefly in question (174–178).[22]
Perhaps the answer would not very much affect our overall understanding of the situation, even if it would contribute in obvious ways
to our picture of Justus.

So much for the literature. We know that Justus attacked Josephus
in writing as a warmonger; presumably, therefore, he emphasized
his own pacific role in the chain of events that preceded Vespasian's
invasion of Galilee. But what had the Tiberian intriguer in fact been
up to? In seeking an answer, we depend, naturally enough, upon
the words of Josephus. In this there is nothing unusual; our position
is the same for almost every aspect of the Jewish War, for, just as
in the case of the Peloponnesian War half a millennium earlier, the
vagaries of the survival and destruction of ancient texts have left the
record of the Great Revolt of 66–73/74 in the hands of its one
major historian, who is the only contemporary one extant. I have
argued in my book on Josephus that in general the problems are
superable; it is possible to extract some check on the historian from
internal coherence and external plausibility. However, this method

---

[21] Drexler 1925: 277–312; Schalit 1933: 67–95.
[22] Cohen 1979: 135.

breaks down in one particular sphere, and that is where Josephus is writing about any personality with whom he was actively involved, be it friend (such as Titus) or foe (such as John of Gischala). The case of Justus falls under this head: we have to take great care in reading anything that Josephus says about him and be ever ready to suspend belief.

However, this does not mean that all of what Josephus offers on the subject falls under suspicion. His reader is protected by one consideration: that outright invention on the writer's part would have earned the scorn of surviving witnesses of the original events; it is a protection which holds good even in cases, such as this one, where personal attitudes come into play. What is more, while people with accurate memories of those times will have been rarer in the nineties than they had been when the *War* was issued, there must still have been enough of them to occasion and to entertain such a debate and to attend both to Justus' writings on the war and to Josephus' *Life*. Therefore, we must take it that the stories found in the *Life* are not fabrications; we should direct our mistrust mainly towards explanations of motive and towards the author's distorting selectivity. It would be wrong to forget altogether that the *Life* is meant as a polemic; it does not even claim the objectivity pretended to by the *War*.

With these principles in mind, we may now consider the actions which Josephus ascribes to Justus and see if it is possible to reach a conclusion about Justus' true role in the events of 66–67. What happened—or rather what is said to have happened—can be easily summarized, and the circumstantial detail is such that the incidents must be deemed real. What is harder to gauge is the level and quality of Justus' involvement as an individual, especially as our impression of that depends often enough on alleged statements or even upon imputed desires or aspirations. Yet it is upon assessment of these that the verdict on his position over the question of war or peace will hang.

Josephus' charge against Justus is, as we have seen, a replica of Justus' objection against Josephus—that he had caused Tiberias to revolt from Rome. Even the most enthusiastic upholder of Josephus' veracity must admit that this charge is never adequately substantiated in the body of the narrative. Josephus' first visit to Tiberias reveals Justus as a waverer but nothing more extreme than that (32 ff.); he is the leader, together with his father, Pistus, of a middle party, lying between the prosperous pacifists with their Herodian names (33) and the ordinary people, a nameless group who wanted war. Even at this stage, then, Justus could not be presented as having sought revolt from Rome. The middle party is shown as pretending to hesitate, but being really bent on a revolutionary change which could enhance its own power. Such slurs are valueless as evidence; what is telling is that the speeches and actions here laid at Justus' door testify that he was militant to a degree, yet not quite enough for it to amount to definite disaffection from Rome. For the middle party was concerned with prosecuting local feuds, in particular with whipping up the Tiberians against the rival city of Sepphoris, which was now the Galilaean capital (Nero had added Tiberias to the territory of Agrippa II [37]). And Justus' activities resulted in the marauding raid by Tiberias against frontier villages belonging to three Decapolis places, where there had already been large-scale trouble between Jewish and Syrian Greek inhabitants (*V* 42; *BJ* II 466–478).[23]

We do not need to follow Schalit and Cohen[24] in their dismissal of the very existence of a third party in Tiberias (it is never desirable to rewrite Josephus in such a thoroughgoing fashion) in order to accept that Justus was not in any real sense pro-war. Indeed, at this point in time, it was entirely unclear which way the war would go, and what happened in Galilee was something separate: everywhere, local tensions and feuds were unleashed, now that there was a license to take up arms. On the other hand, it should be noted that Justus' verbal assault on Sepphoris did entail rejection of the obedience owed to Agrippa, and we are told in addition that the king was much abused by Justus (39). If the latter is true, then so will be Josephus' assertion that Justus was at this stage poised to go either way, towards war or towards peace. For Agrippa, having failed to dissuade the Jerusalemites from provoking Rome, had been expelled from Jerusalem before the Roman sacrifices had been stopped in the Temple, had helped the procurator Florus to crush disturbance in the city in the summer of 66, and had himself led a military detachment that joined the invading legion of Cestius Gallus in the autumn (*BJ* II 407, 417 ff., 500–503). To damage Agrippa could be a challenge also to Rome. So, neither doubting nor accepting every word

---

[23] On the distinction between action against Gentile Greeks and action against Rome, see Rappaport 1982.

[24] Schalit 1933; Cohen 1979.

in Josephus, we have to grant that in the early days Justus did indeed sit on the fence. His reason for doing so is another matter, be it prudence, politics, ambitions, or genuine perplexity. Either way, we cannot accept that he took Tiberias all the way to war, especially as the city was still to change sides four times in the course of the coming months (82).

Justus, then, emerges as an ambivalent character not unlike Josephus himself. To accept this requires not naive credulity but simply a straight reading of the *Life*, and when such a reading has been rejected, it has been largely in the interests of proving an underlying point about Josephus.[25] The contrast with Josephus springs from the differing importance of the two men. Josephus, whatever doubts he personally felt about the revolt, had more than merely local significance; he was (at least until his rejection) part of a provisional government which had taken over the action in an attempt by its members to keep the lid on the ferment, to stall as long as possible and to save themselves from the class hatred of their more militant compatriots.[26] Once they had done this, they had to go through with at least the semblance of resistance to Rome. Justus was a simple local politician, and such associates as he had appear to have been drawn first and foremost from his family; not only were there his father and brother, but he included among his relatives by marriage a man known as Philip, son of Jacimus, who was a maverick agent of Agrippa II (177–178). Beyond this, Justus was to an extent in harmony with his fellow members of the town council of Tiberias, but we cannot suppose that they always constituted a united body. Justus thus had to reach his own decisions sooner than Josephus, and it no doubt became easier to make up his mind after his brother was mutilated by militant 'Galilaeans' at Gamala (177).

So for Justus the period of uncertainty may have been rather shorter (although the chronological picture to be derived from Josephus is not at all clear). Josephus mentions him and his father in passing, as being eager to join John of Gischala's movement against Josephus' leadership (87). That happened when the Galilaean patriot first went to Tiberias; whether or not it implies hostility to Rome

---

[25] Thus Cohen's purpose is to argue that Josephus in the *Life* was bent on concealing his erstwhile militancy; for this the evidence had to be systematically distorted, which required denying Justus' true position as essentially a pacifist.

[26] This is explained in the *War*; see *BJ* II 449, 562 ff.

depends upon our assessment of John's position: some would see him as a moderate, though I have been inclined to interpret his position as a rebellious one throughout.[27] At any rate, nothing came of the attempted coup, since it was anticipated by Josephus; John ran away and there is no further mention of Justus' plans. No great weight should be put on so slight a statement (88) by Josephus that Justus and his father sought to join John. Though perhaps suspect, in that it contributes to Josephus' objective of pinning the blame for the Tiberian troubles on Justus, there is nothing inherently implausible about it, and it fits in well with the confusion and uncertainty of this early period, as well as with our impression that Justus and Josephus had already conceived an intense personal dislike of one another. Josephus felt that Justus had aspirations to power of his own in Galilee (37, 391).

On the other hand, Justus did not repeat his rash challenge to Agrippa. His change of heart did not come a moment too soon, for he was before long to depend upon Agrippa's favour for rescue from a death sentence imposed by Vespasian, at the prompting of indignant Greeks of the Decapolis (342–343). The change of heart is first revealed when Justus is found among those who resist official demands for Agrippa's Tiberian palace to be destroyed because it bore pictorial representations of animals unacceptable to some of the strictest Jews. In fact, the mob took the law into its own hands, before any formal action could be adopted. Here again, Justus' presence among the leading men of Tiberias (64) is given a brief mention; there is some slight room for doubt, but little is to be gained by treating the inclusion of Justus as a libellous fabrication by Josephus. The leader's action is, in any case, one of civilized moderation, not necessarily implying a particular stance towards the war.

As we have indicated, the city of Tiberias seesawed in its allegiance as different elements took control of its democratic organs or managed to gain an ascendancy over its mob. Josephus' displeasing task continued to be to prevent the city from declaring for Agrippa and to keep it within the revolt; this is what he did, however contrary it may have been to his deepest sympathies and instincts. Justus was, of course, playing a different game, and was, with his father, among the councillors and leading commoners arrested by Josephus

---

[27] See Revised Schürer 1973: 1, 480–483.

after he had suppressed the city's disloyalty by means of a mock
fleet and a trick (169, 174). An interesting episode is related in which
Josephus, so he says, gave dinner to Justus and Pistus and advised
them to accept his authority. 'I remarked that I was well aware
myself of the unrivalled might of the Roman arms, but, on account
of the brigands, kept my knowledge to myself' (175). The little vignette
would hardly have been worth inventing; its implication is that Justus
and Pistus should have been well able to understand Josephus' predicament, and would have approached the war from a standpoint
sufficiently similar, to enable them to grasp both its undesirability
and the good sense there was in playing along with the rebels.

Caution, however, took Justus in a different direction, and his
opportunity for desertion came before any fighting, during a second
bid by his city to get Agrippa to come in and take over (381). There
was a serious risk of violent reprisals by the Galilaean hordes, a risk
from which Josephus, in boastful vein, claims to have saved the city
through his influence with the rebels (389). In fact, Justus' decision
to communicate with the client king through his agent Crispus, who
was then present, and afterwards to make his escape, is quite understandable as a bid for safety; we may overlook the disappointed
ambition and the fear of Josephus, which are named, somewhat
absurdly, as the main motives (390–393). For Josephus' aim is to
rob Justus of any credit he might acquire as a respectable pacifist:
'but you, Justus, will urge that you at least were no enemy [of Rome]
because in those early days you sought refuge with the king. I reply
that it was fear of me which drove you to do so' (357). Nor is there
anything surprising in Justus attaching himself to Agrippa: the association through members of Justus' family will have made up for
early disloyalty to the king.

The 'great digression' is not the place to look for accurate representations of Justus' position, and least of all in the case of so
personal a statement as this one. It looks as though we should also
treat with a pinch of salt a rather wild paragraph which precedes
these accusations of fear and which has often gone unnoticed. In it
Josephus claims a considerably greater and longer resistance on the
part of Justus than is borne out by the rest of his narrative, allegations that it was in the later stages of revolt that Justus was active
at Tiberias, that he was still anti-Roman after the fall of Jotapata
(in the summer of 67), and that he laid down arms only when
Vespasian was at the walls of Tiberias (349–352). Yet only a little
later, we have Josephus insisting that Justus could not have under-

stood the campaign in Galilee, let alone the events at Jotapata, because he was at Berytus with Agrippa during this whole period (357). We can suppose only that Josephus wrote the earlier paragraph before he had looked into the facts of Justus' flight and failed to alter it afterwards. Were the claims tenable, he would have had every reason to exploit them more fully, as they could have made a major contribution to his case that Justus had been the true warmonger.

The *Life* exposes a number of loose ends and puzzling little problems. Nonetheless, we have been able to derive with a fair degree of certainty a sketch of Justus before the war as a pro-peace individual who had made some pro-war noises. In this he emerges as a pale shadow of Josephus, just as he does in his writing. It is remarkable that even the circumstances of their respective defections enhance this impression: in Justus' case, after rescue from Vespasian's death sentence, he returns to Agrippa and eventually to a secretaryship with the client king of a marginal kingdom, in Josephus' case, a defection to Vespasian and Titus, and, after imprisonment, to the friendship of emperors and to residence in an imperial property in Rome itself. The scope and talents of Josephus are highlighted through the comparison.

The later years of both men are shrouded in obscurity; with Josephus we have the writings, it is true, but regrettably little biographical background against which to set them. For Justus, we have Josephus' jaundiced statement that he fell out of favour several times with Agrippa, being twice imprisoned, twice exiled, once sentenced to death, and eventually banished after a fraud charge (355–357). Yet even the activities and powers of the client king are for this period unknown to us,[28] let alone the doings of his secretary.

What can, however, be divined is an interesting similarity of cultural attitudes and goals between the two writers—again, writ larger in the case of Josephus. In each case, political ambivalence has its cultural correlative: the indications are that, like Josephus, Justus tried to bridge Hellenism and Judaism through historiography. In his early days he had been something of an orator (*V* 40). The medium for this still may have been his native Aramaic or even Hebrew, rather than Greek.[29] But the techniques will have been sharpened by the Greek education of which, according to Josephus, Justus had had at

---

[28] See Dan 1982: 61 and n. 12.
[29] On Hebrew and Aramaic as Josephus' native languages, see Rajak *Josephus*, appendix I.

least a smattering. And it is Josephus, a man who, after all, had every reason to understand the situation, who says that it was pride in this facility which later induced the Tiberian to set himself up as a historian. In what Justus wrote about the war he evidently treated Jewish politics in a Greek language narrative. In the text on the 'Jewish kings' he presumably followed Hellenistic-Jewish precedent in working out a chronology for biblical antiquities: genealogical reconstruction made it possible to relate the Greek mythical past to the Jewish, and, if only by implication, to demonstrate the superior historicity and greater length of Jewish tradition. It is interesting that works to which the same title was at least sometimes applied had earlier been produced by two Hellenistic-Jewish writers, Demetrius, an Alexandrian, probably in the third century B.C.,[30] and Eupolemus, perhaps from Palestine and of the second century B.C.[31] The few fragments of Demetrius to survive are skeleton resumes of biblical stories; Eupolemus seems to have been more of a chronographer. Justus may well have taken such treatment down to the present, with the Herodian dynasty in whose pay and service he himself was placed.

The royal secretaryship, too, which will have offered some opportunity for political involvement as well as for writing, must have combined Justus' Jewish with his Greek interests. Agrippa, like his predecessors, had been granted a general tutelage over the Jewish people in addition to his kingdom around the margins of Palestine. But Agrippa's main sphere of operations—again like his predecessor's—was on the larger stage of the Hellenized Greek East, a world of cities (to which Agrippa's great-grandfather Herod had made such notable benefactions), and, above all, of client kingdoms. Agrippa's secretary, too, would have had to appear on both the smaller stage and the larger. In this respect there is no exact parallel with Josephus so far as we know; but another prototype springs to mind, and he is Nicolaus of Damascus, who had been Herod's minister and a Greek historian, as well as being a staunch advocate of the Jewish cause (though he himself was in fact a pagan).[32] Again, Justus was by a long way the lesser in stature, both as writer and politician.

---

[30] For Demetrius' fragments, see *FGrH* III C, 722, and now Holladay *Fragments*: 51–91, or Walter 1975: 280–292.

[31] For Eupolemus' fragments, see *FGrH* III C, 723; Holladay *Fragments*: 93–156; Walter 1976: 93–108; and Wacholder *Eupolemus*. It was Clement of Alexandria (*Strom.* I 153.4) who gave this title to Eupolemus' book.

[32] On Nicolaus, see Wacholder 1962.

In general terms, then, Justus can become a comprehensible, even a predictable figure. Nor does further study and interpretation of the detail require any change in the overall assessment which I made on concluding my original study of Justus and Josephus: the modern historian's predicament can best be defined by saying that we have to learn from Josephus about Justus, and then, through observing Justus, we can come to improve upon our grasp of Josephus. In this way, the two men's disputes have turned, in the end, to a kind of mutual support.

BIBLIOGRAPHY

Barish, D.A. 1978. 'The *Autobiography* of Josephus and the Hypothesis of a Second Edition of His *Antiquities*', *HTR* 71: 61–75.

Cohen, S.J.D. 1979. *Josephus in Galilee and Rome: His Vita and Development as a Historian.* Leiden.

Dan, Y. 1982. 'Josephus and Justus of Tiberias', in U. Rappaport (ed.), *Josephus Flavius: Historian of Eretz-Israel in the Hellenistic Roman Period* (Hebrew). Yad Izhak ben Zvi. Jerusalem.

Drexler, H. 1925. 'Untersuchungen zu Josephus und zur Geschichte des Jüdischen Aufstandes 66–70,' *Klio* 9 n.s. 1: 277–312.

Gelzer, H. 1880–98. *Sextus Julius Africanus und die byzantinische Chronographie*, 2 vols. Leipzig.

Gelzer, M. 1952. 'Die Vita des Josephos,' *Hermes* 80: 67–90 = *Kleine Schriften* III, Wiesbaden, 1964.

Hägg, T. 1973. *Photios als Vermittler antiker Literatur.* Uppsala.

Luther, H. 1910. *Josephus und Justus von Tiberias: Ein Beitrag zur Geschichte des jüdischen Aufstandes.* Halle.

Otto, W. 1913. 'Herodes', in *RE*, suppl. ii: 1–200.

Rajak, T. 1973. 'Justus of Tiberias', *CQ* n.s. 23: 345–368 = Ch. 9 in part.

Rappaport, U. 1982. 'John of Gischala: From Galilee to Jerusalem', *JJS* 33: 479–493 = G. Vermes and J. Neusner (eds), *Essays in Honour of Yigael Yadin.* Totowa, New Jersey.

Rühl, F. 1916. 'Justus von Tiberias,' *RhM* 71: 289–308.

Schalit, A. 1933. 'Josephus und Justus: Studien zur Vita des Josephus,' *Klio* 26: 67–95.

Wacholder, B.Z. 1962. *Nicolaus of Damascus.* Berkeley.

Walter, N. 1976. *Fragmente jüdisch-hellenistischer Historiker.* JSHRZ I 2. Gütersloh.

—— 1975. *Fragmente jüdisch-hellenistischer Exegeten.* JSHRZ III 2. Gütersloh.

Wilson, N.G. 1968. 'The Composition of Photius' *Bibliotheca*', *GRBS* 9: 451–455.

Woodman, A.J. 1975. 'Questions of Date, Genre, and Style in Velleius: Some Literary Answers', *CQ* 25: 272–395.

CHAPTER ELEVEN

THE *AGAINST APION* AND THE CONTINUITIES
IN JOSEPHUS' POLITICAL THOUGHT

Introduction: political thought in Josephus

Among Josephus' various *personae* in the conduct of the polemic in
Against Apion is that of political thinker. The signal merits of the
Jewish politico-religious order are invoked as part of the defence of
Judaism against his opponents, that clutch of (named) detractors from
previous generations the foremost of whom was the Alexandrian
intellectual Apion. While the first of the two books demonstrates the
superiority of the Jewish nation by proving its antiquity, the second
book is devoted specifically to the refutation of slanders, and in the
process it concerns itself with defining, interpreting and defending
the *politeia* of the Jews, in the sense of the Jewish constitution with
its prescriptions for the life of the community. Here, Josephus' political thought is distilled and systematically set out without the need,
present in his historical writings, to engage with specific time-bound
events.[1]

It is implicit in the discussion that the Jewish version is to be
judged in terms of the aims and attributes of Greek constitutions.
The defence is upbeat: the system emerges not only as a worthy com-
petitor but as superior: it is held out for inspection as a realized
Utopia, available for emulation by the rest of humanity. Already this
has proved itself to be widely admired by philosophers, copied by
legislators, and sought after by ordinary people (*CA* II 279 ff.). Even
Plato, when he excludes unedifying representations of deities, is its
imitator (II 257). The impression given to the reader is that the Jews
live in an ideal state—at a time, we may observe, when in reality
they were stateless.

But political ideas occupy a significant place elsewhere too in

---

[1] On the entire *Against Apion* discussion, see especially Vermes 1982. Amir 1985–88:
84–85 regards the *Antiquities* material as an earlier stage in Josephus' development.

Josephus' writings. Closest to *Against Apion* is the brief Jewish 'constitution' in the *Antiquities*, embedded in what is formally a digression within the Deuteronomic account of the death of Moses (*AJ* IV 196–301). Public and domestic regulations from Deuteronomy are there combined with material from Leviticus to generate a systematic account. Then again, other of the author's thoughts on the subject of the *politeia* and of the conduct of political life are dispersed through the biblical part of the *Antiquities* and especially through the extensive Mosaic sections (II 217—IV 331). There comments arise for the most part out of particular narrative contexts and they cluster especially around analyses of Moses' leadership.

When it comes to those books which are concerned with recent or current events, that is to say the *Jewish War* and the second half of the *Antiquities*, Josephus theorizes less about politics. None the less, his writing is suffused with political judgements. Like many of the Greek and Roman historians, he is preoccupied with these matters. The turbulent times about which he wrote, times during which the Jews were exposed to extreme vicissitudes from both external and internal forces, were such as to demand a political interpretation quite as much as did any world dominated by rulers, empires or great battles. Indeed, Josephus himself claims just this, when at the very opening of the *Jewish War*, he promotes his subject by declaring, in the manner of Thucydides, that the Jewish revolt was more or less the greatest conflict in human history (I 1).

In addition, there is the human factor. Josephus accepted a position of leadership in the Jewish revolt against Rome of A.D. 66–73/4, but, notoriously, he deserted at an early stage from the revolutionary side and associated himself closely with Titus. With the emperor-to-be he witnessed and, for his own part, lamented the fall of Jerusalem, and he was somehow active behind the scenes during the rise of the Flavian dynasty to power at Rome. These activities were apparently well-known in Josephus' own day: that is no doubt why he found it expedient to tell all in the so-called *Life* which he appended to his *Antiquities*, creating for himself an opportunity to put his own spin on events. The personal history was a powerful stimulus to political analysis. And Josephus' interpretation of contemporary history emerges as in large measure coherent, despite the inevitable emotive charge behind his writing, the strong (if intermittent) element in it of personal *apologia*,[2] and moments of inconsistency.

---

[2] On Josephus as apologist, Sterling 1992: ch. 6.

The composition of Josephus' works extended over a long period, with the *Jewish War*, or most of it, written in the 70's A.D., the *Antiquities* and the *Life* appearing in the 90's, and *Against Apion* after that. Their subject matter, as we have seen, also diverges radically, ranging from the rewriting of the Bible in the first half of the *Antiquities*, to the day-by-day account of the historian's personal conduct as a regional commander in the *Life*. Yet there were important continuities. Significant among them, I would suggest, was the character of Josephus' core readership. He said he wrote *The Jewish War* for the inhabitants of the Roman world, and the *Antiquities* for Greeks, but content and approach suggest that the audience was always expected to consist as much of Jews who knew Greek, that is to say Jewish residents of the cities of the Roman empire. It is hard to explain on any other basis the note of lamentation which runs through the *War*, or the attachment of the immensely detailed *Life* to the *Antiquities* as an appendix. As for the *Against Apion*, it fulfils the function, like all apologetic literature, of bringing new heart to those under attack and providing them with an armoury for their defence.[3]

The question of the various continuities in Josephus' writings is a difficult one. Indeed, there are major differences of opinion among modern scholars as to how far the historian's judgments on Judaism and on Jewish society underwent change with the drastic alterations first in his personal situation, from Jerusalem priest to Diaspora Jew and Flavian client, and second in that of the Jewish people, from being the proud possessors of a renowned Temple and erstwhile allies of Rome, to a vanquished, dispersed and humiliated nation whose mother city had been burnt to a cinder.[4] The differences in modern assessment focus on Josephus' valuation and presentation of the Jewish sects and especially on his later self-presentation as a Pharisee.

That debate remains open. So it is perhaps worth transferring the enquiry, in order to consider on a wider front how far Josephus' religious, moral and social values, or, at least, his expressed opinions,

---

[3] Some scholars, it should be noted, are prepared simply to take Josephus' professions of reaching out to a Greco-Roman audience at face value, e.g. Bilde 1988: 200.

[4] Some scholars prefer, however, to emphasize evidence of development. See especially Cohen's (1979) version of Morton Smith's widely-accepted theory, that Josephus' much-vaunted early affiliation with the Pharisees is retrojected from the 90's. But for a denial that Josephus ever meant to identify himself with Pharisaism, see Mason 1991.

develop over time. In this paper, the question is posed in relation
to Josephus' political thought. It is tackled by way of enquiring what
continuities, and also what disjunctions, are to be found between the
final, developed system of the *Against Apion*, on the one hand, and
Josephus' earlier ideas in the *War* and the *Antiquities*, whether explicitly expressed or implicit, on the other hand. Differences between
the latter two are also noted and discussed, but the main emphasis
is on locating correctly the ideas of Josephus' last work, the *Against
Apion*. Distinctions of genre and of literary framework have, of course,
to be taken into account in such an enquiry. Josephus' leading ideas
are examined one by one and the method adopted is to start where
possible with the end-product and then to look back to earlier texts.
But first the ideas of the *Against Apion* need to be set in context.

Greek-Jewish political thought

Josephus drew on an extensive corpus of political ideas and concepts.
The books of the Bible offered a range of doctrines and *exempla* concerned with government and decision-making. It appears that Josephus
was familiar with the Bible in Greek as well as in Hebrew. The
Greek translation, especially that of some of the later books, offered
above all a ready and peculiarly abundant vocabulary for describing
power, be it that of human rulers or that of God, correctly reflecting
the Hebrew Bible's preoccupation with the subject. δυναστεία, βασιλεία,
ἀρχή, ἐξουσία, κράτος and δύναμις are all consistently employed, and
they have overlapping senses. Different translators within the corpus
have their own preferences. Josephus incorporates the full range of
terminology, though he does not apply every one of these terms to
Divine power, as do the Septuagint translators. ἐξουσία for him
means simply authority or competence, δυναστεία supreme power
or rule of one kind or another, and ἀρχή empire, sovereignty or
office. Josephus, for his part, shows a particular predilection for the
various senses of δύναμις. While sometimes, the application is merely
to a military force of one kind or another, especially, as might be
expected, in the *Jewish War*, or else to human capacity, when it just
means the ability to do something, still many of the word's approximately 500 appearances, carry a religio-political or a simple political significance. This is a preference of the *Antiquities* more than of
the *Against Apion*.

Correspondingly, in the Septuagint, the people of Israel was God's slave, *doulos*; this latter formulation was also adopted, but more rarely, by the cautious historian, perhaps aware that too much belittling of his people could be dangerous. None the less, examples of the usage can be found in his different works.[5]

Greek-Jewish literature was created under the impact of the changing national fortunes of the Jews: exile, Persian suzerainty, the rise of the high priesthood as a political force, the revolt of the Maccabees against the Seleucids, a state under Seleucid suzerainty, the independent Hasmonean monarchy, the declining authority of that monarchy, civil war, the Roman conquest, the hardening of sectarianism, revolt and the loss of Temple and capital city. One consequence of this experience was a growing capacity to describe and analyse political change, manifested above all, in the literature which was written in Greek, since the language was, by the Hellenistic period, deeply attuned to the discussion of political matters.[6] Jewish-Greek political thought is a creative fusion of a non-Greek literary culture with Greek ideas. Interpreters have debated the proportions in the mix; the truth is that the elements are inseparable.[7] This was Josephus' inheritance.

Josephus was, more specifically, the successor to Philo as the exponent of a political theory centred on Judaism and expressed in Greek. The two writers are intellectually far apart, and Josephus had little penchant for philosophical speculation. None the less, their backgrounds and experience are comparable. From a base within the small Jewish social elite of the Roman east, each acted for a period as political leader, defender of the Jews and delegate to the emperor; in Josephus' case, the mission to Rome marked the beginning of his career. Josephus' literary output, almost as much as Philo's, belongs to the Diaspora: transfering from Jerusalem to Rome, he addressed readers around the empire. Admittedly, unlike Philo, who probably knew no Hebrew, Josephus, who was of priestly and royal stock and brought up in an Aramaic/Hebrew milieu, had to labour,

---

[5] Gibbs and Feldman 1986: 289–290.

[6] On these developments and their impact on Jewish culture, see Bickerman 1988, with attention to both Greek and Aramaic milieux. Also, Mendels 1992; Rajak 1996 = Ch. 3.

[7] See especially Attridge 1976 for an analysis of the Jewish dimension in the biblical *Antiquities*.

he informs us, to perfect his grasp of the language in which he
wrote.[8] This he successfully did, and we should regard him as in full
command of the political vocabulary and of the concepts he deploys.

There are indications that Josephus knew and exploited Philo, and
it is commonly accepted that this was the case. Thus, part of the
discussion of Jewish practices in the *Against Apion* reveals a close
dependence on Philo's now fragmentary *Hypothetica*.[9] Indicative parallels include the prohibitions on destroying a fleeing animal and on
killing an animal with its young or a bird in its nest. There is food
for thought, too, in the fact that Josephus' main butt in this work,
the grammarian, teacher and rhetor Apion, not only belonged to
Philo's generation, but confronted him directly before Caligula in
Rome, when the two participated in rival delegations from Alexandria
after the anti-Jewish riots there. Elsewhere in Josephus, for the simple
reason that the bulk of his extensive output, unlike Philo's, is historical, the influence is less detectable.

To admit Philonic influence is to allow that Josephus wrote within
a tradition and that he worked with some well-established ideas; not,
however, to suggest that his exposition is other than his own. Neither
Philo nor any other prior author, so far as we know, chose to discuss
Jewish practice within a polemical framework and there are no known
parallels for the structure of *Against Apion* or for many of Josephus'
themes. We may safely take Josephus' ideas as his own and discuss
them on that basis.

1. *The Jewish* πολιτεία *in Josephus*

Josephus in his later writings, and especially in the *Against Apion*,
accepted the common Jewish-Greek interpretation of Judaism as a
politeia (πολιτεία), a constitution in the broadest sense. This application is of course quite distinct from the use of πολιτεία with the
meaning of citizenship which figures, with notorious ambiguity, in
Josephus' narratives concerning Jewish status at Alexandria. Occasion-

---

[8] On all these points, Rajak *Josephus*.
[9] Fragments in Eusebius, *Praep. Ev.* 8.15. On the parallels, see Terian 1985:
142–146. On Philo's *Hypothetica* in Josephus: Troiani 1978, and, rejecting direct
dependence, Carras 1993. Asserting Philo's general influence on Josephus' construction of an ideal constitution, Kasher 1996: vol. 2, 438. Schwartz 1990: 40–43
and 52–54, is less persuasive in seeking to reduce to a minimum Josephus' knowledge of Philo.

ally in the *Against Apion* Josephus uses as a variant the term πολίτευμα, a term which means, strictly, a constitutional entity, but which in this context bears much the same sense as πολιτεία.[10]

Although the Jews were a dispersed race (γένος) the majority of whom no longer resided in their homeland of Judaea, the continuing appropriateness of defining their religious way of life as a πολιτεία came from the central role in Jewish existence of the Torah, that is to say the Pentateuchal texts together with the code of law and practice set out in them. The πολιτεία is indeed sometimes said to be enshrined in a book, both in the *Against Apion* and in the constitution set out in the *Antiquities*.[11] The definition had the advantage also of evoking vaguely a certain moral and social cohesion of Jewish communities within the non-Jewish civic structures surrounding them.[12]

The Jewish πολιτεία of the writers, however, is often in large measure theoretical, virtually a city of God, as we shall see in Josephus' case.

This interpretation of Judaism as a πολιτεία is notably absent from the *Jewish War*; neither the word πολιτεία nor the word πολίτευμα figure in that work. There the only categorization offered is the famous one in terms of three, or four, philosophies (which is not absent from the *Antiquities*). πολίτευμα still makes no appearance in the Mosaic sections of the *Antiquities*. Clearly, then, at this level of generalization, Josephus' language did develop over time or was, at the very least, adapted to the nature of the work he was writing: that may have been the result of wider reading, or perhaps of greater experience; or perhaps, again, the driving force was the literary exigencies of the moment.

2. *Theocracy and monotheism*

To Josephus falls the distinction of adding a new concept to political thought. This he presents as a bold innovation, an addition to the accepted Greek framework of the three basic types of political

---

[10] Josephus uses πολίτευμα for πολιτεία at *CA* II 145; 164; 165; 184; 250; 257.

[11] *AJ* IV 194; 302 ff.; *CA* II 295 etc. Lebram 1974 stresses instead antecedents from Hellenistic Utopias. But the parallels in Strabo and Diodorus account for only a small part of Josephus' conception.

[12] On the synonymity of the two terms, see Kasher 1996: 450, n. *ad* II 165. The term πολίτευμα, taken by some scholars (notably Kasher, elsewhere) as the formal definition of the Jewish entity within certain Greek cities, is never used by Josephus in this sense. For doubts as to the formal significance of the term, see Zuckerman 1985–88; Lüderitz 1994: 222; and now Honigman 1997: 62–65.

rule, autocracy (or tyranny or monarchy), oligarchy (or aristocracy) and democracy. Josephus speaks, indeed, of 'twisting the language' when he presents the new concept (*CA* II 165). This might incline us to believe that the word, if not the idea as well, is invented by Josephus, though, of course, the possibility that the whole discussion is lifted from a source cannot be formally excluded. Josephus' concept, which has endured, is θεοκρατία, the sovereign rule of God (II 185).[13]

It is curious that the newly-minted abstract noun is deployed by the author just this once in the *Against Apion*, and nowhere else. However, the idea it conveys does receive some expansion. The lawgiver is said to have placed in divine hands 'all sovereignty [ἀρχή] and power' (II 167). Alternatively, and more often, supremacy rests with the Deity, and the Mosaic constitution is described as one framed in accordance with God's will (184), or as deriving from knowledge of God's true nature (250), or even just as emanating from God, much as divine origins are ascribed by Plato to Greek constitutions at the opening of the *Laws*. There is no reason to think that theocracy is here intended by Josephus as incompatible with human rule under God's supervision, although the formulation has been taken to imply that. Were that strong claim intended, then the *Against Apion* would indeed be drastically out of line with the rest of Josephus. But there is no hint of such an extreme position at any point.

It would be absurd to suppose that Josephus was ever anywhere near the uncompromising theocratic doctrine he ascribes to the revolutionary groups of 66–73/4, who refused to recognize any other master than God, although that is what might be regardedas full theocracy.[14] The originators of that doctrine, the followers of the so-called Fourth Philosophy (the coinage is probably Josephus' own), are said to diverge from the Pharisees precisely on that point. Josephus abhors their extremism and he blames the destruction of his nation on the heirs of the Fourth Philosophy.[15]

---

[13] For the view that Josephus' coinage is original but not the idea, with a discussion of the previous literature and of the broader issues of interpretation, see Kasher 1996: 450–454.

[14] *BJ* II 117–119; VII 323, 410, 418; *AJ* XVIII 23; Hengel 1989: 76 and 90 ff.

[15] Josephus also seems to imply, however, that later, during the rebellion, the revolutionary leader Menahem was hailed as a would-be Messianic king. See Mendels 1992: 222 and 352, n.

Sole rulership by a wholly self-sufficient deity is, we are told, embodied in the first commandment (II 167; 190). This generates a governing principle in the world, that of unity (II 179), a principle which had always been important to Josephus on a number of levels. The unity of the godhead is pictured as replicated in the structure of the world and equally in human institutions: thence springs the unique status of the Jews, God's only people, and, in turn, the central-ity for them of Jerusalem and of the Temple (II 193). At *Antiquities* IV 199–201, when Josephus introduces the Mosaic code, the same idea is forcefully expressed: 'let there be one holy city in the most beautiful spot in the land of Canaan . . . and let there be one Temple in it and one altar of unworked stones . . . . let there be no altar or temple in any other city, for there is one God and one race of Hebrews.'

However, the unique status of the Temple seems to have mat-tered rather less to Josephus earlier on. For the digression in the *Jewish War* about the temple of Onias at Leontopolis in Egypt, which Vespasian closed in A.D. 73, explains its foundation as a rival to the Jerusalem cult, fails conspicuously to offer any criticism of this alter-native cult place, and, indeed, cites Isaiah's prediction as offering apparent justification for the existence in Egypt of a second 'altar to the Lord' (*BJ* VII 420–436). The same is true of the brief men-tion of the Leontopolis temple in connection with the appearance of Onias in the survey of the high priesthood at the end of the *Antiquities* (*AJ* XX 236–237).

Also derived from the principle of unity are the fundamentally desirable and characteristically Josephan goals of ὁμόνοια, social unity, and συμφωνία, unanimity of opinion (II 179–180). These are under-stood as social values which were guarantees against στάσις, civil strife.[16] It is not the business of the *Against Apion* that those funda-mental values had not always been regarded. In the *Jewish War*, Josephus depicts the warring rebel groups as finally realizing, under the urgent pressure of the Roman siege, that they can only continue in business if they lay aside their differences. That is a pragmatic conclusion; but these evildoers are also aware that real ὁμόνοια, a true and lasting concord, is something very different, that it can come only from God and that it will not be a favour that is granted

---

[16] On unity, see especially *CA* II 193. Vermes 1982: 295; Kasher 1996: 465–466. On στάσις, see below.

to them (*BJ* V 278). They had found, however, by a horrible inversion, unanimity in the practice of the grotesque impieties so eloquently denounced by Josephus (V 441). But it remains the case that *stasis*, civil war, which is the rebels' stock-in-trade, is the diametric opposite of concord (*BJ* VI 216).

3. *The virtues in the Jewish politeia*

In Josephus' definition, in the *Antiquities* as well as in the *Against Apion*, a constitution fixes the framework of life, its κατασκευή (*CA* II 156) or διάταξις (*AJ* IV 198) or κόσμος (*AJ* III 84). The πολιτεία, thus broadly defined, tends to include the entire Jewish code. It is therefore easy for the historian to follow the standard Platonic-Aristotelian line, that a πολιτεία promotes the virtues through education. By contrast, he recalls that the anti-Semites Apollonius Molon and Lysimachus had alleged Jewish laws to be instructors in vice, κακία: *CA* II 145. In the *Antiquities* (IV 179), Moses before his death bequeaths the laws to the people, not only as an eternal possession, but also, again echoing philosophical sources, as a generator of happiness.

At the opening of his defence against the anti-Semites (*CA* II 145), Josephus lists the cardinal virtues recognized in Jewish philosophy as follows: piety (εὐσέβεια), fellowship (κοινωνία), universal goodwill (τὴν καθόλου φιλανθρωπίαν), and, by way of additions, justice, supreme perseverance and a contempt for death. Lists of cardinal virtues were commonplaces in Greek philosophical writing. But several points are noteworthy in this particular hierarchy: the primary position of piety, the relegation of justice to the secondary list,[17] the emphasis on communitarian values, and the expectation of persecution. The analysis is clearly influenced by the charges requiring refutation in the *Against Apion*,[18] and it is manifestly an analysis appropriate to an embattled group.

The list of cardinal virtues proves somewhat fluid in the *Apion*. This may suggest some looseness of thought on Josephus' part, a cavalier attitude towards his argument, a concern perhaps with superficial impressiveness above coherence. But it should be remembered that greater philosophers than Josephus, among them Philo, evinced a degree of flexibility in their approach to the roster of

---

[17] In his biblical narrative, Josephus does emphasize justice as a commendable attribute in certain monarchs, though still not as a pre-eminent quality. See, e.g., on Josiah, Feldman 1993b: 123–124.

[18] See *CA* II 147–148.

virtues. In the *Against Apion*, the formula is slightly different on its second appearance. Piety, εὐσέβεια, is further accentuated, and we are told by Josephus that it takes the position occupied by ἀρετή in the Greek schemes, becoming the overarching category; the elements which make up piety are then the Platonic virtues in their Jewish adaptation: justice, temperance (σωφροσύνη), perseverance, and, lastly, harmony (συμφωνία). The latter, intensely Josephan value squeezes out the expected Platonic and Aristotelian φρόνησις or practical wisdom (171).

The definition of the cardinal virtues is an appropriate topic for the philosophically-orientated second book of the *Against Apion*. But the lists are quite consistent with the value-system of the *Antiquities*, from which they might be seen as extrapolations. εὐσέβεια is indisputably the essential virtue ascribable to individuals, not only in the biblical half of that work but throughout.

The two versions of the list of virtues in the *Against Apion* have in common not only the emphasis on piety but also the prominence of the value of communal harmony as a good. We learn that even women, whose subservience is necessary to a well-run society[19] fall into line (181). But such group loyalty, it is stressed, need not be incompatible with openness to outsiders: the Spartan expulsions of foreigners are undesirable, and Jews, by contrast, are never misanthropic (261). Hostility to outsiders was the most often repeated criticism of Judaism, made even by authors as favourable as Hecataeus of Abdera, let alone by those who were hostile, and Josephus is on the defensive.

The interesting comparison with Sparta recurs when Jewish perseverance is said to outdo Spartan; their repeatedly-vaunted tenacity thus confers upon the constitution of the Jews another attribute highly valued in Greek political thought, and exemplified by Sparta, that of stability. And Josephus observes that even the Spartan system had succumbed to its own defects in the end (222 ff.; 272 ff.). It may be said, too, that Josephus lends an extra dimension to the claim of stability by repeatedly stressing his people's distinctive readiness to undergo martyrdom for the sake of the law; this is the ultimate guarantor of its preservation.[20] A law which is promised as eternal must outdo all others.

---

[19] *CA* II 201. Regarded as an interpolation by Niese, however.
[20] *CA* II 232; 272; 277–278; the point about dying for the law is made also in

Josephus' assertion of the stability inherent in the Jewish πολιτεία applies to its internal character: the laws cannot be replaced or even modified and the Jewish way of life will not change. Transgressions are not even worth discussing (II 277–278). The physical fate of the Jews is a different matter, and here their recent catastrophe is fleetingly admitted: 'Even if we are deprived of resources, of cities, of all advantages, our Law remains immortal' (II 277). But these events are of little relevance to the project of the *Against Apion*.

By contrast, the ups-and-downs of history are central in Josephus' historical writing, whose subject matter is naturally largely confined to temporal events. For him, these are part of a world-historical process. In essentially biblical terms, the destinies of nations are seen as ordained by God, and as triggered by the moral conduct of human beings. In the *Jewish War*, the notion of the shift of divine favour from the Jews to Rome, and, specifically, to the Flavian dynasty, is a key explanatory tool, going far beyond the historian's personal need to exculpate himself from charges of betraying the anti-Roman movement.[21] In the *Antiquities*, the doctrine finds expression in the historian's rendering of Daniel's prophecy of the succession of kingdoms, where he appears to imply, but avoids mentioning, the pre-destined ultimate supersession of Roman power as well.[22]

This central idea of instability harmonizes well with the view of other nations and their laws expressed in the *Against Apion*, although, again, it is remote from the concerns of that work. There is a considerable distance from Josephus' earlier writings, but no inconsistency.

4. *The law and the legislator*

νόμος or its plural are the ubiquitous Greek-Jewish terms for the Jewish law. Josephus' preference is for the plural. In *Against Apion*, laws are deemed the mark of civilization, by contrast with rule by edict and custom; and since the Jewish code is an ancient one, even perhaps the most ancient, the Jews emerge as highly civilized. Josephus,

---

the excerpt ascribed to Hecataeus at *CA* I 191–193, where illustrations are offered; cf. below n. 32. On the motif in general: Gafni 1989: 124–125. See also Rajak 1997 = Ch. 6. The word used for the eternity of the law is ἀθάνατος; cf. *AJ* IV 179: ἀΐδιον.

[21] *BJ* II 261; IV 353; V 19; V 367; *AJ* XX 166 etc. Linder 1972: 42–48; Rajak *Josephus*: 99.

[22] *AJ* X 210. Investigated anew by Mason 1994: 172–176.

as is well-known, noticed the absence of the word νόμος from the Homeric poems (*CA* II 155). The exact reference of νόμοι, in the Jewish context, is no clearer in Josephus than in any other Greek-Jewish text. In broad terms, the laws must be equated with Torah; but it is impossible to discern whether Josephus, where he speaks of a written source (for example at *AJ* IV 194), has in mind the ten commandments, the Pentateuchal law codes, the entire Pentateuch, or even the Pentateuch together with all that already existed by way of oral law, which came to be understood as integral to the written Torah. The term can be used synonymously with πολιτεία by Josephus, as in the recurring pleonastic phrase 'the laws and the constitution' (e.g. *CA* II 222; 264; 287 and already at *AJ* IV 194). At one point, in the *Antiquities* however, Josephus is more precise, announcing that he will discuss those Mosaic laws which are specifically relevant to the politevia. One might suppose that this delimitation is envisaged as covering those laws and regulations which are concerned with government and social regulation. In fact, the laws then set out turn out to be not particularly of this kind, but rather to include the basic prescriptions for purity in private life, as well as various public arrangements which were less matters of social organization than of cultic practice, notably the conduct of the festivals and the mechanics of tithing.[23] It seems that when Josephus wrote the *Antiquities* his conception of the Jewish πολιτεία was not yet fully settled.

Moses, as legislator, is the sole human architect of the Jewish way of life, a system written and promulgated by him as a body of legislation, a νομοθεσία (*CA* II 160 ff.; *AJ* IV 319 ff.). He is set firmly in a comparative context when he is pitted against Lycurgus, Solon and Zaleucus of Locri; once, too, Minos is introduced (II 161). The lawgiver is, we learn again, the educator of the nation, and Moses' institution of weekly readings ensured complete familiarity with the provisions on the part of the (male) population (175–178).[24] Moses understood, as many did not, that education had to be both theoretical and practical, with the dietary laws, in particular, offering the desirable element of ἄσκησις. The law is also said to educate as a

---

[23] *AJ* IV 199–291. For this point, see Troiani 1994.
[24] The comparison with other lawgivers echoes the opening of Plato's *Laws*. While the emphasis on education is also Platonic, Josephus is more specifically concerned with instruction in the system of law. See Feldman 1993b: 118–120, on this idea in relation to Josephus' presentation in the *Antiquities* of King Josiah as teacher.

father and mother educate (174), and especially through the medium
of Sabbath reading (175).

In *Against Apion* Josephus delineates in brief Moses' great qualities
of leadership, to back up the claims of the Jewish lawgiver to rival
Minos and other Greeks (II 156 ff.): Moses is a brave general, a
shrewd counsellor, and a selfless protector. Although he is effectively
in sole control, and often lonely in power, Moses' behaviour stands
out, we are told, as the opposite of tyrannical. But we remain in no
doubt that his subjection to the divine will is what ultimately permits Moses to outstrip all the others in the competition. Here, Josephus
is drawing on themes he had dealt with earlier and *in extenso*. Embedded
in the narrative of the *Antiquities*, and particularly in the biblical history, with its strong moralizing and apologetic tendencies, appear
thumbnail sketches of political skill in action and of the correct or
faulty exercize of power.[25] And it is Moses who stands out unchallenged as the perfect model. His supreme ἀρετή incorporates all the
virtues, and above all of them, sagacity and wisdom.[26] The encomium
on his death in book IV emphasizes his control of the passions, the
power of his oratory, his generalship; but also, as the climax, his
prophetic identity as the man through whom God spoke (*AJ* IV
328–329). This last theme is not taken up in the *Against Apion*.

5. *Priestly rule*

That the Jewish polity is what we would call a hierocracy, a system
of priestly rule, with a hereditary high priest (*CA* II 193–194) at its
head, is another central principle for Josephus, deriving from his
understanding of θεοκρατία (*CA* II 185–187). This was the system
established by Moses. And this is the system Josephus regularly
endorses, subsuming the dominance of the high-priestly families under
the technical heading of aristocracy, or aristocracy-cum-oligarchy (*AJ*
XI 111). Sometimes, he assigns a non-technical spokesmanship or representative leadership in the state (προστασία or ἡγεμονία) to the high
priesthood; this seems to be a way of describing the aristocratic model
of a society controlled by a pre-eminent, notionally hereditary group
of superior men.[27]

---

[25] For the terms in which leaders and prominent personalities are praised, see
Villalba i Varneda 1986: 200–203.
[26] See especially Feldman 1992.
[27] On hierocracy in Judaean theory and practice, see Goodblatt 1994: 30–56,

Hierocracy came about because God as the supreme ruler of the universe delegated power to the priesthood. The original priestly title had been allocated according to the skills and aptitudes of those selected, thus generating an aristocracy in the true sense. In a notionally inalterable system, centred on holiness, the priesthood, and above all the high priesthood, is entrusted with the permanent protection of the legal *status quo*, as well as with civil and criminal jurisdiction (*CA* II 187). The omission here of any mention of a lay judiciary has been noted.[28] Nor are the interpretative activities of a rabbinic or proto-rabbinic class allowed for in this timeless Greek version of an ideal Jewish polity.

The sanction of tradition for the rule of the high priests is spelled out in the concluding part of the *Antiquities*, where Josephus informs readers that an Aaronite high priesthood had existed for 2,000 years, with Aaron as the first in the line (*AJ* XX 224; 261). The *Antiquities* excursus on the high priestly succession offers a more complicated account of the succession of constitutions which qualifies, and might seem to contradict, the simplification of the *Against Apion*. Between the return from Babylon and some point in the late Seleucid period,[29] the fifteen successive high priests are said to have held office within a democracy, presumably because they had to account for themselves before assemblies of the people. Monarchy followed, under the Hasmoneans and the Herodians, and the high priesthood, whose hereditary continuity Herod had destroyed, only came to be at the head of an aristocracy after the death of Archelaus (*AJ* XX 251). The ideal system of the *Against Apion*, presented there as universal, is thus in fact the system which prevailed at Jerusalem during Josephus' own youth and early manhood.[30]

In other ways, too, the *Contra Apionem* account is remarkably schematized. Discussion is conducted on a plane where precise questions such as the manner of appointment of the high priest in charge, the preferred succession, or the exact leadership role of the high-priestly

---

arguing for pre-Hasmonean origins. In relation to Josephus' theory: Amir 1985–88. On προστασία: Schwartz 1983–84: 33–38 and note especially *AJ* XX 251.

[28] Vermes 1982: 295.

[29] The chronology is a little confused: see Feldman's note *ad AJ* XX 234 in the Loeb edition.

[30] On this and other versions of the sequence of Judaean constitutions, see Schwartz 1983–84.

aristocracy simply do not arise.[31] This approach is perhaps fore-
shadowed in the *Antiquities*, where, from the entire, extended excursus
on the high-priestly succession (XX 224–251), we learn just that an
office once held for life gave way to limited tenure (XX 229).

Furthermore, we can hardly fail to observe that both the texts we
are considering were written long after 70. but that Josephus—understandably—fails to point out that the high priesthood is by then
defunct, the resurrection of its dominance in a rebuilt Temple at
best a remote hope.

From the *Antiquities*, it emerges that Josephus approved also of the
form of government, in effect monarchic, in which an autonomous
Jewish state was controlled by a high priest, whether as king (like
the later Hasmoneans) or not (like the earlier Hasmoneans). He also
looked back favourably to the individual dominance of Moses, Joshua
(VI 84; XX 229) and the judges.[32] Certain types of μοναρχία (the
rule of one) could thus be acceptable, although there was less to
commend in the exclusively kingly rule of Saul or of most of the
Davidic dynasty, still less of Herod, who had been responsible for a
profound devaluation of the high priesthood (XX 247). These refinements are lost in the blanket statement of the *Against Apion* that the
Jews' mode of government was an aristocracy.

It is relevant to our investigation that Josephus' overwhelming
predilection for the priesthood in its various manifestations is at least
partly personal in origin. His priestly descent was a major source of
pride, something of which, in his *Life*, he made even more of than
he did of his royal origins. His detailed knowledge of the role of the
priests and of the high priests, inside and outside the Temple, is not
open to doubt. Greek writers on Judaism also made much of the
priests. But Josephus was deeply interested in their role in the state
before ever he came to write the *Against Apion* and his elevation of
the priesthood and the high priesthood even when schematized, as
it is in the *Against Apion*, stands apart from that of any other writer.
Thus, the excursus on the Jews excerpted from the *Aegyptiaka* of the
fourth century B.C. author Hecataeus of Abdera has the Temple and

---

[31] Cf. Thoma 1989: 201: 'Josephus evades the question how much political power
might be given to the high priest.'
[32] VI 84, XX 261; however, the judges seem to be defined as monarchs at XI
112 and XX 230. See Schwartz 1983–84: 39.

the high priesthood at the centre of the state founded by Moses, yet
Hecataeus' picture is hazy and he erroneously believes that the high
priest was chosen (by whom?) out of the entire priesthood for his
pre-eminent qualities and that the priests were all allocated large
tracts of land.[33]

6. *Foreign rulers*

World rulers may be put in position by God, as part of His scheme
for the rise and fall of nations, but the distinction between that idea
and any claim to divinity by those rulers, ordained or not, is carefully preserved by Josephus. It is striking that in the *Against Apion* he
takes the trouble to spell out in a sentence the distinction between
sacrifices offered by Jews to the Roman emperors and sacrifices
offered simply for their welfare, in response to Apion's criticism
that the Jews are culpable in failing to make statues of the emperor
(*CA* II 73–77). It is interesting that this accusation of Apion's is specifically mentioned in the *Antiquities*, in connection with his role in the
Alexandrian delegation to Caligula (XVIII 257–258). We may also
adduce here the *Jewish War* account of the rejection of foreign gifts
or sacrifices by the Temple officials, the event which signalled the
outbreak of revolt in A.D. 66 (*BJ* II 409–417). There too the narrative makes it quite clear that what is crucially at stake is sacrifice
offered on behalf of the Romans and the emperor (*BJ* II 409; 416).

In the *Antiquities*, Josephus distances himself from emperor worship by his unconcealed identification with the Jews who opposed
actions such as Pilate's importation of Roman military standards carrying the imperial bust into Jerusalem—'for our law forbids the making of images'—and the erection of Caligula's cult statue in the city.[34]
It may be recalled that the rejection of idolatry, important already

---

[33] On Josephus' personal relationship with the priesthood: *Vita* 1–2; Rajak *Josephus*:
14–20. On Josephus' hierocracy generally, Vermes 1982: 294–296; Amir 1985–89:
88–92; Cancik 1987: 67–74; Thoma 1989. On Hecataeus, as cited in Diodorus
40.3.3–5 (from Photius), see the text and commentary in Stern 1974: no. 11, 23–35;
Goodblatt 1994: 31–35; Sterling 1992: 78–91; Bar-Kochva 1996. I do not comment here on Ezekias, the otherwise unknown high priest who is prominent in the
fragment of so-called Pseudo-Hecataeus at *CA* I 183–204: opinions are divided as
to whether the fragment is a Jewish falsification; but cf. n.19 above.

[34] *AJ* XVIII 55–59; 261 ff. It has, however, been noted that the earlier erection
by Caligula of the altar at Jamnia (Philo, *Leg.* 200–203) is omitted by Josephus.

in the later books of the Bible, is a central theme in post-exilic writing, and such material is highly visible in both Aramaic and Greek texts of the period. Autocratic rulers, especially oriental despots, are regularly associated with idols: these figures, often grotesque or intimidating, represent either the rulers themselves as gods or else their favoured deities. Here, then, is a distinctly Jewish reflection on monarchy, but one expressed in graphic form rather than as theory. Josephus, in the *Antiquities* adaptation of the book of Daniel, gives full coverage to the golden image, sixty cubits by six, set up by Nebuchadnezzar in the great plain of Babylon, to which all but the Jews bowed down at the sound of the trumpet (*AJ* X 213–214).

7. *The masses*

A blanket contempt for the masses (πλῆθος or δῆμος) runs through Josephus' thinking. We may detect it in the *Against Apion* when a statement of Plato (*Timaeus* 28c) is paraphrased as asserting that it is not safe to expose the truth about God to the ignorance of the masses (*CA* II 224). Josephus does, however, allow that one virtue exists which is open to all—subservience to the Law and abstention from any attempt to change it (*CA* II 153). This assertion scarcely displays confidence in the common people. Moses' final oration in the *Antiquities* similarly exhorts them to be, above all, obedient, both to their masters and to the Law (*AJ* IV 187).

We hear in these sentiments the old Josephus of the *Jewish War*, with all his disgust for the masses, whom he identified with the rebels. There, the rebel ideology of the zealots (in the narrow sense) and the *sicarii* (knifemen), is presented as the polar opposite to the stance of respectable elements in society. Josephus' unrestrained loathing for all the dissidents is rooted in his personal experience of the catastrophe; his conviction that they had brought it about was absolute. Those formulae for mob behaviour which he derived from Greek political thought stand him in good stead in communicating his loathing And it is worth remembering that the irresponsibility and capriciousness of the mob was a regular preoccupation of the Greek world under Rome, some of whose literature will have assisted Josephus in the composition of the *War*.

For Josephus, civil discord, στάσις, was the prime cause of the Jewish revolt. This is the agent which undermines consensus, breeding violence, sacrilege and other forms of madness, and, in the *Jewish*

War, the conflict is for the most part fought out between the rich and the poor. The damage done by discord is a theme taken up again in the *Antiquities*, especially in book 4, in which Korah's rebellion and other protests against Moses are recounted. The influence of Thucydides, that most political of historians, whose great set-piece on στάσις in Corcyra (3.81–83) was highly influential, is here unmistakeable; however, Josephus' observations do not aspire to the universality of those of Thucydides.[35]

8. *The idea of freedom*

When he argues with Apion, Josephus uses the word *douleuein* of the condition of subjection to Rome (*CA* II 125), just as he had in Agrippa's and his own orations in the *Jewish War* (II 355–356; IV 364). In similar vein, it has been effectively shown that in his version of 1 Maccabees in the *Antiquities*, Josephus' minor changes serve to endorse the Hasmonean war of liberation as a meritorious human act.[36] It is perhaps unexpected, that Josephus was always ready to label foreign rule enslavement and to take for granted the positive value of national liberation.[37] It is fair to say that, throughout, the Roman empire like every other, may be an acceptable necessity, but is never a positive good.[38] It might be said that the Jewish historian was doing no more than updating the message of the Exodus, precisely as every Jew is enjoined to do.

Freedom, ἐλευθερία, was the stated political aim of rebel groups in the Great Revolt. Perhaps on account of the resonances of this abstraction for both Greek and Roman readers, Josephus, in the *Jewish War*, does not wholly disguise this one admirable aspect of the revolutionary ideal. On the rock of Masada, before the mass suicide of the last of the Jewish resistance, the rebel leader Eleazar ben Yair, is allowed two speeches in which to laud death over political subjection, defining the latter simply as slavery. The ideals are depicted

---

[35] Cf. also *AJ* I 117 (the tower of Babel); VIII 205 ff. (Jeroboam). On στάσις in the *Jewish War*, Brunt 1977; Rajak *Josephus*: 91–94; in the *Antiquities*, Feldman 1993a: 43–51.

[36] Gafni 1989.

[37] See e.g. *AJ* III 20; III 44; III 64; III 300; IV 42. On this, Feldman 1993d: 316. In the *Jewish War*, the reality of enslavement is by no means glossed over in the pacifying speech of Agrippa II to the Jerusalemites: *BJ* II 345–401.

[38] Stern 1987; Rajak 1991: 129–134 = Ch. 8: 154–158.

in distinctly Hellenizing terms, and it is indisputable that they stand
out starkly, and unchallenged, even if modern historians continue to
differ about Josephus' underlying attitude to the episode.[39]

Political freedom also figures in Josephus in a wholly different context. It is a fact no less remarkable for being well-known that the
Jewish historian made the deliberate choice of incorporating a long
narrative (the only one to survive) of the assassination at Rome of
the emperor Caligula into book XIX of his *Antiquities*. The episode
is presented as an act of liberation from tyranny of the highest order:
Josephus takes care to stress that 'freedom' was the conscious goal,
as well as the achievement, of the conspirators, and he highlights
the role of Cassius Chaerea, 'who planned for our liberty in the time
of tyranny', and whose password was ἐλευθερία.[40]

But Josephus was acutely aware of the dangers of liberty and a
careful distinction is drawn, in Moses' parting words to the people
(*AJ* IV 187–189), between liberty on the one hand, and on the other
insubordination, offensive arrogance (ὑβρίζειν) and license (παρρησία).
Here, again, the historian exploits a familiar Greek distinction. Ultimately, however, we remain in no doubt that for him liberty was
more than a political value. A religious ideal was in his mind, intrinsic to Judaism as he presented it, and naturally therefore attainable
only through the Law.[41] Freedom is God's reward to those who abide
by his precepts, enslavement his punishment. Liberty must thus be
recognized as the product of discipline and submission. To this long-
lasting doctrine Josephus undoubtedly remained constant.

Conclusion

The interests of the *Against Apion* are not those of Josephus' other
works. Even the Mosaic constitution in the *Antiquities* does not share
the later work's requirement for abstraction, simplification and generalization. The argument could scarcely be conducted in any other
terms. Furthermore, because the *Apion* is a response to Greek intel-

---

[39] Ladouceur 1987 stresses Josephus' reservations about the ideals behind the
suicide of Masada, seeking to connect the historian's attitude with Stoic and Cynic
discussions in Flavian Rome.
[40] *AJ* XIX 11–273; see especially Sentius Saturninus' senatorial oration on tyranny:
167–184, culminating in the proposal of honours for Chaerea: 182–184.
[41] Feldman 1993d: 317.

lectuals, it partakes more fully than the rest of Josephus' *oeuvre* in the Greek culture of its time: that culture was permeated with philosophy at all levels, and this to some extent explains Josephus' involvement with philosophical commonplaces in the *Apion*; Philo's influence is clearly another factor. Polemic, finally, was a branch of rhetoric, and the *Against Apion* is the most rhetorical of Josephus' works. In the light of all this, it is scarcely surprising that the political thought of the *Apion* is more schematized than anything else in Josephus. The Jewish πολιτεία has to be presented as a clearcut entity, and made parallel with Greek systems, before its individual virtues can be highlighted and its quintessential merits extracted. The terms operative in Greek political thought, especially in Plato, along with the characteristic mix of real and ideal found in the philosophers were seized upon by Josephus.

These considerations help us to understand such discrepancies as have emerged between the Josephus of the *Against Apion* and the earlier Josephus. The innovations of the late work can now be reviewed. There, Josephus consolidates an existing preference for portraying the Jews as living within their own *politeia*: the whole of Judaism is there explained in these terms. So frequently is the conception invoked that *politeuma* is pulled in, as an alternative term, to create variety. Furthermore, the definition of Judaism as a theocracy is new. It might be seen as implicit in the control over leaders and their actions repeatedly ascribed to God in the *Antiquities*, but now we have a stronger claim. It is also a claim which could not have been made in the *Jewish War*, where Josephus' theocratic ideal would have been easily confused with the very different ideology of the zealots. Again, the insistence in *Against Apion* on the essential uniqueness and exclusivity of the by-then-defunct Temple also post-dates the *Jewish War*, although it is firmly present in the *Antiquities*. The definition of the Jewish constitution as a permanent aristocracy is also confined to the *Against Apion*.

By contrast, all of Josephus' works share the insistence on God's omnipotence and of the importance of standing in a right relationship with Him, the conviction that the Law is to be unchanging and eternal, the high valuation put upon unity in all spheres, a preoccupation with political concord and a hatred of στάσις, an interest in asserting and boosting the importance of the high priesthood in society—without always a clear picture of what its role might be— a generally aristocratic outlook, allied to a contempt for masses, a realistic respect for the ruling power within the limits of a total abhorrence of idolatry, and a positive attitude to freedom, understood not as public license but as liberty under and through the Law.

The common ground between *Against Apion* and the later works would thus seem to be extensive and significant, and we may conclude that our author did not undergo any fundamental change of heart about the nature of Jewish society and about the way it ought to be governed.

BIBLIOGRAPHY

Amir, Y. 1985–88. '*Theokratia* as a Concept of Political Philosophy: Josephus' Presentation of Moses' *Politeia*', *SCI* 8–9: 83–105.

Attridge, H.W. 1976. *The Interpretation of Biblical History in the Antiquitates Judaicae of Flavius Josephus*. Missoula, Montana.

Bar-Kochva, B. 1996. *Pseudo-Hecataeus on the Jews: Legitimizing the Jewish Diaspora*. Berkeley, CA.

Bickerman, E.J. 1988. *The Jews in the Greek Age*. Cambridge, Mass. and London.

Bilde, P. 1988. *Flavius Josephus between Jerusalem and Rome: His Life, his Works and their Importance*. Sheffield.

Brunt, P.A. 1977. 'Josephus on Social Conflicts in Roman Judaea', *Klio* 59: 149–153.

Cancik, H. 1987. 'Theokratie und Priesterherrschaft. Die mosaische Verfassung bei Flavius Josephus contra Apionem 2. 157–198', in J. Taubes (ed.), *Theokratie. Religionstheorie und politische Theologie* 2, 65–77.

Carras, G.P. 1993. 'Dependence or Common Tradition in Philo *Hypothetica* 8.6.10–7.20 and Josephus *Contra Apionem* 2.190–219', *Studia Philonica Annual* 5: 24–57.

Cohen, S.J.D. 1979. *Josephus in Galilee and Rome. His Vita and Development as a Historian*. Columbia Studies in the Classical Tradition 8. Leiden.

Feldman, L.H. 1992. 'Josephus' Portrait of Moses', part 1, *JQR* 82: 285–328.

—— 1993a. 'Josephus' Portrait of Jeroboam', *Andrews University Seminary Studies* 31: 29–51.

—— 1993b. 'Josephus' Portrait of Josiah', *Louvain Studies* 18: 110–130.

—— 1993c. 'Josephus' Portrait of Moses', part 2, *JQR* 83: 7–50.

—— 1993d. 'Josephus' Portrait of Moses', part 3, *JQR* 83: 301–330.

Gafni, I.M. 1989. 'Josephus and I Maccabees', in L.H. Feldman, L.H. & G. Hata (eds), *Josephus, the Bible and History*. Detroit, 116–131.

Gibbs, J.H. & Feldman, L.H. 1986. 'Josephus' Vocabulary for Slavery', *JQR* 76: 281–310.

Goodblatt, D. 1994. *The Monarchic Principle. Studies in Jewish Self-Government in Antiquity*. Texte und Studien zum Antiken Judentum 38. Tübingen.

Goodman, M. 1994. 'Josephus as Roman Citizen', in F. Parente & J. Sievers (eds), *Josephus and the History of the Greco-Roman Period. Essays in Memory of Morton Smith*. Studia Post-Biblica 41. Leiden, 329–338.

Hengel, M. 1989 (German eds 1961; 1976). *The Zealots. Investigations into the Jewish Freedom Movement in the Period from Herod I until 70 A.D.* Transl. D. Smith. Edinburgh.

Honigman, S. 1997. 'Philo, Flavius Josèphe, et la citoyenneté alexandrine: vers une utopie politique', *JJS* 48: 62–90.

Kasher, A. 1996. *Josephus Flavius: Against Apion. A New Hebrew Translation and Commentary*, 2 vols. Jerusalem.

Ladouceur, D.J. 1987. 'Josephus and Masada', in L.H. Feldman & G. Hata (eds), *Josephus, Judaism and Christianity*. Detroit, 95–114.

Lebram, J.C.H. 1974. 'Der Idealstaat der Juden', in O. Betz, K. Haacker & M. Hengel (eds), *Josephus-Studien. Untersuchungen zu Josephus, dem antiken Judentum und den neuen Testament, Otto Michel zum 70 Geburtstag gewidmet*. Göttingen, 233–253.

Linder, H. 1972. *Die Geschichtsauffassung des Flavius Josephus im Bellum Judaicum. Gleichzeitig ein Beitrag zur Quellenfrage*. Arbeiten zur Geschichte des antiken Judentum und des Urchristentums 12. Leiden.

Lüderitz, G. 1994. 'What is the Politeuma?', in J.W. van Henten & P.W. van der Horst (eds), *Studies in Early Jewish Epigraphy*. Arbeiten zur Geschichte des Antiken Judentums und des Urchristentums 21. Leiden, 183–225.

Mason, S. 1991. *Flavius Josephus on the Pharisees*. Leiden.

—— 1994. 'Josephus, Daniel and the Flavian House', in Parente, F. and Sievers, J. (eds), *Josephus and the History of the Greco-Roman Period. Essays in Memory of Morton Smith*. Studia Post-Biblica 41. Leiden, 161–191.

Mendels, D. 1992. *The Rise and Fall of Jewish Nationalism. Jewish and Christian Ethnicity in Ancient Palestine*. Anchor Bible Reference Library. New York etc.

Rajak, T. 1991. 'Friends, Romans, Subjects: Agrippa II's Speech in Josephus' Jewish War', in L. Alexander (ed.), *Images of Empire*. Journal for the Study of the Old Testament Supplement Series 12. Sheffield, 122–134 = Ch. 8 in this volume.

—— 1996. 'Hasmonean Kingship and the Invention of Tradition', in P. Bilde *et al.* (eds), *Aspects of Hellenistic Kingship*. Studies in Hellenistic Civilization 7 (Aarhus), 99–115 = Ch. 3 in this volume.

—— 1997. 'Dying for the Law: The Martyr's Portrait in Jewish-Greek Literature', in M.J. Edwards & S. Swain (eds), *Portraits: Biographical Reprsentation in the Greek and Latin literature of the Roman Empire*. Oxford, 39–67 = Ch. 6 in this volume.

Schwartz, D.R. 1983–84. 'Josephus on the Jewish Constitution and Community', *SCI* 7: 30–52.

Schwartz, S. 1990. *Josephus and Judaean Politics*. Columbia Studies in the Classical Tradition 18. Leiden.

Sterling, G.E. 1992. *Historiography and Self-Definition: Josephos, Luke-Acts and Apologetic Historiography*. Leiden.

Stern, M. 1974. *Greek and Latin Authors on Jews and Judaism: Edited with Introductions, Translations and Commentary*, vol. 1. Jerusalem.

—— 1987. 'Josephus and the Roman Empire as Reflected in the Jewish War', in L.H. Feldman & G. Hata (eds), *Josephus, Judaism and Christianity* Detroit, 71–80.

Terian, A. 1985. 'Some Stock Arguments for the Magnanimity of the Law in Hellenistic Jewish Apologetics', in B. Jackson (ed.), *Jewish Law Association Studies* 1. Chico, California, 141–150.

Thoma, C. 1989. 'The High Priesthood in the Judgment of Josephus', in Feldman, L.H. and Hata, G. (eds), *Josephus, the Bible and History*. Detroit, 196–215.

Troiani, L. 1978. 'Osservazioni sopra l'Apologia di Filone: gli Hypothetica', *Athenaeum* 56: 304–314.

—— 1994. 'The Politeia of Israel in the Greco-Roman Age' in F. Parente & J. Sievers (eds), *Josephus and the History of the Greco-Roman Period. Essays in Memory of Morton Smith*. Studia Post-Biblica 41. Leiden, 11–22.

Vermes, G. 1982. 'A Summary of the Law by Flavius Josephus', *Novum Testamentum* 24.4: 289–303.

Villalba I Varneda, P. 1986. *The Historical Method of Flavius Josephus*. Leiden.

Yavetz, Z. 1975. 'Reflections on Titus and Josephus', *GRBS* 16: 411–432.

Zuckerman, C. 1985–88. 'Hellenistic *politeumata* and the Jews: A Reconsideration', *SCI* 8–9: 171–185.

CHAPTER TWELVE

CIÒ CHE FLAVIO GIUSEPPE VIDE:
JOSEPHUS AND THE ESSENES

Josephus' descriptions of one of the Jewish sects will, I hope, be an appropriate subject for a memorial tribute to Morton Smith. Smith's brilliant and provocative reading of the historian's statements about the Pharisees in the *Antiquities* (1956), which he saw as a retrojection to the pre-war period of the religio-political needs of the 90's, has had a major impact on scholarship. As we all know, it was developed in various ways, especially by Jacob Neusner (1972) and by Shaye Cohen (1979). It became almost an orthodoxy. Now Steve Mason (1991) has moved sidewise, with his own theory that Josephus never claimed to be a Pharisee. I myself have never been comfortable with Morton Smith's reading, for a variety of reasons,[1] but its fruitfulness is not in doubt.

Even more to our purpose, as I was reading for this paper, I recalled that it was Morton Smith (1958) who first queried the precise connection between the notice on the Essenes in Hippolytus of Rome (Smith preferred to refer simply to the anonymous *Philosophoumena*) and Josephus' remarks on the subject. I shall have occasion to consider this study later. There, Smith produced a summary of Josephus' early career which perhaps says all that needs to be said on the subject: 'he was able . . . to spend three years with a hermit (evidently, therefore, not an Essene, in spite of the fact that he bathed every day) and returned to Jerusalem by the age of 19, no doubt tired of asceticism and ready for the pleasures of Rome, where he moved in the circle of the Empress Poppaea (who also bathed every day, but was probably not an Essene)'.[2]

The Essenes have another claim to our attention here. We are, hopefully, mapping the present and the future state of Josephus-studies, and it seems to me that one of the most important challenges that lie ahead is to redefine the writer's Judaism, in the light

---

[1] In brief, Rajak *Josephus* 33–34.
[2] Smith 1958: 277–278.

of transformed perspectives in Jewish studies. First and foremost, no one has yet brought the full wealth of the material from Qumran and with it our new view of the spectrum of Second Temple thought, to bear systematically and on a broad front on the study of Josephus' religious ideas. I should, however, like to signal the important study by Rebecca Gray as a large step in the right direction (Gray 1992). Her study demonstrates that Josephus shared fully in the mental world of contemporary Judaism, whatever he made of it for his own purposes. This paper is no more than a skirmish on the margins of those concerns.

1. *The problem*

Some extraordinary claims have been made about Josephus' two excursuses on the Essenes. Before the Dead Sea Scrolls were known, it was possible to argue, as no less a scholar than W. Bauer did in the long entry on the Essenes in Pauly's *Realencyclopädie* (1924), that all of Josephus' data on the subject in the *Jewish War* excursus was an idealizing invention of Greek-Jewish writing, an ethnographic fantasy derived—one need hardly say—from some 'source' or other, probably Philo.[3] Well after 1947, del Medico could still maintain that, while the name 'Essene' was Philo's, the descriptions in our Josephus were interpolations by a precursor of the Slavonic translator (1952).

Also quietened today are those vigorous debates about the relation of the literary Essenes to the Dead Sea sect, which marked the first Qumran research, even if 'the establishment Essene theory' is a target for occasional snipers.[4] In Beall's comparative study (1988), the identity of the two groups is taken as a working hypothesis. Beall's commentary serves, among other purposes, to highlight the high level of congruence in points of detail between the Essenes of Josephus and the sect of the sectarian scrolls.

Here, too, it will be supposed that Josephus was describing Jewish ascetics who were, at the very least, part of the same tradition as those who, over the generations, wrote the sectarian scrolls from Qumran, even if the correlation is not exact; and that the portrait is based upon those who occupied, in one fashion or another, at

---

[3] Such thinking persists, on which, see Petit 1992: 142, n. 9.
[4] Eisenman & Wise 1992: 5, 11, 273, 275.

one stage or another, the installations at Qumran. Josephus, as is well known, does not mention the Dead Sea area in connection with his description. The Essenes of Josephus are, however, linked with that area through the mention in Pliny the Elder's short notice on the 'Esseni', of the striking, if not one hundred percent correct geographical specification 'infra hos Engada oppidum fuit . . . inde Masada castellum in rupe, et ipsum haut procul Asphaltite' (*Natural History* 5.17.4).

To proceed cautiously, we can see from Beall that Josephus had a decent knowledge of a sect which shared practice and doctrine with the people of Qumran. We certainly cannot deny that he supplies genuine information. E.P. Sanders' recent conclusions sum up this position succinctly: 'The scrolls allow us to comment on Josephus and also on the relationship between primary sources and secondary description. Josephus was quite a good historian; that is, he had good sources plus some personal knowledge, and he got a remarkable number of things right . . . When it comes to theology, we find him a little less trustworthy. Certainly, his description does not convey adequately the flavour of the scrolls'.[5] Sanders' last point will require further comment.

Josephus' excursuses on the Essenes are, then, due for a fresh investigation, in the light of recent scholarly concerns. The complexity of the Qumran material should not deter us. Josephus' remarks are still intermittently important to scrolls research. Issues such as the sectaries' commitment to celibacy and their attitude to sacrifice are discussed by scholars in relation to what Josephus says: those are the terms in which the problems are often posed. Moreover, we are again confronted with radical re-interpretations of the Qumran site, by which even its monastic character is being called into question; from this point of view too it will be important to know how we should view Josephus' remarks about the Essene lifestyle.

Apart from any agenda dictated by Qumran scholarship, with which I cannot deal directly in this paper, there is also the challenge simply of understanding Josephus on his own terms; and nobody familiar with Josephus needs persuading of the value of that. In this context, too, the Essenes are an important test case: to find that Josephus knows more or less what he is talking about is certainly not an end of the matter.

---

[5] Sanders 1992: 379.

A collection of new translations (Vermes & Goodman 1989) brings the texts from different authors together, conveniently reminding scholar and student alike that the texts are more than just repositories of disparate observations.[6] Brief footnotes offer Qumran parallels; these, and, more especially Beall's book (mentioned above), which sets out the parallels in detail, invite us to look at the relationship between Josephus' statements and the Qumran texts more closely. It becomes necessary to take these convergences seriously and to think afresh about Josephus' knowledge and its origins.

For all our acceptance of Josephus as a witness, there are limitations in his account, which spring from his *modus operandi* as a historian and from the formal aspects of his text. Josephus' expositions display, as has often been noted, many features typical of the moralizing ethnographical digressions favoured by ancient writers.[7] Yet they are also unusual. Writing ancient ethnography usually presupposed knowing rather little about what you were talking about, because, apparently, it was not felt that there was any decipherment to be done.[8] Here, by contrast, we have, as we presume, an author who both had seen for himself and had the capacity to decipher.

It is reasonable to presume, as Sanders does, and as many early commentators did, that Josephus' information has a connection with his personal experience: his statement in the *Life* (56), that he had taken a lot of trouble to try out the regime of all three Jewish sects, can be given some credence even in the case of the Essenes. I have shown that the story is not chronologically impossible, and I would stress again the observation that for the description of the three sects to be an established *topos* is not incompatible with veracity.[9] However, those who remain uncomfortable with Josephus' autobiographical assertions have still to give some weight to the consideration that the Jerusalem priestly establishment could hardly have afforded to be wholly ignorant of what radical Jewish sectaries a stone's throw from Jerusalem were thinking and doing. There was no language barrier to stop them finding out.

The significance of this paper's title should now be clear: the eyewitness element in the descriptions of the Essenes is in my view a

---

[6] Another collection is Adam 1972; cf. also Dupont-Sommer 1961.
[7] Trüdinger 1918: esp. 133–145; Müller 1972, 1980.
[8] Momigliano 1975; J.Z. Smith 1985: 20–21.
[9] Rajak *Josephus*: 34–39. For a different defence, Feldman 1984: 81–82.

very important feature of them. It will not have escaped you that I
have inverted a famous title of Arnaldo Momigliano's. In fact, my
position, is not far removed the one he took in the essay entitled
'Ciò che Flavio Giuseppe non vide' (Momigliano 1980; 1987): for
there the focus lay precisely in aspects of Judaism which, in Momigliano's view, Josephus must have been quite aware of, but which
somehow he chose not to register—the synagogue, on the one hand,
and apocalyptic currents on the other. Here, too, we are thinking
about how and why a particular picture of a species of Judaism has
been fashioned by an author who could have said so much more.
At the same time, Momigliano's interpretation of Josephus' silences
was, I think, implicitly psychological and personal—like so much of
what is written about Josephus—while mine operates on a literary
level and has the aim of explaining how the nature of the narrative
limits what is or can be stated.

The position may be summed up by saying that we are dealing
not with an *either/or*, as tends to be supposed (*either* ethnographic
fiction *or* a realistic account), but with a *both/and*. Josephus' digressions on the Essenes are texts which *both* conform to historiographical canons *and* draw upon the author's experience.[10] There is nothing
impossible in that. The difficulty lies in understanding how the two
elements interact.

The distinctive feature of Josephus' descriptions of the Essenes,
especially the longest version, in book II of the *Jewish War*, is precisely this mix of real information with quite considerable modelling
and idealization. For both of Josephus' excursuses do, after all, form
part of that well known, stylized reading in which he analyses Judaism
in terms of three 'philosophies', with differing views on fate, and in
structure and attitude these excursuses are far from representing
unmediated information. Some would describe them as 'Hellenized'.[11]
In a different context, where he introduces Menahem's prophecy of
Herod's kingship, Josephus claims that the Essenes followed the
Pythagorean way of life (*AJ* XV 371).

The Essene digressions are thus very much part of a 'text' (in
today's sense of that term). But in connection with this sect, in contrast to the other two, our knowledge of the Qumran literature serves

---

[10] For Feldman 1984: 416–417, the assumption that personal experience was the
'chief source' excludes any use of Philo.
[11] Moore 1929; Wächter 1969.

as a control on the process, albeit one which needs careful handling. If we can understand what Josephus is up to here, we may obtain some leverage on what he is doing in more opaque areas of his writing. This is a chance to watch Josephus at work. The enterprise becomes even more promising when we take into account the fact that Josephus left us not one excursus on the subject in question, but two; and, again, when we remember that his great precursor Philo had also (in all probability) written at least twice about the Essenes, whom he calls *Essaioi* (while Josephus uses equally the form *Essenoi* and in *AJ* XV 371–379 even combines the two in one passage). The first Philonic account, in intricate Greek, is in the Stoically-influenced discussion *Quod omnis probus liber sit* (75–91) contained in Eusebius (*Praep. Ev.* VIII 12) and ascribed by him to Philo, and the other in the *Hypothetica*, also preserved, in fragmentary form, in the same book of Eusebius (*Praep. Ev.* VIII 6–7). Both Philonic accounts must have been known by Josephus.

2. *Contrasts between the War and the Antiquities*

In *Jewish War* II 119–161, Josephus describes the Essenes at far greater length than he does the Pharisaic and Sadducean 'philosophies', and he also puts them before the others. There is undoubtedly some imbalance in this design, even if Sanders (who locates 'common Judaism' around the Temple) misleads in speaking of 'a tiny and fairly marginal sect':[12] the urban and village Essenes may quite well have made a significant impact on Jewish society, especially those living in Jerusalem, of whom Sanders himself has a fair amount to say. His undervaluing of the Essenes may, perhaps, be influenced by their absence from New Testament literature. Furthermore, there is no reason to think that thoroughgoing Pharisees, still less Sadducees, were more than a minority in the population as a whole: many 'common Jews' will probably have not been affiliates of any grouping.

The Essenes, then, may have had quite a high visibility. For all that, the manner in which Josephus parades them shows that he was well aware of the appeal of the most 'philosophical' of the sects to a Greco-Roman readership.[13] Philo had acclimatized the subject to

---

[12] Sanders 1992: 341.
[13] Paul 1992: 131 suggests that Josephus wished to depict the Essenes to Romans as the quintessential Jews.

Greek literature and Pliny the Elder had alerted a Roman readership. Pliny, it would seem, was not unaware of the Jewish revolt and its consequences for the region, since elsewhere he mentioned Vespasian's post-war colonization, and noticed Gamala (*Natural History* 5.69). Nor is it is out of the question that Tacitus, in the lost part of *Histories* book 5, had included the grim fate of the Essenes which Josephus details towards the end of his excursus: 'the war against the Romans fully revealed their souls. During it their limbs were twisted and broken, burned and shattered . . .' (II 152, Vermes & Goodman's translation). So the Essenes were undoubtedly a suitable case for treatment, and especially so in the 70's.

When it comes to the *Antiquities*, the order in which the sects are handled is reversed, and the balance between them is regularized. What is now in need of explanation is the new dependence on Philo, especially on the extended *Quod omnis probus* account. This is associated with the loss of much that was specific and immediate in Josephus' earlier version. The Philonic account is highly philosophical, to the extent where it views Judaism from the outside, and its focus is on extolling a virtuous and free life, lived in community, as designed in accordance with divine inspiration. Distinctly Philonic in Josephus are the attribution to the Essenes of opposition to slavery (21), a characteristic which Hellenistic writers had fathered on various little known peoples (for example, Megasthenes on the Indians), and on which the Qumran literature seems to be silent either way (Beall 1988: 129);[14] the high valuation on agriculture, which goes together with reservations about all or some crafts (19); and a degree of detachment about the normal sacrificial ritual (19).[15] Josephus' celebrated analysis of the sects in terms of their views of divine providence connects with his making Essene determinism his first defining characteristic here, and this may be anticipated in Philo's 'the Deity is the cause of all good but of no evil' (*QOP* 84).

These themes in themselves might not seem to be treated sufficiently similarly by the respective authors to assure us of a connection, especially given the textual problems in the Josephus passage. But the

---

[14] Slavery appears explicitly only in the Damascus Document.

[15] For this purpose, it is unnecessary to discuss the exact statements of either author. There are textual difficulties in both cases, and in Josephus the presence of a negative in the Latin text makes it unclear if Essenes are alleged to have sent sacrifices to the Jerusalem Temple: Vermes & Goodman: 36–37, 55.

total figure of 4,000 for the Essenes which appears in both places
clinches the dependance. When one considers Josephus' acceptance
of Philo in the *Antiquities*, one cannot help wondering what the historian could have made of the confident assertion in the *Hypothetica*
(3) that the Essenes allowed no adolescents or young men near them,
when he himself had, so he tells us, sampled life in the sect when
he was at most seventeen.

Equally, it is reasonable to say that there is remarkably little information unique to the *Antiquities* account. The statement about Essene
sacrifices is garbled, whatever its meaning, and textual problems
apart. Then there is the observation that priests have a special role
in the community, and that they are engaged in the preparation of
food (22). And here we recall that the attribution of a high position
to religious leaders is a familiar element in the Greek portrayal of
various strange peoples, as for example the Celtic Druids in the
sketch in Diodorus which is ascribed to Posidonius (Diodorus V 31;
Momigliano 1975: 69–70). Whatever were the actual functions of
priests at Qumran, and whatever the commitment there to preparing food in purity, Josephus' culinary priests are plainly bizarre.

Had Josephus, assuming that he was writing from memory, forgotten what he had known perfectly well all those years ago? Was
he just less interested, because the subject was now rather stale to
outside readers? Or, was it that Pharisees were by then claiming the
attention of the Jewish world? Or, perhaps, was Josephus at this
stage reserving material for the projected, but never written work
On Customs and Causes? Or, again, had our author just found that a
previously unfamiliar section of Philo was wonderfully to his purpose, just as he was to make good use of the *Hypothetica* when it
came to writing the *Against Apion*? (Philo, ed. Colson 1941: 409). This
last explanation perhaps seems the least likely, since a limited influence
of the *Quod omnis probus* may already be suspected in the *War* version, especially on the theme of the sectarians' resilience in the face
of torments inflicted by tyrants (89–91), where Josephus seems to
offer an update. Further than this, I cannot see any sensible basis
for choice between these hypotheses.

Morton Smith identified the problem of the gap in content and
quality between the two Josephan accounts, and grappled with it.
He allowed that the *War* version shows 'considerable knowledge of
the Essenes'.[16] But his conclusion was that Josephus could not have

---

[16] 1958: 276–278.

written either account: 'for had Josephus himself written the account in the War he would probably not, when he came to write the *Antiquities*, have replaced his work by a copy or condensation of somebody else's. Therefore the account in the *War* must also have been a copy or condensation of some outside source.' This reasoning, perhaps compelling in the case of a modern author, takes insufficient account of the demand for sheer variety and of the high valuation put on form by ancient authors.

In any case, the consequence of Josephus' decision is that the earlier version is the important one for us, and not just by virtue of its length. It is the more interesting, and, I would argue, it is the more Josephan—which does not mean that it is the less stylized. If I am right, then it becomes unnecessary to struggle to reconcile the two accounts in terms of real changes over time or of variations in practice in the Qumran community, as some observant investigators have suggested.[17]

3. *The framework of BJ II §§ 120–161*

Returning to *Jewish War* II, it is instructive to consider the overall structure before looking at individual features in the portrayal of the Essenes there. Individual 'Hellenizations' tend to catch the eye of commentators, but this structural element is generally overlooked. That is hardly surprising, for at first sight, there is a puzzling lack of order. But the key is, I suggest, that the themes are those favoured in descriptions of ideal states in Greek political thought, and that the organization corresponds to a progression appropriate in studying a polity. Greek ethnographic writing, with its large component of idealization and eulogy, was heavily influenced by the philosophers, and Josephus' Essene communities are depicted, like those of other writers on the subject, as a form of ideal society.

The themes may be listed as follows in the order in which they appear. Since the context is inappropriate for geography or topography, first comes the family: the distaste for marriage (but we should note the qualification in Josephus' afterthought, discussed below), the securing of increase through the adoption of children, and a general misogynistic observation on the unfaithfulness of women, which is

---

[17] Vermes 1981. Of course, some discrepancies between sources on the Essenes do invite explanation in terms of variation or change in practice, in the terms indicated by Vermes.

regrettably quite in keeping with Josephus' own thinking on the subject.[18] The destructive charms of women are also a feature in Philo,
where they are given greater scope (*Hypothet.* 13–17), but his problem does not seem to lie with their promiscuity.

Next we learn about the household, where the economy, in its
literal sense belongs: wealth is despised, while assets are held com-
munally and thus equalized. Dress follows from this, as part of the
basic fabric of domestic life: not only the white clothing but also the
abhorrence of oil on the skin. The city is the next level up: we are
told that Essenes live in various towns, offering hospitality to one
another. The subject of cities leads on to exchange and trade; but
here a negative is recorded, since the Essenes of course permit no
buying and selling among themselves, and they even avoid buying
clothes until their old ones are in tatters.

Cultic habits come in only after all these matters: while not neglected, religious practices rarely have pride of place in Greek writing:
we learn about the daily regime of the sect in relation to purity and
holiness, starting from the early morning prayers and culminating in
the quietness of the cultic meal with the accompanying blessings
from the priests. The social hierarchy follows, when the great powers
of the overseers are described, with charitable deeds being mentioned
as the only area where the individual's freedom of action is preserved.
Here, the authority of the traditional texts is also stressed. Education
is then represented by the stages of Essene initiation; within this
topic comes quite a detailed description of the attitudes and conduct
expected of a fully qualified member, as enunciated in his initiation
oath. The political and legal system of the Essenes involves total
obedience to authority, and the formidable disciplinary requirements,
with relentless accompanying punishments, are expanded upon with
a rhetorical flourish.

Character—ἦθος—is the beginning and end of any civic organization according to both Plato and Aristotle. Later Greek philosophers thought no differently. Here, the essential virtues required and
enhanced by the system are described as courage and wisdom, the
latter especially in relation to the good of the soul. Firm convictions
about the afterlife are the underpinning, and so a pleasing doctrine
of the immortality of the soul is sketched.

---

[18] Brown 1992.

The headings which I have teased out are naturally not explicit in Josephus. But what looks at first sight like a random collection falls into place under this ordering. We can understand, too, the otherwise baffling placing of some of the details in Josephus, such as the Essene presence in cities or the hostility to olive oil. Expansion of individual topics is possible up to a point, and Josephus dwells especially on the cultic meals and the content of the initiation oaths. Eating habits, it is worth remembering, are a topic favoured by Greek ethnographers, and Posidonius appears to have written with particular gusto about the feasts of the Celts.[19] Philo's account of the ascetic Egyptian *therapeutai* in *de vita contemplativa* (64–89) centres on the sect's banquets, in what is an ironic reversal of the familiar, at which he expects his audience to scoff: those banquets are non-banquets, where satisfaction comes from the decorous and joyful singing of the Divinity's praises, and from drinking water, rather than from consumption and carousing.

Yet it is arguable that other important matters, especially in the area of Essene religious practices and beliefs—even the all-important sectarian solar calendar—are given very short shrift or omitted by Josephus, for the simple reason that the scheme does not readily accommodate them.

Where does this analysis originate? The various themes under which the model city is discussed in Plato's *Republic* and in his *Laws*, together with the analysis of the elements of the city in Aristotle's *Politics* (from couple to household to city and so on), probably lie behind all such designs, although the philosophers operate, of course, on a much bigger scale than any ethnographic work seems to have done. Much ethnography appeared in digressions comparable in length to Josephus' miniature composition. The constructions of the philosophers influenced the historians.

To talk of a Platonic lineage in the case of Josephus is by no means fanciful. For if we turn our attention for a moment from structure to content, it is hard to avoid detecting Platonic echoes in Josephus' concluding depiction of the liberation of the souls of the blessed from the bodies in which they have been entangled: we scarcely need the Jewish historian to tell us that the 'sons of the Greeks' would be in agreement with the Essenes on the subject, because we already know.

---

[19] Momigliano 1975: 69.

4. *A source for the account in The Jewish War?*

But how and why should Josephus hit upon this kind of analysis?
No one is going to entertain the idea that he was busily reading the
Republic at the stage in his life when he was composing the *War*.
One solution is to postulate a source for Josephus, and in particu-
lar to look to the Platonist Philo.

Such ideas used to be much in favour in Josephus scholarship,
and this one is not new. It is therefore worth dispelling at the outset the notion that any external data demands the assumption. A
description of the Essenes close in substance to that of Josephus is
to be found in the *Refutation of All the Heresies*, ascribed to the third
century Roman Christian writer Hippolytus, and the obvious possibility that these similarities are to be explained in terms of a common source, used by both Josephus and Hippolytus, is the main
support for the claim that Josephus lifted much of what he says from
an earlier writer.

Hippolytus contains strikingly Josephan details, such as his statement that expelled Essenes often starve to death. But why should
Hippolytus' account not derive directly from Josephus himself? The
acid test is whether there is significant information, coherently struc-
tured, that is present in Hippolytus but absent from Josephus: should
there be reason to think that this information cannot have been
added by either Hippolytus or any other late writer upon whom he
depended, and, further, to assume that Hippolytus is likely to have
used one source alone, then it follows that there was a common
source from which Hippolytus took certain details which Josephus
chose to omit.

It was Morton Smith who saw the value of making a detailed
comparison of Hippolytus and Josephus; and the key divergences in
content are now briefly indicated in Vermes & Goodman. Smith
sought to establish the case for a common (he believed Semitic)
source—a case, it should be noted, of which his judgment on the
Josephus passages had already independently (and in my view mistakenly) persuaded him. Yet, for all his endeavours, nothing of substance emerges. The disparities are entirely explanatory comment,
until chapter 26, whose pronouncements can be simply described as
a mixture of nonsense and anti-Judaism. The additional details are
characteristic of Jews generally, especially the strict Sabbath observance which even forbids carrying coins—a point hardly appropri-

ate to people without private possessions. Zealots are wrongly identified with *sicarii*; and Hippolytus goes so far as to assert that the sectaries will kill any uncircumcised person caught discussing God or his laws. The vocabulary of the additions is in keeping with Hippolytus generally.[20] In chapter 27, the resurrection of the body has replaced some of Josephus' Platonizing account of immortality as the soul's survival. This change is part of a tendency in Hippolytus to 'vary', as Smith puts it, 'in the direction of Jewish piety.' But, at points, some Christianization is also detectable.[21]

For those who doubt that Hippolytus himself altered Josephus—in general he does not seem to have reshaped his sources—the hypothesis that he used an earlier Christian rewrite serves to explain all the changes. Baumgarten has claimed (1984) that, in describing the Pharisees, Hippolytus must have had a favourable Jewish source apart from Josephus; but this intended 'test case' has no relevance to the visibly unfavourable Essene excursus.

5. *Philo and Josephus*

While the arguments from Hippolytus have to be dismissed, it cannot be denied that Josephus had some familiarity with what predecessors wrote about the Essenes. He undoubtedly had parts of Philo to hand, and we have detected the earlier author's influence on the *Antiquities* notice.

So it would in theory be not inconceivable for Philo to have originated the framework in the *War*. Moralistic themes comparable to those in Josephus figure in the two Philonic accounts of the Essenes. Yet the thrust in Philo is quite distinct. In both of his descriptions of the Essenes, we find a greater emphasis on the ethical virtues and less on social organization. Community of property and of living bulks particularly large in Philo, and this feature of life is linked with a highly moral stance on avarice (*Hypothet.* 11.8) and on the corrupting influence of cities (*QOP* 12.75–76, in contradiction to what Josephus writes and also, seemingly, to Philo's own statement, *Hypothet.* 11). It can hardly escape notice that avarice, as πλεονεξία, is one of Plato's *bêtes noires*, and it is in Plato, too (*Laws* 743e etc.) that the

---

[20] Burchard 1977.
[21] Burchard 1977.

agricultural society is labelled the best. So Philo's judgment of the
Essenes, not unexpectedly, carries marked Platonic echoes.

I do not wish to claim that these specific Philonic themes are
entirely absent from the *War*. They are not. Josephus does not overlook the standard moral topics,—the rejection of pleasure in favour
of moderation (*BJ* II 120), sobriety and self-control as an escape
from the passions (II 161). But Josephus' Essenes are by no means
Philo's 'athletes of virtue' (*QOP* 89; cf. *Hypothet.* 6). they are not
seekers of freedom. Josephus' moral assessments are not presented
in the same way as Philo's. What is more, on a general level, such
assessments find a place even in the scrolls: not only the *Damascus
Document* but *hodayot* and the *pesharim* contain ringing denunciations
of riches and of their acquisition, if not precisely of greed.[22] Disapproval
of wine is also a feature of the *Damascus Document*.[23]

The supposition that Josephus got his *War* framework from a
different account of the Essenes by Philo, one that was part of a
work which is now lost, is thus a possible but not an attractive solution. The loss of a third and longer Philonic account, perhaps an
entire treatise which preceded the surviving *de Vita Contemplativa*, where
there is mention of a passage on the Essenes, was argued by Bauer
and has been often been taken as a fact.[24] But there are other difficulties in turning this conjectural treatise into Josephus' source. For
I believe that it makes little sense to ascribe the immediate detail of
the *War* account to Philo, above Josephus himself, whose knowledge
should have been considerably more direct and more extensive.

The nature and derivation of Philo's information on the Essenes
is, if anything, an even more vexed question than that of Josephus.
That the Alexandrian is the first in the line of surviving writers to
find the sect important enough to dwell on is certainly a fact worthy of comment. And unlike Josephus, Philo never incorporates his
discussions of the Essenes into any account of the three Jewish groupings: the Essenes stand alone, and they are entirely *sui generis*, as Petit
has pointed out.[25] Both Philonic accounts centre on the welfare of
the soul. But whether Philo, for his basic information, drew on oral
tradition, on what he learnt on his pilgrimage to Jerusalem, or, in

---

[22] Beall 1988: 43–44.
[23] Beall 1988: 62.
[24] Petit 1992: 141.
[25] 1992: 139.

his own turn, on a written source, Jewish or non-Jewish, is not a question which we have any means of resolving, and Petit's investigation remains wholly inconclusive. The difficulty is, it seems to me, compounded by the impression given in the *de Vita Contemplativa* (Vermes & Goodman: 75–79) that Philo, for all his stylization,[26] did have a firsthand acquaintance with the ascetic *therapeutai* of Lake Maraeotis, who are distinctly similar in many respects to the Qumran sect. But the identity of the *therapeutai* is a separate problem.

Here, I would suggest that the contribution of Philo to Josephus did not lie in what the Alexandrian *knew* about the Essenes, but in his literary presentation and in some concepts. Furthermore, while Philo's philosophy was occasionally echoed by the historian, even much of that was unsuitable. Philo could be of only limited use to the writer of the *War* account.

An observation may now be drawn from the relation of framework to content: if much of the substantive information offered by Josephus, especially in the relatively long *BJ* II passage is taken to reflect the author's own experience, then it is preferable to lay the organization and shaping of the whole at his door as well. It is, quite simply, difficult to conceive of Josephus taking over a structure from an earlier author and then packing this with his own content.

If it is not to be a source, then we have to think of Josephus himself. For him to have supplied a structure, we must suppose that by the time of writing of book II of the *War*, he had read and absorbed something of that literature in Greek which included portraits of foreign peoples: he could have gone back to the great Posidonius, or he might have been content with reading more recent writing, by Strabo perhaps or by Nicolaus of Damascus. It is interesting that, by way of conclusion to the *Antiquities* account, an explicit comparison is drawn between the Essenes and the Dacians, which suggests that by then, at any rate, Josephus had a familiarity with such literature.[27]

For the *War* account, Josephus did not need a source, but he did need sources of ideas and techniques. When so much of Greek historiography is lost, the temptation to speculate on the identity of Josephus' models should be resisted. The important point is that there is no difficulty in principle. After all, what the preparation for

---

[26] van der Horst 1984: 56.
[27] Note, however, that the Greek text in all MSS is unacceptable as it stands, and, among the emendations proposed, some eliminate the Dacians: Beall 1988: 121–122.

writing the *War* necessitated was precisely immersion in the historians.

In an investigation of the tale of Moses' military expedition against the Ethiopians in *AJ* II 238–253,[28] a dependance upon Greek ethnographical traditions became apparent from the topography and from other small details of the Josephan narrative. There, I posited an Alexandrian source for Josephus. Here, the impact lies in the method more than in the detail. And in this case, although we are concerned not with the *Antiquities*, but with the *War*, written so much earlier, it seems to me appropriate for the reasons I have given to envisage Josephus himself as the author.

6. *The information in Josephus*

The constraints of structure do not prevent Josephus from giving revealing—even if consciously picturesque—information about Essene practices. Details of customs are the other element in all the best ethnographic writing: again we may point to the Celtic descriptions. In the *War* excursus, the details are numerous and they regularly echo Qumran literature. Included are observations on the early morning prayer,[29] purifications, the strictness of Sabbath observance, the distinctive meal-times in which the dining room is seen as a shrine, the cultivation of silence, the respect for God's name and for that of Moses, the abhorrence of oaths and the formidable initiation oaths (though not the contents of these) together with the stages of initiation—in fact, we have a fair summary of many of the basic elements of sectarian living. Overseers are mentioned (*BJ* II 123), a reflection, presumably, of the important figure of the guardian (מבקר) in Qumran literature, even if the obedience of the sectaries to them is interestingly compared, in a nice literary touch, to that of children to their παιδαγωγοί (*BJ* II 126). What would seem to be the council of the community also figures, for a council of more than one hundred members acts as the stern administrator of justice.

The three-year phased initiation procedure in the *War*, as is well known, does not correspond exactly with the arrangements described either in the *Damascus Document* or in the *Community Rule*. The stages

---

[28] Rajak 1978 = Ch. 14.

[29] The implication of sun-worship which has been read into these words is a red-herring; the Mishnaic benediction of the light which precedes the morning Shema is a convincing parallel: Beall: 52, with n. 89, citing the revised Schürer.

specified by Josephus show clear parallels to both provisions, and especially to the latter; but the oaths there appear to come at the end of the initiation process and not at its beginning.[30] There is no reason why all three versions could not have represented sectarian practice at some stage of its development.

Especially powerful is Josephus' formidable story of those who are punished by expulsion and then all but starve to death out of continued devotion to the purity laws to which they had sworn allegiance; here he goes somewhat further than the *Community Rule*, which talks of deprivation of the pure food (1QS 5.15–16; Beall: 90). At these points, the portrayal of an ideal community gives way to a different kind of rhetorical representation, apparently based in reality, but highlighted for effect.

Contemporary life appears also to obtrude, momentarily at least, in the reference to the torments inflicted during the war with Rome, which Tacitus, perhaps dependant on Josephus, also mentions. This is generally taken to refer to events surrounding the Roman seizure of the site at Qumran. Philo (*QOP* 89–91) has an obscure passage about oppressive kings who had torn Essenes limb from limb, but had eventually had their come-uppance. But what Josephus volunteers in this line, is specific and up-to-date.

Again, we find what is effectively a correction concerning a different group of married Essenes, tagged on to the end of the *War* excursus, as if Josephus wants to get the record straight. This is an interesting case where the evidence wins out in a struggle against the stereotype. It is still not agreed, after much discussion, whether marriage was ever permitted at Qumran itself, though the *Damascus Document* refers to it repeatedly and other texts do not wholly ignore the subject.[31] Josephus offers us a very important modification to t he impression of Essene celibacy given earlier. He also gives us here unique and valuable indications of a negative attitude to sexuality within marriage in a Jewish sect, for, we are told, 'they observe their women for three years. When they have purified themselves three times . . . then they marry them. And when they are pregnant, they have no intercourse with them, thereby showing that they do not marry for pleasure but because it is necessary to have children.' The position of this qualification as a special afterthought, and its factual importance

---

[30] Beall 1988: 74–78; Vermes 1982: 129.
[31] Beall 1988: 38–42.

suggest that it should not be read merely as further exploitation of that theme of asceticism that so fascinated Greek readers of philosophical bent.

7. *Josephus' omissions*

But there are significant features of the sect which are not in Josephus and which may be deemed a casualty of the interplay between Josephus the eyewitness and Josephus the Greek theorist. What is missing adds up to what Sanders rightly identified as the 'flavour' of the scrolls. It scarcely needs saying that many fundamental features of the Qumran thought-world are absent from Josephus, even if our author does take care to assure us of the Essenes' strong concern for the inherited texts (*BJ* II 136). And it is hardly to be credited that Josephus simply could not grasp Essene thought, even if this ultimate outsider may have been kept away from some of the sectarian texts—an experience not unfamiliar to the modern scholar. It is somewhat more probable that Josephus perceived what was involved in Essene theology as wholly tainted by dangerously apocalyptic notions. But I hope I have shown that there are other issues involved.

The world of belief was less readily accommodated to the Greek model than the world of social organization and practice. And it is only fair to add that the former was not readily transferred from one language to another. We are, as I have said, told in a sentence about Essene respect for the secret names of the angels (*BJ* II 142), a small but clear allusion to the complex world of Qumran angelology.[32] We learn that Essenes made predictions about the future. We are also made aware of the ferocity of Essene sabbath observance. And the intensity of their conviction makes an appearance in the curious phrase πίστεως πρόστάται (*BJ* II 135).

But what we seek in vain is any notion of the Qumran sectaries' dualism, of their powerful awareness of evil, of their concentration on the future, or of their joy in praising God: this last, it should be said, is beautifully captured in Philo's account of the θεραπευταί (*de vita contempl.* 80 ff.). We miss, too, in Josephus, much of a sense of the distinctiveness of Judaism: among Josephus' Essenes, there is no covenant, there is no sequence of the festivals, there are no tribes,

---

[32] For a good brief exposition, see Hengel *Judaism*: I, 231–234.

there are priests but no Levites.[33] We learn nothing of any Essene stance towards the rest of Jewry, even though the sectaries are defined by Josephus as being Jews by birth (*BJ* II 119), in contrast to Pliny's description of them as a *gens* in themselves, or, again, to Philo's partial explanation that they live in Judaea, but are not a γένος, just volunteers.

'What Josephus did not see' should therefore perhaps best be reformulated as 'what Josephus did see but could not write about.' For there were strong constraints upon him, the constraints not (as is so often suggested) of patronage or of dishonesty, not even just those of his own temperament, but something equally pervasive—the constraints of literary form, the tyranny of text.

I do not wish to seem to espouse the naive position that realistic reportage, even if squeezed, can survive such onslaughts intact and be extracted, in nuggets, from a narrative. The relationship between the two elements is necessarily more complex, for they influence one another continuously. That is why it has not been profitable to subject each Josephan claim in either *War* or *Antiquities* to a test of truth or falsehood, even if there are moments when scholars need to do this over particular claims. For our purposes, it is sufficient to grasp how an eye-witness description can also be a highly literary artefact, and then what impact this has upon content. Some kind of negotiation between the two pure types is, after all, what writing history is about.

In the case of Josephus, it is arguable that the demands of literary form are, all things considered, the largest single determinant in his presentation of Jewish history.

8. *Conclusion*

My starting point was two statements that cannot reasonably be denied: on the one hand, Josephus knew a fair amount about the Essenes while, on the other, he drew on Greek models. My aim has then been to pursue a closer definition of the Greek literary component in the *War* account. I see it as a structural, and therefore a pervasive and also a limiting feature. Such an analysis offers at least some explanation of what Josephus reveals and of what he overlooks

---

[33] However, some take the four groups of *BJ* II 150, to refer to the divisions of priests, levites, laity and novices: Beall 1988: 99.

in explaining the Qumran sect to his readers. It also points the way
to an approach to Josephus' historiography generally, where we
often find that literary form controls content to a surprising extent.

I have argued that the long *War* excursus is substantially the
author's own, rather than a predecessor's. This is not a matter sus-
ceptible of proof, but there is much to support such a conclusion.
It does not mean that Josephus had not seen other accounts. The
conclusion entails a degree of competence in manipulating Greek
forms on the part of the Josephus of the *War* period, beyond what
was directly required by the composition of a military history. The
underlying structure of the Essene notice is quite sophisticated, conceived in terms of certain categories taken from Greek political thought
into ethnographic analysis.

A marked disparity in quality has emerged between the two
Josephan accounts, *BJ* II and *AJ* XVIII, even allowing for the difference in scale. Whether or not my explanation of it be accepted,
this phenomenon should, I think, be taken into account by Qumran
scholars, who have perhaps been unduly perplexed by various difficulties
in the *Antiquities* account—notably, the troublesome assertion that (on
the more usual reading) the community sent sacrifices to Jerusalem.
These difficult statements cannot, of course, be wholly ignored, but
their context must be kept in mind. For students of Josephus, the
contrast between the two accounts is surely a fascinating one.

Perhaps I may be permitted to end on a speculative note. To
judge by the case in hand, the Josephus of the *Antiquities* lacked the
communicative passion of the aspiring younger man. His Palestinian
roots had been dislodged; what he had seen counted for less and
less, and the Essenes, our present topic, had certainly ceased to matter very much. It was still *de rigueur* to write about them—traditional
themes die hard in Greek historiography—but he had little that was
new to offer: he shortened the account considerably; but also, for
most of his later description he drew, somewhat lazily it may be
thought, on a few stereotypes, and he fell back on Philo.

So, finally, I have not managed entirely to escape an analysis in
personal terms. And thus we come round again to Momigliano. For
we may recall the essay of which I have already talked, and the
seductive portrayal conjured up there of a Josephus who, in his
declining years in exile, appears caught between times and places,
culturally isolated, somehow out of touch. The immediacy of the
War was long gone. And so were the realities of Palestine.

BIBLIOGRAPHY

Adam, A. 1972. *Antike Berichte über die Essener*. Kleine Texte für Vorlesungen und Übungen 182. 2nd edition. Berlin.

Bauer, W. 1924. 'Essener', in *RE* supplement IV, 386–430.

Baumgarten, A.I. 1984. 'Josephus and Hippolytus on the Pharisees', *HUCA* 55: 1–25.

Beall, T.S. 1988. *Josephus' Description of the Essenes Illustrated by the Dead Sea Scrolls*. Society for New Testament Studies Monograph Series 58. Cambridge.

Black, M. 1956. 'The Account of the Essenes in Hippolytus and Josephus', in by W.D. Davies & D. Daube (eds), *The Background of the New Testament and its Eschatology, in honour of Charles Harold Dodd*. Cambridge, 172–175 = Appx. B. in M. Black. 1961. *The Scrolls and Christian Origins. Studies in the Jewish Background of the New Testament*. London, 187–191.

Brown, C.A. 1992 *No Longer be Silent: First Century Jewish Portraits of Biblical Women. Studies in Pseudo-Philo's 'Biblical Antiquities' and Josephus' 'Jewish Antiquities'*. Gender and the Biblical Tradition. Louisville, Kentucky.

Burchard, C. 1977. 'Die Essener bei Hippolyt', *JSJ* 8: 1–41.

Cohen, S.J.D. 1979. *Josephus in Galilee and Rome. His Vita and Development as a Historian*. Columbia Studies in the Classical Tradition 8. Leiden.

Dupont-Sommer, A. 1960. *The Essene Writings from Qumran*. 2nd edition. Trans. G. Vermes. Oxford.

Eisenman R.H., and Wise, M. 1992. *The Dead Sea Scrolls Uncovered. The First Complete Translation and Interpretation of 50 Key Documents Withheld for Over 35 Years*. Shaftesbury, Dorset etc.

Feldman, L.H. 1984. *Josephus and Modern Scholarship (1937–80)*. Berlin/New York.

Gray, R. 1993. *Prophetic Figures in Late Second Temple Jewish Palestine: the Evidence from Josephus*. Oxford.

Horst, P.W. van der. 1984. *Chaeremon: Egyptian Priest and Stoic Philosopher. The Fragments Collected and Translated with Explanatory Notes*. EPRO 101. Leiden.

Mason, S. 1991. *Flavius Josephus on the Pharisees: a Composition-Critical Study*. Studia Post-Biblica 39. Leiden.

Medico, H.E. del 1952. 'Les Esséniens dans l'oeuvre de Flavius Josèphe', *Byzantinoslavica* 13: 1–45; 189–226.

Momigliano, A. 1975. *Alien Wisdom: the Limits of Hellenization*. Cambridge

—— 1980. 'Ciò che Flavio Giuseppe non vide', Intro. to Ital. trans., *Il buon uso del tradimento*, of P. Vidal Naquet, *Flavius Josèphe ou du bon usage de la trahison*. Rome, 305–317 in *Settimo contributo alla storia degli studi classici e del mondo antico*. 1984. Rome.

—— 1987. 'What Josephus Did Not See', in *On Pagans, Jews and Christians*. Middletown, CT, 108–119 = trans. of Momigliano 1980 by J. Weinberg.

Müller, K.E. 1972, 1980. *Geschichte der antiken Ethnographie und Ethnologische Theoriebildung*. Vols. 1 and 2. Wiesbaden.

Neusner, J. 1972. 'Josephus' Pharisees', in C.J. Bleeker, S.G.F. Brandon, & M. Simon (eds), *Ex Orbe Religionum: Studia Geo Widengren Oblata*. Supplements to Numen = Studies in the History of Religions 21–22. Leiden, 224–244.

Paul, A. 1992. 'Flavius Josèphe et les Esséniens', in D. Dimant & U. Rappaport (eds), *The Dead Sea Scrolls: Forty Years of Research*, Leiden/Jerusalem, 126–138.

Petit, M. 1992. 'Les Esséens de Philon d'Alexandrie et les Esséniens', in D. Dimant & U. Rappaport (eds), *The Dead Sea Scrolls: Forty Years of Research*, Leiden/Jerusalem, 139–155.

Philo, *Hypothetica* and *Quod Omnis Probus Liber Sit* in Loeb Classical Library IX 1941. London.

Rajak, T. 1978. 'Moses in Ethiopia: Legend and Literature', *JJS* 29.2: 111–122 = Ch. 14 in this volume.

Sanders, E.P. 1992. *Judaism: Practice and Belief 63 B.C.E.–66 C.E.* London/Philadelphia.

Smith, M. 1956. 'Palestinian Judaism in the First Century', in M. Davis (ed.) *Israel: its Role in Civilization.* New York, 67–81. Repr. in *Essays in Greco-Roman and Related Talmudic Literature.* 1977. New York, 183–197.

—— 1958. 'The Description of the Essenes in Josephus and the Philosophoumena', *HUCA* 29: 273–313.

Smith, J.Z. 1985. 'What a Difference a Difference Makes', in J. Neusner & E.S. Frerichs (eds), *'To See Ourselves as Others See Us': Christians, Jews, 'Others' in Late Antiquity.* Scholars Press Studies in the Humanities. Chico, CA, 3–48.

Trüdinger, K. 1918. *Studien zur Geschichte der griechisch-römischen Ethnographie.* Diss. Basel.

Vermes, G. 1981. 'The Essenes and History', *JJS* 32,1: 18–31.

—— 1982. *The Dead Sea Scrolls: Qumran in Perspective.* Revised edition. London.

Vermes, G. & Goodman, M.D. (eds). 1989 *The Essenes according to the Classical Sources.* Oxford Centre Textbooks 1. Sheffield.

Wächter, L. 1969. 'Die unterschiedliche Haltung der Pharisäer, Sadduzäer und Essener zur Heimarmene nach dem Bericht des Josephus', *Zeitschrift für Religions- und Geistesgeschichte* 21: 97–114.

CHAPTER THIRTEEN

JOSEPHUS AND THE 'ARCHAEOLOGY' OF THE JEWS

Josephus' *Jewish Antiquities*, like his surviving *Jewish War*, is not only a history written in Greek, but one apparently Greek in conception and form. This substantial product of Josephus' later years was composed at Rome, where he lived as an expatriate, assisted to some extent by the emperor Domitian, and encouraged and perhaps subsidized by a Greek freedman, Epaphroditus. Yet the question arises how close the *Antiquities* are at a deeper level to the Greek historiography of their time. Should we treat them as Greek history?

This question can be, and has been approached along various lines, through analysis of parts, or of aspects of the text: of such features as narrative technique, the treatment of individuals and their reactions, rhetorical devices, the author's attitude to the course of history and to the role of divine Providence, or his view of the miraculous.[1] Here I shall consider Josephus' project in a more general way. I shall ask what was understood in Greco-Roman culture by *antiquitates* or rather, to use the Greek term, *archaiologia*; and then whether Josephus' book conforms to those expectations. It has been taken for granted that, in writing a work to which that label was attached, the author was operating within a Greek framework. In a limited sense, this is obviously true. But, if we look further, doubts occur, and interesting contrasts emerge. We shall see that the answers to our question are to be sought within the first, Biblical part of the *Antiquities,* which truly constitutes the 'archaeology'. Examination of the largely political history in the second half of the work might well lead, by another route, to a not entirely dissimilar conclusion, but that is for a different occasion.

Archaiologia, the description Josephus himself gives of the theme of his work,[2] is a word with a clear meaning and an established usage in Greek. At its simplest, it can of course signify nothing more than

---

[1] Some of the more recent studies are: Collomp 1947; Feldman 1968a; id. 1968b; id. 1970; Attridge 1976.

[2] *AJ* XX 259, 267; *V* 430; *CA* I 1, 2, 54, 127; II 136; 287.

'an old story'; and that is how Strabo uses it when he tells of an
Armenian legend that Armenus went with Jason to Armenia (XI 14,
12, 530). But it had been employed in an extended sense already
by Plato, and roughly defined in his dialogue *Hippias Maior* (285d),[3]
where Hippias the sophist talks of *archaiologia* as a subject about which
the Spartans are prepared to learn from him, and which includes
the genealogies of heroes and of ordinary men, and stories of the
foundation of cities. This becomes an established usage in the Roman
period, at least by the reign of Augustus.[4] As the way of referring
to a literary product, we find the label in Diogenes Laertius' history
of philosophy (VII, 175), listed already among the numerous pro-
ductions of the Hellenistic philosopher Cleanthes:[5] the work in question may have been primarily a cosmogony.

Dionysius of Halicarnassus, the first century B.C. rhetorician, styl-
ist and historical scholar, wrote a history of the Romans from the
pre-Trojan, 'aboriginal' period down to the beginning of the first
Punic War (*Rom. Ant.* I 8, 2), and he describes his theme as the
archaiologia of Rome; this is how his book is now known. The name,
and its arrangement in twenty books, makes it, on the surface, the
closest parallel to Josephus, so that Dionysius is often regarded—
rather misleadingly—as the Jewish historian's model.[6] In Latin, there
were, in the first century B.C., M. Terentius Varro's forty-one books
Antiquitatum Rerum Humanarum et Divinarum,[7] of which twenty-five were
devoted to human affairs—people, places, times and things—and sixteen to divine; but these were not chronological history, and were
perhaps more like the book about the nature of God and Jewish
laws and customs which Josephus had considered writing after the
Antiquities (*AJ* XX 268).

Other works of the same period shared with Dionysius the characteristic of starting with the most distant knowable (or supposedly
knowable) events and coming down to quite recent history: we think,
say, of Livy, or of Diodorus Siculus and his Universal History; both

---

[3] Norden 1923: 46, n. 1.
[4] See, e.g. Diod, I 4, 6; Dion. Hal. I 4, 2. There appears to have been a special interest in such matters at that time: we may recall the interest of the age in
the Greek logographers, noticed by Pearson 1939: 12–13.
[5] Norden 1956: 373, n. 1.
[6] The comparison is developed by Shutt 1961: 97–101; Thackeray 1929: 56 ff.;
Attridge 1976: 43–70. Contrasts are elaborated by Collomp 1947. The influence is
well assessed by Schalit 1955: XXII–XXVI.
[7] See Schanz-Hosius 1927: 564–565, and n. 55.

of these included their own lifetimes. Josephus, a century later, followed a similar scheme for the history of the Jews. As in the case
of Dionysius, the label *archaiologia* applies only to the first half (roughly)
of his work. Even this apparently peculiar usage seems to be not
abnormal. With Cato the Elder's seven-book work on the history of
Italy, the name *Origines* is strictly applicable to the first three books,
where the origins of different cities are discussed; but theories that
the author changed his intention in midstream, or that two separate
works were combined, have now rightly been rejected; support is
offered for this rejection by other works whose title really applies
only to their first part, such as Xenophon's *Cyropaedia* and *Anabasis*.
Another somewhat curious phenomenon, the tendency of ancient
books to lack formal titles,[8] to some extent accounts for all this; in
default of suitable opening words, a work could conveniently be
referred to by a name applicable to its first part, or indeed to any
distinctive portion of it. It should be added that Josephus can also
use *archaiologia* even more narrowly than might be expected; and in
his introduction he distinguishes between two major themes, the
Jewish *archaiologia*, and the formation of the Jewish constitution (*politeuma*) (*AJ* I 5).

Now the earliest history of Greeks, and on the whole of Romans
too (partly in imitation of Greeks), was embodied in myths which
told of their wanderings, their heroes and the foundation of their
cities. Myths were the principal source for *archaiologia*. This state of
affairs is nicely demonstrated by the use of the word *archaiologos* to
mean an actor, which occurs in an Attic inscription:[9] for tragic actors
were concerned, precisely, with the representation of myth. The limitations of the available material were recognized by Varro in his
schematic threefold division of the past, in which the first of the
three eras was the 'mythical', the second was a dark age, and only the
third earned the title 'historical'.[10] And when historians incorporated
such material into their works, some of them at least cherished no

---

[8] See *RE* Suppl. XII (1960), 1108–1109, s.v. 'Thukydides'.
[9] See Robert 1969: 671–674. The inscription of the second or third century
A.D., is *IG* II² 2153. Robert confirmed this meaning in a late Latin-Greek glos-
sary, where *archaiologoi* translates 'Atellani'. For the reading, cf. Mitsos 1974: 120.
[10] The division is described by Censorinus, *de Die Nat.* 21, 1:1 'mythical'—from
the beginning to the first cataclysm, an unknown length of time. 2. 'obscure' (*adelon*)—
from the first cataclysm to the first Olympiad, 1,600 years. 3. 'historical'—'quia res
in eo gestae veris historiis continentur'.

illusions about it, as we can see in Livy's appealing justification (and
he was not the most critical of writers): 'what is transmitted from
before the foundation and establishment of the city is more appropriate to poetic tales than to the solid structures of history, and it
is not my intention to confirm or deny these things. Let the license
be granted to hoary tradition, of mixing the divine with the human,
so that the city beginnings might be made more dignified' (praef 6).
Apology or no apology, it came naturally to historians to treat prehistory as their province.[11] They were perhaps encouraged by the
example of Thucydides' willingness, in what became known as his
archaiologia, to look in myths for certain proofs (*tekmêriah*) from which
he could make inferences about how things had once been; he talks
of Hellen son of Deucalion as the man who united the Hellenes in
an alliance and gave them their name (I 3), and speculates as to the
power of Minos (I 4) and of Agamemnon (I 9). In fact, it was wrong
of Dionysius of Halicarnassus, in his study of Thucydides (*de Thuc.* 7),
to say that Thucydides had altogether excluded the mythical from
his history. The few fragments of Polybius' so-called *archaiologia* of
early Rome (VI 11a) show signs of a similar procedure, for Pallas,
son of Hercules and Lavinia, is there discussed as an historical figure.[12]
The opponents of this approach did not manage to hold the fied
for long; Diodorus (IV 1, 1–5) vigorously defended the incorporation of myths in an hisotrical work against the scepticism of those
who claimed that the traditions in them could neither be proved nor
disproved and were mutually contradictory; and, in contrast to the
practice of fourth century historians like Ephorus, he announced his
policy of presenting ancient legends and honouring the heroes and
demi-gods of old.

It was, one might say, the defeat of the sceptics which allowed
Josephus to make the remote past of the Jews, that is to say Biblical
traditions, the material for the first half of his *Antiquities.* In a sense,
Moses, Joseph, David and the rest were Jewish heroes. The stories
would not look very different from those which readers were used
to, especially after they had received Josephus' enlivening treatment,

---

[11] On myth as a subject for history, see Jacoby 1949: 136; Walbank 1960: 221 ff.;
Wardman 1960; 403–413, esp. 408 ff.; Finley 1975.

[12] Neither Thucydides nor Polybius, however, considered such subject-matter suitable for a whole work: see Momigliano 1966a: 130–131.

through the addition of a degree of realism, of psychological interpretation and of sentiment.[13]

But the similarity is a superifical one. In a variety of respects, Josephus is performing a task different from the Greek and Roman writers. It is noticeable that he never uses the words *mythologia* or *mythos* with reference to his own nation's past. He himself points out the important ways in which the Jewish *archaiologia* was distinguished and in his view superior to others, above all to the Greek *archaiologia* (he did not discuss that of the Romans). First, there was the comparative antiquity of Jewish traditions. Josephus insists, both in the *Antiquities* (I 13) and in the defensive *Contra Apionem* (I 1 ff.), where he backs up the *Antiquities* and often makes explicit what is latent there, that the Jews had a history going back five thousand years, which made them an older people than the Greeks, and also that they had adequate records of the earliest period of their history. The number five thousand is a somewhat exaggerated approximation to the total of Josephus' figures, based largely on the Biblical generations, for the lengths of the different eras of Jewish history; from Adam to the flood; from the flood to Abraham; from Abraham to the Exodus; from the Exodus to Solomon's Temple; from the building of Solmon's Temple to its destruction; the seventy years of the Babylonian captivity; and finally from Cyrus to his own day. The work of Hellenistic Jewish chronographers may have assisted this calculation.[14] In the *Antiquities*, as contrasted with the Contra Apionem, external attestations for the chronological claims are not felt to be necessary; nor are explicit and detailed synchronisations with other events in world history.[15] But Josephus is in no doubt that he has an impressive claim to make. And indeed, the estimated five thousand years compares favourably with anything the classical world could offer. The last two of Varro's periods taken together total only some two thousand years. For Josephus, the supposedly historical

---

[13] Josephus' 'psychologizing' is assessed by Attridge 1976: 40, with examples in nn. 3 and 4.

[14] *AJ* I 82, 148, 318; VIII 61–62; X 146; XI 1. Two inconsistent but not greatly divergent systems of calculation seem to be employed by Josephus which may, but need not (it seems to me) be due to the use of two different sources. See Thackeray's notes, Loeb *Josephus, ad loc.*

[15] *CA* I 93 ff. is the key passage in Josephus for such synchronizations. See Wacholder 1968.

period extended into what for Greeks was the mythical. This advantage over the Greeks was something which many Eastern peoples shared with the Jews; in respect of antiquity, Greeks were used to finding themselves unfavourably compared with the Orientals.[16]

Then apart from the question of the age of the traditions involved (which might be seen as merely a difference of degree), there was a fundamental distinction between the kind of task which Greek writers of early history had to perform and that which lay before Josephus. The work of Greek historians of the remote past consisted in collecting ancient memories, which would exist in a variety of forms and versions and might be of a recondite character, and in combining, sifting and criticizing them. Josephus would not have worked in this way. It is true that the Bible may have seemed to be a remote and inaccessible tradition to Josephus' intended readers,[17] and in that way he may have been for *them* unearthing abstruse information. But that was not, of course, the real situation. For Jews, the collection had been made.

In this case, therefore, there was no need for the material to be discovered; nor was there any room for the examination of it, which to many Greeks was so important. Hecataeus of Miletus, the predecessor of Herodotus, had already approached the mythological material which he had gathered in a critical spirit.[18] Much later, it was virtually automatic among Greeks to adopt a questioning stance, even if the actual questioning done was superficial.[19] The main criterion used to sift the accumulated learning, whether explicitly or implicitly,[20] was naturally that of plausibility. Thus Dionysius of Halicarnassus in *de Thucydide* (5) criticizes the forerunners of Thucydides for their naivety in accepting many incredible myths. And to give an example from his own work, he dismisses fanciful suggestions about an apotheosis of Romulus, and prefers the more realistic story that the king was assassinated by some of his subjects (*Rom. Ant.* 11.56). The pejorative implications of the very word 'myth' made it

[16] See Momigliano 1969: 33–34. Awareness of this unfavourable comparison goes back to Hecataeus of Miletus.
[17] On their unfamiliarity with it, see below.
[18] As announced in the famous opening of his *Genealogies: FGrH* 1, Fl. See Momigliano 1966b: 323–353 and 1966c: 211–213.
[19] Which it could not but be, in the absence of much documentary material: see the remarks of Momigliano 1966a: 135–136.
[20] See Wardman 1960: 409–410.

necessary to tread with care. On the whole, a residual uncertainty about many points was acknowledged in Greek writing, as, for example, in Plutarch's statements about Theseus' battle with the Amazons (*Theseus* 26). Josephus takes pleasure in pointing out the dubiousness of Greek sources and the contradictions contained in them, and makes the multiplicity of the tradition into grounds for disparagement and contempt. Ironically, his remarks are somewhat reminiscent of the criticisms ascribed by Diodorus to predecessors who had altogether opposed the inclusion of myth in history (4.1.1): 'May one not easily discover from the writers themselves that they wrote without secure knowledge of any one fact, but in accordance with conjectures on the subject? For the most part they confute one another in their books, not hesitating to give the most contradictory accounts of the same matter' (*CA* I 15). Among the Jews on the other hand, the fact that the records are the product not of human hand but of prophetic utterance under divine inspiration, means that there exists no multitude of inconsistent, warring texts (*CA* I 38). Thus Josephus sees the Jewish tradition, so he tells us, as one which may not, and at the same time need not be, questioned. It was unique and incomparably superior to Greek traditions; in fact, it was all true. The Bible was worlds apart from Greek myth. Nor is the position significantly altered by the fact that the author does introduce extra-Biblical, Aggadic material into his narration.[21] For it would have been equally inappropriate to investigate this kind of material on the factual level— to consider how far different exegeses or legends were mutually contradictory, or individually plausible. A basic characteristic of *Aggadah* is that it can accommodate such contradictions.[22]

Again, it is not a serious departure from his principles when Josephus invokes extra-Biblical, non-Jewish authors, as he does occasionally in his narrative, above all in book I, to confirm some point in the Biblical tradition. For they are used not to check but only to reinforce the latter.[23] Thus we are told that the flood and Noah's ark are also to be found in the work of Berossus, of Hieronymus of Egypt (otherwise unknown) and of Nicolaus of Damascus (I 93–94); or (I 158 ff.) that Berossus knew but did not name Abraham, while Hecataeus of Abdera wrote a book about him (probably, in fact, a

---

[21] Discussed below.
[22] See Heinemann 1954: 1 ff.
[23] For a full list, see Schürer 1973: 49, n. 3; or Schalit 1955: XLIII–XLIV.

Jewish forgery), and Nicolaus made him king of Damascus (a tradition on whose validity Josephus offers no comment). It is clear that although Josephus took the trouble to ransack the obscure corners of Greek literature for this sort of material — and there is no reason to think he used an anthology[24]—this has made not the slightest difference to what he has to say, but serves only as embellishment: the accumulation of authors' names confirms the infallibility of the Bible. Greek and Roman historians tend to do exactly the opposite, not naming their predecessors or citing their points of view except where they disagree with them or want to indicate that there is a dispute between them.

Of so little importance are these outside sources to Josephus that he feels able to claim his work to be an exact version of the sacred texts in their original language; it is interpreted from the Hebrew (I 5). The point is made with some emphasis: 'the narrative will proceed through the Scriptures, rendering them accurately in their original ordering. For I have already undertaken to do so throughout this whole work, without adding or removing anything' (I 5; cf. X 218). The claim that an historian had neither added to, nor subtracted from, the facts has, as one might expect, parallels in Greek writers. But to have transmitted texts unaltered was a different matter.[25] True, we find one instance of this, too, in a Greek context: a process of faithful reproduction similar to that claimed by Josephus was ascribed by Dionysius of Halicarnassus to the earliest Greek antiquarians, the so-called 'logographers', who had compiled local histories, both Greek and foreign (de Thuc. 5). But these fall outside the mainstream of Greek historiography. And even in their case, there have been doubts as to whether the task was merely one of publishing existing archives. Gomme's comment is worth repeating: 'It is clear, I think, that the main object of the chief writers of his class was not reproducing local records of epic legends in prose, but re-arrangement (which would of itself imply much correction) and, above all, criticism'.[26]

[24] As Schalit argues 1955: XLIV–XLVII, precisely from the fact that these authors were not of material interest to Josephus. Their reappearance in the Contra Apionem suggests, rather, that he was genuinely familiar with them. Josephus' assertion there (I 16) that his readers would be better placed than himself to judge the reliability of Greek historians is not to be taken as a confession of real ignorance of his part.
[25] Van Unnik 1978: 26–40, overlooks this distinction. In general, his attempt to assimilate Josephus' formula with isolated classical Greek instances, and to associate its implications with Tacitus' claim of being without personal partisanship ('sine ira et studio') fails to convince.
[26] Cited by Pritchett 1975: 54, n. 20.

In practice, however, the Greek precedent had very little in common with Josephus' case. The real home of the sort of claim which he makes about accurate reproduction of a sacred tradition seems to be among the later Greek exponents of Oriental cultures. And we can see that these writers of the Hellenistic and post-Hellenistic period, generally native in origin but using the Greek language, are altogether closer to Josephus in function than the students of early Greek tradition. Their work is distinctive, and in some cases unusually reliable, precisely because they drew extensively on genuine records. Thus, according to Josephus, Manetho, the Egyptian priest and a contemporary of Ptolemy Philadelphus, 'wrote his native history in the Greek language, translating it, so he himself says from sacred tables' (*CA* I 73; cf. I 288).[27] Likewise, the somewhat less sound Greek writer, Hecataeus of Abdera, had slightly earlier consulted priestly authorities and writings for his work on Egypt: 'Those things which have been set down by Egyptian priests in their sacred writings we shall assiduously collect together and publish' (Diod I 69.7).[28] In a comparable way, Berossus the Babylonian astronomer and priest of Bel, in a work dedicated to Antiochus I, assures his readers that he has preserved and used old documents;[29] with their help he refutes many false notions of Herodotus. In all probability, later writers, now lost, continued the same tradition. There was Ptolemy of Mendes, an Egyptian priest who wrote a chronology used by Apion and whom Josephus specially commends for telling each nation's history from its own written records (*CA* I 116; *AJ* VIII 283); or Menander of Ephesus, who translated the archives of Tyre (*AJ* VIII 144; 324; IX 283); or various other Phoenician historians, such as Dion, whose accuracy Josephus praises (*CA* I 112; *AJ* VIII 147).[30] Perhaps the roots of this approach are in Herodotus, for he

---

[27] Manetho was thus able to lay the foundations for the study of Greek chronology. The fragments: Jacoby, *FGrH* IIIC 609. On Manetho's priestly sources, see first the brief account in Waddell's Loeb Classical Library edition (1940), intr. xxi ff. For a good general survey see Fraser 1973: I, 505–510; for some bibliography, Fraser 1973: II, 727, n. 93.

[28] *FGrH* IIIA 264. On his sources, Jacoby, IIIA Comm., 82 ff. For a vindication of the general supposition that Diodorus' first book is taken from Hecataeus, and an assessment of Hecataeus' methods and reliability, see Murray 1970: 144–171, together with the criticisms of Fraser 1973: II, 1116, n. 11; and Fraser 1973: I, 496–505.

[29] *FGrH* IIIC 680. On his sources, see Schnabel 1923: esp. 172–173; Drews 1975: 39–55. General comments and bibliography, in Murray 1972: 208–209.

[30] Ptolemy: see *RE* XXIII, 2 (1959), 1861, Ptolemaios no. 74. The dates of Menander and Dion are unknown, although Menander has sometimes been thought

repeatedly supplements his own observation with native tradition and reports on many interviews in Babylon and Egypt, especially with priests, some of whom read to him from written records.[31] It is significant that most of what we know about the later authors who employed this method comes to us from none other than Josephus; clearly, this was a branch of Greek literature which was very much alive to him, however remote is seemed to real Greeks.[32]

Josephus, then, has much in common with those native historians, and it is in this tradition that he is explicitly putting himself with his claim of following sacred sources verbatim. Yet his function is different even from theirs. For even such writers as Manetho and Berossus used, it appears, a variety of sources of different kinds, many of them more in the nature of bare records than literary texts; and for them the task of selection and compilation was not eliminated. Josephus had only the freedom of selecting within the Bible. In fact, of course, he did make omissions and even additions. But the operations performed by him are of a kind endorsed by Jewish tradition, compatible with a pious reverence for the text. The procedure for omissions is the same as that of later synagogue readers, and consequently Targumists, who by Rabbinic prescription avoided dangerous or discreditable passages; it does not matter that not all of Josephus' omissions actually coincide with those mentioned in the Mishnah.[33] As for his additions, they may be described as Aggadic or of Aggadic type, and it is well known that many of them reappear in later Midrashic literature; this kind of exegesis was seen as an extension of the Book itself.[34] Thus Josephus' modifications in no way signified a departure from Scripture. His respect for the Bible was unbounded; for him this one source was possessed of a greater

---

to be the pupil of Eratosthenes mentioned by the *Suda:* see on him Fraser 1973: II, 735 nn. 130 and 131.

[31] See e.g. II 100. This is not to say that he was not frequently misled by his informants. That presumably is why Manetho wrote a pamphlet attacking him: *FGrH* IIIC 609 F13; *CA* I 73. On this aspect of Herodotus, see Drews 1973, especially 78–81.

[32] On the neglect of Manetho and Berossus, cf. Drews 1973: 208, n. 81.

[33] Analyzed by Feldman 1968b. Of five passages which *b.Megillah* 25a recommends for reading without translation, Josephus omits three, including the golden calf episode.

[34] On Josephus' Aggadic additions, see Bloch 1879: 23–53 (but he believed them to represent Hellenistic and Babylonian traditions); Guttmann 1928: 16 ff.; Rappaport 1930. On Midrash as an extension of the text: Vermes 1973: 176–177; Kasher 1953: introd. xiii–xiv, discussing the term 'whole Torah'.

sanctity than anything else in existence. No other collection of documents known to him, even among those treasured by priests or
deposited in temples, enjoyed the same status as did the Bible in the
eyes of the people of the Book, which for countless generations no-
one had dared touch (*CA* I 42). Only the Jews had shown themselves prepared to die for their Law (*CA* I 43).

Before Josephus, there had been other Jews who had contributed
in a minor way to Greek literature, exploiting Biblical themes. We
might be tempted to think that at least in this limited way our
author's *archaiologia* fits comfortably into a Hellenized historiographical tradition. But it is remarkable that he refers on only one single
occasion—and that in the *Contra Apionem*—to any Hellenistic Greek
rewritings of parts of the Bible. And there his purpose is to assert
that while 'Demetrius of Phalerum, Philo the Elder and Eupolemus'
may have known the history better than some, 'they were not in a
position to follow our texts with complete accuracy' (*CA* I 218). He
is apparently so ill-informed about those writers that he can confuse
Demetrius the historian with his better-known Greek namesake, the
politician and librarian, and can assume all three to be non-Jews.
He did not, then, regard Hellenistic Jewish historians as his precursors;
and in reality such authors can hardly have shared Josephus' broad
objectives. It has been concluded that Demetrius (in the third century B.C.) was interested mainly in chronological arguments, and the
other chronicler, Eupolemus, in reproducing such inventions as King
Solomon's correspondence. Philo was an epic poet, exploiting Biblical
material. In general, the main concern was manipulation rather than
restatement. Only in one respect were these writers like Josephus:
they addressed themselves (at least in part) to an outside audience, and
their writing, like his, was possessed of a strong apologetic purpose.[35]

The justification for Josephus' own re-writing had been made
quite plain. It was that his national treasure had been ignored by
pagans. It had received even less recognition than other Eastern traditions. Here, again, Josephus stands apart. His approach is in the
sharpest contrast with such pagan writers as had concerned themselves, in excursuses or in whole works, with the origins of the Jewish
people, or with some phase of their early history (generally the exodus or the Mosaic constitution). For it is clear that it was not so

---

[35] On these writers see Freudenthal 1874; Fraser 1973; Wacholder Eupolemus;
Bickerman 1975: 72ff.; Walter 1976.

much ignorance or the difficulty of access to information which made writers like Strabo, Diodorus and (even after Josephus) Tacitus collect and repeat absurd and garbled stories about these matters. The Bible existed in Greek. The answer to the question why pagans did not consult the Septuagint is not that they simply did not happen to see it. They would not have been impressed with its contents if they had.[36] For they showed little or no willingness to ascribe special value to what this contemptible nation thought about its own past; and, indeed, no very great willingness to consider what any nation thought about itself.[37] As far as the main Greek and Roman authors were concerned, it was writers from a milieu close to their own who appeared to them reliable. Thus, to select the best known example, Tacitus presents six conflicting accounts of the origins of the Jews—that they were Cretans from Ida, Ethiopians, the surplus Egyptian population, Assyrians, Homer's Solymi or a diseased part of the Egyptian people—and it is clear that he takes them all quite seriously, although he does not care to choose between them.[38] Yet he does not reflect upon what the Jews thought of the matter. Perhaps our own attitudes to peoples whom we regard as barbarous are not so very different: we expect our own scholarship to produce better answers than indigenous traditions. It is interesting that one of the many contrasts between Dionysius of Halicarnassus and Josephus lies in this very area: even though Dionysius admired the Romans, his way of making them respectable was by integrating them into Greek myth and giving them the pedigree of Arcadian descent. Josephus, on the other hand, justifies the Jews essentially on their own terms.

To suggest that Greeks and Romans did not care about Jewish traditions is not to say that all important pagan writers disapproved of Judaism; but even those who admired some aspects of it, or held mixed attitudes—Hecataeus of Abdera, Theophrastus, or, most probably, Posidonius—gave curious and garbled accounts, substituting Utopianism for calumny.[39] The only possible exception is that appar-

---

[36] That they did not read the Septuagint is clear. See the still valid discussion of I. Heinemann, *RE* Suppl. V (1931), s.v. 'Antisemitismus'; and now Momigliano 1975: 91ff.

[37] See Bickermann 1952: 65–81, who maintains (75 f.) that Caesar's approach to the Gauls was a rare exception; and Dihle 1961: 207–239, especially 233–234.

[38] Cf. Bickermann 1952: 68ff. For Tacitus on the Jews, see Lévy 1946: 331 ff.; Hosper-Jansen 1949; and above all the recent commentary of Stern 1980: 1–93.

[39] According to Hecataeus, Moses the wise lawgiver founded a state in which purity was jealously guarded, youth was trained for deeds of valour, and land was

ently remarkable polymath who flourished in the 40's B.C., Alexander Polyhistor.[40] Probably under the impact of Pompeius' conquests—although not, it seems, in any direct relationship with them[41]—Polyhistor collected information about many peoples and regions. His *On the Jews*, about which we know a certain amount from book IX of Eusebius' *Praeparatio Evangelica*, was a compendium of extracts from Hellenistic Jewish writers, from Greeks like Apollonius Molon, and from other stranger figures such as a man whom Josephus calls 'Cleodemus the prophet, also called Malchus' (*AJ* I 240), who is thought to have been a Samaritan. Polyhistor does not appear to have used the Bible directly, but some of the authors he cited—Demetrius the chronographer for example—probably did. Be that as it may, since Polyhistor also gave space to Greek views, we may infer that even he did not assign pre-eminence to the native version.

In general, there was wilful ignorance about the Jews. It was this cast of mind which Josephus had set himself to shake when he presented the historical portions of the Bible in Greek dress, as an 'archaeology', to the attention of Greek readers. He was in this sense quite aware that he was in a class apart from the Greek and Roman antiquarians and that they provided no more than a formal precedent for him. The composition of the *Contra Apionem* some years later shows, as clearly as does Tacitus' attitude, that Josephus felt that he had not succeeded; the work is an admission of defeat, for in book I, as we have seen, Josephus combs a number of *non-Jewish* authorities to try and convince his readers once again of the antiquity of the Jewish people. They had not, he says, been persuaded

---

inalienable. For Theophrastus, the Jews were philosophers who pondered the nature of God, watched the stars and sacrificed at night. For Posidonius, as cited (it is commonly agreed) in Strabo's *Geography*, Moses and his people were uncompromising monotheists who therefore founded their own state, so well-governed that their neighbours were drawn to it (until corruption set in). I have discussed pagan ignorance of the real character of Judaism in connection with Stern's source-book in Rajak 1977: 20–29.

[40] On Polyhistor, see Freudenthal 1874: 16–35; Ed. Schwartz in *RE* I, 2 (1894), 1449; Jacoby, IIIA Comm. (1954), 248 ff. As to the date, Servius *ad Aeneid* X, 388 describes Polyhistor as a freedman of Sulla; the *Suda* says he flourished during and after the period of Sulla; the forties are indicated by the information in Suetonius, *de Gramm. el Rhet.* 20 that Hyginus, the Augustan freedman, had heard Polyhistor, when we know that Hyginus was brought to Rome in the mid-forties, cf. Jacoby, *FGrH loc. cit.* 248–250.

[41] Not all the works seem to have described peoples conquered by Pompeius: there was one about Caria, and probably one about India: see Jacoby, *loc. cit.* 256–257; *FGrH* IIIA F18 and 21–28.

by his previous writings: 'Since I observed many people, influenced by the malicious slanders of certain individuals, distrusting what I said in my *archaiologia*, and adducing as a proof that our nation is young the fact that the most famous Greek historians did not see fit to mention it, I thought I should write briefly on this whole subject' (*CA* I 2). In book II, Josephus attacks the statements of Apion about the Jews; these were the product of a previous generation, but evidently still heeded in spite of the publication of the *Antiquities* (*CA* II 4). Still, the historian's failure to achieve what was perhaps an impossible task should not obscure the importance and originality of what he had tried to do in the archaeological part of his *Antiquities*. There is no parallel for it in the Graeco-Roman world.

It would be wrong, in the end, to dismiss as insignificant the Greek form in which Josephus' product is clothed; after all, to achieve a kind of Hellenization is central to his whole enterprise, and a reconciliation of the two nations is, as we know, his ultimate aim. But we cannot escape the conclusion that, at least in the way he conceives of the Biblical part of his undertaking, this Jewish writer is less of a Greek historian than he appears at first sight, and that he expects the Greeks among his readers to accept the early history of the Jews on his terms, and not on theirs. The pill may be sugared, but it remains a pill.

BIBLIOGRAPHY

Attridge, H.W. 1976. *The Interpretation of Biblical History in the Antiquities Judaicae of Flavius Josephus*. Harvard Dissertations in Religion 7. Missoula, Montana.

Bickermann, E.J. 1952. 'Origines gentium', *CP* 47: 65–81.

——— 1975. 'The Jewish Historian Demetrius', in J. Neusner (ed.), *Christianity, Judaism and other Greco-Roman cults: Studies for Morton Smith at Sixty* III. Leiden, 72–84.

Bloch, H. 1879. *Die Quellen des Flavius Josephus in seiner Archäologie*. Leipzig.

Collomp, P. 1947. 'La place de Josèphe dans la technique de l'historiographie hellénistique'. *Études historiques de la Faculté des Lettres de Strasbourg*, 106: *Mélanges* 1945, 3, *Études Historiques*. Paris, 81–92.

Dihle, A. 1961.'Zur hellenistischen Ethnographic' (followed by discussion), *Grecs et Barbares: Entretiens Hardt* VIII. Geneva, 207–239.

Drews, R. 1973. *The Greek Accounts of Eastern History*. Cambridge, Mass.

——— 1975. 'The Babylonian Chronicles and Berossus', *Iraq* 37: 39–55.

Feldman, L.H. 1968a. 'Abraham the Greek Philosopher in Josephus', *TAPA* 99: 143–156.

——— 1968b. 'Hellenizations in Josephus' Portrayal of Man's Decline', in J. Neusner (ed.), *Religions in Antiquity: Studies in Honor of E.R. Goodenough*. Leiden, 336–353.

——— 1970. 'Hellenizations in Josephus' Version of Esther (*Ant. Jud.* 11, 185–295)', *TAPA* 101: 143–170.

Finley, M.I. 1975. 'Myth, Memory and History', in *The Use and Abuse of History*. London, 11–34.

Fraser, P.M. 1973. *Ptolemaic Alexandria*. Oxford.

Freudenthal, J. 1874. *Alexander Polyhistor und die von ihm erhältenen Reste jüdischer und samaritanischer Geschichtswerke*. Breslau.

Guttmann, H. 1928. *Die Darstellung der jüdischen Religion bei Flavius Josephus*. Breslau.

Heinemann, I. 1954. *The Methods of the Aggadah*, 2nd edn (in Hebrew). Jerusalem.

Hosper-Jansen, A.M.A. 1949. *Tacitus over de Joden*. Diss. Utrecht; with English summary.

Jacoby, F. 1949. *Atthis*. Oxford.

Kasher, M.M. 1953. *Torah Shelemah*, in English as *Encyclopedia of Biblical Interpretation: a Millennial Anthology* I. York.

Lévy, I. 1946. 'Tacite et l'origine du peuple juif', *Latomus* 5: 331–340.

Mitsos, M.Th. 1974. in *Phoros: Tribute to Benjamin Dean Meritt*. New York.

Momigliano, A. 1966a 'The Place of Herodotus in the History of Historiography', in *Studies in Historiography*. London, 127–142.

——— 1966b. 'Il razionalismo di Ecateo di Mileto', *Terzo Contributo alla storia degli studi classici e del mondo antico*. Rome, 323–353.

——— 1966c. 'Historiography on Written Tradition and Historiography on Oral Tradition', in *Studies in Historiography*. London, 211–220.

——— 1969. 'Time in Ancient Historiography', in *Quatro contributo alla storia degli studi classici e del mondo antico*. Rome.

——— 1975. *Alien Wisdom: The Limits of Hellenization*. Cambridge.

Murray, O. 1970. 'Hecataeus of Abdera and Pharaonic Kingship', *JEA* 56:144–171.

——— 1972. 'Herodotus and Hellenistic Culture'. *CQ* 22: 208–209.

Norden, E. 1923. *Die Germanische Urgeschichte in Tacitus' Germania*, 3rd edn. Berlin.

——— 1956. *Agnostos Theos*. Stuttgart.

Pearson, L. 1939. *The Early Ionian Historians*. Oxford.

Pritchett, W. Kendrick. 1975. *Dionysius of Halicarnassus on Thucydides*. California.

Rajak, T. 1977. 'The Unknown God', *JJS* 28: 20–29.

Rappaport, S. 1930. *Agada und Exegese bei Flavius Josephus*. Vienna.

Robert, L. 1969. *Opera Minora Selecta* I. Amsterdam.

Schalit, A. 1955. *The Jewish Antiquities* (Hebrew translation), I. *Introduction and Books I–VI*. Jerusalem; Hebrew.

Schanz-Hosius, M. 1927. *Geschichte der römischen Literatur*, I. Munich.

Schnabel, P. 1923. *Berossos und die babylonisch-hellenistische Literatur*. Berlin

Schürer, E. 1973. *The History of the Jewish People in the Time of Jesus Christ*, revised and edited by Geza Vermes & Fergus Millar, vol. 1. Edinburgh.

Shutt, R.J.H. 1961. *Studies in Josephus*. London.

Stern, M. 1980. *Greek and Latin Authors on the Jews and Judaism*, vol. 2. Jerusalem.

Thackeray, H.St.J. 1929. *Josephus the Man and the Historian*. New York.

van Unnik, W.C. 1978. 'Die Formel "nichts wegnehmen, nichts hinzufügen" bei Josephus', in *Flavius Josephus als historiker Schrifsteller*. Heidelberg.

Vermes, G. 1973. *Scripture and Tradition in Judaism*, 2nd edn. Leiden.

Wacholder, B.Z. 1968. 'Biblical Chronology in the Hellenistic World Chronicles', *HTR* 61: 451–481.

Walbank, F.W. 1960. 'History and Tragedy', *Historia* 9: 216–234.

Walter, N. 1976. *Fragmente jüdisch-hellenistischer Historiker*. Gütersloh.

Wardman, A.E. 1960. 'Myth in Greek Historiography', *Historia* 9: 403–413.

CHAPTER FOURTEEN

MOSES IN ETHIOPIA: LEGEND AND LITERATURE

In his *Antiquities*, Josephus introduces many Aggadic amplifications into the Biblical narrative. But the story he tells of Moses' military expedition against the Ethiopians is the most extensive, and the most divergent from the Bible—though still never incompatible with it. Its character and origins deserve enquiry, both in order to explain Josephus' choice, and in order to shed some light on a Jewish legend and its transmission. It will emerge, on the one hand, that Josephus himself seems to have had a ready literary source for the story, on the other, that it was by no means a literary creation, and is likely to have existed also on other levels.

Josephus recounts (*AJ* II 242 ff.) how, at Pharaoh's urgent request, his daughter agreed to allow Moses to go and lead an army against the invading Ethiopians. Travelling cross-country, he negotiated, with the help of ibises in baskets, a hazardous route crowded with serpents, crushed the enemy army, besieged the survivors at Meroë, was passionately loved by the king's daughter Tharbis who had watched him from the battlements, and, after marrying her, returned to Egypt and to the jealousy and hatred of the Egyptians. Similar stories occur elsewhere.[1] First, in the curious and undated Hellenistic-Jewish writer Artapanus, fragments of whose account of Moses have been preserved in citations by Eusebius from the 1st century B.C., compendium of Alexander Polyhistor.[2] Then in several variant forms in Jewish texts of a much later date, sadly neglected by scholars. Of these there are at least three:

---

[1] On the different versions, see in general Lévy 1907: 201–202; Ginzberg 1925: 407–411; Vermes 1955: 53–92. For a somewhat different approach, with more concentration on Artapanus, see Silver 1973: 123–153.

[2] Eusebius, *Praep. Ev.* IX, 18, 1; Jacoby, *FGrH* IIIC 726, F3. On Artapanus in general see Freudenthal 1874: 143 ff.; Fraser 1973: I, 704–706—but Fraser views Artapanus' work, including his version of the Moses in Ethiopia story, as primarily a counterblast to Manetho. There is no doubt that some of the ingredients of Artapanus are reversals of Manetho, but his whole story can hardly be explained as originating in that way, especially in view of the Sesostris elements discussed below.

a) *The book of Yashar (Sepher ha-Yashar)*, a chronicle running from Adam to the Judges (and including material as diverse as the story of Hannibal and Hasdrubal!) existing in several MSS. The tentative assignation of an eleventh to twelfth century date is not based on secure foundations; the *editio princeps* was in 1553.[3]

b) *The Chronicle of Moses (Dibrei ha-Yamim shel Mosheh)*, containing a shorter version of the Ethiopian story in Yashar. Their relationship has not been explored. That Yashar is mentioned in the conclusion to the *Chronicle* need not mean that it was written earlier, for the reference could simply be to the book of Jashar mentioned in the Bible.[4] Zunz dated the *Chronicler* between 840 and 1100 on criteria, largely linguistic, which appear far from adequate.[5]

c) A collection of apocryphal, pseudepigraphical, historical, scientific liturgical and poetical books claiming to be the work of one Yerahmeel ben Shelomoh, and known from a single Bodleian MS.[6] M. Gaster, who first investigated it extensively, believed it was substantially a document from as early as the first century A.D.; but, again, without good reason.[7] Yerahmeel is not likely to be a particularly early compilation, since the author describes himself as rescuing from oblivion many old works.[8] The question of the age of the traditions in these writings is of course separate from that of the times and places when they themselves were written. One thing would seem probable; that the first two works, even if not Yerahmeel, were produced in the form we have them at a time when their contents still seemed important and interesting. It is certainly legitimate, and sufficient for our purposes, to say that, many centuries after Josephus, versions of the story of Moses in Ethiopia were in some sense current.

Finally, there are other Mediaeval appearances, of less service to our enquiry. The pre-ninth century Byzantine Chronicle, *Palaea Historica*,

---

[3] Some notes in Strack 1931: 226 and n. 14; see also Abraham 1925: intr. The work was edited by L. Goldschmidt (1923); there is an English translation by M.M. Noah (New York, 1940).

[4] Joshua 10:13; 2 Sam. 1:18.

[5] The text in Jellinek 1853: 1–22; translated and discussed by Rankin 1956, ch. 1.

[6] No. 2797 in Neubauer's Catalogue—a MS copied by one Eleazar ben Asher.

[7] The first part was translated by Gaster 1899; some discussion by Neubauer 1970: pref., xix ff. and 1898–99: 364–386: see also Reiner 1969–70: 134–137.

[8] If poems ascribed in a different Bodleian MS (2079) to Yerahmeel are his, then he appears to be the contemporary of eleventh century Rabbis. See Reiner 1969–70: 135, n. 31.

studied by Flusser,[9] gives a version (perhaps influenced by the career of Alexander the Great) in which Moses' expedition is by the land route to India, and which is otherwise similar to the Mediaeval Jewish adaptations. And in the *Historica Scholastica* of the twelfth century French Biblical scholar Peter Comestor there is a version deriving directly from Josephus, who has in fact been named in the preceding paragraph.[10]

It is evident that the starting point of the anecdote is the problematic verse Num. 12:1: 'And Miriam and Aaron spoke against Moses because of the Cushite woman whom he had married: for he had married a Cushite woman'. Peter Comestor saw the connection clearly, concluding his narration of the Ethiopian incident with 'inde est quod Maria et Aaron jurgati sunt adversus Moysen pro uxore eius Aethiopissa'. Since this Ethiopian wife was nowhere else mentioned, there were two possibilities: either to identify her with Zipporah (as was generally done), or to invent a different context.[11] Thus, Moses was brought to Ethiopia. The story belongs to the realm of *Aggadah*. But it is not really a *Midrash*—an exegesis of a difficult text. Though it originates from a Bible passage, it moves very far away from it, expanded, it would appear, for its own sake. If we take as a working description of the characteristics of Midrash the five points named by Bloch and Vermes,[12] it will be clear that in some respects our story does not conform:

1. The point of departure is Scripture.
2. Midrash is homiletical.
3. It makes a punctilious analysis of the text in order to illuminate obscurities.
4. The Biblical message is adapted to contemporary needs.
5. According to the nature of the text, the Midrash either tries to discover the basic principles inherent in the legal sections (*Halakhah*), or to find the significance of events in the narrative (*Aggadah*).

Criteria 3 and 5 are not fulfilled in our case. This will stand out through contrast with a well-known Aggadic *Midrash*, how the baby Moses, dandled by Pharaoh, picked up Pharaoh's crown and put it

---

[9] Flusser 1971: 28–79.
[10] PL 198, 1144.
[11] See the excellent exposition of Lévy 1907.
[12] Vermes 1973: 7.

on his own head (or, in the other version, dropped it on the ground),
thus presaging his future destruction of Pharaoh. The anecdote, in
different forms, occurs in Josephus, in Midrash Rabbah to Exodus
and in Midrash Tanhuma.[13] It meets the Biblical narrative at various points, for it fills out the statement that Moses was brought up
as the son of Pharaoh's daughter (Ex. 2:4); it foreshadows Pharaoh's
fate; and it is linked, in the fullest version (Ex. Rabbah), with another
Biblical datum, Moses' stammer, for the sequel there is that the
child's understanding of what it was doing was tested by offering it
gold at the same time as a glowing coal, whereupon it picked up
the coal and put it in its mouth. It is understandable why the
Ethiopian story, unlike this one, did not find its way into Midrashic
treatises. Admittedly, *Aggadah* differs from *Halakhah* in that there are
no rigid limits as to what is an authoritative interpretation;[14] but it
is still significant that Moses' expedition to Ethiopia remained peripheral to the field of Jewish Bible commentary.[15] None of the texts
which preserve it are in any sense Rabbinic texts, in spite of the
fact that they do have some relationship with Rabbinic exegesis. It
remains a theoretical possibility that the tradition, in its early stages,
did play an important part in serious Jewish teaching and interpretation; it is often, as here, the case that we can only speculate about
the career of a tradition before its appearance in Josephus. But our
investigation will not suggest quite those origins for this story.

All this is in no way to suggest that the story was not alive in the
popular imagination. Indeed, that the contrary is the case is suggested by its long and varied history. We shall try to discover what
sort of story it is which Josephus chose to insert in the Biblical narrative. To describe the material contained in the tradition we must
examine its different forms. Some distinctive features of Josephus'
narrative will first be picked out and analysed.

1. Moses is presented as a heroic figure, performer of great exploits:
that is the main point of the whole digression. However, it looks as
though from underneath this representation another emerges, one
which is closer to the implication of the Bible, where Moses is in a

---

[13] Josephus, *AJ* II 233–234; Midrash Rabba Exodus I 26; Midrash Tanhuma
Exodus 8 (but, the incident seems to have been omitted in the MS used in Buber's
Vilna edition). See also Flusser's discussion, 1971: 63 ff.

[14] See *Enc.Jud.* (1971), I, 354 ff.; Zunz 1892: 61.

[15] As shown by the way in which it is only elliptically alluded to in Targums:
see the ensuing discussion.

very vulnerable position and Pharaoh is anxious to do away with him (Ex. 2:18). And, on both sides of the Ethiopian incident, Josephus' narrative has the same emphasis. It is also perceptible in quaint inconsistencies within the incident itself. Thus, Josephus writes that the Egyptians hoped both to defeat their foes through the valour of Moses, and by the same stratagem to do away with him (II 243). But it would hardly be possible for the Egyptians to arrange both to win the war through the agency of Moses *and* to destroy Moses in the process. Again, it is stated that when Moses is besieging Meroë he is in despair because of the inactivity of his army and at the same time performs great feats of valour at the walls of the besieged city. Here too Moses is both the man in an extremely perilous predicament and the great hero; but at this point both aspects play a part in the romantic story—the Ethiopian Princess had both to rescue Moses from a hopeless situation and to be impressed with his valour. The first inconsistency is perhaps more suggestive than the second of the earlier stages in the development of the story. It shows that there was a movement away from a story which was closer to the original Biblical narrative. But this did not happen equally everywhere. It is interesting that the persecuted Moses is a prominent feature in Artapanus' narrative (see below), and still in the later versions, where Moses' exploits are subsequent to the killing of the Egyptian, and thus come at a time when he is already a refugee.

The new figure of the victorious Moses which we find in Josephus must have emerged in Egypt, presumably in Alexandria. For it was to Egyptians that Ethiopia had a special significance, the permanent enemy on Egypt's border. Since the *raison d'être* of the story is the connection with Ethiopia, we may conclude that an earlier and different Palestinian version could not have played any part in the first stages of the tradition.[16]

2. Sesostris: an Egyptian (and Greek) tradition ascribed to Sesostris (or Sesonchosis or Sesoosis) the subjugation and control of the whole of Ethiopia (in actual fact, Nubia). This Pharaoh, based, it is thought, on a conflation of real figures in Egyptian history,[17] was built up into the greatest of Egypt's legendary national heroes, the prototype of the heroic world conqueror. After Herodotus, his exploits were a commonplace in Greek literature. He was a subject for those tales

---

[16] As Rappaport 1930: 116, n. 38, believes.
[17] See Sethe 1900, on the historical realities.

of romance and adventure which were so popular in the Hellenistic period; and a fragment of a papyrus romance about Sesonchosis and his son survives. The earliest versions of the Alexander Romance are thought to have been influenced by and to have influenced what was told of Sesostris, while in some texts of Pseudo-Callisthenes Alexander is actually declared a new, world-conquering Sesonchosis.[18] The claim that a different hero, the leader of the Jews, had conquered Ethiopia for the Egyptians, was thus a direct challenge to Egyptian national traditions. That is what underlies the story found in Josephus. In Artapanus' version, some of the specific achievements ascribed to Moses are exactly those with which Sesostris was credited: military success in youth, the invention of weapons, the creation of 36 nomes, and the spread of the habit of circumcision;[19] at the same time, Moses is also credited in Artapanus with the achievements of Osiris and other legendary figures. In Josephus, the Sesostris connection is less evident, unless the ascription earlier in his narrative of a prophetic dream to the hero's father (instead of, as elsewhere, to Miriam) recalls what we read of Sesostris (*AJ* II 212; Diod. 1.53.9). In the late versions, one of the sons of Balaam is named Sesostris; and Moses had nine years of campaigning, as did Sesostris.

We need not suppose such reinterpretations originally to have been literary in impetus, although it was in a literary context that they underwent some development. The Jewish claims for Moses, it is interesting (and not surprising) to note, did not win widespread acceptance: Braun[20] points out the significance of the omission of Moses from the list of Oriental national heroes given by Plutarch (*de Is. et Os.* 24, 360 P). It is, then, in this battle that Josephus or his source strikes a blow by presenting Moses as the conqueror of Ethiopia.

---

[18] Her. II 101 ff.; Diod. I 53 ff.; Strabo 769. Cf. Braun 1938: 5 and 13 ff. For the papyrus romance, Zimmermann 1936: 36–39. = POxy 1826 (apparently a conversation between father and son) and POxy 2466 (part of a sober account of a war against the Arabs). That the two belong to the same text is shown by another fragment, in the same hand as the second, concerning the romantic involvements of Sesonchosis. I am indebted to an unpublished paper of Dr. S. West for this information. On Sesostris and the Alexander Romance, Pfister 1946: 56–58. On such creations in general, Fraser 1973: I, 674–687.

[19] The connection between Artapanus' Moses and Sesostris was already seen by Willrich 1900: 14; by Lévy 1907: 208; and by Braun 1938: 17 ff. Braun compares the Ethiopian exploits with those with which the Assyrian Queen Semiramis was credited.

[20] 1938: 5.

3. Ethiopia: Josephus describes aspects of the route to Ethiopia and of Meroë in terms very close to those of some Greek historians.

a) Moses was attacked *en route* by winged serpents, which he put to flight with ibises. This is a clear reminiscence of the phenomenon discussed by Herodotus (2.75), that the winged serpent of Arabia is met by ibises on its way to Egypt and killed by them: hence the Egyptian reverence for the ibis. The Herodotean background seems to be actually alluded to when Josephus writes: καὶ περί μὲν τούτων (sc. the ibis) παρίημι νῦν γράφειν οὐκ ἀγνοούντων τῶν Ἑλλήνων τῆς ἴβιδος τὸ εἶδος (*AJ* II 247), 'And about this I omit to write now, since Greeks are not unacquainted with the nature of the ibis.' It was first and foremost Herodotus who had said what there was to say about the ibis. This remark shows very clearly the genre of writing to which the whole excursus belongs— the kind of historical-cum-ethnographical work in which a description of the ibis as a natural curiosity, and of its significance to the natives, would be in place. Whether Josephus himself wrote the remark because he was making an omission from his source, or whether, as is far more likely, the source himself had written it, finding nothing new to say about the ibis, the sentence constitutes evidence that this part of Josephus' narrative derives from an historian, or from a writer in some way influenced by Hellenistic historiography, working in a tradition in which it was accepted to profess ethnographical interests.

b) Meroë: Josephus' explanation of the name and nature of the most notable town in Ethiopia has close Greek parallels. As part of Diodorus' description of the Nile (1.33), probably taken, like the rest of his first book, from Hecataeus of Abdera,[21] Meroë is written up in very similar terms. It is named after Cambyses' mother, Meroë (Josephus says his sister); it is an island, one side of which is washed by the Nile (Josephus is more exact and says that it resembles an island). The same type of description is to be found in Strabo,[22] who in some details is closer to Josephus: Meroë was Cambyses' sister (though some say his wife, says Strabo); three rivers have their confluence on the south side of the island. Again in this case the Herodotean ancestry is unmistakeable, for Herodotus'

---

[21] On this generally accepted assumption, see Murray 1970: 144 ff.
[22] Strabo 790 and 821.

description of the Ethiopian campaign of Cambyses is the starting point for all these descriptions (3.25 ff.); this is closely followed, in the *History*, by the story of how the mad Cambyses
murdered his sister-wife in Egypt. The actual description of Meroë
is new, due perhaps to Hecataeus, perhaps to another of the
Greek authors referred to by Diodorus (3.11) as having written
about Ethiopia. Josephus' (or his source's) contribution is that the
place was earlier named Saba; and this must be related to the
identification of the Queen of Sheba's homeland with Ethiopia,
which Josephus himself adopts (*AJ* VIII 165), and which perhaps
was not confined to Jews.[23]

c) A few details of Moses' military campaigns are carefully described
and read like the account of a narrator in the habit of describing warfare (II 248):

τοῦτον οὖν ὁδεύσας τὸν τρόπον οὐδὲ προμαθοῦσι παρῆν τοῖς Αἰθίοψι,
καὶ συμβαλὼν αὐτοῖς κρατεῖ τῇ μάχῃ καὶ τῶν ἐλπίδων, ἃς εἶχον
ἐπὶ τοὺς Αἰγυπτίους, ἀφαιρεῖται τάς τε πόλεις αὐτῶν ἐπῄει κατασ-
τρεφόμενος. 'And having travelled in this way, he took the Ethiopians
unawares, and, joining battle, defeated them and deprived them
of the hopes they had of success against the Egyptians, and attacked
and reduced their cities so that there was great carnage among
the Ethiopians.' We are even told how Moses reduced the Ethiopian
towns, after his defeat of the main army. Such elaboration is also
characteristic of Josephus, however, so that these details may simply be due to him.[24]

4. Tharbis: Moses' romance is described briefly but in recognizable
Hellenistic terms—the woman's passion from afar, her offer of marriage etc. Martin Braun argued that an important part was played by
such material in Hellenistic historiography, and emphasized Josephus'
predilection for it.[25] This particular story is, he suggested one of a
type common all over the ancient world, and based on the Scylla
legend.[26] Indeed, one long-standing view of the origin of the Greek
romance is that it arose from a degenerate historiography, which

---

[23] See Ullendorff 1968: 25.
[24] Cf. *AJ* III 44 ff. and IV 89–95.
[25] 1934: especially 11–17. He perhaps exaggerates Josephus' interest in the love
motif (romance, in the narrow sense) as distinct from adventure and emotional experience in general.
[26] 1938: 97 ff.

would bring the two types of writing even closer together. Whatever the precise relationship between the genres, there is no doubt that what we have here is a familiar type of Hellenistic concoction.

Now it is probable, even if not certain, that the above ingredients were in this case combined in a source used by Josephus for the Ethiopian adventure. Quite simply, for Josephus to have formed the elements, linked them and grafted them on to the basic legend would have involved disproportionate labour, in the case of a few peripheral pages in a long work. What is more, some of the material does not suit Josephus at all well, for it is unlikely that he carried in his head knowledge of Greek writers' views about ibises, Ethiopia and Meroë, nor that he was aware enough of them to look them up. Nothing in his works suggests that he had intimate knowledge of Hecataeus and Agatharchides (or even Diodorus and Strabo who had used them). The author whom Josephus followed will have been an Alexandrian Jew, in touch with contemporary historiography, whose aim was, no doubt, to bring a Jewish 'hero' into the sphere of Greek historical or quasi-historical writing, and who took considerable pains to do this plausibly, developing in a Greek way a current Jewish legend. A readership at least partly non-Jewish could have been intended. The works of pseudo-Hecataeus, and, to a lesser extent of Aristeas, provide a parallel.[27] There would seem to be no chance of putting a name to our author—he may indeed have been pseudonymous—or of discovering more about him. He is perhaps best placed in the early Ptolemaic period, when Jews still felt it was worth competing with their neighbours. One wonders whether Josephus compressed a longer story, or whether the little Moses adventure we find in the *Antiquities* was originally part of some bigger work of a different kind. A study of the rest of Josephus' Moses narrative does not suggest that he was so closely indebted elsewhere to an Alexandrian, or indeed to any post-Biblical written source. But the Ethiopian excursus will have had obvious appeal for him because of the relatively polished form into which it had already been cast. It must be

---

[27] Lévy (following an idea which Willrich had suggested and subsequently discarded) took pseudo-Hecataeus to be the source of the Artapanus story, on the basis of the similarities between some of Artapanus' statements and those in the real Hecataeus (*apud* Diodorus). But there are also differences in approach, in particular the persistent stress on religious aspects in Artapanus. There is no evidence that pseudo-Hecataeus covered the Mosaic period, and Jacoby (*FGrH* IIIA Comm., 64) believed that he did not include early history.

added to the short but significant list of Josephan debts to Hellenistic-
Jewish literary predecessors.

We have now analysed the story in Josephus. What remains is to
bring into the picture other versions of the tradition. First, for the
sake of perspective, it is worth recording that the account which
made Moses conqueror of Ethiopia did not have a monopoly among
Hellenistic Jewish writers. It was still possible to adhere to the conservative identification of the Ethiopian wife with the Midianite one.
This was the course adopted by Ezekiel the tragedian, who made
Midian and Ethiopia one and the same place. This both conformed
to his generally strict treatment of Scripture, and, no doubt, seemed
dramatically convenient, creating one scenario for the whole play.[28]

For Artapanus, our legend was full of possibilities. Even more than
the Josephan author, he has put the legend to new use. Indeed, in
doing so, he has moved very far away from it. The Ethiopian wife,
for whose sake it came into being, has disappeared (it is unlikely
that Polyhistor or Eusebius missed her out in summarizing). Μωϋσος,
alias Musaeus (the teacher of Orpheus), alias Hermes, was sent by
Pharaoh Chenephres of Egypt with an army of farmers against the
Ethiopians, because Chenephres wanted to destroy Moses, in spite
of the fact that Moses had taught the Egyptians most of the arts of
civilized life and invented the Egyptian religion (like the Osiris of
Diodorus). The war lasted ten years and Moses established his men
in Heliopolis, founding a cult of the ibis. Chenephres arrived in
Memphis, set up the Apis bull as an object of worship, built temples,
and again tried to get rid of Moses. After this, Moses left together
with one Chanethothes in order to bury Merris, Pharaoh's daughter. Her tomb was made at Meroë where she was worshipped as
much as Isis. Moses tried to flee to Arabia, but Chanethothes laid
an ambush, so Moses killed him. (The last incident is perhaps an
echo of Moses' killing of the Egyptian).

What is striking at first sight are Artapanus' own syncretistic and
anthropological elaborations (which would deserve a separate investigation). At the same time, there appears to be a different basic version of the story behind his narrative; the ten year war, the names
of Chenephres and Chanethothes seem to be details from a different

---

[28] For a short assessment of, and bibliography on Ezekiel, see Fraser 1973: I,
707–708 and II, 987, n. 203.

tradition. But we also find in Artapanus garbled versions of elements which occur in Josephus: thus, either Josephus' source or some of the material known to Josephus' source must have been known to the maker of the Artapanus narrative. It is clear that the Josephan elements are prior to the handling in Artapanus.

a) The name Merris for Pharaoh's daughter, not found elsewhere, must have arisen after Moses had been linked with Meroë.[29] That the Thermuthis of Josephus was a traditional name is clear from its appearance in the Book of *Jubilees*.[30]

b) Moses' institution of the cult of the ibis would seem to have developed from what we hear in Josephus of Moses' use of ibises. Indeed, it has been plausibly maintained by Freudenthal that the Artapanus account of the establishment of the ibis cult presupposes the Josephus story as its basis and is not fully intelligible without it.[31] In spite of this insight, Freudenthal offered the unacceptable general analysis, that Artapanus was the source of Josephus. Lévy talked of a common source of Josephus and Artapanus, and, insofar as so mechanistic an explanation is applicable to the complex processes of transmission of material of this kind, that is nearer the truth. But even then, it would be an over-simplification, in view of the great difference between the two stories. The archetype cannot have been similar both to Josephus and to Artapanus, and yet we have not supposed it likely that Josephus made drastic changes in what he received. Thus the source we have posited for Josephus hardly be ascribed to Artapanus, unless we also attribute to Artapanus access to other material and far more originality than Lévy does, in which case the notion of Artapanus' 'source' retains very little content. All we can say is that some of Josephus' material is the same as some of Artapanus' material.

What is more significant is the intangible form of transmission which occurs side by side with the literary succession. Josephus, we have supposed, took the story from a literary source. But this source and

---

[29] Heinemann's suggestion in *RE* XVI, p. 372 (s.v. Moses) that Josephus' etymology of 'Meroë' is a polemic against Artapanus is far-fetched.

[30] *Jubilees* 48.

[31] 1874: 160 n. and p. 169. Freudenthal thought Artapanus had been abridged. Silver 1973: part III, regards Artapanus as prior, but needs to posit an early syncretistic cult of Moses to explain the ibis association.

Artapanus probably drew on a common fund of oral material (as well as, possibly, on literature): that is the best way of explaining their complex relationship, and the rich, inventive detail found in both. The functions of such oral tradition in Hellenistic—or any other past—society cannot be fully grasped by us, but contexts for it can readily be imagined. Comparative material might have a role to play here. It looks, furthermore, as though the legend continued to retain its place among living *Aggadot* of the more peripheral kind. For its continued existence in this form is strongly suggested by the later versions. These certainly contain elements which seem to be in origin Josephan: the marriage to Ethiopian royalty (in this case, the widowed queen); the defeat of serpents with birds (the ibis, unfamiliar outside Egypt, has become the stork and the context of the stratagem has been shifted to the later stages of the war itself). Other elements seem to descend from Artapanus: a nine year war (instead of ten years); garbled names—the name of the Menecrus who ultimately ousts Moses as king of Qush in the *Yashar* version is probably a corruption of Chenephres; the death and burial of Qiqanos king of Qush, parallelling Merris' death and burial in Artapanus. Josephus (as distinct from Yosippon) may conceivably have been read by some few Jews in the early Middle Ages;[32] Artapanus certainly was not. There are, therefore, two possibilities. Either we must postulate that the elements deriving from Artapanus were preserved in popular memory,[33] or our hypothesis may be one of a literary transmission of Artapanus (presumably through the Byzantines) to the Mediaeval Jewish writers, and a fusion by them of our two known sources. Certain details support the former view: the name Sesostris for one of Balaam's sons could only be a recollection of some Alexandrian tradition, but the actual name is not mentioned by either Josephus or Artapanus.[34] It must have been remembered separately. The tradition that Moses would not touch his Ethiopian wife is again an old one, but not from either of the two authors (see below). However, the latter explanation cannot be entirely excluded in the

---

[32] Lévy assumes that this was the case and takes the late versions to derive solely from Josephus. However, though Yerahmeel, depends on the *Antiquities*, these are cited in an early form of the history of Yosippon reproduced by him. See Reiner 1969–70: 141–146. The picture is still far from clear.

[33] On hypotheses of such a process, see Vermes 1973: 122.

[34] 1973: 79, n. 109, and *passim*.

light of Flusser's conviction that now lost Hellenistic-Jewish literature was known and used in the Byzantine period, and his demonstration of mutual influence between Christian and Jewish rewritings of the Bible.[35]

On either view, the tenacity of legend, even when uprooted from its native Alexandrian soil, is remarkable. Some understandable modifications in this story occurred: the ibises became storks; the war was no longer on behalf of the Egyptians against the Ethiopians but on behalf of the Ethiopian king, who had been ousted by Balaam—outside Egypt it would hardly be to Moses' credit that he had fought for the Egyptians. The legend has been extended: Moses ruled Qush for forty years, made war on Aram etc. But in effect, it is the old story. It is certainly not unreasonable to assume a continuous tradition from the Hellenistic period.

The tradition also touched Palestine at an early date, and is alluded to in the Palestinian Targum: Pseudo-Jonathan to Num. 12:1[36] interprets the 'Cushite woman' as the Queen of Qush whom Moses had been given but had sent away. How much knowledge of the Ethiopian story this assumes it is hard to say; but the brevity of the allusion suggests that the hearers were expected to know what was being referred to. Perhaps any further detail was eschewed because the emotional aspect of the story cast little credit on Moses. The Fragmentary Targum gives less, but points in the same direction in its assertion that the 'Cushite woman' was not Zipporah (actually, she was a creature different from all other women).[37] Neophyti is very close to the Fragmentary Targum.[38] Whether the story gained any prominence in Palestine, and whether the main transmission was through Palestine cannot be known. But the link with Palestine is in any case an interesting and suggestive one, for it raises the possibility that the story had already been familiar to Josephus in that milieu, and shows, yet again, that it is impossible rigidly to separate Palestinian from Alexandrian Jewish culture.

---

[35] Josephus does not mention Sesostris in connection with the defeat of Rehoboam, but ascribes it to another Pharaoh, Isokos, and explicitly corrects Herodotus: *AJ* VIII 253.

[36] See the edition of Ginsburger 1903: 248. Translation: Etheridge 1968: 377. Cf. now Reider 1974: 209.

[37] See Ginsburger 1899 and Etheridge 1968.

[38] See Díez Macho 1974. This reading was kindly checked for me from the photograph of *Neophyti I Numbers* by P.S. Alexander.

There are, we have ascertained, two important aspects to the digression presented by Josephus. It is a literary account, influenced by Greek ethnographical traditions, such as would please a reader familiar with Greek literature. A reader of this kind would be sensitive to the strong apologetic purpose inherent in making Moses conqueror of Ethiopia. But at the same time this account seems to be just a convenient adaptation of a story familiar to Jews, and obviously liked by the people, even if not by the Rabbis. In that sense, Josephus' digression is not extraneous material, a literary extravaganza, but corresponds to the conception which many Jews must really have had of the figure of Moses, and this will have rendered quite acceptable his inclusion of it in his Bible.

We have found it necessary to hold that our story existed in a variety of forms before Josephus' source and Artapanus ever came to it; and we have also observed it to be seemingly alive (rather than artificially resurrected) long after Josephus. Such a pattern of transmission has suggested that the story was often narrated and subject to repeated modification just because of its popularity. Its appearance in a work as bookish as Josephus' *Antiquities*, or in writing as recherché, apparently eccentric and consciously polemical as that of Artapanus should not obscure its real roots in popular imagination, on which literature fed, and in turn was able to feed. We have further suggested that the underground process was one of oral transmission; and it does seem most reasonable to envisage such activity in the case of material which has in it a distinctive folk-tale element. For the Jewish milieu at least we need have no doubts about the possibility and potential of an oral tradition: the literal meaning of 'Aggadah' should not be forgotten. Within non-Jewish Hellenistic culture, which has produced texts (to which we have alluded in passing) not dissimilar in type from our little story (and perhaps early Mediaeval literature too), the possibility of this kind of tradition seems to have been insufficiently considered, even for material of the most popular and humble appearance.[39] This may be a misjudgement, resulting from scholars' professional preoccupation with books.

Our conclusion, then, is that talk and literature influenced one another, and therefore the relationship of one recorded legend to another is by no means as straightforward as scholars would like to

---

[39] Fraser 1973: 681, writing on native Egyptian literature in demotic, does raise the question; but he comes to a tentative negative conclusion.

believe. To accept this means to realize that certainty about the mingling and travelling of traditions will often be impossible to achieve; but also to appreciate that, if we handle what survives with delicacy, it can yield valuable clues to aspects of ancient thought more pervasive, and in a way more fundamental, than those embodied in any formal literature. Yet, finally, we should give literature, too, its due, remembering that were it not for Josephus' inclusion of the Ethiopian episode in his narrative, and, presumably, for its earlier re-working by a Hellenistic-Jewish author, our investigation could not have proceeded at all.[40]

BIBLIOGRAPHY

Abraham, M. 1925. *Légendes juives apocryphes sur la vie de Moïse*. Paris.
Braun, M. 1934. *Griechischer Roman und Hellenistische Geschichtschreibung*. Frankfurt.
―――― 1938. *History and Romance in Graeco-Oriental Literature*. Oxford.
Díez Macho, A. 1974. *Neophyti I, Targum Palestinense MS de la Biblioteca Vaticana*, IV. Madrid/Barcelona.
Etheridge, J.W. 1862; repr. 1968. *The Targums of Onkelos and Jonathan ben Uzziel on the Pentateuch, with the Fragments of the Jerusalem Targum. From the Chaldee*. New York.
Flusser, D. 1971. 'Palaea Historica', *Scripta Hierosolymitana* 22: 28–79.
Fraser, P.M. 1973. *Ptolemaic Alexandria*, 2 vols. Oxford.
Freudenthal, J. 1874. *Alexander Polyhistor*. Breslau.
Gaster, M. 1899. *The Chronicles of Jerahmeel*. London.
Ginsburger, M. 1899. *Das Fragmententhargum: Thargum Jeruschalmi zum Pentateuch*. Berlin.
―――― 1903. *Thargum-Jonathan ben Usiel zum Pentateuch nach der Londoner Handschrift*. Berlin.
Ginzberg, L. 1925. *Legends of the Jews*, vol. 5. Philadelphia.
Goldschmidt, L. 1923. *Sefer Hajaschar, das Heldenbuch*. Berlin.
Jellinek, A. 1853. *Bet ha-Midrash*, vol. 2. Leipzig.
Lévy, I. 1907. 'Moïse en Ethiopie', *REJ* 53: 201–2011.
Murray, O. 1970. 'Hecataeus of Abdera and Pharaonic Kingship', *JEA* 56: 144–171.
Neubauer, A. 1970. Mediaeval Jewish Chronicles. Oxford, 1887–95; reprinted. 1970.
―――― 1898–99. 'Yerahmeel ben Shelomoh', *JQR* 11: 364–386.
Pfister, F. 1946. 'Studien zum Alexander Roman', *Würzburger Jahrbücher für die Altertumswissenschaft* 1: 29–66.
Rankin, O.S. 1956. *Jewish Religious Polemic*. Edinburgh.
Rappaport, S. 1930. *Agada und Exegese bei Flavius Josephus*. Vienna.
Reider, D. 1974. *Pseudo-Jonathan. Targum Jonathan Ben Uziel on the Pentateuch*. Jerusalem.
Reiner, J. 1969–70. 'The original Hebrew Yosippon in the Chronicle of Yerahmeel', *JQR* 60: 134–137.
Sethe, K. 1900. 'Sesostris', in *Untersuchungen zur Geschichte und Alterumskunde Aegyptens*, II. Leipzig.
Silver, D.J. 1973. 'Moses and Hungry Birds', *JQR* 64: 123–153.

―――――――――

[40] Nor could it have proceeded as successfully as it has without the remarks made by Oswyn Murray and David Lewis at an earlier stage.

Strack, H.L. 1931. *Introduction to the Talmud and Midrash.* Philadelphia.
Ullendorff, E. 1968. *Ethiopia and the Bible.* London.
Vermes, G. 1955. 'La figure de Moïse au tournant des deux testaments', in *Moïse, l'Homme de l'Alliance.* Cahiers Sioniens. Paris, 53–92.
—— 1973. *Scripture and Tradition in Judaism,* 2nd edn. Leiden.
Willrich, H. 1900. *Judaica.* Gottingen.
Zimmermann, F. 1936. *Griechische Roman-Papyri und verwandte Texte.* Heidelberg.
Zunz, L. 1892. *Die gottesdienstlichen Vorträge der Juden.* Frankfurt.

CHAPTER FIFTEEN

THE PARTHIANS IN JOSEPHUS

Introduction

Flavius Josephus wrote his surviving histories in Greek and was based at Rome during his entire writing career. We might simply reckon him as one of a number of Greek and Roman historians who deal with Parthia in relation to Rome. At the same time, as a Jewish historian, he stands in a rather different relation to the Parthian empire and to its inhabitants from other Greco-Roman writers; it is this identity which makes his work particularly interesting for us. For although Josephus is most often discussed in what might be called a Mediterranean context, as a figure poised between Jews and Romans, or between Hellenism (since he was a Greek writer) and Judaism (his personal affiliation and his subject matter), or between Palestine (where he started) and the Jewish diaspora (where he ended), he is also an author poised between east and west. Born in Palestine, but residing from the early 70's A.D. outside his homeland, Josephus is essentially a writer of and for the Jewish diaspora. And that diaspora, in the so-called Greco-Roman period, was not confined to the Roman empire. Its focal points were, over many centuries, located not only in the west, but across the near east, so as to include important communities in the Parthian territories. Josephus' biggest work, the *Jewish Antiquities*, issued probably in A.D. 93–94, is concerned with the doings of the Jewish people wherever they were to be found, insofar as the historian had sources, written or oral, about that history. There indeed is no reason why a history of the Jews should respect the boundaries of the Roman empire.

Thus, not only does Josephus quite naturally incorporate what we may loosely call Parthian material into the *Antiquities*, but he does so, more unusually, as an author who has personal and ideological links with subjects of Parthia. The existence of Jews in large numbers in many of the regions beyond the Euphrates, seen as descending from the ten tribes which were taken into exile from Samaria (*AJ* XI 133), figured in the political consciousness of Jews in the

Second Temple period. Herod, anxious to create a new high priesthood which would be loyal to him, made an obscure Babylonian
Jew called Ananel his first high priest (*AJ* XV 22). Hillel, the most
famous teacher of the period, was also said to have come from
Babylon.[1] More explicit evidence is supplied by Philo who, in connection with opposition to the implementation of Caligula's plan to
put his own statue in the Temple, invokes Jewish prominence not
only in Babylon but, he claims, in many other satrapies. The potential power of these exiles is emphasized first in the deliberations
ascribed to the Roman governor Petronius and then again in Agrippa
I's letter to Caligula.[2] That the exiled Jews were indeed widely dispersed is already attested in the second book of Kings (2 Kings 17:6;
18:11), which speaks of the deportation of Israelites from Samaria
to places in Assyria and to cities in Media.

But there are also firm linguistic links. Josephus' native language,
what he calls his *patria glosse*, is evidently Aramaic, even if he is also
capable of addressing his compatriots in Hebrew.[3] It is likely, as we
shall see, that he was able to deal with Jewish source material in
Eastern Aramaic and to absorb it into his history. This is not a usual
phenomenon among authors writing in Greek under the Roman
empire. Indeed, I do not believe there to be evidence of others doing
likewise, even among those who might have been expected to, for
example, Lucian of Samosata, who wrote a century or so later than
Josephus.

There is more. Josephus' knowledge of Palestinian Aramaic, a particular branch of middle Aramaic, apparently made it possible for
him to write a work aimed at readers within the Parthian empire. This
was an earlier version of his extant Greek history of the *Jewish War*,
or so he tells us in his preface. Alas, that version of the *Jewish War*
does not survive. Had it done so, we would have known rather more
than we do about the culture of at least one element among the
inhabitants of the Parthian empire.

I shall begin by looking at the implications of Josephus' remarks
about that earlier version. I shall then move on to the *Antiquities*,
with an eye to assessing the impact on his writing of the author's
affinity with Parthian subjects. It is worth asking what Josephus wrote

---

[1] On these two episodes, see Neusner 1969: 37–41.
[2] Philo, *Legatio* 216; 282.
[3] Rajak, *Josephus*: appx. 1.

that could not have been written by a Greek writer? Does he appear to have privileged sources of information? Is he able to give us insights unparalleled elsewhere? Close analysis of the text is virtually our only avenue of approach. But we should note the existence of later Jewish traditions which bear on some of the Josephan material; these may assist in putting Josephus' Jewish orientation into perspective.

Addressees of the Aramaic version of the Jewish War

Josephus describes the target of his very first work as 'the barbarians of the interior' (*BJ* I 5–6), using the term 'barbarians' here in a fashion designed to satisfy his Greek readers in reference to all who are non-Greeks. Even his own nation is included among them, as emerges a few sentences later, when he breaks the category down into its components: Parthians, Babylonians and the furthest Arabians, along with the Jews who lived across the Euphrates and the people of Adiabene. It is not entirely clear from the shape of the sentence whether the latter are classed by him as Jews or not.

I have argued that Josephus' sweeping claims about the readership of this early work are to be taken with a pinch of salt: he makes comparable impressionistic claims for his later history, the *Antiquities*, this time in relation to a broad Greek readership. If the Aramaic *War* was a relatively brief account of how and why the Temple fell, in the nature, perhaps, of a report for those who had no contact with the events, then it will not have carried remotely the same interest to ethnic Parthians or Babylonians as it will have been to the Jewish inhabitants of that world.[4]

However that may be, Josephus' statement is in itself significant. It is remarkable that an author patronized by the Flavians freely admits involvement with the Parthian world in a work in which Roman activities and Roman concerns are consistently highlighted. This openness has been connected by some scholars with the rapprochement between Rome and Parthia during the reign of Vespasian: Vologaeses offered 70,000 Parthian horse to assist the Romans in the *Jewish War* (Tacitus, *Histories* II 82; IV 51) and later sent Titus a golden crown to mark the Judaean victory. In 75, Vologaeses, notoriously, requested Roman help against the Alan invasion of Media

---

[4] Rajak *Josephus*: 176.

(*Jewish War* VII 244–251; Suetonius *Domitian* 2.2; Dio *Epitome* 66.11.3). That was a passing phase.

Yet the Roman conception of Parthia and the Parthians remained largely negative and, rather than promoting Flavian policy, it would seem, on the contrary, that our historian taking a risk. The suspicions incurred by the author's treatment of Parthia as an insider among Romans readers who would perceive him as sympathizing with aliens stood a good chance of discrediting him. We should therefore look to Josephus' Jewish stance as the more decisive factor in determining the character of the Parthian passages in his work.

That links between the Jewish world in the east were real in his day and not confined to Josephus alone emerges in the first instance from references in his own text to the expectations before and during the revolt in Palestine that help would be sent by the Jews in the Parthian empire. Again, the fact that only Adiabenian support materialized (*BJ* II 520; V 474) does not obviate the strength of the ties between the communities suggested by the request itself (*BJ* I 5). The Jewish ruler Agrippa II is made by Josephus to say in his long, pacifying speech that Parthia would not allow such help to be sent— not that those appealed to would not wish to send it (*BJ* II 388–9).

Less explicit in Josephus, but still suggested on several occasions, are ties, past and present, between Jews and members of the Parthian ruling dynasty. Modern scholarship has made much of this alliance,[5] and, even if its consistency has been over-stressed, we must allow that it was a recurring feature of the landscape. The first major Hasmonean ruler Hyrcanus I, an ancestor, as it happens, of Josephus, in fact took the anti-Parthian side: he accompanied the Seleucid Antiochus VII Sidetes, whom he had previously fought, in his major, fatal expedition against the Parthians in the 130's B.C. (*AJ* XIII 249 253), and there is nothing to suggest that Hyrcanus went under compulsion or reluctantly.[6] Indeed. Josephus proudly asserts that the Seleucid expedition was willingly delayed by its commander for two days in deference to the Jewish sabbath followed by the festival of Shavuot (Pentecost). But the pattern of alignments shifted. Links

---

[5] See Widengren 1957: 205–206 and especially Neusner 1969: 24 ff., who maintains that there was a continuing community of interest between the Hasmoneans and the Parthians in opposing Seleucids interests and finds 'inferential evidence that a formal Parthian-Hasmonean entente was recognized.'

[6] As Neusner 1969 would have it.

between Hasmoneans and Parthian rulers reached a climax at the moment when the ill-fated last Hasmonean Mattathias Antigonus, in a context of civil war, made himself a Parthian protégé. He owed his installation and brief tenure of power in the early 40's A.D. entirely to the incursion into Palestine of Pakoros son of Orodes, together with the satrap Barzaphanes, and to their temporary victory over Herod and his brother (*BJ* I 248 ff.; *AJ* XIV 330 ff.). Moreover, when Hyrcanus, a rival Hasmonean (and for a long time Herod's ally), was carried off as a prisoner to Parthia, he was treated with marked respect by Phraates (IV) and allowed to take up residence within the Babylonian Jewish communities (*AJ* XV 14 ff.). According to the *Jewish War*, he was released in 30 B.C. and sent home because of the intercession of the Jews with Phraates (*BJ* I 434). In the *Antiquities*, we learn that Herod, by that time in control in Palestine, sent gifts to Phraates to secure Hyrcanus' return, while the journey was subsidized by the local Jews (*AJ* XV 19–21). Either way, a closeness between the communities, the Parthian throne, and, now, Herod, is presupposed by the events.

To claim that the Jews could always be seen by the Parthians as a reliable ally against Rome[7] is to oversimplify. Soon after Josephus' death, there was to be the manifestation of a synchronized and perhaps even a concerted resistance to Trajan's expedition between the Parthians and the Jews of Mesopotamia. It is, furthermore, possible that the involvement of the Jews in this major conflict sparked off the concurrent Jewish revolt against Roman rule and their Greek neighbours in various diaspora centres within the Roman empire.[8]

Intermittent as Parthian-Jewish co-operation may have been, it occurred regularly enough to have a real political significance. Whether these ties extended beyond the rulers to any level of the population among whom the Jews lived was another matter. We notice that it is rather a pattern of negative relationships between Jews and certain native peoples which is summed up by Josephus at *AJ* XVIII 371: Babylonians hate Jews because of the *enantiosis*, opposition, of their respective laws: whichever group was the stronger would attack, says Josephus. We shall look later at the troubles in Seleukeia and Ktesiphon which led the historian to make this remark.

---

[7] So Neusner 1969: 34 ff.
[8] Argued most recently by Barnes 1989 on chronological grounds. Objections in Horbury 1996.

The Parthian material in Josephus

Josephus' additions to our knowledge of dealings between Rome and Parthia are familiar and have been recently reviewed.[9] It is fairly clear that such information reached Josephus from the two Greek (non-Jewish) works, now lost, which served as his major sources for the later books of his *Antiquities*, the *Histories* of Strabo and the *Universal History* of Nicolaus of Damascus. In relation to Josephus' selection of material, it is worth noting that Jewish dynasts, whether Hasmoneans or Herodians, play a part in most of the relevant narratives, operating sometimes on one side or the other, sometimes as intermediaries. Thus, Josephus sheds extra light upon Roman-Parthian relations under Tiberius and Nero (*AJ* XVIII 96–105), when he summarizes Artabanos II's attempted annexation of Armenia, Tiberius' counterattack with the help of the kings of Albania and Iberia, and Artabanos' flight, exile and eventual victorious return. Josephus adds one significant episode to the information in Tacitus (Tac. *Ann.* 6.31 ff.) and this is part of his unusual perspective on the story. For he makes much of the signal service provided by Herod Antipas, the ruler of Galilee, at its conclusion, telling how, when L. Vitellius, the Roman commander, needed to settle with the restored Parthian king, it was Antipas who brought off a coup by bringing together no less than the emperor Tiberius and Artabanos for a feast on a purpose-built bridge across the Euphrates. And it was Artabanos who presented Tiberius with a Jewish giant (118.103).[10]

Even in describing Roman-Parthian dealings, then, our author's particular angle bears fruit. My concern here, however, is rather with those excursuses where Josephus, in pursuit of a Jewish theme, concentrates on the internal affairs of the Parthian empire.[11] Here we find much material which is virtually unique to Josephus. These are narratives whose texture and literary flavour are of a looser and less formal kind. But to register that Josephus can offer us something more like an insider's view of the Parthian empire than the generality of Greek and Roman writers is only a starting point. We

---

[9] Täubler 1904; Colpe 1974.

[10] Josephus' information about the role of Antipas makes his ascription of the episode to Tiberius preferable to Dio's dating to Caligula's reign (59.17.5). In Suetonius (*Vitellius* 2), the time is unspecified. See Schottky 1991: 83.

[11] Colpe 1974: 107–108 laments the absence of any such perspective in Josephus' treatment of the Arsacids, but does not take into account the two excursuses discussed here.

must ask what effect this has on his histories, either through any access to unusual sources, whether Jewish or Parthian, and to the oral reminiscences of his compatriots, or else through his personal knowledge. We need therefore to take a close look at the narratives themselves and to observe their character. Within them, we shall pay special attention to Josephus' grasp of the Parthian kingship and state and of Parthian society.

These two excursuses have characteristics in common and there should be advantage in looking at both together. In part historical, they have the air of drawing on traditional stories as well: they focus on the activities and adventures of individuals presented as in one way or another heroic, even if they are shown as less than morally spotless. One kind of morality is, none the less, strongly emphasized: this is found in the observance, or at least the awareness of the Jewish law by the protagonists. For all that, the episodes may be called novelistic, and they have something of a picaresque flavour: there embody dramatic sequences of events, some of them military, with colourful reversals and twists of fate, as well as, in each case, the involvement of women and, in one case, a minor erotic element. Direct speech and the occasional colourful dialogue add to the effect.

These narratives share certain literary features with other short novelistic narratives within the *Antiquities*, mostly set within the Roman ambit. Notably, there is a common tendency to explain major historical events in terms of personal relationships without considering other causes, and a particular liking for making the religiosity of women a causative factor. We may cite the interpretation of Tiberius' executions and expulsion of priests of Isis at Rome as arising out of the entrapment of a high-born Roman woman, Paulina, on behalf of her passionate admirer, the knight Decius Mundus, through the agency of a freedwoman and the connivance of the priests (*AJ* XVIII 65–80); or, again, more briefly, the explanation for the expulsion of the Jews from Rome, also under Tiberius, as occasioned by the embezzling by Jewish crooks of the Temple contributions of a proselyte of high-rank, Fulvia, wife of a certain Saturninus (*AJ* XVIII 81–84). We may also cite a Parthian instance, the representation of the concubine Thesmousa (or Thermousa),[12] formerly an Italian slave, as responsible for persuading king Phraates (IV) to send his children

---

[12] Part at least of this story is confirmed by a range of coins from various locations on which Thesmousa figures with Phraatakes as Thea Musa: Karras-Klapproth 1988: 95; Schottky 1991: 62, n. 8.

to Rome as hostages and then as getting her own son Phraatakes—
allegedly her incestuous lover—to conspire (unsuccessfully) against
his father (*AJ* XX 39–41).

But our two Parthian-Jewish narratives are distinguished by their
broad geographical and historical canvas: the bulk of their subject
matter is political drama, and they highlight adventure which may
be military, or may at the very least be extreme risk, as in the second
episode. There may be something of Parthian taste in this.

These two Parthia-based excursuses have a further interesting
dimension in being directly concerned with the fate of the monarchy:
the extraordinary vicissitudes in the fortunes of Artabanus II are a
central element.[13] A closeness between the Jewish protagonists and
a monarchic figure is an important feature, and services performed
for the latter by the former are highlighted. The amount of detail
suggests, *prima facie*, a degree of historical veracity in these transactions; and this, as we shall see, can be to some extent confirmed,
even if the few chronological indicators offered by the author leave
us with a number of problems. At the same time, we should not
forget that the motif of the successful, self-made Jew assisting a royal
master is a deeply traditional one, harking back to the biblical stories of Joseph, of Mordecai and of Daniel. The motif served as a
paradigm for diaspora communities whose destinies could, indeed,
be determined by their ability to win and retain the favour of the
ruling power. It is unlikely that the motif will not have influenced
our narratives.

Anilaios and Asinaios (AJ XVIII 310–379)

Josephus sets out to give the background to a massacre of unprecedented proportions which befell the Jews in Mesopotamia, and principally, he specifies, those of Babylonia. He explains that the Jews
of the region banked their Temple contributions at the major city
of Neardea on the Euphrates as well as in another well-fortified
Babylonian city, Nisibis,[14] whence the money was conducted by con-
voy to Jerusalem, thus avoiding, in Josephus' view, the possibility of

---

[13] Called Artabanos III in deference to von Gutschmid's genealogy. For a full
discussion of the numbering, Schottky 1991: 78–81.

[14] On the problem of locating this town, see below, p. 284.

interference by the Parthian controllers of the region (rather, be it noted, than by Babylonians).

We then turn to two orphaned Jewish boys from Neardea who were apprenticed to a weaver, a not undignified craft for men in those parts. Sore at a punishment meted out to them, they fled, turned to banditry and protection-racketeering and thus became wealthy 'robber barons'. Attacked suddenly by the local satrap's large force of Parthians and Babylonians in their stronghold at 'the parting of the rivers', they reluctantly took up arms on the sabbath. Josephus includes a dialogue in which Asinaios, one of the brothers, and his scouts agonize about this. Their overwhelming victory attracts the attention of the King Artabanos (II), who offers repeated pledges of safety, holds out an offer of power and gets each brother in turn to his court.[15] Here Josephus' narrative becomes rather detailed. The King's motivation is explained: to neutralize Asinaios and to curb rebellion and intended rebellion among the satraps (330–331). Asinaios' short stature is said to be a source of surprise. The tale now told, of the resentful chief-of-staff, Abgadases, is designed to shed light on monarchic shrewdness, for the King, while insisting that he is honouring his pledges to the brothers by refusing to allow them to be killed then proceeds to incite Abgadases to redeem Parthia's honour and to display his own courage by setting upon the returning Asinaios 'without my knowledge' (336); yet at the same time he issues a secret warning to Asinaios, whom he loads with gifts, to avoid the generals' jealousy by making a quick getaway. The Jew emerges as favoured even above a general so powerful that to cross him overtly would be dangerous for the King.

Asinaios, whose rise has (we are told) been uniquely rapid, remained in control for fifteen years, securing himself now with fixed strongholds. Babylonian honours proving inadequate, Parthian generals were encouraged to pay their respects. But the regime of the Jewish leader became tyrannical and arbitrary (as might be expected). Also to be expected, perhaps, is that its downfall comes about through the intervention of a glamorous female protagonist. For the beautiful

---

[15] Artabanos was earlier introduced (*AJ* XVIII 48). Josephus is informative on the career of this monarch, even if he differs from Tacitus (*Ann.* VI 36.4; VI 42.3) in some small particulars: for Josephus Artabanos is originally king of Media rather than of Atropatene, and he does not say that the King was only on his maternal side an Arsacid: see Schottky 1991: 63–4.

wife of his brother Anilaios, whom the latter had taken after mur-
dering her previous husband, was an idolater whose practices became
more and more open. Complaints were made about the husband's
transgressions of the Law and his licentiousness, and curses were laid
on both brothers by an individual (unnamed), who was condemned
to death for speaking up in the name of the Law. Although, even
in the face of open worship of Parthian deities, Asinaios loyally
refused to intervene against his brother, the idolatrous wife took
fright and poisoned her brother-in-law.

Anilaios continued in the old ways, of which the author seems to
have a clear understanding. Rashly raiding villages controlled by
Artabanos' son-in-law, Mithridates, he was warned of an impending
attack by a 'Syrian' and he saved the day with a pre-emptive sabbath strike. He captured and humiliated Mithridates but spared his
life. A debate between Anilaios and his friends on the advantages
of doing so is reported. Mithridates' successful retaliation is the result
of his wife's goading—the story's second influential wife, we observe—
into whose mouth Josephus puts an angry threat to divorce him. To
be outdone by a Jew is, it emerges, a particular disgrace. Supported
in the end by a band of criminal types (presumably regarded as
non-Jewish), Anilaios, still active in the destruction of Babylonian villages, was eventually driven into a corner and killed by local people. But the Jews of Neardea, whose interest in the 'robber barons'
is here mentioned for the first time, appear to have been held responsible for his actions, in spite of their attempts to bring about a general reconciliation. Josephus thus offers a picture of cohesion between
the disparate groups of Jews in Babylonia.

Epilogue: Seleukeia on the Tigris (AJ XVIII 372–378)

This is a pendant to the saga of the 'robber barons', but it is composed in the sober, matter-of-fact style of a 'pragmatic' historian. To
some scholars this quite reasonably suggests a separate source. It is
also noteworthy that the Jews emerge here as victims, and the tone
elsewhere characteristic of so much of Josephus' *Antiquities*, one of
vigorous and confident apologetic, is far away at this point. We learn
that Babylonian Jews moved to Seleukeia on the Tigris, to escape
persecution after the destruction of Anilaios' power, the advantage
being that in this major city they would live among Macedonians,

Greeks, and so-called Syrians, all of them holding citizen rights, rather than Babylonians; yet it turns out that the Jews have gone from the frying pan into the fire. The two major groups in the city are at loggerheads, and after five years they unite to turn on the Jewish element, massacring, it is claimed, 50,000 of them, with only a few escaping to Ktesiphon, a city described as the King's winter retreat and baggage store. Pursued thither by Seleucians and Syrians as well as by the Babylonians, the Jews had to move on to Neardea (which we are to presume is now safe) and to Nisibis, where the protection of strong men, whose affiliation is unspecified, was supposedly available.

Anilaios and Asinaios: dating and historical context

These events, though not temporally anchored by Josephus, can be convincingly slotted into a historical situation known from other sources. Thus the migration of the Jews to Seleukeia has been reasonably connected with the revolt and defection of this Greek city from the Parthian throne which began during the troubled last years of Artabanos II and was only suppressed by Vardanes.[16] With the help of numismatic evidence the seven-year revolt (Tacitus, *Annals* 11.9) is normally dated to A.D. 36–42. The Jews are said to have had five years of quiet in Seleukeia before they ran into trouble (*AJ* XVIII 373). Tacitus ascribes Seleucian support for the Roman protégé Tiridates to internal dissension in the city (*Ann.* 6.41 ff.): the conclusion of the revolt will thus have involved a rapprochement between the warring parties within the city at the expense of the Jews. Furthermore, it has been suggested that Josephus' account of a voluntary move by the Jews may well conceal what was in fact a deportation carried out by Artabanos in an attempt to alter the population balance of the city in his favour.[17] But deportations were rare under the Parthians,[18] and it seems equally possible, however, that, through the war against Mithridates, who was a member of Artabanos'

---

[16] On the tie-up with the Seleukeia revolt: Schippmann 1980: 52; Dabrowa 1994: 191 ff. A few scholars have found difficulty with reconciling the two events: recently, Goodblatt 1987: 617–618.

[17] Dabrowa 1994: 194; Wolski: 158, n. 54.

[18] Kettenhofen 1994: 297–298.

close family, the Jews of this region had finally incurred Artabanos'
disapproval, and that by moving to Seleukeia they were in fact aligning themselves with the opposition to him.

As to the power of the 'robber barons', two plausible interpretations have been offered. We may envisage a deeply 'Parthianized'
and 'feudalized' Jewry, containing its fair share of great landowners
who will have lived much as Parthians did and will have been
accepted as a part of the nobility.[19] It must be acknowledged, however, that evidence for this picture derives in large measure precisely
from the Anilaios-Asinaios saga itself and that it ought not, strictly,
to be used to explain it. Others have argued for a period of anarchy in the region in the years leading up to the revolt of Seleukeia
and this is supported by Josephus' statement about Artabanos' fear
of Anilaios and of the satraps, some of whom were in rebellion
(XVIII 330). The city's revolt would then be explicable as part of
a much wider disturbance. And the rise of the 'robber barons' would
be set against a context of increasing lawlessness and the disintegra-
tion of central control.[20]

Geography and peoples (AJ XVIII 312)

The position of Neardea, a town surrounded by the Euphrates, is
carefully documented; and also the dense population of the city's
territory (not just of the city itself). Perhaps Josephus' awareness of
the site reflects widespread Jewish interest in the collecting points for
the Temple tax.[21] For he is then led to name the second main collecting point as Nisibis, and to locate this town too in relation to
the river, even if in language which is less than clear to us (XVIII
372–378).[22]

---

[19] So Widengren 1957: 205; Neusner 1969: 16 ff. Background in Wolski 1989.
[20] The case is developed by McDowell 1935: 225, on the basis of the absence
of coins of the city in the years leading up to A.D. 36. Cf. Oppenheimer 1983:
218–219.
[21] Cf. Philo, *Legatio* 216, and also Acts 2:9 on Jerusalem residents originating in
these parts.
[22] The current preference, e.g. Oppenheimer 1983, s.v. Nisibis, for attaching
Josephus' reference to an otherwise unknown southern town also called Nisibis, is
scarcely warranted. Josephus' phrase at *AJ* XVIII 312, *kata ton auton tou potamou perir-
roun* remains obscure, but may perhaps simply mean that Nisibis too is between
rivers, i.e. in Mesopotamia. A northern collecting point to balance Neardea in the
south would make sense. Neusner 1969: 47, n. 2, argues succinctly for one Nisibis.

Ktesiphon had less importance to Jewry, although there was a community there, as in virtually all the urban centres in the Parthian empire.[23] Josephus is aware of the town's role as a winter and baggage capital for the Parthian kings. He also records some details of rural geography: the brothers' first stronghold is at a place called 'parting of the rivers' (XVIII 315).

On the ethnic groups inhabiting Seleukeia, Josephus supplies unique evidence, dividing the populace not just into Greeks and 'others', but distinguishing a Semitic element ('Syrians') from a non-Semitic ('Babylonian') and separating Greeks from Macedonians.[24] Tacitus by contrast stresses the gap between the senate and people there: Josephus' alertness to ethnic differences serves us well.

The monarchy

The value placed on the King's pledge, expressed by oaths in the name of the 'ancestral gods', by gifts and by proffering his right hand, is clearly brought out (XVIII 328). There is authentic information here about the gesture of *dexiosis*. The power of the ever-jealous generals emerges clearly. Anilaios' rash public shaming of his opponent, Mithridates, who is made to ride on an ass is graphically represented; and this may well represent Parthian practice.[25]

Local customs

Josephus, in a useful aside, explains the standing of the wool trade in Neardea (XVIII 314). The observation has a literary function, since it enhances the status of the youthful heroes. At the same time, it witnesses to a degree of anthropological awareness on the author's part, since to accord high status to craftsmen runs contrary to the norms of Greco-Roman society. The pastoral character of the region of Babylon is also understood (XVIII 315–317). Settled villages appear to be a part of the landscape (XX 368).

---

[23] Dabrowa 1994: 194. For documentation, Oppenheimer 1983.

[24] Dabrowa 1994 takes this seriously. The problems in Seleukeia were clearly not due simply to the hostility of 'Greeks' to 'natives'. Goodblatt 1987: 606, n. 3 argues that by 'Syrians' Josephus means Hellenized Babylonians.

[25] Though one might suspect an inversion here of the Persian practice recorded in Esther 6:6–11, where the 'man whom the King wishes to honour' (who turns out to be Mordecai) is led through the streets on the king's horse.

Character of the story

The narrative is vivid, and it is enhanced by direct speech. So, for example, Asinaios, lying idle on the grass with his men on the sabbath, weapons discarded, reports that he has caught the sound of neighing: not, he declares, a sound like that which would emanate from grazing horses, but rather from those whose riders are jangling their bridles (XVIII 320). Then his scouts return to report that they have all been caught unawares exactly like grazing animals.

But this is considerably more than a good tale. There is a marked assertion of Jewish identity: it enhances Jewish rather than Parthian prestige and the native Babylonians are given short shrift. The perspectives of diaspora Jewry are embedded in the very structure of the story, documenting as it does the ups-and-downs of the fortunes of a community which takes pride in an unprecedented success and in the public acceptance of its pair of outstanding heroes. Great stress is laid on observance of the Laws (the less usual plural is used here) and on respect for God (*theou tou autois sebasmiou*—XVIII 350). More than this, there is a marked emphasis on *halakhic* (legal) issues, whether for the serious edification of committed readers or merely as a sort of highbrow entertaiment it is hard for us to gauge. Thus the issue of Asinaios (the virtuous brother) defending himself on the sabbath against the attack of the satrap of Babylonia is treated at some length and with precision: transgression of the Law was justified by necessity (XVIII 323) and was in fact more lawful, *nomimoteron*. The author's engagement with this issue may be compared with the concern about the topic in a different milieu, as reflected in the first book of Maccabees. Furthermore, a lively emphasis is laid on the box of idols (*aphidrumata*) with which Anilaios' immorally-gotten wife appears in his house and with which she insists on travelling. We learn that these arouse enormous antagonism as a contravention of the Law: a Gentile (*allophulos*) wife could not but neglect the precise rulings (*akribeia*) on rites and sacrifices. And so Josephus goes on, with a champion of the Law put to death, and the conflict between Parthian gods and the Jewish God building up to a crescendo.

The conversion of the ruling dynasty of Adiabene (AJ XX 17–96)

Opening the narrative, Josephus spells out his purpose as being to explain the reason for the adoption of the Jewish way-of-life (*ethe*) by the ruler Izates and his mother Helena. Before we come to the conversion, the devices by which the unexpected succession of Izates, favourite of his father Monobazos, was secured by his mother are recounted. We see here a touch of the same (admiring?) interest in the deviousness of rulers as was reflected in the earlier account of the dealings between Artabanos, the general Abgadases and Asinaios, For Helena, we are told, sees the necessity of consulting with the generals, manages to stave off their recommendation to put Monobazos' other sons to death, but accedes to the suggestion that her eldest son occupy the throne until Izates returns from the territory, Carron,[26] which he governs. There is a follow-up to this theme further on, when Izates deals smartly with the embarrassing problem of his chained relatives by sending them off as hostages, some to Claudius, some to Artabanos. The patent diplomatic functions of such a move are ignored by the historian.

The real subject, the conversion of the royal household, is dealt with in stages. It is indicated that Ananias, a Jewish merchant, had begun his work among the king's wives before the succession of Izates, at that time still at Charax Spasinou, where he had been living since his boyhood. Then the merchant moved on to Izates, with the women's help, while 'another Jew' was engaging Helena. Josephus is explicit about the role of the women, and especially that of Helena: her conversion spurred Izates on. At the same time, the broader picture remains undefined; thus we are in the dark as to whether those two effective individuals were dedicated Jewish missionaries, or rather, as is perfectly possible, individual religious enthusiasts. It is worth mentioning in passing that, for want of better information, layer upon layer of modern scholarly claims about Jewish missionary activity has been built upon the former assumption.

The thrust of the episode is visible in the amount of space allocated to Izates' acute problem of whether or not to get circumcised, a move to which his mother is vehemently opposed, as, remarkably, is the missionary Ananias himself, fearing trouble for himself (XX 89–91). For the nobles of Adiabene had objected in the first place to Izates' and his brother Monobazos' conversion (it is the first we hear of the latter), and the nobles have to be kept happy. The danger from these quarters was indeed to materialize in due course: the

---

[26] See below about the problems of identification.

revolt of the Adiabenian nobility towards the end of the reign is ascribed precisely to their resentment at their ruler's foreign ways and beliefs (XX 76 ff.). Josephus seems to imply that there was no Judaism amongst the Adiabenian population, but nothing is said about anyone other than the nobles. Regrettably, we are never told whether the kingdom contained born Jews, though it is not impossible that some descendants of those originally deported by the Assyrians were still to be found there, not to mention newcomers. Josephus' story is simply that of the royal family. Still, the debate as presented revolves not only around pragmatic considerations but also around questions of Jewish law and theology, of what is required of a convert and whether it is possible to honour God while ignoring one of the commandments, that of circumcision.

Josephus is not unaware of Izates' role as the vassal of the Parthian king beyond the Tigris (and later also in territories further west). Izates' restoration of the deposed Artabanos to throne is told as a story of royal comradeship, though the author does not forget to draw our attention to Izates' well-judged respect for Artabanos. As a result, Izates in turn was treated with high honour and we learn that Nisibis was added to his territories.

Izates had many lucky escapes and much is made of the role of divine assistance in this good fortune. But it emerges that shrewdness also played its part, for he refused to fight against Rome, insisting always on Roman power and acchievements, and so was attacked by Vardanes, successor to Artabanos (according to Josephus: XX 69–74). However, Vardanes was executed soon afterwards. Here, be it noted, a positive orientation towards Rome creeps into Josephus' narrative. Again, speed of reaction prevented Izates' rebellious nobility fromunseating him, even after (allegedly) bribing the Arab king Abias to invade with a large force and then deserting to the Arab side in mid-battle (XX 77 ff.). Later, Vologaeses, also at the invitation of his discontented aristocracy, provoked and attacked Izates. Another nice calculation on Izates' part—that whatever compliant gestures he made would not stave off an attack—together with his stout resistance opened the door to further divine intervention in response to the family's fasting and prayer. The twin values of political shrewdness and Jewish piety come together dramatically here: Vologaeses miracululously withdrew to meet trouble from Scythian tribes, about which he had received communications that very night'.

A parallellism has been suggested with the account of Hezekiah's rescue when attacked by Sennacherib.[27]

Izates died soon after this miraculous escape, predeceasing his mother, the depth of whose grief is explained in terms of the unusual piety of the son she had lost (XX 94). The transfer of both their bones to Jerusalem after her death is recorded and the tomb described.

Dating and historical context

This episode is inserted into Josephus' narrative in the reign of Claudius and within procuratorship of Fadus, A.D. 44–46. In fact, the conversion must fall considerably earlier, since Izates' assistance to Artabanos, occurring in the mid-30's, must be placed at least a few years into Izates' reign. It can be associated with what we know of the difficulties of Artabanos from elsewhere. At the same time, Izates' last reported dealings are with Vologaeses and belong to the early 50's. If we accept Josephus' narrative, the dates of Izates' twenty-four year rule (*AJ* XX 92) will be c. A.D. 33–57. One might wish to see Josephus drawing together Artabanos' involvement with the Adiabenian dynasty, on the one hand, and the King's relationship with Anilaios and with the Jews who settled in Seleukeia, on the other. In fact, although this Parthian king plays so large a part in the *Antiquities*, no coherent picture emerges of his relationship with Mesopotamian Jewry. But that would perhaps be too much to ask of a historian who is not in the habit of connecting the diverse extracts which make up the fabric of his history.

Josephus does have a general grasp of developments in the Parthian state during this period. Among surviving sources, he alone knows about Kinnamos the pretender, who after a brief tenure returned the throne back to Artabanos (XX 63–65).[28] Josephus sets out the Parthian dynastic succession in brief: Vardanes, the successor to Artabanos was assassinated by conspirators; he was succeeded by Gotarzes, who met the same fate. Then came the great Vologaeses, in association with his brothers Pakoros and Tiridates (XX 69–75). It is not uncharacteristic that Josephus, while registering Gotarzes, fails, unlike Tacitus (*Ann.* XIII 1; XIV 1), to note Izates' association

---

[27] So Taübler 1904.
[28] Karras-Klapproth 1988, s.v. Kinnamos.

with Gotarzes' campaign when the latter marched through Adiabene, which would have been material to his purpose.[29] Josephus has also omitted a first brief tenure of the throne by Gotarzes, which, according to Tacitus, preceded Vardanes' accession (*AJ* XX 69–74; Tacitus, *Annals* 11.6–10).[30]

Geography and peoples

Josephus knows that Izates' wife Symmacho was the daughter of Abennerigos of Charax Spasinou (XX 22–23). The latter personage is known from coins of Charax of the years 10/11, where he is Abinerglos or Adinerglos.[31] Josephus also purports to know that missionary work radiated from there.

A district was given to Izates by his father Monobazos and its name is given as Carron. The place is otherwise unknown. But Josephus mentions a Jewish tradition, that this was the resting place of Noah's ark. The name of one of Izates' fortresses is known to Josephus as Arsamos (XVIII 80).

The monarchy

A number of distinctive customs pertaining to the Parthian monarchy figure in this text. The regalia of sovereignty bestowed on the younger Monobazos are described as the diadem, his father's signet ring and 'what is called the sampsera' which remains unexplained. This may suggest that Josephus took the name from his source and simply did not know what it referred to. Again, Artabanos performs the traditional *proskunesis* in front of Izates while the latter still does not recognize him. The protocol in the further exchanges between Izates and Artabanos is also carefully delineated. Thus Izates goes on foot as the lesser king while Artabanos is mounted; but Artabanos then insists on a reversal, since he, a refugee, is no more than a private individual (XX 56–61). At home, Izates gives Artabanos a place of honour at council meetings and at banquets. Then, after his restoration, permission to wear the tiara upright and to sleep on a golden bed is given by Artabanos to Izates—*gera kai semeia ton parthon basileia* (XX 68). The first of these privileges, authenticated in Parthian

---

[29] Stern 1980: 73–74.
[30] Karras-Klapproth 1988, s.v. Gotarzes.
[31] Kahrstedt 1950: 54; cf. Debevoise 1938: 164.

iconography, is some guarantee of the quality of Josephus' data on Parthia. When Vologaeses wants to provoke Izates into war, he demands the return of the royal 'marks of honour' (*timas*; XX 82).

The King's dependence on the aristocracy is understood, as in the case of the pledges made when Izates, urging 'the Parthians' to restore Artabanos to the throne, offers on Artabanos' behalf his right hand and oaths that there will be no reprisals: the gestures are the same as Artabanos had made to Anilaios. Izates' role in this restoration is generally accepted as historical by modern scholars.

The confidence and arrogance of Izates' own nobility emerges in the need for Helena to placate the 'great men and satraps' at the succession of Izates (XX 26 ff.) and later in the general anxiety produced by their indignation at his conversion and in their inviting the Arab king to support their armed reprisals. Foiled once, they are able to persuade Vologaeses himself to come to their rescue. The Adiabenian court is thus depicted, quite plausibly, as modelled on the Parthian.

Character of the story

Although what is involved is the remarkable conversion of an entire dynasty, the focus throughout is on the single figure of Izates, lending the narrative a dramatic unity which it would otherwise lack. His mother, the more famous figure in the Jewish world, gets some coverage but always as his mother. Josephus promises to narrate at a later stage the achievements of Izates' successor Monobazos (XX 96), but this promise remains unfulfilled. The choice of focus is all the more telling when we take into account the fact that early Rabbinic (Tannaitic) sources reflect considerable awareness of the Adiabenian Jewish dynasty, but incorporate material which is very different from that of Josephus. Mishnah (Nazir 3:6) and Tosefta (Sukkah 1:1; Megillah 3:30; Pe'ah 4:18), both compiled in the third century A.D., although embodying earlier traditions and teachings, concern themselves with Monbaz, that is Monobazos, presumably the second of that name who was the brother and successor of Izates: they describe his relations with Palestine, they know nothing of Adiabene, they offer no conversion story[32] and they do not mention

---

[32] For that we have to turn to later, Midrashic material: in the context of a discussion of circumcision, a conversion story about Munbaz and his brother appears

Izates; they also ignore the Parthian connections. Perhaps the name Monobazos is remembered because it was also the name of the founder of the dynasty and therefore a natural way of referring to the dynasty itself; or perhaps events ascribed to Izates by Josephus were in popular memory linked with his successor. It should not be forgotten that, by contrast with Josephus, the rabbinic texts do not purport to be historical; indeed, they incorporate many garbled recollections and fantastic distortions of the Second Temple period. Against them, Josephus is almost always to be preferred. But the important point for us lies in the sharp contrast with Josephus' wholly Izates-centred narrative, which in its own way bears the marks of substantial literary shaping.

There is equivalent material in the Izates narrative to the *halakhic* concerns of the Anilaios and Asinaios narrative. This lies in the extended exploration of the appropriateness and problems of circumcision for converts of this type. Helena hears that her son feels he will only be securely a Jew (*bebaios*) when circumcised, and both she and her teacher employ every means in their power to make him see that his subjects will not tolerate their king engaging in these foreign practices. Izates tries to convince himself that zeal is more important than circumcision and that God would forgives choices made under constraint. But a fresh arrival, Eleazar, a hard-line teacher from the Galilee, finds the king reading the Law and tells him that he must also obey it. This tips the balance in favour of Izates' circumcision; a doctor is summoned. While ambiguities permit various interpretations of the understanding of conversion implied by the narrative, the author's expansiveness on religious matters is undeniable. Moreover, a real dispute about observance is reflected, tackled by the rabbis and, in a different dimension, by Paul and the early Christian church.[33] One is inclined to suppose that Josephus' source will already have carried this emphasis. More revealing about Judaism than about the Mesopotamian environment, the debate is directly relevant to the moral underpinning of the whole Izates narrative: God forthwith extends his protection to this hard-pressed ruler.

In addition, this narrative, unlike our previous one, but like the dynasty itself, has important connections with Judaea. Emphasis is

at Genesis Rabbah 46.11. This is not germane to our purpose here, but see Schiffman 1987: 301–302.

[33] Broer 1994; Schwartz 1996.

laid upon the visit, the benefactions, *philanthropiai*, during the famine and the death and burial there of Helena (XX 49–53; 94–95). It is also recorded that Izates sent five of his twenty-four sons and twenty-four daughters (XX 92)[34] to learn Hebrew, the ancestral language, and to acquire the Hebraic *paideia* in Palestine (XX 71).[35]

Sources of the two narratives

Attempts to specify sources for the narratives have yielded little more than speculation. Whatever these sources were, there is no reason to think that Josephus copied from them verbatim. The Adiabenian excursus is introduced by *kata touton de ton kairon*, Josephus' customary introductory words to a digression, and it has been argued[36] that this formula, together with the three unfulfilled Josephan promises in the excursus to treat of a particular subject in the future, suggest Josephus' slavish dependance on his source. But such unfulfilled promises occur in a number of places in the *Antiquities*.[37]

We can say, however, that the distinctive character of the narratives almost certainly derives from their sources. Jewish texts which incorporated a real grasp of Parthian matters seem to have been available to our historian. Josephus may, of course, have intensified their religious twist. One would not wish to foist any narrow purpose onto this source material, whether it be pro-monarchic propaganda or the promotion of conversion to Judaism. Its concern with Jewish practice could have been aimed mainly at satisfying readers and, indeed, the pure story element is so prominent that this could have provided quite enough justification in itself for the telling.

Oral input is not to be excluded. It is worth noting that most of the historical events involved occurred during Josephus' lifetime and some of them were of major importance to Jewry. The massacre at Seleukeia was surely a well-known incident. Josephus may well have met the Adiabenian prisoners/hostages in Rome and heard of the exploits of Izates from them.[38]

---

[34] Broer 1994: 150 suggests the figure is mythical.
[35] Neusner's suggestion: 1969: 66–67; 1976: 64–66, that the Adiabenian dynasty dreamt of ruling a great Jewish state and would have been in line to govern Judaea if the revolt of A.D. 66 had succeeded is not substantiated by any evidence.
[36] Schiffman 1987.
[37] See the list in Petersen 1958.
[38] So Neusner 1964: 60.

A single source for the Anilaios and Asinaios and the Adiabenian episodes has been proposed. Schalit (1975) categorized the entire document as propaganda on behalf of the house of Adiabene, demonstrating the divine favour which preserved them and their special claims as virtuous proselytes, and he conjectured that this material reached Josephus via the Herodian Agrippa II, with whose family the Adiabenian dynasty might conceivably have intermarried. We have seen that the episodes display common traits. But the argument for a single Adiabenian source is not sustainable, when there is no mention whatsoever of Adiabene in the Anilaios and Asinaios material. It should also be noted that Agrippa II and the Adiabenian royal family were on opposite sides in the Great Revolt.

Schalit further maintained that, while the supposed text reached Josephus in Greek, an Aramaic source lay behind it. He based himself on an ingenious interpretation of an unintelligible Greek word appearing in the majority manuscripts in connection with Anilaios' decision to do away with the husband of the woman he desired (XVIII 343). This word, *ktilion*, which qualifies *aner*, was traced to the Aramaic expression *ktila* in the idiom *gavra ktila*, 'a slain man', i.e. one who was fair game for all.[39] If that were correct, it would validate not the complete single-source hypothesis, but at least the conjecture of a source written in Aramaic close behind this portion of the material. However, for all the proposal's appeal, we are bound to ask how Josephus, writing fluent Greek, could suddenly and uniquely have swept an isolated Aramaic word into his composition. So, while general considerations make an Aramaic source highly likely, its existence is not demonstrable.

An older view[40] has it that Josephus drew on Parthian royal annals or chronicles to supply his chronology, his data on the kings and other material, but also on Jewish 'missionary literature' for the Adiabene narrative. Few scholars now see reason to believe in the existence of the latter genre, either in a Greek or in a near eastern context. We might rather suggest that some sort of popular royal biography from Adiabene, focussing on Izates, lies behind this part of the *Antiquities*. Such features as the attendance of the hero's birth

---

[39] Schalit 1975, supported by Cohen 1976, but criticized by Schiffman 1987: 309, n. 7, who also scotches the argument from a phrase of Daniel in Izates' prayer. Further doubts in Goodblatt 1987; Broer 1994.

[40] Widengren 1957, agreeing with Täubler 1904.

by a divine voice point to a biographical format:[41] perhaps the deploy-
ment of that motif served to gloss over the awkward fact, in Jewish
terms, that Izates' parents were brother and sister.

Assessment

The scholarly emphasis has been on investigating the possible lines
of transmission of these narratives. To study the material itself seems
more profitable. It may be useful to sum up our findings. On dynastic and other historical matters, Josephus' data is quite detailed and
reasonably accurate. It is preferable to be able to confirm his statements from other sources, but he has been found acceptable even
where that is not possible. On geography, he transmits some valuable information, but he fails, sometimes, to set this in a wide enough
context to make it fully intelligible. On court and aristocratic practice, he offers an engaging general impression and some plausible
detail, in which he shows a certain interest. Overall, he has rather
more ethnographical awareness than Tacitus and is more open-
minded. It is fair to bear in mind that Josephus is, after all, writing
Antiquities. The history of a people can scarcely do without an ethnographical element, even if Josephus found as he wrote that he needed
repeatedly to defer descriptive material to a forthcoming work to
which he referred as 'On Customs and Causes'.[42] This approach to
his own people perhaps leads to an increased alertness to the *mores*
of others.

Josephus' attitude to the Jews in Babylonia emerges as one of
identification. As for Parthian rule, it is an established fact and individual rulers may be friends or enemies, or, often enough, turn from
one to the other. To the Parthian aristocracy he tends to be hostile
and suspicious. For the native population, whether Babylonians,
Semites or Greeks, he has no special sympathy. In spite of this authorial distance, the Jews emerge as an active constituent of the Parthian
empire, a potential political and military force to weigh against others,
a valuable support for at least one monarch.

Finally, what can we say of the Parthian-Jewish traditions which

---

[41] On this as another legendary motif, Broer 1994: 152–154, rejecting, however,
any specifically Iranian affinities.
[42] Petersen 1958.

supplied our stories? The relationship between Jews, individually or collectively, and Parthian rulers, both failed and successful, is a key theme in the *Antiquities* excursuses, and this does, of course, reflect real diaspora preoccupations and anxieties. We are specifically reminded of the court material in the biblical books of Esther and Daniel, both of which are reflections of the Persian court. Here the material is Parthian. But it is tempting to ask whether the Jewish literature on which Josephus drew conceptualized the Parthian court in terms similar to those which had been used for depicting the Persian one, so as to be able to grasp and describe the fluctuations in the Jews' relationship with the monarchy in terms of the older literature.[43]

Yet we have detected a number of probable Parthian elements as well, and it is likely that these were originally embedded in narratives which, at the least, will have had a Parthian flavour as well as an Iranian element—inasmuch as the two can be separated.[44] I have sought to define what we possess. The picture is still far from clear. It is, however, in exploring the local roots and connections of these traditions, so as better to explain their genre and structure, their literary idiosyncrasies and their particular blend of fact and fiction, that further work might, I suspect, be productive.

BIBLIOGRAPHY

Barnes, T.D. 1989. 'Trajan and the Jews', *JJS* 40: 145–162.
Broer, I. 1994. 'Die Konversion des Königshauses von Adiabene nach Josephus', in C. Mayer, K. Müller, G. Schmalenberg (eds), *Nach den Anfängen Fragen*, Giessen, 133–162.
Cohen, N.G. 1976. 'Anilaeus and Asinaeus', *ASTI* 10: 30–37.
Colpe, C. 1974. 'Die Arsakidennachrichten bei Josephus', in O. Betz, M. Hengel, C. Haacker (eds), *Josephus-Studien. Untersuchungen zu Josephus, dem antiken Judentum und dem Neuen Testament, Otto Michel zum 70. Geburtstag gewidmet*, Göttingen, 97–108.
Dabrowa, E. 1994. 'Dall'autonomia alla dipendenza: le città greche e gli Arsacidi nella prima metà del I secolo D.C.', *Mesopotamia* 29: 185–198.
Debevoise, N.C. 1938. *A Political History of Parthia*, Chicago.
Goodblatt, D. 1987. 'Josephus on Parthian Babylonia (*Antiquities* 18.310–379)', *JAOS* 107.4: 605–622.
Horbury, W. 1996. 'The Beginnings of the Jewish Revolt under Trajan', in: P. Schäfer (ed.), *Geschichte—Tradition—Reflexion. Festschrift für Martin Hengel zum 70. Geburtstag. 1 Judentum*. Tübingen, 283–304.

---

[43] Widengren 1957 traces Iranian linguistic and other elements in Parthian culture.
[44] Thus Widengren 1957 sees the apocryphal book of Tobit as reflecting Parthian conditions as well as Iranian influences. The genre and subject matter of Tobit are, however, very different from those of Josephus' excursuses.

Kahrstedt, U. 1950. *Artabanos III und seine Erben*. Dissertationes Bernenses 1.2. Bern.

Karras-Klapproth, M. 1988. *Prosopographische Studien zur Geschichte des Partherreiches auf der Grundlage antiker literarischer Überlieferung*, Bonn.

Kettenhofen, E. 1994. 'Deportations' in *Encyclopaedia Iranica* 7.3. Costa Mesa, California, 297–308.

McDowell, R.H. 1935. *Coins from Seleucia on the Tigris*. Ann Arbor.

Neusner, J. 1964. 'The Conversion of Adiabene to Judaism', *JBL* 83: 60–66.

—— 1969. *A History of the Jews in Babylonia*. 1 *The Parthian Period*, 2nd edn. Leiden.

Neusner, J. 1976. 'The Jews East of the Euphrates and the Roman Empire 1st to 3rd Centuries A.D.', *ANRW* 9.1: 46–69.

Oppenheimer, A. 1983. *Babylonia Judaica in the Talmudic Period*. Beihefte zum Tübinger Atlas des Vorderen Orients, Reihe B, 47. Wiesbaden.

Petersen, H. 1958. 'Real and Alleged Projects of Flavius Josephus', *AJP* 79: 259–274.

Schalit A. 1975. 'Evidence of an Aramaic Source in Josephus. *Antiquities of the Jews*', *ASTI* 4: 163–188.

Schiffman, L.H. 1987. 'The Conversion of the Royal House of Adiabene in Josephus and Rabbinic Sources', in L.H. Feldman & G. Hata (eds), *Josephus, Judaism and Christianity*, 293–312.

Schippmann, K. 1980. *Grundzüge der parthischen Geschichte*. Grundzüge Bd. 39. Darmstadt.

Schottky, M. 1991. 'Parther, Meder und Hyrkaner. Eine Untersuchung der dynastischen und geographischen Verflechtungen im Iran des 1 Jhs. n. Chr.', *Archaeologische Mitteilungen aus Iran* 24: 61–134.

Schwartz, D.R. 1996. 'God, Gentiles and Jewish Law: On Acts 15 and Josephus' Adiabene Narrative', in: P. Schäfer (ed.), *Geschichte—Tradition—Reflexion. Festschrift für Martin Hengel zum 70. Geburtstag*. 1 *Judentum*. Tübingen, 263–282.

Stern, M. 1980. *Greek and Latin Authors on the Jews and Judaism*. 2 *From Tacitus to Simplicius*. Jerusalem.

Täubler, E. 1904. *Die Parthernachrichten bei Josephus*. Berlin.

Widengren, G. 1957. 'Quelques rapports entre Juifs et Iraniens à l'époque des Parthes', in *Volume du Congres. Strasbourg 1956*. VT suppl. 4. Leiden, 197–241.

Wolski, J. 1989. 'Die gesellschaftliche und politische Stellung der grossen parthischen Familien', *Tyche* 4: 221–227.

—— 1993. *L'empire des Arsacides*. Acta Iranica 32. Louvain.

PART THREE

THE JEWISH DIASPORA AND JEWISH EPIGRAPHY

CHAPTER SIXTEEN

WAS THERE A ROMAN CHARTER FOR THE JEWS?

In the cities of the pre-Christian Roman empire, Jewish groups were in general free to pursue their own religious and social practices and, at any rate until Hadrian, they were not persecuted by the Roman government; even the exceptional and provocative demands for worship which came from a tyrannical emperor such as Gaius Caligula do not amount to planned persecution. There is a contrast with the subsequent fate of the early Christians, whose cult was, of course, often suppressed by the emperor and his governors. There is also a contrast with the later plight of the Jews themselves under Christian rule.

Since, at the local level, Jews on the one hand and Greeks and natives on the other were often profoundly hostile to one another, the fact that the central government was on the whole proof against anti-Jewish pressure coming from below is indeed noteworthy. The edict of L. Flaccus as proconsul of Asia, by which in 62/1 B.C. he had confiscated the Jewish Temple contributions collected for export from his province, was never repeated, so far as we know (Cic., *Flac.* 66–69). Not only that: the Romans appear at times to have chosen to put their influence behind Jewish communities in dispute with their neighbours, as occurred to some extent in the cases which we shall discuss here, and did not cease even after A.D. 70.

One way—the traditional way—of depicting the situation is to say that the Jews happened to be protected by a special legal status, first conferred by Julius Caesar and then regularly renewed for over a century. On this view, Judaism was put in a supposed formal category of *religio licita* (the term originates with Tertullian), and the Jews had their special privileges (or rights) enshrined in a charter. Behind the picture perhaps lies the implicit analogy of the status of the Mediaeval Jew, which was indubitably defined by royal charters; royal protection gave the outsider the sole right to live where he did and to function in the economy. However, for the Roman world, this model is inappropriate. We shall see that, as a matter of fact, such a charter did not exist. But it is also in the nature of the situation that the Jews did not require it; for they were not intrinsically

alien bodies within homogeneous *poleis*; the later Hellenistic *polis* may
still have reserved the prizes of citizenship or political office for a
select number, but it accommodated considerable diversity of population and did not demand conformity. And we know that, with
the exception of overt participation in emperor worship, Jews could
and did involve themselves in the life of their cities—even, in some
cases, with the theatre and the gymnasium.

What Jewish communities needed was not the award of a special
status, but, more simply, public backing with muscle behind it. That
this was forthcoming will be seen to be largely due to political pressure and diplomacy on the part of the Jewish representatives and
especially of some powerful intermediaries, such as certain members
and adherents of the Herodian dynasty, whose other services were
of manifest value to Rome. The early Christians were to lack—perhaps they deliberately shunned—this kind of worldly protagonist and
as a result the balance is reversed in their case; the cities managed
to impel the Roman authorities (whose deeper instincts were by no
means wholly tolerant when it came to strange oriental cults) to take
action against distasteful trouble-makers.

For the most part, I would suggest, Jewish *nomoi* were not formally incompatible with city requirements, though they could become
contentious if the populace or the officials wanted to make life awkward. That was when the authorities might create difficulties about
Sabbath observance, close special food markets, deny ownership of
meeting places, prevent the export of funds. But it was not in the
very nature of the *polis* to exclude such activities and in the normal
course of events they must have proceeded without question. It is
for this reason that it is unsatisfactory to talk of the permanent need
for *privilegia* from Rome, while it is right to stress the repeated necessity for outside, i.e. Roman help. The citations of documents studied here will expose the distinction and assist in defining more closely
not only the dealings of Rome with the Jews but also, which is perhaps more difficult, the structural relationship between the Jewish
community and the city.

The Hellenistic background

Communities of Jews were among the many groups of resident aliens
to be found in the cities of the Greek East during the Hellenistic
period. Some were established early; at Alexandria and Antioch they

regarded themselves as among the founders of the city, while at Ephesus and elsewhere in Ionia they were believed, at least in some quarters, to have come as military colonists in the service of the Seleucid monarchy, whose holdings they were protecting.[1]

Setting aside apologetic claims of this kind, little can be known of their status; reconstructions have depended upon analogy, hypothesis and retrospection from the Roman era. Their historian, V. Tcherikover, quite reasonably maintained that these Jews came into the class of *katoikoi*, settlements of aliens with a measure of self-determination and technically separate from the city, but he believed that they were somewhat different from others in this category, in that they alone required an exemption from participation in the city cults. Since he could find no evidence of any such thing, he took it to be a matter which could not be explicitly expressed. But he still held that an implicit 'charter' of this kind, deriving from the monarch, underlay Jewish co-existence with the Greeks.[2] A letter of Antiochus III to an official named Ptolemy, apparently his governor of Coele-Syria, is quoted by Josephus in his *Antiquities* (XII 138 ff.); its genuineness was forcibly argued by Bickermann;[3] it is mainly concerned with the restoration and privileges of the Temple at Jerusalem, but it includes also the permission to have a government 'according to their ancestral laws'. And a similar expression is found in the second document of Antiochus III quoted by Josephus, which is addressed to his governor Zeuxis and deals with instructions for a two-thousand-strong Babylonian-Jewish military colony in Phrygia, that is to say, with a Diaspora community (*AJ* XII 147–153). Zeuxis is here told that the Jews are to be allowed νόμοις . . . χρῆσθαι τοῖς ἰδίοις.[4] The formula is unspecific; it would have entailed permission to follow the Mosaic law, together with a degree of separate political organization; though, as Tcherikover pointed out, only the beneficiaries will have given it real content. But we cannot follow Tcherikover in extrapolating from these two gestures, which concern would-be autonomous units, to conclusions about the terms on which Jews cohabited with others in or around new or established cities (except possibly in the special case of Alexandria); all the less so in that these declarations seem to be unparalleled until we get to the Romans.

---

[1] *AJ* XII 199 ff.; *CA* II 39.
[2] Tcherikover 1959: 82–89; 296–332.
[3] Bickermann 1935.
[4] Schalit 1959–60: 289–318.

In documents of the Roman period, a similar general formula is often repeated, both in association with further, specific provisions and by itself. The Seleucid legacy is indisputable. But that the situation inherited by the Romans was one in which special conditions for Jewish communal existence in the cities were already defined and familiar cannot be asserted. The Romans inherited a formula and retained the general *status quo*. But the implications of that formula and the precise nature of the previous arrangements are not readily discernible. The coming of Roman control to the East is not reflected in any surviving statement about the status or privileges of Jewish communities, and evidence of Roman involvement in such matters begins a good time after Roman rule in any area. This is noteworthy in the case of Asia Minor, where established communities at Ephesus and elsewhere in Ionia came into Rome's orbit with the creation of the province of Asia in 129 B.C.; yet it is not until two generations later that, as we shall see, we first hear of Roman intervention over Jewish difficulties. The inference to be drawn is not that relations were always smooth between the Jews and their pagan neighbours, but, more likely, that formal arrangements were generally not at issue; with the advent of a new power in direct control of the region, there was no question of seeking a new general definition of the position of the Jew in the *polis*, probably because there had not been any such generally understood definition in the past.

The documents in Josephus

For c. 50 B.C. onwards, there exists a body of evidence, in the shape of some thirty decrees and letters cited by Josephus, at several points in his *Antiquities*, concerning Jewish rights and privileges. The *Antiquities* are designed to recommend Judaism to the Greeks, and Josephus' purpose in offering these citations is overtly propagandist, and part of a tradition of apologetic, as we shall see. This in itself makes the documents difficult to handle; and partly because of the very considerable technical problems involved in interpreting them, they have received close scholarly scrutiny for over two centuries.[5] There are

---

[5] For a survey of the scholarship, which goes back to Protestant-Catholic controversies in the eighteenth century, see Bickermann 1953. See now Pucci Ben Zeev 1998.

numerous technical stumbling blocks: the order in which they are arranged is puzzling, their text is often corrupt and their dating sometimes uncertain. One response has been to doubt their authenticity altogether; but, although this kind of scepticism, which fell away with Mommsen's work on the Roman archives,[6] has recently been revived, every new investigation (even by the most sceptical of researchers) serves to confirm that the formal features of the documents are correct for genre and period, to a degree which makes it very difficult to conceive of them as forgeries.[7] Amidst much precise and learned discussion, the overall interpretation of the purpose and significance of what is in the dossiers tended to lag behind.

There are further reasons, too, for this neglect. The first lies in the overshadowing effect of one major uncertainty, that of the meaning of Jewish claims to citizenship in certain cities, notably at Alexandria. This is a complex and perhaps insoluble question; perhaps for that very reason it has appeared to offer a key to the fundamental issue, to be the basis of any definition of the Jewish situation.[8] By contrast, the descriptions of rights and privileges which emerge from our documents have assumed a secondary position in the overall assessment of 'the Jewish problem' in the ancient city. Yet citizenship as such was, at most, rarely claimed; and if by such claims the independent standing of a separate Jewish *politeuma* within a politically plural *polis* was meant (a view to which opinion has recently inclined),[9] that is unlikely to have arisen outside Alexandria, and its dependency Cyrene, for these two closely related cities had an unusual structure, not duplicated elsewhere. I shall not here contribute to the debates on citizenship, but rather aim to bring wider issues into the discussion.

The second reason why the documents in Josephus have not been adequately interpreted lies, I think, in the pervasive legalism of the standard approach. Jean Juster, the historian of Jewish institutions in the Roman Empire (himself trained as a lawyer), exemplified and

---

[6] Mommsen 1858.

[7] Thus Moehring 1975, exposes the formal features of the *acta* as in general appropriate to type and period, but proceeds to rest his revival of the case that they are apologetic Jewish forgeries on minor aberrations and corruption in the texts. For a discussion of indices of authenticity and the importance of correct diplomatic formulae, see Bickermann 1953: 33 ff.

[8] On this, see Tcherikover 1959: 309 ff. (with a guide to the extensive earlier literature); Applebaum 1974; Smallwood 1976: 124 ff.

[9] Applebaum 1974; Smallwood 1976; Kasher 1978.

promoted this tendency;[10] the relevant material is classed by him entirely under the heading 'Sources Juridiques'. We find the documents, or at any rate those associated with Julius Caesar, described as charters of Jewish rights, indeed as the 'Jewish Magna Carta'.[11] We shall see that, on close examination, they are less than this and do not add up to an overall definition of Jewish religious liberty. All in all, their legal power has been exaggerated, to the neglect of other prominent features. Yet it is perhaps as political statements that they are most important.

Omitting Seleucid decrees, the principal documentary material falls into three blocks, introduced at three separate points in Josephus' narrative, two in book XIV of the *Antiquities* and one in book XVI. We shall also bring in to the discussion the three Claudian edicts inserted by Josephus into book XIX of the *Antiquities*, two of the emperor himself and one of P. Petronius, the Syrian legate (280–291; 303–310). The last are more extensive texts of broader scope. They involve special problems of authenticity at certain points, problems which can only be touched upon in this paper. But they belong to the line of development begun by the earlier grants.

The first dossier, arising from the interest of Julius Caesar and, among the Jews, with Hyrcanus II, the Hasmonean high priest and ethnarch, comes from the years 49–43 (*AJ* XIV 185–267). Hyrcanus' involvement in the issuing of these documents is considerable, in spite of the fact that a range of different cities is concerned. The point at which Josephus introduces them into his narrative (XIV 185) is with Caesar at Rome, preparing for the war in Africa, i.e. summer 47 B.C.: a request reaches him from Hyrcanus, for confirmation of τὴν πρὸς αὐτὸν φιλίαν καὶ συμμαχίαν. A digression is then announced: 'it seemed necessary to me to set out all the honours and alliances made with our nation by the Roman people and by their emperors' (*AJ* XIV 186). What follows is not the comprehensive catalogue loosely promised here, but material relating to Hyrcanus of between the years 49 and c. 43 B.C.; this serves, among other things, to show something of the diplomatic connection between the Romans and the Jewish ethnarch in the period immediately pre-

---

[10] Juster 1914: vol. 1, 132–158, 213 ff. Juster's interpretation is analysed and reassessed by Rabello 1980: 662–762, from which it emerges clearly that the old framework is still widely accepted.

[11] 1914: vol. 1, 217; cf. Smallwood 1976; Grant 1973: 59; Rabello 1980: 692.

ceding the embassy described at XIV 185, as well as the confirmation of the relationship after Caesar's death (XIV 217 ff.).

The second small group in book XIV contains three documents associated with Antony's operations in the East during the early triumviral era (301–323) and is directed to Phoenician cities. Josephus cites these as demonstrating Roman pronoiva for the Jews (323). In fact, apart from abusing the tyrannicides, they aim to undo Cassius' acts in the region, which involved restoring Galilean Jewish property (especially that of Hyrcanus II, the ethnarch) lost to Tyre, and the release of enslaved Jewish captives.

In book XVI (160–178), decrees of Augustus, M. Agrippa and two proconsuls to cities in Asia and to Cyrene are reproduced, with the aim, as we shall see below, of showing Greeks (of his own day) that the ruling power had in the past treated its Jewish subjects well and granted them explicitly the right to follow their ancestral laws, customs and religion. No overt connection is made between the six citations given here, and an earlier famous episode, the narrative with which book XVI had opened, in which the appeal of the Jews of Ionia to Agrippa in 14 B.C. is reported. There the historian and minister of Herod, Nicolaus of Damascus, informs Agrippa and his council (this included kings and princes of the region as well as the Romans who were in authority) that these Jewish communities had been hindered in following their Law, and justifies their claim to Roman protection and to freedom. The speech ascribed to him by Josephus (XVI 31–57) is largely on the plane of theory, but includes allusions to earlier instances of Roman benefactions, mentioning specifically the honours paid by Caesar to Antipater, minister of Hyrcanus II and father of Herod the Great, in return for services rendered during the war in Egypt. No *ipsissima verba* are cited, but it is possible that some of the documentary material in the three Josephus dossiers we have mentioned was gathered together for the purpose of this defence; and probably (though there is no explicit evidence) it was cited by Nicolaus in that context in books 123 and 124 of his own Universal History, where we should expect to find a full record of his own achievements.[12]

---

[12] On Nicolaus' probable reproduction of the *acta*, Niese 1876; Viereck 1888: 91 ff., both of which claim Nicolaus as Josephus' sole source on the subject. For an early rejection of the latter view, see Mendelssohn 1877: 249–258. It is accepted by Momigliano 1934: 10 ff. See also Juster 1914: 154–155 and nn. A balanced

However, the somewhat haphazard order of the material and some strange intrusions would point to a mixed origin and suggest that it has been through various vicissitudes in the process of transmission, perhaps confirming in some cases Josephus' own claim to be citing documents which he himself found engraved on bronze tablets on the Capitol;[13] if this is true, it does not preclude some use of Nicolaus as well, which will be relevant when we come to discuss Josephus' personal understanding of the material he cites.

There is at least one case of a grotesque misfit, at XIV 247 ff., where a Pergamene decree incorporating a *senatus consultum* about territory taken from 'the high priest Hyrcanus' by 'Antiochus son of Antiochus' appears; this clearly relates to the international situation during the reign of Hyrcanus *the First*, i.e. John Hyrcanus, and Antiochus IX Cyzicenus is most likely to be the Seleucid monarch referred to. The document is in fact a sequel to the *senatus consultum* about Antiochus VII Sidetes, given in book XIII of the *Antiquities* (259–266), and has nothing at all to do with the Hyrcanus II dossier.[14]

Among the documents with which we are concerned, a minority are precisely datable, by Caesar's titulature or by the names of magistrates. But even within this category, apparently secure chronological indications have been doubted for external or technical reasons. Thus Julius Caesar's principal decree, confirming the high priesthood of Hyrcanus and his sons (*AJ* XIV 196–198), emanates from 'Gaius Caesar, Imperator, Dictator and Consul'; that leaves open which dictatorship and which consulship are intended and has allowed dates of 48, 46, 45 and 44 to be claimed for this important decree. However, it should be made clear that an impression of this kind is unsurprising, as the result of a complex transmission process, and

---

general assessment of Josephus' debt to Nicolaus, in Hebrew: Stern 1971: 375–394, and, more briefly, 1974: 227–233.

[13] *AJ* XIV 188; 265–267. Moehring 1975: 129–131, rashly rejects this claim with the assertion that no decrees will have survived the conflagration of A.D. 69 (Suet., *Vesp.* 8). Josephus may well have used local archives *in addition*: contact with Jews around the Greek world and visits are likely during more than twenty years spent at Rome. On both kinds of archive, see Laqueur 1920: 221–230.

[14] Juster 1914: 134–135. The matter in the document, principally concerned with directing a Seleucid monarch to restore Judaean territory, is appropriate to the reign of John Hyrcanus I and wholly inappropriate to the circumstances of Hyrcanus II. On the Hyrcanus I documents see Rajak 1981: 65–81, esp. 79 = Ch. 5 in this volume. There is no reason to refer any other documents to the earlier monarch on the basis of the one intrusion in *AJ* XIV as Th. Reinach does.

does not constitute an argument for the spuriousness of the text. Indeed, from a later period, that of Trajan, we have explicit evidence that some provincial texts of imperial edicts and letters sent to cities and proconsuls by previous emperors (Augustus, Vespasian and Titus) were considered 'parum emendata et non certae fidei'. It was for this reason that Pliny (*Ep.* X 65) requested from Trajan (or Trajan's clerks) that better versions of judgements concerning foundlings be extracted from the imperial archives (*scrinia*) and sent to him.

Among the proconsuls mentioned in our documents, some are not otherwise attested as long as the MSS reading be sustained; for example, the Publius Servilius Galba son of Publius, who appears at the head of a letter to the Milesians reporting a decision taken at the Tralles assize, permitting Jewish Sabbath observance and practices (*AJ* XII 244–246). Others, such as L. Lentulus Crus, who writes to the Ephesians about having exempted Jews who were Roman citizens in a hearing before his tribunal, and on whose decision a number of other rulings are based, are reasonably well-known (*AJ* XIV 228–229).[15] The names of officials appear to be the principal casualties of the transmission and to have a strong propensity to confusion and corruption. All in all, amongst over thirty documents, the text of seven alone is entirely acceptable and can stand as it is; the rest have required refurbishing of one kind or another, and sometimes substantive emendation. And even among the good texts, some cannot be attached to a particular year and internal evidence allows us only to put them within a general context.[16]

The geographical scope of the collections is worth some comment. The first one is principally concerned with the province of Asia and some Greek islands, the Antony material with Syria (Phoenicia) and book XVI with Asia and Cyrene. Overall, the dossiers range widely, involving at one point or at more several of the main regions of Jewish occupation at the time—Judaea (questions of tax reduction and possession of the port of Joppa), the coast of Palestine (Askalon), Phoenicia (Tyre and Sidon and Aradus), the Greek islands (Delos

---

[15] It is possible that P. Servilius Isauricus, *procos.* of Asia in 46 B.C., is referred to, as conjectured by Bergmann. For L. Cornelius Lentulus Crus, see *MRR* II, 256 and 276: consul in 49 B.C., he left Italy early in the civil war, to recruit troops in Asia for Pompeius, for whom he later fought at Pharsalus: a case of an anti-Caesarian forwarding Jewish claims.

[16] Full discussion in Juster 1914. For an analysis which seeks to relate the material concerning Palestine to the power politics of the period, see Momigliano 1934.

and Cos), coastal and inland Asia Minor (Parium, Ephesus, Sardis, Laodicea, Miletus, Tralles, Halicarnassus), Syria (Antioch) and Cyrenaica (Cyrene). Ephesus, as the chief city of Asia, makes repeated appearances, and several other cities figure as the recipients of more than one communication: Tyre, Sidon, Sardis and Antioch.[17] On the other hand, that a major Jewish centre, as Cyrene was, should make just one isolated appearance, is puzzling. Again, guided by our observation of St. Paul's journeys, as well as of later history, we note the absence of Cyprus and of cities of mainland Greece, not to mention Tarsus and Damascus. This peculiar selection could be an accident of survival, merely a reflection of the small proportion available to Josephus of what had once existed; also, it may be, of what he saw fit (perhaps with a degree of inattention) to reproduce for the Greek readers at whom his work was ostensibly directed (or for the Hellenised Jewish readers whom he no doubt also bore in mind). He does in fact say that he could, had he wished, have given us more of the same (*AJ* XIV 265). But there is perhaps another factor, for we should expect an arbitrary spread of geographical provenance to arise from the political process of appeal and *ad hoc* decision which lies behind the documents and which will be discussed below.

In type the documents are also diverse. Josephus categorizes those in book XIV as (1) decrees of senate and emperors; (2) resolutions of cities; (3) 'rescripts sent in reply to letters about our rights directed to provincial governors' (XIV 265). These categories are not in order of frequency or importance. Nor do they reflect Josephus' chosen sequence which, in the major collection in book XIV is *roughly* to put Caesar's decrees first, then letters of provincial governors, then city decrees—as is logical. He seems equally interested in all three

---

[17] Judaea: XIV 200–201; 202–210.

Other parts of Palestine: XIV 196–198 (decrees about Hyrcanus to be set up at Ascalon); XIV 323 (Aradus).

Phoenicia: XIV 190–195 (Sidon); 196–198 (Sidon and Tyre); 313 (Tyre); 319–322 (Tyre); 323 (Sidon); XIX 303–311 (Dora).

Islands: XIV 213–216 (Delos); 231–232 (Delos); 233 (Cos).

Syria: XIV 232 (Antioch).

Province of Asia: XIV 213–216 (Parium—but Paros, following Schürer); 233 (general provision); 225–227 (Ephesus); 235 (Sardis); 238–240 (Ephesus); 241–243 (Laodicea, Tralles); 244–246 (Miletus); 256–258 (Halicarnassus); 259–261 (Sardis); 262–264 (Ephesus); XVI 160–161 (Asia); 162–165 (Asia, Ancyra); 166, 167–168 (Ephesus).

Cyrene: XVI 160–161; 169–170.

Alexandria: XIX 286–291.

types. The spread is: one *senatus consultum* (the confirmation of Caesar's *acta*), eleven gubernatorial communications, not all of equal importance, seven letters of Julius Caesar, three letters of Mark Antony, of which one cites an edict (and the existence of other letters is mentioned), two edicts of Augustus, two of Claudius and five decrees of city councils or popular assemblies.[18] It is likely that Josephus chose to offer as wide and representative a sample as he could of the kinds of source from which favours to the Jews had emanated. From our point of view, what stands out is the variety of routes through which pro-Jewish decrees must have been processed. For a community of Jews there can have been no one obvious way of seeking what it wanted on such matters; and this is just what we should expect, given what we know about the administration of the provinces of Rome during the Caesarian, triumviral and early imperial eras.

The significance of the documents

The question is whether any of this material had, in the Romans' perception, a general application or any validity as precedent, beyond the specific context. What the Jews, *qua* claimants, tried to make of it should be considered only later. The former is not an easy question to answer. Once more book X of Pliny's correspondence shows a structurally comparable situation, over a different kind of issue, at a considerably later date. On the question, again, of foundlings, we there see Trajan distinguishing between imperial rulings which could be meant to apply over the whole empire, and ones intended for certain provinces: 'There is nothing to be found in the records of my predecessors which could have applied to all provinces. There are, it is true, letters from Domitian to Avidius Nigrinus and Armenius

---

[18] *Senatus consulta*: XIV 219–222 (ratifying Caesar's *acta*).

Communications of governors: XIV 225–227; 228–229; 230; 233; 234; 235; 237–240; 244–246; XVI 171; 172–173; XIX 303–311.

Edicts and letters of Julius Caesar: XIV 190–195 (letter containing a decree to be set up); 196–198; 199; 200–201; 202–210; 211–212 (speech); 213–216.

Letters of Mark Antony: XIV 306–313; 214–218; 319–322; 323 (reference only).

Edicts of Emperors: XVI 162–165 (Augustus); 166 (Augustus); XIX 280–285; 286–291 (Claudius).

Edicts of M. Agrippa: XVI 167–168; 160–170.

Decrees of cities: XIV 231–232 (Delos); XIV 241–243 (Laodicea); 256–258 (Halicarnassus); 259–261 (Sardis); 262–264 (Ephesus).

Brocchus, which ought perhaps to be followed, but Bithynia is not one of the provinces with which his rescript deals' (*Ep* 10.66.1–2).[19]

To strengthen his case, Josephus at times introduces documents with something of a nourish, *as though* they concerned Jewish status universally; for example, at XIV 228 ff. he writes, 'these then are the favours which Dolabella granted to our people when Hyrcanus sent an envoy to him'. But what is in the texts often belies the sweeping introduction; in the instance just given, the wording is: 'Those Jews who are Roman citizens and observe Jewish rites and practise them in Ephesus, I released from military service before the tribunal . . .'. Here Ephesus evidently figures as the chief city of Asia, and this document is just one within a series about the same issue and the same area. The province as a whole is deemed bound by it, and its officials (224) as well as other cities (227) are to be notified. But it goes no further. If we consider the texts themselves, we are hard put to it to find any with an entirely general reference. Even Julius Caesar's edict of exemption of the Jews from his ban on *collegia*, which appears by way of reference within the citation of his letter to Parium (*AJ* XIV 215),[20] is given in a form which refers only to 'the city', i.e. Rome, so that its extension to the empire would seem to be a matter of interpretation. The *senatus consultum* posthumously validating his ruling on the Jews (περὶ ὧν . . . ὑπὲρ Ἰουδαίων ἔκρινε καὶ εἰς τὸ ταμιεῖον οὐκ ἔφθασεν ἀνενεχθῆναι—*AJ* XIV 221) is entirely vague as to its reach.

It is among the edicts in the corpus that we might expect to find statements of general principle, but even those fall short.[21] An edict of Mark Antony as triumvir (XIV 369 ff.)[22] issued in both Greek and Latin, about the restoration of Jewish property previously sold (which

---

[19] Following the Aldine reading: see Sherwin-White 1966: n. ad loc. Cf. X 109, for a reference to laws covering only Pontus-Bithynia.

[20] Παριανῶν is normally taken to mean the people of Parium, in the Troad. Schürer conjectured Παρίων, to refer to Paros, because dealings with the Jews of Delos are reported in this same document. On the measure, see Smallwood 1976: 135, n. 52.

[21] See Millar 1977: 255–259. Unlike other forms of imperial pronouncement, edicts had, in principle, no addressee and were not always merely responses to individual initiatives; if they laid down general rules, these remained in force after the death of their author; none the less, some just gave instructions related to particular circumstances. In the case of the Jews, this factor is acknowledged by Juster 1914 215–218, but does not influence his assessment of the 'legal' issues.

[22] Which can be dated to 41 B.C., when Antony was regulating the affairs of Asia and raising support in the East.

is in any case not really concerned with Jewish rights) appears unrestricted in scope, but in fact addresses itself specifically to the city of Tyre and is dealing with the undoing of Cassius' arrangements or violations. A more hopeful candidate is the letter of Augustus about the Jews of Asia, reporting a decision of himself and his council 'under oath' and stating that 'the Jews are to follow their own customs in accordance with their ancestral laws . . . and that their sacred funds are to be inviolable and may be sent up to Jerusalem and that they need not offer bonds on the Sabbath or on the eve of it after the ninth hour. And if anyone is caught stealing their sacred books . . . he shall be deemed sacrilegious and his property shall be requisitioned by the Roman people's treasury' (*AJ* XVI 162 ff.). Yet this is clearly limited in its addressee and by its concluding instruction that it is to be conspicuously displayed in the Temple dedicated to the imperial cult by the *koinon* of Asia. What is more, the decision is a response to complaints of ill-treatment from Asia and Cyrenaica, brought to Augustus by envoys (it is unclear whether the two issues arose at precisely the same time or were separate), and the council-meeting from which it emanated would therefore have been convoked to consider these complaints, not to address itself to the Jewish question in general.[23] There follows, in the narrative of Josephus, an earlier letter to Norbanus Flaccus (probably consul in 24 B.C.) which *looks* entirely general: 'Let the Jews, however many they be, who have been in the habit of following their traditional practice and contributing sacred money for despatch to Jerusalem, carry this out without obstruction' (*AJ* XVI 166). But the next items quoted, a letter from Agrippa to Ephesus, and then one from him to Cyrene, are presented as though they dealt with the same problem as the Norbanus Flaccus letter and therefore with Asia in particular.[24]

---

[23] This document is often dated to A.D. 2–3 by a reference in it to an honorific vote for C. Marcius Censorinus, *cos.* 8 B.C. and subsequently *procos.* of Asia, where he died, at the same time as M. Lollius, in A.D. 2. However, his proconsulate is likely to have been a few years earlier: Syme 1984: 872. Bowersock 1964: 207–208, adopts the date given on the marginal note in the Latin Josephus which has XI beside the *trib. pot.* of Augustus, and supposes that Censorinus was in the East also in 12 B.C. (not as proconsul). The inscription would be set up at Pergamum (not Ancyra, as suggested in Scaliger's ingenious but unjustified emendation).

[24] To be dated within his stay in the East between 17 and 13 B.C., and probably after Nicolaus' pleadings of 14 B.C. One C. Norbanus Flaccus was consul in 38 B.C., the other in 24 B.C., and there is no evidence to show which became proconsul of Asia. The consul of 38 is more often identified with this Flaccus, on the weak grounds that the documents in Philo and Josephus, which refer to Augustus

In Philo's *Legatio ad Gaium*, Augustus' goodness to the Jews is set
out by way of example for his great-grandson (309–319). The first
princeps' philosophical bent of mind, it is said (he had not merely
sipped but feasted upon philosophy daily!), led him to admire the
Jerusalem Temple. He expressed his benevolence by telling the governors of Asia to let the Jews alone hold meetings (since their gath-
erings were schools of temperance and justice) and send contributions
and envoys to Jerusalem. Here a letter of Norbanus Flaccus is inserted,
one which was sent to the Ephesian archons and which itself cited
in indirect speech Augustus' letter to him: 'the Jews, wherever they
may be, are in the habit, following tradition, of assembling and contributing money for despatch to Jerusalem. He did not want them
to be obstructed from so doing. He therefore wrote to us so that
you might know that he orders things to be done in this way'. With
this indirect form of citation, we should not expect complete accuracy,
and Philo is evidently drawing at one remove on the same letter to
Flaccus as Josephus was to use. We have seen that Josephus may
well have exploited Nicolaus of Damascus' material at this point,[25]
and it is highly likely that Philo had the same source for his document (unlike Josephus, he does not even claim first-hand knowledge
of any archives or inscriptions). What Philo says about this does not
disturb our conclusion that the matter is one of Asia alone. Indeed,
Philo is unequivocal. We should not be misled by the words 'the
Jews, wherever they may be' which refer not to the new ruling, but
to the age-old Jewish practice of the Temple levy. Augustus, appre-
ciating that the Jews were ubiquitous, no doubt saw that he had a
general problem on his hands, but, quite characteristically, was not
impelled to formulate a policy to cover all cases.

It is perhaps significant that the problem with which the Augustan
statements are mainly concerned is that of *collecting funds for Jerusalem*.
That may be not only because the issue had become particularly
controversial, but also because this particular facility was a con-

---

as 'Caesar', are seemingly pre-27. For counter-examples, see Smallwood 1970: 309,
n. *ad* 315. The later consul can be assigned to a vacant governorship of Asia at a
date which makes it possible to retain the association of his activities with the appeal
of the Jews of Ionia, between 17 and 13 B.C., and is therefore preferable. So
Smallwood 1970 (though her chronological argument that Josephus recounts the
appeal of the deputations from Asia and Africa after describing the rebuilding of
Caesarea is tenuous). Syme 1979: 267, prefers the consul of 28 as the proconsul of
Asia, on the grounds of Augustus' titulature in Josephus' edicts.
[25] See above, n. 12.

comitant of Julius Caesar's licence for Jewish associations: this connection emerges clearly from the decrees to Parium, where it is stated
that the Jews alone had been allowed by Caesar to form *thiasoi* or
to *collect money* in Rome, or to have common meals (*AJ* XIV 216).
Here Augustus had an important Caesarian ruling to be guided by,
which he chose to interpret as relevant to the provinces.

The early decisions about Asia and Cyrene were important and
encouraging for Jews, but what happened in other provinces was
still wholly undetermined. For all we know, it remained so in many
cases.

From the papyrus text of Claudius' letter to the Alexandrians, it
appears that Augustus may have also granted to the Jews of Alexandria
the right to pursue their own customs.[26] This presumably refers to
a specific enactment, and, as Tcherikover points out, it is reasonable to expect Augustus to have dealt with the Jewish-Greek conflict
in Alexandria after the annexation of Egypt.[27] Still, we may wonder
why Claudius refers to the Augustan precedent in such vague terms:
'I conjure the Alexandrians to behave gently and kindly to the Jews,
who have lived in the same city for a long time, and not to dese-
crate any of the religious practices associated with the cult of their
God but to let them observe their customs as they did under Augustus'
(85–87). We cannot put any weight on the fact that Claudius' edict
to Alexandria, in the version of Josephus, refers specifically to Augustus'
continuation of the Jewish ethnarchy and to the preservation of equal
Jewish citizenship by his prefects.[28] For both these alternative claims
are suspect. The one about the ethnarchy contradicts Philo's statement that a *gerousia* was established after the ethnarch died (*Flac.* 74),
and that about citizenship seems (at least on most interpretations) to
contradict the papyrus letter.[29] Thus the two assertions about Augustus
cannot be relied upon and we must accept the common verdict that
the edict, though in all probability a largely genuine document (and
not just a version of the letter), has been falsified in places.

---

[26] *P. Lond.* 1912 = *CPJ* II, No. 153, I. 87.

[27] *CPJ* II, No. 153, nn. *ad* 82–88, p. 49.

[28] In the edict the Jews are Ἀλεξανδρεῖς (an official designation for citizens) and
had ἴση πολιτεία with the Alexandrians: in the letter, they are said to dwell 'in a
city not their own'. See *CPJ* I, 70, n. 45.

[29] *CPJ* I, *loc. cit.*, 'parts of the edict which are in accordance with the letter are
to be regarded as authentic; those that are in direct contradiction are to be looked
upon as forged and so should be disregarded'.

This Josephan edict is in fact suspect at one further point material to our argument, when it ascribes an articulated policy of general tolerance to Augustus (*AJ* XIX 283), saying that he wished 'the separate peoples to be subject to their own customs and not to be compelled to violate the religion of their fathers'. The latter is probably a Jewish elaboration on a less ambitious original, for this picture of the empire as a consciously plural and tolerant society finds its parallel only in another claim made by Jews, the assertion of Nicolaus of Damascus, as composed by Josephus, that 'the happiness which the whole human race now enjoys through you, we can measure by the fact that it is possible for people in every country to go through life and prosper while valuing their own ethnic traditions' (*AJ* XVI 37). Yet even Nicolaus did not go as far as to claim that the *princeps* himself had deliberately sought to foster ethnic traditions, only pointing out that this was a valuable *consequence* of empire.

We are left with very little; and Augustus' dealings with Alexandrian Jewry should therefore not be overestimated.

Finally, we may hope to find some trace of an overall policy of Augustus in the second of the two Claudian edicts cited by Josephus, that directed to 'the rest of the world'. Claudius does not want to withdraw in any Greek city Jewish rights which had been protected by Augustus: μάλιστα δὲ δίκαιον κρίνων μηδεμίαν μηδὲ Ἑλληνίδα πόλιν τῶν δικαίων τούτων ἀποτυγχάνειν, ἐπειδὴ καὶ ἐπὶ τοῦ θείου Σεβαστοῦ αὐταῖς ἦν τετηρημένα (*AJ* XIX 289). He goes on, therefore, to say that Jews ἐν παντὶ τῷ ὑφ' ἡμᾶς κόσμῳ should follow their traditions unimpeded, and, in return for this *philanthropia*, should moderate their own behaviour. But what is actually suggested is just that Augustus had made decisions city by city. It is rather the emperor Claudius who puts it all together—for the first time—and arrives, in his own peculiar way, at a new kind of sweeping pronouncement. This edict of Claudius, datable to the years A.D. 41/2, is shortly afterwards invoked by P. Petronius, his governor of Syria, in a reproof to the people of Dora in Phoenicia who had put a statue of the emperor in the synagogue there. The Claudian enactment, described as an edict, which permits the Jews to live according to their own customs, τοῖς ἰδίοις ἔθεσι (*AJ* XIX 299–307), and as the Greeks' fellow citizens, συμπολιτεύεσθαι, is given considerable prominence by this benevolent governor who, like Claudius, regarded himself as a friend of the Herodian dynast Agrippa I. Petronius' edict is some confirmation for certain parts of Josephus' version of Claudius' general edict.[30] We are led to ascribe innovation to the emperor Claudius; soon after his accession, he was evidently shaken by the pressures of those Greek-Jewish crises in both Palestine and Alexandria, which his predecessor Gaius had created and he had to resolve, to utter in his own inimitable way a general policy of toleration (if we may call it that) for Jewish observances. Even now, however, the policy is not elaborated, and the pious phrases are given no specific content in the general edict. It is fair to say that Claudius is not doing much more than expressing his goodwill towards the practice of the Jewish cult and establishing a lead for Greek cities to follow. This still falls well short of being the 'Jewish Magna Carta'.

Before Claudius, the rulings are generally on specific issues, with sometimes the addition of the familiar general formula—that the Jews are to be allowed to pursue their own ancestral laws or customs (νόμοι or ἔθη).[31] In such cases, the formula is certainly no more than a fine-sounding verbal gesture: even Juster recognized that no prescription flowed from it automatically.[32] As for the specific matter included, that depends, evidently, upon the particular points at issue in the dispute which has given rise to the enactment. There are bones of contention which recur, doubtless, not only as a result of the common situation, but also because what happened in one place had an influence upon others. The most noteworthy concessions are: exemption of Jews who are Roman citizens from military service, with which the first dossier is principally concerned;[33] the freedom to perform customary rites without interference and to observe the Sabbath; the right not to appear in court on the Sabbath, which is a particular aspect of the preceding grant; the right to collect and despatch the Temple tax, which is the main issue in book XVI;[34] and permission to have a separate meeting place or market,

---

[30] Petronius' edict twice alludes to Augustus: to an edict from him (307) and to privileges granted by him (311). The legate's knowledge evidently derives from Claudius' edict, and he overvalues the Augustan example offered there.

[31] The formula also occurs earliest in modified or weakened forms, especially in the subordinate clause κατὰ τὰ πάτρια αὐτῶν ἔθη.

[32] Yet this is contradicted by his interpretation of the liberty of worship clause as a universal edict of toleration. An edict of toleration requires identifiable prescriptions.

[33] Military exemption: XIV 223 (Asia); 226 (the same decision, Ephesus); 228 (Ephesus); 230 (Asia, Ephesus); 234 (Ephesus); 236, 237–240 (Ephesus). Cf. Rabello 1980: 741, n. 320. That this exemption was sought in some cases does not mean that Jews found it contrary to religious prescription to serve under any circumstances.

[34] Freedom of worship, collection and Sabbath observance; XIV 216 (Parium

and a measure of judicial autonomy (though this may be specific to Sardis, where there seems to be a long tradition of acceptance of the Jews).[35] There is considerable variation in the constituents of the package even within a province, in spite of the normal applicability of precedent from city to city.

Exchanges of beneficia

To explain this, we turn, at last, to some observations on the transactions behind the texts. This is not a matter discussed directly by Josephus, apart from the episode in book xvi about Nicolaus' advocacy of the Jews of Ionia, and the problems under Claudius. On the whole, Josephus' documents are largely disembodied. But internal evidence taken from the decrees, together with some very brief surrounding material, offers important clues. The first—and again this is not unexpected—is the personal nature of the dealings. Every batch of documents is part of an exchange of beneficia, and in most cases this exchange arises ultimately from and caters to a personal connection which involves gratitude and mutual esteem. The distribution of privileges to cities, communities, or shrines as tokens of esteem for meritorious individuals is a familiar pattern in the Roman empire.[36] And it may be suggested that, while such origins should not in any way formally limit or invalidate what is decided, they do impart a degree of potential impermanence or instability. There is a telling denial of this in the speech ascribed by Josephus to Nicolaus of Damascus as advocate of the Jews of Ionia, when he is made to insist that earlier Roman grants to the Jews were an acknowledgement of Jewish loyalty, but would have been valid quite apart from this (XVI 48). The denial reveals precisely that the matter was in some doubt. For no amicitia can be entirely secure and any clientela may turn sour. Revocation of the decrees would not, of course, have

---

and Delos—assembling and feasting); 235 (Sardis—meeting and market place); 242 (Laodicea, Tralles); 244–246 (Miletus—Sabbath, rites and food); 259–261 (Sardis); 262–264 (Ephesus—sacred funds. Sabbath, etc.); XVI 162–5 (Sabbath, sacred funds); 167–168 (Sabbath, sacred funds); 169–170 (sacred funds); 171 (sacred funds); 172–173. Another privilege is exemption from having troops billeted or for paying for this.

[35] At a later date, archaeological evidence suggests that the Jews had a prominent place there. See Kraabel 1979: 83–88.

[36] See Millar 1983: esp. 77–78, for valuable remarks on the operation of centrally-granted beneficia.

to follow, but their authority could suffer. In one sense, therefore, they are things of the moment.

The starting point is the career of Hyrcanus II, the weak Hasmonean ruler, whose succession in Judaea to his mother Salome Alexandra had immediately been met with an armed challenge in 67 by his brother Aristobulus II. Though Hyrcanus seems then to have given up power and the high priesthood, his nagging ambitions were continually revived by a resolute minister, Antipater, father of the future Herod the Great. Pompey's annexation of Judaea in 63—encouraged by the Jewish aristocracy—had been followed by the restoration of Hyrcanus' nominal control (perhaps now as 'ethnarch' rather than king). However, the Jewish state had been severely reduced and Judaea itself was effectively under direct rule, organized in toparchies; thus, apart from the high priesthood, it was not easy to discern a real role for Hyrcanus. Aristobulus was still popular, and in 49 B.C. was released (not for the first time) from internment, as part of an abortive scheme designed to achieve Caesarian support in the East. The failure of this scheme drew Caesar to Hyrcanus, but their new and precarious relationship evidently required to be cemented by means of mutual assistance and favours.[37] Hyrcanus (with Antipater) could offer military help and Jewish loyalty. What he needed was not merely confirmation of his titles, as high priest and ethnarch, not merely dignity, which came in the alliance made in 47 under Caesar's auspices, between the Romans and himself (*AJ* XIV 187; 194–197),[38] but also a clearly-defined role. Palestine became more hazardous for him than ever with the rise of the young Herod in the 40s B.C. What better, then, than for Hyrcanus' ethnarchy to be interpreted as a tutelage over *all Jews everywhere*; for its potential as the protection of the Diaspora, τῶν Ἰουδαίων προϊστῆται τῶν ἀδικουμένων, to be highlighted (*AJ* XIV 197)?[39]

---

[37] For reconstructions of these events (which have to derive almost exclusively from the narrative of Josephus' *Antiquities*) see Revised Schürer: I, 267–276; Smallwood 1976: 30–43. On Caesar rewarding Hyrcanus and the Jews' εὔνοια to him, see *AJ* XIV 212. At 216, the εὔνοια and ἀρετή are ascribed to the Jews alone, but Hyrcanus is perhaps alluded to (as well as Jewish assistance to Caesar at Alexandria).

[38] According to Josephus' text, Hyrcanus personally is here party to the alliance, not the Jewish people, as Smallwood 1976: 42, suggests.

[39] The first series of Hyrcanus documents, deriving from Julius Caesar himself, concerns concessions to Palestine; but the Herodian king remains almost as prominent in the Diaspora transactions.

The main group of documents in book XIV is introduced by
Josephus as an expansion of the narrative at the point where Hyrcanus
is shown seeking a confirmation of Caesar's friendship, φιλία καὶ
συμμαχία, with him (*AJ* XIV 185). The first document, a Caesarian
letter to Sidon, contains the text of a decree, to be set up in Latin
and Greek, describing Hyrcanus' devotion and his contribution of
1,500 troops to the Alexandrian war, and confirming his ethnarchy
and high priesthood and the friendship between him and his sons
and Julius Caesar. 'And if, during this time, any problem shall arise
concerning the Jews' way of life, it is my pleasure that the decision
should rest with them' (195). There is a surprising end-piece, which
shows as clearly as anything can the curiously casual way in which
particular issues make their appearance: 'I do not approve of troops
being given winter-quarters (with them) or of money being exacted
(from them)'. Bronze tablets setting out Hyrcanus' powers are to be
set up in the Capitol, and at Sidon, Tyre and Askalon, and the
decree is to be sent to quaestors and magistrates in the cities (it is
unclear whether the same cities or others are meant) (199).

A decree, apparently of 44 b.c., about tax reductions for the Jews
(we cannot tell where) is linked to the permission to Hyrcanus to
fortify and control Jerusalem (200). Further honorific decrees for
Hyrcanus, containing also tax and other concessions for the Jews of
Palestine and Phoenicia precede, in Josephus' narrative, the important letter to Parium containing Caesar's ruling on *collegia*.

After Caesar, P. Dolabella (whom he had chosen as consul for
44)[40] wrote to Ephesus in response to a communication of Hyrcanus
which had explained that Jewish soldiers could not fight on the
Sabbath and needed special food. Dolabella accepted this and also
allowed them to follow native custom and to assemble and make
Temple contributions (223–227). Precedents from within the province
of Asia and also a decree of Delos, on the question of the levy, are
appended to this document; none the less, in 44, the crucial initiative had evidently come from Hyrcanus. We learn that Sardis followed the lead of the Ephesians (227–232).

With the coming of Antony to the East, the picture remains the
same, except that now Herod is described by Josephus as appear-

---

[40] *MRR* II 317 and 344: he took Syria as a consular province, but, in Asia, killed
C. Trebonius, and on reaching his province was cornered by Cassius.

ing beside the long-lasting Hyrcanus in the negotiations with Antony, largely for the purpose of sustaining himself against his Palestinian enemies (*AJ* XIV 301 ff.). However, Antony's decrees make mention only of the ethnarch Hyrcanus, in the manner which had become habitual. These decrees, which expand freely on the triumvir's military and political circumstances, appear to welcome the gestures and crowns offered at Ephesus by Hyrcanus' envoys (who arrive via Rome); the restoration of Jewish property supposedly lost to the Tyrians during Cassius' period of control is a *quid pro quo* (*AJ* XIX 297 ff.). A generation later, when Nicolaus of Damascus appeals on behalf of the Jews of Ionia to Agrippa and his council, he invokes in similar vein the services once performed by Antipater on behalf of Caesar, services deserving to be recompensed not only by honours to the individual but also by benevolence to his people and a confirmation of the old alliance (*AJ* XVI 51 ff.). Hyrcanus, for whom Antipater had worked, is not mentioned by name: Nicolaus naturally prefers to concentrate attention on the father of his own master, Herod. After half a century, when Claudius issued his second edict, he presented it as an act of consent to a petition of 'my dearest friends Agrippa (I) and Herod (of Chalcis)'. Agrippa's role in the accession of the emperor should not be overlooked when these transactions are assessed : according to Josephus it had been the Herodian who advised Claudius to accept the guards' offer of the empire and then reported to him on the senate's state of truculent disarray (*AJ* XIX 236 ff.; cf. Dio 60.8.2).

The personal factors which I have outlined are not simply a background to the documents; these factors are relevant not merely to an account of their genesis, but must be seen also as influences on the character of the decrees themselves and on their functioning, so far as we can envisage it.

The decrees in operation

In other respects, too, it is helpful to construe the *acta* as part of a political process and not just as the bare, ambiguous and unsatisfactory legal statements which they appear to be on the page. If not sought by the Jews' patrons (for a mixture of motives) then concessions will have been pursued, preserved and publicized by the communities themselves or their envoys. At Sardis (XIV 235), it was

'Jewish citizens' who approached L. Antonius with the claim that they had always had their own meeting place and separate juris-diction in internal matters. They were perhaps prompted by news from Ephesus of the decision of L. Lentulus of 49 B.C. exempting Jews from army service.[41] In Cos, the praetor tells the local magis-trates that he had received envoys from the Jews asking to see copies of certain senatorial decrees in their favour; he recommends safe conduct for the envoys (XIV 233). Further instances of this behav-iour will be visible in other cases discussed below. It is all entirely in keeping with the normal stimulus-response pattern of Roman administrative decision-making. There are good examples among the triumviral documents from Aphrodisias of official decisions being made available to interested parties other than those to whom they are addressed: the initiative evidently had to come from the gov-erned, not from the authorities.[42]

But in the case of Jewish rights, the phenomenon is even more marked, for several reasons. First, the frequent alienation of Jews from their neighbours served only to strengthen the natural ties between Diaspora communities,[43] and those ties facilitated the effective diffusion of texts and encouraged appeal to precedent. Secondly, the Jews in the cities were constantly dependent upon Roman support in any struggle to hold their own against Greek authorities whose attitude was often hostile. A vicious circle was soon no doubt cre-ated, in which renewed appeal to Roman intervention served to incur further local hostility. Thus their eyes were directed Romewards more than those of other groups. This was especially so during peri-ods of political instability in Roman politics, when they will have reacted to the threat of losing their protection, and that is in part the explanation for the burgeoning of grants of privilege during the civil war and triumviral periods when Rome might have been expected to be more, rather than less, neglectful. Third, this tripartite rela-tionship meant that Roman directives could well go by default. It is

---

[41] Juster 1914: 142–144, distinguishes a series of several Asian documents depend-ent upon Lentulus' original exemption edict, including the Sardis decision, which contains different privileges, but perhaps comes as a consequence; this would explain why it is sandwiched between exemption decrees in Josephus.

[42] Reynolds 1981: Nos. 10–12.

[43] As an instance of such ties, consider the personal life of the historian Josephus, who married first a Palestinian captive, then a Jewess from Alexandria, and lastly one from Crete (*V* 414–415; 426–427).

to be expected that the cities would sometimes slide out of their obligations, and the evidence suggests that they did, for we have instances both of recalcitrant recipients and of trouble recurring in one and the same place. Events which concerned Laodicea (in Caria) during the 40s offer a useful demonstration (XIV 241–243). The magistrates, ἄρχοντες, write to the proconsul of the province,[44] saying they have a letter from him which an envoy of Hyrcanus (one Sopatrus) had brought them. This stated that Hyrcanus had sent documents claiming for the Jews rights of Sabbath observance and freedom of worship, and that no one was to do the Jews an injury because they were the Romans' friends and allies. The letter went on to state that an objection to these claims had already been lodged in person before the governor by the Trallians' representatives, but that he had overridden the objections and insisted that the instructions be carried out. The Laodiceans were accepting the letter and would deposit it in their files, εἰς τὰ δημόσια ἡμῶν γράμματα. They conclude with the non-committal sentence 'and as to *the other matters* on which you have instructed us, we shall take care that we are free from blame'. What stands out is, on the one hand, the *double* involvement of Hyrcanus' emissaries in the business, first in sending documents to the governor, and second in bringing the gubernatorial letter to the Laodicean magistrates; and on the other hand, the *overt rejection* by the Trallians of the claims embodied in Hyrcanus' documents and transmitted by the governor, together with the indications that the Laodiceans too were intending to drag their feet and offering no clear sign of obedience with regard to the Jewish matter. The general impression given by the document, as Josephus cites it, is favourable to the Jews; a careful reading of the text and reconstruction of the situation show it to be less so.

Another development at a Trallian assize, as we learn from a proconsular letter (XIV 244–246), was that a Milesian citizen, one Prytanis, son of Hermas, (it is not indicated that he was himself Jewish) appeared before the proconsul[45] and said that Jews were being attacked at Miletus, and prevented from observing the Sabbath,

[44] The proconsul's name in the MSS is C. Rabellius son of Gaius; the emendation Rabirius is perhaps desirable, but still does not yield a known official in the province. There is no apparent way of dating the document.
[45] This time he is the P. Servilius Galba of n. 15 above. This letter must not be taken with the Pergamene decree which follows it directly.

and their own rites and their dietary laws, *in spite of this governor's previous instructions*. The arguments of both sides were rehearsed again and the governor's terse conclusion was that the Jews were not to be impeded from following their customs. Again, then, there is something like a continuous dispute going on, with the Jews actively invoking an earlier favourable decision which had been disregarded.

The story at Ephesus reveals troubles extending over a much longer period. L. Lentulus, the consul of 49 B.C., exempted certain Jews who were Roman citizens from military service before his tribunal (XIV 228–299; 234). Some time later, perhaps in 42 (if the proconsul's name mentioned at XIV 263 is to be read as M. Brutus), the assembly, on the proposal of the magistrates, passed a decree enforcing the governor's instructions that Jewish observances were not to be interfered with: the decree stated that no one should be prevented from or fined for keeping the Sabbath, and this gives us an interesting glimpse into what had previously been going on. It concluded with the ineffectual exhortation that 'the Jews should be permitted to do everything that was in accordance with their laws'. But, around 14 B.C. M. Agrippa had to write to Ephesus, to say that the Jews should have control over their Temple funds, in accordance with ancestral customs, and that any men who stole from these should be treated as temple robbers by law and dragged away from asylum. We see from this that the Jewish cult had not been granted the same recognition as other cults. Finally, Agrippa has written to the praetor to say that no one is to make the Jews appear in court on the Sabbath; here is direct evidence that the city's decree of (?) 42 had been contravened, and apparently with impunity.

Only when we get to P. Petronius' edict to Dora, do we find, at any rate in Josephus' florid version, a severe castigation by the legate of the 'insanity' shown by the city's leaders in disregarding Claudius' edict, and the threat that they themselves will be treated as implicated in any offence committed, if they do not hand over wrongdoers to the legate's centurion, so that they can be brought to trial (*AJ* XIX 303–308). When we bear in mind that Josephus, whose purposes, as we shall see, are avowedly partisan, presents only what looks relatively advantageous to the Jews and puts it in as favourable a light as he can, we realize that the decrees left much to be desired from the point of view of their beneficiaries. Furthermore, of Jewish claims lost to the record, many must have been rejected, whether *ab initio*, by the Roman authorities, or at the second stage, in the

Greek cities. The record has been preserved by Jews, because the documents were valuable to them, and they will not have been interested in reports of proposed decrees which failed or ones which were ignored. And that is quite apart from the question of how the city populations reacted to decrees which *were* passed by their own councils or in assembly—how often they chose to flout them. Penalties are specified at Halicarnassus: 'and if anyone, whether magistrate or private citizen prevents them, he shall be liable to the following fine and owe it to the city' (*AJ* XIV 258).[46] But how often were the fines imposed? The later insistence of P. Petronius is lacking at this earlier stage. Much will have depended on the state of community relations in particular places at particular times. In the face of overwhelming hostility, such tenuous support as the *acta* were intended to supply can have been of little avail.

None the less, the decrees were all that the Jews had and they clung to them tenaciously and relied on them vigorously in their political battles. Under threat, they could call on records which they regarded as containing established rights—δικαία, δικαιώματα, ἀξιώματα—which could be described, in other contexts, as privileges—φιλάνθρωπα, δεδομένα, συγκεχωρημένα[47]—the difference in wording reflecting only a difference in attitude or emphasis. We can see how this might have worked from Josephus' report of the case argued by Nicolaus of Damascus before Marcus Agrippa on behalf of the Jews of Ionia (*AJ* XVI 275). The complaints were the usual ones: they could not observe their own *nomoi* because of being hauled into court on the Sabbath, the contributions destined for the Temple had been taken away from them, they were being made to perform military duties in spite of previous exemption. Nicolaus' speech in Josephus is a plea for relief from ill-treatment of all kinds, presented in a broad perspective. Favourable decrees from Rome of a former period are the basis of the claim; yet these are invoked in a sweeping allusion, without legal precision, and used to buttress the case as a whole, not individual heads: 'we therefore hold, mighty Agrippa, that we should not suffer harm, nor be ill-treated, nor prevented from observing our customs, nor have forced upon us by these people what we

---

[46] On the difficulty of imposing sanctions in this kind of situation, Juster 1914: 238–239.

[47] For the vocabulary of rights, privileges and concessions, see Juster's valuable list, 1914: 222, n. 2. Josephus' distinctions are not rigorous—rights are termed privileges if the stress is on their coming from a donor.

do not force upon them. For that is not only just, but was earlier granted by you. Moreover, we could read out to you many decrees of the Senate, and tablets deposited in the Capitol, which were clearly issued after our loyalty to you had been tested, and which would be valid even without any such circumstances' (*AJ* XVI 47–48). Josephus' wording implies that documents were *not* read out on this grand occasion, that to conjure with them was enough. While we must allow that this is a historian's version of the speech and of the occasion—two historians', in fact, for before Josephus, Nicolaus will already have written up the events in his own works—it is likely that the shape of the occasion is realistically reported. Josephus tells us categorically that 'the Jews were not arguing about set points, as in a court of law, but it was a plea about the violence they were enduring' (57).

What is remarkable is that the documents were thought to have a key role to play even in an avowedly non-legal dispute. They were not valued for their specific content, but as symbols of respect for the Jews; not as exact precedents to be analysed, but as encouragements to good treatment, of a kind which could be particularly meaningful for a conservative administration, such as the Roman empire indisputably was.

Josephus' understanding of the documents

It is also to be noted that it is in exactly the same spirit that the decrees are exploited by Josephus in his *Antiquities,* an openly apologetic history with a purpose relevant to his own time.[48] In the well-known conclusion to the dossier in book XVI, he apologizes thus: 'if I often mention these texts, it is in order to reconcile the nations and to remove the causes of hatred which have taken root in the thoughtless among us and among them'. With this aim in mind he has produced evidence that 'in earlier times we were treated with every respect and were not prevented by those in power from practising any of our ancestral customs, but were even assisted by them in our cult and in honouring God' (XVI 174–175). Thus the worth

---

[48] For remarks on Josephus as defender of the Jews of the Diaspora in the 80s and 90s, see Rajak *Josephus*: Epilogue. A study of the apologetic thrust in Josephus' later writings is wanting.

of the texts to him is not that they uphold precise privileges which might be under threat, or assert distinct rights which had been challenged, but rather, through a reminder of the attitudes underlying earlier grants, make a large case for the acceptance by pagans of the practice of Judaism (as well as of paganism by Jews).

A further indication that Josephus is more concerned with the general theme of esteem for the Jews than with the details of Jewish status is to be found in another of his expressions of intent, the preamble to the book XIV dossier (187–188): 'and here it seems to be necessary to make public all the honours given our nation and the alliances made with them by the Romans and their emperors, in order that the other nations may not fail to recognize that the kings both of Asia and of Europe have had respect for us and admired our courage and loyalty. But since many people refuse out of malice to believe *what has been written about us by Persians and Macedonians*, because these texts are not found everywhere and are not deposited in public places, but exist only among us and some other barbarian peoples, whereas there is nothing that can be said against the Roman decrees, for they are positioned in public places in cities and are still to be found engraved on bronze tablets on the Capitol . . . it is from the latter documents that I shall take my demonstrations.' In other words, the author claims, and is proud, to be making the same point as had been made about other periods with different proofs, one which he could perfectly well have made now with that same older material. In this, he is in part expressing a literary self-identification, aligning himself with the tradition in post-exilic Jewish writing of quoting documents, especially the texts of treaties and concessions between foreign rulers or nations and communities of Jews.[49] Citation of documents is not entirely alien to Greek historiography—witness the late Thucydides—but it is particularly a hall-mark of near-Eastern writing, starting with Ezra's decrees of Cyrus, and making a pronounced appearance in the Roman treaties and Seleucid decrees of Maccabees 1 and 2.[50] Josephus refers to these very antecedents when he speaks about what was written by Persians and Macedonians and

---

[49] See Momigliano 1977: 31–33.
[50] Ezra 1:2–4; 4:9–22; 5:8–17; 6:3–12; 7:12–26; 1 Macc. 8:23–30 (alliance with Rome); 10:18–20, 26–45; 11:30–37; 13:36–40; 40:20–23 (letter from Sparta), 27–47 (inscription put up by the Jews); 15:1–9, 16–21 (letter from the Romans); 2 Macc. 9:19–27; 11:17–39 (letters of Antiochus and of the Romans). Some of these documents are authentic, others patently falsified.

he allows himself some liberty in suggesting that their apologetic goals had been just the same as his.

But the literary context is not all. Josephus writes with an eye to the present, and interprets the Roman documents in the light of his own experience. He finds them a valuable support to his general argument; indeed, on the hypothesis which we have accepted, that their provenance is varied and that Josephus did not simply reproduce a literary source (such as Nicolaus), the labour was not inconsiderable. He must have known what he wanted. At the same time, he is somewhat cavalier about detail, in a way which should not be put down simply to the 'sloppiness' for which some scholars condemn him;[51] this comes out in the impenetrable ordering of the documents, where some small groups form sequences, while others, as we have said, appear chronologically haphazard, with no apparent rhyme or reason; and the difficulties are demonstrated by Juster. I would suggest that we may best account for this phenomenon with the explanation that Josephus, like the original recipients of the grants, was concerned with their use in political argument and not very interested in their exact legal content. His viewpoint and his concerns are, in fact, not very different from theirs, and this is natural enough, for there is continuity as well as development between their Diaspora and his. He will have been a small child at the time of the Claudian decrees, he was an emissary from Jerusalem to Rome in A.D. 64, and from 71 he himself was a Diaspora resident.

An incident which occurred in that very year and is reported in the *Jewish War* (written in the 70s) bridges the gap between Claudius and the publication in the 90s of the *Jewish Antiquities*. It shows that specific rights were still (or perhaps even more) important in the aftermath of the fall of the Temple. It reveals the Jewish population clinging desperately to a small privilege which had evidently come to represent security for them. The pagan citizens of Antioch, doubtless emboldened by the failure of the revolt in Palestine, tried to expel the Jews from the city. When Titus objected, they proposed instead to destroy the bronze tablets on which Jewish rights, δικαιώματα, were inscribed (*BJ* VII 100–111). It is in another Josephan context that we hear incidentally what those rights were. For in *Antiquities* 12 (119–123) it is alleged that Seleucus I Nicator gave the Jews

---

[51] Especially Cohen 1979.

πολιτεία and made them ἰσότιμοι; as proof, one specific and limited privilege is offered—that the gymnasiarchs gave the community financial assistance to enable it to purchase its own oil. There follows a prospective statement to the effect that *this* was the privilege which the Antiochenes first sought to revoke during the Jewish revolt, and that Mucianus had upheld it; later, at some unspecified time after A.D. 70, they challenged Jewish πολιτεία more fundamentally. I shall not speculate upon what is meant by that. What matters is that Josephus is unequivocal about the supreme importance for the Jews of the oil privilege, in spite of a certain vagueness about exactly what was inscribed on the tablets. Perhaps he did not know.

Thus the structure of the situation was not fundamentally altered by the revolt, even with Jewish fears intensified and Roman disapproval now in the air and to some extent expressed in the removal to the *fiscus Iudaicus* of the former two-drachma Temple contribution. There is still every reason to suppose that, in looking back to the period when the pattern was established, and then to its Augustan and Claudian sequel, Josephus would have had no difficulty in grasping its essentials, and would have adequately understood the meaning and function of the pro-Jewish decrees, and the nature of the politics behind them.

The decrees were weapons in a polemic which was often intense and fierce. Josephus, by his literary labours, contributed consciously to that polemic. It is not surprising if in his presentation he overestimates respect for the Jews, exaggerates the scope of grants in their favour and tells us nothing of the times when Roman support was denied.

The Jewish need for protection

There is no doubt that the Jews, as organized communities, were often at odds with their Greek neighbours and eager for Roman backing which could forestall or terminate trouble. To say this is not to suggest that relations were always and everywhere bad, nor to deny the existence of Greeks who were well-disposed; there was also successful integration of individual Jews into their environment (even without apostasy), and even a degree of Hellenization and cultural assimilation by most Jewish groups. Paradoxically, Josephus, in arguing for harmonious co-existence, highlights situations of tension, because those situations often conclude in the legal or quasi-legal interventions which constitute the only tangible evidence he can produce of good treatment of the Jews. In arguing his case, he tends also to be suggesting its opposite.

To enquire into the causes of conflict requires a separate analysis, which would centre not on the places that figure in the documents (about whose Jews, for the most part, we know almost nothing), but on the familiar episodes from Alexandria and from the Greek cities in and around Palestine and occasionally further afield, as at Antioch, before and after the first revolt; and it would take into its purview the Trajanic revolt in the Diaspora. What must be said is that the *manifestations* of the conflict took the form of direct attacks, both by the city populations and by their authorities (there was no great gap between the two in a Greek city) upon Jewish cult practices. Paganism is often said to have been tolerant and accommodating. But it was not so towards a monotheistic religion centred upon an invisible God, a religion which could not readily be assimilated, in the usual fashion, into the existing system. From the provisions of the decrees, the problem might be taken as being simply that the Jews did not "fit in" to the cities where they lived: they were an anomaly and an inconvenience, for example in being unavailable on the Sabbath; and a drain on the cities' finances and solidarity, especially through their collections for Jerusalem. To those who are willing now to accept more or less at face value the ancient pagan charges of Jewish misanthropy, such an interpretation of the decrees will come readily; for, on this view, the essential feature of the situation is the intractable exclusiveness of a people different from others and always difficult and inflexible.[52] A milder version of this approach lies behind Juster's formulation of the Jewish predicament in the Greek city—'persecutions ou privileges';[53] the implication here is that exemptions were intrinsically necessary, as Judaism prevented the fulfilment of essential obligations in the *polis*: not to make special concession to the Jews *was* to persecute them. It is a mere assumption that the Jews of the cities needed or sought such complete separation or that they always insisted upon special arrangements; and it is an assumption which should be examined.

---

[52] So e.g. Smallwood 1976: 123–124; Pucci [Ben Zeev] 1981:15; Sherwin-White 1967: 93; Balsdon 1979: 67.

[53] 213–214.

As far as the evidence of the decrees goes, it looks rather as though in many cases they became necessary only because of deliberately engineered attacks on Jewish practices. It seems that Jews were made to appear in court on the Sabbath not by accident, but as a provocation, precisely because it was known that this would cause offence. The money destined for Jerusalem was, as we have seen, sometimes seized by the cities: not, surely, as an administrative act, because the collection was deemed illegal, but as one form of violent assault; out of this arose the need for a special grant of explicit entitlement and protection. Simple dislike came first: this need cause no surprise. Moreover, as far as the Greeks went, this dislike attached itself to the apparent oddity of Jewish religious practices. The rhetoric in Josephus' version of Nicolaus' speech before Agrippa is instructive: Jewish customs are to be praised for their excellence and antiquity, but 'it is these customs which they would outrageously deprive us of by snatching away the money which we contribute in the name of God, and by openly committing sacrilegious theft, by imposing taxes upon us and taking us to court and other public business on our feast days, not because this is required by the contracts, but to insult our cult, towards which they feel a hatred which—they know it as well as we do—is neither just nor legitimate' (XIV 45). The speaker is partisan and his language indignant; those on whose behalf he speaks may have had an exaggerated sense of being persecuted. None the less, his representation is both credible and fully consonant with what we have gleaned from the documentary evidence, and that makes it worthy of serious attention.

It may also be noted that Roman administrative tolerance—the term is regularly applied here too—also had severe limits. It was not difficult as an administrative measure to direct others sometimes towards enforced toleration; on home ground, it was another matter, and the reign of Tiberius saw the Jews expelled from the city. It is true that Nicolaus' speech envisages the Roman empire as deliberately favouring ethnic diversity; but this, we have suggested, was a Jewish, not a Roman interpretation.

The *acta* then, are the product of struggles, and of animosities within Greek cities of a kind which we know (as at Alexandria and in the conflicts of 66–73 in many cities) could issue in serious and bloody riots. That is why Josephus, in his last work, *Against Apion*, is able to distinguish the Law of the Jews from that of Greeks by the fact that Jews are prepared to die rather than abandon any part of theirs.[54] We can readily see that for those who lived in such circumstances and with such convictions, every battle for rights and privileges was a battle for their Law and therefore, potentially, for their physical survival.[55]

BIBLIOGRAPHY

Applebaum, S. 1974. 'The Organization of the Jewish Communities in the Diaspora', in S. Safrai & M. Stern (eds), *The Jewish People in the First Century*. Compendia Iudaicarum ad Novum Testamentum I.1. Assen/Philadelphia, 464–503.

Balsdon, J.P.V.D. 1979. *Romans and Aliens*. London.

Bickermann, E. 1935. 'La charte Seleucide de Jerusalem', *REJ* 100: 4–35 = E. Bickermann, *Studies in Jewish and Christian History* II (1980), 44–85.

—— 1953. 'Une question d'authenticité: les privilèges Juifs', *Annuaire de l'Institut de Philol. et d'Hist. Orient.* 13. Brussels, 11–34 = *Studies in Jewish and Christian History* II (1980), 24–43.

Bowersock, G.W. 1964. 'C. Marcius Censorinus, Legatus Caesaris', *HSCPh* 68: 207–210.

Cohen, S.J.D. 1979. *Josephus in Galilee and Rome: His Vita and Development as a Historian.* Columbia Studies in the Classical Tradition 8. Leiden.

Grant, M. 1973. *The Jews in the Roman World*. London.

Juster, J. 1914. *Les Juifs dans l'Empire romain: Leur condition juridique, économique et sociale*, 2 vols. Paris.

Kasher, A. 1978. *The Jews in Hellenistic and Roman Egypt* (Hebrew, with English summary). Tel Aviv.

Kraabel, A.T. 1979. 'The Diaspora Synagogue: Archaeological and Epigraphic Evidence since Sukenik', *ANRW* II, 19.1: 81–88, 477–510.

Laqueur, R. 1920. *Der jüdische Historiker Flavius Josephus*. Giessen, 221–230 = A. Schalit (ed.), *Zur Josephus-Forschung*. Wege der Forschung 84. Darmstadt (1973), 104–112.

Mendelssohn, L. 1877. 'Zu den Urkunden bei Josephus', *Rhein. Mus.* 32: 249–258.

Millar, F. 1977. *The Emperor in the Roman World (31 B.C.–A.D. 337)*. London.

—— 1983. 'Empire and City, Augustus to Julian; Obligations, Excuses and Status', *JRS* 73: 76–96.

Moehring, H.R. 1975. 'The *Acta pro Judaeis* in the *Antiquities* of Flavius Josephus; a study in Hellenistic and Modern Apologetic Historiography', in J. Neusner (ed.), *Christianity, Judaism and other Greco-Roman Cults: Studies for Morton Smith at Sixty*, vol. 3. Leiden, 125–158.

Momigliano, A. 1934. 'Ricerche sull'organizzazione della Giudea sotto il dominio romano', *Ann. della Reale Scuola Normale Superiors di Pisa, Lettere, Storia e Filosofia*, ser. 1, vol. 3. Pisa, 183–231 (repr. Amsterdam, 1967).

—— 1977. 'Eastern Elements in Post-Exilic Jewish, and Greek, Historiography', in *Essays in Ancient and Modern Historiography*. Oxford.

---

[54] *CA* I 43; II 219, 233. Josephus appears to speak of martyrdoms for the Law within living memory. And, whatever these were, his strong interest in the matter shows it to have active significance for him in this polemical work.

[55] I am grateful to Michael Crawford and to members of the Editorial Committee of *JRS*, especially Fergus Millar, for improving this paper; to Alan Wardman for valuable assistance; and to Arnaldo Momigliano for responding to an earlier draft.

Mommsen, Th. 1858. 'Sui modi usati da' Romani nel conservare e pubblicare le leggi ed i senatusconsuiti', *Annali dell'Instituto di Corrispondenza Archeologica* 30: 181–212 = *Gesammelte Schriften* III (1907), 290–313.

Niese, B. 1876. 'Bemerkungen über die Urkunden bei Josephus Archaeol. B. xiii. xiv. xvi', *Hermes* 11: 466–488.

Pucci [Ben Zeev], M. 1981. *La Rivolta ebraica al tempo di Traiano*. Pisa.

—— 1998. *Jewish Rights in the Roman World. The Greek and Roman Documents Quoted by Josephus Flavius*. Tente und Studien zum Antiken Judentum 74. Tübingen.

Rabello, A.M. 1980. 'The Legal Condition of the Jews in the Roman Empire', *ANRW* II, 13: 662–762.

Rajak, T. 1981. 'Roman Intervention in a Seleucid Siege of Jerusalem?' *GRBS* 22: 65–81 = A.5 in this volume.

Reynolds, J. 1982. *Aphrodisias and Rome: Documents from the Excavation of the Theatre at Aphrodisias*. Journal of Roman Studies Monographs 1. London.

Schalit, A. 1959–60. 'The letter of Antiochus III to Zeuxis regarding the establishment of Jewish military colonies in Phrygia and Lydia', *JQR* 50: 289–318.

Sherwin-White, A.N. 1966. *The Letters of Pliny*. Oxford.

—— 1967. *Racial Prejudice in Imperial Rome*. Cambridge.

Smallwood, E.M. 1970. *Philonis Alexandrini Legatio ad Gaium*, 2nd edn. Leiden.

—— 1976. *The Jews under Roman Rule from Pompey to Diocletian: A Study in Political Relations*. Studies in Judaism in Late Antiquity 20. Leiden.

Stern, M. 1971. 'Nicolaus of Damascus as a Source for Jewish History in the Herodian and Hasmonean Periods', *Studies in Bible and Jewish History Dedicated to the Memory of Jacob Liver* (in Hebrew). Tel Aviv, 375–394.

Stern, M. 1974. *Greek and Latin Authors on Jews and Judaism*, 2 vols. Jerusalem.

Syme, R. 1979. *Roman Papers*, edited by E. Badian, vol. 1. Oxford.

—— 1984. *Roman Papers*, edited by E. Badian, vol. 3. Oxford.

Tcherikover, V. 1959. *Hellenistic Civilisation and the Jews*, trans. by S. Applebaum. Philadelphia.

Viereck, P. 1888. *Sermo Graecus*. Göttingen.

CHAPTER SEVENTEEN

THE JEWISH COMMUNITY AND ITS BOUNDARIES

The Jewish Diaspora

After rejecting the theological animus, as well as the historical absurdity, in claims that Judaism effectively vanished when Christianity arose, we may still wonder whether the followers of a faith apparently organized around self-separation could really play a full part in any plural society. And yet we see the Jews doing just that in the post-70 era, as already before it. This discussion examines that seeming contradiction, suggesting reasons why it may in fact be inappropriate to speak of Diaspora Jews as separated from their neighbours by metaphorical high walls and, on the other hand, enquiring about the meaning and the limits of the types of interaction known to us.

In Acts, Peter offers the centurion Cornelius a grossly unfair representation of the Jews as forbidden by their religion 'to visit or associate with a man of another race' (Acts 10:28). Discounting the exaggeration, we may still be inclined to feel that there is an element of truth here. We may recall that pagan outsiders, even more than Christian, saw Jews as misanthropic, self-sufficient, unwilling to share a table with any but their own kind or even to render basic human assistance.[1] This is indeed the regular, virtually automatic response of Roman writers to Jews, or to the thought of them, and before that of certain Hellenistic Greek writers. Take away the hostility, and here too there may remain a degree of verisimilitude. After all, Balaam had long-ago prophesied for Israel a future as 'a people that dwells alone, that has not made itself one with the nations' (Numbers 23:9). And Philo's comment (*Life of Moses* I 278) had explained this in terms of the distinctiveness of Jewish customs. Modern experience readily leads us to believe that the life-arrangements required by completely orthodox Judaism, as we today know it, presuppose an intensely communal existence and scarcely leave room for more than superficial mixing.

---

[1] Stern 1974: 1980.

It is undeniable that the crystallization and the increasing influence of rabbinic Judaism constituted by far the most prominent development in Jewish life and thought over the first five centuries of the Christian era. From the inside, this is usually viewed as a supreme achievement (which it undoubtedly was, by any intellectual standards); from the outside, often with wilful ignorance, as a regrettable, even a culpable, narrowing. The fact, either way, cannot be forgotten; yet what it means for the communities under consideration is by no means self-evident.

The communities of Jews who lived in the cities of the Roman Empire were in no sense a marginal phenomenon. The first-century authors Philo and Josephus tell us that in their day there existed already a large and ubiquitous Jewish Diaspora. In some places its origins went back to long before Alexander the Great. We may perhaps distrust their exaggerations, as also the supposed citation from Strabo about the Jewish people (Josephus, *Antiquities* XIV 115) that 'it has already made its way into every city, and it is not easy to find any place in the habitable world which has not taken this race in and which it does not dominate'. Josephus appears to have picked up a nasty remark in Strabo (or else quoted from Strabo) and then attempted to turn it to his own purpose.[2] Josephus' statement in the *Jewish War* (II 462–463) that, at the war's outbreak in 66 A.D., every city in Syria had in it both Jews and Judaizers, has a somewhat greater claim on our attention. However, we do not have to rest on these subjective utterances to be confident that Jews were to be found in number in many of the cities of the eastern empire, and of course in Rome, and tentatively to suggest that they are likely to have spread around the west as well by the mid-first century A.D. Inscriptions attest urban settlement; while we cannot say much about rural settlement, it has been suspected for Cyrenaica, where an inscription refers to the Jews of the region,[3] and is clearly demonstrated by papyri for Egyptian villages. There is no need to enter into discussion here about highly speculative figures.

Diaspora communities were grouped around the institution of the συναγωγή, also called προσευχή, of which there would be more than

---

[2] In annotation in the Loeb edition of Josephus (Vol. 7: 509), Marcus suggests that ἐπικρατεῖται ὑπ' αὐτοῦ means 'makes its power felt' in quite a neutral sense, rather than 'is dominated by', but this does not accurately render the Greek.

[3] Applebaum 1979.

one in a large city—eleven are attested for Rome in the catacomb epitaphs.[4] Inscriptions reveal synagogue officials to have been promi- nent figures. But the word συναγωγή, which means assembly, unlike προσευχή, meaning prayer, carries an important ambiguity, and we cannot always tell whether a building is intended, or merely the par- ticular community, viewed as an association, *conventus*, or σύνοδος in Greek.[5] Nor is it impossible for both implications to be carried at the same time. Thus, while we can readily say that the synagogue was central to Diaspora Judaism, we are in no position to say how far the religious life of individuals expressed itself through the syn- agogue. Furthermore, we have clear knowledge from inscriptions that synagogues might consist of more than just halls for the reading of the Law and the recital of prayers, and might, as at Macedonian Stobi[6] or in the Theodotus synagogue of pre-70 Jerusalem,[7] contain also dining-halls (Stobi had a *triclinium*) or hostelries or other com- munal facilities. Therefore, the labelling of an individual as belong- ing to a particular synagogue becomes even less easy to interpret.

If the role of synagogue affiliation and the demarcation there between the religious and the social are opaque to us, the practices and observances of Diaspora Jews in their daily lives are also hard to penetrate. But we can make an attempt to discern something of the implications of rabbinic Judaism for their world, and then to conclude whether it is indeed likely that the demands of that sys- tem will have cut them off from the life of the city around them.

Rabbinic Judaism

A rough and uncontroversial description of rabbinic Judaism must be the starting-point. Rabbinic Judaism is that form of religion which took shape after the failure of the first revolt against Rome and the destruction of the Temple in 70 A.D., and in some measure in response to those events; its foundations, however, had been earlier laid by the Pharisees. In Palestine, this replaced the sectarianism which had marked the period between the Maccabees and the destruction, even if the ideal unity that rabbinic literature likes sometimes to depict

---

[4] Leon 1960.
[5] Applebaum 1974: 490.
[6] *CIJ* 694; Lifschitz 1967, no. 10; Hengel 1966.
[7] *CIJ* 1404; Liftschitz 1967: 79; Levine 1987: 17.

was not achieved. The emphasis of the rabbis was on study of the Torah (the Pentateuch) and its interpretation, in an ever-increasing body of oral doctrine, whose main thrust was towards norms of behaviour (*halakhah*), though its range was in fact much wider. The production of written texts began with the Mishnah, a summary of practice in commentary form which was composed in about 200 A.D., and was supplemented by the longer Tosefta, perhaps a generation later; the process reached its climax, though in no sense its conclusion, with the massive and heterogeneous compilation of the sixth century, known to us as the Babylonian Talmud. It is noteworthy that this was produced not in Palestine but in the Aramaic-speaking Diaspora. The institution of the synagogue, with its regular Torah readings, and (in Palestine) its Aramaic translation, had emerged already before 70; but it assumed a new importance in the absence of the Temple cult (which had drawn many pilgrims) and ensured that the sacred text was widely familiar. It is probably right to see the development of rabbinic Judaism, and perhaps also its beginnings, as in some way a response to the Christian challenge, a sharpening of self-definition (a fashionable term in this field); yet it is highly significant that no such purpose is made explicit: everything in the system is explained in its own terms, with ultimate recourse to divine requirements. Some see the concern of the rabbis with purity and with establishing correct action in every particular as the construction of a fortification against fatal erosion or undermining through compromise of essentials. 'The Rabbis', wrote Momigliano, 'humane and alert as they were, chose or were driven to create a new Jewish culture, which touched only the fringes of Greek culture.'[8]

No less significant than the content of rabbinic Judaism, was the centralized authority structure, based first at Yavneh (or Jamnia), on the coast of Judaea, but later elsewhere; this may be described as a strengthened replacement of the focal point that Jerusalem had been. The rabbinic academy (*beth midrash*), the court of law associated with it,[9] the ordination of one another by the rabbis, who might also be spoken of as *hakhamim* or sages,[10] and the prestige of these scholar-

---

[8] 1987: 401.

[9] Levine (1989: 76–83) argues that the sources do not attest the existence of a 'Great Sanhedrin' after 70, contrary to common opinion, and he allows only local courts associated with specific rabbis.

[10] Levine 1989: 141–142.

teachers as individuals and as a collective elite, were the components of rabbinic Judaism. The Patriarch (*Nasi*) was the leader of Palestinian Jewry (and perhaps of other Jews too) and in the eyes of the Roman government; he had supreme status by the beginning of the third century if not before, and he was always the upholder of rabbinic authority. Rabbis who were especially esteemed issued ordinances (*takkanot*) and prohibitions, but those were few at first. The evolution, elucidation and transmission of a much larger and more complex (even sometimes contradictory) network of *halakhot* (which we might call accepted rulings) was the main part of the rabbis' business. Practical rulings about the calendar (which determined the observance of the festivals and many other aspects of Jewish life) were among both the earliest and the most fundamental of the powers assumed by the central institutions. Jewish piety, as understood by the rabbis, rested on the fulfillment of a very large number of approved acts, *mitzvot*, of either a ritual or an ethical character; it was indispensable that these be performed in a spirit of love. They could account, in their totality, for all areas of an individual's life. All activities were seen as sanctified, but study was strongly promoted as a value in itself; one may detect an element of professional interest in the latter. This ever-growing system was generated by way of the spoken word. Large-scale literary formulation of principles was not undertaken until the Mishnah was completed.[11]

We can discern that the authority of the rabbis did not establish itself immediately; naturally, however, the setbacks suffered by the earlier leaders were not preserved for the record by their successors. For all periods, it is a matter of uncertainty how much of the *halakhah* which the rabbis debated so enthusiastically was seen as theoretical. There were other limitations too. Those *mitzvot* which were to do with land-use (tithing, sabbatical year, etc.) were applicable only to the area regarded as being within the notional confines of the land of Israel. But even there, throughout the Mishnaic period and probably beyond, a whole section of the population, known as *amei ha-aretz* (literally, peoples of the land) appear to have ignored them, with no worse consequences than incurring the snobbish contempt or the abusive comments of the rabbinic class.[12] For the Galilee, it

---

[11] Stemberger 1991: 31–44; Safrai 1987: 71–81.
[12] Oppenheimer 1977; Levine 1989: 112–117.

has been argued[13] that, before the third century, the rabbis attempted to control the population only in matters of specifically *religious* observance, and not at all in practical matters, and that even in the first sphere they were largely unsuccessful. Although there was, on this view, universal observance of the basic requirements of Judaism— the sabbath, circumcision, the festivals, the regulations about sexual cleanness and uncleanness, and widespread practice of the basic dietary laws, that was something which occurred independently of the rabbis. And even that may be too strong a statement: it relies largely on the negative evidence of absence of complaint by Tannaitic (i.e. pre-Talmudic) rabbis on those cardinal issues. During the third and fourth centuries the situation must have changed somewhat, since Galilee became the heartland of Jewish settlement in Palestine, but it is unclear how this happened.

In the literature, attributions of doctrine or utterance to particular rabbis are often highly dubious;[14] none the less, there has been enough investigation to reveal that, far from a unified view, there existed a spectrum of opinion among prominent rabbis on major questions, and this is visible in the case of approaches to the outside world, to association with Gentiles and to levels of permitted contact.[15] The Mishnaic tractate on idolatry, *Avodah Zarah*, exposes a number of such divergences. Palestine, of course, contained its own Greek cities where such problems could be pressing, and the rabbis seem often to have regarded places like Caesarea, Scythopolis and Sepphoris as within their purview.[16] However, while it would be wrong to treat the rabbis as a monolithic group, the possibility which opens before us, in questioning their connection with Diaspora Jewry, is a radical one which makes the matter of their diversity of stance less significant. If the Jewries of the Graeco-Roman Diaspora were far removed from the refined debates taking place in Palestine (or Babylon), they need not have accepted the combination of premises from which those debates started and, therefore, would have had as little interest in tolerant rabbinic positions as in hard-line ones. In their lives, self-separation for the achievement of purity may not have been perceived as an issue in the same terms.

---

[13] Goodman 1983: 93–118.
[14] Neusner 1984.
[15] Levine 1989: 83–97.
[16] See Elmsley's edn (1911). Sheppard (1979: 170) comments on the absence in

The Diaspora and the Rabbis

What, then, can we say about how the rabbis viewed the Diaspora and the Diaspora the rabbis? Those rabbinic sources which contain some kind of answer to the first question, have to be read with the greatest caution, as they have a marked tendency to prefer imaginary constructs of the past to real descriptions. But what at any rate emerges from those texts is that rabbinic interest, at least at times, extended to the dispersed communities. The institution of *shelikhim* (ἀπόστολοι, emissaries) is attested also in Christian writers and in the Theodosian code.[17] Talmudic reports ascribe especially hectic travels establish themselves. Journeys like these, or the ones attributed to Rabbi Akiba (who died under Hadrian), took rabbis to Rome, Gaul, Africa, Arabia, Antioch (in Syria), Cilicia, Cappadocia, Babylonia and Media, and could clearly involve visiting Jewish communities and also preaching in synagogues.[18] But the journeys also had a political dimension, where negotiations with local or imperial authorities might be required; and we should not forget fund-raising; at a certain stage the patriarchate may have been strong enough to exact taxes from Jews abroad; and if the visitors were acceptably received, and, indeed, contributions paid without any compulsion being applied, we may conclude that the rabbis were accorded some respect. This form of contact, if indeed we should take it as historical, would demonstrate that the rabbis of Palestine meant something in the Diaspora; but not, of course, that the system for Jewish living promoted by the rabbis was meaningful there in its entirety or their learning grasped.[19]

The prime rabbinic values of study and teaching are not absent from Diaspora Jewry. Josephus maintained that detailed knowledge of the Torah (which he rendered as νομός, law) was derived from regular reading (*CA* II 175), and was a determining characteristic of all Jews, at any rate by the time he wrote the *Against Apion* (towards

Mishnah *Avodah Zarah* of any discussion about the permissibility of Jews being town councillors (which would involve at the very least being present at pagan rituals; see Rajak 1985: 256–257 = Ch. 18: 365–366). Perhaps the matter was simply out of the question in Palestine, and this then would constitute further evidence that the rabbis did not look any further.

[17] Safrai 1974; cf. Millar 1992: 98.
[18] Safrai 1974: 208–210; Feldman 1989: 301–302.
[19] Kraabel 1982: 454.

100 A.D.). Epitaphs commemorate, from Rome, a μαθητὴς σοφῶν (the exact Greek equivalent of the Hebrew, *talmid hakham*), a *didaskalos* and a *nomodidaskalos*; from near Rome, a God-fearer (Rufinus) who was ἁγίων τε νόμων σοφίης τε συνίστωρ (Reynolds & Tannenbaum 1987: 31), from Athens, a πρόσχολος (*CIJ* 333; 1158; 201; 715b), and, from Larissa, a σχολαστικός, perhaps of the first century A.D. (*SEG* XXIX, 197: 537).[20] But here it is only fair to point out that in Greek culture the latter term could mean a 'professor' of rhetoric or even an advocate.[21] The inscription from Aphrodisias has now revealed a group (δεκανία) of φιλομαθῶν, lovers of learning. No literature survives to expose the preoccupations of any of those scholars. Their total number in known inscriptions cannot be said to be high, in proportion to our evidence; and geographically they are also rather confined. Their appearance does seem to reveal, once again, a link with the distant rabbis. At the same time, it is quite possible that the positions and activities they represent were but pale imitations of their counterparts in Palestine. I ignore here any appearances of the term 'rabbi'; this should not be taken as indicative since the term can also serve as a form of respectful address, with no technical meaning.[22] I do not know whether one should add to the collection Juvenal's begging Jewess who was an 'interpreter of the laws of Jerusalem', as well as being a 'high priestess of the tree' and a decoder of dreams.[23] The joke there was perhaps meant to be compounded by ascribing legal expertise to a woman.

For the period between about 200 and 350 A.D., there is archaeological evidence of an association in death between Palestinian rabbis and members of Diaspora communities. It became desirable to be interred in the Holy Land. The rock-cut necropolis at Beth She'arim (near modern Haifa) already housed the sarcophagus of the Patriarch R. Judah I, author of the Mishnah, and a number of rabbis after him.[24] Here were brought the bodies of many wealthy lay individuals, especially from Phoenicia and from Syria, but also from places further afield, such as Pamphylia. All were buried in the same manner, and the use of the Greek language (some 80 percent

---

[20] On these terms, see also Fergus Millar's discussion, 1992: 110–111.
[21] Loewe 1974.
[22] Levine 1989.
[23] *Satire VI*, 524–527; Stern 1980, no. 299.
[24] Schwabe and Lifschitz 1974.

of the inscriptions are in Greek) and of figurative designs, including the occasional one from Greek mythology, seems equally acceptable to all groups. It is hard to say how far this indicates shared practices among the living. The existence, to our knowledge, of one single synagogue within reach of the site, constructed towards the end of the third century, may perhaps be taken as a pointer in this direction, if it is right to take it as a place of worship for all who had occasion to stay there. On the other hand, we should remember that the synagogue should, according to Jewish Law, have had nothing to do with the cemetery, and the requisite prayers for the deposition of the sarcophagi would have been pronounced not in any synagogue but in the necropolis itself.

To observe the presence or absence of rabbinic influence or authority anywhere in the Diaspora, we should need to know more than we do about the texture of life, since that is where the principles found their full expression. The sources are inadequate for this; descriptions of practice in them are limited, yet it would be wrong to draw conclusions from this negative evidence. Had Josephus written his promised work 'on Customs and Causes (*Antiquities* IV 198), we might have been better off. The second book of the *Against Apion* contains an interesting summary of Judaism's salient features, written in the 90s A.D., just at the time when rabbinic Judaism was beginning to take shape in Palestine; but the thrust of this account is ethical, serving the work's apologetic argument.[25] For the rest, what we find in such Diaspora Jewish writing as we have, are brief remarks, with that in Philo's *On the Creation of the World* (170–172) being the most notable.[26]

By far the best-documented practice, which also caught the attention of Roman writers, is the keeping of the sabbath, with its lighting of lamps; and from what is said we can infer that enough Jews treated it seriously as a day of withdrawal from public life, of rest and prayer, to make it stand out as a distinguishing feature.[27] It is, interestingly enough, in a speech ascribed to the hostile Roman prefect of Egypt, Avilius Flaccus, that Philo gives a memorable vignette of how a Jewish sabbath might have looked: the Jews should abandon the observance, says Flaccus; if invasion or disaster were to strike

---

[25] Vermes 1982.
[26] Mendelson 1988: 29–49.
[27] Goldenberg 1979; Rabello 1984.

on that day, would they really continue to walk around the streets with their hands in their pockets as usual, or stay in their synagogues, and not budge an inch (*On Dreams* 123–129)? We also learn from Philo that there were problems for Jewish recipients if the Roman grain distribution was made on a Saturday (*Embassy to Gaius* 23, 158). Exemptions from military service because of its incompatibility with sabbath observance are sought in letters cited by Josephus, from Roman officials of the triumviral period to the city authorities of Ephesus and Miletus. The Jews of Ionia regard it as a form of harassment that they are asked to appear before tribunals on the sabbath and (interestingly) on festivals, and this is one of the principal complaints that they lay before Marcus Agrippa as arbiter in 14 B.C. (Josephus, *Antiquities* XIV 27). The consequent exemption granted by Augustus appeared still in the Theodosian Code (II 8,6 = VIII 8, 8; XVI 8, 2). There is no reason to envisage much change over time in this area, and the impression given in the fourth century by John Chrysostom and in the Laodicea Council canons, of the Jewish sabbath as a happy day, set apart for Bible-reading and repose, has the ring of truth about it.

The sabbath was central to the identity of Jews living among Gentiles. It is possible in similar fashion to track down other basic practices from a combination of sources, with the additional help of Christian literature.[28] Circumcision, ritual immersion and the wearing of *tephillin* (phylacteries) are well attested. Among the festivals, Passover and Tabernacles appear to have been prominent, and an assembly held during the latter is mentioned explicitly in a first-century A.D. decree in Greek where the Jewish community of Cyrene honours a Roman official.[29]

For the question of boundaries, the dietary laws might be of special significance, since in their very nature they would appear to encourage, even if not necessitating, separate eating: consuming food and drink together with others is an important way of breaking down barriers; and a community's eating habits are a major social distinguishing mark. We need look no further than Josephus to be assured that Diaspora Jews observed at least some of the Levitical regulations, and, indeed, he claims that 'many of our prohibitions in the matter of food' have become widespread (*CA* II 123). Equally, how-

---

[28] Meeks and Wilken 1978: 64–65.
[29] Lüderitz 1983, no. 71.

ever, this very remark, with its implication that the dietary laws were accessible, suggests that a limited form of observance may have been in question. Certainly, the complicated regulations about preparing and mixing food and about contamination of vessels and utensils, which play so large a part in Talmudic discussions, need not be read into the world of the Graeco-Roman city. In any case it is not inevitable that special dietary laws compel people to eat away from others, even if they may encourage such habits, as well as being best preserved by them. All sorts of arrangements are feasible, where there is a social reason to make them. And again, where we do suspect a high level of punctiliousness in eating habits, it would be wrong on this basis simply to assume a high degree of self-segregation from outsiders in every sphere. There is no necessary connection, and practices at any particular moment in history do not always form a harmonious unity.

What we know of Diaspora observance need not point beyond what might be called a minimal Judaism, comparable, perhaps, with that ascribed by Goodman to the Galileans in the Mishnaic age.[30] For the Diaspora, such an interpretation is not entirely new. Feldman has suggested that in the third century the Jews of non-coastal Asia Minor were particularly cut-off from rabbinic influence.[31] Kraabel has argued primarily on the basis of architecture and iconography for a non-halakhic Diaspora Judaism.[32] It is the implications of such a view that are interesting: a Judaism of the kind proposed does not in itself need to induce a tightly enclosed community. The most that can be said is that the system may tend that way in certain circumstances. Any group needs some boundary, or its identity will vanish. Special practices make a group distinct and also provide a way of making entry meaningful and the membership somewhat select. Equally, any group needs some contact with the world in which it is located, in order to secure its existence, its livelihood and some new blood. Jewish communities will undoubtedly have occupied different places along that continuum which runs from having boundaries that are almost closed to manifesting a high degree of openness.[33] They must also have reacted to circumstances and adapted.

---

[30] Goodman 1983.
[31] 1989: 300–305.
[32] 1981; 1982. Goodenough's *magnum opus* (1953–) provides the inspiration for such interpretations of the iconography, though its ascription of a special form of mystical Judaism to the Diaspora is now no longer tenable.
[33] Cohen 1989.

Here, the aim is not to illuminate the diversity of possibilities but rather to look at shared characteristics, to determine some leading features. The notion of the typical community has its uses. I shall focus on two aspects which emerge from recent publications. One has been much discussed on a technical level, but its implications perhaps shirked; the other now demands an explanation.

Activity on the Boundaries

The first feature to be highlighted is the intensity of activity on the boundaries: the ease with which it was possible to enter Judaism and the availability of forms of partial membership which were often taken up, it would appear, by both pagans and Christians. Indeed, Marcel Simon, who, in a work perhaps more noticed by theologians than by historians,[34] was the first systematically to demonstrate the vitality of Judaism between the second and the fifth centuries, spoke of Jewish involvement in a universal syncretism. That concept is in fact best confined to real religious fusions, such as the cult of Zeus the Most High (Zeus Hypsistos) led by an ἀρχισυνάγωγος (a term occasionally used for the leader of a pagan club) at Pydna in Macedonia.[35] But the manifestations which led Simon to invoke the concept widely are very real. He was preoccupied principally with Jewish–Christian relations, and so he made a special study of Christian Judaizers, those individuals who incurred the wrath of their bishops by maintaining Jewish habits and rituals alongside their Christianity; these extended to the use of phylacteries and the celebration of Jewish festivals together with their Jewish neighbours. Pagan Judaizers are, however, equally important, though perhaps more obscure to us. We have already seen references in Philo and Josephus to the attractions of Judaism. We also meet in Josephus individuals described as 'worshippers of God' (θεοσεβεῖς), normally translated as 'God-fearers' or 'sympathizers'. They appear to correspond with those who are similarly described, though with a slightly different verbal formation, in Acts; and they figure in some inscriptions. Greek and Latin authors have various ways of alluding to sympathizers with Judaism. Rabbinic literature appears to echo the same formulae.[36] Clearly, those par-

---

[34] 1964; 1986.
[35] Cormack 1974: 51–55.
[36] See now Feldman 1989: 274–282.

tial adherents were distinguished from proselytes and yet they were publicly associated with Judaism, in benefaction, possibly in burial and also, we may suppose, in at least some forms of worship.[37] Apparently, they were not generally deemed impure. Josephus evidently approves them.[38]

The major inscription recently discovered in the excavation of Aphrodisias in Caria[39] makes it evident, after years of inconclusive debate, that the God-fearers were indeed a category of half-way proselytes, even if the terms have a range of uses beyond that quasi-technical one. It is unnecessary to recall the debate here. The inscription of a dedication for some sort of memorial created by an association (δεκανία) of Jews, perhaps in the early third century. On its second face (which may be later than the first), there appears a list giving the names of fifty-two people described at the top as θεοσεβίς (sic); these include nine Aphrodisian town-councillors (βουλευταί), members of the city's elite. The δεκανία, which is described in a perplexing introduction on the first side, is that of the φιλομαθῶν and (apparently) παντευλογήτων ('lovers of wisdom' and 'all-blessed' or 'all-blessing') of which we have I already spoken.[40] The names listed on the first side are presumably those of its full members. There is no necessity to take the Godfearers as also belonging to the club, though it is possible that they did do so and they are linked with it here. At the very least we find them closely associated in a common philanthropic activity with the full Jews, and subscribing, presumably, to the same semi-private memorial.

There emerges the picture of a category of adherent that was kept distinct for formal purposes, but scarcely one that was held at arm's length. The opposite, indeed, would seem to be true, since the picture is complicated by the appearance of two θεοσεβεῖς, Antonios and Emmonios, on the first face, among the Jews. Perhaps they were allowed entry because they were closer to Judaism than the θεοσεβεῖς

[37] Kant 1987: 688.
[38] Rajak 1985: 257–259 = Ch. 18: 366–368.
[39] Reynolds & Tannenbaum 1987.
[40] The exact nature of the δεκανία is uncertain, the name being unparalleled for a Jewish association. The reading, however, ought to stand, though see Feldman (1989: 280). There is even more doubt about the nature of the so-called πάτελλα, perhaps some kind of charitable foundation, with which the δεκανία is linked. The exact formation φιλομαθῶν appears only here in Jewish epigraphy but is common in Philo and LXX; παντευλογ(. . ων) (the word is damaged in the text) is more contentious: see Reynolds & Tannenbaum 1987: 30–36.

on the second face, and this then would raise the interesting possibility that varying degrees of adherence had different standing;[41] or perhaps this happened for quite other reasons. Josephus' formulation, when he tells us of the throngs of Greeks at Antioch in Syria who were in his day attracted to Jewish worship and goes on to say that the Jews had 'in a fashion made them a part of themselves' (*Jewish War* VII 45), seems aptly to describe the situation visible at Aphrodisias.

Also among the eighteen names on the first face of the inscription, there are three proselytes, so designated; these bear Jewish names, Samuel, Joses and Joseph. Presumably, they were circumcised[42] and were deemed to have abandoned pagan practices, having 'made the journey to a better home' (Philo, *On the Virtues* 102). This does not mean that all their fellow Jews will have accepted them as entire equals: both in Qumran texts and in the Mishnah some distinctions are drawn between proselytes and Jews.[43] To cross the boundary wholly no doubt required a decisive and not altogether easy act; though we notice that, even then, not everyone choosing to label himself or herself in an inscription as *Ioudaios* or *Ioudaia* or the like seems fully to have achieved the transition. A pagan-style Latin dedication to an interesting collectivity of deities entitled Iunones was erected by Annia, an Italian freedwoman, who is able to describe herself quite simply as 'Iuda', 'Jewess'.[44] In any case, we can safely say, on the basis of the Aphrodisian categories, that a clear distinction between proselytes and God-fearers was quite operable, whether or not there was some spectrum of degrees of affiliation to be found among proselytes. And we may add that, when it comes to God-fearers, there need be no uncertainty on the latter point: for them it was possible to sit astride the boundary in comfort, temporarily and probably even permanently.

---

[41] Cf. Cohen 1989.

[42] There is no evidence that a ban on Gentile circumcision operated in practice, following Antoninus Pius' modification of Hadrian's total prohibition of the act (Reynolds and Tannenbaum 1987: 43–45; Linder 1987: 100). A reiteration by Septimius Severus is not securely attested.

[43] Cohen 1989: 27–29; cf. Goodman 1983: 71.

[44] *CIJ* 77; Kraemer 1989: 42. See possible examples of similar 'Jewish paganism' in Feldman (1989: 304).

Women benefactors and community practices

The second issue to be discussed concerns the principles by which Diaspora Jews characteristically conducted their affairs. A prime reason for maintaining closed boundaries is to preserve a particular value system intact, allowing the values and practices of outsiders only limited access. Can the surviving inscriptions, in their fragmentary state, tell us anything of the community life of Greek-speaking (or Latin-speaking) Jews? Again, our purpose is to look for patterns within the local and chronological diversity.

A challenging proposal which has aroused considerable interest is the subject of a book by Bernadette Brooten on woman synagogue leaders.[45] On her view, some very peculiar and certainly unrabbinic practices were to be found in Diaspora communities. Even if the thesis has flaws, the observed phenomenon requires an explanation and leads us to consider the ideology of the Jews in relation to their environment. On the basis of a detailed study of nineteen Greek and Latin inscriptions of varying or sometimes unknown date (together with some supporting material), all of which name a woman as some type of community or synagogue leader, Brooten argues for the existence in the Diaspora of a form of Judaism which allowed women an active role in the religious life of the synagogue. They appear as ἀρχισυνάγωγοι as 'elders', as 'mothers' of the synagogue, and, in all these capacities, they can be benefactresses; they might even, it would appear, be categorized as priests. She therefore argues that responsibility for every major facet of synagogue life, including instruction and the ritual itself, might, in principle, have been assigned to a woman. She vigorously contests the traditional explanation of these inscriptions, that the stated offices were honorific in nature, claiming that such explanations can either be shown or suspected to originate in an a priori assumption: the view has been that women simply could not have played the roles ascribed to them by the names of their offices. That such prejudices were constantly and illegitimately entertained by male scholars need hardly be doubted. The belief seems to have been that women held purely honorific offices while men held proper ones, and for this there is no justification. The problem, however, is that there are also independent, strong arguments

---

[45] Brooten 1982.

for taking the posts named in the inscriptions as essentially honorific
for *all* types of holder. First, it should be observed that Brooten discusses, but fails to account for, the presence of children among the
office-holders. Kallistos, an *archisynagogos* at Venosa, was aged 3 years
and 3 months, while at Rome there was a youthful (νήπιος) ἄρχων
(*CIJ* 120; 587). These children can hardly be regarded as having
been functional in their posts. Second, and more fundamentally, she
does not take serious account of the parallelism between the honorands of the synagogue inscriptions, and the larger world, where
holders of municipal office were regularly honoured with inscriptions. There too, at any rate in Asia Minor, women and children
were to be found, among a vast preponderance of men.[46] Both in
the larger and in the smaller world, the individuals in question may
or may not have been functional in the capacities ascribed to them.
This was of secondary importance, and the significant thing about
them, whether they were men, women or children, was evidently
that they had benefited, or were connected with those who had
benefited, the honouring institution by their munificence or their
patronage. They may have been owners of property in their own
right. They are linked into a wider pattern of exchange of benefits
between powerful individuals and communities which has come to
be known as euergetism. Payment, obligatory or voluntary, by the
office-holder for the privilege of office-holding is a crucial part of
this system. In the case of the synagogue, these features of office-
holding explain well why there are sometimes in the same institution a surprising number of seemingly overlapping offices, and why
the post of ἀρχισυνάγωγος may have multiple holders. Brooten vastly
overestimates the amount of administrative activity that would have
surrounded an ancient institution, and her picture of dedicated female
rabbis of progressive persuasion, concerned with everything from
liturgy to repairs, introduces an anachronistic note.

None the less, Brooten's questioning exposes an important phenomenon: the mirroring of the city's social framework, with its implicit
values, within a Jewish context. Those values, by which status and
power were tied to demonstrative wealth, obviously ran counter to
certain Jewish principles.[47] This mirroring is striking in relation to
the post of ἀρχισυνάγωγος, rightly described by Brooten as the most

---

[46] van Bremen 1983.
[47] See Ch. 19 in this volume.

widely known Jewish title in the ancient world. What deserves comment is the distance this name has travelled. It would seem to have
originated in Hebrew, for it is a literal Greek translation of the
Hebrew *rosh kneset*, assembly head: hence the rather odd Greek formation, where the second part of the word does not designate a position, as in ἀρχιερεύς and other such titles, but an institution (Brooten
1982: 5). But ἀρχισυνάγωγος eventually embedded itself comfortably
in the context where we find it when we read the Greek and Latin
inscriptions. That context was, in essence, the honour-based system
of administration which characterized the cities of the Roman Empire.
It may be added that such a change in meaning had surely been
facilitated by the fact that Jews, like the nine councillors at Aphrodisias,
themselves took a part in that administration: that is attested already
for the first century A.D. and occurred widely after Septimius Severus
early in the third century.[48] To some extent, they must have internalized its values.

The appearance of women and children as synagogue leaders is
the clue which leads us to a plausible and fruitful interpretation of
the titulature and the pattern of office-holding in the Jewish community. It will require further testing. If it is correct, then we observe
also the hint of an important social mechanism. For the connection
of the Jewish world with the patronal system of the city will have
provided an easy way in for those who wished to transfer (or partly
to transfer) from one side of the boundary to the other. And the
interconnection also suggests an obvious source of pressure on some
pagan citizens to do lust that: if the Jews were prominent in a city,
the claims of patronage or of the exchange of benefits could have
dictated the move. This, then, would be a powerful force for keeping boundaries open.

There is another observation to be made. If the social pattern surrounding the synagogue not only was intelligible to outsiders, but
also rested on the same base of patronage and munificence as their
own institutions, then it will have been of use to outsiders to be
benefactors of synagogues. And some undoubtedly were, the most
notable being the distinguished Julia Severa, a pagan priestess in
Acmonia, Phrygia, recorded in an inscription from the time of the
Emperor Nero. This priestess used sometimes to be taken by scholars

---

[48] Rajak 1985 = Ch. 18; Linder 1987, no. 2.

as a syncretizing Jewess, but she has now been firmly put in her place as a great pagan lady; she may, but need not, have been a sympathizer with Judaism.[49] It was Julia Severa who built the synagogue in Acmonia. Exactly why she might have done so, must remain a subject for speculation.

Epilogue

The institutional and social familiarity of the synagogue world will also have made it easier for those whose motivation was more private to enter this world, whether wholly or partly. The ἀρχισυνάγωγοι will surely have made entrants welcome, whatever the degree of their involvement or the irreproachability of their lives. And the rabbis in remote Palestine will not have been consulted.

Closeness, of course, produced tension too, and the major explosions of violence that occurred intermittently over the period are all too well known. But eventually, neither pagan nor Jewish but Christian anxieties were to be responsible for constructing new barriers. And soon, Jewry itself was virtually to forget a remarkable phase of its existence, to an extent where it has become hard to believe that the rabbinic age was for many Jews not a period of looking inward, but rather a time when the world opened out.

BIBLIOGRAPHY

Applebaum, S. 1974. 'The Organization of the Jewish Communities in the Diaspora' in S. Safrai & M. Stern (eds), *The Jewish People in the First Century*. Compendia Rerum Iudaicarum ad Novum Testamentum 1, 1. Assen, 464–503.
Applebaum, S. 1979. *Jews and Greeks in Ancient Cyrene*. Leiden.
Bremen, R. van 1983. 'Women and Wealth' in A. Cameron & A. Kuhrt (eds), *Images of Women in Antiquity*. London/Sydney, 223–242.
Brooten, B. 1982. *Women Leaders in the Ancient Synagogue*. Brown Judaic Studies 36. Chico, Calif.
Cohen, S.J.D. 1981. 'Patriarchs and Scholarchs', *PAAJR* 48: 57–85.
——— 1989. 'Crossing the Boundary and Becoming a Jew', *HTR* 82: 13–33.
Cormack. J. 1974. 'Zeus Hypsistos at Pydna', in *Mélanges Helleniques offerts à Georges Daux*. Paris, 51–55.
Elmsley, W.A.L. 1911. *The Mishnah on Idolatry: 'Aboda Zara*. Texts and Studies 8, 2. Cambridge.

---

[49] *CIJ* 766; Revised Schürer: 3.1, 30; Sheppard 1979: 170.

Feldman, L.H. 1989. 'Proselytes and "Sympathizers" in the Light of the New Inscription from Aphrodisias', *REJ* 148: 265–305.

Forkman, G. 1972. *The Limits of the Religious Community*. London.

Goldenberg, R. 1979. 'The Jewish Sabbath in the Roman World up to the Time of Constantine the Great', *ANRW* II, 19, 1: Berlin and New York, 414–447.

Goodenough, E.R. 1953–. *Jewish Symbols in the Greco-Roman Period*, Vols 1–11. Bollingen Series 37. New York.

Goodman, M. 1983. *State and Society in Roman Galilee, A.D. 132–212*. Totowa, N.J.

Hengel, M. 1966. 'Die Synagogeninschrift von Stobi', *ZNTW* 57: 145–183.

Kant, L.H. 1987. 'Jewish Inscriptions in Greek and Latin', *ANRW* II, 20, 2: Berlin and New York, 671–713.

Kraabel, A.T. 1979. 'The Diaspora Synagogue', *ANRW* II, 19, 2: Berlin and New York, 477–510.

—— 1981. 'Social Systems of Six Diaspora Synagogues', in J. Gutmann (ed.), *Ancient Synagogues: The State of Research*. Chico, Calif.

—— 1982. 'The Roman Diaspora: Six Questionable Assumptions', *JJS* 33: 445–464.

Kraemer, R.S. 1989. 'On the Meaning of the Term "Jew" in GrecoRoman Inscriptions' *HTR* 82: 35–53.

Leon, H.J. 1960. *The Jews of Ancient Rome*. Philadelphia, Pa.

Levine, L.I. 1979. 'The Jewish Patriarch (Nasi) in Third Century Palestine', *ANRW* II, 19, 2: Berlin and New York, 650–688.

—— (ed.). 1987. *The Synagogue in Late Antiquity*. Philadelphia, Pa.

—— 1989. *The Rabbinic Class of Roman Palestine in Late Antiquity*. Jerusalem/New York.

Lifschitz, B. 1967. *Donateurs et fondateurs dans les synagogues juives*. Paris.

Linder, A. 1987. *The Jews in Roman Imperial Legislation*. Detroit, Mich./Jerusalem.

Loewe, R. 1974. 'Rabbi Joshua ben Hananiah: LLD. or D.Litt?', *JJS* 25: 137–154.

Lüderitz, G. 1983. *Corpus jüdischer Zeugnisse aus der Cyrenaika. Mit einem Anhang von J.M. Reynolds*. Tubingen.

Meeks, W.A. & Wilken, R.I. 1978. *Jews and Christians in Antioch in the First Four Centuries of the Common Era*. SBL Sources for Biblical Study 13. Missoula, Mont.

Mendelson, A. 1988. *Philo's Jewish Identity*. Brown Judaic Studies 161. Atlanta, Georgia.

Millar, F. 1992. 'The Jews of the Graeco-Roman Diaspora between Paganism and Christianity, A.D. 312–438', in J. Lieu, J. North & T. Rajak (eds). *The Jews among Pagans and Christians, In the Roman Empire*. London/New York, 97–123.

Momigliano, A.D. 1987. Review of Meeks, *The First Urban Christians*, in *Ottavo Contributo alla Storia degli Studi Classici e del Mondo Antico*, Rome: 399–402.

Neusner, J. 1973. *The Idea of Purity in Ancient Judaism*. The Haskell Lectures. Leiden.

—— 1981. *Judaism: The Evidence of the Mishnah*. Chicago/London.

—— 1984. *In Search of Talmudic Biography. The Problem of the Attributed Saying*. Brown Judaic Studies 70. Chico, Calif.

Oppenheimer, A. 1977. *The 'Am Ha-aretz*. Leiden.

Rabello, A.M. 1984. 'L'observance des fêtes juives dans l'empire romain', *ANRW* II, 21, 2:1288–1312.

Rajak. T. 1984. 'Was there a Roman Charter for the Jews?', *Journal of Roman Studies* 74: 107–123 = C.1 in this volume.

—— 1985. 'Jews and Christians as Groups in a Pagan World', in J. Neusner & E.S. Frerichs (eds) *'To See Ourselves as Others See Us': Christians, Jews, 'Others' in Late Antiquity*, Chico, Calif., 247–262 = C.3 in this volume.

Reynolds, J. & Tannenbaum, R. 1987. *Jews and Godfearers at Aphrodisias*. Cambridge Philological Society, Supplementary Volume 12. Cambridge.

Safrai, S. 1974. 'Relations between the Diaspora and the Land of Israel', in S. Safrai and M. Stern (eds) *The Jewish People in the First Century*. Compendia Rerum Iudaicarum ad Novum Testamentum 1, 1. Assen, 184–215.

—— (ed). 1987. *The Literature of the* Sages. Compendia Rerum Iudaicarum ad Novum Testamentum 2, 3, 1. Assen/Philadelphia, Pa.

Sanders, E.P., Baumgarten, A. & Mendelson, A. (eds). 1981. *Jewish and Christian Self-Definition*, vol. 2. London.

Schwabe, M. & Lifschitz, B. 1974. *Beth Shearim*, vol. 2. Jerusalem.

Sheppard, A.R.R. 1979. 'Jews, Christians and Heretics in Acmonia and Eumeneia', *Anatolian Studies* 29: 169–180.

Simon, M. 1964. *Verus Israel. etudes sur les relations entre Chrétiens et Juifs dans l'empire romain (135–425)*, Paris; English translation (1986). Oxford.

Stemberger, G. 1991. *Introduction to the Talmud and Midrash*, translated by M. Bockmuehl. Edinburgh.

Stern, M. 1974, 1980, 1984. *Greek and Latin Authors on Jews and Judaism*, Vols 1, 2 and 3. Jerusalem.

Vermes, G. 1982. 'A Summary of the Law by Flavius Josephus', *Novum Testamentum* 24: 289–303.

CHAPTER EIGHTEEN

JEWS AND CHRISTIANS AS GROUPS
IN A PAGAN WORLD

'The other' is certainly most threatening when he is proximate. But
there is also a force of attraction: while the two sides fend one
another off (not necessarily in a balanced or equal way), they are
also drawn together. I am concerned less with theories of 'the other'
as such, than with theory as expressed in values and in behaviour—
the patterns of life of people or groups of people. But the two—
theory and action—have, of course, an intimate (if not a parasitic)
relationship, and when we know how people act we can find a new
meaning in their theories. The main theme at this point is Jewish
groups, with the early Christians figuring by way of comparison and
contrast, in respect of the way they face a pagan outside world and
refer both inwards and outwards. Although Jewish-Christian relations
are a leading theme in scholarship today, this paper casts the pagan
Gentile in the role of outsider, looking at the Jewish Diaspora in the
Greek world of the first centuries A.D.

A Greek synagogue inscription found in 1931 by excavation at
Stobi in Macedonia, and dating, it seems, from some time in the
third century A.D. records the benefaction of one Claudius Tiberius
Polycharmus, son of Achyrios. In fulfillment of a personal vow, this
man, by his name a Roman citizen but evidently a Jew, has apparently donated a building he owns for use as a synagogue. The institution will have a dining room and meeting hall attached (τρίκλεινον =
triclinium, and τετρασροόν), and he and his heirs will retain the
upper storey for their own purposes. No one is to interfere with
these arrangements, on pain of being fined by the 'patriarch'.[1]

Perhaps the most revealing and unexpected statement is Polycharmus' opening description of himself—ὁ πατὴρ τῆς ἐν Στόβοις
συναγωγῆς ὃς πολιτευσάμενος πᾶσαν πολιτείαν κατὰ τὸν Ἰουδαισμὸν.
This is not readily translatable, but in the light of Martin Hengel's

---

[1] *CIJ* I, 694; see Hengel 1966: 145–183; also in Gutmann 1975:110 ff.; for further bibliography, see Hengel n. 2, and (especially on the site), Kraabel 1979: 495.

interpretation, it might be rendered as 'father of the Stobi synagogue, who has been fully active in communal affairs for the purposes of Judaism'. Of course, the word used for the man's sphere
of operation, πολιτεία, has deeper implications than are suggested
by the English. Though it can have both a strong and a weaker
sense, the connection with *polis* is inescapable, and the connotation
of an independent, self-contained and constitutionally-defined unit is
always there.

I am not going to make assertions now about Jewish citizenship,
at Stobi or elsewhere, or to put forward claims about a separate and
autonomous Jewish political body, the so-called πολίτευμα, which has
become a popular subject for scholarly theorizing.[2] Incidentally,
Hengel too avoids putting his feet into that morass. I am not concerned here with the technical question of Jewish status at all. But
what Hengel has established leads to other interesting implications
and consequences; that is, that the sentence must at any rate be a
way of referring to the donor's involvement with the Jewish religion
and not at all a matter of acting in the interests of Judaism within
the larger *politeia*, the city in which Polycharmus lives. There is no
very close verbal parallel to be cited for this use of the term *politeia*,
but the sense should not be doubted. The expression is in fact somewhat clumsy. Nonetheless, there is significance in the odd choice of
words, for a *politeia* is a complete political and moral framework for
a citizen, not just a set of external rules, and to be engaged in 'politics' is part of the fabric of the life of a Greek. Here, therefore,
'Judaism' appears as an alternative framework, as it were, supplying
a Jew with a substitute *polis*.

How far in the Stobi case that *politeia* is to be identified as resting on the single institution of the Stobi synagogue is not clear,
though what does emerge from the inscription is that the synagogue
was (or was claiming to be) the only establishment of the kind in
that city and that, with its eating facilities and hall, it was considerably more than just a place of worship. This corporate body, then,
would appear to constitute a primary group affiliation for Polycharmus,
to the exclusion, we might be tempted to think, of the pagan city
around him.

Such an impression is derived in less vivid but equally distinct
ways from a multitude of Diaspora Jewish inscriptions coming from

---

[2] See Kasher 1978; Applebaum 1974: ch. 9; Smallwood 1976: 359–361 etc.

the Greek-speaking east of the Roman empire (Stobi, incidentally, is somewhat anomalous in being, as Hengel points out, a primarily Latin-speaking town, in spite of the Greek language of our inscription). One thinks of graves, for example, which bear a valedictory formula such as τῷ λαῷ χαίρειν, hailing the deceased's co-religionists and identifying him until the end, or rather, beyond it, as a member of that 'people' (a group of whom—not all, even within his own city—must of course have been personally known to him).[3] One thinks, too, of the separate and explicit hierarchy of status and office associated with a community or an individual synagogue, and of the way an individual's place within it is so often attached to his name, for example: *archisynagogos, archon, prostates*, or perhaps 'father of the synagogue' as in the case of Polycharmus. These partly honorific titles may even be assigned to women or small children, and in that respect they operate in a manner strikingly analogous to the titles of civic office in the Greek city at large.[4] The appearance is therefore one of a parallel alternative society. It is a phenomenon which can be more fully delineated within another, not unrelated grouping, that of Pauline Christianity. Indeed, this has recently attracted interest, especially that of Wayne Meeks in *The First Urban Christians*. Meeks writes of the Christian groups' conception of themselves as an *ekklesia*—a term, in fact, scarcely found within Diaspora Judaism or paganism—and studies the 'language of separation' which Pauline groups used to distinguish those who did not belong from those who did.[5]

But there are revealing differences. It is paradoxical that while Christianity discarded the (supposed) rigours of the law and of Jewish purity requirements (I shall come back shortly to some doubts about these), it was among Pauline Christians that the drawing of boundaries appears sharper and more complete, the alternative language, value-system and structure more overwhelming. That, at any rate, is the impression we get, although we do have to make allowances for the imbalance of our sources, since we possess a Pauline literature, but virtually no Diaspora-Jewish one for this period. The second apparent difference is also difficult to assess, and for the same reason. The Pauline communities seem often to be most conscious of themselves not so much as part of a big movement, but as small

---

[3] See Robert 1946.
[4] See now Brooten 1982.
[5] Meeks 1983: 84–96.

sub-groups, especially as individual households or families. This division into small units or cells is entirely intelligible in terms of the way Christianity grew from small beginnings and spread in the cities. And in these terms, too, it makes sense that Jewish groups should be more centralized. Still, the pattern was probably quite varied among the Jews, and larger cities such as Antioch certainly had more than one synagogue; in that instance, we do not know whether the worshippers' basis of distribution was purely geographical or not.[6]

My purpose, however, is to try to correct another imbalance brought about by our sources. For these are produced in and for sectarian contexts, and aim, broadly, at mutual encouragement (what today might be called 'consciousness-raising'). So they deliberately stress self-differentiation and group identity. What they are responding to, in fact, is a contrary pull which is always there—that exerted from the outside by the wider community. Again, this must have affected Christians and Jews in contrasting ways, for among the early Christians, most would have come directly out of the world of the Gentile city and have been linked with it by many ties of affinity, habit and sentiment. This is perhaps why they need stronger marks of separation. The Jews, apart from proselytes and 'God-fearers', have a different past; theirs goes right back to early Hellenistic times when the Greek cities were often ethnically exclusive, closed units. There was a pattern of separate Jewish communal development, but with inclinations on the part of some to participate in the general community as, for example, those who sought entrance to the gymnasium (and probably to citizenship) at Alexandria under Claudius. Such people were probably secure in their identity and had worked out a balance of loyalties over generations. Still, this same general point applies to both Jews and Christians: the impression of total apartness is illusory, so what in fact we must look for is an interplay between group identity on the one hand and a relationship (perhaps ambivalent) with the Greek city on the other. Clearly, this will not be a simple matter.

It is the outward-looking tendencies which I wish to explore and, in particular, one aspect of the relation between monotheists and the world around them. Let me introduce this by recalling that on the day of a pagan festival it was considered undesirable for a Jew

---

[6] On households, etc., see Meeks 1983: 29–31; 75–77; on the synagogues at Antioch, Meeks & Wilken 1978: 8–9.

to banter with a Gentile (*Tosefta Av.Zar.* 1.2). The rationale, evidently, is that one thing leads to another and, before he knows where he is, the gregarious Jew may find himself taken up in the festival crowd. Of course, the recommendation was meant for Eretz Israel and there, in Galilee at least, Jews lived surrounded by a Jewish majority (as Martin Goodman has emphasized).[7] So perhaps it would not have been too difficult to reserve one's humour for one's co-religionists. But in the Diaspora the situation is entirely reversed. Pagans could not be so easily avoided, and it is hard to see how the normal casual intercourse could have been artificially suppressed without grave damage to good manners and good relations.

This is all the more true since the round of festivals was continuous, and pagan occasions were woven thickly into the fabric of the Greek city's year, especially during the period of the Roman empire. One could not put it better than Gibbon does, writing about the predicament of the Christian (in his 15th chapter): 'the innumerable deities and rites of polytheism were closely interwoven with every circumstances of business or pleasure, of public or private life; and it seemed impossible to escape the observance of them without, at the same time, renouncing the commerce of mankind and all the offices and amusements of society.' And again, 'the dangerous temptations which on every side lurked in ambush to surprise the unguarded, he (the Christian) believed, assailed him with redoubled violence on the days of solemn festivals.'[8] It was not merely a question of temple ceremonial; athletic and musical contests for professionals and for locals, oratory and theatrical performances, clowning and pantomime, public feasts and processions, all were included among the festivities dedicated to the local deities, to major gods, or to the divine emperor—or to all three. Not only temples, theatres and stadia, but even the town squares would be taken over. Sacrifice was an integral part of these public celebrations, just as libation was part of any private festive occasion. With the latter, too, Gibbon has some fun at the expense of early Christian Puritanism (such disapproving attitudes were, be it noted, rarely shared by the Jews, though the pressures were the same for both groups): 'The Christian, who with pious horror avoided the abominations of the circus or the theatre, found himself encompassed with infernal snares in every convivial

[7] Goodman 1983: ch. 4.
[8] Gibbon, ch. 15.

entertainment, as often as his friends, invoking the hospitable deities, poured out libations to each other's happiness.'

Festivals dominated the city. In one way, this had a symbolic value. In the 2nd century A.D. the orator Dio of Prusa, in a speech to the Rhodians, could say that the celebration of civic festivals (along with sitting in council) was part of the Greeks' traditional way of life and by it, they could show themselves better than the rest of the world. This was best of all if the games made their city dignified (σεμνήν), with the spectators watching quietly and applauding only by smacking their lips (ποππυσμός, *Oration* 31, 162–163); for cities were represented at one another's festivals and also competed in the splendour of these occasions.[9] Festivals were also of material importance. They generated market trade (this earned Olympia the name *mercatus Olympicus*);[10] they occasioned distribution of money and (sacrificial) meat; and at least until the third century A.D., they stimulated the flow of funds from the community's benefactors, who received in exchange personal prominence and prestigious office. In the case of competitive games, a special official (often called the *agonothetes*) administered and presided; on other occasions city magistrates, who were in many ways involved with the local cults were in the forefront. For such people, these were highly significant opportunities to make grand appearances.[11]

To be outside all this was to be effectively outside the city—which is exactly how some of the early churchmen, especially Tertullian, exhorted their flocks to see themselves. Is that where we are to locate the Jewish communities of the Diaspora of the Hellenistic-Roman world?

While it was utterly incompatible with Judaism to participate in a sacrifice, let alone to touch sacrificial meat, what did being present as an uninvolved spectator signify? What if one was present as a dignitary? What if one was a performer in a contest ultimately dedicated to a deity? Are we to interpret the familiar cry of misanthropy found in so many pagan authors to mean that the Jews utterly absented themselves from the city's best moments, that they substituted the rhythms of their own calendar and their own ritual, and operated purely as self-contained groups?

---

[9] Price 1984: 128.
[10] MacMullen 1981: 26.
[11] Price 1984: 122.

If the Rabbis of Palestine and their emissaries (*shelikhim*) were influential, then the answer is to an extent determined. For the aims and presuppositions of the code in Mishnah and Tosefta, *Avodah Zarah*, are to create not, admittedly, hostility to idolatry, but still a clear distancing from anything associated with it or the appearance of it.[12] This extremely protective form of separation was built, as usual, into an intricate system of purity regulations, whose dynamic we are beginning to grasp through the work of Jacob Neusner.'[13] The Rabbis were not in entire agreement, but the differences between the milder opinion and the more severe on any issue was only a matter of degree, with the premises unchanged. Thus, while it will have made a substantial difference to trade which view prevailed: either R. Ishmael's view that 'for three days before their festivals and for three days after them it is forbidden [to have any business with them]' or the Sages' (*hakhamim*) view that 'before their festivals it is forbidden, but after their festivals it is not forbidden'—either way it was transparently clear that the objective was this: to give the festival a wide berth and avoid being pulled into it (Mishnah *Av.Zar.* 1.2). Likewise, the necessity of avoiding contact with libation wine was overriding, leading to the rule that 'if libation wine fell into the vat, it is forbidden to have any benefit at all from any of it' (Mishnah *Av.Zar.* 5.10), and the concession of Rabban Simeon b. Gamaliel, that 'it may all be sold to the Gentiles excepting the value of the libation wine that is in it' was no more than a slight softening.

We may be disposed to believe the stories about the travels of Rabban Gamaliel and his fellow scholars from Jamnia, but even if we do, and are prepared to accept the pleasant notion that they preached and argued *halakhah* in the synagogues of Rome (Ex. Rabbah 30.9 etc.) there is still, I think, no reason to take it that outside Israel those same stringent standard of purity were set, or that the Rabbinic *halakhah*, so far as it had been formed, was transferred there.[14]

It is interesting that the Mishnah has a provocative question on idolatry put to the 'elders in Rome' (*Av.Zar.* 4.7). 'If God does not wish an idol to exist, why does He not destroy it?' suggests, perhaps, that the Roman Jews tossed aside Rabbinic ideas on the subject.

[12] See Elmsley 1911; Hadas-Lebel 1979: 397–485, esp. 426–441.
[13] See Neusner 1973, together with id. 1974–77.
[14] See Safrai 1974: 209.

The answer was as follows: 'If idolators worshipped an object not essential to the world, He would destroy the idol. But they worship the Sun, Moon, Stars and Planets. Is He to destroy the world because of fools?' And there was more, for even that did not, apparently, put an end to the interrogation: 'Even if it be so, He ought to destroy those objects which are not essential to the world and leave those which it requires.' They replied, 'Then He would just be supporting the beliefs of the worshippers of these things, in that they would say 'Know that these are gods, for look, they are not destroyed.'

Judaism in the Hellenized Diaspora can have been adequately defined by the cult's basic components—Sabbath observance (of one kind or another),[15] circumcision (though even this, perhaps, with reservations),[16] study of the Torah, the keeping of the feasts, and ritual washing.[17]

The evidence of the Pauline Epistles (together with Acts), while putting a heavy stress on the burdensome aspects of the law of Moses, in fact does not suggest that the observance of Diaspora Jews amounted to more than the essentials. These basic requirements in themselves, had they been imposed on Christians, would have been trouble enough for a Gentile convert. It is true that Paul's complex instructions about the consumption of meat from idols, which he did not ban for Christians but from which they were none the less exhorted to abstain for the sake of the weaker brethren,[18] make great play with stressing the more restrictive approach of the Jews (1 Cor. 9:20–25). But it is not surprising for us to learn that such meat (or any un-kosher meat) was strictly forbidden to Jews. What we should note is rather that nothing further is suggested by Paul about Jews shunning the many manifestations of paganism around them. Yet I suspect that at the same time, the *Tendenz* of these Christian texts is in fact the cause, or part cause, of the vague but widespread notion that Diaspora Jews led rigidly closed-in lives, separating themselves uncompromisingly from the normal forms of existence.

Whether the Palestinian Rabbis perceived the adherents of such a basic Judaism as *minim* (heretics) or as mere *ammei ha-aretz* (uneducated peasants) I would not venture to say, but, at any rate, a

---

[15] On the question of the Sabbath, see Goldenberg 1979: 414–447, esp. 429.

[16] So Collins 1985.

[17] On these components, see Goodman 1983: 102, where he neatly cites Mekhilta together with Justin Martyr.

[18] See Theissen 1982.

baraita in the name of either R. Ishmael or R. Simeon ben Eleazar
makes it clear that the opinion was not favourable. 'Israel outside
the land (of Israel) are idolators. In what way? If a gentile held a
banquet for his son and invited all the Jews in his town . . ., notwithstanding that they eat their own food and drink their own wine and
are served by their own servant, the scripture charges them, as if
they had eaten of the sacrifices to the dead, as it is written (Ex. 34:
15): "And they call thee and then eat of their sacrifice"' (*b.Av.Zar.*
8a; *Tos. Av.Zar.* 4(5).6).[19] It *may*, further, be the case that we should
read the iconographic remains of this Diaspora Jewry as suggesting
special leanings to symbolic mysticism, in the way that E.R. Goodenough did. (This is a question which deserves more attention than
it has received, but which is now beyond my scope.) Here I wish
to see what light is shed by epigraphic evidence, not directly on the
beliefs of those who produced the inscriptions, but simply on their
behaviour within the city.

I am not presenting any entirely new material and much of what
is relevant has long been available. But let me turn to a document
of major importance.[20] This is the long dedicatory inscription of a
memorial (μνῆμα) invoking divine aid (θεὸς βοηθός) erected by a society (πάτελλα) of Jews and sympathizers or God-worshippers (θεοσεβεῖς) from Aphrodisias in Caria. These men (and one woman—Yael
a προστάτης, 'leader') are in some sense responsible to (ὑποτεταγμένοι)
a further grouping, a δεκανία (*minyan?*), of those described as φιλομαθῶν (hakhamim?) and παντευλογ(ητῶν). (The import of that is less
clear.) They are, it would appear, an exclusive and inward-looking
group, with their own values and, almost, a sub-language; they have
made this dedication out of their own funds, and it is an entirely
private phenomenon. We do not know where the stone originally
stood, nor do we know its date, though it has to come from after
the middle of the second century and may belong to the early third
(with the reverse possibly added even later). This uncertainty is unfortunate; still, even for a late inscription, what we have here is noteworthy as evidence not only of the separate corporate identity (for
certain activities) of a group of Aphrodisian Jews and quasi-Jews, but
also for its opposite—their involvement in the city. This emerges not

---

[19] Cf. the Christian discussions at the Ancyra council of A.D. 314 (can. 7): see
Baer 1961: 90 and n. 38.
[20] Reynolds & Tannenbaum 1987.

only from the first list of subscribers, who appear to be full Jews, together with three proselytes and two isolated *theosebeis* (for some reason), but also from the second section, headed καὶ ὅσοι θεοσεβῖς (sic). In this group, none of whose names are markedly Jewish, we have no fewer than nine individuals labelled as councillors (βουλευτής). As befits their importance, they appear at the head of the list. Further down we have what seems to be a boxer ('Aλέξανδρος πύ[κτης]), though some have doubted the supplement, and a man whose profession is certainly listed as athlete. (For reasons which are uncertain, some but not all of those listed are given a professional description.)

While it may be significant that no councillors or sportsmen are to be found among the fully committed, it is to my mind equally deserving of comment that, together with Jews, we find here registered as participating members of one and the same organization (for study, prayer, eating or burial?) a number of 'Sympathizers'—outsiders who have simply attached themselves to Judaism. For there can be no doubt that at the very least the 'God-worshippers' named in the first list have been allowed to belong. And it is probable that those of the second list are also a part of the club since, after all, they contribute to the same private memorial. Yet the second list contains men who still describe themselves proudly as city councillors, and presumably operate as such. It also contains men who perform professionally in the games. And all this, it should not be forgotten, was in a city dedicated to and enthusiastic about the cult of the goddess after whom it was named, a city which in the second century A.D. boasted a great number of traditional agonistic events. Nor does there appear to be any embarrassment or difficulty for the councillors about identifying themselves openly with a Jewish group[21] We should remember that in a Greek city the council house itself might well contain an imperial altar (as at Miletus and Ephesus).

There exist other known cases of persons who have names usually regarded as Jewish and who are councillors and city officials—again mostly from the first half of the third century A.D. In the Sardis synagogue were found several fragmentary inscriptions recording the fulfilment of vows by men who are titled βουλευταί and, in two cases, also Σαρδιανοί, citizens of Sardis.[22] Unfortunately, many other inscriptions from the Sardis synagogue remain unpublished. For

---

[21] As pointed out by Joyce Reynolds.
[22] Robert 1964: 55–56.

Corycus, Cilicia, there is a sarcophagus bearing an incised menorah and the name Αὐρ(ηλίου) Εὐσανβατίου Μέανδρου Κωρυκιώτου Βουλευτοῦ. This could be dated after A.D. 212, because of the name 'Aurelius'. And here too the man is not only citizen but also councillor.[23]

Two Phrygian tombs, which Robert traces back to the Jewish community of Acmonia in Phrygia, are identified as Jewish by the imprecations they carry. The first calls down 'the curses of Deuteronomy' on anyone who tries to intrude upon the burial.[24] It belongs to Aurelios Phrougianus son of Menocritus and his wife. His offices are listed at the side as *agoranomos, sitones, paraphylax, strategos*, and furthermore, 'he has carried out all the magistracies and liturgies.' The second is also erected for a couple, and the man has been a councillor and archon and has lived virtuously (ζήσας καλῶς). Since it is not the custom for Jews to identify themselves verbally on such monuments as Jews, it is theoretically possible that all these individuals were *theosebeis*, like the Aphrodisias councillors—though to my knowledge this has not been suggested. Against this view, a name like Eusambatios is parallelled by similar constructions among the Jews in the Aphrodisias inscription but not among the God-worshippers. The councillors with Jewish names are probably, then, Jews. How many God-fearers or sympathizers might figure in the epigraphic records, as councillors and in other capacities, without being identifiable as such, we cannot tell, but we should remember that in this direction our knowledge is seriously incomplete.

A wholly Jewish official is the 'curialis' (πολιτευόμενος) spoken of by Malalas (290), one Asabinus, who, around A.D. 190, sold his property so that a municipal building could be erected on it. Here the obvious fact is underlined that he, like all the councillors and city dignitaries we have mentioned, was a man of means. In fact, that may have been partly why these people were pressed into service at a time when there were fewer public benefactors coming forward in the cities. It has even been suggested to me that some of these individuals may have made the liturgical (in the Greek sense) contributions appropriate to their office without actually performing as officials—in the way that some Christians appear to have done for pagan priesthoods in early fourth century Spain, as we learn

---

[23] Robert 1964; *CIJ* II 788, corrected slightly in *Bulletin épigraphique* 24 (1954), 103–104.

[24] Robert 1955: 249–251.

from the records of the Council of Elvira.[25] Whether there were corresponding developments in the integration of non-elite Jews, indeed
whether we are to see them as sharing the same circumstances at
all, is probably an unanswerable question.

With the problem of the Sympathizers, and their relation to the
proper Jews, we may perhaps hope for some further advance. For
it will by now have become evident that the Aphrodisias inscription
sheds new light on the meaning of that problematic term θεοσεβῖς.
There is no doubt that what they are here is a separate and distinct category of people, less fully Jewish than the others (it is not
merely a question of origins, for the proselytes have evidently taken
new Jewish names) and bearing the epithet as a special label. Yet
this is exactly the sense of the term which has been disputed by
those who wished to see it merely as a description which might be
used to qualify 'Jews' by stressing their monotheistic piety.[26] It has
to be admitted that at least sometimes the word means more—or
rather less—than that, and that there exists such a thing as a semi-
proselyte. It is reasonable to go further and take it that the 'God-
fearers' referred to eleven times in Acts (as φοβούμενοι or σεβόμενοι
τὸν θεόν) are members of that same class of the partially-committed,
in spite of the minor divergence in terminology.

This takes us straight to the inscription, found many years ago *in
situ* on the seats of the theatre at Miletus, which comes from the
Roman period but cannot be closely dated (a dating of second to
third century A.D. would seem right on epigraphic grounds). Here,
Schürer's idea that in τόπος Εἰουδέων τῶν καὶ θεοσεβίον (sic), which
strictly means 'place of the Jews who also are called God-worshippers,' we should read τόπος Εἰουδέων καὶ τῶν θεοσεβίον—'place of
the Jews and of the God-worshippers'—now gains in appeal.[27] There
are two sub-groups named here. Although the Greek, taken as it
stands, is incorrectly formulated for this meaning, it is not unusual
to find ungrammatical constructions, improper idioms and simple
errors of word transposition in this kind of provincial notice. In my
view, the text should be interpreted in the light of parallel evidence

---

[25] In A.D. 306; see Jonkers 1974: no. 1, can. 3. I owe this suggestion to A.E.
Wardman.
[26] As Feldman 1950; Robert 1964: 41–45; Kraabel 1981. For bibliography on
the subject, see Kraabel 1981: 124, n. 7.
[27] *CIJ* 748; Schürer 1909: III 174; Hommel 1975: 167–195.

and especially, now, of the clear statement from Aphrodisias. These few Milesian words offer, in a way, almost as much food for thought as the longer inscription. For again, we have the two groups taken as one, this time not by self-identification but by the external agency which allocated to them the privilege of special seats in the civic theatre. And we have unequivocal testimony to the fact that both groups were regular, prominent and respected among the theatre audiences. They would of course have watched not only plays embodying pagan mythological scenes, but also mime, farce and dance of every kind. Sometimes they would have seen gladiatorial shows (Dio of Prusa, *Or.* 31, 121), sometimes pagan religious ceremonial as well. And all were dedicated, as Tertullian insisted (*de Spect.* 95 ff.) to 'those degenerate gods, Venus and Liber', with the path to the theatre coming directly 'from the temples and altars, from that miserable mess of incense and blood, to the tune of flutes and trumpets'.[28]

An even more telling association of the two groups (the Jews and God-fearers), in actual worship can also be demonstrated, though it appears in an inscription which originates in a part of the empire more remote from Mediterranean custom. One of the interesting first century A.D. Jewish manumission inscriptions from Panticapaeum on the North coast of the Black Sea (part of the Pontic kingdom, and once Mithridates' stronghold, but also subject to Hellenic influence since the days of early Greek colonization) concludes with the usual formula that the freed slave, who is to be untrammelled by any obligation except to continue with Jewish worship, will be under the care of the synagogue of the Jews and God-fearers (ἐπιτροπευούους τῆς συναγωγῆς τῆς Ἰουδαίων καὶ θεὸν σέβων).[29] Whether this is the same institution as the one mentioned in other inscriptions[30] and described as just τῆς συναγωγῆς τῆς Ἰουδαίων, we cannot say.

It is worth mentioning at this point that two other Bosphoran inscription (of A.D. 41) from Gorgippia, appear to show Jewish manumitters subscribing to the customary pagan oath formula, 'by Zeus, earth and sun.'[31] But we should not lean too heavily on this testimony, first because the text of the first was apparently tampered with at some stage and, secondly, because the dedication is always

---

[28] Loeb translation.
[29] *CIRB* no. 71.
[30] Ibid. nos. 70, 72, 73.
[31] Ibid. 1123 = *CIJ* 690; Lifschitz 1964: 157–161.

to the Most High, Omnipotent God, who may or may not be a version of the Jewish deity; even the reference in the first inscription
to a house of prayer (usually a synagogue) is quite compatible with
this being at the very least a pagan production written 'under the
influence of Judaism' as Schürer thought, rather than a truly Jewish
inscription. Still, it should be registered that the latter explanation
is generally favored, and rightly so, insofar as the distinction is an
operable one.[32]

Moreover, we do know that city Jews were not always averse from
associating themselves with a pagan oath. This emerges strikingly
from the important Cyrene ephebic inscription, and, even though
there it is a case of passive association with, rather than active adoption of a formula, still it goes well beyond what we might have
expected a priori. This document[33] is part of a list of ephebes—
young men in training—attached to the gymnasium of the major
city of Cyrene in the years A.D. 3/4, and carries with it some additional graffiti. It contains Jewish names of a kind which seem not
open to argument—Ἰούλιος Ἰησουτος, Ἐλασζαρ Ἐλαζαρος, Χαιρέας
Ἰουδα, Ἀγαθοκλῆς Ἐλαζαρος—and there are also three or four such
in the graffiti. It is evident that at the end of the second column
came the customary dedication to the gods of the gymnasium, Hermes
and Heracles. It is not much consolation to remember that, according to 2 Maccabees, the Hellenizing high priest Jason had been keen
to send ambassadors and contributions to the five-yearly festival of
Heracles Melkart at Tyre, nor to note, with Hengel, that the Hellenistic-
Jewish historian Cleodemus-Malchus made Heracles marry a grand-
daughter of Abraham.[34] Applebaum[35] believed that the Jewish ephebes
of Cyrene were bent primarily on securing a special half-way-house
brand of citizenship, not on sport. Still the gymnasium's simple pleasures, if not its educational centrality, should not be overlooked, especially in the light of two more distinctly Jewish names in fragmentary
ephebic lists—Ἰουδας from Iasos in Caria, noted by Robert, and
Αὐρ. Ἰωσης from a third century A.D. list from Coronea, Messenia

---

[32] Schürer 1909: III, 24. Nock, who minimizes the Jewish connection, still sees
the epithets *pantokrator* and especially *eulogetos*, as decisive in favour of Jewishness in
this case (1972: 474). So also Stern 1974: 156, n. 4.
[33] See Lüderitz 1983: no. 7.
[34] Hengel *Judaism*: I, 74; Cleodemus-Malchus—*FGrH* 727 = Holladay *Fragments*:
frag. I B, 1.20.
[35] Applebaum 1964: 291–307.

(in mainland Greece).[36] In addition, H.A. Harris speaks of a possible Menorah scratched on the wall of what was probably the gymnasium changing room, and found by excavation at Priene, but he does not give chapter and verse and, in any case, one can conceive of many possible explanations of this figure—it looks to me more like a fir-tree.[37]

The Sardis synagogue's topography is equivocal in a different way. The synagogue was built (probably towards the end of the second century A.D., though it was much refurbished afterwards), to adjoin the *palaestra*, on a prime site in the centre of the city.[38] We cannot infer a common clientele, but we must suppose at least that such a degree of external contact was not offensive to the founders or to the worshippers, and that this was so although (as has been shown, once more, by excavation) an institution of this sort could well contain within it rooms housing cult statues—including those of the divine emperor, as at Pergamum.

From one point of view, to be among the ephebes was already an achievement. We can see this in the emperor Claudius' injunction to the Alexandrian Jews 'not to intrude themselves into the games presided over by the *gymnasiarchoi* and the *kosmetai*'.[39] But eventually—though not until A.D. 304—a man with a Jewish name becomes himself a gymnasiarch in Egypt. An Egyptian woman issues a tax receipt on papyrus, and is represented by her husband, Joannes Aurelius, who is described as γυμν(ασίαρχος).[40] The editors comment 'to judge from his name, Joannes was a Jew, though, as it seems, a lax one, if indeed he acted as gymnasiarch, a post hardly compatible with strict adherence to the Jewish faith'! The question is, which brand of the Jewish faith.

If this is the first gymnasiarch to appear so far in surviving records, it does not, of course, follow that there were none before. Another point to bear in mind is that change is likely to have occurred at different rates in different places—the relatively early date of the Cyrene ephebe list deserves emphasis.

It is at Cyrene, interestingly enough, that we find also a Jewish city official of the first century (A.D. 59–61). He thus precedes the

---

[36] *Hellenica* 1940: 29; 1937: 80; *IG* V, 1, 1398.
[37] Harris 1976: 93 and Plate I.
[38] For assessment and bibliography, see Kraabel 1979: 83–88; also, Seager 1972.
[39] *CPJ* II, no. 153, 11. 92–93 = P. Lond 1912.
[40] *CPJ* III, no. 474, 11. 1–3.

Asian councillors by almost two hundred years. So let us leave the gymnasium to cast a concluding eye over the Cyrenaic list of the law-guardians (*nomophylakes*).[41] (This was studied fully by Applebaum.)[42] Among the names is an unequivocal Ἐλαζα(ρ) (Ἰ)ασονος. So this man, presumably a Jew, figures among a small number of officers who supervised law-enforcement and the constitution for a now aristocratic government. Other inscriptions erected by the people of Cyrene are dedicated to Good Fortune, Apollo Nomios, Homonoia (Concord) and Aphrodite. Robert[43] accepts Ἐλαζα(ρ) as Jewish. I suppose it remains theoretically possible that such characters had in fact abandoned their faith but, in the then not wholly unfriendly atmosphere of Cyrene, felt no need to alter their names. Yet that they were Jews, of one kind or another, is the more natural explanation. Were they uneasy about what they were doing? Or was it entirely acceptable within the terms of the Judaism they practised? Among their other limitations, inscriptions are poor evidence for the subtler nuances of personal attitude. Perhaps, after all, it was the former; and perhaps the compromise was not without certain tensions. We may fancy that our law guardians and ephebes might be the ancestors of some of those desperate people who were eventually driven, during the Jewish revolt under Trajan, to set upon and vandalize the temples of Hecate, Apollo and Zeus, as well as that of the imperial cult, and probably those of Artemis, Demeter, Isis and the Dioscuri too,[44] and who thus express an underlying resentment about the pagan cults which had formerly been allowed to encroach upon their lives. In their iconoclasm, they may have been taking literally the Deuteronomic injunction—'and ye shall overthrow their altars and break their pillars' (11:3); yet, after centuries of co-existence, such an outburst must be taken above all as expressing pent-up fury, as the eventual product of old restraints and tensions.

---

[41] *CJZC* no. 8.
[42] Applebaum 1964.
[43] Robert & Robert 1962: 218.
[44] The evidence is mainly archaeological; see Applebaum 1979: 272–285; Pucci 1981: 45–46; and for an excellent summary of the evidence, with references, Smallwood 1976: 397–398, with n. 25.

BIBLIOGRAPHY

Applebaum, S. 1964. 'Jewish Status at Cyrene in the Roman Period', *La Parola del Passato* 19: 291–307.
—— 1979. *Jews and Greeks in Ancient Cyrene*. Leiden.
Baer, Y. 1961. 'Israel, the Christian Church, and the Roman Empire', *Scripta Hierosolymitana* 7: 79–149.
Brooten, B.J. 1982. *Women Leaders in the Ancient Synagogue*. Brown Judaic Studies 36. Chico, California.
Collins, J.J. 1985. in J. Neusner & E.S. Frerichs (eds), 'A Symbol of Other ness: Circumcision and Salvation in the First Century', *"To see ourselves as others see us": Christians, Jews, "others" in late antiquity*. Scholars Press Studies in the Humanities Series. Chico, California, 163–186.
Elmsley, W.A.L. 1911. *The Mishna on Idolatry: 'Aboda Zara*. Cambridge.
Feldman, L.H. 1950. 'Jewish 'Sympathizers' in Classical Literature and Inscriptions', *TAPA* 81: 200–208.
Gibbon, E. *The Decline and Fall of the Roman Empire*, chap. 15.
Goldenberg, R. 1979. 'The Jewish Sabbath in the Roman World', *ANRW* II, 19, 1: 414–447.
Goodman, M. 1983. *State and Society in Roman Galilee 132–212*. Totowa, New Jersey.
Gutmann, J. (ed). 1975. *The Synagogue: Studies in Origins, Archaeology and Architecture, selected with a prolegomenon*. New York.
Hadas-Lebel, M. 1979. 'Le paganisme à travers les sources rabbiniques des IIe et IIIe siècles. Contribution à l'étude du syncrétisme dans l'Empire romain', *ANRW* II, 19.2: 397–485.
Harris, H.A. 1976. *Greek Athletics and the Jews*. Cardiff.
Hengel, M. 1966. 'Die Synagogeninschrift von Stobi', *ZNTW* 57: 145–183.
Hommel, H. 1975. 'Juden und Christen im kaiserzeitlichen Milet', *Istanbuler Mitteilungen* 25: 167–195.
Jonkers E.J. (ed). 1974. *Acta et symbola conciliorum quae saeculo quarto habita sunt*. Leiden.
Kasher, A. 1978. *The Jews in Hellenistic and Roman Egypt* (Hebrew with English summary). Tel Aviv.
Kraabel, A.T. 1979. 'The Diaspora Synagogue: Archaeological and Epigraphic Evidence since Sukenik', *ANRW* II, 19.1: 477–510.
—— 1981. 'The Disappearance of the God-fearers', *Numen* 28: 113–126.
Lifschitz, B. 1964. 'Le culte du Dieu Très Haut à Gorgippia', *Rivista di Filologia* 92: 157–161.
Lüderitz, C. 1983. *Corpus judischer Zeugnisse aus der Cyrenaika*. Beihefte zum Tübinger Atlas des vorderen Orients Reihe B, 53. Wiesbaden.
Meeks, W.A. 1983. *The First Urban Christians: The Social World of the Apostle Paul*. New Haven.
Meeks W.A. & Wilken, R.L. 1978. *Jews and Christians in Antioch in the First Four Centuries of the Common Era*. Sources for Biblical Study 1. Missoula.
MacMullen, R. 1981. *Paganism in the Roman Empire*. New Haven.
Neusner, J. 1973. *The Idea of Purity in Ancient Judaism*. Studies in Judaism in Late Antiquity 1. Leiden.
—— 1974–77. *A History of the Mishnaic Law of Purities*, vols. 1–22. Studies in Judaism in Late Antiquity. Leiden.
Nock, A.D. 1972. *Essays on Religion and the Ancient World*. Oxford.
Price, S.R.F. 1984. *Rituals and Power: The Roman Imperial Cult in Asia Minor*, 128. Cambridge.
Pucci, M. 1981. *La Rivolta ebraica al tempo di Traiano*. Pisa.
Reynolds, J. & Tannenbaum, R. 1987. Jews and God-Fearers at Aphrodisias: Greek

Inscriptions with Commentary. Cambridge Philological Society, Supplementary 12. Cambridge.

Robert, L. 1937. 'Un corpus des inscriptions juives', *REJ* 101: 73–86.

—— 1940. *Hellenica*, vol. 1. Paris.

—— 1946. *Hellenica*, vol. 3. Paris.

—— 1955. *Hellenica*, vol. 10. Paris.

—— 1964. *Nouvelles inscriptions de Sardes*. Paris.

Robert, J. & Robert, L. 1962. 'Bulletin épigraphique', *REG* 75: 130–226.

Safrai, S. 1974. 'Relations between the Diaspora and the Land of Israel', in S. Safrai & M. Stern (eds), *The Jewish People in the First Century*. Compendia Iudaicarum ad Novum Testamentum I.1. Assen/Philadelphia, 184–215.

Schürer, E. 1909. *Geschichte des jüdischen Volkes im Zeitalter Jesu Christi*, 4th edn., vol. 3. Leipzig.

Seager, A.P. 1972. 'The Building History of the Sardis Synagogue', *AJA* 76: 425–435.

Smallwood, E.M. 1976. *The Jews under Roman Rule*. Studies in Judaism in Late Antiquity 20. Leiden.

Stern, M. 1974. 'The Jewish Diaspora', in S. Safrai & M. Stern (eds), *The Jewish People in the First Century*. Compendia Iudaicarum ad Novum Testamentum I.1. Assen/Philadelphia, 117–183.

Theissen, G. 1982. 'The Strong and the Weak in Corinth: a Sociological Analysis of a Theological Quarrel', in J.H. Schutz (ed.), *The Social Setting of Pauline Christianity: Essays on Corinth* (transl.). Studies in the New Testament and Its World. Edinburgh.

CHAPTER NINETEEN

BENEFACTORS IN THE GRECO-JEWISH DIASPORA

Philo opens his book *On the Decalogue* by asking why Moses gave the laws in the desert rather than in a polis. The answer is concerned with the evils of city-life.' In cities there arises that most insidious of foes, pride (τῦφος), and some people admire it and bow down to empty appearances of distinction and make it important by means of golden crowns and purple robes.' He declares that 'pride is the creator of many other evils: boastfulness, haughtiness, inequality;[1] and these are the sources of war, both foreign and civil'. He also makes the fundamental claim that 'pride brings divine things into contempt, although these ought to receive the highest honour (τιμή)' (*de Decal.* I 4–7).

Josephus writes in similar vein in *Against Apion*, belittling the award of crowns and public announcements of honours: 'for those who live by our laws, the reward is not silver or gold or a crown of olive or of parsley or any such proclamation.' (*CA* II 217–218). The allusion is surely not just to the time-honoured way of treating victors in the Olympic and other great games of Greece, as Thackeray's note suggests,[2] but rather to the modes of recognition of the powerful and the munificent in the Greek civic milieu of Josephus' own day and age. The writer is making an ideological point, sharpening a distinction between Jews and pagans to establish an ethical contrast between two world views. He would not have needed, in this moralizing context, to take account of an awkward case like that of a man from Leontopolis in Egypt, perhaps a near contemporary of the historian. This was the most blessed Abraham, Ἄβραμος ὁ μακαριότατος, who was 'not without honour' (ἀγέραστος) in his city but, in the interesting metaphor of his verse epitaph, 'wore the wreath of magistracy for the whole people, in his wisdom.'[3]

---

[1] Or perhaps 'impiety', depending on the manuscript reading adopted (Colson prefers ἀνισοτητος, as in R, to ἀνοσιοτητος: see Loeb Philo VII, n. *ad. loc.*).

[2] Loeb Josephus I, n. *ad. loc.*

[3] *CPJ* III 1530A.

Once more in *Against Apion*, Josephus reminds readers that Jews, unlike Greeks, do not believe in making statues of those they like or admire (*CA* II 74). Here, of course, the second commandment is at least as much a consideration as distrust of honours. And finally, at yet another point in that work, in a discussion of death, it is asserted by Josephus that 'the Jewish law does not allow for expensive funerals or the erection of conspicuous monuments.' (*CA* II 205). This is another way in which the display values of the late Greek polis are undercut, at least in theory. In fact, we may be inclined to think that the tombs of the high priests in Jerusalem, still visible in the Kedron valley, told another story; but it might then be suggested that, in Jerusalem, Jewish self-differentiation from Greco-Roman values was less necessary. In any case, we need not be wholly surprised to find practice diverging from principle.

Visible abstention from social competition and from its various manifestations was a way of marking out a community from its civic environment and binding it together. This at least partly explains the stress laid upon such ideas by another diaspora Jew, Paul of Tarsus, as he sought to define a place in society for the developing Christian church.[4] The Epistle to the Romans (12:3) offers, appropriately enough, a particularly clear statement: 'I say to everyone among you: do not be conceited or think too highly of yourself; but think your way to a sober estimate based on the measure of faith that God has dealt to each of you. For just as in a single human body there are many limbs and organs, all with different functions, so all of us, united with Christ, form one body.'

It is instructive, and also ironic, to note that these critiques are expressed in terms indebted to Greek culture itself, even if they are fuelled, ultimately, by a biblical sense of justice. For there is a familiar *topos* favoured by writers of Stoic inclination—though not necessarily of modest lifestyle—which bears a clear resemblance to our theme, especially as Josephus expresses it. Plutarch, a near-contemporary, has this *topos* on occasion. But particularly with Dio Chrysostom, the second-century orator from Prusa, it is a characteristic stance to denounce the pursuit of public popularity. For him the absurdities of honours offer an excellent subject for satire or vituperation. So,

---

[4] I owe to Professor Halvor Moxnes the suggested connections between this strand in Paul's thought, and civic patronage, made in a paper given in Aarhus University, Denmark.

Dio describes how cities 'led their victims about with a sprig of green, as men lead cattle, or clapped upon their heads a crown or a ribbon' (*Or.* 66.2). Some men might be equipped with any number of crowns: olive, oak, ivy, myrtle. Yet, he says, the cost of getting a purple mantle from the dyers is less than that of getting it by public award. No nanny-goat would hurl herself over a cliff for the sake of a sprig of wild olive, and no sane person would walk around with his head bound unless he had suffered a fracture (*Or.* 66.4–5). But with Dio, the whole issue is given a Stoic twist which is crucial to his philosophical position: to pursue δόξα, fame, is to be the victim of a passion like any other, and thus to be at the mercy of people and events and so unable to achieve true happiness.[5] This conclusion puts an entirely different complexion on the matter from that in Philo and Josephus.

The various practices from which the two major Jewish-Greek writers distance themselves are ones which, at any rate from the Hellenistic period, were deeply ingrained in the fabric of city life around the Greek world and in areas influenced by it. We need to define it more closely, if we are to understand the Jewish reaction.[6] The bestowal of lavish honours on those who had power, which might be manifested through office-holding, through personal connections, through family prominence, or, most often, through all three, and nearly always with the accompaniment of conspicuous wealth, was one of the most visible features in the life of a city. Those honours were the repayment for an expenditure of a large part of that wealth within the public domain, for supposed benefits, demonstratively conferred on the citizens. And they were a not-too-subtle statement to the donor that he had a reputation which could only be kept up by further benefaction.

So, those who were honoured were honoured not just for what they were or even for what they had achieved, but by way of trade-off for what they had done or given or were going to do or to give, for the enhancement of the city and for the advantage of its gods or its people. In a watered-down form, such phenomena are perfectly

---

[5] On these themes in the speeches of Dio Chrysostom, who still endorsed generosity to one's city, see Jones 1978: 110 ff.

[6] For an excellent discussion of the system of benefaction in relation to synagogue construction, see White 1990: ch. 4. M. Lewis discusses male as well as female benefactors in a Roman context in Haas 1992. Cf. Rajak & Noy 1993 = Ch. 20 in this volume.

familiar today. But in the Greco-Roman world, they made up a tighter structure, with patterns that were more fixed, and they were also more crucial to the working of the cities and to social relations. Paul Veyne regards the unusual combination of apparently contradictory features, a sense of constraint on the one hand, and a measure of spontaneity, as the distinguishing mark of Greco-Roman euergetism.[7] Public buildings and works, provisioning, politics and diplomacy, entertainment and festivals, religious life, medicine: all these a city was likely to owe to its benefactors, who were usually prominent citizens, but occasionally interested outsiders. The process was also, as Philo and Josephus well appreciated, an intrinsic part of the moral formation of the pagan elites: benefactors were praised in the highest terms, and the φιλανθρωπία or μεγαλοψυχία which were understood to have motivated their actions were deemed supreme virtues.

It is because the system was both distinctive and central that recent historians have labelled it, evolving the term 'euergetism', from the Greek εὐεργέτης, a benefactor.[8] The manifestations of classical euergetism are familiar to us largely through an extensive and increasing epigraphic record.[9] Euergetism, indeed, went hand in hand with the 'epigraphic habit', since, in the first place, it was advantageous to donors to put their donations on public record, while, from the other side, honours could be made meaningful by being perpetuated in stone by a grateful recipient community or its representatives. Thus the act of giving best be made to serve not just the donor but his children and descendants, and the social standing of an entire family could be enhanced.

Honorific decrees are often framed in the most lavish of terms. Moreover, a city council's resolution that decrees should be inscribed on a stele in a prominent place is itself sometimes listed as one of the honours accorded to the honorand. It has been aptly pointed out that there is a careful reciprocation in the transactions, with honours being seen as due payment for services rendered. In fact, honours might well be spoken of as having to be commensurate in

---

[7] Veyne 1990: 103.

[8] Veyne's landmark study appeared in French in 1976. Cf. Hands 1968: ch. 2; Gauthier 1985. Other important studies tend to focus on individual foundations: recently, and with bibliography, see Rogers 1991: 91–100. See also a collection of translated texts primarily for students of the New Testament: Danker 1982.

[9] MacMullen 1982: 233–246; Meyer 1990: 74–96.

quantity and quality with the benefactions, as well as with the importance of the individual in question. Honours ranged from crowns, wreaths, and titles, to front seats at ceremonial occasions (προεδρία), the linking of parts of festivals or of whole festivals to the name of the donor, statues in precious metals, freedom from obligations, further and higher offices, and perpetuation to eternity of some or all of these benefits.

There were evidently local and temporal variations in custom (it would seem that honours became more elaborate as time went on), but on the whole the system surprises us with its uniformity. One typical instance—so typical, indeed, as to be described as 'banale' by its editor—will therefore suffice for illustration. In the decree of the city of Kyme now in the J. Paul Getty Museum,[10] which probably dates from the Augustan period and which honours the πρύτανις Kleanax, it is on record that this man's ancestral nobility of character (ἀμθιθάλεια, εὐγένηα *sic*) and his goodwill toward the people, aimed εἰς φιλοδοξίαν (love of glory) had made him overlook no opportunity of conferring benefit upon them. This φιλοδοξία combined with εὐσέβεια had ensured extensive subvention of the mysteries of Dionysus, with public banquets and, of course, wine. His education of his son (obviously a future benefactor) merited special comment. The imperial cult had been well served. Altogether, an open and shut case for a gold crown. It is not clear, due to defects in the stone, what other rewards Kleanax received. It is worth pointing out that Kleanax does not appear to have belonged to the very highest social stratum in Kyme.

To get the honours right was vital in order to secure future services, from the donor in question or from others, and sometimes the gifts expected in the future are even spelled out in an inscription. Also, we find a number of formulae in which the donor is described as an example to others; and the actual inscription itself may also be explained as being intended to inspire emulation. Indeed, it is in this light that the various terms of praise for the generosity and the moral qualities of the donor should be seen, especially the stress on

---

[10] The inscription is published by Hodot 1982: 165–180. I owe my acquaintance with it to an unpublished seminar paper given by Riet van Bremen at the Institute of Classical Studies, London.

the virtues of devotion to honour or to glory—precisely those attributes which Jews professed to disregard.[11]

An additional feature to be observed in certain inscriptions is that
there exists an opportunity for self-congratulation even for the givers-
of-thanks: to pay due acknowledgement is itself an act within the
sphere of public morality.[12]

It is clear that in the civic context and even more widely, on the
regional and imperial levels, euergetism played a major economic
role, though how far it is right to analyse it ultimately in those terms
is a matter of disagreement: Paul Veyne would say rather little, stressing that the self-gratification of the donor, and the accumulation of
honour and of power, are basic commodities in this kind of transaction, which needs therefore to be analysed in terms of social relationships and not of economic rationality. I shall not to enter into
these theoretical questions here. What is more to the point is to
notice that the same patterns of language and behaviour operated
also on a smaller scale, within the clubs and associations with which
the cities proliferated. These too had their patrons, their notables
and their benefactors, and they too honoured them in a variety of
ways.[13] We recall Polybius' unforgettable remarks about those wealthy
families in Boeotia who had distributed the greater part of their fortunes among the clubs, so that many Boeotians had more dinners
in the month than there were days in the calendar (20.6–7). In such
a context, we quite often see individuals of moderate means acting
out the roles of the good and the great.

Thus two major questions arise, when we come to consider the
Jews. First, did they have any role to play in the civic euergetism
of their environments, or rather was their reluctance to accept its
principles a factor which contributed to marginalizing them? Second,
did they take on board any aspect of these practices within their
own organizations, and if they did, are there any signs of limits being
set to their adoption? The protests of Philo and Josephus offer a
background against which to ask these questions.

The foreground, as with the study of pagan euergetism, is necessarily epigraphic. Neither Diaspora Jews, nor in due course those of

---

[11] On *philotimia* manifested by gods when they are honoured, see the interesting
remarks of Versnel 1981: 51.

[12] A striking example is Danker no. 15, from Iasos.

[13] See Hands 1968: 49–53.

Palestine, proved immune from the 'epigraphic habit' and, as is well known, we have a body of inscriptions concerning benefactions within a Jewish or Judaizing context. Baruch Lifshitz[14] collected the majority of them, a total of 102. His valuable collection with its commentary is the basis for this study and, indeed, a stimulus to it. Those rare cases where the benefaction is not synagogue-related, or ones where the benefactor appears not to be a Jew, as well as those in languages other than Greek, and of course those surfacing since 1967, are not included in the volume. In contrast to Lifshitz, I shall take into account the small number of relevant Latin inscriptions along with the Greek, though it is hard sometimes to avoid the shorthand 'Greek inscriptions', because that is what the bulk of them are. Aramaic and Hebrew material will appear here only peripherally.

I have chosen to focus on the Jewish Diaspora. But it has to be recognized that this delimitation introduces a certain arbitrary element when it comes to inscriptions, and, indeed, to Jewish communities, since there is no hard-and-fast distinction between a Diaspora Greek city, a city within Palestine but with a cosmopolitan population, like Caesarea, one on the fringes of Palestine such as Gadara, and one a little further afield but still within the same cultural world, for example, Beirut. One might adopt the Talmudic definitions of what was a Jewish city, but that would not advance matters very far. If we stop for a moment to consider Jerusalem itself, we recall that it is the provenance of one our most important donor inscriptions, the text about the refurbishment by Theodotus son of Vettenus of the synagogue founded by his forbears (Lifshitz 79; *CIJ* II, 1404). We also recall that the apparently Roman name 'Vettenus' has encouraged a *communis opinio* that this was a family of returnees from Rome; that, then, is where the father and grandfather will have been *archisynagogoi*. It becomes arbitrary to exclude even the Theodotus inscription. Then again, in terms of cultural patterns, Syria seems to be closer to Palestine sometimes than to what is regarded as the Diaspora. We shall see an example of this later. A further complication is that, when it comes to synagogue building within Palestine, donors are recorded in the Galilean villages of the later Roman empire, and not only in cities and towns, so we are no longer dealing with a civic phenomenon; these inscriptions are more often in Hebrew or Aramaic than in Greek.

---

[14] 1967.

These are very real problems and I do not pretend that I can see exactly how they should be dealt with. They affect discussion of the Greco-Roman Diaspora over a wide range of issues, and they suggest that the Diaspora-Palestine distinction may not always be the most useful one with which to operate, in writing the Jewish history of this period. Now, however, I shall keep the subject within limits, restricting the main discussion to texts in Greek or Latin, and directing the focus onto those which technically originate from outside Palestine.

There survive four reasonably extended texts concerning individual benefactions in a Jewish context, apart from the Theodotus inscription. One (from Berenice in Cyrenaica) in fact involves a non-Jewish patron of the Jewish community. The Aphrodisias inscription, which is the longest known Jewish inscription, concerns two groups of contributors to a foundation, including both Jews (among them proselytes) and sympathizers. Significant groups of benefactors are listed in the fourth major text, once again from Berenice. Groups also appear in a series of small inscriptions, as contributors to a mosaic floor in late fourth century Apamea in Syria, and at Sardis where they contribute to the wall-paintings of the synagogue, in much the same period. In the synagogue of Naro (Hammam Lif), the mosaic was also paved collectively.[15] The group at Hammath Tiberias does not concern us.

A few middle-length inscriptions are of enormous interest, especially, perhaps, that concerning a woman called Tation in Phocaea, Ionia—whose Jewishness has also been doubted; that of the refurbishers of Julia Severa's synagogue at Acmonia, Phrygia, where the builder herself had been a pagan priestess; and that of Polycharmus, the *archisynagogos* at Stobi, Macedonia.

Short texts are occasionally of special note, as is the dedication of Publius Rutilius Ioses (thus disentangled by L. Robert, from the letters PROUTIOSES), ἀξιολογώτατος ἀρχισυνάγωγος in Teos in Ionia (Lifshitz 16; *CIJ* II, 744). Often enough, we are just dealing with scraps, perhaps a name or a couple of names and a formula. All this is, in fact, very far from the verbose world of pagan epigraphic benefaction and honour. It may seem surprising, then, that I should claim the possibility of drawing any conclusions at all about

---

[15] See Le Bohec 1981: 165–170.

Jews and euergetism. Yet a careful study, in which the dossier is considered as a whole rather than as individual items, throws up some striking possibilities.

For this purpose, a body of 94 inscriptions was studied. This number excludes those from Palestine, which Lifshitz included, but adds to his list several items in the categories already mentioned, including the Aphrodisias inscription, two items from Egypt, one Ptolemaic and one Roman, some short texts from Hammam Lif and Utica in Africa, an inscription from Ostia, and one from Philippopolis (Plovdiv) in Thrace. While not every one of these can receive individual discussion here, my general observations and tentative conclusions are based on this corpus. I have not been able to take into account material from Sardis, beyond what was known to Lifshitz, though when all of this is eventually published, it will obviously be of very great importance. A pair of inscriptions from the Samaritan community on Delos, who, as is well known, describe themselves as Israelites from Shechem, have here to be excluded from the reckoning, though not because they are undeserving of attention.

The overwhelming majority of inscriptions, while giving the names and sometimes the offices of donors, do not describe honours accorded to them. If we compare the non-Jewish epigraphy, this is already a striking fact, even taking into account the accidents of survival. Six post-third century Syrian inscriptions might be deemed an exception in that they confer blessings on the donors or on their memories and in one case on their children too; this pattern is also found in nine late texts from Palestine, but nowhere else.

What of honours proper? Is there evidence that benefactors in the Diaspora Jewish milieu were repaid with visible honours, as was normal in a euergetistic system, but as should have been discouraged, if the principles of Philo and Josephus meant anything?

It does seem to be the case that Jews did not honour one another with statues. There is one possible exception, but it is a very dubious one. This is an Egyptian fragment now in the Hermitage (Lifshitz 98), in which one Artemon son of Nikon, eleven times a προστάτης, is recorded, apparently, as having given something to a synagogue (probably that term is to be taken in the sense of 'community'). This inscription in fact derives from a statue base, no doubt belonging to Artemon's honorific statue (a fact seemingly unknown to Lifshitz). However, it seems that we should probably discount altogether any Jewish attachment. A *synagoge* can also be a pagan grouping in Egypt and other places, and there are no other indicators of Jewishness, even if both Artemon and Nikon are names used by Jews. Were this to be taken as a Jewish inscription, it would constitute a striking exception. on existing evidence.[16]

We now need to consider other kinds of honours conferred on benefactors. There are five clear-cut instances, three from Cyrenaica. It is important to note that all five may be described as in some sense marginal. I use the word 'marginal' neutrally, without begging any questions, and its implications will emerge in the course of discussion.

One of the inscriptions from Berenice, now in Toulouse,[17] is a virtually complete decree made at the *sukkoth* convention (σύλλογος) honouring a certain M. Tittius, son of Sestus, evidently a Roman official (ἔπαρχος), who has been a patron both to the Jewish πολίτευμα and to individual members. He is to receive an olive wreath and a wool fillet at each assembly (σύνοδος) and at each new moon, and the archons are to have the decree itself inscribed on marble in the most prominent position in the amphitheatre. The garlanding may well presuppose the existence of a statue. Tittius himself is described as a man καλὸς καὶ ἀγαθός, but no further praise is offered. Arguably, no more would be expected, however, at so early a date as this: the inscription is perhaps even as early as the first century B.C., but more likely belongs to the first half of the first century A.D.[18] In general terms, we see here a Jewish community honouring a pagan benefactor in the established Greek way. The question arises whether the amphitheatre was that of the city, in which the Jews as a group could conceivably have had a share and perhaps their own patch, or an oval building of their own, as was already proposed by Applebaum.[19]

Applebaum's solution would seem to be demanded by the sister inscription, where the amphitheatre of Berenice figures prominently. This decree honours M. Valerius Dionysius, also a Roman citizen, as the *tria nomina* indicate (though no tribe is given) and it is now

---

[16] For arguments against the Jewishness of this inscription, see JIGRE no. 20, where it is now newly edited. Cf. no. 26, for an even more dubious case of what may have been a statue connected with a possibly judaizing association.

[17] Lüderitz 1983: no. 71.

[18] The identification of the dating era remains uncertain. For the early dating, see Baldwin Bowsky 1987: 495–510.

[19] Applebaum 1979: 164–167.

to be found in Carpentras, of all places.[20] For Dionysius had sur-
faced the amphitheatre's floor and decorated its walls. His rewards
are comparable, with the addition of freedom from liturgies. But
since those liturgies can only be understood as those paid to the
Jewish πολίτευμα (such terminology can be parallelled in pagan epigraphy in the context of clubs and associations), Dionysius is normally
taken as a member of that πολίτευμα and therefore as a Jew. I cannot see any way round this conclusion: we otherwise have to go to
the lengths of supposing that Dionysius has refurbished the *city's*
amphitheatre, that he has been honoured by the city's archons for
it (the largely pagan names given for the archons might support this)
and that the Jewish πολίτευμα, being a constituent part of the city,
has joined with the archons in endorsing those honours, as part of
the give-and-take process in a highly integrated city.[21] If we do not
accept this last, rather strained reconstruction, then we have here a
case of a Hellenized and Romanized Jew honoured in Greek style.
just possibly even with a statue, though that, it should be stressed,
is nowhere mentioned in what survives of the text. The alternative
reconstruction would show us the Jews as a community operating
freely within the Greek euergetistic pattern, in relation to an outsider and to the affairs of the city. Both scenarios would be remarkable and the Berenice community was indubitably a remarkable
community. But we should treat it not as a unique case to be
explained away, but as a fortunate surviving instance of what could
be possible in certain circumstances.

At Acmonia in Phrygia, an interesting mixed environment of a
different kind,[22] the three first century restorers of the synagogue earlier established by Julia Severa were honoured by the community
for their virtuous benevolence and zeal with a golden shield (Lifshitz
33; *CIJ* II, 766). The honour is a familiar one; so too are the virtues;
but in the Jewish world they stand out. The donations are explained
as having been made ἐκ τῶν ἰδίων, from the individuals' own resources.
Of the dedicators, one is a Roman citizen, P. Turronius Cladus; he
and Lucius son of Lucius are *archisynagogoi*, the former for life (διὰ

[20] *CJZC* 70, with bibliography.
[21] I am grateful to Joyce Reynolds for discussing this problem with me.
[22] On this environment, see Sheppard 1979: 169–180; Trebilco 1991: 58–84.
There is much that is still of value in Ramsay 1897, who perhaps over-estimates
actual Jewish involvement in the society.

βίου),²³ and the third individual is described as an archon. Julia Severa, the foundress, is attested as a pagan priestess on the city's coinage, while the Turronii were a well-known family in pagan Acmonia. The presumption is that this Turronius Cladus, being an *archisynagogos* is attached to the Jewish community (I deliberately put it no more strongly than this). It makes sense that in such circles, the honour system should be firmly rooted. It is noteworthy, on the other hand, that a degree of restraint is observable in its application: there is no statue mentioned, and the praise is modest.

In the old Greek colony of Phocaea, in Ionia, Tation daughter of Straton, who was the son of Empedon, was honoured by the synagogue for favours to the Jews (Lifshitz 13; *CIJ* II,738). Some have taken this formulation to suggest that she herself was not in any real sense Jewish, which is certainly not to be excluded.²⁴ If this were the case, then the construction of a meeting place (οἶκος) and courtyard for which she was honoured with a gold crown and προεδρία (a front seat) would be another instance of Jewish involvement in the wider honour system of the city. We would be witnessing a mutual exchange of courtesies, with Tation appearing on occasion in the synagogue to take up her front seat. If Tation was Jewish, which is more likely, then the gold crown is something to be remarked on; but so, too, perhaps, is the absence of encomium. It is worth pointing out, however, that Jewish communities appear to have had no difficulty about awarding gold crowns to rulers who were benefactors, and even displaying them in (or perhaps in the entrance to) synagogues.²⁵

There are also two honorific decrees of a very fragmentary nature. One from Samos, of which three fragments survive, is apparently a decree by the presbyters of the Jews, and its concern seems to be with honours. We can make out here some of the characteristic language of the conferring of honours.²⁶ The second is a damaged Latin

---

²³ On the significance of this title, see Rajak & Noy 1993: 75–93 = Ch. 20.

²⁴ See Trebilco 1991: 230, n. 34. On Tation, see also Brooten 1982: 143–144.

²⁵ See Philo, *Legatio* 133, with discussion in Smallwood 1961: n. *ad. loc.*, 220–221. To Smallwood's list of Jewish honours to rulers from the Roman period, add Scheiber 1983: no. 3: a soldier who seems to be an *archisynagogos*, for the safety of Alexander Severus.

²⁶ ἐτίμησαν ... πάσης δόξης ... ἀνεθήκαν. For the inscription see B. Lifshitz in *CIJ* I, ed. 2, Prolegomenon, 89 (731f).

text from Castel Porziano, south east of Ostia, in which the word 'universitas' has been supplemented before 'Iudaeorum' and a plot of land is given to a *gerousiarch*, for a family tomb; this is done presumably, though not explicitly, as a recompense for his services (*CIJ* 533).

An interesting and difficult document from Tlos in Lycia (*CIJ* 757) has a citizen called Ptolemaios Leukios setting up a tomb for his family, under public protection, though at his own expense, as a consequence of his having held office—ὑπὲρ ἀρχοντείας τελουμένης. In this formula, the office-holder is conceived of as a *euergetes*, who is owed something by the city.

Now it is a possibility which we have to acknowledge that the donors in the bulk of our inscriptions were simply not big enough people to receive crowns, shields or garlands: had they been wealthy enough to give on a large scale they might, it could be argued, have done so. The lack of awards and eulogies would then tell us more about the economic status of Jewish communities than about their values and beliefs. And indeed many donations seem to be moderate, consisting in portions of a synagogue floor or wall, or perhaps an accoutrement or vessel. Perhaps one third of donors are not specified as title-holders.

Where there are groups of donors, the cost of an operation is split, and separate names or groups of names may be recorded, but that record, as one among many, is the only visible honour conferred. In the case of the Berenice group of A.D. 56 (*CJZC* 72), where sums of money are, uniquely, given, these range from ten drachmas from each of ten archons of the community, and from one priest, to twenty eight from one individual without office and twenty five from each of two others. Further names are missing. The great new Aphrodisias inscription, which lists those responsible for a mysterious memorial, gives a large number of names, perhaps the entire roster of the equally opaque δεκάνια, which may or may not have included also the sympathizers on the second face of the stone.[27]

It is tempting to argue that these and other group donations are nothing less than another strategy to minimize the impact of the donor and his or her wealth within the Jewish community, by asserting the act of giving as a communal and equalizing activity, not a

---

[27] Reynolds & Tannenbaum 1987.

field for display, for the exercize of power or the accumulation of privilege. The identity of the sums given by each and every one of the listed Berenice archons might support this case. Office-holding in that society carried its obligations, but was scarcely a route to outshining others. Lists of group donations are not unique to Jewish communities,[28] but they do seem to have taken root in the Jewish environment.

Our last major inscription, a 32–line text known since 1931, suggests another strategy for taking the donor out of the limelight, and that is to link the donation into the sphere of religious obligation. Claudius Tiberius Polycharmus of Stobi in Macedonia could have been no mean donor. This is suggested both by his Roman citizenship, evidently predating A.D. 212 and by what he owned: a property with a courtyard in the city large enough for him to hand over a major part of it, so that its downstairs could serve as a synagogue and a communal facility. He has the respected position of being father of the synagogue. But he makes over the gift εὐχῆς ἕνεκα, in fulfilment of a vow. That being so, self-advertisement might not seem in order, and we do not find any in the text. The detailed record of the donation appears to designed largely to clarify the legal position, enshrining the right of Polycharmus and his heirs to the upper storey of the house, and securing against any change to the arrangements by the imposition of a fine to be paid to the patriarch (presumably a local Jewish official). More recent excavations have established something of an archaeological context for the inscription, though its date remains controversial. Fresco fragments in red on white repeat Polycharmus' name, with the formula Τιβέριος ὁ πατὴρ εὐχήν.

The vow formula is repeated in numerous small inscriptions, to be precise, we find it in 42 of them, in one form or another. In inscriptions that can be established as later in date, the formula ὑπὲρ σωτηρίας (*pro salute*) tends to take over, but to have the same implications. So standard are they that it is hard to decide whether a real vow was to be seen as underlying the donation in every case. These votive formulae are perfectly well-known in pagan contexts, where they are normally associated with various smaller or larger thank-offering dedications to deities. But the high correlation of votive

---

[28] See Hands 1968: 51, for examples of collective donations in the Greek world.

formulae with essential building projects seems to be a distinctive feature of the Jewish epigraphy.[29]

Yet another such strategy is what might be called the Sardis formula, where a contribution, instead of being described as coming from the individual's own resources in the customary fashion, is rather specified as the gift of God, or, more often, of the divine *pronoia*. This formula appears in Lifshitz 20, where the editor adduces later Christian material; we now know, from circulated but unpublished texts, that it was widespread in the city. There is one parallel from Aegina (*CIJ* 722). Sardian variants are, ἐκ τῶν τῆς προνοίας δομάτων and ἐκ τῶν δωρεῶν τοῦ παντοκράτορος θεοῦ and, more concisely, just ἐκ τῶν τῆς προνοίας. Kraabel has associated the formula with the cultured neo-Platonist milieu of late Roman Sardis; but the term *pronoia* for the deity is rooted in Greek-Jewish thought, being quite at home in Josephus.[30]

The ultimate strategy comes in a late inscription from Scythopolis (Beth She'an).[31] This might be thought to represent a more extreme self-effacement than anything from the Greco-Roman Diaspora, because here the contributors to a sixth-century mosaic floor are anonymous and we are explicitly informed that their names are known to God. Perhaps those names were not entirely unknown to friends and neighbours either! Such a formula has affiliations, on the one hand, with the Palestinian Aramaic synagogue dedications, with their characteristic Semitic request that the donor be remembered for good: there is obvious mutual influence between the Aramaic and Greek styles in Palestinian dedications, but the directions of influence are not easy to disentangle.[32] On the other hand, the formula points forward to Christian epigraphy, which takes it up: a little text from Grado in northern Italy, for example, *both* gives us the name of a donor and then solemnly says 'cuius nomen deus escit'. We might also compare the wording of the Aramaic inscription from

---

[29] On votive formulae, cf. Roth-Gerson 1987a. For the pagan context, Rouse 1902.

[30] On the synagogue inscriptions, see Hanfmann 1964; Mitten 1965; cf. Kraabel 1983: 178–190.

[31] See Roth-Gerson 1987b: no. 9; Huttenmeister & Reeg 1977: 62, no. 4.

[32] For discussion of Greek influence on the Hebrew/Aramaic formulae, see Roth-Gerson 1987a; for another angle on the formulae, Foerster 1981: 12–46. For donation in Palestine, Kindler 1987: 55–56; also in Hachlili 1989. For Aramaic and Hebrew texts, see Naveh 1979.

the synagogue of Severus at Hammath Tiberias: 'may peace be to all those who donated in this holy place and who in the future will donate.'[33]

The different strategies I have pointed to will not have been employed with equal enthusiasm in all communities at all times. Local patterns can be dimly discerned. Yet it is not fanciful to detect also a certain consistency of principle, limits beyond which Jewish communities could not allow themselves to go in adopting local modes of giving and of honouring, limits which allow us to suggest that somewhere in this area lay one of the defining marks which were seen by Diaspora Jews as distinguishing them from their neighbours. If this suggestion is right, then they will have been striking an extremely delicate balance, doing things the Greek way up to a point, but stopping short where it mattered to them. It is the setting of that sticking point which constitutes the art of Diaspora living, and perhaps the art of being an ethnic or religious minority of any kind.

We might go further, and suggest that there are some practices of features of life in the host community which will acquire a symbolic value. They are perceived as a danger area, standing for what is alien, controversial, impermissible. this conscious distancing from selected items in a culture is as significant a part of acculturation as the corresponding, and more often remarked on, process of selective appropriation.

Jews in the cities were not outside the framework of euergetism. Indeed, within it they manifested a complex interaction with the society around them. Through its agency, important political gestures were made. A pagan woman might build a synagogue; so might a centurion in Palestine, who sympathized with Judaism (Acts 10–11). A Roman administrator might be honoured in an amphitheatre. There are even possible instances of Jews making contributions to pagan cults: at Iasos, a Jerusalemite called Niketas son of Jason, specified as a metic, μέτοικος, contributed to the Dionysia, and two further donors are described as Iouda (*CIJ* 749). At Smyrna, οἱ πότε Ἰουδαῖοι participate in honouring Hadrian, appearing in a 45-line list of donors (*CIJ* 742). This last phrase is particularly intriguing.

At the same time, it is hard to believe that the absence in the Jewish epigraphy of virtually all the language in which the transac-

---

[33] See Dothan 1967.

tions of euergetism can be conducted can be no accident. To enter the Jewish world, as a sympathizer or proselyte, would have been to learn a new dialect of a familiar language.

For Paul Veyne, Christian society substituted charity for euergetism—to his mind, an entirely different concept,[34] involving a radical redefinition of philanthropy. In the new version, individual self-gratification is no longer the leading motivation, and reward is not precisely measured out in the currency of privilege. Veyne suggests more than once that the changed concept had its roots in Judaism; and in a general sense this must be true. But I am not sure that the sharp dichotomy can deal adequately with a very complex process of change. As far as the Jews of the Greco-Roman Diaspora go, the evidence for charitable foundations is slight indeed. Admittedly, we can now say that if the πάτελλα of the Aphrodisias inscription was indeed a soup kitchen (tamhui), as Reynolds & Tannenbaum, its editors, inventively propose,[35] then we would have, through that one word, extraordinary epigraphic evidence of a real alternative to civic pride and self-aggrandizement, set in a judaizing context, yet close to the heart of the city, and involving even town councillors of pagan Aphrodisias. We have to confess, however, that uncertainty still reigns over the identification of the Aphrodisias club. Our other epigraphic evidence for Diaspora Jewish arrangements suggests, as we have seen, forms of organization rather closer to, if still distinguished from, those of the city at large.[36]

BIBLIOGRAPHY

Applebaum, S. 1979. *Jews and Greeks in Ancient Cyrene.* Leiden.
Baldwin Bowsky, M.W. 1987. 'M. Tittius Sex. F. Aem. and the Jews of Berenice (Cyrenaica)', *AJP* 108: 495–510.
Brooten, B.J. 1982. *Women Leaders in the Ancient Synagogue.* Brown Judaic Studies 36. Chico, California, 143–144.

---

[34] 1990: 19–34.
[35] 1991: 26–28.
[36] For the database and breakdowns on which this paper is based and for other help, I am much indebted to Dr David Noy. Joyce Reynolds was a kind and generous adviser on the material from Berenice. A paper on this subject was read at a conference on the Jewish Diaspora held in the Rosenberg School of Jewish Studies, Tel-Aviv University, in January 1991, and I thank the organizers, Professors B. Isaac and A. Oppenheimer, and also the other participants, for a most congenial forum in which to discuss these ideas.

Danker, F.W. 1982. *Benefactor: Epigraphic Study of a Graeco-Roman and New Testament Semantic Field*. St Louis.

Dothan, M. 1967. 'The Aramaic Inscription from the Synagogue of Severus at Hamat Tiberias', *Eretz Israel* 8: 183–185. (Hebrew); 73–74 (English).

Foerster, G. 1981. 'Ancient Synagogue Inscriptions and their Relation to Prayers and Blessings', *Kathedra* 19: 12–46.

Gauthier, P. 1985. *Les cités grecques et leurs bienfaiteurs (IVᵉ–Iᵉʳ siècle avant J-C)*. Bulletin de Correspondence Hellénique Supplément 12. Athens.

Haas, P.J. (ed.). 1992. *Recovering the Role of Women. Power and Authority in Rabbinic Jewish Society*. South Florida Studies in the History of Judaism 95. Atlanta.

Hachlili, R. 1989. (ed.), *Ancient Synagogues in Israel. Third-Seventh Century C.E.* BAR International Series 499. Oxford.

Hands, A.R. 1968. *Charities and Social Aid in Greece and Rome*. London.

Hanfmann, G.M.A. 1964. 'The Sixth Campaign at Sardis (1963)', *BASOR* 174: 3–58.

Hodot, R. 1982. *Journal of the J. Paul Getty Museum* 9: 165–180.

Huttenmeister, F. & Reeg, G. 1977. *Die antiken Synagogen in Israel*, vol. 1. Wiesbaden.

Jones, C.P. 1978. *The Roman World of Dio Chrysostom*. Cambridge.

Kindler, A. 1987. 'Donations and Taxes in the Society of the Jewish Villages in Eretz Israel during the Third to Sixth Centuries C.E.', in A. Kasher, A. Oppenheimer, U. Rappaport (eds), *Synagogues in Antiquity*. Jerusalem (in Hebrew).

Kraabel, A.T. 1983. 'Impact of the Discovery of the Sardis Synagogue', in G.M.A. Hanfmann (ed.), *Sardis from Prehistoric to Roman Times. Results of the Archaeological Exploration of Sardis 1958–75*. Cambridge, Mass.,178–190.

Le Bohec, Y. 1981. 'Inscriptions juives et judaisantes de l'Afrique romaine', *Antiquités Africaines* 17: 165–170.

Lifschitz, B. 1967. *Donateurs et fondateurs dans les synagogues juives*. Paris.

Lüderitz, G. 1983. *Corpus jüdischer Zeugnisse aus der Cyrenaika, mit einem Anhang von Joyce M. Reynolds*. Beihefte zum Tübinger Atlas des vorderen Orients Reihe B, 53. Wiesbaden.

MacMullen, R. 1982. 'The Epigraphic Habit in the Roman Empire', *AJP* 103: 233–246.

Meyer, E.A. 1990. 'Explaining the Epigraphic Habit in the Roman Empire: the Evidence of Epitaphs' *JRS* 80: 74–96.

Mitten, D.G. 1965. *The Ancient Synagogue of Sardis. Published for Private Circulation by The Committee to Preserve the Ancient Synagogue of Sardis. On Behalf of the Archaeological Exploration of Sardis*. New York.

Naveh, J. 1979. *On Stone and Mosaic* (Hebrew). Tel-Aviv.

Rajak, T. & Noy, D. 1993. '*Archisynagogoi*: Office, Title and Social Status in the Greco-Jewish Synagogue', *JRS* 83: 75–93 = Ch. 20 in this volume.

Ramsay, W.M. 1897. *The Cities and Bishoprics of Phrygia*, vol. I, part 2. Oxford.

Reynolds, J. & Tannenbaum, R. 1991. *Jews and Godfearers at Aphrodisias*. Cambridge Philological Society, supplementary volume 12. Cambridge.

Rogers, G.M. 1991. 'Demosthenes of Oenoanda and Models of Euergetism', *JRS* 81: 91–100.

Roth-Gerson, L. 1987a. 'Similiarities and Differences in Greek Synagogue Inscriptions of Eretz-Israel and the Diaspora', in A. Kasher, A. Oppenheimer, U. Rappaport (eds), *Synagogues in Antiquity*. Jerusalem, 133–146.

—— 1987b. *The Greek Inscriptions from the Synagogues in Eretz-Israel* (Hebrew). Jerusalem.

Rouse, W.H.D. 1902. *Greek Votive Offerings*. Cambridge.

Scheiber, A. 1983. *Jewish Inscriptions in Hungary*. Budapest.

Sheppard, A.R.R. 1970. 'Jews, Christians and Heretics in Acmonia and Eumeneia', *Anatolian Studies* 29: 169–180.

Smallwood, E.M. 1961. *Philonis Alexandrini Legatio ad Gaium*. Leiden.

Trebilco, P. 1991. *Jewish Communities in Asia Minor*. Cambridge.
Versnel, H.S. 1981. 'Religious Mentality in Ancient Prayer', in H. Versnel (ed.), *Faith, Hope and Worship: Aspects of Religious Mentality in the Ancient World*. Leiden.
Veyne, P. 1976. *Le pain et le cirque: sociologie historique d'un pluralisme politique*. Paris.
—— 1990. *Bread and Circuses*. Abridged English translation, London.
White, L.M. 1990. *Building God's House in the Roman World: Architectural Adaptation among Pagans, Jews and Christians*. Baltimore/London.

CHAPTER TWENTY

ARCHISYNAGOGOI: OFFICE, TITLE AND SOCIAL STATUS IN THE GRECO-JEWISH SYNAGOGUE

1. *Pluralism in the cities of the Roman Empire*

The cities of the Roman Empire were, on the whole, plural societies, which had in them significant sub-groups, ethnic, religious, or, indeed, both together—for the two categories were still only sometimes distinguishable. Such an environment carries many resonances for us and it is surprising to realize its neglect as a subject for study. The classical Greek *polis* had been a theoretically homogeneous institution of look-alike citizens, with outsiders excluded or enslaved. The notional Roman approach was, in the early days, to deal with outsiders by assimilating them. When we look at the cities of the Hellenistic kingdoms, we observe that they often did consist of several racial elements, though how these were accommodated has been for some time an issue for debate, and this remains an open question. But beyond that, our concern seems to stop.[1] Probably, we have been dazzled (if that does not flatter the subject unduly) by the uniform veneer of Greek culture which spread over the cities of the East during the high Empire. And, in general, the imperialistic processes of Hellenization and Romanization have been given pride of place in historical analysis, for reasons which derive from cultural preferences current until quite recently. And yet, as John North has made us aware, the direction of change in religious history was towards a society of choice in the late Empire (until Christian intolerance closed it down).[2]

The increasing visibility of Jewish and Christian elements in city life (and death) is thus a leading theme in the history of the Roman Empire, but it can only be effectively grasped within the perspective of civic pluralism. In the case of the Jews, who are, after all,

---

[1] But see Millar 1987. The approach in MacMullen 1981: chs 4 and 5, is also worth noting.
[2] See North 1992: 174–193. Kraabel 1987: 53 speaks in terms of a 'need for community in a bewildering larger world'—bewildering, apparently, because of the demise of the *polis.*

the starting point and exemplar for the Christians, our problems are particularly acute. Although the fact that the Jewish communities of the Diaspora (and, indeed, in some cities in Palestine) were key participants in the great process of change is now less often forgotten than it used to be,[3] severe deficiencies in the evidence, and the absence to date of any framework for discussion, not to mention the tenacity of the age-old habit of marginalizing Jewry, all conspire to obfuscate the implications of their presence. Here, our aim is to explore a central feature in the intermeshing of Jewish communities with the societies in which they were located, by reinterpreting the most visible office among them, that of *archisynagogos*. This reading locates the communities firmly within their society. A reassessment of the meaning of Greco-Roman office-holding is therefore central to it; against this the Jewish material makes sense.

At the heart of any enquiry about the survival of communities within a wider framework lie the issues of group cohesion and group distinctiveness. Given that a group must of necessity demarcate itself somehow from its environment, basic questions arise of how far group ethos emphasizes solidarity and separation, and how these are achieved by any group.[4] Characteristic social and moral values and, indeed, all the visible aspects of an apparently distinct culture can be constructively seen as symbolic indicators of separate identity. Of course, the response of the larger unit also comes constantly into play; a group's claims to allegiance are threatening to social control, and the group may in turn find itself, or perceive itself, to be threatened in one way or another. There are intricate and interesting correlations between any group's definitions of its own identity and its relations with the larger whole in which it exists.

2. *Group identity and the syngagogue*

For Diaspora Jewry in the Greco-Roman world, the community was undoubtedly of overriding importance; as, indeed, it has generally been through history. The term συναγαωγή comes to be overwhelmingly

---

[3] It is hoped that Lieu, North & Rajak 1992 has contributed to a new awareness. We cannot share the optimism of Seth Schwartz's review, *Bryn Mawr Classical Review* 3, 3 (1992), 1–4, that the point is now widely grasped.

[4] See Meeks 1983: 74–75, 84–85; and, for an introduction to the sociological issues, Homans 1968: 258–265.

dominant in our record, although we do not find complete uniformity in the naming either of the united Jews of a city, or of smaller units inside a place. Alternatives to *synagoge* are known; and, on the other hand, we encounter such associations as the mysterious δεκανία, not to mention the πάτελλα of the Aphrodisias inscription.[5] Another significant feature of the concept *synagoge* is that it retains a double application, referring also to a building, the physical home of the 'congregation' or community. For that purpose, too, words other than *synagoge* were employed, but they seem, again, to have been gradually squeezed out. Thus, προσευχή—(place of) prayer—had currency at first,[6] but both οἶκος (house) and ἅγιος τόπος (sacred place) are found too.

Archaeological discoveries have meant that there has been more interest in the nature of the synagogue as building than in its role as community. Architectural and formal developments have been much discussed, especially in the light of the more copious Palestinian remains, and something of the range of possibilities in style and conception is emerging. There has also been research into the development of the sequence of service and of the liturgy.[7]

The synagogue as a social institution is altogether more problematic, and basic matters are obscure to us. Pagan authors, Josephus and the Rabbis are all oddly uninformative about it,[8] and the Pauline epistles are equally unhelpful. The question of how far synagogue organization became co-extensive with community structure has not been seriously raised, except in older discussions about Rome, the only place where we have definite evidence—the catacomb epitaphs—of more than one Jewish synagogue, apart from Philo's Alexandria.[9] Often, the question seems unanswerable. What do we know of the relation between the *dekania* and the *patella* at Aphrodisias to any synagogue which there might have been in the city?[10] But, above all, we should be asking what sort of a grouping the Jewish synagogue

---

[5] *Synodos* and *syllogos* are attested, as well as just οἱ Ἰουδαῖοι. For Aphrodisias, see Reynolds & Tannenbaum 1987: *passim*.

[6] Hengel 1975, argues that the use of the term *synagoge* for a building began in first-century A.D. Palestine and gradually spread to the Diaspora.

[7] See, for an introduction, Gutmann 1975 and also Levine 1987.

[8] Cohen 1987: 50–60; Momigliano 1989: 108–119.

[9] See Leon 1960: 135–166. An unpublished inscription refers to synagogues at Salonica, and the Side synagogue is described as 'first' (*CIJ* 781). An approach to the problems is in Kraabel 1975: 79–91.

[10] Reynolds & Tannenbaum, 26–30.

itself was. What group identity might it have assumed, in different contexts? And what range of individual identities did it offer to members? How much of individuals' lives might it absorb?

In discussions of the first churches, the Jewish communities of the Diaspora have been disposed of quite summarily. And yet the situation of the two groups was in many ways strikingly similar and there were obvious interconnections. Even Wayne Meeks,[11] who reflects upon the synagogue as a possible model for Pauline churches and points to analogies in their activities, quite quickly rejects the model because of the surprising lack of explicit evidence in the Pauline letters for any Christian imitation of the synagogue in behaviour or organization. And yet conscious imitation is not the only form of influence to matter. Not just habits—scripture-reading, hymn-singing, prayers, common meals—were shared by Jews and Christians, but also many problems of principle and practice arising from participation in city life and interaction with idolatrous 'pagans'. Both religions—or should we say 'peoples'?—had to grapple constantly with the question of boundaries.

We may refer at this point to John North's comments on the articulation of religious associations in the ancient world, for a workable set of criteria by which to evaluate what amounts to the 'groupness' of groups: the focus is not on beliefs or aspirations but rather on socio-religious behaviour.[12] These criteria, as North expresses them, are:

1. Existence as autonomous groups with their own organization or authority structure.
2. A level of commitment asked of the members of the group in terms of loyalty to the cult or the rejection of other or past modes of behaviour.
3. The existence of separate values and principles, unacceptable to other members of the society but required of members.
4. A degree of separation from the normal life of the city, to be marked by different rituals, different calendars, different dietary rules.

---

[11] Meeks 1983: 80–91.
[12] North 1992: 183–184.

What North's analysis highlights is that the definition and distribution of status and authority within a group is itself important information about that group: it is a pointer to the place of that group on a scale of openness/closedness or separation/assimilation. Patterns of status and authority are potentially relevant to all four of the suggested criteria, but especially to the first and third. Given the nature of our evidence for the Diaspora Jewish communities, this is particularly helpful, as we shall see shortly.

After the closing years of the first century, a small corpus of inscriptions, architectural remains, and the angled statements of pagan and Christian outsiders are virtually the only surviving evidence to tell us about the Jewish solution to the problem of being a minority. The internal literary tradition now becomes entirely unhistorical in character, and almost wholly undatable, consisting of Bible-derived pseudepigrapha and apocalypses that survive often in translated or modified form. They can make no contribution to our study. The Talmudic tradition—itself, of course, profoundly ahistorical—touches directly on Diaspora life (and then outside the Roman Empire) only with the compilation of the Babylonian Talmud in the fifth century or even later.

On the problem which concerns us, the nature of the Greco-Roman synagogue hierarchy, there exists a consensus which has gone wholly unchallenged; this gives primacy to the literary evidence, while drawing sporadically on impressions gleaned from inscriptions. Our approach, by contrast, is to re-read the literary texts with a proper recognition of their character as texts; and, at the same time, adequately to exploit the epigraphic evidence with the help of a hypothesis derived from Greek parallels. Much of the epigraphy consists of names of individuals, figuring in epitaphs or as donors, and those names often go with titles, not only that of *archisynagogos*, but also *archon, gerousiarch, presbyter*, father or mother of the synagogue, *grammateus, phrontistes*, and occasionally others. These evidently represent a spectrum of positions within the community. The titles give us some leverage on the communities which generated them.[13]

---

[13] Trebilco 1991: 4, expresses the excellent objective of not 'approaching the evidence with an agenda from research in the NT or in Rabbinic literature in mind'; but we may be less comfortable about the definition of the alternative goal—'to let the issues addressed arise from the material itself'.

Our choice of focus, the key post of *archisynagogos* (roughly trans-latable as 'head of the synagogue'), does not require long justification. The title is the one most widely represented in the ancient literature in association with the synagogue, and it is revealed there as the best known to outsiders. In inscriptions, the title figures prominently over a long stretch of time and a broad geographical span; the rel-evant inscriptions are collected in Appendix I. With most other titles, the Roman evidence predominates. This title is almost exclusively Jewish in its application, unlike other comparable titles. Its mode of operation will emerge as no different in principle from others in the set, and they will be considered where appropriate. But in the case of the *archisynagogos* there is the most work to be done, in examin-ing and clearing away old and influential interpretations. We might also add, that, if our purpose is to make new sense of the syna-gogue, it is particularly appropriate to be able to offer a new angle on the office which, after all, appears to incorporate verbally the very concept itself.

3. *Literary representations*

In external perception, as reflected in literature, the *archisynagogos* is the synagogue notable *par excellence*, seen (at first unofficially, and later, it seems, officially too) as responsible for what went on in the community. Only the patriarch, who was right outside the syna-gogues and located far away in Palestine, could in due course come to be thought of as having precedence over the *archisynagogos*. A pow-erful emotive component is demonstrably present in such represen-tations. They are reflections, direct or indirect, of Christian anti-Judaism, and should not be read literally as straight evidence on synagogue arrangements.[14]

We might ask why writers were apt to seize upon the *archisynago-gos* as specially representative of the Jewish leadership. The real role of *archisynagogoi* is scarcely reflected in the choice. First of all, here to hand was a title with a distinctly Jewish flavour, whose very sound conjured up the synagogue. This could scarcely be said of archon or presbyter. Then, *archisynagogos* was, we discover, an almost exclu-

---

[14] On literary anti-Judaism in the early Church, see Lieu 1992: 70–96; Kraabel 1985: 219–246.

sively Jewish term. Indeed, we find an even stronger exclusivity here than in the word 'synagogue' itself. For very few *archisynagogoi* indeed are visible in non-Jewish contexts, and those few tend to be restricted to a confined geographical area; yet meetings of various kinds, quite unconnected with Jews, might be called in Greek *synagogai*.[15]

The handful of epigraphic, pagan *archisynagogoi* known to us appears in Appendix II. They emerge as an esoteric collection, for we see that these inscriptions originate (apart from one or two highly dubious instances) from the coastlands of the north Aegean—Perinthus, Salonica, Olynthus, Pydna, and Beroea. They date from between the first and third centuries A.D. We note that, in that locality, the title was given to the principal sponsor, or perhaps even the founder, of a religious or craft association. In each case, the *archisynagogos* seems to stand apart from the other officers mentioned, and in three of the texts the formula 'those around' (οἱ περί) the *archisynagogos* indicates that the whole group was identified with him. In No. 6, the *archisynagogos* is made more important than the other officers by a curious prepositional phrase using ὑπό with the accusative case, which is presumably intended to mean 'under the control of'. A pagan cultic character emerges clearly from details in the texts such as the mention of an altar. The exception is No. 5, which has no such detail, and which has therefore, been occasionally regarded as Jewish; its use of the οἱ περί formulation, however, brings it close to the others in the group. The Zeus Hypsistos cult at Pydna (No. 6) has perhaps, in its epithet for the supreme deity, Jewish resonances, but scarcely on that account a Jewish identity. Our provisional judgement must be that, while Jewish influence behind this curious clutch of clubs is not excluded, there are at present no persuasive arguments for accepting it;[16] if, however, such suspicions were to prove justified, that would only go to reinforce the already overwhelmingly Jewish character of the archisynagogate.

In literature, the association of the *archisynagogos* with Judaism is fixed, from the Gospels on. In Mark and Luke, we encounter just two individual *archisynagogoi*; and synagogue heads play an incipient, but still fairly minor exemplary role in that Gospel demonology which is peopled by the Pharisees, the scribes and the high priests, a

---

[15] See Schrage 1971: 798–841, for a survey of the evidence.

[16] Poland 1909: 358, points out that Theos Hypsistos and Sabbatistes are deities close to the Jewish God.

demonology to which later Christian literature admits the *archisyna-gogoi* as well. However, there is reason to think that even those brief Gospel appearances are not straight representations of a Palestinian reality, but rather embody assumptions which the authors have brought from their own contexts; these, of course, may not be Palestinian and are almost certainly from the second half of the first century. At best, the use of the titulature is somewhat impressionistic. For Jairus, the *archisynagogos* whose daughter was healed by Jesus, is regularly described by Mark as *archisynagogos* (5:22, 35, 36, 38), and by Luke once thus (8:49) but once, just a few verses earlier, as ἄρχων τῆς συναγωγῆς (8:41). Matthew (9:18, 23) uses an abbreviated form of the second version, ἄρχων *tout court*. It may be that Matthew is trying to gloss over Jairus' connection with the synagogue, but that does not explain Luke's inconsistency.[17]

But there is more to it, for our second individual appears in Luke alone (13:14), where he is castigated as hypocritical when he objects to Jesus, who had been teaching in the synagogue, offering a cure on the sabbath to a woman who had had a 'spirit of infirmity' for eighteen years. Here, a representative function for the Jewish religious leadership as a whole is assigned to this Galilean *archisynagogos*, in a section of Luke marked by its criticism of the Pharisees, and at a point where the author is preparing us for Jesus' journey to Jerusalem, 'the city that murders the prophets and stones the messengers sent to her' (Luke 13:34).

It is again Luke, in Acts, who shows us *archisynagogoi* in action, apparently managing religious life in the synagogue. At Pisidian Antioch they invite Paul and Barnabas to address the people on the sabbath and then ask them back for the following week (13:15, 42); here they seem to operate as a collectivity. At Corinth, two *archisynagogoi* are named: Crispus becomes a Christian, but Sosthenes heads a complaint to the proconsul Gallio and is beaten up (18:8, 17). As far as the author is concerned, these are important men (literary *archisynagogoi* are never women), who are emblematic of the Jewish community. Finally, a textual variant in Codex Bezae has Acts 14:2 claiming that the *archisynagogoi* of the Jews and the archons of the synagogues (in place of the 'unbelieving Jews') stirred up the Gentiles against Paul at Iconium. This appears to be late in origin.

---

[17] We know of individuals in Italy who were both *archon* and *archisynagogos*: Appendix I, Nos. 1, 6. So the titles were not generally interchangeable.

There is no doubt that these images of *archisynagogoi* influenced later representations, for patristic writers readily incorporate New Testament allusion, and their image of the synagogue is visibly dependent on the Gospels.[18] But the literary prominence of *archisynagogoi* has now increased, relative to Pharisees and the rest, and this would seem to reflect the later synagogue, as the authors saw it.[19] A particularly striking statement of Justin Martyr reveals both New Testament antecedents and a new awareness of the existence of *archisynagogoi* (who no doubt had proliferated), when he links synagogue leaders with Pharisees in an all-too familiar formula, supposedly urging Jewish readers not to 'agree to abuse the son of God, nor follow the Pharisees as teachers in jesting at the king of Israel, as your *archisynagogoi* teach you after the prayer' (*Dial. with Trypho* 137). Justin, a Samaritan by origin, was certainly well-informed about Judaism; but an intensely polemical passage of this kind is no proof that the *archisynagogoi* were either actual teachers or leaders of prayer.

Epiphanius (*Haer.* 30.11) tells a story, attributed to the time of Constantine, about the *comes* Joseph who, while he was still an emissary of the Jewish patriarch, was caught reading the gospels and was attacked by other Jews: his enemies were led by '*archisynagogoi* and priests and presbyters and hazzans'—a curious and scarcely coherent collection of seemingly token titles. For Epiphanius himself, the presence of *archisynagogoi* can serve as a distinguishing mark between Christian and Jewish communities: he says of the Jewish-Christian Ebionites that they are people who have presbyters and *archisynagogoi* and that they call their church a synagogue and not a church (*Pan.* 30.18.2).[20] In a work dubiously ascribed to John Chrysostom (*de Eleemosyna* = PG 60.709), Paul (or rather Saul) is said to have been despatched by the *archisynagogoi* with instructions about taking Christians prisoner. Similarly, the author of the *Martyrdom of Peter and Paul* asserts that it was the Jewish *archisynagogoi* and pagan priests who resisted the apostles' message at Rome.[21] Scarcely less stylized, in spite of its seeming precision, is the statement in the life of Chrysostom attributed to Palladius that 'the corrupt and false patriarch of the Jews changes the *archisynagogoi* each year or even within the year in his

---

[18] See Cohen 1987: 160.
[19] On such realism, see Millar 1992: 117.
[20] For Epiphanius' view of Jewish 'heresies', see Lieu 1988.
[21] §10 = Lipsius 1959: 128.

pursuit of silver' (*PG* 47.51). It is questionable whether the patriarch in Palestine, even at the height of his powers, could have intervened so actively in local appointments, and we shall see that even imperial legislation was capable of a gross misrepresentation of the relationship between the patriarch and the *archisynagogoi*.[22]

However, a significant change is reflected in this last, Palladian passage. The advent of the Christian empire produced, from Constantine on, a stream of laws concerning the Jews. The rigidly hierarchical structure of the late empire meant that the upper echelons of the Jewish hierarchy acquired importance in the eyes of the imperial authorities, as responsible for implementing the legislation; to match this, they got a new status, because they were repaid with honours and, especially, with exemption from municipal burdens.

One might, then, expect full precision about titulature in legislation, but this we do not get. We seem to find no more than a generalized awareness of the relevant Jewish officialdom in the varied descriptions of status which are incorporated in the laws. *Archisynagogoi* figure in a shifting pattern of reference to the Jewish leaders.

There are two important passages in the Theodosian Code which relate to exemption from municipal burdens. In the first case, in Constantine's law of 330, the application is said to be 'to the priests and *archisynagogoi* and fathers of the synagogues and others who serve in the same place' (*C.Th.* 16.8.4).[23] The final, catch-all phrase covers any errors or ignorance there may be on the part of the legislators about what goes on in the synagogue, and ensures that Jewish communities using different titles (or at least some of them) will not be excluded. It may be observed that 'priests' are unlikely to have been central to synagogue practice so long after the end of the Temple cult, and that they most probably bore a limited symbolic role similar to that of today. Constantine appears ill-informed.

The version of the exemption law promulgated by Arcadius and Honorius (A.D. 397) is recorded as being applicable 'to those who are subject to the rule of the illustrious patriarchs, that is the *archisynagogoi* and patriarchs and presbyters and others who are involved in the rites of that religion' (*C.Th.* 16.8.13; Linder no. 27). The same protection is included and there is the same lack of exactitude, with

---

[22] See below, p. 409. The unsupported patristic evidence for the patriarch's power to appoint *archisynagogoi* is accepted by Avi-Yonah 1976: 62.

[23] Linder 1987: no. 9, version B.

a different set of titles being offered this time. Other imperial legislation, which does not include *archisynagogoi*, selects yet other sets of titles.[24] Another law of Arcadius and Honorius, dated to A.D. 399 but revoked in 404 (*C.Th.* 16.8.14, 17; Linder nos. 30, 34) prohibits the delegates of the patriarch from collecting money from synagogues, and defines those delegates as *archisynagogoi* and *apostoloi* (emissaries). Only the latter can be correctly described as the patriarch's representatives, as Linder points out,[25] and the error is striking.

This time the culprit would seem to be less a New Testament-based understanding of Jewish leadership, than an inadequate grasp of its character. The legislation seems to assume an authority structure in synagogues comparable to that in the typical church. Admittedly, the legislators could well have brought about the paradoxical result of solidifying the position and enhancing the role of those very title-holders whom they had pinpointed. This process we cannot recover. Their vagueness, by contrast, stands out in their formulations. Apart from incompetence and ill-will, we may suggest an additional explanation for this vagueness: the real lack of fixed hierarchy in synagogues. By this we mean not just variation in nomenclature at different places, but a looseness in the use of titles and a lack of specificity about their functions. This is a point whose significance will emerge later.

Ordinary non-Christians, too, came to hear of *archisynagogoi*: here was a catchword which could evoke Judaism as a typical oriental religion, with suitable derision. There is plausibility in the well-known story told in the *Historia Augusta* of Alexander Severus' mobbing (the exact location of the incident is distinctly unclear): 'at a certain festival, the Antiochenes, Egyptians and Alexandrians, as is their custom, had hurled insults at him, calling him the Syrian archisynagogus and high priest' (*HA* Alex.Sev.28). The ruler liked to deny his Syrian origins, which are here flung in his face; at the same time his noted tolerance to the Jews and his supposed interest in Jewish and Christian teaching are mocked. As Momigliano put it, the juxtaposition produces a double insult.[26] It is worth noting that this outburst by a largely pagan crowd is assigned (by a fourth-century author) to a

---

[24] E.g. *C.Th.* 16.8.29: *primates*; *Nov.Just.* 146.1: *archipherekitai*, *presbyteroi* or *didaskaloi*.
[25] See Linder 1987: 215.
[26] On Alexander Severus and Judaism, see Stern 1980: vol. 2, 629–633; Momigliano 1934: 151–153.

date earlier than those fourth-century legal developments which drew public attention to the Jewish hierarchy.

Then, in the life of Saturninus (*Quad.Tyr.*8), a letter spuriously ascribed to Hadrian comments negatively on the religious climate in Egypt, observing that 'no *archisynagogus* of the Jews, no Samaritan, no presbyter of the Christians is not an astrologer or soothsayer or wrestling master.' These sweeping words, whatever their origin, demonstrate, once again, how the stereotype of the *archisynagogos* had penetrated popular consciousness.

4. *Reconstructions, old and new*

The external literary tradition thus reveals that *archisynagogoi* had a high profile in the eyes of outsiders, for largely extraneous reasons. This literature embodies garbled images of the Jewish community but very little of its reality. What is perhaps more disturbing is the widespread modern assumption of precise knowledge. Scholars have thought it a straightforward proposition to define the functions of the *archisynagogos*, by a process of joining together dubious evidence, which they read wholly literally, extrapolating from the combination, and filling in the gaps with anachronisms. These reconstructions have acquired and retained the status of fact. And those who made the reconstructions had no reason to doubt that they could grasp what the *archisynagogos* was, since they saw no problem in understanding the nature of the ancient synagogue itself. They modernized unconsciously, and their implicit models were often the places of Jewish worship familiar to them, within the contemporary type of western community which they had come across. Judaism, after all, was reputedly unchangeable after the advent of Christianity, and that damaging theological doctrine is even detectable in interpretations of Jewish history or society by non-Christians.

A nineteenth- or twentieth-century synagogue (or indeed a church) located in a developed society will have multifarious responsibilities: a highly wrought and formalized sequence of religious services must be laid on; a high level of communal support for a membership with highly-differentiated social needs is expected; and the infrastructure, including property rights and the fabric of the buildings themselves, will require care and management—all within the framework of a highly complex society. All three branches of activity may have been represented in the ancient synagogue, but the necessarily rudimentary and therefore qualitatively different level of each is clear. As far as ritual goes, recent debates on the development of the synagogue service are not relevant here; but, on any account, the set sequence of prayer and poetry was still severely restricted, leaving Torah reading, short formal prayers and some sermonizing as the dominant acts.[27]

Emil Schürer evoked a picture of a specialized officialdom for the ancient synagogue, to match the synagogue's imagined functions, and this stands largely intact in the pages of the revised Schürer.[28] Samuel Krauss' learned and wide-ranging study[29] contributed a Talmudic slant and new refinement. Between Schürer and Krauss in date came Jean Juster's heavily legalistic approach.[30] There, it is perhaps easiest to see what was being constructed. A number of rigid distinctions are drawn by Juster. First, centralized institutions under the patriarchate are delineated.[31] Then, descending to the communal level, a wholly anachronistic separation is made between, on the one hand, lay leaders such as gerusiarchs and archons, and on the other, 'the clergy'. *Archisynagogoi* head the 'clergy'. We even discover how they get their jobs—there are tough qualifying examinations in law and medicine (*à la française*). For that assertion the leading item of evidence is, astonishingly, an offensive statement in a letter of Jerome, where the Christian polemicist discredits rabbis by satirizing the rabbinic regulations on sexual purity: 'They have in charge of the synagogues very wise men too, who are appointed to the foul work of judging by tasting, if they cannot decide with their eyes, whether the blood of a virgin or menstruating woman is pure or impure' (*Ep.* 121.10). To this is added a comment of Ambrose, together with the passage we have already encountered from the 'Hadrianic' letter about the dubious proclivities of religious leaders in Egypt.

Schürer's logic should not detain us much longer than Juster's. On the restricted basis of the first century inscriptions from Cyrenaica, it is argued that 'the *archontes* were the chiefs of the congregations

---

[27] See for example, Shinan 1987: 97–110.
[28] Revised Schürer: 2, 423–453.
[29] Krauss 1922.
[30] Juster 1914: vol. 1, 450–453.
[31] In fact, there is no compelling reason to posit even notional patriarchal control over Diaspora synagogues until the late fourth century: Kraabel 1982: 454; Cohen 1987: 170–175; Millar 1992: 98. For a full study of the patriarchate, see Levine 1979.

[every congregation?] and responsible for their direction in general.'[32] Since some archons in inscriptions have the title of *archisynagogos* too, 'the office of *archisynagogus* was therefore different from theirs. But he cannot have been the chief of the *archontes* either, since that person was known as a *gerousiarches* [always?]. He had accordingly nothing whatever to do with the direction of the congregation in general. Instead, his special responsibility was to attend to public worship . . .' And, again, 'an officer was needed to supervise the arrangements of divine worship and the business of the synagogue as a whole.' This reasoning rests on the assumption that titles represent consistently defined, specialized roles within a developed administrative system.

A fantasy realm opens out, of uniform, neat and tidy communities across the Jewish world, with serried ranks of officials, each with a clearly demarcated job to do. Some evidence is also adduced in support, but we have to ask what the force of this evidence is. We meet, again, the *archisynagogos* who invites Paul and Barnabas to speak at Pisidian Antioch (Acts 13:15). Then an inscription from Aegina (App. I no. 17) has an *archisynagogos* 'directing' the building of a synagogue, as Schürer renders οἰκοδόμησα: in fact, the verb is a standard one in inscriptions for recording the name of the person who paid for a building.[33]

Schürer's most detailed support comes, however, from the Rabbinic world. The Mishnah (c. A.D. 200) assumes the existence of an office-holder designated in Hebrew as *rosh ha-kneseth*, 'head of the congregation or synagogue'. In a pair of parallel passages, this individual appears as officiating in an imagined version of a service of the reading of the Law in an imagined synagogue on the Temple Mount.[34] The descriptions are distinctly stylized: 'the *hazzan* of the congregation (*kneseth*) takes the scroll of the Law and gives it to the head of the synagogue and the head of the synagogue gives it to the deputy and the deputy gives it to the high priest; the high priest stands up and receives it and reads it standing' (Yoma 7.1, Sota 7.7). What stands out in the Mishnah is the conflation of contexts in these passages: the presence of the high priest is meant to evoke the golden age of pre-70 Jerusalem, but the synagogue and its con-

---

[32] Revised Schürer: 2, 435.
[33] Cf. Luke 7:3–5, where the word is used for the centurion who has a synagogue built.
[34] On the imaginary nature of this synagogue, see Hoenig 1975: 55–71.

gregation belong to an era when synagogues had become the religious focal points of Palestine, not much before the time of the Mishnah itself. There is also a text in the roughly contemporaneous Tosefta (Meg. 4.21) which states that the 'head of the synagogue' should not read from scripture until others have told him that there is no one to read. We may be disposed to take such texts, garbled as they are, to be indicating that the 'head of a synagogue' regularly had an important liturgical function in the Mishnaic milieu, although even this would be open to argument. There is obviously still less justification in extrapolating from the Hebrew to the Greek version of the title, and from Palestine to a pre-rabbinic Diaspora whose Judaism was quite independent at this time, and probably very different in character.[35] Schürer adds the support of the great commentator on the Mishnah, Rashi, and of another mediaeval Mishnah commentary, but these scarcely carry independent weight on a historical matter of this kind.

More recent authors have followed wholly in the footsteps of Schürer, Juster and Krauss: that reconstruction is unquestioningly accepted as the basis of Schrage's entry in an authoritative theological dictionary, and is now reiterated in van der Horst's guide to Jewish epitaphs.[36] It is a reconstruction with far-reaching implications. Our whole perception of the Diaspora community will be coloured by a supposition that its highest and best-known leaders, by whom it was defined, were people who made prayer their business and who were assigned to the sphere of the sacred. If, on the other hand, piety is located less visibly in the community, say with teachers or charismatics, then a more complex picture is suggested, with perhaps a greater degree of tension between competing values, and certainly with more potential for responsiveness to the outside world.

It is striking that Brooten's challenging study of women synagogue leaders takes a traditional line on the question of functions, and ascribes to *archisynagogoi* (whether male or female) the familiar dual role of liturgical prominence combined with practical duties.[37] For Brooten, the fact that *archisynagogoi* are commonly found in donor

---

[35] In fact, even the rabbinic *rosh ha-knesset* is a term more varied in its application than these authors have allowed: for a convenient collection, see Marmorstein 1921: 24–26.

[36] Schrage 1971; van der Horst 1991.

[37] Brooten 1982: 23–24 etc.

inscriptions to have constructed or paid for building portions of synagogues or restoring synagogues, serves to confirm the second of the
two functions—which she describes in a revealingly modernizing way
as responsibility for the 'plant of the synagogue'. Brooten too draws
on the rabbinic evidence, emphasizing especially substantive religious
aspects of the role, which she is eager to ascribe to women office-
holders equally. 'Women synagogue heads, like their male counterparts, were active in administration and exhortation . . . Perhaps they
looked after the financial affairs of the synagogue . . .; perhaps they
exhorted their congregations . . . We must assume that they had knowledge of the Torah in order to be able to teach and exhort others
in it.' (p. 32). As testimony to the scholarly character of the *archisynagogoi*, she makes much of a list in the Babylonian Talmud (*Pesahim*
49b; sixth century, but with earlier material): 'Our rabbis taught: let
a man always sell all he has and marry the daughter of a scholar.
If he does not find the daughter of a scholar, let him marry (one
of) the great men of the generation. If he does not find the daughter of (one of) the great men of the generation, let him marry the
daughter of a head of synagogues'—after that comes the organizer
of a charity and below that an elementary school teacher. If the synagogue head is to be deemed a man of learning on this basis, as
Brooten proposes, then what are we to make of the social grandees,
'the great men of the generation'? In any case, we are clearly dealing here with a thoroughly rabbinized view of the social order, with
more than a whiff of wishful thinking about it.

Brooten offers an interesting etymological argument for the priority of the Hebrew term and the Hebrew institution over the Greek,
which would seem to justify extrapolation from the rabbinic world
to the Greco-Roman Diaspora. She classifies the Greek verbal formation *archisynagogos* as irregular, because the second part of the word
does not designate a post or occupation, as in *archiereus* (chief priest)
and other such common titles, but an institution (with the termination adapted appropriately).[38] That irregularity would be explained
if the term had originated as an attempt at a literal rendering of
the Hebrew *rosh ha-kneseth*. We might then be inclined to suppose
that the Palestinian hierarchy, as glimpsed in the Mishnah, served

---

[38] Brooten 1982: 5. In Rajak 1992: 24 = Ch. 17: 349, Brooten's argument is
cautiously accepted.

as the pattern for the Diaspora; and this is implicit in Brooten's treatment.

It is more plausible, however, that the Hebrew term was secondary rather than primary. First, *archisynagogos* is not so odd a formation as suggested, given the existence in the pagan world of the titles *synagogos* and *synagogeus*. The former seems to have been particularly common in cult associations from the Black Sea area,[39] though there are a few fragmentary appearances elsewhere (none of them from the zone which produced the pagan *archisynagogoi*).[40] The latter appears to have been a slightly more popular title, marking individuals of somewhat greater importance. It is occasionally related to contexts with some affinity to Judaism.[41] It is understandable that the Jews did not adopt either of those terms: as words they are easily confused with *synagoge* and they lack weight (by comparison, say, with *archiereus* or Asiarch).

Archisynagogos, a more imposing word, can be understood as compounded of *archi-* and *synagogos* rather than as derived from *synagoge*. This undermines Brooten's premise. Second, a different line of formation, from ἄρχων τῆς συναγωγῆς is conceivable, given the use of that term at Luke 8:41 to describe Jairus, who has been presented in the same narrative also as an *archisynagogos* (and in Matth. 9:18 and 23 as an archon).[42] Third, as we have seen, the designation has a solid and respectable pagan existence in one geographical region: not such as to lead us to conclusions about direct influence either way, but such at least as to demonstrate the word as quite at home in a Greek context.

Horsley[43] reviews the evidence in the wake of Brooten's discussion and argues instead for *rosh ha-kneseth* as a back-formation from *archisynagogos*. This is an attractive suggestion, though to test it would require intensive analysis of rabbinic data on the synagogue. If it were correct, there would be different implications to consider: Diaspora-Palestine interaction need not be a question of one-way traffic; perhaps

---

[39] Latyschev 1890: nos. 19, 60–64; iv (1901), nos. 207–208, 210–212, 469; from Tomi: G.C. Tocilescu, *Arch-epig. Mitth. aus Öst.* 6 (1882), 19–20.

[40] E.g. Chios: G. Dunst, *APF* 16 (1958), 172–127. Egypt: *JIGRE* no. 26.

[41] Lucian, *Peregr.* 11. Delos: G. Fougères, *BCH* 11 (1887), 256. Istria near Tomi, A.D. 138: *SEG* 1.330. Moesia, 2nd century: *SEG* 24.1055. Cilicia, Augustan period or soon after: *OGIS* 573, a decree of 'the companions and *Sabbatistai* of the *theos Sabbatistes*', includes the crowning of Aithibelios (?) the *synagogeus*.

[42] Cf. above, 399–400, and Brooten 1982: 15.

[43] Horsley 1987: 214–217.

410   CHAPTER TWENTY

the Jews of the Rabbinic world took at least certain external forms of organization from their co-religionists in other societies.[44]

5. *Archisynagogoi and Greek honorific titles*

It should now be apparent that light on the Greco-Jewish *archisynagogoi* must come from within their own context. And there we shall confront a certain contradiction in the role, as it emerges from the inscriptions. For as we have seen, we are dealing with a term which is more or less specific to Jewry. And yet, the application evokes the Greco-Roman status distinctions in which standard civic inscriptions abound, and investigation reinforces those parallels.

Associations proliferated in Greek and Roman cities—and increasingly so as time went on. Whether religious groups, trade guilds or burial clubs, they show a tendency to replicate in miniature the organization and government of the cities themselves. Similar names for councils and offices may appear and also sometimes similar mechanisms for self-government.[45] Jewish synagogues or other community groupings have often been treated as instances of this kind of association, and not inappropriately; and the archonship is an example of a civic title transferred to the Jewish context.[46] Not only names and methods are transferable, however, but, more importantly, an ethos. We find in many clubs and associations echoes of that honour-driven pattern of office-distribution which increasingly characterizes the cities themselves. What this means is not, of course, that titles and positions were necessarily void of content, or that they were in their nature purely honorary, in the sense that empty titles were bestowed on some while others did the work. What is involved is in fact a fundamental and obvious feature of Greco-Roman society, which may be summarized under four heads:

---

[44] Cf. White 1990: ch. 4. However, the *hazzan* referred to by Epiphanius, above, and parallelled in a Greek inscription, *CIJ* 805 from Apamea, is a real example of a loanword in Greek and of a post whose point of origin would seem to lie in Palestine.

[45] For this phenomenon already in a classical Athenian context, see Osborne 1990.

[46] See especially, Meeks 1983: 32–40. It does not follow, however, from manifestations such as the Jewish archonships that Jewish communities had the special formal status of *politeumata* operating as legal cities within cities, a view maintained in, e.g., Smallwood 1976: 359–360.

1. Administrative 'jobs' required little expertise or investment of time compared with modern assignments.
2. The primary criterion for appointment was not competence; any definition of recognized merit would have to incorporate extraneous, social factors.
3. There was a markedly close correlation between social standing and appointment to high position.
4. Beneficence played a major role in getting chosen and in the performance of the office itself, making wealth a *sine qua non*.[47]

There are some interesting and extreme consequences of these principles among the inscriptions which are our main evidence on civic office-holding in the Roman Empire and, in fact, virtually our only evidence on the doings of associations. Complete outsiders could be appointed, especially powerful outsiders like the emperor.[48] Women could hold titles even if they were not otherwise group-members or holders of full citizen rights.[49] Children could be appointed.[50] In fact, people could hold titles without even being alive: the recently deceased sometimes received posts. And it was not even necessary to have existed in the first place: gods were occasionally elected.[51] Such office-holders clearly had something to contribute which outweighed their lack of full civic status: influence, family connections, prestige or (presumably most important) wealth.

Other notable features of honour-driven hierarchies are fluidity, inconsistency and elasticity in the number and formulation of titles; these are natural consequences of the valuing of honour over function. It is, indeed, the indeterminacy of such systems, rather than shortage of evidence, which might explain our own difficulties in interpreting them. For example, epigraphists have been hard put to judge whether the prestigious office of Asiarch in the province of Asia was identical with that elsewhere called the High Priest of Asia, or a separate office:[52] some have thought that the Asiarch was

---

[47] Cf. Saller 1982: 94 ff., on merit in relation to imperial appointments.
[48] E.g. from Cyzicus (*SEG* 33.1056): 'When the Emperor Hadrian was hipparchos for the second time . . .'.
[49] Evidence for Asia Minor is collected by Trebilco 1991: 116–126.
[50] E.g. H. Pleket, *Epigraphica* 2, no. 34, first century A.D.: 'The city of Epidaurus honoured Cn. Cornelius Pulcher, son of Gnaeus, aged 4, former gymnasiarch, former agoranomos at the sacred festivals, for his virtue and goodwill towards the city.'
[51] Magie 1950: 470, 515, 650, 839 n. 24, 1508 n. 34.
[52] The issues are well set out by Horsley 1987: 48 ff.

appointed Asiarch for the duration of a festival of the *koinon* of Asia;
others that the title was gained after the holder's term of office as
chief priest and retained in perpetuity; others again that the title was
one quite distinct from that of chief priest. It is perhaps unexpected
that office-holding within the Jewish group shows clear signs of being
governed by the same honour-driven principles; and it is particularly instructive to note indications of this in the case of the post
which we are reviewing, the archetypally Jewish and supposedly cler-
ical post of *archisynagogos*.

The sample of available inscriptions (Appendix I) is small, with
32 apparently Jewish texts mentioning some 40 *archisynagogoi*.[53] But
this is enough to allow distinct patterns to emerge. *Archisynagogoi* do,
at least, outnumber other posts, with the exception of the archonship, whose frequency is to be accounted for by the importance of
the archonship in the synagogues of Rome, from which (thanks to
the early exploration of the catacombs) a disproportionate number
of inscriptions emanate.[54] The sample is also geographically and
chronologically diverse. It covers Africa, Spain, Italy, Pannonia,
Moesia, Greece, Crete, Cyprus, Asia Minor, Syria and Palestine, and
it stretches from the first century down to the sixth. Local variation
and development over the years were admittedly significant: it is, for
example, striking that the archisynagogate had little or no presence
in Greco-Jewish Egypt, and, again, that the three major Jewish
inscriptions from Berenice in Cyrenaica, which come from the early
to mid-first century A.D., list archons but no *archisynagogoi*, although
two of them are formal decrees of the Jews in the city and the third
does mention a *synagoge*.[55] But our concern is with a general pattern
existing within a reasonably homogeneous Greco-Roman culture, and
therefore we need not be too concerned about such divergences.

The first indication of a strong honorific component in the
epigraphic titles is the phenomenon of office-holding in perpetuity,
διὰ βίου, a later Greek practice which echoes Roman *perpetuus* appointments. Among the Jewish *archisynagogoi*, we find two who are explicitly

---

[53] This excludes the following very fragmentary texts where either there is no
clear evidence of Jewish connections, or restoration is very dubious, or only a single word is preserved: *CIJ* 638, 759; *BE* (1980) 230.30; *BS* II 212. Also the fragmentary honorific inscription from Alexandria mentioned above, *JIGRE* no. 18.

[54] See Leon 1960: ch. 2.

[55] Lüderitz 1983: nos. 70–72.

described as appointed for life, Appendix I, Nos. 18 and 20.[56] At Acmonia (No. 20), in the early imperial period, the restoration of Julia Severa's synagogue was achieved by the *archisynagogos* for life, together with an ordinary *archisynagogos* and an archon. The *tria nomina* suggest that the first-named alone was a Roman citizen, as too was his second or third century counterpart at Teos (No. 18). It would have to be clear even to the most gerontocratic society that real continued competence can scarcely be guaranteed with a life appointment, and what is important in such an appointment must be the strong desire of those who honour to underline and prolong a temporary pre-eminence. This certainly demonstrates an important association between office and status. But it does not, we must admit, exclude the possibility that primarily honorific titles, such as these perpetual ones, could exist alongside annual appointments which were more functional and which were intended for lesser individuals.

There can be an inbuilt ambiguity in cases where a formula expressing status is added to a title, leaving a reader unsure whether the extra distinction belongs to the specific case or is rather a statement of the honour which is normally understood to inhere in the title. It should be noted that extra designations of honour are not confined to *archisynagogoi*.[57] That the honour is a concomitant of the title would seem to be suggested in the dating formula of the Apamea synagogue mosaic (No. 21), where ἐπί is followed by the names of three *archisynagogoi*, a gerousiarch and two presbyters—the presbyters, like the *archisynagogoi*, are designated τιμιώτατοι. The date is 391, and the liberality of designation here ought perhaps to be seen as echoing that hierarchy of formal modes of address which characterize late Roman imperial society. This is also apparent in the use of λαμπρότατος in the fifth-century inscription from Sepphoris in Palestine (No. 26): the Greek cities of the region in this respect come close to Diaspora practice. Rather earlier, at Beth She'arim, also in Palestine (No. 13), Eusebios from Beirut is already λαμπρότατος. At Rome (No. 1), we encounter Stafylus, an *archisynagogos* and archon who is

---

[56] The existence of other Jewish honorands for life should also be noted, either simply displaying the formula διὰ βίου in some form (*CIJ* 266, 398, 416, 417, 503 (Rome); 533 (Ostia); 575, 589 (?) (Venosa), or carrying the formula attached to another title: 561 (Puteoli, gerusiarch); 720 (Mantinea, πατὴρ λαοῦ).

[57] In addition to the instances below and the officers 'for life', note *CIJ* 85, 216, 324, 337 from Rome: archons πάσης τιμῆς.

said to have 'held all the honours'. We may quite reasonably suppose that in such a case the title of archon was held simultaneously with that of *archisynagogos*, and perhaps far beyond any fixed term. In fact, we should take the suggestion of a formal *cursus honorum* a little less than literally.

We have already learned that a proliferation of names for officials ought not to surprise us. A community might simply have enlisted more titles when it sprouted more notables. When we find individuals described as holders of more than one office (e.g. Nos. 17, 24), or else holders of different offices listed as having presided together over a benefaction, we are more likely to be confronting records of accumulated honour and privilege than descriptions of precisely defined jobs held at precise times, as Schürer thought. As in the case of Stafylus, we cannot always know whether the titles held by an individual were held sequentially or simultaneously.

It may also be a function of the titular nature of the offices that both *archisynagogos* and other designations tend to stand unqualified, without any anchorage in a particular place; though there are exceptions in the cases of the *archisynagogos* of the Vernaculi and the *archisynagogos* Isaac at Rome, where affiliation to one of the eleven synagogues seems to have mattered (Nos. 4, 2).[58]

At both ends of the chronological spectrum, we find the title of *archisynagogos* running in families. In the Theodotus inscription which was found in Jerusalem, and which presumably from before A.D. 70, the restorer of the synagogue and its hostelry declares himself a priest and the son and grandson of *archisynagogoi*. The name of the founder's father, Vettenus, has led to the speculation that this was an enslaved family freed in Rome,[59] though where we are then to suppose that Vettenus acquired his archisynagogal title is unclear. Among the latest inscriptions there are also father and son *archisynagogoi* at Sepphoris and Venosa (nos. 25, 26, 8). There is, of course, no reason to suggest that hereditary transmission operated in such cases.

Nor need the explanation of inheritance be used to account for the female title-holders who have aroused interest in recent years.[60]

---

[58] At Beth She'arim, place of origin is indicated because the dead were buried far from their home countries. See Schwabe & Lifshitz 1974.

[59] Notably Vincent 1921, who sought to identify the synagogue with the 'synagogue of the Libertines' in Acts 6:9.

[60] Brooten 1982: ch. 1. There is also epigraphic attestation of a small number

Three of them figure among the *archisynagogoi*. Theopempte from Myndos in Caria figures together with her son Eusebios in a text which is apparently a dedication of a chancel-screen (No. 19). Sophia of Gortyn is described on her tomb as πρεσβυτέρα κὲ ἀρχισυναγωγίσσα (No. 11). Rufina of Smyrna, called Ἰουδαία[61] and *archisynagogos*, built a tomb for her ex-slaves and so was clearly a woman of substance, head of a Jewish household (No. 12).

Child title-holders raise some of the same questions as women, and ought probably to be considered together with them. At Venosa, a three-year old managed to become *archisynagogos* (No. 7).[62]

The parallel with the familiar civic inscriptions from Asia Minor where women and children appear as major donors, as holders of the highest titles in the male sphere and as prominent honorands, is an inescapable one. And if we wish to look outside Asia Minor, we may invoke the 15-year-old son of a freedman who is a dedicatee at Pompeii.[63]

The question which arises in the Jewish context (scarcely addressed by Brooten) is whether these figures are, like the great pagan women, owners of wealth in their own right, who gain titles and honours because they are able to be benefactors, or whether they are merely inheritors, *faute de mieux*, of titles which happen to be hereditary. The evidence for female land ownership presented by van Bremen is strong, and there is no *prima facie* reason to expect the situation of Jewish women living in comparable urban milieux to be different on account of their Judaism. We have only to think of Babatha, that now renowned second-century Jewish lady from the provincia Arabia, whose property and complex dealings are revealed in her papyrus archive.[64] In the case of Rufina at least, we have epigraphic proof that she had means of her own to dispose of. The first interpretation therefore commends itself. There also arises the question of whether women office-holders functioned, *qua* office-holders, exactly

---

of women who hold other offices in the community: Brooten 1982: chs. 2–4. Trebilco 1991: ch. 5, brings together the Jewish and pagan evidence for Asia Minor.

[61] Cf. Kraemer 1989 for the possible meanings of this term, which may designate here and elsewhere a pagan adherent to Judaism.

[62] Cf. the case of the twelve-year old *grammateus* and *mellarchon* from Rome, *CIJ* 284.

[63] See van Bremen 1983. For Pompeii: *CIL* 10.846; White 1990: 31, makes the interesting suggestion that preferment not open to the freedman father was available to the son.

[64] See Lewis 1989.

as did their male counterparts. Brooten's claim of functional equality is acceptable (though perhaps less so in the case of the small children), but the synagogue service is not the correct setting for that
equality, and the contribution of women, just as that of men, must
be envisaged as patronal and perhaps ceremonial rather than religious.[65] No doubt, too, the public behaviour of these women, like
that of the benefactors of Asia Minor, 'was still defined and con-
strained by the . . . traditional ideology'.[66]

6. *Archisynagogoi as benefactors*

In many cases, Jewish officials are explicit benefactors. That of course
is why they seem to be linked with the fabric of the synagogues—
not because they looked after the 'plant'. *Archisynagogoi* are found as
donors of whole synagogue buildings (Appendix I, Nos. 17, 18, 25),
restorers of buildings (No. 20), or donors of parts of buildings: mosaic
floors (Nos. 21, 22, 24), a chancel screen (No. 19), columns (No. 23).
These Jewish benefactors operate essentially like Greco-Roman benefactors within a 'euergetistic' framework of giving benefits and receiv-
ing honours, though it has been possible to demonstrate certain
limitations within Jewish groups on the full adoption of the value-
system inherent in that framework: not only honorific statues seem
to have been generally eschewed, but also lesser visible payments of
honour such as shields, as well as elaborate verbal eulogies. Group
benefactions were relatively common, and gifts relating to the physical
structure of synagogues seem to have been the only kind of benefaction made.[67]

Archisynagogoi share their role as benefactors of synagogues with
other title-holders. This is to be expected, since, on our view, the
major Jewish titles shared the same social functions. The exception
is the *grammateus*, who may well have been a true functionary. It is
impossible to offer meaningful comparative quantification of the
records of the different post-holders as donors, since our initially
small samples for the different posts are hopelessly skewed by the

---

[65] On this point, see Rajak 1992: 23–25 = Ch. 17: 350–352; also White 1990:
179, n. 50.

[66] Van Bremen 1983: 236.

[67] With the possible exception of the Aphrodisias inscription, where the editors
tentatively identify a 'soup-kitchen' (Reynolds & Tannenbaum 1987: 26–28); see
also Rajak 1996 = Ch. 19 in this volume.

domination of archons and, to a lesser extent, gerousiarchs, both of whom appear in the epitaphs of the Roman catacombs, where they naturally could not be recorded as donors. We cannot judge whether *archisynagogoi* were regularly the most illustrious of the title-holders, and this perhaps does not matter very much. But we notice that they do stand well as benefactors. The figure of 9 *archisynagogoi* who are donors (out of the total of some 40 names) is suggestive. For comparison, only one gerousiarch is known as a donor, while four archons figure in such a role. Furthermore, we have seen that *archisynagogoi* tend to be associated with what, in synagogue terms, are substantial gifts.[68]

To suggest that *archisynagogoi* were people of scope and standing in their own communities is not to say that all or even most of them were possessors of large-scale wealth by the standards of their cities, let alone in empire-wide terms. Even the donation of a whole synagogue building could not compare with the strings of massive benefactions attributed to great donors in the Roman east. The real means of Jewish benefactors evidently varied greatly, not only according to the character of the city they inhabited, but also, no doubt, according to the history and circumstances of the Jewish community within it (and communities suffered many vicissitudes in all centuries). While most donations may appear modest, it is not easy to get an accurate picture, given the apparent inclination of Jewish communities to play down the act of giving. The point is, at any rate, that archisynagogal status could not have been acquired without resources.

7. Archisynagogoi as patrons

The *archisynagogos* was a patronal figure. With his wealth, his standing, and the advantage of a title which the outside world could recognize instantly, he had the wherewithal to act as mediator for the community. It is conceivable, indeed, that you did not have to be

---

[68] Most of the other apparently Jewish individual or family donors of whole buildings are named without titles: Alypus in Egypt (*JIGRE* no.13, probably 37 B.C.); Papous in Egypt (*JIGRE* no. 126, 1st century A.D.); Tation at Phocaea (Lifshitz no. 13, probably 3rd century); two brothers and their father at Tafas in Syria (Lifshitz no. 63, probably 4th century). There is one case of the holder of another title donating a whole building: Ti. Claudius Polycharmos the πατὴρ τῆς . . . συναγωγῆς at Stobi in Macedonia (Lifshitz no. 10, probably 3rd century). In Cyprus, a presbyter and his son restored a whole synagogue (Lifshitz no. 82, probably 4th century).

Jewish to be an *archisynagogos*. It may have been enough to take a patronal interest in a Jewish community. Such may be the case with at least one of the refurbishers of Julia Severa's synagogue in Acmonia, those men who were honoured for their improvements to the original building (Appendix I, No. 20). It has been noted that P. Turronius Cladus, the *archisynagogos* for life, has the same *nomen* as prominent pagans in Akmonia: a C. Turronius Rapon had been high priest together with Julia Severa. And Julia Severa herself, though a high priestess in the imperial cult and a very grand lady, had seen fit to build a synagogue or at least to donate a house to the Jews.[69] In parts of Phrygia, Judaism had a high religious profile,[70] and we need not be surprised to see this echoed in social contacts and mutual esteem. It is striking that the two *archisynagogoi* and the archon who are together honoured in the renovation inscription are presented with gilded shields, which is a form of recognition quite uncharacteristic of Jewish epigraphy.

There is no real problem in conceiving of a non-Jew being given archisynagogal standing. Momigliano's depiction of Alexander Severus quite literally as an *archisynagogos*, although it lacks supporting evidence,[71] is an ingenious and plausible one. For, after all, nothing by way of Judaism or Jewish knowledge need have been required to be a satisfactory *archisynagogos*, beyond the capacity to display benevolent concern for the group. The *archisynagogos*, we may be inclined to say, was what he or she was, rather more than what he or she did.

8. *Conclusion*

The echoing of the city's status system within the Jewish group represents at the very least an external acceptance within the group of

---

[69] Julia Severa, who originally erected the building, is known to have been active in the 50s and 60s. The inscription records the restoration of the building, and while this might have happened as early as the 80s or 90s, as is usually assumed, it could have been considerably later. White 1990: 81, suggests that the renovations were what made the house into a synagogue. On Julia Severa's connections and on the improbability of her being in any real sense a Jew, see Trebilco 1991: 58–60; Sheppard 1979; W. Ramsay, *Cities and Bishoprics of Phrygia* (1897), 639, 650–1, 673, curiously reconstructed the whole family as Jewish.

[70] The milieu is nicely characterized by Sheppard 1979.

[71] Momigliano 1934. He cites an inscription from Rome (*CIJ* 501) apparently referring to a woman ἀπο τῆς συναγ(ωγῆς) Ἀρκ[ου Λι]βανου which was Alexander's birthplace.

civic political values. These echoes would necessarily be both the result and the facilitator of interaction. The result of redefining the archisynagogate in terms of a sound understanding of Greek civic titles, is thus to conclude that it belonged in an outward-looking type of community, which did not see fit to run its affairs in isolation, even if it might parade its cultural distinctiveness in chosen ways.

Nor does the loosely proliferating officialdom of the synagogue, with its polite designations and its reliance on benefaction, suggest a powerful authority structure with a strong hold on its members, such as existed in certain early Christian communities and such as is visible in ultra-orthodox Jewish groupings today. If there were any such strong figures in the Jewish communities of the Roman empire, then they were not the *archisynagogoi* but others, perhaps prophets or charismatics, hidden from our view. The communities need not have been monolithic, and we do not pretend that the title-holders are the whole story. But they are an important part of it, over a long period: and the brief inscriptions produced by community members themselves, viewed without preconception, serve to locate the *archisynagogoi* in an intelligible civic context which we could never have divined from literary allusion alone. After discarding the old certainties about Jewish titles, we are in a position to understand not less, but more. The synagogue of Julia Severa is brought to life.[72]

BIBLIOGRAPHY

Avi-Yonah, M. 1976. *The Jews of Palestine: A Political History from the Bar Kokhba War to the Arab Conquest*. Oxford.
Brooten, B.J. 1982. *Women Leaders in the Ancient Synagogues*. Chico, California.
Cohen, S.J.D. 1987. 'Pagan and Christian Evidence on the Ancient Synagogue', in L.I. Levine (ed.), *The Synagogue in Late Antiquity*. Philadelphia, 50–60.
Gutmann, J. (ed.). 1975. *The Synagogue: Studies in Origins, Archaeology and Architecture*. New York.
Hengel, M. 1975. 'Proseuche und Synagoge', in J. Gutmann (ed.). *The Synagogue: Studies in Origins, Archaeology and Architecture*. New York.

---

[72] Short versions of this paper were given to an interdisciplinary colloquium on 'groups' held at King's College, London, under the auspices of Dr Judith Lieu; and to seminars in the Faculties of Oriental Studies in Oxford and Cambridge. We are grateful to the various participants for constructive comments, as also to the Editorial Committee. Composition was aided by a grant from the British Academy; and consideration of the subject was begun during the first author's tenure of the Woolley Fellowship at Somerville College, Oxford. The facilities of the Cambridge Jewish Inscriptions Project, where David Noy worked, have been invaluable; for the encouragement to exploit these we thank William Horbury.

Hoenig, S.B. 1975. 'The Suppositious Temple-Synagogue', in J. Gutmann (ed.). *The Synagogue: Studies in Origins, Archaeology and Architecture.* New York, 55–71.

Homans, G.C. 1968. 'The Study of Groups', in *International Encyclopedia of the Social Sciences*, vol. 6. New York, 258–265.

Horsley, G.H.R. 1982. *New Documents Illustrating Early Christianity*, vol. 2: 1977. Sydney.

—— 1987. *New Documents Illustrating Early Christianity*, vol. 6: 1979. Sydney.

Juster, J. 1914. *Les Juifs dans l'empire romain.* Paris.

Kraabel, A.T. 1975. 'Social Systems of Six Diaspora Synagogues', in Gutmann, J. (ed.). 1975. *The Synagogue: Studies in Origins, Archaeology and Architecture.* New York, 79–91; repr. in Overman & MacLennan 1992: 257–269.

—— 1982. 'The Roman Diaspora: Six Questionable Assumptions', *JJS* 33: 445–464.

—— 1985. '*Synagoga caeca*: Systematic Distortion in Gentile Interpretation of Evidence for Judaism in the Early Christian Period', in J. Neusner & E.S. Frerichs (eds), '*To See Ourselves as Others See Us*': *Christians, Jews, 'Others' in Late Antiquity.* Chico, Califronia, 219–246; repr. in Overman & MacLennan 1992: 35–62.

—— 1987. 'Unity and Diversity among Diaspora Synagogues', in L.I. Levine (ed.), *The Synagogue in Late Antiquity.* Philadelphia, 49–60; repr. in Overman & MacLennan 1992: 21–33.

Kraemer, R. 1989. 'On the Meaning of the term 'Jew' in Greco-Roman Inscriptions, *HTR* 82: 35–54 repr. in Overman & MacLennan 1992: 311–330.

Krauss, S. 1922. *Synagogale Altertümer.* Berlin.

Latyschev, B. 1890. *Inscriptiones Regni Bosporani*, vol. 2. Petropoli.

Leon, H. 1960. *The Jews of Ancient Rome.* Philadelphia.

Levine, L.I. 1979. 'The Jewish Patriarch (Nasi) in Third Century Palestine', *ANRW* II.19.2: 649–688.

—— (ed.). 1987. *The Synagogue in Late Antiquity.* Philadelphia.

Lieu, J. 1988. 'Epiphanius on the Scribes and Pharisees (*Pan.* 15.1–16.4), *JTS* 39: 509–524.

—— 1992. 'History and Theology in Christian Views of Judaism', in Lieu, North & Rajak 1992: 70–96.

Lieu, J., North, J. & Rajak, T. (eds). 1992. *The Jews among Pagans and Christians.* London.

Lewis, N. (ed.). 1989. *The Documents from the Bar-Kokhba Period in the Cave of Letters: Greek Papyri.* Jerusalem.

Lifshitz, B. 1967. *Donateurs et fondateurs dans les synagogues juives.* Paris.

Linder, A. 1987. *The Jews in Roman Imperial Legislation.* Detroit.

Lipsius, R.A. (ed.). 1959. *Acta Apostolorum Apocrypha.* Hildesheim.

Lüderitz, G. 1983. *Corpus jüdischer zeugnisse aus Cyrenaika.* Wiesbaden.

Magie, D. 1950. *Roman Rule in Asia Minor to the End of the Third Century after Christ.* Princeton.

Marmorstein, S. 1921. 'The Inscription of Theodotus', *Palestine Exploration Fund Quarterly Statement*, 24–26.

Meeks, W. 1983. *The First Urban Christians: the Social World of the Apostle Paul.* New Haven.

MacMullen, R. 1981. *Paganism in the Roman Empire.* New Haven/London.

Millar, F. 1987. 'Empire, Community and Culture in the Roman Near East: Greeks, Syrians, Jews and Arabs', *JJS* 38: 143–164.

—— 1992. 'The Jews of the Graeco-Roman Diaspora between Paganism and Christianity, AD 312–438', in Lieu, North & Rajak 1992: 97–123.

Momigliano, A. 1989. 'What Josephus Did Not See', in *On Pagans, Jews and Christians.* Middletown, CT, 108–119.

—— 1934. 'Severo Alessandro archisynagogus. Una conferma alla Historia Augusta', *Athenaeum* 12: 151–153.

North, J. 1992. 'The Development of Religious Pluralism', in Lieu, North & Rajak. 1992: 174–193.

Noy, D. 1993. *Jewish Inscriptions of Western Europe*, vol. 1. Cambridge.
Osborne, R. 1990. 'The *Demos* and its Divisions in Classical Athens', in S. Price & O. Murray (eds). *The Greek City from Homer to Alexander*. Oxford, 265–295.
Overmann, J.A. & MacLennan, R.S. (eds). 1992. *Diaspora Jews and Judaism. Essays in Honor of, and in Dialogue with, A. Thomas Kraabel*. South Florida Studies in the History of Judaism 41. Atlanta, Georgia.
Poland, F. 1909. *Geschichte des griechischen Vereinswesens*. Leipzig.
Rajak, T. 1992. 'The Jewish Community and its Boundaries', in Lieu, North & Rajak 1992, 9–29 = Ch. 2 in this volume.
——— 1996. 'Benefactors in the Greco-Jewish Diaspora' in P. Schäfer (ed.), *Geschichte–Tradition–Reflexion. Festschrift für Martin Hengel zum 70 Geburtstag*, vol. 1. *Judentum*. Tübingen, 305–319 = Ch. 4 in this volume.
Reynolds, J.M. & Tannenbaum, R. 1987. *Jews and God-Fearers at Aphrodisias*. Cambridge.
Robert, L. 1940. *Hellenica* vol. 1. Paris.
Saller, R. 1982. *Personal Patronage under the Early Empire*. Cambridge.
Schrage, W. 1971. '*Synagoge* etc', in G. Kittel *et al.* (eds), *Theological Dictionary of the New Testament*, 7. Grand Rapids, 798–841.
Schwabe, M. & Lifshitz, B. 1974. *Beth She'arim*, vol. 2. English edn. Jerusalem.
Sheppard, A.R.R. 1979. 'Jews, Christians and Heretics in Acmonia and Eumeneia', *Anatolian Studies* 29: 169–180
Shinan, A. 1987. 'Sermons, Targums and the Reading from Scriptures in the Ancient Synagogues', in L.I. Levine (ed.), *The Synagogue in Late Antiquity*. Philadelphia, 97–110.
Smallwood, E.M. 1976. *The Jews under Roman Rule: from Pompey to Diocletian: a Study in Political Relations*. Studies in Judaism in Late Antiquity 20. Leiden.
Stern, M. 1980. *Greek and Latin Authors on the Jews and Judaism*. Jerusalem.
Trebilco, P. 1991. *Jewish Communities in Asia Minor*. Cambridge.
van Bremen, R. 1983. 'Women and Wealth', in A. Cameron & A. Kuhrt (eds), *Images of Women in Antiquity*. London, 233–242.
van der Horst, P.W. 1991. *Ancient Jewish Epitaphs: an Introductory Survey of a Millenniun of Jewish Funerary Epigraphy (300 B.C.E.–700 C.E.)*. Kampen.
Vincent, R. 1921. 'La découverte de la synagogue des affranchis à Jérusalem', *RB* 30: 247–277
White, L.M. 1990. *Building God's House in the Roman World*. Valley Forge, PA.

APPENDIX I

JEWISH TEXTS MENTIONING *ARCHISYNAGOGOI*[73]

Epitaphs of Archisynagogoi

1. Rome, via Appia: *CIJ* 265. 2nd–4th century.
Stafylo arconti et archisynagogo honoribus omnibus fu<n>ctus, Restituta coniux benemerenti fecit. ἐν εἰρήνῃ ἡ κοίμησίς σου.

---

[73] Accepted dates are given for the inscriptions in most cases. A number of the texts given here have been re-edited for Noy 1993, cited below as *JIWE* I, under the auspices of the Jewish Inscriptions Project, University of Cambridge.

To the well-deserving Stafylus, archon and *archisynagogus*, who held all the honours. Restituta his wife made (the monument). In peace your sleep.

2. Rome, via Appia: *CIJ* 282; Leon 1960: 306. 2nd–4th century.

[- -] καὶ Ἰσαακ [- - ἀρχισυν]άγωγος [- -] συναγωγῆ[ς - -] ἐπλήρωσ[εν ἔτη - -] . . .

. . . and Isaac . . . *archisynagogos* . . . of the synagogue . . . he completed . . . years . . .

3. Rome, via Portuenses: *CIJ* 336; Leon 1960: 314. 1st–3rd century.

ἐνθάδε κεῖτε Εὐφράσις ἀρχισυναγώγης ὁ κα[λῶς βιώσας ?].

Here lies Euphrasis, archisynagogos, who lived a good life (?).

4. Rome, via Portuensis: *CIJ* 383: Leon 1960: 322. 1st–3rd century.

[ἐν]θάδε κεῖτε Πολυ[. .]νις ἀρχισυναγωγὸς [συ]αγωγῆς Βερνα[κλ]ων ἐτῶν νγ΄. [ἐν] εἰρήνη ἡ κοίμησις αὐτοῦ.

Here lies Poly . . nis, *archisynagogos* of the synagogue of the Vernaclians, aged 53. In peace his sleep.

5. Ostia: M. Squarciapino, *Rassegna mensile di Israel* 36.7–9 (1970), 183–191; *JIWE* I, 14. 1st–2nd century.

Plotio Fortunate archisyn(agogo) fec(erunt) Plotius Ampliatus Secundinus Secunda P T N et Ofilia Basilia coiugi b(ene) m(erenti).

For Plotius Fortunatus, *archisynagogus*. Plotius Ampliatus, Secundinus (and) Secunda made (the monument) . . ., and Ofilia Basilia to her well-deserving husband.

6. Capua: *CIJ* 553; *JIWE* I, 20. 2nd–4th century.

P. Alfius Iuda arcon arcosynagogus, q(ui) vi(xit) ann(is) LXX mesib(us) VII dieb(us) X. Alfia Soteris cum q(ua) <vixit> an(nis) XXXXVIII coiugi incomparabil(i) bene merenti fecit.

P(?) Alfius Iuda, archon and *archisynagogos*, who lived 70 years 7 months 10 days. Alfia Soteris, with whom he lived 48 years, made (the monument) for her incomparable, well-deserving husband.

7. Venosa: *CIJ* 587; *JIWE* I, 53. 5th century.

τάφος Καλλίστου νιπίου ἀρχοσσιναγωγοῦ, ἐτῶν γ΄ [μη]νῶν γ΄. ἐν [εἰ]ρέ[νη ἡ] κόμη[σις αὐτοῦ.]

Tomb of Kallistos, child, *archisynagogos*, aged 3 years 3 months. In peace his sleep.

8. Venosa: *CIJ* 584; *JIWE* I, 70. 5th century.

τάφως· Ἰοσὴφ ἀρχησυναγώγως υἱὸς Ἰωσὴφ ἀρχησυναγογοῦ. [ש]לום. אל [משכנך].

Tomb. Joseph, *archisynagogos*, son of Joseph, *archisynagogos*. Peace upon his resting-place.

9. Venosa: *CIJ* 596; JIWE I, 64. 5th–early 6th century.
τάφως ACHΛONOYA ἀρχοσηνωγούγου ἐτῶν πεντῆντα. שאלום.
Tomb of . . . the *archisynagogos*, aged fifty. Peace.

10. Oescus, Moesia: CIJ 681; A. Scheiber, *Jewish Inscriptions in Hungary* (1983), no. 10. 4th century (?).
Ioses arcisina[go] gos et principales, filius Maximini Pannoni, sibi et Qyriae coiugi sui vivo suo memoria dedicavit.
Joses the *archisynagogus* and leading decurion, son of Maximinus the Pannonian, to himself and Kyria his wife, dedicated the memorial while he was alive.

11. Kastelli Kissamou, Crete: *CIJ* 731c; Brooten, 11. 4th–5th century.
Σοφία Γορτυνία πρεσβυτέρα κὲ ἀρχισυναγωγίσσα Κισάμου ἔνθα. μνήμη δικέας ἰς ἐώνα. ἀμήν.
Sophia of Gortyn, elder and *archisynagogissa* of Kisamos (lies) here. The memory of a just one (is) for ever. Amen.

12. Smyrna: *CIJ* 741; *I.Smyrna* I, 295. 3rd century or later.
Ῥουφεῖνα Ἰουδαία ἀρχισυνάγωγος κατεσκεύασεν τὸ ἐνσόριον τοῖς ἀπελευθέροις καὶ θρέμασιν [followed by provisions against violation].
Rufina the Jewess, *archisynagogos*, built the tomb for her freedmen and home-bred slaves.

13. Beirut: M. Schwabe & B. Lifshitz, *Beth She'arim* II (English edn, 1974), 164. 3rd–early 4th century.
ἐνθάδε κῖτε Εὐσέβις ὁ λαμπρότατος ἀρχσυνάγωγος ὢν Βηριτῶ[ν].
Here lies the most distinguished Eusebis, being *archisynagogos* of Beirut.

14. Caesarea: Schwabe & Lifshitz, 203. 3rd–early 4th century.
Ἰακὼς Καισαρεὺς ἀρχισυνάγωγος Παμφυλίας. שלום.
Iakos the Caesarian, *archisynagogos* of Pamphylia. Peace.

15. Sidon: B. Lifshitz, *ZDPV* 82 (1966), 57 (from Beth She'arim). 3rd–early 4th century.
Ἰωσῆ ἀρχισυναγώγου Σίδονος.
(Tomb of) Ioses, *archisynagogos* of Sidon.

16. Jerusalem: *CIJ* 1414. Restoration and date uncertain.
ῥαββὶ Σαμου[ὴλ] ἀρχησ[υνάγωγος Φ]ρύγιος Δο[ρυλαεύς?]. δοξάσ⟨ε⟩ι α[ὐτὸν ἡ] ο⟨ἰ⟩κου[μένη]. שלום [ע]ל מישכבך.
Rabbi Samuel, *archisynagogos* of Dorylaea in Phrygia. The world will honour him (?). Peace upon your resting-place.

Archisynagogoi as donors

17. Aegina: *CIJ* 722; Lifshitz, no. 1. 4th century (?); restoration uncertain.

Θεόδωρος ἀρχ[ισυνάγωγ(ος) φ]ροντίσας ἔτη τέσσερα ἐχ θεμελίων τὴν σ[υναγωγ(ὴν)] οἰκοδόμησα· προσοδεύθ(ησαν) χρύσινοι πε' καὶ ἐκ τῶν τοῦ Θ(εοῦ) δωρεῶν χρύσινοι ρε'.

I, Theodoros, *archisynagogos*, *phrontistes* for four years, built the synagogue from its foundations. 95 gold pieces were received[74] and 105 gold pieces from the gifts of God.

18. Teos: *CIJ* 744; Lifshitz, no. 16. 2nd–3rd century.

Π. Ῥουτ(ίλιος) Ἰωσῆς ὁ ἀξιολογώτατος ὁ διὰ βίου ἀρχισυνάγω[γος] σὺν Βισιννίᾳ Δημῷ τῇ συνβίῳ αὐτοῦ ἐκ θεμελίων ἐκ τῶν ἰ[δίων].

P. Rutilius Joses[75] the most respectable *archisynagogos* for life, with Bisinnia Demo his wife, (built it) from the foundations, from his own money.

19. Myndos, Caria: *CIJ* 756; Brooten, 13. 4th–5th century or later.

[Ἀπὸ Θ]εωπέμπτης [ἀρ]χισυν(αγώγου) κὲ τοῦ υἱοῦ αὐτῆς Εὐσεβίου.

From Theopempte, *archisyn(agogos)*, and her son Eusebios.

20. Acmonia: *CIJ* 766 Lifshitz, no. 33. Probably late 1st century A.D.

τὸν κατασκευασθέντα οἶκον ὑπὸ Ἰουλίας Σεουήρας· Π. Τυρρώνιος Κλάδος ὁ διὰ βίου ἀρχισυνάγωγος καί Λούκιος Λουκίου ἀρχισυνάγωγος καὶ Ποπίλιος Ζωτικὸς ἄρχων ἐπεσκεύασαν ἔκ τῶν ἰδίων καὶ τῶν συνκαταθεμένων καὶ ἔγραψαν τοὺς τοίχους καὶ τὴν ὀροφὴν καὶ ἐποίησαν τὴν τῶν θυρίδων ἀσφάλειαν καὶ τὸν λυπὸν πάντα κόσμον, οὕστινας καὶ ἡ συναγωγὴ ἐτείμησεν ὅπλῳ ἐπιχρύσῳ διὰ τὴν ἐνάρετον αὐτῶν δ[ι]άθ[ε]σιν καὶ τὴν πρὸς τὴν συναγωγὴν εὔνοιάν τε καὶ σπουδήν.

The building was erected by Julia Severa. P. Tyrronius Cladus the *archisynagogos* for life and Lucius son of Lucius the *archisynagogos* and Popilius Zotikos the *archon* restored it with their own money and with what had been deposited. They painted the murals and ceiling, and made the reinforcements for the windows and all the other decoration. The community honoured

---

[74] Lifschitz gives this word the unparallelled meaning 'spent'.
[75] The interpretation of the name was made by Robert 1940: 27–28.

them with a gilded shield for their virtuous disposition and their goodwill and zeal towards the community.

21. Apamea: *CIJ* 803; Lifshitz, no. 38. A.D. 391; also includes dating formula.

ἐπὶ τῶν τιμιωτάτων ἀρχισυνα[γώ]γων Εὐσεβίου καὶ Νεμέου καὶ Φινέου καὶ Θεοδώρου γερουσιάρχου καὶ τῶν τιμιοτάτων πρεσβυτέρων Εἰσακίου καὶ Σαούλου καὶ λοιπῶν, Ἰλάσιος ἀρχισυνάγωγος Ἀντιοχέων ἐποίησεν τὴν ἴσοδον τοῦ ψηφίου πό(δας) ρν΄, ἔτους γψ΄ Εὐδνέου ζ΄. εὐλογία πᾶσι.

Under the most honoured *archisynagogoi* Eusebios and Nemeos and Phineas, and Theodoros the gerousiarch, and the most honoured presbyters Isaac and Saul and others, Ilasios, *archisynagogos* of Antioch, made the entrance, 150 feet of mosaic. In the year 703, Audunaios 7. Blessing to all.

22. Apamea: *CIJ* 804; Lifshitz, no. 39. A.D. 391; same donor as No. 21.

Ἰλασίου Εἰσακίου ἀρχισυνάγωγος Ἀντιοχέων, ὑπὲρ σωτηρίας Φωτίου συμβίου καὶ τέκνων καὶ ὑπὲρ σωτηρίας Εὐσταθίας πενθερᾶς, καὶ ὑπὲρ μνίας Εἰσακίου καὶ Ἐδεσίου καὶ Ἡσυχίου προγόνων, ἐποίησεν τὴν ψήφωσιν τῆς ἰσόδου. εἰρήνη καὶ ἔλεος ἐπὶ πᾶν τὸ ἡγιασμένον ὑμῶν πλῆθος.

Ilasios son of Isaac, *archisynagogos* of Antioch, for the well-being of Photion his wife and of his children, and for the well-being of Eustathia his mother-in-law, and in memory of Isaac and Aidesios and Hesychion his forebears, made the mosaic of the entrance. Peace and mercy on all your hallowed community.

23. Salamis, Cyprus: Lifshitz, no. 85 (inscribed on a marble column). Date uncertain.

[---] πεντ(άκις) ἀρχι(συναγώγου) υἱοῦ Ἀνανία δὶς ἄρχοντ(ος).

... of ... five times *archisynagogos*, son of Ananias who was twice archon.

24. Caesarea: Lifshitz, no. 66. 6th century.

Βη[ρ]ύλλος ἀρχισ(υνάγωγος) καὶ φροντιστὴς υἱὸς Ἰούτου, ἐποίησε τὴν ψηφοθεσίαν τοῦ τρικλίνου τῷ ἰδίῳ.

Beryllos the *archisynagogos andphrontistes*, son of Ioutos, made the mosaic of the *triclinium* with his own resources.

25. Jerusalem: *CIJ* 1404, Lifshitz, no. 79. Before A.D. 70.

Θεόδοτος Οὐεττήνου, ἱερεὺς καὶ ἀρχισυνάγωγος, υἱὸς ἀρχισυναγώγου, υἱωνὸς ἀρχισυναγώγου, ᾠκοδόμησε τὴν συναγωγὴν εἰς ἀνάγνωσιν νόμου καὶ εἰς διδαχὴν ἐντολῶν, καὶ τὸν ξενῶνα, καὶ τὰ δώματα καὶ τὰ χρηστήρια τῶν ὑδάτων εἰς κατάλυμα τοῖς χρῄζουσιν ἀπὸ τῆς ξένης, ἥν ἐθεμελίωσαν οἱ πατέρες αὐτοῦ καὶ οἱ πρεσβύτεροι καὶ Σιμωνίδης.

Theodotos son of Vettenus, priest and *archisynagogos*, son and grandson of *archisynagogoi*, built the synagogue for reading the law and teaching the commandments, and the guest-house and the rooms and the water provisions, as accommodation for those who need it from abroad. His fathers and the presbyters and Simonides founded the synagogue.

Archisynagogoi named in a dating formula (cf. No. 21)

26. Sepphoris-Diocaesarea: *CIJ* 991; Lifshitz, no. 74. 5th century.
(ἐπὶ) Ὑελασίου σχο(λαστικοῦ) κώ(μητος) λαμ(προτάτου) υείοῦ Ἀετίου τοῦ κό(μητος) Εἰούδα (ἀ)ρχισυναγώγου Σιδονίου ἀρχισυναγώγου ΠΕΡΙΕΡΘΟΟΝΤΑΔ Συβεριανο(ῦ) Ἄφρο(υ) ἀρχισυναγώγου Τύρου λαμπρ(οτάτου).

Under Gelasios the scholastikos and most distinguished count, son of Aetios the count, and Iuda, *archisynagogos* of Sidon, . . . Severianus Afer, most illustrious *archisynagogos* of Tyre.

Archisynagogos in a votive inscription

27. Intercisa, Pannonia: A. Scheiber, *Jewish Inscriptions in Hungary*, no. 3. A.D. 222–235.
Deo aeterno pro sal(ute) d(omini) n(ostri) Sev(eri) A[lex(andri)] P(ii) F(elicis) Aug(usti) e[t Iul(iae) Mamae]ae Aug(ustae) m(atris) Aug(usti) v(otum) red(dit) l(ibens) Cosmius pr(aepositus) sta(tionis) Spondill a(rchi)synag(ogus) Iudeor(um).

To the eternal God, for the safety of our lord Severus Alexander Pius Felix Augustus and of Julia Mamaea Augusta the emperor's mother, Cosmius the superintendent of the guard-post of Spondill (and) *archisynagogus* of the Jew's willingly repaid his vow.

Archisynagogoi named in patronymics (cf. Nos. 9, 25)

28. Rome: *CIJ* 504. 2nd–4th century.
ἐνθάδε κεῖτε Ἰουλιανὸς ἱερευσάρχων Καλκαρησίων υἱὸς Ἰουλιάνου ἀρχισυναγώγου.
Here lies Julianus, gerousiarch (?) of the Calcaresians, son of Julianus, *archisynagogos*.

29. Hamman Lif, North Africa: Brooten, 164, no. 38. Date wholly uncertain.
Asterius filius Rustici arcosinagogi (et) Margarita Riddei partem portici tesselavit.
Asterius, son of Rusticus the *archisynagogus*, and Margarita daughter of Riddeus paved with mosaic part of the portico.

30. Side: Lifshitz, no. 37. 5th–6th century; restoration uncertain.
[ἐ]πι Λεοντίου πρεσβ(υτέρου) καὶ ζυγ(οστάτου) [κ]αὶ φροντιστοῦ υεἱοῦ Ἰακὼβ ἀρχ(ισυναγώγου) καὶ ζυγ(οστάτου) ἐγένετο ἡ κρήνη σὺν τῷ μεσαύλῳ· ἰνδ(ικτίονι) γ′ μη(νὶ) ζ′.
Under Leontios, presbyter and weight-checker and *phrontistes*, son of Jacob, *archisynagogos* and weight-checker (?), the fountain was installed with the inner court. Year 3 of the indiction-cycle, month 7.

Inscriptions of uncertain nature

31. Tarragona: W.P. Bowers, *JTS* 26 (1975), 395–402; G. Alföldy, *Die römischen Inschriften von Tarraco* (1975), no. 1075; *JIWE* 1, 186. 5th–6th century(?).
Fragments of an epitaph in Latin and Greek: ll. 7–12 read
ἔνθα κατακ[εῖται] ῥαβ Λατουστ [- -] ΡΑ τοῦ μακ[αρίσ(?)]του ΚΜ[. .]Ε[- -] ἀρχησυν[αγωγοῦ/ος - -] Κυζηκο[νου/ος(?) - -]

32. Ephesus: *I.Ephesos* iv. 1251. Date uncertain.
τῶν ἀρχι⟨σ⟩υναγωγ⟨ῶ⟩ν καὶ τῶν πρεσβ(υτέρων) πολλὰ τὰ ἔτη.

APPENDIX II

NON-JEWISH ARCHISYNAGOGOI TEXTS

1. Perinthus, Thrace: E. Kalinken, *Arch-Epig. Mitth. aus Öst-Ung.* 19 (1896), 67. Early 1st century A.D. (?).[76]

   [- - - ὁ] διοικητὴς κ[αὶ Μά]ρκος Πομπήι[ος Κωμ?]ικὸς κω[......]ος τὸν βω[μ]ὸν τῇ συν⟨α⟩γω[γ]ῇ τῶν κουρέω[ν π]ερὶ ἀρχισυνάγ[ωγ]ον Γ. Ἰούλιον [Ο]ὐάλεντα δῶ[ρ]ον ἀποκατέστη[σα]ν καὶ τὸν τόπο[ν παρεσκεύ]ασα[ν.]

   ... the *dioiketes* and M. Pompeius Komikos (?)... (They) restored the altar for the *synagoge* of the barbers around the *archisynagogos* C. Iulius Valens as a gift and fitted out the place.

2. Salonica: IGx.ii.i No. 288. A.D. 155.[77]

   οἱ συνήθε[ις] τοῦ Ἡρακλέος Εὐφρά[νορ]ι τῷ συνήθει μνήμης χά[ριν] ἀρχισυναγωγοῦντος Κωτυος Εἰρήνης, γραματεόντων Μ. Κασσ[ί]ου Ἕρμωνος τοῦ καὶ Δημᾶ καὶ Πριμιγᾶ ἐπιμελητοῦ Πύθωνος Λουκειλίας Θεσσαλονικέος.

   The companions of Herakles to the companion Euphranor as a memorial, when Kotys son of Eirene was *archisynagogos*, M. Cassius Hermon, also known as Demas, and Primigas were *grammateis*, overseen by Python son of Lucilia of Thessalonica.

3. Salonica: *BE* (1972), No. 263; G. Horsley, *New Documents Illustrating Early Christianity* 4 (1979), 215.[78] A.D. 75(?).

   ... ἡ συνήθια Ἥρωνος Αὐλωνίτου Γ. Ἰουλίῳ Κρήσκεντι· οἱ περὶ ἀρχισύναγωγον Ἀρτέμωνα ζυγοποιὸν, ἱερῆ Τρύφωνα, τὰ ἐκ τοῦ γλωσσοκόμου γινόμενα αὐτῷ μνίας χάριν.

   ... The association of Heron Aulonites to C. Iulius Crescens. Those around the *archisynagogos* Artemon the yoke-maker, (and) the priest Tryphon (paid for) the costs arising from the sarcophagus for him as a memorial.

4. Olynthus, Chalcidice: *CIG* II. 2007f. 1st–2nd century A.D.

   Αἰλιανὸς Νείκων ὁ ἀρχισυνάγωγος θεοῦ ἥρωος καὶ τὸ κολλ⟨ή⟩γιον Βειβίῳ Ἀντωνίῳ ἀνέστησαν τὸν βωμόν. τὸν δὲ πίνακα ἀδέστησε γαμβρὸς αὐτοῦ Ἀσιδάρης.

---

[76] Schrage 1971: 8 f, suggests 1st century B.C.

[77] *IG* no. 299 is very fragmentary but seems to follow the same formula: [ἀρχισυνα]γογοῦντος [Κωτ]υος Εἰρήνης, [γραμματ]ευόντων Αὔλου[...].

[78] From Ph. Petsas, *Arch. Deltion* 24 (1969), Chron. 300–301.

Aelianus Nicon the *archisynagogos* of the Hero god and the college set up the altar for Vibius Antonius. His son-in-law Asidares set up the tablet.

5. Beroea, Macedonia: G. Horsley, *New Documents Illustrating Early Christianity* 4 (1979), 215; SEG xxvii. 267.[79] Imperial period.

'Αμμία ἡ γυνὴ καὶ Κουαρτίων ὁ ὑὸς Γεμέλλῳ μνήμης χάριν καὶ οἱ συνήθεις οἱ περὶ Ποσιδῶνιν τὸν ἀρχισυνάγωγον.

His wife Ammia and his son Quartion to Gemellus as a memorial, and the companions around Posidonis the *archisynagogos*.

6. Pydna, Macedonia: J.M.R. Cormack, *Mélanges offerts à Georges Daux* (1974), 51–55.[80] A.D. 250.

... οἱ συνελθόντες θρησκευταὶ ἐπὶ θεοῦ Διὸς 'Υψίστου ἔθεντο τήνδε τὴν στήλην, λογιστεύοντος Οὐρβανιανοῦ Βιλίστου, ἄρξοντος Αὐρ. Νιγερίωνος ὑπὸ ἀρχισυνάγωγον Αὐρ. Κηπίωνα τὸν πρὶν Πιερίωνος καὶ προστάτου Αὐρ. Σεβήρου καὶ γραμματέως Αὐρηλίου Θεοφίλου τοῦ πρὶν Πιερίωνος καὶ οἱ λοιποὶ θρησκευταὶ οἱ ὑπογεγραμμένοι. ...

... The assembled worshippers of the god Zeus Hypsistos put up the stele, when Urbanianus Bilistus was *logistes*, Aurelius Nigerion was *archon* under the *archisynagogos* Aurelius Cepion formerly of Pierion, and Aurelius Severus was *prostates*, and Aurelius Theophilos formerly of Pierion was *grammateus*, and the other worshippers who are written below ... [list of twenty nine names, including three women and two slaves. On the side of the stele: 'Overseers Theophilos and Aurelius Cepion formerly of Pierion.']

[79] Following A. Romiopolou, *Arch. Delt.* 28 (1973), Chron. 439.
[80] Discussed by Horsley 1982: 26–71.

CHAPTER TWENTY-ONE

INSCRIPTION AND CONTEXT:
READING THE JEWISH CATACOMBS OF ROME

Epigraphy, as we all know, is the 'handmaid' of history. Yet in Jewish epigraphy, as in the study of inscriptions generally, it is usual to analyse texts as disembodied entities, divorced from any spatial and visual context, related for the most part to one another, sometimes to literature. Often enough, this is unavoidable. But in the Rome catacombs, whence not far short of half of all known Jewish inscriptions emanate, we are offered a very remarkable context, a visual world which cries out to be considered together with the written word within it. It is a new consideration of this context which currently holds out, I would suggest, our most hopeful route to a better understanding of the inscriptions. Here, I offer no more than a preparatory investigation, in which I shall look at some of the major problems of interpretation, and through which I shall hope to indicate areas where further work is likely to be fruitful. The focus will be on a number of historical questions rather than on the material *per se*. Another direction in which our view of the texts might be widened with the help of visual data is by incorporating the symbols and designs which appear with many epitaphs into our discussion of the verbal element. That, however, has to be the subject of a separate study, although we shall have occasion to touch on the question of representation.

The disjunction between text and context did not always exist, and, as may be imagined, tunnels, decorations and texts alike were avidly scoured by the earliest explorers of both Christian and Jewish catacombs, starting with Bosio, 'the Columbus of the catacombs', whose *La Roma Soterranea* was published posthumously in 1632, going through Marucchi, and in a sense including even Father Frey, the indefatigable, if not quite infallible editor of the *Corpus Inscriptionum Iudaicarum* (for which the significant work was, we are told, completed before the second world war, in spite of a later publication date).[1] This tradition in Christian archaeology at Rome has not been

---

[1] See van der Horst 1991: 12.

lost, as we shall see when we come to discuss Fasola's recent work at the Villa Torlonia site.

Inscriptions and excavations

The history of the excavations of the Jewish catacombs of Rome has been very well told by Leon and I shall only mention some relevant points here.[2] The situation is that, while we are in the position of being able to relate most of the extant inscriptions, with the exception of those on sarcophagi, to the particular catacomb from which they come (just a few have turned up in odd locations in or outside Rome), it is much harder to place them in an exact context. Six or seven Jewish catacombs are known, with four apparently no longer in existence, but the bulk of our material derives from two extant sites and one non-extant site, one of the former comprising two separate burial systems.

We are presented with contrasting situations. The catacomb of Monteverde, beside the Janiculum (sometimes known by its topographical location, as Via Portuense) is now built over. The bulk of its inscriptions was taken off to collections at various times, most of them to the Lateran where a Jewish room was set up, and they were recorded by Nikolaus Müller.[3] For any notion of their original location within the overall plan of the catacomb, it is on the old records that we depend. On the other hand, in the Vigna Randanini, it is still possible to enter the main Jewish catacomb of the Via Appia area, discovered in 1859, with a good number of inscriptions still in the walls, though probably not *in situ*; further exploration could be fruitful. Finally, the two extensive burial complexes (known also as the Via Nomentana catacombs) in the garden of Mussolini's residence at the Villa Torlonia, were discovered in 1920 and have been systematically explored in recent years by U. Fasola, with the lower catacomb yielding 90 texts, some very fragmentary, and the upper 24. The small and now lost Vigna Cimarra hypogeum has produced six Greek inscriptions. From Via Labicana, outside the Porta Maggiore, where now a new road runs (strikingly photographed in Leon's book),[4]

---

[2] Leon 1960. For more details, Vismara 1986: 2.351–355.
[3] It is still necessary to refer to Müller & Bees 1919.
[4] Leon 1960: fig. 1.

came five or six items, and also two Hebrew scrawls, fancifully restored by Marucchi and rightly dismissed by Leon; and from Via Appia Pignatelli, a site which was once proposed as Jewish, two highly dubious texts. It is helpful at the start to recall that c. 75% of the total of some six hundred known texts is in Greek. Of the distribution of paintings and visual material, something will be said later. The problems and limits of the excavations deserve some words now.

It would be foolish to expect too much from any early exploration or excavation. It is also a wholly familiar story for tomb robbers to have empied much of a site, as is reported for a number of galleries at Villa Torlonia. None the less, in this case, we have an additional set of disadvantages. It is not unfair to say that the Jewish tombs have been, quite simply, the poor relation in Christian archaeology. While arousing intermittent interest and curiosity, they could not compete with the venerated shrines of Christian saints and martyrs. The consequences are apparent in the record of work cut off in mid-course, and in the ready abandonment of Jewish sites. The prime case of such neglect is, of course, the Monteverde catacomb, and Müller vividly evokes for us his desperate attempts to get the permits which would allow him to complete his investigations.[5] This was a site which had been known from the earliest phase of catacomb exploration, for Bosio had already ascribed it to the 'ancient Hebrews'; it is a reasonable surmise that at its full extent, this burial area would have been at least as large as the Villa Torlonia complex. Quarrying and the resultant weakness of the *tufo*, resulted eventually in a total collapse of the system, and this time it is blocks of flats constructed on part of the site which Leon had the pleasure of photographing.[6]

The obvious consequence of this sad story is the near certainty that material of inestimable value has been destroyed. But I am concerned with some less obvious, and perhaps more interesting consequences. It will be helpful to list them here as a preliminary.

1. It is unlikely that the entire constellation of galleries and chambers which made up any Jewish catacomb were ever excavated in their entirety. Lost peripheral material may have had a special importance, as we shall see.

---

[5] 1912: preface.
[6] Fig. 7.

2. We are in a position to ascribe inscriptions to catacombs; but not
   to areas within them. The organization of burials is opaque to
   us. This deficiency could be amongst the original accounts, published and unpublished, but it remains to be seen how great the
   returns might be.[7]
3. Disentangling the relative phases of a catacomb's construction is
   an essential preliminary to evolving any kind of hypotheses about
   actual dating. The complexities of such a task have been demonstrated by U. Fasola in exemplary fashion but within a limited
   scope at the Villa Torlonia site.[8] He has shown very clearly that
   we need to think in terms of *sections* of catacomb complexes.
   Through a study of their meeting point and of the methods of
   the diggers, the upper and lower catacombs have been delineated
   as separate systems. A study of the construction suggests the likelihood that the two systems were being developed simultaneously
   during their peak period, which will have been in the third century. Part of the lower catacomb had been expanded several times
   before what is apparently the first visible gallery of the upper catacomb was begun. Two interactive operations within the upper
   catacomb itself are detectable, with a new section being started
   before the first section was deepened. A spur to this first section
   may, however, on the basis of small finds, have been a post-Dio-
   cletianic expansion. After all this, the sad fact emerges that one of
   the hardest sections to place, even in relative terms, is, as chance
   would have it, the epigraphically richest part of the lower catacomb. The general picture, then, is one of numerous interrelated
   phases, and this makes it extraordinarily difficult to date any particular item from a catacomb without very precise knowledge.
   It is highly dubious whether even this kind of analysis will be
   possible in relation to Monteverde, where we depend on reports
   alone, nor even at the Vigna Randanini, given the present state
   of the catacomb, where several bouts of 'tidying up' seem to have
   taken place.
4. Not having access to the story of any one catacomb's development, we are tempted to take the easy route and simply to treat

[7] David Noy's edition of the Roman inscriptions has undoubtedly made matters
clearer (1995). I am grateful to him for assistance which facilitated the writing of
this paper.
[8] Fasola 1976.

them as a unit when we discuss their inscriptions; then we generalize about the Jews of Rome. Yet, if anything is clear, it is the emptiness of such generalizations.

Diverse Jewish milieux

We should rather ask whether, on the available evidence, we can say anything meaningful about the differences between Jews buried in different locations. Scholars have found at least some reason to identify such distinctions, and have deemed them either date- or culture-related. But these are crude and impressionistic readings. However, the linked questions as to whether we may detect differing levels of assimilation or of acculturation in different parts of the Jewish community, and how these might relate to changes in Jewish society over time, are central to any grasp of the community. So the first step must be to re-examine the old distinctions.

First, there is the interpretation, current since Nikolaus Müller, and endorsed by Erwin Goodenough,[9] that the Jews buried at Monteverde were in some sense more 'conservative' in their Judaism. It has been observed that the Vigna Randanini texts have no Hebrew. The only exception is a decorative *shalom*, of little significance, on a sarcophagus from the vicinity, belonging to Faustina, and decorated with masks which have led some to decide she was an actress.[10] But what Hebrew was found at Monteverde? Leon can report three inscriptions (reckoned by him as of 1.4%!), a figure which he rightly describes as 'almost negligible';[11] all three carry a basic *shalom* formula, one merely scratched in the stucco. There is simply not enough for quantification to make any sense. In any case, where a significant showing of formulaic Hebrew in a funerary context does occur, as at Venosa,[12] it is to be connected with broad processes of linguistic change in the Diaspora, linked probably to rabbinization, and occurring at a late date; not to Palestinian roots or to special closeness to the religious mainstream.

---

[9] Goodenough 1953–68: 2.4 ff.
[10] Konikoff 1990: III–15, with discussion on p. 42.
[11] Leon 1960: 76–77.
[12] Leon 1954 is basic. For more recent developments, see especially Colafemmina 1981; Meyers 1983.

Image has been associated with language in this type of argument. When it comes to ornament, it has been noted that there are notably fewer representations of living beings (three according to Goodenough) in Monteverde than in Vigna Randanini.[13] The argument from representation is altogether insecure: the copious material has come to light in Palestininian synagogues, and even more in the Rabbinic cemetery at Beth-She'arim, makes it clear that during the Rabbinic period,[14] when the Roman catacombs were in use, a relaxed attitude to the second commandment prevailed even in the most halakhically stringent circles. The point needs no elaboration, and the conclusion must be that the numerical disparity here has no implications in terms of Jewish orthodoxy.

Goodenough, as often, has scrutinized the evidence more searchingly than anyone else and has asked important questions. He merits more attention than he currently receives. However, his notorious preoccupation with reconstructing a comprehensive non-orthodox Diaspora Judaism which expressed its ideas through mystical symbolism has led to distortions.[15] In any case, the problem of the distribution of figurativeThe problem awaits an explanation, and one in terms of chronology is not to be excluded, for we must suppose that, the prohibition on images, which was taken rather strictly in various Jewish circles during the Second Temple period, was relaxed by a gradual progression after A.D. 70.

Then there is the question of what has been called 'Romanization' of the Jews. Variations on this scale are seen to be reflected in the balance of Latin against Greek in the epitaphs, with Leon estimating that at Vigna Randanini over a third of the epitaphs are Latin, and at Monteverde about a fifth, while at Villa Torlonia there are only four Latin texts, and those on distinctive marble plaques. Such divergences seem immediately significant, but we need to remember the very partial sample on which the figures are based: we are most unlikely to be dealing with complete catacombs.[16]

---

[13] Goodenough 1953–68: 2.15 ff.

[14] Basic discussion in Gutmann 1971: xiii–xxxx; 3–16; also in id. 1970: 1–14; and id. 1961.

[15] See the editor's forward to Goodenough 1988: xi–xxxiv, where the critiques of Nock and Morton Smith are also discussed. For Beth She'arim, see especially Avigad 1976.

[16] Leon 1960: 77.

We have also to bear in mind, once again, that the surviving or known material from any particular catacomb probably represents burials over a considerable period, even if not over the whole time that the catacomb will have been in use. The evidence of brick stamps, which provide at least a *terminus post quem*, has been ably re-assessed by Rutgers, and this suggests a concentration of building in the Severan era, but some activity at both Monteverde and Villa Torlonia (as we have seen) stretching back to the second and on into the fourth century. The Vigna Randanini cemetery appears to have yielded only seven brick stamps, of which five are certainly Severan.[17] But the chronological distribution of surviving epitaphs will not necessarily be the same for different catacombs.

We cannot judge, then, whether we are dealing with different types of Jews or with changes over time. Greek was commonly used among the Roman plebs,[18] but Greek was also the language of the Bible and of prayer for diaspora Jews. There is no direct evidence for a Latin Hebrew Bible.[19] Whether, therefore, the use of Latin connotes a lower level of Jewish education, a greater distance from Judaism, or simply a modest social advance in Roman terms cannot easily be decided; nor may a higher frequency of Latin be automatically assumed to be a later development. These questions will have to be asked against the perspective of patterns of language usage among the Roman plebs generally, and it may well be that the Jewish pattern will be seen simply to follow those trends. If so, a longstanding Jewish conformity to the immediate pagan environment, would be suggested, with the Jews as a proper constituent element of the Roman plebs (which is still in many respects an unknown quantity to us).

Organization of burials

A major issue is the organization of the burials within a catacomb, which, were it ascertainable, could give us vital information about family and synagogue groupings. The archaeologists have tended to

---

[17] Rutgers 1990: 158–159.
[18] Kajanto 1963.
[19] Deissmann 1927: 447, argues that the hexametric Regina inscription from Monteverde (*CIJ* 1.476), with its echoes of the Vulgate, is an indication of the existence of a Latin Jewish Bible.

regard individual *cubicula*, wherever they be, as occupied by household or family units of one kind or another. But we have as yet, so
far as I can see, no evidence of contiguous burial by the members
of any one family at Rome, though this phenomenon can be seen
in the (largely later) Jewish catacombs of Venosa (Venusia) in ancient
Apulia.[20] Family *cubicula* are known in the Christian catacombs, of
Rome; indeed, the entire Via Latina structure, with its remarkable
paintings, has been ascribed to one family unit.[21] For the Jews, the
alternative arrangement of burial by synagogue is probably to be
excluded within catacombs; all we can say with confidence is that
several synagogues used the same catacomb complex. Still other
models are, of course, conceivable: the simplest of all would be that
for each deceased the next space along was allocated, or purchased
(which it was remains unknown) in a convenient catacomb currently
operative. At the Vigna Randanini, a fair number of marble or plaster tomb closures carrying epitaphs are today to be seen in the walls
of the catacomb, but it would appear that many have been moved
from their original locations, and we may not draw any conclusions
about arrangements in that catacomb without tracking down the history of the work within it.

Burial and social level

How to locate the Jews of Rome within the social spectrum is a
more teasing problem than has normally been acknowledged, and
one on which little light is shed by the vituperation of Roman writers.
The archaeological evidence is far more important. Leon maintained
without much hesitation that the catacombs reflected the low status
of those Jews, in the simplicity of their tombs, the general poor quality of the script in the usually rudimentary epitaphs, and the poverty
of a good proportion of the *loculi* closures, which are plaster more
often than marble. He admits a few prosperous individuals, but allows
them to disappear from view after surveying the relevant artefacts,
without allowing them to affect the overall picture.[22] Leaving aside
Jewish objections to elaborate burial places (articulated several times

---

[20] See Noy 1994.
[21] So Toynbee 1971: 242. On this catacomb, Ferrua 1991.
[22] Leon 1960: 203–224; Solin 1983: 713–20.

by both Philo and Josephus),[23] two types of visual evidence in particular raise, challenge the first impression derived from our written
epitaphs, and suggest that elite practices and values were not absent
from the Jewish community. This implication has not gone unnoticed, but it has been stated rather than explored.

First, marble sarcophagi were found in the vicinity of the catacombs, and also marble sarcophagus fragments within the galleries.
Others with Jewish characteristics were found in various locations
around the city. None of these have so far proved securely restor-
able to their exact original locations, though Konikoff's publication
gives some impression of the discoverers' reports and of the known
findspots.[24] The tendency to regard sarcophagi as intrusive pagan
material was sharply attacked by Goodenough and is now generally
receding. Twenty two such items are associated with the Jewish catacombs, only four carrying explicit Jewish imagery, in the shape of
a menorah. In the well-known fragment of a Jewish 'seasons' sarcophagus (provenance unknown), the menorah replaces the usual
portrait in the central roundel, and of this Jocelyn Toynbee nicely
said, 'there could scarcely be a more impressive piece of evidence
of a Jewish patron's deliberate choice of a pagan setting for his most
revered religious symbol'.[25] The norm is to draw on the common
stock of designs, including, of course, human representations such as
the figures of the seasons, and mythological motifs such as the Muse
Urania, or cupids picking grapes. The assumption is that all emanated
from the normal local workshops.[26] Sarcophagi were in use in the
West from the second century, and among the Christians from the
third.[27] It is worth noting that they were in established Jewish use
in Palestine at the necropolis of Beth She'arim during this same
period.

The tendency for such attractive items to be appropriated and re-
used, for example as troughs, together with the total absence of
Jewish imagery on many of them, means that further Jewish sarcophagi are likely to have travelled around the city and their fragments to be now unrecognisable. That fragments have lain unnoticed

[23] See Rajak 1996 = Ch. 19.
[24] See above, n. 10.
[25] Konikoff 1990: III–14; Toynbee 1971: 238.
[26] On workshops, see Rutgers 1992: 104–106.
[27] Toynbee 1971: 270–277.

even within the catacombs is suggested by Rutgers' recent claim to have found, at Vigna Randanini, fractions of the Muse Urania sarcophagus identified from an old photograph in the Bodleian Library.[28]

Nine sarcophagus inscriptions refer to synagogue posts.[29] Twelve sarcophagi, including the long lost coffin of the proselyte and synagogue mother of two congregations, Beturia Paulina alias Sara, and the lost sarcophagus of the Gerousiarch (?) Julianus,[30] bear or bore inscriptions whose formulae and titles are wholly in line with the epigraphy of the Jewish catacombs.[31] It is worth observing that in most cases the writing itself is of the same primitive level as the epitaphs from the simpler burials within the catacombs. Since sarcophagus burial is evidently not a cheap option, the interesting possibility is raised that the crudity of the texts may be a culturally rather than an economically determined phenomenon. Jewish clients and Jewish masons may by this have chosen to distance themselves from the epigraphic habit of the surrounding culture, with all its connotations of display.

As well as noting the vulnerability of sarcophagi, we must remember that the failure which we have discussed to excavate Jewish catacombs to the limits, and the liability of exposed parts to landslides, renders likely a disproportionate loss in the burials of important and prosperous individuals and families: these may well have located themselves on the periphery in areas which could be marked off, especially as the immigrant community became more rooted in Rome and its social structure therefore more differentiated. Toynbee endorses the suggestion that at Vigna Randanini, the three small rooms between the current entrance on the Via Appia Pignatelli and the catacomb proper were used for the burial of 'special persons'.[32] These happen to have survived because they are a means of access; other such in other places are likely to have perished.

The evidence of the sarcophagi should be given its full weight. It then becomes not unreasonable to posit for the Jewish community of Rome in the imperial period a ratio of rich to poor comparable with that in the steeply graduated social pyramid of Roman society

---

[28] Konikoff 1990: II–4.2; Rutgers 1988.
[29] Konikoff 1990 I–1,2,3,6; III–17,18,19,20,21.
[30] *CIJ* I.523 and 504.
[31] In addition to the above, Konikoff 1990: II–5 (a painter); III–15,16; III–12 speaks of Julia Irene Arista as 'iustam legem colens'.
[32] 1971: 238.

generally.[33] Major questions remain. Above all, we have to face the problem that, while synagogue titles are well-represented in the surviving sarcophagi, it is also the case that title-holders of what would seem to be every level figure amply amongst the ordinary epitaphs, including five *archisynagogoi* and some forty seven archons. Some of these, but by no means all, have superior *loculus* closures made of marble. Should we, then, conceive of a significant social distance between those interred in sarcophagi and the other community notables? And if the archisynagogate was in fact, as we have reason to believe,[34] a title of some eminence, we would have to conclude that social distinctions were not invariably made visible in tomb types? And yet it seems that sometimes they were displayed. Were we to be able to trace difference of practice through different periods we should undoubtedly have a clearer picture of the meaning of these social distinctions, but we should not assume that the solution to the conundrum lies entirely in change over time.

Tomb paintings are also widely regarded as an index of prosperity. We cannot tell what has been lost, but we can now feel comfortable about restoring to the Jewish ambit the four rooms in the western part of the Vigna Randanini catacomb which are quite nicely decorated with so-called 'pagan' symbolism: Victory garlanding a nude youth who carries a branch and, perhaps, a quiver, with peacocks and other birds (room 1); Fortuna with cornucopia, cupids, dolphins, hippocampus, flowers etc. (room 2) (The date palms in the four corners of room 4 may argue for Jewishness). Strenuous and long-standing claims from among the Christian archaeologists that these were chambers from an earlier hypogeum, incorporated in the Jewish catacomb by the *fossores* and passively accepted by the Jews, were already persuasively dismissed by Goodenough; further investigation of the construction of the galleries would be needed to lay the old theories finally to rest.

The paintings are, then, an indication of the resources and aspirations of the communities which were users of this burial place, if not of individual or of family means. The synagogues of the Siburesians and the Campesians are named in inscriptions from this catacomb;[35] and

---

[33] On this, see MacMullen 1974: 88–120.
[34] See Rajak & Noy 1993 = Ch. 20 in this volume.
[35] Synagogue affiliation in the different catacombs is helpfully set out in table E in Vismara 1986: 388.

even if these had once served poor inhabitants of the Suburra and Campus Martius districts, there is no reason to suppose that their circumstances were unchanging. It is to be noted that a fine sarcophagus from the garden of the Villa Torlonia, its ends decorated with griffins, has a crudely cut inscription, first read by Leon, which names 'Caelia Omnina, wife of Julianus, archon of the Siburasians'.[36]

The Villa Torlonia catacombs also held paintings, and to these Beyer and Lietzmann have given generous treatment.[37] Three *cubicula*, all with *arcosolia*, depicted with considerable panache and elegance pagan mythological and Jewish motifs, including a flaming menorah and dolphins twisted around a trident. Both groups of paintings are directly comparable in design and technique with the decorated rooms of a number of Christian catacombs: this is visible even to the casual observer, and the parallels have been well explored by Rutgers.[38]

More broadly, we need to give content to any proposed social stratification and to try to relate the Jewish hierarchy to the surrounding society. What sort of a figure could a prominent Roman Jew ever hope to cut in the city at large? Could he ever be more than a mere Trimalchio? How far above and beyond him were the members of the senatorial class? To pursue the Roman Jewish elite further, it becomes necessary to evolve a model for the social structure of the community as a whole. And there we become involved in central problems of Roman social history, the question of the 'middle class' (including its freedmen), and, as I have said, the composition of the Roman plebs.[39]

Religious exclusivity

A context-related problem with wide implications is that of religious exclusivity within Jewish burial areas. This has a bearing on our conception of the tripartite interaction between Jews, Christians and pagans: a much more open situation than used to be envisaged is now favoured in many quarters.[40] Evidently, the Roman catacombs were Jewish burial areas, and many Jews chose to be buried among

---

[36] Konikoff 1990: III–21.
[37] Beyer & Lietzmann 1930; for bibliography, see Leon 1960: 207 and n. 1.
[38] Rutgers 1990: 145–151; cf. Gutmann 1984.
[39] For an epigraphic approach, see Huttunen 1974.
[40] See Lieu, North & Rajak 1992: introduction.

their co-religionists. But have we any grounds for seeing the separation of Jews in death either as total, or as dogmatic? I have collected material on mixed burials from various Diaspora sites, and had come to conclusions very similar to those now admirably presented in Rutgers' recent study.[41] His work makes it unnecessary to traverse this ground in detail here. The difficulty, and above all at Rome, is that we come up against distortions in the record. It is not fanciful to ascribe these to deep-seated preconceptions about Judaism and Jews, as Rutgers perceives. To grasp what is involved, one cannot do better than refer to Bosio's assurance to his readers referred to by Leon,[42] that the sacred cemeteries of the Christians were never profaned or contaminated by bodies of Jews. To this we may add the highly emotive reaction to the Jewish catacombs expressed by an author (admittedly not necessarily a scholarly one) in the *Catholic World* of 1879 and cited by Rutgers:[43] 'there is a cold cheerless look about the place very different from that of any neighbouring Christian catacomb, so full of the warmth of faith and hope'. In other words, the Jewish catacombs are seen as a place entirely apart—whether from Christian or from pagan space.

The obvious consequence of such attitudes is that material which appears to be unJewish in the supposedly exclusive Jewish catacombs has been systematically relegated to appendices, such as those of dubiously Jewish inscriptions, carrying D(is) M(anibus) or the Greek equivalent, in Frey's *Corpus*. They are explained away, like rooms 3 and 4 of the Vigna Randanini catacomb. In fact, Frey regularly accounts for the presence in a Jewish catacomb of any text or fragment which to him has an 'allure paienne' with the claim of secondary use as the closure of a Jewish *loculus*. Some apparently eccentric texts may well have been simply disregarded when the first records were made in a catacomb and the material in it first organized. A handful of DM texts, for no very good reason, have found their way into the main body of Frey's collection.[44]

---

[41] Rutgers 1992; on mixed Christian-pagan burial in Christian catacombs, see Pergola 1986.
[42] Leon 1960: 47.
[43] 1992: 101.
[44] Appendix material: *CIJ* 1, ed. 2, 535–574. Accepted DM texts: *CIJ* 1.464; 524 (a 'metuens'); 531 (a vegetable-seller near the *proseuche*). DM texts were found in Christian catacombs, too: see e.g. Ferrua 1991: 44. Against acceptance: Solin 1983: 657.

To determine in advance what is Jewish and what is not (or even 'probably' not) is to operate with a preconception of Jewish identity, when our task is, precisely, to seek to define that identity. The relative infrequency of such material, as against material which can readily be taken as Jewish, does not mean that the marginal material is unimportant.

The interpretation of 'unJewish' material (a very different phenomenon from the plentiful inscriptions, amounting to some one hundred and twenty, which are not visibly Jewish and can only be defined as such by their context) is obviously a complicated matter. Are we dealing with the adoption of a Roman formula which, however much this may surprise us, was not unacceptable to Jews, even if it was not widely favoured? Or are we seeing traces of marginal, misguided or even 'bad' Jews? Or, again, still allowing all such texts a real attachment to the catacombs where they were found, should they perhaps be linked to pagans who were in some way associated with Jews, perhaps by family ties, or with sympathizers of one sort or another? That such material is indeed intrusive, having dropped into the catacombs or been somehow imported, is not, admittedly, an impossibility, yet it should not be allowed as an assumption.

The implications of re-instating such texts into the catacombs at all times, except where there is a specific reason not to do so, are important. We move again nearer to the view that Jewish epitaphs are part of a world in which there were various forms of close association between some Jews and some non-Jews. This, as Rutgers observes,[45] need not have lessened the Jews' sense of ethnic identity.

Conclusion

A discussion such as this requires no long conclusion, since its purpose is to ask questions, to reflect on how we might go about answering some of them, to indicate areas of obscurity in the evidence or of methodological difficulty in interpreting it, and to serve as a pointer for work that lies ahead. If, however, we are to sum up those areas where it appears that progress might be made, then the following should be singled out: the archaeology of the catacomb in the Vigna Randanini; the comparison of the language pattern in the Jewish

---

[45] 1992: 117.

epitaphs with that among the Roman plebs; the sharpening of our social analysis of the Roman Jews in the context of changing social patterns in the city; the comparison of Jewish with Christian patterns on all fronts; and the investigation of the various categories of 'dubiously Jewish' or supposedly non-Jewish material found in the catacombs.

The Jewish inscriptions of Rome, taken together with their context in the catacombs, do not belong exclusively to Jewish history, though to judge by a widespread neglect of Leon's excellent book on the part of Roman historians, one might think that this was the case. The inscriptions in context are a first rate, cohesive collection of data on an ethnic group who, from Julius Caesar to the conquest of Christianity, were a characteristic element in the life of the city; and archaeology can play a crucial part now in our reconstruction of that life.

BIBLIOGRAPHY

Avigad, N. 1976. *Beth She'arim. Report on the Excavations during 1953–68*, 3. Jerusalem.

Beyer H.W. & Lietzmann, H. 1930. *Die jüdische Katakombe der Villa Torlonia in Rom.* Berlin and Leipzig.

Colafemmina, C. 1981. 'Saggio di scavo in località 'Collina della Maddalena' a Venosa', *Vetera Christianorum* 18: 443–451.

Deissmann, A. 1927. *Light from the Ancient Near East*, 4th edn. London.

Fasola, U. 1976. 'Le due catacombe ebraiche di Villa Torlonia', *Rivista di Archeologia Cristiana* 52: 7–62.

Ferrua, A. 1991. *The Unknown Catacomb: A Unique Discovery of Christian Art.* New Lanark.

Goodenough, E.R. 1953–68. *Jewish Symbols in the Greco-Roman Period.* New York.

——— 1988. *Jewish Symbols in the Greco-Roman Periodi.* Abridged Edition, ed. J. Neusner. Princeton.

Gutmann, J. 1961. 'The "Second Commandment" and the Image in Judaism', *HUCA* 32: 161–174.

——— 1970. *Beauty in Holiness: Studies in Jewish Custom and Ceremonial Art* (New York.

——— 1971. 'The "Second Commandment" and the Image in Judaism', J. Gutmann (ed.), *No Graven Images: Studies in Art and the Hebrew Bible.* New York, xiii–xxxx; 3–16.

——— 1984. 'Early Synagogue and Jewish Catacomb Art in its Relation to Christian Art', *Aufstieg und Niedergang der römischen Welt* 2.21.2 (ed. H. Temporini and W. Haase). Berlin, 1313–1342.

Huttunen, P. 1974. *The Social Strata in the Imperial City of Rome: a Quantitative Study of the Social Representation in the Epitaphs Published in the 'Corpus Inscriptionum Latinarum' volume 6.* Oulu.

Kajanto, I. 1963. *A Study of the Greek Epitaphs of Rome.* Acta Instituti Romani Finlandiae 2.3. Helsinki.

Konikoff, A. 1990. *Sarcophagi from the Jewish Catacombs of Ancient Rome: a Catalogue Raisonné.* Stuttgart.

Leon, H.J. 1954. 'The Jews of Venusia', *JQR* n.s. 44: 267–284.

—— 1960. *The Jews of Ancient Rome*. Philadelphia.
Lieu, J., North, J. & Rajak, T. (eds). 1992. *The Jews among Pagans and Christians in the Roman Empire*. London/New York.
MacMullen, R. 1974. *Roman Social Relations*. New Haven/London.
Meyers, E.M. 1983. 'Report on the Excavations at the Venosa Catacombs 1981', *Vetera Christianorum* 20: 445–459.
Müller, N. 1912. *Die jüdische Katakombe am Monteverde zu Rom*. Leipzig.
Müller, N. & Bees, N.A. 1919. *Die Inschriften der jüdischen Katakombe am Monteverde zu Rom*. Leipzig.
Noy, D. 1994. 'The Jewish communities of Leontopolis and Venosa', in J.W. van Henten & P.W. van der Horst (eds), *Studies in Early Jewish Epigraphy*. Leiden, 162–182.
—— 1995. *Jewish Inscriptions of Western Europe, vol. 2: The City of Rome*. Cambridge.
Pergola, P. 1986. 'Le catacombe romane, miti e realtà (a proposito del cimitero del Domitilla', *Società romana e impero tardoantico* 2 (ed. A. Giardina). Rome/Bari, 332–350.
Rajak, T. & Noy, D. 1993. '*Archisynagogoi*: Office, Title, and Social Status in the Greco-Jewish Synagogue', *JRS* 83: 75–93 = C.5 in this volume.
Rajak, T. 1996. 'Benefactors in the Greco-Jewish Diaspora', in H. Cancik, H. Lichtenberger, Hermann & P. Schäfer (eds), *Geschichte—Tradition—Reflexion. Festschrift für Martin Hengel zum 70. Geburtstag*. Band I: Judentum. Tübingen: 305–319 = C.4 in this volume.
Rutgers, L.V. 1988. 'Ein in situ erhaltenes Sarkophagfragment in der jüdischen Katakombe an der Via Appia', *Jewish Art* 14: 16–27.
—— 1990. 'Überlegungen zu den jüdischen Katakomben Roms', *JAC* 33: 140–157.
—— 1992. 'Archaeological Evidence for the Interaction of Jews and non-Jews in Late Antiquity', *AJA* 96; repr. in Rutgers, L.V. 1998. *The Hidden Heritage of Diaspora Judaism*, 2nd edn. Leuven.
Solin, H. 1983. 'Juden und Syrer im westlichen Teil der römischen Welt. Ein ethnisch-demographische Studie mit besonderer Berücksichtigung der sprachliche Zustände', *Aufstieg und Niedergang der römischen Welt* 2.29.2: 713–720.
Toynbee, J.M.C. 1971. *Death and Burial in the Roman World*. London.
van der Horst, P.W. 1991. *Ancient Jewish Epitaphs*. Kampen.
Vismara, C. 1986. 'I cimiteri ebraici di Roma', in A. Giardina (ed.), *Società romana e impero tardoantico*. Rome/Bari.

CHAPTER TWENTY-TWO

JEWS, PAGANS AND CHRISTIANS IN LATE ANTIQUE SARDIS: MODELS OF INTERACTION

In thinking about religious groups in the Roman world, historians often cast the Jews as a people set religiously and socially apart, largely, one suspects, under the influence of ancient literary caricatures and what we know—or think we know—of later European history. Yet it is apparent that in Asia Minor, right through the Roman period, Jews were numbered among the most prominent residents and they were also well-integrated into the city or village environments where they lived. The picture has now sharpened up considerably, both because we have fresh material, notably the now famous long inscription from Carian Aphrodisias, put up by a club of local Jewish and God-fearing tradesmen, and because there has been a crop of important new studies.

We must suppose that the Jews did not fundamentally compromise their monotheistic faith, or lose sight of the rhythms of their own way of life, with its own pattern of festivals and its own shape to the week, or cease adhering to their own permitted diet. We are not taking about syncretism, the fusion of different cults into one; nor about complete assimilation, the merging of one group with another.

So how did they express what was distinctly Jewish about them? And what social arrangements encouraged their retention of their distinctive group values? There is a great deal we do not know and cannot know, on the basis of evidence which consists mainly of ruins and short, fragmentary inscriptions.

Still, we are perhaps in a position to ask what is in effect a sociological question about the nature of their interaction with other groups? How did these Jews establish boundaries and define their difference, as every ethnic or religious group needs to do to maintain itself, whatever the strength of its bonds with other?

One of the most rewarding environments in which to look for answers is in the great and very ancient city of Sardis, erstwhile capital of the Lydian empire, lying some 60 miles inland from the coast

of Asia Minor at Smyrna. Its Jewish community had had a continuous presence in its place of residence over many generations, in
fact from the days of the first exile.[1] The community had almost
certainly been enlarged in the Hellenistic period by Antiochus III's
establishment of 2,000 Jewish military settlers in Phrygia and Lydia.[2]
By the decree of a Roman governor, the Jews of Sardis had been
granted the privilege of managing their own affairs, allowed to settle
their own disputes and to meet in a 'place' of their own.[3] These
rights had been confirmed by decrees of the city, with the emphasis
on the city's donation to them, in response to their request for somewhere to congregate and to pray. Mention is made of legal autonomy in the matter of their own disputes and city officials are made
responsible for importing appropriate food.[4] Privileges stretching back
many years are alluded to in the preamble to this civic document,
and it may be significant that the Jews are referred to in this decree
as 'Sardians'.[5] By a decree of Augustus, the right of Sardian Jews to
collect temple tax was upheld.[6]

The community thus maintained its separate identity over many
years, and, however much assimilated, it was not submerged. Nor
is there much temptation to apply to them the over-used concept of
religious syncretism:[7] in this case there appears to be no merger of
different cults. But terms such as 'acculturation', 'integration' and
'accommodation' have all seemed appropriate to the relationship
between Sardian Jewry and the host society.

Literary evidence, as usual for the diaspora Judaism of this period,
fails us—or virtually so. The only relevant text is considerably earlier than the synagogue. This is a poem by the prolific mid-second-

---

[1] Obadiah 20.

[2] Josephus, *AJ* XII 147–153 cites Antiochus' letter.

[3] See *AJ* XIV 235 for the decree of L. Antonius of 49 B.C. Commentary in Pucci
Ben Zeev 1998: No. 14.

[4] AJ XIV 259–261. The civic decree curiously mentions sacrifice along with
prayer. See Pucci Ben Zeev 1998: No. 20.

[5] *Politai* technically means Sardian citizens, a description hardly applicable to the
status of the city's entire Jewish population. We have either to interpret the designation non-technically, or to suppose that it refers to incorporation of the Jewish
entity as a whole within the city. That the document has been 'improved' in Jewish
hands is also not impossible. See further the discussion by Pucci Ben Zeev 1998:
219–220.

[6] *AJ* XVI 171. On the decrees in general, see Ch. 16 in this volume.

[7] For a full discussion of the problems surrounding the concept of syncretism,
see Levinskaya 1996: 197–205.

century anti-Jewish bishop Melito, his only work to have come down to us in nearly complete form. As might be expected, moreover, Melito's paschal homily deals with theological and spiritual matters: the contemporary information to be gleaned from the poem is essentially no more than that the synagogue still held a powerful attraction for the Christians of his day, causing considerable anxiety to the local leaders of the church.[8] The temptation to pull together such evidence as we have by pushing the archaeological data back in time to the age of Melito has proved hard to resist. Our problem is rather to read that rich body of evidence on its own terms.

The great late antique synagogue of Sardis is now substantially reconstructed and it is one of the most prominent features of the city's ruined urban landscape. This synagogue has come to symbolize the integration of a major, Jewish community of considerable antiquity into its polis environment.[9] A community of standing is conjured up, allocated as its synagogue a former civic basilica, in the heart of the city, hard up against a huge civic bath-gymnasium complex. The hall was 59 metres in length and held up to 1,000 people. Proceedings were conducted amidst painted marble and rich mosaic, under the illumination, probably, of a host of decorative candelabra. It was a community which served the city, producing, in the surviving epigraphic record alone, nine Sardian councillors among some 30 donors, and many Sardian citizens.[10]

Among the synagogue's more remarkable artefacts was an elaborate, free-standing marble menorah on which was carved at the top left-hand corner the one evocative name Socrates, generally taken to be the name of a Jewish artesan who was its maker.[11] And among the later appurtenances of the hall was an impressive and unusual marble table resting on a base of thunderbolt-bearing eagles and flanked by a pair of (perhaps Sardian) lions.[12] God-fearers, probably to be understood as Gentiles associated with Jewish life, that is to say affiliates of some sort, emerge as an active part of the community, with six

---

[8] Kraabel in Overman & MacLennan (eds): 197–208.
[9] For descriptions of the synagogue, see Seager 1974; 1981 and Trebilco 1991: 37–54. For interpretation, see especially Kraabel 1983.
[10] For the figures, see Hanfmann 1972.
[11] Kroll number. But for the possibility that Socrates was a donor, see now Williams 1998: 25, I.93. Nor is it safe to assume that he was a Jew.
[12] The sculptures are thought to be re-used in the synagogue, the eagles possibly coming from a Roman monumant: Seager 1974: 8 and n. 9.

of them recorded as benefactors on the same terms as others.[13] We find them in a comparable role in a similar Asia Minor milieu, at Aphrodisias.[14] Sardis epitomizes that world and the high visibility of its Jewry.[15] The synagogue has become a byword.

Apart from the building itself, there is one unusual resource: the Harvard-Cornell excavations of 1958–75 produced a unique corpus of 79 texts naming over 30 donors of sections of the marble wall-revetments, of other sections of wall-decoration, of the mosaic floor of the main hall and porch (eleven separate texts), of an ornamental balustrade from the forecourt and of some individual items connected with the cult. All the texts are very brief; those from the marble revetments, which are the majority, had to be laboriously pieced together from minute fragments, a task rendered possible by the formulaic character of many of the dedications. Still, a good number remain incomplete, and some lack the donors' names. Only a few have been published. They are now, however, in the public domain on an informal basis and I can refer them here thanks to the kindness of their restorer and editor John H. Kroll.[16]

One donor stands out as responsible for a major donation. The rest have made contributions of varying modesty. In Jewish epigraphy, the phenomenon of the composite donation, involving relatively small donors, either in a list or, more often, inserting their names in a mosaic floor or decorated wall or on columns, is readily parallelled, notably, from Berenice in Cyrenaica (a single list), from the mosaics at Apamea in Syria (with lengths of flooring specified), and from Hammath Tiberias and other sites in Palestine. This is by no means a specifically Jewish phenomenon, and there are also pagan parallels (for example the columns in the great piazza at Gerasa in Syria) and an abundance of Christian ones. But Jewish communities seem to me to show a partiality for such equalizing modes of recording benefactions which fit in with other quiet but detectable strategies to cut benefactors down to size.[17]

---

[13] Moreover, we can observe that identification as a God-fearer is not always recorded: one such, Aurelius Hermogenes, has a second dedication which omits the label (Kroll 37 and 66).

[14] Reynolds and Tannenbaum 1987; note that theosebeis are not confined to the list on face b: two are to be found among the Jews on face a.

[15] Though see now Barclay 1996, especially 82–98, for some well-drawn distinctions between the latter two concepts as applied to the Jewish diaspora.

[16] Kroll's numbering is used throughout for unpublished material.

[17] This phenomenon is explored in Rajak 1996. Cf. also the comments of Bonz 1993: 150–152.

We feel we know the Jews of Sardis. An image was crystallized early, in the first excavation reports and developed in the discussions that followed, notably those of Kraabel.[18] The overall interpretation locates the whole development firmly in its late-antique setting and the interpretation presupposes that late philosophical paganism rather than Christianity dictated the cultural tone of the city through the fourth century. Such a state of affairs supposedly allowed a particularly fruitful bonding to evolve between Jews and spiritually-minded pagans. An important contention of Kraabel's is that influence tends to be two-way: we should envisage not only Greek influence on Jewish practice but also Jewish influence on the pagan culture of Sardian society.[19]

Another cornerstone of that picture is the open-door character of the synagogue. A delightful image is conjured up: this way for a work-out, this way for a quick prayer, no track suits please. Here too the site falls short when we re-examine it. The synagogue as reconstructed gives onto the public street on the east side of the complex, not far from the entrance of the bath-gymnasium. Not only the courtyard but also the synagogue behind it were, we are informed, open in aspect and welcoming to passers-by. Much is made of the courtyard fountain in the shape of a huge crater, which is understood as a watering place open to the public. But the support for all this is tenuous: essentially, the appearance of the synagogue fountain in a list of such provisions in the city's cult places and civic spaces transcribed from a broken and now long-lost stone.[20] We may observe that, if this list is, as its editors maintained, an inventory designed to facilitate water-management and possibly its rationing in the city, then no conclusion can be drawn about the public status of the synagogue fountain beyond the fact of its being known by the authorities and taken into account in their reckonings. Other fountains in the list belong to private groupings. How they were used we cannot say.

More generally, the challenge of presenting a remarkable building to the public may be suspected as having dominated the later stages of excavation and coloured the results. The story of the Sardis synagogue has always been the story of its donors. In the United

---

[18] See Kraabel 1983 and the other papers by Kraabel in Overman & MacLennan (eds). 1992.
[19] See especially Kraabel 1978.
[20] Buckler & Robinson 1932: no. 17. *CIJ* 2.751. The text seems undateable.

States, funds were raised from the public not very long after the discovery of the building. Naturally, thenceforward, preservation and reconstruction went hand in hand. In the process, hypotheses about the synagogue's shape were rather soon set in stone.

This physical reconstruction is crucial to the judgment that the Jews of Sardis were a particularly assertive and self-confident community, so positioned in society as to exert a real influence on their neighbours.[21] In reality, rather less than this emerges from the site. What we can say with some confidence about the Jews who frequented it is that they were both tolerated and tolerant. They were tolerated at least inasmuch as their presence was accepted in an important civic space. They were tolerant in that they apparently did not regard the presence in the immediate vicinity of quintessentially Greek (and pagan) activity as compromising their purity or the synagogue's sanctity. These were very far from the isolated misanthropes of that time-honoured caricature, the demolition of which was understandably one of Kraabel's primary motivations. This community does not seem insecure; its members were at least highly energetic. Moreover, they expressed themselves in the language of the wider community and deployed the stylistic norms prevalent in the local culture.

Furthermore, if we look at the synagogue as a whole, what stands out is indeed the high degree of its acculturation to the environment of its users. Thus, apart from the frequent menorah representations (a dozen or so images or fragments were found), the synagogue's remains offered rather few of the indicators of Jewish identity familiar to us from elsewhere. It is no surprise that there were no more than a few inscribed fragments of Hebrew found.[22]

And it is noteworthy that there were only two biblical names, Samuel and Samoe among the donors, and the donation of a νομοφυλάκιον ('place which guards the Law') is attested, referring, clearly, to the ark (*aron*) in which the scrolls were housed. Identification of the function of the two pavillion-like shrines which stood at the east end of the hall as the synagogue's twin Torah arks was encouraged

---

[21] Clear evidence of the influence of Jews on others is scarce, but see the Acmonia curse texts. See also Williams 1998: 111-2, on the coin type from Acmonia in Phrygia which depicts Noah's ark.

[22] Seager 1974: 10.

by the discovery near one of them of a plaque which, along with a menorah, carries the standard iconography of lulav, shofar and what seem to be scrolls.[23] It was this plaque, in fact, which had in the first place suggested to its discoverers that the building was a synagogue. The floor mosaics and marble decorations represent vines, peacocks, and various floral and geometric designs, including pomegranates and fish.

Such is the degree of acculturation, indeed, that one careful observer has been moved to doubt altogether the Jewishness of the synagogue's congregation, at any rate until into the fifth century A.D. (Goodman 1994). This challenge responds to various unique architectural and other features in the synagogue, notably the presence of the two Torah shrines in place of the usual one, and the 'unJewish' eagle-table, which is unparallelled as a piece of synagogue furniture and unexpected in its decoration. So strange an edifice, it is argued, looks more like the meeting-place or cult-place of syncretizing monotheists, a species of 'God-fearers' or sympathizers with Judaism. The confiscation of the meeting-places of a group described as '*caelicolae*', 'heaven-worshippers', is required in legislation of A.D. 407 recorded in Justinian's codex and in a law of 409 found in the Theodosian Code:[24] they are possible candidates.

This, however, is an interpretation which creates more problems than it solves. Nevertheless, such a radical response to the ambiguities in the material serves very well the intended purpose of bringing home the limitations of our knowledge. It is healthy to be reminded of the strong element of conjecture in the archaeology-based picture which we have come to accept. This picture, with its admixture of reasonable speculation, has proved a compelling one. But now, nearly thirty years after the discovery, a little scepticism will be helpful in considering this glowing portrayal of co-existence. The Jews' involvement with the city's Gentile population may well have had its limits; there is good reason to put a certain distance between the two groups. It may not be helpful and not entirely irrelevant to bear in mind a modern comparison: we may reflect how,

---

[23] Shiloh 1968; Seager 1974: 9. Cf. also fragments of a lintel representing the ritual objects, Kroll (unpublished) no. 72 and of an inscribed medallion with the same, Kroll (unpublished) no. 76.

[24] Goodman 1994: 216.

in the very different circumstances of the late nineteenth and twentieth centuries, the members of a Jewry as numerous and as highly
assimilated as that of pre-war Germany still had a ceiling set on
their social advancement, by way both of formal restrictions and
political prejudice. I have recently been lecturing in Berlin and living
beside the golden dome of the restored Neue Synagoge in Oranien-
burger Strasse, constructed in 1864. I was struck by the numerous
parallels. This edifice too is repeatedly taken as a demonstration of
the Berlin community's pride and acceptability. It seems to vie for
attention on the city's skyline with the vast and imposing Wilhelmine
hulk of the Berliner Dom, though it is actually very much smaller.
Inside the services were heavily influenced by Protestant practice.
The organ caused a major controversy when introduced, but became
indispensible to the delivery of a modernized, concert-style liturgy in
the idiom of Schubert. A picture of successful assimilation, one might
think. Yet the records reveal that the members struggled long and
hard to find a reasonably central site that they could use, and several were vetoed by the municipal authorities. The permitted street
frontage is too small in relation to the proportions of the hall inside,
which had to some 3,000 on the High Holydays, demanding special ingenuity from the (non-Jewish) architects. Not all was rosy in
the relationship between Jews and their city.

Similarly, the contiguity of the Sardis synagogue with the bath-
gymnasium complex is there for all to see. But how much should
be deduced from the spatial impression? Recently, the standard interpretation of the site has been subjected to some hard questioning.
One interesting suggestion, made in the light of archaeological indications that the Jews' place of worship had in the early third century been a Sardian civic structure, is that the transfer of the basilica
to the Jewish community occurred when and because the city came
under serious pressure, as a result of the economic crisis which hit
the Roman empire at the end of the third century (Bonz 1990;
1993). This transaction already would put a somewhat different complexion on the juxtaposition of the two institutions. Compulsion,
rather than a warm welcome, could lie behind the handover. We
need to note, too, that by this time, the civic decurionate was becoming set in the slow decline which was to render it wholly insignificant
by the time of Justinian. Service as a *bouleutes*, town-councillor, naturally lost its attractions as government posts became not only
financially more burdensome but also, as a consequence, more freely
available. We should not be over-impressed by the Sardian Jewish

town councillors, for they may in fact have had quite a mediocre ranking in the social hierarchy.[25]

Another recent reading, based on reassessment of the chronology of the site, has suggested that the closeness of Jewish to pagan activity on the site may not be all it seems. A simple question needed asking. Must the two institutions be fully contemporaneous?[26] The corpus of inscriptions was ascribed by the excavators of the synagogue to the third and fourth centuries A.D. and the dedications were understood as emanating from at least three generations of Sardian donors. Renovation of the building still seems to have occurred as late as A.D. 500. While it is clear that the decorative programme was completed in stages, with a corresponding series of changes and developments in epigraphic technique, the dating of the beginning of the process is more difficult. The origins of the synagogue as a synagogue were first ascribed to the Severan period. In fact, however, the third-century dating for the earliest of the inscriptions relies on the slender foundations of the find of a single coin under the mosaic of one bay, together with the presence of Aurelian names among the dedicators. It is now accepted that such names continued in use well beyond the time of their acquisition through Caracalla's edict. J.H. Kroll's unpublished comments on the numismatic evidence now also support a lower chronology, with a mid-fourth-century start. Nothing compels us to think that the building functioned as a synagogue until the last of the four stages assigned to its development. This, we may note, would put the foundation well into the Christian empire. There is ample evidence for the continuation of synagogue construction during this period regardless of legal prohibitions.[27]

The consequence of such redating is to distance the synagogue to some extent from the peak period of the next-door bath-gymnasium's functioning. For while the baths seem to have operated until the widespread devastation which took place in the city in 616, the gymnasium, like others, will have acquired a new role at a considerably earlier date, perhaps becoming a simple bath house. The large internal space which served as the *palaestra*, seems to have been refurbished and put to some other civic purpose.[28] Thus it is a fair surmise that

---

[25] On the decline in the decurionate, see Jones 1966: 192–210.
[26] Questioned by Boterman 1990.
[27] Boterman 1990: 119.
[28] Foss 1976: 40–41; Hanfmann & Buchwald in Hanfmann 1983: 195; Yegül 1986: 16.

the bath-gymnasium complex was no longer central to city life at the moment when the synagogue got going.

At the same, the standard picture has major omissions. Enquiry into the links between the Jews and the third element in the city, the Christian element, has so far been allowed to remain in the background. It is true that paganism was long-lasting in Sardis and that, although the city housed one of the Seven Churches in the book of Revelation, we can discern the manner of the spread of Christianity there only hazily. The Christian quarter, when it came to be built under Constantine and his sons, was located outside the city gates. None the less the Byzantine shops on the east side of the synagogue have yielded artefacts bearing Christian symbols as well as Jewish and pagan ones.[29] Good relations between Jews and Christians at a late period, continuing to the 616 destruction, have been inferred from these minor finds.[30] The general resemblance of the synagogue plan to that of contemporary Christian basilicas has also been pointed out and taken as 'an illustration of the adaptation of the Sardian Jews to their Greek environment.'[31] An early church apparently stood some half a mile from the synagogue, in which re-used masonry was found matching that of the synagogue.[32]

Further glimpses of lost relationships may, I believe, be found in the epigraphic evidence, which I can mention only briefly today, though I may perhaps be allowed to refer you to my published discussion of it. Although these are in many ways standard donor inscriptions, we can, if we look closely, find in them support for a revised historical reconstruction along the lines which I have been suggesting. The authors of these small texts, in a context whose Jewishness was unemphatic, to say the least, did choose to differentiate themselves by means of certain formulae from the pagan world. And at the same time those formulae point to common ground between Jewish and Christian religious values.

A notable feature of twelve of the texts in the unpublished corpus is a formula which states that a financial contribution to a part of the building made by a named individual, in some cases together with his family, emanates from the gifts of God or of Providence.

[29] Hanfmann & Buchwald in Hanfmann 1983: 192–194.
[30] Foss 1976: 43; Crawford 1996.
[31] Foss 1976: 42.
[32] Seager 1974: 12.

Two such donors are described as councillors and two as God-fearers. This formula gives a twist to the texts which is alien to their pagan counterparts from similar contexts. The best expression of the theme is one which stands out from the others. (Kroll no. 29) Here a certain unnamed donor, claims credit, along with his wife, named Regina, and their children, for the marble-facing (σκύτλωσις) of some area of wall and for the painting (probably on the wall above the facing). But he adds the phrase 'from the gifts of almighty God', here called θεὸς παντοκράτωρ. Exactly how the manifestation of divine favour is to be understood is not self-evident. It is most likely, I think, that the formula is general and conventional in this context and so does not require a specific application in each case: the capacity to be a donor, like all else, is a God-given capacity. In the Jewish context, the conception (assuming that I have correctly interpreted it) is in keeping with that recurring spirit in Jewish benefactions, the tendency to indicate, by one means or another, a degree of reserve about munificence and to undercut the claims of donors (Rajak 1996 = Ch. 19). This is a spirit for which general biblical models can be found in the many passages which stress that God is the ultimate source of wealth as of all other goods.

What stands out is the reversal of the expected. The usual run of Greek donors, in any of the cities of the Roman empire, declare themselves proudly as donating from their own private resources, ἐκ τῶν ἰδίων, or the like, and expect to be thanked for it. These even include some Jewish donors.[33] The gifts of emperors or generals can also be referred to by an 'out of the gifts of' (ἐκ δωρεάς) formulae. It can only be a wholly deliberate departure when the Jews of Sardis declare that the Almighty is the correct recipient of acknowledgement.

Now, as Robert did not fail to notice in his original publication, there are numerous Christian versions of the same idea, especially in the Byzantine period. Thus, for example, a text from Tralles in Lydia records the foundation of a cemetery by Gennadios son of Elias 'from what God gave him', ἐξ ὧν αὐτῷ ὁ θεὸς ἔδωκε (Robert 1964). Further development of the motif seems, moreover, to have occurred in Christian quarters. So, it was sometimes expressed in a

---

[33] Notably Polycharmos of Stobi, who uses the phrase ἐκ τῶν οἰκείων χρήματων (CIJ 694; Lifshitz 10). Cf. also CIJ 2. 244, from Teos, the three donors in the Julia Severa inscription (see n. 12) and the Ostia dedication.

neat form which has liturgical echoes τὰ σὰ ἐκ τῶν σῶν προφέρομεν[34] 'we offer yours from yours'. There the further notion is spelled out of giving back to God some of what was originally his: in other words, the transaction is presented as the direct return of assets to their owner.

Given the sentiment, it is not surprising that this type of expression belongs largely in the Jewish and Christian spheres. We need not necessarily think of usage by Christians as an act of appropriation from the Jewish milieu: traffic in the other direction is equally possible and what is really at issue is a process of cross-fertilization, now quite unrecoverable. This openness will, however, have had its limits and it looks as though the usage of the common formulae evolve somewhat differently in the different milieux. The τὰ σὰ ἐκ τῶν σῶν formula is not found in any clearly Jewish contexts. It is tempting to deem this version characteristically Christian. However that may be the 'gifts of God' formula brings together Jews and Christians. Its use in the Sardis synagogue thus gives us a glimpse of interconnection in the city between these two elements, and at the same time, one might suggest, of distancing.

This depressingly limited parallel has its importance, once again, shifting the focus of discussion. On first inspection, our inscriptions belong nicely into the world of the late Greek city, as will have become clear. The studies done hitherto, by Tom Kraabel, Trebilco and myself, have explored in some depth the Greek character of the dedication. Kraabel, in particular, offers a broad-ranging discussion of those eleven Sardian πρόνοια texts where the term 'providence' substitutes for the divine name, and places them in the context of the culture of this great cosmopolitan city. He associates this version of the formula with the understanding of Providence which plays a prominent role in neo-Platonic speculation: πρόνοια was 'in the air' as he puts it.[35] The role of Sardis as a significant educational centre for the mix of rhetoric, philosophy and mysticism which was characteristic of the period is adduced. Prominent cultural figures lived and worked there, and the city housed an offshoot of the Pergamene

---

[34] Discussed by Robert 1954: 228, p. 167; 1964: 45. Cf. *SEG* 19 (old series; 1963), 719, a Christian monument from Lydia, probably fourth century, and Robert, *BE* 73 (1960), 196 and n. 364; *IGLS*: Jordan 2.81.

[35] Cf. for some of the many late Greek philosophical and cultural ramifications of the concept, Sharples 1995.

school. Notable were the charismatic ascetic Flavius Chrysanthius (*floruit* 350–375) with whom the emperor Julian studied in A.D. 351, and the influential home-grown rhetor Eunapius (c. 310–390) who wrote biographies of sophists.[36] Before that, the distinguished Neoplatonist Proclus had cultivated Sardian friendships.[37] Kraabel seeks to identify a single source of influence and so he argues for the exclusivity of the pagan philosophical dimension.

However, this leaves room for considerable doubt, in view of the good Jewish-Greek literary pedigree of πρόνοια as a way of describing divine benevolence.[38] For, although the concept is virtually absent from the translated books of the Greek bible and from the books of the New Testament (except as ascribed to Gallio the proconsul), it occupies a prominent position within other branches of the tradition. Kraabel himself provides ample documentation and even some enumeration, but he is then at pains to marginalize the material on the very grounds of its scope and diversity. In Josephus, the term is a common circumlocution for the name of God as beneficent planner and overseer, what we might call 'the management'. The form used is generally ἡ τοῦ θεοῦ πρόνοια, or ἡ θεία πρόνοια. Occasionally, the adjective δαιμόνιος instead refers to the divine component. Thus, faced with conspiracy and revolt, Moses calls on God to demonstrate that all happens by his Providence—ὅτι πάντα σῇ προνοίᾳ διοικεῖται (*AJ* IV 47). The plot against Joseph by his brothers profaned, in Reuben's view, God's ubiquitous Providence—μιανάντας αὐτοῦ τὴν πανταχοῦ παροῦσαν πρόνοιαν (*AJ* II 24). That Josephus is also able to use πρόνοια in its regular Greek application to human action can scarcely be relevant to any consideration of the theological usage.[39] Instances prior to Philo and Josephus have been assembled, which show how well-rooted the concept is in Jewish-Greek thought.[40] These are to be found in Hellenistic literature, both in the biblical book of Daniel, in the *Letter of Aristeas* (201), where a Greek philosopher, Menedemus of Eritrea, hails the Jewish conception of Providence, and in 2 Maccabees. From the Roman period, the closest and perhaps the most relevant parallels are provided by the appearances of πρόνοιαν in 4 Maccabees, a first or second century A.D. text which

[36] See Foss 1976: 22–27.
[37] See Marinus, Vita Procli 15. Cf. Hanfmann 1983: 209 and 291, n. 43.
[38] Discussed more fully in Rajak 1998.
[39] The opposite view is taken by Kraabel 1996: 86.
[40] Trebilco 1991: 41–43 and nn. *ad loc.*

combines a gruesome martyrological narrative and a series of rhetorical displays with philosophical homily, and which probably originates from Antioch in Syria. Their presence there is particularly significant for Sardis because the milieux are comparable.[41] One of the martyred sons, as he dies at the torturer's hands, prays that 'the just Providence of our ancestors (πάτριος) will punish the 'tyrant' (9:24). In this formulation, Providence stands alone and unqualified, as in the Sardis inscriptions. In the other instances in this text (13:19; 17:22), θεία πρόνοια instructs the new-born, in the one case, and redeems Israel, in the other. Jewish literature has therefore brought us within range of the inscriptions, but not right up to them.

To this background, we may add the consideration that the context of benefaction may be seen as encouraging the use of the particular term πρόνοια, since, the word itself is familiar in donor epigraphy as a designation for the care and concern of benefactors, be it emperors or generals or other leading individuals.[42] Is it entirely fanciful to read the synagogue formulae as consciously re-allocating the beneficence, giving current Greek terminology, which they must have known well, a deliberate and value-laden twist?

Here, then, is an alternative set of contexts which greatly weakens, if it does not negate, the philosophical ramifications of πρόνοια highlighted by Kraabel. We remain at best able to adopt a compromise position along the lines suggested by Trebilco who takes πρόνοια in the Sardis dedications as a typical example of Diaspora language, a Janus-faced usage with a convenient double identity. If it is right that πρόνοια was both a powerful late Greek and an established Jewish conception, it could be expected precisely because of this duality to fit the bill for Sardis Jewry.[43] Yet even this compromise leaves us with a problem, that of explaining the appearance of the formula in a recently discovered mosaic text from a synagogue in far away Philippopolis, today Plovdiv in Bulgaria, a new find men-

---

[41] For the strong possibility of a second-century date, and on the Antiochene provenance of 4 Maccabees, see the full discussion in van Henten 1998: 58–82.

[42] Favoured over a long period in the Hauran region and in Arabia (see e.g. from Bosra, *IGLS* 13. 9108; 9111 and p. 134; *SEG* 41.590; *IGLS*: Jordan 2.53). But instances from elsewh᷍ ᷍c are not lacking. Cf. also *CIJ* 2.682, in relation to a Jewish *thiasos* from Olbia.

[43] Trebilco 1991.

tioned by Kraabel in passing, but as apparently yet without appreciation of the challenge this poses to his contextualization of πρόνοια.[44] Yet Plovdiv must break the firm connection of the concept as it appears in the inscriptions with the special cultural world of Sardis. And the link with Christian formulations which I have here suggested serves, perhaps, further to detach the Jews from that pagan high ground on which Kraabel sought to secure them.

So what model do we put in place of the old one? We approach the synagogue now with greater chronological precision and also with more methodological caution when it comes to interpreting the spatial meaning of the excavated ruins and extrapolating from them. In reading the inscriptions, we are alert to marks of separation as well as to parallels. We are not cajoled by the literary evidence from late antique Sardis into looking in one direction only. Our premise is that relationships between religious groups carry an inbuilt ambivalence. In other words, bond and boundary are inseparable. The Sardis synagogue stands as a demonstration of just that. The close bonding of its Jews with their society, Christian as well as pagan, had its necessary limits. Close observation allows us still to detect expressions of separation. That these are found in matters of style as much as substance does not diminish their significance.

BIBLIOGRAPHY

Barclay, J.M.G. 1996. *Jews in the Mediterranean Diaspora. From Alexander to Trajan (323 B.C.E.–117 C.E.).* Edinburgh.
Bonz, M.P. 1990. 'The Jewish Community of Ancient Sardis: A Reassessment of its Rise to Prominence', *HSCPh* 93: 343–359.
—— 1993. 'Differing Approaches to Religious Benefaction: The Late Third-Century Acquisition of the Sardis Synagogue', *HTR* 86.2: 139–154.
Boterman, H. 1990. 'Die Synagoge von Sardes: Eine Synagoge aus dem 4. Jahrhundert?', *ZNTW* 81: 103–121.
Buckler, W.H. & Robinson, D.M. 1932. *Sardis: Publications of the American Society for the Excavation of Sardis.* Vol. 7: Greek and Latin inscriptions: Part 1. Leiden.
Crawford, J.S. 1996. 'Jews and Christians Live, Work and Worship Side by Side', *Biblical Archaeology Review* 22/5: 38–47.
Foss, C. 1976. *Byzantine and Turkish Sardis.* Cambridge, Mass.
Frey, J-B. 1936–52. *Corpus Inscriptionum Iudaicarum* 1–2, Rome; reprint of vol. 1 with prolegomena by B. Lifshitz, 1956. New York.

---

[44] Kraabel 1996: 87, n. 27. Kesjakova 1989.

Goodman, M. 1994. 'Jews and Judaism in the Mediterranean Diaspora in the Late-Roman Period: The Limitations of Evidence', *Journal of Mediterranean Studies* 4.2: 208–224.

Hanfmann, G.M.A. 1972. *Letters from Sardis*. Cambridge, Mass.

—— 1983. *Sardis from Prehistoric to Roman Times. Results of the Archaeological Expedition of Sardis 1958–75*. Cambridge, Mass. and London.

Hanfmann, G.M.A. & Bloom, J.B. 1987. 'Samoe, Priest and Teacher of Wisdom', *IEJ* 19: 10–14.

Jones, A.H.M. 1966. *The Greek City: from Alexander to Justinian*. Oxford.

Kesjakova, E. 1989. 'The Ancient Synagogue of Philippopolis', *Archeologia* 1: 20–33 (with French summary).

Kraabel, A.T. 1978. 'Paganism and Judaism: the Sardis Evidence' in *Paganisme, Judaïsme, Christianisme: Influences et affrontements dans le monde antique*. Mélanges Offerts à Marcel Simon. Paris: 13–33; repr. in A. Overman & J. MacLennan (eds). 1992: 237–255.

—— 1983. 'The Impact of the Discovery of the Sardis Synagogue', in Hanfmann 1983, 178–190 = Overman & MacLennan (eds), 269–292.

—— 1996. 'Pronoia at Sardis' in B. Isaac and A. Oppenheimer (eds), *Studies on the Jewish Diaspora in the Hellenistic and Roman Periods*. Te'uda 12. Tel-Aviv: 75–96.

Levinskaya, I. 1996. *The Book of Acts in its Diaspora Setting*. Grand Rapids, Mich./Carlisle.

Overman, J.A. & MacLennan, R.S. 1992. *Diaspora Jews and Judaism: Essays in Honor of and in Dialogue with A. Thomas Kraabel*. South Florida Studies in the History of Judaism, 41. Atlanta. Georgia.

Penella, R.J. 1990. *Greek Philosophers and Sophists. Studies in Eunapius of Sardis*. Leeds.

Pucci Ben Zeev, M. 1998. *Jewish Rights in the Roman World. The Greek and Roman Documents Quoted by Josephus Flavius*. Texte und Studien zum Antiken Judentum 74. Tübingen.

Rajak, T. 1996. 'Benefactors in the Greco-Jewish Diaspora' in P. Schäfer (ed.), *Geschichte-Tradition-Reflexion. Festschrift für Martin Hengel zum 70 Geburtstag*, Band 1. Tübingen, 305–323 = Ch. 19 in this volume.

—— 1998. 'The Gifts of God at Sardis', in M. Goodman (ed.), *Jews in a Greco-Roman World*. Oxford: 229–239.

Reynolds, J. and Tannenbaum, R. 1987. *Jews and Godfearers at Aphrodisias*. Cambridge Philological Society, Supplementary vol. 12. Cambridge.

Robert, L. 1964. *Nouvelles Inscriptions de Sardes*. Paris.

Rutgers, L.V. 1998. *The Hidden Heritage of Diaspora Judaism*. Leuven.

Seager, A.R. 1974. *Archaeology at the Ancient Synagogue of Sardis, Turkey: Judaism in a Major Roman City*. Ball State Faculty Lecture Series. Muncie, Indiana.

—— 1981. 'The Synagogue at Sardis', in L.I. Levine (ed.). *Ancient Synagogues Revealed*. Jerusalem, 178–184.

Sharples, R.W. 1995. *World under Management? Details, Delegation and Divine Providence, 400 B.C.–A.D. 1200*. Inaugural Lecture given at University College, London.

Shiloh, Y. 1968. 'Torah scrolls and the Menorah plaque from Sardis', *IEJ* 18: 54–57.

Trebilco, P. 1991. *Jewish Communities in Asia Minor*. Cambridge.

van Henten, J.W. 1997. *The Maccabean Martyrs as Saviours of the Jewish People. A Study of 2 and 4 Maccabees*. Supplements to the Journal for the Study of Judaism 57. Leiden.

Williams, M.H. 1998. *The Jews among the Greeks and Romans: A Diasporan Sourcebook*. London.

Yegül, F.K. 1986. *The Bath-Gymnasium Complex at Sardis*, with contributions by M.C. Bolgil and C. Foss. Archaeological exploration of Sardis, Report 3. Cambridge/London.

CHAPTER TWENTY-THREE

THE SYNAGOGUE IN THE GRECO-ROMAN CITY

The synagogues of the Greco-Roman diaspora are all but lost, as indeed is that diaspora itself. What we know of the synagogue buildings has come to us, of course, through archaeology. And when it comes to the life of those synagogues, the most important source is inscriptions, themselves brought to light by the archaeologist's spade. And so, to bring us a little closer to that world, I shall look closely at two Greek inscriptions from synagogues and then tease out some of their implications. Both are from Asia Minor. The first is a text from the central part of the region.[1] Its precise provenance is Acmonia in Phrygia, a fairly remote part of the Roman province of Asia, lying to the east of Lydia; we happen to know that the city fell within the assize district of the larger city of Apamea.[2] For all its remoteness, Acmonia, whose ruins have not been excavated, had according to William Ramsay,[3] a position of some natural strength, suggesting a regional centre of note. The place scarcely figures in contemporary literature, But such a gap in the written record is what the ancient historian has regularly to contend with.

Like almost all synagogue inscriptions from the Greco-Roman world, this is a donor inscription. Its general character is readily comprehensible: we are today all too familiar with many varieties of advertisement or acknowledgement of munificence. Though quite short, our document is still, sadly, one of the longer Jewish texts in Greek to have survived. It concerns a refurbishment for which three honorands were responsible, but it alludes also to an earlier stage in the building's history, in that the building is called 'the house' (or perhaps 'the hall') built by Julia Severa. This description is not transparent. The Greek word οἶκος in the context could mean 'house of prayer', that is to say 'synagogue', quite a common usage of the word οἶκος, with the text thus indicating that Julia Severa was the

---

[1] *MAMA* VI 264; *CIJ* II 766; Lifshitz 1967 no. 33.
[2] Habicht 1975: 85.
[3] Ramsay 1897: 625.

founder of the synagogue. Otherwise, the word 'house' could refer
to a different kind of building, even to domestic premises, erected
earlier and only later transferred to new ownership and to a new
purpose. Or again, as a third possibility, οἶκος can be used for the
main hall in a building, a sense to which Louis Robert has more
than once drawn our attention[4] and for which some recent translators of this text have opted.[5] On the latter interpretation, Julia Severa
will have built and paid for the central area of the synagogue, and
her successors will have refurbished it.

But if we take the word οἶκος in its regular sense, as 'house', then
two of the possible scenarios remain. The second was that a structure
erected by Severa for some quite other purpose, whether civic or
private, may have been acquired for a synagogue. It could then be
suggested that Severa herself, far from being a conscious benefactor,
was in no way connected with the synagogue. We would then also
take into account the fact that the lady appears as part of a participial clause, with her name in the accusative case. The designation
of the house as hers would amount merely to a method of identification. However, the very fact of Severa's mention by name might rather
lead us to expect a more substantial relationship between the lady
and the synagogue, and to look therefore to the first scenario, in
which Julia Severa is genuinely involved in the synagogue's foundation. And indeed, most translators[6] makes this supposition explicit
by turning the opening participial clause into a separate sentence.

If we do conclude that Severa is likely to have been pulled in
with a view to marking her out, along with the individuals named
after her, as an honoured donor, then the most natural implication
is that Severa had the 'house' built for the community.[7] It may be
observed that, since a later generation associated this 'house' with
her and attached her name to it, the whole edifice rather than the
central hall is rather more likely to be at issue. The details of the
transaction, no doubt perfectly familiar to the Acmonians and therefore not requiring to be spelled out, must remain for us shrouded
in mystery. But the speculation may be permitted that one or more
inscriptions exclusively concerned with Julia Severa were once to be

---

[4] See White 1997: 308, n. 47.
[5] Brooten (1982: 156) adopts this sense in translating our second text, the Tation
inscription.
[6] So Brooten 1982: 158.
[7] κατασκευάζω is 'to build', as in the Tation inscription. Contrast ἐπισκευάζω,
'to repair', lower down in the same text.

seen somewhere around the premises. For this speculation there is
at least a comparative basis. The remains of the famous Sardis synagogue belong to a similar milieu, even if the Sardis edifice was
rather more important and considerably more imposing as well as
significantly later in date. That synagogue contained at least three
inscriptions associated with one single donor, a certain Leontius.[8]
The parallel is helpful in suggesting possibilities for Acmonia, where,
alas, our inscription gives us the sum-total of our firm knowledge
about the synagogue. Apart from this inscription, we have just two
marble architectural fragments found in the vicinity and tentatively
ascribed to Acmonia and to our building, each displaying a menorah and, it appears, a partially unrolled scroll.[9]

Whatever the rationale for the inscribers' decision to bring in
Severa's name, the unusual consequence is that there is a clear chronological marker to guide the modern interpreter. For Severa was so
well-known a figure in Acmonia as to appear on the city's coinage.[10]
This makes hers an early inscription, as far as Jewish-Greek epigraphy is concerned. Thus, for once, we are fortunate in the coincidence
of survival and we can with confidence place Severa in the mid-first
century A.D., and, more precisely, in the reign of Nero. If she is
indeed being actively honoured by her mention in the synagogue
inscription, then the gap between the two events, presentation and
refurbishment, should be small: if not still alive and standing by to
respond to the compliment paid her by the 'synagogue', then we
would expect her at least to belong to living memory.

Julia Severa's name is, of course, Roman. Of the three male donors
who are the central concern of the text, one bears the *tria nomina* of
a Roman citizen, Publius (abbreviated as P) Turronius Cladus, while
the other two are designated by just a part of their Roman names: the
praenomen, Lucius, in the one case and the *nomen* and *cognomen* in the
third, Popilius[11] Zoticus. The first and third have Greek *cognomina*
(whose spelling are Romanized here).[12] All three characters have the

---

[8] I am most grateful to Professor J.H. Kroll for making available to me the
unpublished dossier of inscriptions from the Sardis synagogue.

[9] *MAMA* VI 347 and pl. 60; cf. Trebilco 1991: 60.

[10] See below.

[11] Not Publius, as, for example, in the translation by Brooten 1982: 158. Publius
is rendered in Greek as *Poplios, Pouplios* or, later, *Poublios*: see Dittenberger 1872:
287–289.

[12] Cladus is a widespread Greek name, whose meaning is 'branch'. See Robert
1963: 271–272.

air of being Greek-speaking Romans of a certain standing, typical of the local bourgeoisie in cities such as theirs.[13] All three are designated also in terms of synagogue office—such people tend to like status. They are, respectively, ἀρχισυνάγωγος (synagogue head) for life, ἀρχισυνάγωγος (understood as for a limited period) and ἄρχων. The titles of these three Acmonian male donors are the standard honorific or semi-honorific titles associated with Jewish communities in Greek cities and at Rome.[14] The most unusual is the most prestigious of the three titles, a post as synagogue-head to be held in perpetuity; but even this has a number of parallels, among them cases from the city of Rome. I shall return to the exact significance of the nomenclature and of the titulature.

The second inscription also concerns a woman, this time as the only donor in the text. It comes apparently from the city of Phocaea, an old Greek colony in Ionia.[15] Tation too has built a house and she too has handed it over to the community, which is referred to at the beginning of the inscription as 'the Jews', *Ioudaioi*. In the same way as for the Acmonian trio, Tation's munificence is detailed, again in the third person, and then the honours with which she was repaid are specified.

But there are interesting differences. Tation, unlike Julia Severa, is defined in terms of the man to whom she belongs, Straton son of Empedon, her husband or her father. She is designated by just one name, probably a Greek one, although it could just have local origins. Similar names are known; for example Tatia is a high priestess of Asia at Thyatira and the mother of a dedicator at Apamea; Tatias was a 'daughter of the city' and a priestess of Zeus at Stratonicea; while Tata was a well-known figure, 'mother of the city' at Aphrodisias, who again held the office of high priestess of the imperial cult as well as being a manager and benefactor of the games there.[16] Tation of Phocaea has no synagogue title, unlike the three donors at Acmonia. The considerable expense of a synagogue and

---

[13] Cf. Mitchell 1993: 9. On Romanization in these circles, and in particular at Acmonia, see Robert 1960: 384.

[14] See the discussion of *archisynagogoi* in relation to other office holders in Rajak & Noy 1993 = Ch. 20.

[15] *CIJ* 1.738; Lifshitz 1967, no. 13B.

[16] Documentation for these women in van Bremen 1996: appx. 2. Robert 1963: 348 treats the name Tatia as in no sense indigenous but rather belonging to the class of universal nicknames, 'Lallnamen'.

a courtyard—or just possibly (on Robert's interpretation of the word οἶκος) of a hall and a balustrade around it, was borne by this donor alone, 'out of her own resources.' By contrast, the trio at Acmonia, in addition to being accorded credit for their personal munificence, are also said to have drawn on accumulated funds. This is an interesting detail and we could wish for more information: the reference must be either to funds raised for the specific purpose or to the synagogue's treasury. If the latter is in question, it would suggest that the three had a mainly supervisory or organizational or patronal role in the construction.

Much of what is referred in these texts is familiar to us from the archaeology and the epigraphy of the Greco-Jewish diaspora. Neither synagogue, Acmonia or Phocaea, has left any trace on the ground. The Severa inscription was found in secondary usage and the exact provenance of the Tation text is unknown. But an open courtyard and walls decorated with marble revetments are features quite familiar to us, above all from the later grand, and many times rebuilt, colonnaded synagogue at Sardis, which was contained within the city's gymnasium complex. Marble did not have to be enormously expensive in these parts: the city of Aphrodisias, where, as we shall see, there was an important Jewish community, was one major source. No object connected with the cult itself figures among the gifts in our texts. At Sardis, where there is a large corpus of inscriptions, the epigraphic picture is similar, although there, at a very late stage in the building's history, a plaque mentioning a religious leader by the name of Samoe is thought to relate to the construction of one of the two Torah shrines.[17]

Other features of the texts are less predictable. The honours accorded the donors—golden crown and a front seat, προεδρία, for Tation, a gilded shield for the three men—are wholly familiar in the Greek world, but they break that tendency towards restraint in trumpeting wealth and generosity which is, in my view, detectable in the Greek-Jewish epigraphy as a whole.[18] Crowns, shields, and front seats were, however, part of the basic currency of so-called 'euergetism', that reciprocal system of honours in exchange for benefactions which kept Greco-Roman cities going. The virtues praised in the trio of the Julia Severa inscription are among the standard

---

[17] Seager & Kraabel in Hanfmann 1983: 183; 189.
[18] Rajak 1996 = Ch. 19.

qualities of benefactors in Greek thinking—good will, translated as
solicitude, taking trouble, or zeal, and, mentioned first of all, a generally good disposition, for which a compound of the noun, ἀρετή,
virtue, is used.

In both texts, the term 'synagogue' is used to refer not to the
building with whose fabric the donors were concerned but rather to
the association of Jews linked with it. The texts make one essential
principle of the synagogue's functioning perfectly clear. In common
with other civic associations in a Greek polis, synagogues operate
precisely as miniature versions of the city of which they are part:
not only the underlying social assumptions but also the language of
symbol and gesture in which those assumptions are expressed echo
what goes on in the city. These two little texts could be transferred
to a civic context and ascribed to the local council, the βουλή, without changing anything material, except that they might want expansion. Moreover, such replication on a small scale in a minor unit
within the larger unit is in itself a characteristic of Greek cities. We
can in fact trace it right back to the demes of classical Athens.[19] In
the Roman period the principle extended to an increasing number
of guilds and associations. When a group behaves like this, it is not
setting up an alternative city, which is what a sub-group might well
be expected to do, but rather it is contributing to the functioning
of the whole, as a system of wheels-within-wheels. The code within
the small group endorses and validates that within the larger. Indeed,
it serves to offer a training ground and practice in the operation of
the latter.

Thus, for Jews to run their association in this particular manner
suggests a grasp of and even, we may fancy, a respect for, the collective political processes of the larger unit. It takes just a moment's
thought to realize that only a highly-acculturated Jewry, well-established in a particular milieu, could even think of operating in such
a way, let alone begin to know how to do it. The Jewish communities seem to be an organic part of society in these parts of Asia
Minor. That their unequivocally monotheistic cult is blatantly and
fundamentally unlike others does not undercut their capacity for integration; since the sub-units in a polis are characterized, indeed one
might say defined, precisely by their individual cults, and since reli-

---

[19] Such patterns in classical Athens are examined in Osborne 1990.

gion was central to their existence, holding them together and lending them identity. Judaism could be perceived as just another such cult at the heart of a typical association. The parallel between Jewish or, even more often, Christian groups, and the other private associations, such as trade guilds or religious clubs, which were familiar features of the towns and cities of the empire has been so often noted as to be a commonplace.[20] Here, I am more concerned with the links between the part and the whole.

It is easy to overlook the oddity of having synagogues run themselves like pagan cities. But it is worth pausing to reflect on this phenomenon, the adoption of those behaviour patterns by communities of worshippers whose business was after all the reading and teaching of the holy Torah and the performance, however attenuated, of *mitzvoth*. All of these acts reflect another, intrinsically different value system. The explanation is to be found, I think, not in the character of those Jews but in the nature of the Greco-Roman city. Judaism could be incorporated into the civic context through the inclusion of a synagogal community into the workings of the polis. So the character of that community would inevitably be dictated by the Greco-Roman polis norms. In this way, I would suggest, the Greek political system permanently shaped the evolution of diaspora Judaism.

In the light of what we have seen, I would suggest describing the synagogue in this period and in this context as the interface between the Jews and their city. It was not only that the synagogue had a clear role within the larger unit. There was also the corollary, that the standing of its members could be readily defined in terms of the values of the wider society. This would have a profound impact even on those Jews who, not being citizens, had no real share in the larger unit.

Within the polis, it is likely that the synagogue was defined as a private grouping rather than as a formal, legally-constituted organization. The idea that Jews were permitted by law to form autonomous entities known as πολιτεύματα (literally, 'constitutions') in some or all of the major centres they inhabited, has been much favoured until recently, but it can be discounted.[21] The reality is that, during the Roman imperial period, associations of all kinds proliferated. Most were of a private character. They were, moreover, associations which

---

[20] Meeks (1983: 77–80) examines this type of interpretation.
[21] Zuckerman 1985–88; Lüderitz 1983.

individuals could chose to join or not join, in what we today might call a free market-place, rather than ones whose membership consisted of those born into them, like those of earlier times. The synagogues had their place among these, as of course did the early churches.

Our inscriptions show, however, that, in functional even if not necessarily in legal terms, the synagogues operated as wholly visible units within the civic context. Thus, non-Jews were able to form with them links which were, we must presume, of mutual benefit. For the synagogues, this had one major consequence apart from simply allowing Jews to feel comfortable in their host societies: it enlarged the number of those who could be counted as political supporters or useful connections. Again, there is nothing particularly new in powerful patrons assisting the less privileged but aspiring. But what we learn here is how, precisely by its replication of the city's patterns, the synagogue opened itself to the wider world. Our two chosen texts show beautifully how this process operated.

Can we get any closer to the realities of the situation? The paucity of our information demands ingenuity and imagination: every lead has to be relentlessly followed up. The most valuable clue is the identity of the named Acmonian donors. As I have said, the Julia Severa text is particularly precious in that it carries names known to us from other local contexts. That Julia Severa figures on an inscription from Acmonia as a leading member of the local elite was noticed already by William Ramsay exactly one hundred years ago. Ramsay's fine discussions are still valuable. The text of this inscription was subsequently republished[22] and it has been joined by more material. Our knowledge of the personalities with whom Severa was associated is still evolving as new finds come to light though so far none of it is Jewish.[23] But we do now understand how widely the great lady's connections extended: the ramifications go well beyond Acmonia, into the elites of other cities of Asia Minor.

Julia Severa was recognized by the gerousiva, the senate, at Acmonia, as high priestess of the house of the divine emperors, and also as ἀγωνοθέτης, president of the competitive games.[24] Athletic events were central to the city's life and prestige so their head was rather more

---

[22] *MAMA* VI 263.
[23] Mitchell 1974; van Bremen 1996: 336, appx. 2.
[24] *MAMA* VI 263.

than a gymnastics teacher. Indeed we know that the agonothete in another city (Oenoanda) was privileged to wear a highly elaborate golden crown which deserved a separate description in an inscribed text and was decorated with relief portraits of the emperor and the god Apollo.[25] On a second inscription, Severa appears together with a man called Turronius Rapon and she is the first named of the couple, thus suggesting her importance: another prominent individual and priest in the cult, one Nicias Asclepias is being honoured under the couple's supervision or perhaps during their tenure of office.[26] Severa further appears on three separate issues of Neronian bronze coins of the city, this time jointly with a certain Servenius Capito (who figures on other coins alone).[27] The earlier series includes one type which carries the bust of Nero's mother, Agrippina, her hair bound with ears of corn. An interesting sidelight is that Nero's wife, Poppaea Sabina, designated Poppaea Sebaste, appears on another type, in similar guise.[28] The second and third issues (A.D. 62 and A.D. 65) record three joint tenures of an office described as αρχ,[29] an abbreviation either of the term for the high priest (ἀρχιερεύς), as most scholars think, or, possibly, of the term ἄρχων,[30] the principal city magistracy in some places. A woman in this milieu might hold either office, though she would always be more likely, as here, to be associated in her tenure with a man.

Ramsay thought that both of those with whom Severa shared office were her husbands; in fact, there is no necessary familial link between her and Tyrronius Rapo. On the other hand, the pairing between Severa and Cornutus is recommended by the fragmentary local genealogy, for the couple can be slotted in as the parents of Lucius Servenius Cornutus (son of Lucius),[31] a local high-flier who reached the giddy heights of the senate at Rome under Nero, and of Servenia Cornuta, described as a descendant of kings on a broken stone architrave from Apollonia in neighbouring Galatia.[32] Slightly

---

[25] Millar 1993: 253; referring to the text from Oenoanada published by Wörrle, ll. 52–53. On the high proesthoods in the imperial cult, see Kearsley 1986.

[26] *MAMA* VI 265; only a part of this in Ramsay 1897: 550; but damage to the stone has eradicated some of what could be read in Ramsay's day.

[27] *RPC* I nos. 3170–3177.

[28] *RPC* I nos. 3172 and 3175.

[29] *RPC* I nos. 3174, 3176, 3177.

[30] So the editors of *RPC*. I *Contra* van Bremen 1996: 336.

[31] Halfmann 1979: nos. 5 and 5a.

[32] *MAMA* IV 139.

later, a plausible reconstruction produces family connections with the Julii Severi, prominent in the province of Galatia from Trajan on, and with the Plancii of that same region. The latter were a very well-known, quite aristocratic and very much Rome-orientated family (M. Plancius Varus, governor of Bithynia under Vespasian, was their first major figure).[33]

It is unusual but by no means unknown in this world for a woman like Severa to have so prominent a position in her city. The phenomenon of wealthy women in public office is nicely documented in a number of inscriptions from the broader region into which Acmonia falls.[34] One suggested explanation is that the narrowing gap at this period between the private and the public spheres of activity brought women into a public domain where they had not been before.[35] It may also not be irrelevant that, while placing women in formal political roles seems to be a novelty in terms of ancient societies, female prominence in cults is perfectly familiar. Priestesses are an established feature of Greek religion at all periods, and, equally, a long-standing phenomenon in the native cultures of Asia Minor.

All this goes to describe Julia Severa. And now, on the assumption that she was a true donor, we must ask what she, a protagonist of emperor-worship, a central figure in her city, was doing associating herself with the local synagogue. We are highly unlikely ever to know her motives. The dream-discovery of one of her own dedicatory inscriptions would be profoundly welcome and would no doubt enormously advance our understanding. But we would still, of course, lack all insight into her mind or any grasp of her inner life. We are restricted to external actions, or, rather, to the brief record of an external set of transactions which is left to us. The record, on the interpretation I have adopted, testifies to a philanthropic exchange arising out of a patronal relationship, later built into in a donor inscription as an event in the past. A great pagan lady sees fit to confer benefit upon a particular group. The group clearly has some significance to her and she, in turn, is well-received by them. They speak one another's language.

Severa is an outsider to the synagogue. An imperial priestess can scarcely have been a Jewess and equally she is fairly unlikely to have been in the process of any sort of conversion. Yet she was clearly some sort of friend of the Jews. It is not impossible that she did experience some real attraction towards the God of Israel, like so many women in the Roman near east. In our state of ignorance about her and her like, it would be rash even to hazard a guess as to her spiritual orientation.

Now neither of our inscriptions uses that problematic label 'god-fearer', θεοσεβής. This controversial term almost certainly identifies what we might call 'fellow-travellers' with Judaism, those associated with the community in some way. The view that these constituted a clearly defined category, though cast in doubt by some, is now strongly supported by the evidence of the great Jewish inscription from Aphrodisias in Caria.[36] The double text, found, again, in iso-lation, lists the contributors to some sort of memorial or philan-thropic venture. A grouping called a πάτελλα (literally 'dish' or 'plate') is involved, and also a club called a δεκανία (literally a group of ten men) of the 'lovers of knowledge' and the 'all-praisers'. There the second section of the text on the second face of the column on which names are inscribed lists a bunch of these sympathizers, with nine members of the city council listed first. The sympathizers have for the most part Greek names, such as Zeno, Diogenes, Onesimus and Antiochus, or even Polychronius and Callimorphus, in contrast to the predominance of biblical and other characteristically Jewish names elsewhere in the inscription. We also, puzzlingly, find two of them, Emonius and Antoninus, on the front face, where Jews are listed.[37] The members of this category are usually imagined as having reli-gious leanings towards Judaism. But it is easy to forget that they are likely in the first instance to have sought a social connection with their local Jews. Client-patron relations may have dictated their choice. For there is a whole spectrum of gestures which a Gentile could make to indicate identification with Jews and Judaism.[38] It is reasonable therefore to locate Severa within the broad class of god-fearers. And it is worth pointing out that, had our record been more complete, we might even have found her so described on stone.

The male trio which is the real subject of the Severa inscription

---

[36] Publication by Reynolds & Tannenbaum 1987.
[37] Reynolds & Tannenbaum: 1987: 5. For the evidence on God-fearers and the relevance of the Aphrodisias text, see the survey in Feldman 1993: 342–368.
[38] As Cohen 1989 has noted.

is also interesting. A closer look shows that this may not be a homogeneous group. They are placed here in descending order of rank, and it is Cladus, the ἀρχισυνάγωγος for life who most demands our attention. He alone has the *tria nomina* written out in full. His family name connects him with a distinguished family whose acquaintance we have made, the Tyr(r)onii: a member of this family, it may be recalled, shared coins with Julia Severa. There is a good chance, therefore, that in this man we have another pagan notable with an interest in the synagogue. I can see nothing against understanding the perpetual archisynagogate as a title of honour open to 'righteous Gentiles' (if that is not an abuse of the concept) as well as to Jews. We must not forget how much we just do not know: Cladus need not have been the only Gentile with such a title at Acmonia.

The possibility that Cladus, the ἀρχισυνάγωγος for life, is to be seen as a non-Jew should be assessed in the light of our understanding of the regular *archisynagogos* post. I have claimed that these title-holders had far more to do with patronage and philanthropy than with the cultic life of the synagogue.[39] These office-holders are not to be imagined as leaders of prayer, or as functional equivalents of the *roshei kneseth* of the Talmudic world. In our environment, it is plausible that those who were accorded the office in perpetuity will have had even less to do with religious practice. Indeed, they need never even have held the straight post at all. I myself would readily understand Cladus as another unlabelled god-fearer, of the same type, even if not of the same status, as Julia Severa.

However, an alternative reading of the role of Turronius Cladus must also be reckoned with. He could have acquired his *nomen* as a freedman or as descendant of a freedman of the Tur(r)onii:[40] a Jew, in that case, who had become prominent and was now a figure of some influence. This could explain Julia Severa's patronal interest. It would put Cladus more on a par with Lucius son of Lucius and with the ἄρχων Zoticus, who lack the *tria nomina* and, seeming to be not particularly grand, are rather less likely to be purely patrons and therefore rather more likely to be active members of the community. Tyrronius is a name found in various places in Roman Asia Minor in the Roman imperial period, as well as in Greece and the

---

[39] Rajak 1992 = Ch. 17; 1996 = Ch. 19.
[40] See now White 1997: 310.

Greek islands, and even cropping up at Rome.[41] It appears to have Greek origins, but the view that it is specifically servile has been persuasively resisted.[42] We do not, therefore, have the wherewithal at present to choose between the two interpretations.

Turning now to Phocaea and to Tation, we meet the same ambiguity. The terms in which the announcement about her is cast seem to place her outside the community, for she is said to have given the building 'to the Jews', perhaps suggesting thus that she herself was not one. Admittedly, this is not a point we can press, since the term 'the Jews' may be intended to be wholly unstressed, operating merely as the designation of the community. The term could be synonymous, in fact, with the expression 'synagogue of the Jews', which appears a little lower down, where the return benefits given by the community to Tation are listed. Yet the Tation text does convey a distinct sense of the woman as an outsider. It may also be observed, for what it is worth, that the good Greek names which run in her paternal family are by no means among those known as favoured by Jews.

It will be objected that this lady is granted, as the second of her two rewards, an honorific front seat, προεδρία. Now, to sit in her seat of honour she would have had to go to synagogue, and, it may be said, going to synagogue more than once would have made her at any rate something more than a mere social sympathizer. Furthermore, the presence of a Gentile in the service would, it may reasonably be felt, scarcely have been encouraged. The answer to this objection lies, I believe, in a consideration of what might have gone on in the synagogue. The building was the community's main meeting-place. At Sardis, it is judged that the hall seated over a thousand.[43] At Berenice in Cyrenaica, an inscription suggests the Jews to have been the possessors of an amphitheatre-shaped building, spruced up and decorated by a donor there; while another text from the same north African city speaks of honours conferred on a certain individual during a Tabernacles assembly—presumably held where worship was carried out. In other words, the buildings of the Jewish community were the venue for a range of events. Some of these events will have had a municipal significance. In Phocaea, it is at

---

[41] Robert 1963: 42.
[42] Robert 1963: 271–272 and nn.
[43] On the scale of the Sardis hall, see Seager & Kraabel 1983: 188.

such occasions that semi-outsiders such as (on my interpretation)
Tation will have had a role to play. On other occasions, in her
absence, her golden crown may even have been laid on her front-
row seat to remind those present of her honours.

Only one option was excluded in the synagogue, that of honouring the donor's statue: in a pagan environment, it would have been
accepted form to crown the statue or even to seat an image in the
alotted front seat. Statues in honour of individuals were common
currency in the honours system of the Roman empire and in euergetistic transactions; but there is absolutely no evidence to suggest
that even the laxest of diaspora Jews countenanced the erection of
images of living beings. To engage securely in interaction with outsiders a community needs to maintain some boundaries, and this in
a world of pagan imagery and ubiquitous human representation was
probably the most important of them.

Such nuances become intelligible once we grasp the synagogue as
a zone of group interaction, and apply this understanding both to
the synagogue association, and also, as we have just seen, to the synagogue as place. That is not to say that the synagogue did not have
other meanings to its frequenters, among them its role as the place
for communal religious observance, especially the reading of the
Torah. Those we know all too little about. We are tantalized by
one fragment carrying both Greek and Hebrew. There, six Greek
letters, unintelligible unless a great deal of ingenuity is brought to
bear, are followed by four Hebrew words which are clearly part of
a formula. One line reads 'on Israel and on Jerusalem' while the
second has the one word 'end'. Sukenik suggested to its editors
restoration as a quotation from the liturgy, but other reconstructions
are possible. This inscription has not been dated. But it was almost
certainly written several centuries after Julia Severa's synagogue was
built, and the text is as likely to belong to a grave as to a building.
Still, this bilingual document allows us at least to scent traces of a
deeper Jewish tradition in the region.[44] It is, indeed, highly unusual

---

[44] *MAMA* VI 34; cf. Trebilco 1991: 82; Mitchell 1993: 35 and fig. 17. I do not
discuss here the well-known Greek inscriptions cursing tomb violators which appear,
in varying degrees, to show knowledge of the Greek bible. Some of these clearly
relate to civic personages, but otherwise they are hard to locate in a cultural context. A handful are today generally considered Jewish: see the perhaps over-inclu-
sive roster in Trebilco 1991: 60–77 and the full discussion and documented catalogue
in Strubbe 1994. Three dated texts of their number belong to the mid-third century and thus they too are significantly later than the Severa inscription: Mitchell
1993: 35.

and I would stress, as commentators have failed to do, the absence in the entire epigraphic record of anything comparable: we do not find Hebrew which exceeds brief formulae in any diaspora milieu, including Sardis, until about the sixth century.

Here, then is a glimpse into the future. As far as the earlier period goes, it is fair to say that writing inscriptions about individuals— what has been described as the epigraphic habit—was essentially a Greco-Roman practice. Thus, on the whole, the Jews of the Greco-Roman diaspora showed, as it were, more of their Greco-Roman face when they practised it. That face was at times a highly amenable one, with a friendly smile and a certain eagerness written on it. Greek came out of its mouth. They perhaps had another, different face as well: Diaspora Jews so often live double lives, as we know. I only wish we could access that other face. For today, it will be enough if I have persuaded you that the synagogue in the Greek city retained a smiling face—for as long as it was allowed to smile.

BIBLIOGRAPHY

Barclay, J.M.G. 1996. *Jews in the Mediterranean Diaspora from Alexander to Trajan (323 B.C.E.–117 C.E.)*. Edinburgh.
Bremen, R. van. 1983; 2nd ed. 1993. 'Women and Wealth', in A. Cameron & A. Kuhrt (eds.), *Images of Women in Antiquity*. London, 223–242.
——— 1996. *The Limits of Participation: Women and Civic Life in the Greek East in the Hellenistic and Roman Periods*. Amsterdam.
Brooten, B. 1982. *Women Leaders in the Ancient Synagogue*. Chico, California.
Cohen, S. 1989. 'Crossing the Boundary and Becoming a Jew', *HTR* 82: 13–33.
Dittenberger, W. 1872. 'Römische Namen in griechischen Inschriften und Literaturwerken', *Hermes* 6: 129–155; 280–313.
Feldman, L.H. 1993. *Jew and Gentile in the Ancient World: Attitudes and Interactions from Alexander to Justinian*. Princeton.
Habicht, C. 1975. 'New Evidence on the Province of Asia'. *JRS* 65: 64–91.
Halfmann, H. 1979. *Senatoren aus dem Östlichen Teil des Imperium Romanum*. Hypomnemata 58. Göttingen.
Jameson, S.A. 1965. 'Cornutus Tertullus and the Plancii of Pergae'. *JRS* 55: 54–58.
Kearsley, R.A. 1986. 'Asiarchs, *Archiereis* and the *Archiereiai* of Asia'. *GRBS* 27: 183–192.
Kraemer, R.S. 1992. *Her Share of the Blessings: Women's Religions among Pagans, Jews and Christians in the Greco-Roman World*. New York/Oxford.
Levick, B.M. 1967. *Roman Colonies in Southern Asia Minor*. Oxford.
Lifshitz, B. 1967. *Donateurs et fondateurs dans les synagogues juives*. Cahiers de la Revue Biblique 7. Paris.
Lüderitz, G., with Reynolds, J.M. 1983. *Corpus jüdischer Zeugnisse aus der Cyrenaika. Beihefte zum Tübinger Atlas des vorderen Orients*. Reihe B. 53. Wiesbaden.
Lüderitz, G. 1994. 'What is the Politeuma?', in J.W. van Henten & P.W. van der Horst (eds), *Studies in Early Jewish Epigraphy*. Leiden: Brill, 183–225.
Meeks, W.A. 1983. *The First Urban Christians: The Social World of the Apostle Paul*. Newhaven/London.

Millar, F.G.B. 1993. 'The Greek City in the Roman Period', in M.H. Hansen (ed.), *The Ancient Greek City-State*. [Historisk-filosofiske Meddelser 67]. Copenhagen.
Mitchell, S. 1974. 'The Plancii in Asia Minor'. *JRS* 64: 27–39.
—— 1993. *Anatolia: Land, Men and Gods in Asia Minor* II. *The Rise of the Church*. Oxford.
Osborne, R. 1990. 'The *Demos* and its Divisions in Classical Athens', in O. Murray & S. Price (eds), *The Greek City from Homer to Alexander*. Oxford, 265–293.
Overman, J.A. & Maclennan, R.S. 1992. *Diaspora Jews and Judaism. Essays in Honor of and in Dialogue with A. Thomas Kraabel*. South Florida Studies in the History of Judaism 41. Atlanta, Georgia.
Pleket, H.W. 1969. *Epigraphica* 2. *Texts on the Social History of the Greek World*. Leiden.
Rajak, T. 1992. 'The Jewish Community and its Boundaries', in J. Lieu, J. North & T. Rajak (ed.), *The Jews among Pagans and Christians in the Roman Empire*. London, 9–28 = Ch. 17 in this volume.
—— 1996. 'Benefactors in the Greco-Jewish Diaspora' in P. Schäfer (ed.), *Geschichte-Tradition-Reflexion. Festschrift für Martin Hengel zum 70 Geburtstag*. Vol. 1. *Judentum*. Tübingen, 305–319 = Ch. 19 in this volume.
—— 1998. 'The Gifts of God at Sardis', in M. Goodman (ed.), *Jews in a Greco-Roman World*. Oxford, 229–239.
Rajak, T. & Noy, D. 1993. '*Archisynagogoi*: Office, Title and Social Status in the Greek-Jewish Synagogue'. *JRS* 83, 75–93 = Ch. 20 in this volume.
Ramsay, W.M. 1897. *Cities and Bishoprics of Phrygia*. Vol. 1, Part 2. Oxford.
Reynolds, J. & Tannenbaum, R. 1987. *Jews and Godfearers at Aphrodisias*. Cambridge Philological Society, Supplementary Volume 12. Cambridge.
Robert, L, 1960. *Hellenica. Recueil d'Epigraphie et de Numismatie et d'Antiquité Grecques 10*. Librairie d'Amérique et d'Orient 11–12. Paris.
—— 1963. *Noms Indigènes dans l'Asie-Mineur Gréco-Romaine. Première Partie*. Bibliothèque archéologique et historique de l'Institut Français d'Archéologie d'Istanbul 13. Paris.
Seager, A.R. & Kraabel, A.T. 1983. 'The Synagogue and the Jewish Community', in G.M.A. Hanfmann, *Sardis from Prehistoric to Roman Times. Report of the Archaeological Exploration of Sardis 1958–1975*. Cambridge Mass./London.
Sheppard, A.R.R. 1979. 'Jews, Christians and Heretics in Acmonia and Eumeneia', *Anatolian Studies* 29: 169–180.
Strubbe, J.H.M. 1994. 'Curses against Violation of the Grave in Jewish Epitaphs from Asia Minor', in J.W. van Henten & P.W. van der Horst (eds), *Studies in Early Jewish Epigraphy*. Leiden, 70–128.
Trebilco, P. 1991. *Jewish Communities in Asia Minor*. Cambridge.
White, L.M. 1991. *Building God's House in the Roman World: Architectural Adaptation among Pagans, Jews, and Christians*. Baltimore.
—— 1997. *The Social Origins of Christian Architecture. 2. Texts and Monuments for the Christian Domus Ecclesiae in its Environment*. Harvard Theological Studies 42. Valley Forge, Pennsylvania.
Wörrle, M. 1988. *Stadt und Fest im kaiserzeitlichen Kleinasien: Studien zu einer agonistischen Stiftung aus Oenoanda*. Beck/Munich.
Zuckerman, C. 1985–88. 'Hellenistic *politeumata* and the Jews: A Reconsideration', *SCI* 8–9: 171–185.

CHAPTER TWENTY-FOUR

THE RABBINIC DEAD AND THE DIASPORA
DEAD AT BETH SHE'ARIM

The Beth She'arim necropolis may reasonably be claimed as the
most important material evidence for Jewish religious life in Palestine
in late antiquity. It is centrally placed, in what is geographically a
transitional area, extending across many acres over the gentle southern
slopes of the limestone hills of the lower Galilee, at the western end
of the Jezreel valley. A town, covering, it is thought, some ten acres,
stood beside the necropolis: its basilica-type synagogue and surrounding buildings have been excavated and can still be seen. This
town was, as we know from Talmudic sources, the home of R. Judah
ha-Nasi before his late move to Sepphoris. Of the necropolis, some
thirty extensive catacombs, as well as some separate tombs, were
excavated between 1936 and 1959, dated to between the second and
the fourth centuries, and published in three Hebrew volumes (1973,
1974 and 1976), later translated into English. In spite of damage in
the Arab period, and extensive looting, the remaining contents were
rich. Not all of these catacombs are today accessible. There are
apparently others still unexplored, and likely to remain so for the
time being.

The sheer scale of the cemetery marks Beth She'arim out as a
facility of importance, obviously more than a local provision. The
provenances of the deceased, specified in epitaphs, confirm that
impression. In this world of the dead, Jews from the land of Israel
meet those of the diaspora, urban Jews meet rural residents, users
of Greek meet users of Hebrew, rabbis meet synagogue heads, Jewish
ritual meets Greek myth. Our understanding of those encounters
derives largely from the physical evidence of the excavation, but a
small number of allusions or otherwise relevant statements in rabbinic literature, mainly found in the Yerushalmi, are crucial to its
interpretation. Naturally, such texts create a picture of the burial
areas as a zone dominated by the rabbis' involvement, and often
enough a further step is taken, with the supposition that the whole
operation was in some sense under rabbinic control. Here we shall
see how easy it is to misuse the rabbinic statements.

Furthermore, such burials as relate to diaspora locations are interpreted in this same light. It has become widely accepted that the Jews of the Greek diaspora expressed their Jewishness by seeking to bury their relatives near, and themselves to lie beside, the rabbinic great and good. Their commitment is gauged from their going to the great lengths, as it is supposed, of transporting bones (or, some seem to think, bodies) from afar for this purpose. This side of the equation too will require scrutiny, by way of a review of the extent and spread of diaspora participation in Beth She'arim and a reassessment of the meaning of such participation. What is the basis of the judgement, found time and again, that Beth-She'arim in its heyday, had become 'sacred for many people', 'a famous and hallowed necropolis',[1] that it was 'the central necropolis for Jews throughout Palestine and the diaspora',[2] a kind of Mecca for the Jewish world? Finally, if this judgement is to be questioned, we need to put in its place some new understanding, however tentative, as to who the primary users of the cemetery at Beth She'arim might have been and what factors determined their choice of burial place.

Two straightforward questions present themselves:

1. To what extent, if any, was this extensive cemetery associated with the circle of R. Judah ha-Nasi and his successors?
2. What meaning, if any, had any such association for those outside either patriarchal or rabbinic circles?

The rabbinic presence at Beth She'arim

Without regard to their limitations, the cryptic and ambiguous rabbinic references—or possible references—to Beth She'arim have been allowed to dictate interpretation of the archaeological data. Speculative conclusions have been, as it were, set in stone, acquiring the apparent solidity of the material remains themselves. Now, new perspectives make it easier for us to stand back from those conclusions. In the first place, the problem of the position of the rabbis among the dead of Beth She'arim is part of a large historical problem which has occasioned considerable recent interest, that of the power and influence of the rabbinic class in the land of Israel. It has now been

---

[1] Negev (ed.) 1990: 61.
[2] Levine 1997: 309.

argued in various quarters that the role of this class was very restricted, even within the world of the Galilaean synagogues.[3] In these newer portrayals, the rabbis emerge as specialized groups with their own social system, their own master-pupil networks and to some extent their own norms, aspiring to, but still far from attaining, authority as spiritual leaders and legislators in the wider Jewish society. Such a reading will obviously call into question any maximalist assessment of their impact on the Beth-She'arim necropolis.

Few would deny that, as a minimum, there are graves of rabbis at Beth-She'arim. Published epitaphs are assigned to individuals designated in Hebrew or Aramaic, sometimes transliterated into Greek, as 'rabbi', 'ribbi', or 'rib', variously spelt, or by a simple Greek 'rho' preceding their names. Admittedly, we cannot take it for granted that these designations never represent a straightforward courtesy title in Aramaic for a man of standing. The use would run parallel with the Greek κυρά (elsewhere, κυρία), 'lady', which precedes a number of female names, notably in the Hebrew inscriptions of Mega, wife of the rabbi Joshua ben Levi (III, no. 23) and of Miriam, a rabbi's daughter (219); we also find in one case, the Phoenician Kal(l)iope of Byblos, the unexpected transliteration of the Latin *matrona*.[4] Yet, where the title 'rabbi' occurs in Hebrew in a closely-related group of epitaphs and is applied to some but not all the members of a group, there the intention can scarcely be other than to suggest that those so entitled are rabbis in a formal religious sense. In catacomb 20, all seven Hebrew epitaphs come with the title 'rabbi'. That the title is frequent among the epitaphs of Palmyrene Jews might give some pause for thought. However, in that group we also observe cases where there is both the 'rho' before the name and after it the word *biribbi*, a term marking special rabbinic expertise or occasionally literal rabbinic paternity.[5] It follows that the Palmyrenes too are declaring some of their number as scholars and sages.[6] The

---

[3] Goodman 1983; Levine 1989 (1); Cohen 1992; Levine 1992.

[4] Nos. 136 and 137; this designation, unlike κυρά, does not precede the personal name. Robert, *REG* 69, 1956, *BE* 340, invokes the Talmudic liking for the word *matrona*. For *matrona* in the Greek version of a Latin epitaph, apparently also used loosely, see *CIL* III, 222, from Tarsus, Cilicia (to which my attention was drawn by Professor J.N. Adams). For two further Beth She'arim Greek transliterations from Latin, Millar 1993: 380.

[5] For the latter use, see no. 16 (catacomb 20). For an epigraphic parallel for the double terminology, *CIJ* II, 892 from Jaffa.

[6] Cf. Millar 1993: 380, for some illuminating comments. But see Cohen 1981–82 for a sceptical view of 'epigraphic rabbis'.

appearance of a 17-year old rabbi, Gamaliel son of Eleazar,[7] has occasioned some anxiety, and this case suggests that the title could be accorded to members of rabbinic families (at least on their demise). In any event, a limited variation of usage is scarcely surprising in a corpus of epitaphs with some geographical spread, and one which is undoubtedly—though we do not know exactly how—distributed over time: numismatic evidence points to the destruction of the town of Beth She'arim in 351/2, the year of the local revolt against Gallus Caesar.[8]

By far the most important find related to the rabbinic world are the three graves plausibly connected with the family of Judah ha-Nasi himself, which emerged from catacomb 14 in 1954, the sixth season of excavation. The crudely carved names of Rabbi Gamaliel, R. Shim'on, and R. Anianos were found,[9] the first two in bilingual Hebrew-Greek inscriptions, the third just in Greek, with the added words τοῦ νάνου.[10] These three names coincided dramatically with those of the three appointed successors of Rabbi according to the famous account in the Babylonian Talmud (Ket. 103.72): the first two were Rabbi's sons, Hanina ben Hama was a disciple.[11] While, disappointingly, no grave bearing the name of Rabbi himself was to be found, a prominently-placed unmarked double grave was deemed a likely candidate to house him and his wife.

This striking discovery occasioned unusually widespread interest in the site, and in many minds the graves remain the cemetery's central feature. An extract from the history of the excavation vividly exposes the involvement of the Israeli establishment, lay and religious, as well as that of the public at large, at the time of the discovery. One cannot fail to observe the high significance for the finds for the self-identity of the fledgling Jewish state. In his report, Professor Avigad (III, 13) evoked an extraordinary scene and an atmosphere of excitement which surely exerted an influence on the archaeological operation and its assessment.

[7] III, catacomb 20, no. 26 and sarcophagus 117.
[8] But for recent doubts see Weiss 1992: 371.
[9] Vol. II, nos. 173, 174 and 175 (Greek); vol. III, 8, 9, 10 (Hebrew).
[10] Taken to be a nickname, 'the dwarf' meaning 'the small', but more likely a paternal proper name. For similar names, see *CIJ* II, 909: νόνου; 917: νόννα (a woman).
[11] According to the story, Hanina gave way, in the event, to his elder, one R. Afes, who proceeded to hold the office of 'president' for the short period until his death. The absence of any tomb which might be ascribed to Afes has gone unremarked. On the succession, Cohen 1981: 60–65. Cf. also *j.Ta'anit* 4.2.68a.

This was an excavation season replete with astounding events and exciting discoveries, which aroused great interest among the general public as well. Catacomb 14 was the center of interest, since it was suggested that members of Rabbi Judah ha-Nasi's family were buried there. This possibility fired everyone's imagination. The place bustled with visitors from all sections of the community: the President of Israel ... the Prime Minister, the late David ben Gurion; Mrs Golda Meir (then Minister of Labour); Cabinet Ministers; the Chairman and Members of the Knesseth; the Chairman of the Jewish Agency; the heads of the Hebrew University; teachers and students; citizens and tourists. All wished to view the inscriptions of R. Shim'on and R. Gamaliel, vivid evidence of so important a chapter in Jewish history and a tangible reminder of two outstanding personalities among the spiritual leaders of the people.

Here, it seemed, Talmud and archaeology came together. How could there be room for doubt? Nor is it surprising that the potent historical image crystallized in the catacombs at that moment should have lingered, to exert an influence not only on popular imagination but also on academic interpretation.

A connection between R. Judah ha-Nasi and the Beth She'arim necropolis is attested in the Yerushalmi, where the place is called בית שערים, by a handful of less than transparent statements. In addition, two passages which refer to the practice of taking the coffins of important figures to Eretz-Israel have been brought into connection with Beth She'arim. The texts are as follows, in either translation or summary; abstract discussions of the merits and demerits of burial in the Land do not concern us here and are not included:

1. 'Rabbi allowed the porch [?] at Beth She'arim. How many pillars did it have?' (j.Erubin 1.18c).
2. Rabbi Judah ha-Nasi moved to Sepphoris when his health weakened, but a tomb had been prepared for him at his previous place of residence, Beth She'arim (b.Ketubot 103b), and in due course he was buried there amid much lamentation (j.Kilayim 9.32a–b; Ecclesiastes Rabba, Vilna edition 9.5; b. *ibid.*).
3. 'R. Huna to the brother of R. Juda b. Zabdi 'When does mourning begin? When you take the dead from one city to another, as for those who take their dead [mediaeval gloss: from Caesarea][12] to Beth She'arim?" (j.Mo'ed Katan 3.5.81).
4. R. bar Qoraya and R. Eleazar [ben Pedat] were sitting and studying the Torah in Tiberias when they saw coffins arriving from abroad ... (j.Kilayim 32c; j.Ketubot 12.35b; cf. Genesis Rabbah 96 etc.)

---

[12] See B. Ratner, *Ahavat Zion ve Yerushalaim*, p. 114. That the mention of Caesarea in this passage appears only as a gloss has been overlooked.

5. The coffin of R. Huna the exilarch was brought from Babylon to Eretz-Israel, and its arrival observed by R. Judah ha-Nasi (*j.Ketubot* 12.35a; cf. *Genesis Rabbah* 33.3).

Below are some conclusions which have been derived from these statements and which have supplied a basis for interpretation of the site. It is worth pointing out that consideration of the correct handling of the texts serves not only to assist understanding of Beth She'arim, but also to exemplify the general difficulties we face in exploiting the hazy and sometimes distorted reflections within the Yerushalmi of the material world of Greco-Roman Palestine.

1. It is held that large-scale development at Beth She'arim can be accurately located in the first quarter of the third century, and is explicitly ascribed, not just to the presence of the Sanhedrin there, but to R. Judah ha-Nasi himself, justifying extravagant descriptions such as 'the great builder of Beth She'arim' (III, 263 ff.). Essentially, the grounds for this claim lie in passage 1, the Talmudic suggestion that Rabbi constructed an *exedra*—perhaps a colonnaded structure with anteroom—at this place, and that it was something unusual enough to require special approval. Scholars expatiate on an elaborate edifice. It should be noted that the passage is at least as likely to refer to construction in the town during the significant period of Rabbi's sojourn there as to the necropolis, which is not mentioned in the text. The likelihood of Rabbi's personal ownership of the hillside into which, supposedly, he had the necropolis dug, is further asserted (III, 2), with the tenuous support of the information that much of the neighbouring Jezreel valley was once Herodian royal property, and that Queen Berenice stored corn at Besara (Josephus, *Vita* 119; 126). Indeed, the area might conceivably have passed from them to the patriarchal household, but the evidence is wholly lacking.

2. It is assumed that Rabbi's place of burial became well known, both in and around the land of Israel and further afield, and that it was treated as holy. Apart from the statements about the widespread public mourning at the time of the funeral (passage 2), there is no evidence.

3. The inference is made that Jews from far and wide found it meritorious to bury their nearest and dearest in the vicinity of the sanctified place. Here, interpreters tend to adduce passage 5, the story of the bringing of the coffin of R. Huna, the exilarch, from Babylon to Eretz-Israel, during Judah's lifetime, even though nowhere

there is the precise destination stated as Beth She'arim.[13] Passage 4 relates to the second half of the third century; again, the story is vague and no destination for the coffins is given. Passage 3 is also brought in; this does at least refer to transports to Beth She'arim, but it makes no mention of the Nasi's burial; moreover, if we follow the gloss, it is concerned only with the dead from nearby Caesarea.[14]

4. Chronological inferences follow about the archaeological development of the site over the third century. A sequence proposed in the original publication has taken root. A linchpin of the reconstruction is the assignation to the Nasi's enterprise of the whole of the huge, 26-room catacomb 20, on the hill's northern slope. There, some 130 sarcophagi were found, though only 13 inscriptions (apart from graffiti), and this is the one catacomb normally still made accessible to visitors. In this catacomb, tombs of individuals entitled 'rabbi' dominate, at least among those that survive. Catacomb 14, where the Nasi's successors (as is thought) are buried, and which is sometimes taken as a private burial vault, is the only other area of which this is true: indeed there no single inscription wholly in Greek has been found, although the proportion of Greek to Hebrew in the necropolis as a whole is about 7:1. The case for judging these two catacombs to be contemporary relies upon physical parallelism in the shape of a common architectural pattern, involving an elevated open-air courtyard with benches on one side which was perhaps designed for memorializing of one kind or another; the version of this construction in catacomb 20 is deemed to have been begun but not finished (III, 83 ff.). Those two catacombs are thus taken as representing the beginnings of large-scale ancient digging and construction at the Beth-She'arim necropolis, and therefore they are fixed as representing an early style; this hypothesis essentially relies on reading what is on the ground in the light of insecure literary evidence.

The question of the Nasi's involvement in the cemetery is inseparable from that of the broader issue of rabbinic prominence there. It is necessary to stress that the rabbis are concentrated in these two specific zones, even if not wholly confined to them; with them, I include the patriarchal family, whose leadership was at that time

---

[13] See Gafni 1981: 98 and n. 17.
[14] See n. 12.

indisputably accepted in rabbinic circles. It is extraordinary that until recently the issue of the meaning of this restriction has not been raised. Now Ze'ev Weiss (1992) suggests that the rabbinic group, as an elite class, kept their burials together, instead of spreading them through the vast necropolis. That is a conservative formulation, which succeeds in preserving the traditional view of the rabbis' standing at the summit of the pyramid of status and authority in Jewish society. But the spatial distribution at Beth She'arim rather points to the rabbis as just one kind of special group among others; a group with large aspirations perhaps, but one whose principles and teachings had not yet permeated Jewish society by the time of the Mishnah, and probably not even considerably later. For, while the rabbinic burials are to a limited extent clustered, they are not in any way marked off as exclusive; indeed they are not even separated from those of others in the community.

Indeed, even in catacomb 20, non-rabbinic as well as rabbinic graves are in evidence. Epitaphs and images incorporate themes which may be said to belong to a different Jewish value-system. One brief epitaph there, not ascribed to a rabbi, enjoins passers-by to cheer up, since no one is immortal; while another, perhaps in jest, seems to be concerned with wishing the deceased a successful resurrection: (194). It is a familiar fact, though it startled the first discoverers, that at Beth She'arim the rabbinic dead were surrounded by iconic representations, not excluding human bodies, by classical imagery, and by depictions of less than salubrious mythological themes, such as the well-known depiction of Leda and the swan. Living in a pagan world, and within the Roman empire, the Palestinian rabbis were naturally used to being surrounded by such material; yet we should not imagine that this kind of Jewish environment is precisely the one they would have chosen for the deposition of their venerated leaders, even if we credit them with a blind eye or an attitude of detached acceptance. It is fairly clear that their own style was markedly different and their own dead are not commemorated by Greek epigrams. It looks, therefore, as though the rabbis were not in control: the necropolis was not theirs. Resulting from the simple realities of the situation, if nothing else, they probably they had little say in the operations by which space was allocated or sold there. We may suppose that rabbis had the know-how and the means to acquire catacombs, chambers or sections for their own use; and that they left it at that. If now we turn back now to the archaeological evidence, we cannot but observe that neither the position nor appearance of the graves suggests that even the Nasi's family was singled out for any preferential treatment; to make this observation is not, of course, to cast any doubt on the reports of the impact of his mass funeral (passage 1).

The diaspora at large

In the logic of this rabbi-centred reconstruction, an important part is played by the discovery at Beth She'arim of deceased individuals with identifiable diaspora origins, supposedly brought to the land of Israel for burial. The cemetery is claimed as 'a central Jewish necropolis',[15] an '"international" meeting place for Jews' (III, 2). Presumably the living relatives are referred to here; and they are understood to have chosen Beth She'arim because they aspired to bury their dead as close as possible to the rabbis. There is an underlying expectation of finding rabbinic authority and charisma extending far and wide in the Jewish world, an expectation which the diaspora epitaphs then seem to confirm.

That there was rabbinic debate, at least from the beginning of the Amoraic period, about the special value of burial in Eretz-Israel is not in doubt. The emergence of a conviction that therein lay a short-cut to both effective atonement and rapid resurrection, together with some evidence for the practice in operation, has been well explored by Isaiah Gafni (1981: 96–104; 1997: 79–95), with healthy scepticism as to any pre-Amoraic manifestations. But we might wish to extend some of that scepticism to the period which runs from the early third century onwards: first, because of the doubts expressed above as to the role of Judah ha-Nasi in the whole process; and second, because the evidence as to the custom over the later period is still disturbingly weak.

Much is made of the late third century discussion (passage 4), intriguingly attached to a specified spot in the town of Tiberias,[16]

---

[15] Avigad and Mazar 1993: 236.

[16] There are two variant readings, each problematic. The *istrin* of Yerushalmi seems to be the stadium (a corruption of *istadin* by change of one letter): while one can scarcely think of an odder place for rabbis to sit and study Torah, the specification might make sense as a geographical marker. *Ilisis* or *ilasis*) in *Genesis Rabbah* is obscure: Lieberman devised a Greek word ὑαλῶσις, to mean a glass factory. Might

between R. bar Qoraia and R. Eleazar (ben Pedat), a discussion whose principal appearances are at two points in the Yerushalmi, and in one MS version of Genesis Rabbah 96 (Vatican 30). That interchange, on the subject of the remission of sins, is said to have been prompted by the discutants' sighting of coffins being carried past which were somehow known to have come from abroad. Bar Qoraia disapproves of the whole business, and expresses his disgust in a strongly-worded quotation from Jeremiah (2:7). The tale is told in such a way as to imply that the sight was a familiar one and Gafni infers that the transports were commonplace at the time of the story's dramatic date. But even without questioning the historicity of the episode, we have to admit that the primary redactor is likely to have overstated the extent of the activity, and this for two reasons: in literary terms, this portrayal gives an extra edge to Bar Qoraia's disapproval; while in religious terms, rabbinic writers had a vested interest in overstressing the popularity of a practice they wished increasingly to endorse and encourage. It was natural to suffuse the past with a rosy glow. To take the further step of assuming that the destination of the coffins in the story was Beth She'arim has no justification.

Apart from the arrival of Rab Huna (passage 5), the deceased Babylonian exilarch, no other explicit Talmudic evidence is forthcoming. Huna, as an international leader, was a special case, all the more so as he is said to have asked to be taken to Israel and then to have been buried in the tomb of R. Hiyya, a Babylonian who lived and worked in Tiberias. We must conclude that, while the ideology of burial in the Land, along with various related doctrines (explored by Gafni) seems to have been evolving in the mid-third century, the actual practice of such burial cannot be deduced from literary evidence and may have been confined to a few very special cases.

So much for the background. Coming now to Beth She'arim itself, we come to primary evidence, in the shape of the diaspora inscriptions from the site. Analysis of this corpus should proceed in the first instance without regard to the rabbinic statements. We can estimate that no more than 20% of individuals named in the Beth

---

one look to the name of the Ilissus, that river of Attica which figures memorably in the landscape setting of Plato's two-person dialogue, the *Phaedrus*? On the passage, see Gafni 1981: 96, n. 3.

She'arim epitaphs are either explicitly associated with a location out-side Eretz-Israel or might for particular reasons be ascribed to one, out of a total of some 200 named persons.[17] Since the origins of local Jews are rarely specified, while those of non-local Jews appear regularly to be so, the count perhaps already has some diagnostic value.

However, it is when the locations of all known diaspora burials are mapped out that the picture is telling. The merest glance reveals that these range across the east: not one is located west of Palestine. It is a simple fact that only Jews from (roughly speaking) east of Eretz-Israel found their way as corpses or bones to Beth She'arim. However, while the point has not gone unnoticed, its implications are overlooked. We should further observe that, within this wide belt, few regions are represented in any kind of quantity. Even more significant is the marked concentration of graves connected with the Syro-Phoenician coastline, and there we cannot fail to remark that we are dealing with a region geographically continuous with the Western Galilee. Via Caesarea, the route thence along the Jezreel valley to Beth She'arim is an easy one. When we move from map to data, further doubts arise. Gafni has argued effectively that dias-pora Jews buried in Judaea before A.D. 70 either came originally from or at some stage made their home in the land of Israel: it is worth asking how many later burials there of individuals associated with the diaspora can be understood in the same way.

The most important case is the Palmyrenes, already mentioned. 4 or 5 generations of Palmyrene Jews are interred in catacomb 1, occupying halls C, E, G and K. They are represented by 33 surviv-ing inscriptions, although hall G alone had an estimated 44 burials. There are some Palmyrene names, alongside those of Greek or Jewish character, in three of the four halls, and these names, together with some use of the Palmyrene language there, suggest that the link with Palmyra was reasonably fresh. There are also Palmyrene burials in catacombs 3 and 4; in catacomb 18 we have Zenobia, daughter of Karteria.[18] Palmyra fell to Aurelian in A.D. 272/3. The excavators' hypothesis, insofar as we can disentangle it, seems to be that Palmyrene

---

[17] Precise quantification is impeded by the organization of the three volumes, with the published inscriptions divided between the volumes, and also separated by language. Some readings are unpersuasive.

[18] See below pp. 492–493.

Jews began the practice of transporting bones to a final resting place in the land of Israel at some point earlier in the third century, and that later some families emigrated there as a consequence of the Roman conquest of Palmyra in 272/3. One such, it is asserted, was the family of the Isaac son of Mokimos, whose name is inscribed above the entrance lintel of a hall, in Greek and separately in Hebrew (nos. 18, 19, 20, 23), and who is therefore considered to have owned the hall; it is further proposed that his father Mokim's remains had been carried by the emigrating family to Beth She'arim.

Yet a simpler reconstruction is available: this and other Palmyrene families may well have became resident in the area before rather than after they started using Beth She'arim as their cemetery, and their move need not be connected with the destruction of 272/3. The Palmyrene burials at Beth She'arim span several generations: Julianus son of Leontios and brother of Rabbi Paregori(o)s (no. 61 in hall K), judged by the editors part of a Palmyrene family, is titled *palatinus*, an imperial post which puts him firmly in the fourth century. A predictable process of acculturation is detectable over the period. Thus, altogether, among the surviving texts there are 5 in Hebrew, and among the names, various are biblical; but only hall G contains no surviving inscriptions in Palmyrene. In addition, the designation 'rabbi' recurs: one individual, Isaac son of Joseph, is called *biribbi*.[19] We seem, then, to be dealing with a rabbinized dynasty rather than with a typical Palmyrene family. Rabbinic families are not a known phenomenon in the Greco-Roman diaspora. Palmyra, subject to Babylonian influence, may, admittedly, have been different; but it is more likely that the family turned rabbinic after early settlement in the land of Israel. We should note that, in Palmyra itself, the Jewish community has left scarcely a trace (Schürer III.1 1986: 14–15).

Three diaspora *archisynagogoi* figure among the burials:[20] Eusebios, or Eusebis, from Beirut, designated *lamprotatos* (164), Jose of Sidon (Σιδονος), whose name is painted in red in an arcosolium of catacomb 26 (221), and, finally, Iakos (Jacob) of Caesarea, named on a marble slab found in the town synagogue[21] and described as an

---

[19] 40, in hall G. On the term, see above, p. 481.
[20] On the social significance of the office, Rajak & Noy 1993 = Ch. 20 in this volume.
[21] 203: apparently a tomb, since it ends with the formula *shalom*.

archisynagogos and a Pamphylian. Whether we should attach Iakos' tenure of office to Pamphylia or to Caesarea is unclear, although the original editors opt unhesitatingly for the latter. A fourth *archisynagogos* may have been mentioned in fragmentary text no. 212. In catacomb 12 (nos. 141–143), we find the gerousiarch Aidesios from Antioch, designated *kratistos*; his stone proudly declares that he is surrounded by six of his kinsmen (or their tombs).[22]

Synagogue leaders, especially the heads, *archisynagogoi*, cultivated international connections, just as did their pagan urban counterparts. One of the mosaic texts from the synagogue at Apamea honours an Antiochene gerousiarch, Ilasios, and two of the names of his ascendants, including Aidesios, suggest him to be of the family of the Beth She'arim gerousiarch.[23] So we might find burial in a great necropolis in Palestine an unsurprising outcome for the two notables from along the coast. As for Iakos, he will simply have left Pamphylia (probably the town of Side) to reside at (presumably Palestinian) Caesarea.

The dead of the Phoenician and Syrian coast are clustered in hall B of catacomb 12, which they occupy in its entirety, and in some of catacomb 13. One whole burial room there belongs to a Sidonian called Aristeas. That his tomb is described in the red-paint inscription of his arcosolium (172) by the Greek word μάκρα, a term current in the funerary epigraphy of Syria and related areas, suggests a live connection with his place of origin.[24] Another of the commemorated is a *cohen* (Χωήν) from Beirut (βυρίτιος; 148). Joint action, not only by kinship groups but also by particular communities, may have facilitated both the acquisition of space and the arrangements required for the transportation of bones. Indeed, it is tempting to add the thought that the presence and expected presence of compatriots on the spot will have enhanced the value of investment in an impressive location, even where the funerary monument itself may

---

[22] The word which has been read, κρηπίδες, bases, may be unique to Beth She'arim in this sense. Robert wrote (*REG* 69, 1956, *BE* 340): 'nouveau à Besara et peut-être en général comme nom de la tombe; sans doute dans le Talmud' (!) Cf. now no. 50, a damaged text where κρηπίς seems to appear in the singular form. It may be noted that Aidesios' short inscription has also another word for tomb, ἄψις, which according to Robert may be new in this sense.

[23] Accepted by Revised Schürer: 3.1, 15.

[24] J. and L. Robert, *REG* 69 (1956) 341. They regard Beth She'arim as itself falling naturally within the sphere of Syrian cultural influence.

have been modest. For the exercise diminishes in value if no one is ever there to be a spectator.

But where an ethnic designation represents an isolated case, no general conclusions should be drawn, as in the case of Sarah Maxima of Misene (Meishan) in Babylonia (102) or of the one word painted in red above an arcosolium in catacomb 7 (111; *CIJ* II, 1138). The latter scarcely suffices to justify confident claims that the other three surviving inscriptions in this catacomb are Himyarite.[25] A reasonable supposition is that this one recorded Himyarite individual died while visiting or while residing in Palestine, just as presumably happened to the individual Alexandrians, Egyptians, Cyrenaicans, Tarsians, Cappadocians, and Babylonians who were buried and commemorated in Jaffa.[26] Patently less credible is the bizarre conjecture propounded in relation to an editorial attempt to match up a name on a marble tablet in the synagogue with that in an epitaph from the Palmyrene group, that the deceased lived locally and therefore that 'there were Jews who came to spend their last days in Beth She'arim, in order to be buried there' (III, 3).

The Beth She'arim reports are inclined to ascribe any irregular or awkward data to Jews from the diaspora. For example, the name of Daniel, the son of Adda from Tyre, appears at the entrance to catacomb 19. Avigad (III, 82) surmised that the inscribed tablet was made in Tyre and was brought with his corpse (or bones?) to Palestine, on the grounds that the masons seem not to have known how to execute properly the 'shin' of the final *shalom*,[27] with the consequence that Daniel would then have to be deemed to have died in Tyre. Again, the freedwoman of Procopius in catacomb 20 is gratuitously ascribed to outside Palestine.

In the case of the well-known Greek verse epitaph erected for Karteria on a finely engraved white marble slab, probably as part of a mausoleum, by her daughter Zenobia, 'at her mother's behest',

---

[25] On the Jews of Himyar, see Revised Schürer: 3.1, 15–16. The Himyarite origin of the 'elder', Manae, no. 110, *CIJ* II, 1137, is there accepted, as it is by J. and L. Robert in *REG* 74, 1961, *BE* 808, who simply run his inscription together with the following one; but the report ascribes them to different locations.

[26] For Alexandrians, see *CIJ* II, 895, 928 (a rag-dealer), 934; Egyptians—920 (a centurion); 930 (a priest); and possibly 902 (a Levite); Cappadocian—910; 931 (a Cappadocian linen merchant from Tarsus); a Cyrenaican from the Pentapolis—950. But see Gafni 1997: 90, who takes these as examples of deceased brought for burial.

[27] This inscription is apparently not catalogued in Schwabe and Lifshitz's volume II; the 'shin' is actually quite legible: see plate xxix, no. 5.

and paid for by Zenobia,[28] a text whose Homeric turns of phrase were noted by its editors (II, 157–167), a misleading impression arises from the translation offered. The text, found in 16 fragments, tells us merely that

> This grave contains the perishable remains of noble Karteria, preserving imperishable her glorious memory. Zenobia laid her here, and fulfilling her mother's wish. For you, blessed one, the fruit which you bore from your gentle womb, a pious daughter, has built this, for she always does deeds praiseworthy among mortals, so that, even after life's limits, you may both enjoy new untouched riches.

The word rendered here as 'laid', θήκατο, is translated misleadingly and tendentiously as 'brought' by Schwabe, and others have followed suit.[29] If we allow ourselves to be led by what is written, and to go no further, then the following points emerge. The piety of the daughter lies, it seems, in the provision of the tomb; there does not seem to be any question of transportation over a distance, let alone of any particular cachet in a burial in the Land. Nor, certainly, is there any suggestion that Karteria's deposition at Beth She'arim involved exhumation and reinterment. Zenobia's name, of course, bespeaks a Palmyrene connection. But both could have lived and died at Beth She'arim itself, or at Beth She'an, or else up the road at Sepphoris, or even at Caesarea. It is to be noted that the subject of Beth She'arim's second, even more Homeric, verse epitaph,[30] equally well-inscribed, is a local boy. Justus, son of Leontios whose mother's name is speculatively restored as Sappho.[31] He describes himself as having gone to Hades, a victim of *moira*, while his inconsolable parents remain behind at Besara, Beth She'arim.[32] The family's capacity to deploy the language of Greek mythology is unlikely to have hindered their ability to participate in the life of Beth She'arim's fine synagogue.

Negative arguments are not enough. Having insisted upon what Beth She'arim was not, a depiction of what it may have been is called for. Several considerations favour an understanding of this

---

[28] No. 183. Cf. *SEG* XVI.829.

[29] And also by van der Horst 1991: 152–3, no. 9.

[30] 127; Van der Horst: 151–2, no. 8.

[31] Presumably on the model of the name Sapho (*sic*) which figures in no. 27.

[32] The accepted reading 'his' Besara, οἷς, is pure guesswork. For the gravestone of another inhabitant of Beth She'arim, found out of context at Ben Shemen, and published by Avi-Yonah and Lifshitz in 1941, see L. and J. Robert, *REG* 59, 1946–7, *BE* 220.

extended and elaborate development as a glorified local cemetery, whose catchment area happens to be rather large. First, we should take into account the position of the site within easy reach of the heartland of post-70 Palestinian Judaism, as also of routes north: not only by means of the coast road, but also, via the Jezreel valley, up the centre of the country. Parts of this region, especially the upper Galilee and the Golan, was quite densely populated by Jews; elsewhere the Jewish population was more dispersed. Throughout, Jews were rarely to be found as majorities in cities, or even in their own exclusive villages, but rather they were spread among other inhabitants of various ethnic affiliations and located in a predominantly Hellenized and Romanized society.[33] So concentration of burial will have had obvious convenience, even if, predictably, Jews also continued to be buried where they lived, as we can see from stones found at Jaffa and also at Caesarea and at Tiberias.[34] It is true that extensive catacombs have been discovered, though not explored, in the vicinity of Sepphoris.[35] But in many other places, a purely Jewish burial area will have been unsustainable, at least at certain periods: when local relations were tense, the acquisition of land by a Jewish family or individual will not have been easy.

It is also useful to look back in time. A tradition of centralized burial derived from pre-70 practice in and around Jerusalem. It may be significant that the distinctive system of that area reached Beth She'arim: the catacombs are reported as containing a substantial number of *kokh* burials (III, 261–262), and it seems clear that deposition followed by later secondary burial was practised: no other explanation has been offered for the apparent sharing of one coffin by three individuals announced in inscription no. 21.

Many Beth She'arim epitaphs give no place of origin or residence for the deceased, but specification is evidently more usual in the case of families from abroad; hence our knowledge of a range of provenances. Nevertheless, a few exceptions do exist, of locations which, if correctly identified, are closer to home. Though too few to be more than suggestive, these fall into two interesting groups.[36] There

---

[33] See Millar 1993: 374–86. Sepphoris may, exceptionally, have been a sizeable town which remained predominantly Jewish.

[34] Jaffa: *CIJ* II, 892–60; Caesarea: *CIJ* II, 886–90; Tiberias: *CIJ* II, 984–6.

[35] So I learn from Professor Eric Meyers.

[36] See no. 51: Ἀραπηνῶ = 'from 'Arav'; 81: Βεκηνῶ = 'from the Beka'; 60: Χορήθου = from Havarah or Havariah, near Beth-She'arim; 26: Μενωνίτου = from

is a pair which have been ascribed to the vicinity of Beth She'an (Scythopolis): the first, no. 51, is reasonably securely identified with 'Arav in Galilee; the second, 60, was read by the editors, somewhat dubiously, as a Greek form of Havariah. Beth She'an was not far away and was a predominantly pagan city: further unattributed burials in Beth She'arim might well belong to Jews from its territory. The other group comprises the Beka (81), Phaene, a town in Trachonitis (178), and Yahmur (138–140), also there. These parts of Syria had been ruled by Herodians and had direct access to the Galilee. While the evidence is meagre, these are certainly appropriate catchment areas for Beth She'arim. We may add here the Yerushalmi gloss about the bringing in of the wealthy dead from Caesarea.[37]

Several elements, among them the character of the local environment, relations with neighbours, relative costs and sheer habit will then have contributed to the choice of final resting place; among these factors, we need not altogether exclude some sense of attraction towards the land of Israel. Living close to, yet outside its borders, this was for the inhabitants of the nearer parts of Syria an obvious point of reference, whose pull did not depend on either rabbinic doctrine or on the presence of rabbinic dead.

The construction of the necropolis will have been a sizeable commercial enterprise, involving a range of trades and quite sophisticated skills, as was grasped by its discoverers. There were imported artefacts, such as the lead sarcophagi from Phoenicia and the standard marble types common in the empire, some of which were probably transported by sea, perhaps landing at Caesarea. The importation of this merchandise has been simplistically connected with the putative passage of corpses for reinterment: the former may not be invoked as evidence for the latter. Empty coffins were often finished and decorated on arrival (III, 138): Beth She'arim carving is not overall of a particularly high standard, although there are exceptions, notably the two acanthus sarcophagi (III, 150–153). A distinctively Jewish sarcophagus displaying a menorah comes from catacomb 20. That the town of Beth She'arim benefited from this commerce is not overlooked in

---

Ma'on in Judaea; 178 (cf. III, pp. 70–1): Φαινήσιος = from Phaene in Trachonitis. And from further afield: 119, 121: Ἡσιττῶν, Ἀσίας = perhaps 'from Asia' (i.e. Etzion-Geber); 101: Μισηνή = from Meishan, in Babylonia; 138–140: Ἰαμουρίτης = from Yahmur, east of Sidon.

[37] See above p. 483.

the original publication (III, 263–265); and, indeed, some interpreters ascribe to the burial industry the entire urban development of the place (III, 2). However that may be, the Beth She'arim project was apparently able to keep expanding.

We do not know what the mechanism was for acquiring a family or an individual space within a catacomb. One might hypothesize the existence of some body comparable to the *fossores* who created and sold off space in the Christian catacombs of Rome and whose equivalent were probably responsible for the Jewish catacombs there. A Hebrew epitaph, that of a man who is described as a rabbi and whose name is Hillel son of R. Levi, is painted on the cover of his sarcophagus (ארון no. 28, in catacomb 20): this describes the deceased as 'the one who made this cave'. Avigad argues (III, 251–254) that the reference is to the artisan himself. However, even if such be the case, we cannot say whether 'this cave' המערה הזו means a catacomb, a section, a hall or a niche. Robert suggests that the unusual expression ὅλος οἶκος in connection with Aristeas refers to one *arcosolium* in hall L of catacomb 13.[38] Where names are inscribed on the lintels of the doorways to the burial areas, as is quite common at Beth She'arim, these are normally taken to refer to the owners of the space within. Women too could be owners, as was Thyme in hall C of catacomb 1. A systematic analysis of these marks of ownership has not so far been undertaken.

Weiss (1992: 362–366) reasonably invokes as applicable to this context the rabbinic presumption that burial is a family responsibility, with the poor assisted by clubs or benevolent societies, *havurot*. The process was thus, he suggests, unconnected with any specific urban or synagogal institution. There were probably guilds of professional mourners and eulogists, though precise evidence is lacking. A well-known Greek inscription from the synagogue area (202) commemorates a man, Samuel, described as ὁ συστέλλων and another, Juda, who is called ὁ κοιμῶν, both of these seemingly verbs which refer to aspects of funerary ritual.[39] The suggestion is that such services were available on site together with those of other operatives

---

[38] Cf. below p. 497 and n. 22.

[39] On the original editors' interpretation of these two roles as 'the preparer' and 'the burier', and for Alon's alternative understanding (based on Talmudic terminology) as 'the wrapper in shrouds' and 'the singer of dirges', see Weiss 1992: 363, n. 35. Cf. also L. and J. Robert, in *REG* 74, 1961, *BE* 808.

such as gravediggers and flute players, also (unsurprisingly) mentioned in Talmudic literature.

The details elude us, but the point is clear: with services of this kind in place, and with the sophistication and scale of the set-up, burial at this most developed and best known of sites will have been expeditious to arrange and relatively economical for those within reach, even allowing for some transport costs. It was also attractive in its offer of a degree of permanence—even if not everything could be provided for, as we see from the recurrence at Beth She'arim of the curse-inscriptions which threaten dire consequences to violators of graves and which are ubiquitous in pagan and Jewish worlds alike. There are two in Aramaic (from catacomb 12) and several in Greek, one unusually long. That of Hesychios (catacomb 13) is unique in attacking the miscreants' share in eternal life (129).

While only charity, a client-patron relationship, or prior family provision could have made burial at Beth She'arim available to the really poor, we should not suppose that the majority of the burials we see are those of the seriously rich from far afield, like today's occupants of prominent tombs on the Mount of Olives. There was ample scope for a middling element: most catacombs appear to have been much more crowded than catacombs 14 and to have contained far fewer sarcophagi than catacomb 20. Catacomb 12 was generous in plan, catacomb 13 congested. There is no reason to regard this disparity as necessarily conditioned by chronology. Sarcophagi were often made of limestone rather than marble, and many remains of wooden coffins have been found. There were numerous pit burials in the floors of the catacombs. Occupations of individuals specifically mentioned on the site are a cloth dyer (188), a cloth merchant (189), a physician (81), perfume dealers (79 and 168), a goldsmith (61) and two Palmyrene bankers (92). These were men of substance, perhaps, but that is no doubt precisely why they chose to state what they did, and even so, they scarcely came from the top social echelons. More ordinary men had less cause to mention their trades, or to have them mentioned by their commemorators.

Conclusion

It emerges that neither patriarchs nor rabbis are to be assigned more than a minor part in the development and functioning of the Beth She'arim cemetery. Their burials are concentrated in confined areas,

distinguished by the deliberate use of Hebrew.[40] There is no reason
to think that rabbinic authorities or any powerful groups within rabbinic society were anywhere near controlling the site, in terms either
of practice or of economics. The remarkable evolution of Eretz-
Israel's leading cemetery was a visibly independent process. It is
tempting, indeed, to view the rabbinic role at Beth She'arim as a
sort of physical correlative of the rabbinic role in Jewish society: the
rabbis had to fit in while others called the tune.

It also emerges that Jews from adjacent diaspora locations, but
quite possibly no others, used Beth She'arim as a burial ground.
Stray individuals should be discounted. The diaspora burials are a
highly regional phenomenon. Although that limits the relevance of
the cemetery to the study of the Greco-Roman diaspora. But there
is still much to be learnt. The hint of close links of a special kind
between Eretz-Israel and the Jews of neighbouring regions, in particular the Phoenician cities, but also, it appears, Trachonitis and
Ituraea is of considerable interest, challenging, among other things,
any simple understanding of the Diaspora/Palestine divide, and suggesting, rather, a graduated continuum of Jewish cultures.

It remains hard to say what resonances the land of Israel carried
for the main body of diaspora Jews in the Greco-Roman cities during the third and fourth centuries. It is impossible to establish a
definite link between that world and the doctrines of burial in the
Land. As for those coffins which are supposed to have streamed past
the two rabbis as they studied Torah in some public place in Tiberias,
and which generated their disagreement, we have no idea whence
they are meant to have come or what dead lay inside them. One
might indeed be tempted to deem them fictitious, a transparent device
for bringing a rabbinic debate to life. If that is the case, the fiction
has been a highly successful one, creating precisely the desired impression in the minds of students of succeeding generations.[41]

[40] The language has been judged 'pure Mishnaic', but the fragmentary texts do
not permit confidence.
[41] Pleasant debts have been incurred in the preparation of this paper for publication: to Professor Isaiah Gafni of the Hebrew University, Jerusalem, for his tolerant reactions, and particularly for making available a pre-publication text of his
book; to Dr Sacha Stern of Jews' College, London, for help with checking and cor-
relating Talmudic references by electronic and other means; to Dr Oded Irshai of
the Hebrew University for introducing me to Ratner's collection of mediaeval glosses;
and to Professor Sean Freyne of Trinity College, Dublin, for his responses to my
paper on this subject read at the Royal Irish Academy in spring 1997, as well as
to others who participated in the discussion.

Bibliography

1. Publication of site and inscriptions

A numeral appearing alone refers to an inscription number in volume II of Beth She'arim; where a Roman numeral precedes, the reference is to volume and page.

Avigad, N. 1976. *Beth She'arim* III. *Catacombs 12–23. report on the Excavations during 1953–58.* Jerusalem.
Mazar, B. 1973. *Beth She'arim* I. *Report on the Excavations during 1936–40.* Jerusalem.
Schwabe, M. & Lifshitz, B. 1974. *Beth She'arim* II. *The Greek Inscriptions.* New Brunswick.

2. Other works

Avigad, A. & Mazar, B. 1993. 'Beth She'arim', in E. Stern, A. Lewinson, J. Gilboa & I. Aviram (eds), *The New Encyclopedia of Archaeological Excavations in the Holy Land.* New York.
Cohen, S.J.D. 1981. 'Patriarchs and Scholarchs', *PAAJR* 48: 57–68.
——— 1981–82. 'Epigraphical Rabbis', *JQR* 72: 1–17.
——— 1992. 'The Place of the Rabbi in Jewish Society of the Second Century', in L.I. Levine (ed.), *The Galilee in Late Antiquity.* New York/Jerusalem, 157–74.
Gafni, I. 1981. 'Reinterment in the Land of Israel: Notes on the development of the custom', *The Jerusalem Cathedra*, 96–104.
——— 1997. *Land, Center and Diaspora. Jewish Constructs in Late Antiquity.* Sheffield.
Goodman, M. 1983. State and Society in Roman Galilee A.D. 132–212. Totowa, New Jersey.
van der Horst, P.W. 1991. *Ancient Jewish Epitaphs. An Introductory Survey of a Millennium of Jewish Funerary Epigraphy (300 B.C.E.–700 C.E.).* Contributions to Biblical Exegesis and Theology 2. Kampen.
Levine, L.I. 1985. *The Rabbinic Class of Roman Palestine in Late Antiquity.* Jerusalem/New York.
——— 1989. 'The finds at Beth She'arim and their importance for the study of the Talmudic Period' (Hebrew), *Eretz Israel* 18:277–281.
——— 1997. 'Beth She'arim', in E.M. Meyers (ed.), *The Oxford Encyclopedia of Archaeology in the Near East*, vol. 1. Oxford.
Millar, F. 1993. *The Roman Near East.* Cambridge, Mass./London.
Negev, A. (ed.). 1990. *The Archaeological Encyclopedia of the Holy Land*, 3rd edition. New York.
Rajak, T. & Noy, D. 1993. '*Archisynagogoi*: Office, Title and Social Status in the Greco-Jewish Synagogue', *JRS* 83: 75–93 = C.5 in this volume.
Weiss, Z. 1992. 'Social Aspects of Burial in Beth She'arim: Archaeological finds and Talmudic Sources', in L.I. Levine (ed.), *The Galilee in Late Antiquity.* New York/Jerusalem, 357–372.

PART FOUR

EPILOGUE

CHAPTER TWENTY-FIVE

JEWS, SEMITES AND THEIR CULTURES IN FERGUS MILLAR'S *ROMAN NEAR EAST*

Jewish territory is a tiny part of the vast area explored in Millar's *Roman Near East 31 B.C.–A.D. 337*[1] (henceforward *RNE*). The subject of this monumental study is defined as a 'series of linked regions between the Taurus Mountains and the Red Sea which were progressively subjected to Roman rule', or again as 'the western and northern tip of the Fertile Crescent, the area of cultivable land closely tied to mountain-chains which linked the Mediterranean and Egypt with Babylonia, Iran and the head of the Persian Gulf', and yet again 'approximately, as that part of the Near East which fell to the Islamic invaders of the seventh century'. This geographical scope is wider than might be expected from the title, for it is often overlooked that, during the too-little studied years of the second century A.D., a renewed bout of Roman imperial expansion took in first (in the 160's) a large territory going south along the Euphrates and then (in the 190's) a tract running north east along the river Chabur in the direction of Nisibis. Judaea and Syria-Palestina add up to less than a half of one out of twelve of the sketch maps accompanying the text.

Yet that marginal and unimpressive territory is in many ways at the heart of the book, emerging as crucial to Millar's conceptual understanding of the whole region. There also existed, of course, a significant Jewish presence in many of the other territories under discussion, notably Babylonia, Adiabene (the Assyria of former ages), Antioch and other important cities on the Syrian coast, Roman Arabia. The Jews of those regions do not have much part to play in Millar's study, with the exception of those inhabitants of Arabia whose lives are illuminated by the Babatha archive,[2] and some brief

---

[1] Millar 1993.

[2] In Appendix B, Millar offers a chronological handlist of all the then-available documentary material (including coins) from the area controlled by the Jewish rebels under Bar-Kokhba. This remains very useful, alongside the relevant section of a wider, more recent survey, by the author together with H.M. Cotton and W.E.H.

remarks on the subject matter of the Dura Europus synagogue paintings. Even the revolt under Trajan falls outside its scope. Probably
because the book is in essence a search for local ethnicities and a
discussion of the possibility of finding long-standing continuities, as
well as of the Graeco-Roman attrition of such continuities as there
were, there is little advantage in looking at minority communities
within the ethnic areas. The interaction of the major players is quite
complicated enough in itself. By contrast, however, and almost paradoxically, Jewish life in the Jewish spheres of dominance is analysed
meticulously and invoked as a point of reference.

In its 'take' on Jewish history, the picture which emerges is a
healthily unfashionable one. For the result of placing the Jewry of
Palestine in a highly localized setting is to reinstate a disjunction
from the Diaspora which recent scholarship has been keen to minimize. On the other hand, it is equally against the background of
this localized setting that the remarkable particularity of Jewish society and culture emerges. After reading Millar, one will never again
be able to sink back into comfortable generalizations about Semitic
ways of doing things—firstly, because he goes a long way towards
persuading us that there was no such general category, except in
the linguistic sphere and secondly because of the many ways in which
the Jews do turn out to be in so many respects *sui generis*. This is a
point of view to which Millar has long been attached, sometimes in
explicit argument, as in his influential 'Reflections on the Maccabaean
Revolt' published in this journal,[3] often implicitly. For those of us
who may have been a little reluctant to follow down this path, there
is now much food for thought. The modest purpose of my discussion here is to open a debate on the key arguments in *RNE* about
the particularity of the Jews in their Middle Eastern environment.
It is fair to say that these have scarcely yet been taken on board,
although the book belongs to the early nineties.

One might mention, however, that the issue of the distinctiveness
or otherwise of Judaism in the Classical context was the connecting
thread in a recent collective volume which considers Palestine and
the Diaspora together.[4] There the cumulative evidence is organized

---

Cockle (1995). See also now the subsequent full publication of the Nahal Hever
material in Cotton & Yardeni 1997.
    [3] Millar 1978: 1–21.
    [4] Goodman 1998.

so as to point, perhaps unsurprisingly, in both directions, towards both differences and similarities between Jews and non-Jews. That necessitates a nuanced editorial conclusion but also generates, as a sort of tie-breaker, the editor's thought-provoking hypothesis that the Jews were no more nor less peculiar than other ethnic groups in the Graeco-Roman world, such as Idumaeans, Celts or Numidians, but that they appear to have greater 'oddities' purely because of the weight of our evidence for them, yielded above all by the survival of their own literature. We need not concern ourselves here with the major difficulties for this hypothesis arising from the simple fact that those other peoples simply did not produce literatures on any significant scale, while the Jews (like the Christians) did, and were *ipso facto* 'odder'. What is relevant, however, is to note the worrying absence of any real *comparandum* when the question is put in such broad terms. There is no general statement of who the Jews are supposed to be like or unlike.

This is one way in which *RNE*, the product of immersion in the history and geography of a defined, if extensive, region together with prolonged reflection, offers something distinctly new and why the perspectives offered there deserve to be noticed by historians of Judaism as much as by historians of Rome. Here we can look at the Jews of Palestine against a perfectly concrete background. That this background is, and must remain, very imperfectly known, is made abundantly clear throughout the book: indeed the limitations of our evidence and the insurmountable gaps in our knowledge are in themselves a theme of this—as ever—resolutely empirical scholar. Yet in spite of the gaps, as the story unfolds, we see the divergences shaping up and we are able to perceive many areas in which fuller knowledge would make no difference at all to the overall assessment of where the Jews stand in relation to their neighbours. In fact, once we leave the Second Temple period, the Jews, like their neighbours, are studied in the main from the archaeological evidence (including under this heading the various kinds of documentary material); in particular the author announces at an early stage a methodological rejection of the resources of Talmudic literature. In this way Millar might be said to have anticipated Goodman's proposal and dealt with it.

The underlying theme of *RNE* is the confrontation of a range of peoples with Graeco-Roman 'civilization' and the near-submersion of their own cultures. The discussion operates with a fairly precise and rather inclusive definition of a culture, as 'a tradition, an educational system, a set of customs and above all a collective understanding of the past.' (p. 517). Cultural traffic, it is argued, went almost exclusively one way, and that was eastwards (p. 332). Hellenization was therefore the dominant process through most of this extensive period. By the end of the second century A.D., a fair number of once significant cultures were profoundly attenuated, among them that of the Nabataeans who had produced fairly elaborate legal texts (pp. 507–508; 521). In the Decapolis, East of the Jordan, once a bilingual Greek-Aramaic zone, Semitic-language inscriptions die out in the second century, while Greek texts are abundant (p. 413). Deities of renown, such as Hadad of Damascus who cannot be reliably located inside the well-known later Damascene cult of Zeus, were on their way to being forgotten (pp. 314–316). To that near-submersion the Jews are the great exception. A major discovery in the book is the surprisingly dim presence of any general Syrian cultural identity: an exhaustive search reveals little in common between the different smaller ethnicities, although there is some basis to the commonly held view that aniconic cults, with stones as the cult objects, were characteristic of the entire area, and it is indeed on this theme that Millar's study opens (pp. 12–14; 522). Syriac literature, when it emerged within the Christian ambit, developed not, as it happens, in Syria but further east, for it originated in Mesopotamia before the Roman occupation and spread in Persian territory as much as in Roman (p. 520). Indeed, in Millar's view, no link is demonstrable between Syrian culture and the emergence of Christianity. Again, then, the Jews, with their indisputably unbroken traditions, form an exception.

There were no clear boundaries to the Jewish region, North, South or East, and Jews were often interspersed among others, perhaps living the village existence which was characteristic of the region and desribed as its most important social formation (p. 350), or perhaps inhabitants of mixed cities, of which only a few, such as Lydda, contained Jewish majorities. Like all other peoples, the Jews were exposed to the massive impact of the Roman legions' ever-growing presence in the area, a process which is easily underestimated (chapter 3). After the suppression of the Bar Kokhba revolt in 135, they were subjected to the imposition of two *coloniae* of which one occupied Jerusalem and the Temple site itself, to a high-status consular governor, and to a security force of two entire legions together with a substantial number of auxiliary cohorts. And yet, when assembled, the dossier of Jewish cultural resilience is striking, as it emerges from both the broad sweep of the chronological narratives at the start of the book and from the richly detailed geographical and cultural surveys which follow. A few of the points in this dossier are unfamiliar. Many are not. It is the authority with which Millar can judge them against their background which gives them all a new resonance and which lends power to the cumulative argument.

1. The long retention of Aramaic as a written and spoken language, continuing into a period when many other users have seemingly abandoned it (p. 521).

2. Widespread bilingualism or even, where Hebrew was included, trilingualism. The Syrian town of Palmyra is found to be the other great exception in this respect, and presented as the only other society to produce a large corpus of genuinely bilingual inscriptions testifing to a 'fully-tangible Graeco-Syrian or Graeco-Aramaic culture' (pp. 319–336).

3. The persistence, in the shape of the Bible, of a communally-protected text, more lasting, distinct and political than any other (p. 340). This offered a continuing frame of reference and a repertoire of meanings for current events, in a way in which the Jewish literature of the Hellenistic period seemed not to do in the Roman imperial era.

4. A virtually unique sense of historical continuity, contrasted with the apparent 'amnesia' elsewhere (p. 6). The Dura Europus synagogue paintings are viewed in this light, as expressing a link with a distant past, which is reinforced by their Greek and Aramaic labelling, and which appears to be locally unparallelled except in the modest decorations of the house church of Dura (p. 470). Here, the only possible exception might be Phoenicia, where Philo of Byblos' scholarly production contains some real elements of an inherited national tradition in the shape of some local history, myths, names, and knowledge of deities.

5. The role of Jerusalem, until A.D. 70, as a focal point, the object, for those in the region (as contrasted with the far-flung communities of the Diaspora) of frequent regular visits and the natural place for the celebration of the festivals by all classes of people (pp. 364–365).[5]

---

[5] What happened after 70 is more problematic. Millar's observations on the role of the Temple might now be both reinforced and qualified in the light of the interesting rabbinic attempts by Babylonian Geonim to annex the former authority of

6. The leadership role of the high priests down to A.D. 70, even conceding, as Millar seems to, Martin Goodman's claim that this *arriviste* aristocracy lacked real roots in Jewish society (pp. 361; 365–366).

7. Herod's role as proponent of Hellenism through the Roman empire: contrary to the common assumption, this is not paralleled by the activities of other oriental 'client kings' under Rome (p. 354). Thus, from a Jewish kingdom there emerged a significant innovation in this manner of paying homage to Roman power and to Greek culture while demonstrating continued respect for the home institutions.

8. Two major and unparalleled popular revolts against Rome, taken as a manifestation of national spirit (pp. 69; 352–353).

9. The distinctive socio-religious phenomenon in the post-70 period of rabbinic status, with the use of the title 'rabbi', attested archaeologically if we follow Millar's understanding of several Beth She'arim texts (pp. 381–382).[6]

10. The erection of the peculiar oblong monumental structures which we identify as synagogues—although only rarely do these carry inscriptions identifying what they are, as in Rabbi Eliezer ha-Qappar's Beth-Midrash at Dabbura on the Golan and probably in the Greek inscription from the Qasyon synagogue near Zefat (pp. 381–382).

It cannot be denied that this is a mixed bag. Thus catalogued, these are phenomena which bear witness as much to change in Jewish circumstances as to continuity, and one is led to think that it is perhaps the adaptability of the Jews that deserves further examination. Do these features add up to a 'culture'? In Millar's terms, the fit is neat, yet the nagging question arises as to whether this result might not be due to the shape of the enquiry, whether perhaps the specific Jewish case has not in a sense set the terms for the rest of the investigation, rather than the other way round. In other words, where others appear to have lacked what the Jews had, their culture is seen

---

Jerusalem, especially in assertions that their synagogues were built from Temple rubble. See the discussion by Gafni 1997: 115.

[6] There is some recent support for the title here as designating more than just 'gentleman' in the arguments of Heszer 1997: 60–61; 119–122, with the proviso that rabbinic circles were not necessarily closed or Torah scholars confined to those who figure in Talmudic literature.

as incomplete. The chosen definition of culture fits the Jews so very well that other groups may perhaps be expected to fail at the first hurdle. We might ask, therefore, whether an independent educational system is a *sine qua non*, given that levels of literacy vary greatly between one culture and another, as anthropologists are well aware. Furthermore, we do well to reflect, in passing, on how far such a system can be traced even in Jewish society until well after the first century. Even the importance of group memory, so crucial to Judaism as we understand it, may be cautiously questioned. There are societies where family and individual memory is considerably stronger than it has been in many Jewish environments, but group memory weaker. Might the other kinds of memory not serve in their own way as a force conducive to group preservation? The necessary dominance of Greek values in the whole discussion and the inevitability of hindsight are additional factors which make it hard for us to conceive of alternative structures and ways of doing things, but that is what this enquiry is really about. Millar shows himself highly conscious of the hazards of 'orientalism', in the sense of ascribing to eastern peoples common, stereotypic characteristics. This sensitivity has surely encouraged his caution over grouping together disparate 'Semitic' phenomena or forms of religious behaviour visible in different parts of Syria at different times. Yet it is perhaps not unfair to suggest that he has not succeeded entirely in the enterprise of taking the Near East on its own terms. *RNE* conjures up much of the magic of the region's geography. But perhaps there remains, if one may be permitted to say so, an oriental mystery in its history, which still eludes us. The paradigm of Jewish society takes us only so far.

BIBLIOGRAPHY

Cotton, H.M., Cockle, W.E.H. & Rajak, T. 1995. 'The Papyrology of the Roman Near East: A Survey', *JRS* 85: 214–235.

Cotton H.M. & Yardeni, A. 1997. *Aramaic, Hebrew and Greek Documentary Texts from Nahal Hever and Other Sites. Discoveries in the Judaean Desert* XXVII. Oxford.

Gafni, I. 1997. *Land, Center and Diaspora: Jewish Constructs in Late Antiquity*. Sheffield.

Goodman, M. (ed.). 1998. *The Jews in a Greco-Roman World*. Oxford.

Heszer, C. 1997. *The Social Structure of the Rabbinic Movement in Roman Palestine*. Texte und Studien zum Antiken Judentum 66. Tübingen.

Millar, F. 1978. 'The Background to the Maccabean Revolution: Reflections on Martin Hengel's *Judaism and Hellenism*', *JJS* 29: 1–21.

—— 1993. *The Roman Near East 31 B.C.–A.D. 337*. Cambridge Mass./London.

CHAPTER TWENTY-SIX

TALKING AT TRYPHO: CHRISTIAN
APOLOGETIC AS ANTI-JUDAISM IN JUSTIN'S
DIALOGUE WITH TRYPHO THE JEW

It is not easy to define a work which evokes at its opening the hon-
eyed charm of the first pages of Plato's *Republic*, on which it is loosely
modelled, or perhaps of a Ciceronian dialogue; but which, by its
sixteenth chapter, is hurling a fully-formed charge of deicide at
Trypho, the author's partner in the dialogue, and at his people, the
Jews. Justin opens thus:

> As I was walking about one morning in the porticoes of the covered
> colonnade, a certain man, who was together with some others, met
> me, and said 'hail philosopher'. And, saying this, he turned round,
> and came with me.

The very first word of the whole dialogue, περιπατοῦντι, describes
more than the physical action—it is walking and discussing, the way
philosophers do (and not just peripatetics). The setting is again appropriate—the covered colonnades of a ξυστός, a context for philosophical discussion chosen, this time, not so much by Greek authors,
as by Cicero.[1] This ξυστός is located at Ephesus by Eusebius (*HE*
4.18.6), who is usually followed;[2] but from the text we might infer
the setting to have been Greece, where Trypho is said to have been
spending a lot of time (3).

In the second paragraph, Justin goes on to insist upon the respect
due to those who parade themselves in the philosopher's cloak: the
form of dress symbolizes the interaction of such people, typified by
a teacher-pupil relationship in which both are part of a civilized
exchange and from which both sides can learn.

Yet the largest part of the dialogue is better characterized by the
very different spirit of a passage which appears not much later, whose

---

[1] For ξυστός settings, see Cicero, *Brutus* 3; *Acad.* 2.3.9. In Classical Greece, they
are usually the place for gymnastics.
[2] Goodenough 1958: 90–91 suggests that Eusebius' source may have been the
work's lost prologue.

outright offensiveness is such that courtesy or lack of it is scarcely at issue:

> These things have happened to you properly and with justice, for you killed the just one, and before him his prophets; and now you reject and dishonour as far as you can those who hope in him and in Him who sent him, God the creator and maker of all things. (16)

It is fair to say that both the spirit of the main section of the dialogue is determined by the second extract, not the first. At this very early stage in the history of anti-Jewish polemic, the battleground has been laid out.[3] It is also fair to say that readers have been remarkably unwilling to acknowledge the sheer vituperative dimension of the dialogue.[4]

Justin's writings mark a major step forward in the history of Christian apologetic literature, even if there are various precedents. Justin was a convert to Christianity, from the city of Flavia Neapolis (formerly Shechem; *First Apology* 1.1), who was martyred at Rome in the reign of Marcus Aurelius. He speaks of himself as a Gentile (29), but of the Samaritans as his people (γένος: 120). It is interesting that the corpus which goes under the name of Justin contains works which run the gamut of the various types of apologetic: apart from the subject of this paper, there are the two books which were actually composed (certainly by the author) under the name of *Apologies*, in which Christianity's merits are ostensibly defended in front of emperors and senate;[5] and also the possibly spurious *Cohortatio ad Graecos*,[6] in which worship of the pagan gods is unfavourably compared to belief in the one God. All of these explore new literary frameworks for justifying and promoting Christianity. But the *Trypho*, which refers back to the first *Apology* and is possibly Justin's last work, is the only one devoted to defence (by attack) against Judaism. For such an approach there may have been a precedent in the lost anonymous dialogue between Jason and Papiscus, which probably preceded Justin

---

[3] Taylor 1995 ascribes modern underestimation of the anti-Judaism of much Christian polemic to an overervaluing of Jewish missionary activity, which would render the Christian stance a necessary defensive response.

[4] See now Lieu's acknowledgement, 1996: 145–148; but she finds more respect for the Jewish answer which Justin allows Trypho than the bare text seems to warrant.

[5] See Young's discussion, 1999: 82.

[6] Included, however, among the writings of Justin in the *Anti-Nicene Christian Library* volume. See now the edition by Riedweg 1994.

and was apparently between a Jew and a converted Jew;[7] while arguments about the abolition of the divine covenant with the Jews and
the validation of Old Testament prophecies in Jesus are anticipated
in the Epistle of Barnabas.[8] To muster the arguments from the Bible,
Justin, like Barnabas, probably drew upon collections of proof texts.[9]
None the less, the *Dialogue with Trypho* remains a pathbreaking work.[10]

It is hard to avoid the conclusion that the polemical element, what
we might in crude terms call 'doing down the other side', is intrinsic to defending one's own side in apologetic literature. This is already
very clear in the prototype Jewish apology, Josephus' *Against Apion*,
cast as it is as a vehement refutation of the slanderers and critics of
Judaism.[11] Establishing a polarity, drawing attention to an enemy,
making the most of a conflict are valuable techniques of advocacy.
The effect is more memorable and therefore more persuasive than
merely stating a case. The other side may be a real opponent or a
paper tiger; they may emerge as an immediately threatening com-
petitor, or as an ideological challenge. And the process may acquire
permanence: the enemy may become an intrinsic part of a group's
self-definition: one understands oneself in terms of the 'other', by
insisting upon what one is not. But polemic figures in differing proportions and degrees in various instances of our somewhat nebulous
genre. In the *Trypho*, the polemic is both sustained and intense, even
if punctuated by moments of genuine interaction.

The intensity is hardly surprising. When the protagonists are
Christianity and Judaism, we have adversaries whose very roots are
deeply and disturbingly intertwined. There is a strong emotional
charge. The *Trypho* goes to the heart of the problem: its core, as we
shall see, is the vindication of what today we would call supersces-
sionism, the Christian claim to have inherited Israel's legacy and
supplanted its original recipients. This is a struggle on both the intellectual and the emotional plane; its practical consequences, in his
own time or later, may not have concerned Justin in the least.

---

[7] On the *testimonia* for *Jason and Papiscus*, see Williams 1930: intro., xxi–ii, 28–30;
Krauss-Horbury 1995: 29–30. Origen who had read it did not have a high opinion: *Contra Celsum* 4.52, but such quotations as survive are found in a seventh century author. The information about the disputants comes from Celsus Africanus.
The work is commonly ascribed to Ariston of Pella.
[8] On Barnabas and supersessionism, see Wilson 1995: 127–142.
[9] Skarsaune 1982. See also Chadwick 1965: 282–283.
[10] On apologetic in dialogue form, as directed against the Jews, see Horbury
1988: 740–742.
[11] See Goodman 1999.

The justification of Christianity rested in the promises of the Old Testament, correctly interpreted; but these interpretations were always open to Jewish challenge, striking at the essence of Christian identity. It is not surprising that such a challenge was productive of a defensive-aggressive response as extreme as that which is visible in Justin. What for us must remain shrouded in obscurity are the routes by which that threat was channelled. Thus, the shortage of external evidence makes it hard to judge how much trust should be put in Justin's accusations of organized Jewish opposition to Christianity.[12] It is no easier to assess the strength of the synagogue's attraction over developing Christian communities in the world of the second-century Greek east. Most obscure of all is the possible influence on the situation of the various forms of Jewish-Christianity which we know by name alone. The *Dialogue with Trypho* is ostensibly concerned with friendly discourse between the two sides. Yet its militant super-sessionism undoubtedly contributed to the construction of the fence between Judaism and Christianity. We cannot say what it was that Justin saw outside that fence.

The philosophical chapters

Justin writes in Greek and positions himself within the world of Greek thought, even when he criticizes it. The introduction to the *Trypho*, with its depiction of a city setting and of a quite friendly debating relationship, creates a framework for the tract. It also introduces a complicating third party into the comparison: Greek culture, and, in particular, philosophy. It is clear from the start that the 'barbarian' subject matter—for Jews were, after all, barbarians from a Greek vantage point, and the Bible a barbarian text, while there were even Christian writers who happily embraced the designation[13]—is made more palatable by writing about it in a format borrowed from Greek literature. Justin's dialogue announces this with his carefully-crafted and deliberately relaxed opening. He signals that his presentation is borrowed from Plato. In the rest of his dialogue, a surface similarity continues: the balance between expositor, Justin, and interlocutor,

---

[12] See below.

[13] See especially Tatian, *ad Graecos* 1.1; 29. For the complexities of Christian versions of the barbarian-Greek divide, see Lieu 1996: 166–167. See also Young 1999: 102 and n. 35 on Aristides.

Trypho, in which the latter mixes objections, questions, shifts of
ground, expostulations and admissions of defeat, is based upon the
Platonic model.[14] Even the final outcome bears some resemblance
to the way in which Socrates' adversaries are reduced to silence, but
it is considerably more extreme. Lukyn Williams' assessment is that
Trypho was 'not very ready in repartee'![15]

The six introductory chapters seem to stand apart from the rest
of the work, in terms both of form and content.[16] We have therefore to avoid the trap of allowing these chapters to define the whole
work for us. The characters, as I have said, are introduced with circumstantial detail of a literary kind such as Plato provides for many
of his dialogues. The Jew Trypho lives appropriately enough in
Greece; and this may surely be taken as a metaphor for the cultural
tradition still evoked by the place, given that we have no reason to
suppose Trypho other than a largely invented character. He is there,
he says, to elude Bar Kokhba's war: again, one may suggest that
the war stands, by contrast, for all that is unacceptable in Judaism
in Justin's eyes and for what would discredit the Jews in the eyes of
'civilized' people—intemperate rebellion, misplaced Messianism (yet
another demonstration that the Jews had got this one wrong). Comment
was not required: the two allusions to the war in the *Trypho*, together
with reference to it in the *First Apology* (31.6), make it clear that
Justin's readers, whoever they were, were informed about it. The
allusion, then, establishes a sort of civilized consensus, as well as
hinting at a theological point.

Trypho the Jew, in the same way as Justin himself, is hanging
around town with a group of friends—a quite plausible scenario for
a comfortably-off Greek-speaking Jew in the second century; but that
is not the point. The narrative has to be set up in such a way as
to pull the participants into the ambit of philosophy. The Jew is
attracted by Justin's garb, and thus Trypho too is temporarily constructed as 'one of us'. The atmosphere is friendly, because this is
appropriate to the philosophical section. This friendliness will be

---

[14] See Hoffmann 1966: 16–17, and especially n. 4 on echoes of *Phaedrus*, *Timaeus*
and, especially, *Protagoras*. Voss 1970: 26–28 invoked the Pseudo-Platonic dialogues
Antiochus and *Eryxias* as well as *Protagoras*.

[15] 1930: intro., xxv.

[16] I put the division here, rather than after chapter 7 or chapter 9, because by
the beginning of chapter 7 the spirit is markedly different. On the disjunction
between the two parts: Hoffmann 1966: 15–16; Voss 1970: 36–37.

briefly—and unconvincingly—recaptured in the final chapter of the work. Eusebius claims to know Trypho's identity, asserting that he was the most prominent Jew of his generation. I take this to be an ill-founded guess. What would such a man be doing in Corinth (or Ephesus)?[17] There has been, from Eusebius on, a long tradition of treating this dialogue as a straight historical report. But there is nothing in the text support such a view. A certain amount of circumstantial detail was required by Justin's chosen form.[18]

Trypho is privileged to hear the first-person story of Justin's search for an acceptable philosophy, followed by the manner of his conversion to Christianity. Behind this section, perhaps, lies a hint of the *Apology* of Socrates, where, one might suggest, the motif of the personal search for the truth has its origins. By this period the search had become a *topos*, in which an individual tried out different schools in order to find the best philosophy by which to live. Among its exponents is Josephus in his *Life*. How conventional the theme had become is shown by Lucian's mockery of it in the humorous dialogue, *Philosophies for Sale*.

Why is the world of philosophy so elaborately introduced into a debate between Christian and Jew? In part, we may explain this in terms of Justin's literary personality, of which some picture is obtainable, in spite of the lack of biographical data and of our imperfect knowledge of his output.[19] To judge by Eusebius' résumé of Justin's career in the *Ecclesiastical History*, Justin moved, at least at times, among philosophers; and it was an important purpose, perhaps the major purpose, of his writing career to locate Christianity in rela-

---

[17] The identification with Rabbi Tarfon, which goes back to Schürer, has little to recommend it except the closeness in the names, and is no longer much favoured. See the detailed arguments in Goodenough: 1923: 91–95, and Hyldahl 1956.

[18] On the conventional character of the material in the introduction, as an argument against historicity, Goodenough 1958: 58–61, Hyldahl 1966; Skarsaune 1976: 53–54. But see, earlier, Williams 1930: intro., xxiv: 'The details of the meeting of Justin and Trypho, and of the emotions with which from time to time both they and Trypho's friends are moved, are related too naturally to be fictitious.' Chadwick 1965: 280 also prefers to take the dialogue as historical, as does Krauss-Horbury 1995: 30. Lieu 1996: 104 seeks a middle course: Trypho has too much flesh and blood to be a straw man, Justin must have known and debated with Jews, but the details are 'far from a careful record' of the two-day session.

[19] There is general agreement on the exclusion of numerous works attributed to Justin from the corpus. For a list of these, as well as of lost works, see Wartelle 1987: 24–28.

tion to philosophy, so as to establish the former's superiority. In doing this, he had the advantage, according to Eusebius, of an educated understanding—πεπαιδευμένης διάνοιας (*HE* 4.18), which we may take to mean that Justin could meet the philosophers on their own ground. The ability to handle this kind of discourse was the main mark of education at the time. Again, in reporting on Justin's disputes with the Cynic Crescens, Eusebius takes pains to show how Justin was the truer philosopher: ὁ ταῖς ἀληθείαις φιλόσοφος (literally, 'in relation to true things'). We learn that Crescens, by contrast, for all his pretensions, should be judged no philosopher at all, because he spoke of what he didn't know (*HE* 4.16). These assaults, as it were from the inside, on Crescens and through him on philosophers as a breed, are offered by Eusebius as the cause of Justin's martyrdom.

If we examine the writings, we see that Justin could manage quite effectively a kind of *elenchos*, a cross-examination of the type practised by the Platonic Socrates in the early dialogues; perhaps he even relished its cut-and-thrust. But it is worth pointing out that Justin's use of the term λόγος, the word, as an active ruling force in the *Trypho* is in the Philonic or Johannine tradition, the word of God, and not Platonic.[20] The extent of Justin's education in philosophy, for all that Eusebius says, remains an open question,[21] and an even more debatable point is the content which should be supplied for his later description of himself as a Christian philosopher. Some would see his development in terms of disjunction, others of synthesis.[22] It is a reasonable surmise that Justin continued through life to wear two hats, though given a character of such extremism and intensity (we can see in the dialogue the stuff of which martyrs are made), it is dubious whether the balance was perfectly maintained.

Our concern, in any event, is merely with the author's self-presentation in the *Trypho*, where we may well feel that he pleads too much. He has himself referred to by the old Christian as a *philologos*, a type contrasted with the man of action, and also as a sophist, which amounts to much the same (3). Clearly, establishing the *persona* is

---

[20] For references, and interpretation of Justin's complex uses of λόγος, Edwards 1995. Earlier, Goodenough 1923: 139–175.

[21] Edwards 1991 makes out a strong case for knowledge of Plato through Numenius of Apamea.

[22] See Edwards 1991 for a nuanced reading; Hyldahl 1966: no continuity. Rejected by de Vogel 1978.

important to the literary strategy. But how much does this have to do with the book's argument?

The establishment of Christianity as the best system flows from the *topos* about choice of philosophies. In the *Second Apology* (ch. 12), Justin presents himself as a former Platonist, who had been won over by the spectacle of Christian tenacity in the face of slander, and by the quality of Christian life. Here we note that Justin is converted by an old man whom he meets on the beach. This old man is outside and beyond the other competitors—he looks different and the interaction is of a different quality,[23] even if he too is marked as a member of the upper classes, when he is said to be seeking out lost slaves. As for Judaism, not only does the Jewish way of life fail to figure as one of the philosophies, but it is not presented as remotely an option for Justin. The structural asymmetry in the role of the three Greek systems, on the one hand, and the Jewish one, on the other, nicely exposes the disjunction between the introductory section and the rest of the *Trypho*.

Moreover, we should not forget that even those first chapters are set up not to embrace but to dismiss philosophy, just as Justin is said to have dismissed Crescens. What better *locus standi* from which to do this than that of a philosopher oneself? Platonism is given the most space, in Justin's account of his personal quest, but that is partly because its pretensions were greatest at this period, socially, intellectually and spiritually, and there was the most interest in it. It was also, on the whole, the closest of the late Greek schools to Christian doctrine, and perhaps Justin really had spent some time with it. So Platonic philosophy is momentarily elevated; but only to lend force to the exposure of its pretensions. 'In my stupidity', says Justin, 'I expected [at the end of his studies] to look on God, since that is the goal of Plato's philosophy' (2). We see here how monotheism emerges firmly as the premise behind the whole enquiry. Philosophies could be interesting if they forwarded the search for God.

There are other early indications of what is to come, hints that things aren't what they seem. That solitary old man on the sea shore, dignified but gentle, who brings about Justin's conversion, has the air of a figure of parable. He proceeds to engage in a rather plausible and extended Platonic discussion with Justin, raising issues of

---

[23] He has even been identified as Christ: Hoffmann 1966: 12.

the soul's knowledge and of memory, but bringing the agenda very skilfully round to sin and punishment, the question of a created world and God's management of souls. By this point, Platonism has been entirely undermined.

Like Justin, this tract walks in philosopher's garb. And, in spite of its unsophisticated and unappealing use of the Greek language, it has walked effectively. Readers have hastened to snap up as reality the author's literary *persona*.[24] We can lay the fault at the door of the seductive first six chapters, and their afterglow. One has only to read the general patrological handbooks and the standard Church histories to see that Justin continues to seduce by means of his philosophical posture—so much more pleasing, for almost all, than sitting down with a sermon, an anthology of passages from the prophets, a triumphant justification of the true religion or a vitriolic denunciation of the false one. The lead-in may have appealed to sophisticated Christians, or even to Greek-speaking Jews as much as to Greeks of the pagan variety.[25] One might add a further consideration: since the bulk of the dialogue is to lie within the realm of intricate, theologically-orientated exegesis, its designation as a philosophical debate is not wholly inappropriate. It is hard to think of a better description, in a world where Christian literary forms were as yet undeveloped.

From dialogue to denunciation

For all its charming introduction, to ascribe good-humour, friendliness, even kindness to the dialogue as a whole, is to read highly selectively.[26] One is tempted to think that portions of this highly inflated work escape attention. One interpreter goes so far as to call it the last 'nice' dialogue between Christians and Jews.[27] That the later *adversus Judaeos* literature is more intemperate should not lead us to exaggerate the moderation of the *Trypho*.[28] Moreover, a modern

---

[24] See e.g. Wartelle 1987 intro: 14–21.
[25] Though we may wish to exclude the possibility of a Jewish readership for other reasons. See below.
[26] Rokeah 1982; Sanders 1973.
[27] Rokeah 1982; cf. Sanders 1973: 51; Lieu 1996: 111.
[28] Wilson 1995: 257–60 regards the 'reasoned argument', the tone, which he describes as 'civilized' (283) and the 'discernible voice' allowed to the Jew as distinguishing the dialogue from all later Jewish–Christian controversy.

reader's preference for Trypho's quietness over Justin's assertiveness[29] is hardly likely to have been shared by the ancient audience, with all the fondness of the period for vigorous—and long-winded—rhetoric. And it is undoubtedly illegitimate to take the mere fact of Trypho's centrality in the dialogue as a compliment to the Jews or to conclude any more from it than that Judaism was still central to the forging of Christian thought.[30]

In Chapter 7, the old man's discourse introduces us to the prophets, men beloved of God who are deemed more ancient than the philosophers: they alone can help us move on to understanding. This is an important moment. These are henceforward to be our company, and, although we are still in the conversational section, a new atmosphere reigns. The prophets are not going to be at all like philosophers, so much is clear, though their subject matter is said to be the same. We are now in the realm of revealed truth, and of proof by miracle, a realm shared by Jews and Christians. We have visited the sphere of philosophy only to show how we might leave it. The prayer at the end of the chapter, 'that the gates of light may be opened to you', exposes the new mode.[31] Only God and Christ offer the understanding required for true vision. Justin's conversion to Christianity will not be long delayed.

Trypho dismisses the old man's Messianic fervour, and this induces Justin to elicit from Trypho further criticisms of Christianity which were supposedly current among Jews. These are structurally important exchanges, for through them it emerges that Justin has to deal not with the charges of cannibalism and promiscuity familiar from the Greek and Roman side,[32] but with more serious matters. Furthermore, Trypho is presented as an interested party who has actually read the Christian Gospel (10), and who seems, in spite of some noisy behaviour from his friends, potentially sympathetic. And so the stage is set for the dialogue with the Jew. Our sense of the subject's growing gravity, and of the significance of the relationship between the two parties is accentuated by the use of the authorial first person:

[29] Wilson 1996: 260–261.
[30] As Trakatellis 1986: 294–295 seeks to do.
[31] For serious attempts to define Justin as a 'true philosopher', in the Christian mode, see Skarsaune 1976;
[32] To which defences appear elsewhere in Justin, see *Apology* II.12, and regularly in Christian defences against Greeks and Romans. For intepretation, see Rives 1995: especially 64–65.

there is complete coincidence between author and Christian protagonist. At the same time, by this means the illusion is produced of
the author having no responsibility for the personality he has created.
It is therefore unnecessary here to adopt any device for distinguishing Justin the author from 'Justin' the protagonist. But we might ask
whether this phenomenon perhaps goes to explain the insistence of
generations of readers on finding verisimilitude in this artificial and
erratic construct.

After chapter 8, the tables are rapidly turned. One indication of
how far we have moved formally away from philosophical dialogue
is shown by the fact that the second section, running to chapter 35,
contains virtually no conversation between the two parties. Trypho
will return; but we are introduced first to a completely different mode
of thought, by way of long biblical citations. These include some of
the angriest of prophetic utterances in the Bible, equipped with exegesis designed to spell out the sins of the Jews, the justice of their
suffering and their rejection by God. The prophecies from Isaiah
declare the new order. Powerful influences are brought to bear on
the reader.

At chapter 38, Trypho asserts that his Jewish teachers may well
have been right in forbidding discussion with Christians, on account
of their blasphemous doctrines. For the next ten chapters, where
Judaism is at the centre of the discussion, the Jew asks a number of
questions; these are designed by the author to expose his loss of
ground and his increasing anxiety of the possibility of Justin being
right. At one moment, he tells Justin that must be out of his mind
(39.3); but this confidence that his territory is the territory of reason
does not survive.

At chapter 45, Trypho makes an urgent enquiry concerning the
expectations at the resurrection of those who lived according to the
law of Moses. This leads quite rapidly to an exposition of Christian
eschatology and thence into Christology. The dense discussion of
Christ's divinity and attendant issues, conducted largely, again, from
biblical proof texts, occupies the central portion of the dialogue. It
is punctuated by quiet objections from Trypho, which merely unleash,
each time, a new stream of exposition.

There is a certain variation, indeed an inconsistency, in the spirit
of Trypho's questions. But the general picture is that, by the time
the second day of debate has been reached (85), the courtesies are
wearing thin. Before long, even the debating style of the Jew comes

under fire, in terms which extend the applicability of the slander far
beyond this one individual:

> For like flies you swarm and alight on wounds, and if someone speaks
> ten thousand words well, but some tiny thing were to displease
> you . . . you latch onto the small utterance and rush to construe it as
> an impious offence. (115)

There is, in the end, only one way out. Trypho and his companions should reject their teachers (137, 142) so that they can take
advantage of the possibility of repentance (141). Matters remain in
the air, but, as the sun sets on the second day of the meeting (an
echo of the atmosphere at the opening, we may fancy), Trypho,
astonishingly, expresses his party's gratitude and appreciation. Future
meetings are impossible because Justin is about to sail, but the Jews
will continue to search the scriptures. One can scarcely imagine a
more implausible conclusion than his final declaration of friendship:
'remember us as friends'. In Plato's early Socratic dialogues, Socrates'
worsted opponents, it is true, are also passive in defeat; but in no
Platonic instance have they been the recipients of such invective.

We have here then, a hybrid work, which at least pays its respects
to several intellectual traditions. But the difficult question is how we
interpret the form and content of the bulk of the work, now that
we have detached the introduction. In principle, we might sum up
the *Trypho* as a defence of the Christian religion organized around
an extended engagement with Judaism, an engagement which takes
the dual and inevitable forms of appropriation and assault.

The true Israel

We see how the engagement with Judaism is fundamental to Christian
self-definition (in a different way from any engagement with heresy)
as early as chapters 11–12 of the *Trypho*, where the Christian claim
to share the God of Israel is coupled with the assertion that the old
law for Israel has been abrogated.[33] This is expressed in terms as
resounding and unequivocal as any in which it has ever been uttered:

---

[33] Cf. Lieu 1996: 181–182: 'while continuity may mark the relationship between
the Christians and the prophecies possessed by the Jews, radical discontinuity or
even opposition had to mark that between Jews and Christians.'

> For the law given on Horeb is already old, and is yours alone, but
> this law is for all universally . . . and as an eternal and final law, Christ
> was given, and the covenant is sure, after which there is no law, no
> ordinance, no commandment. (11.2)

The supersessionist claim is made explicitly: 'we are the true Israel
of the spirit and the race of Judah' (11.4). And in the discussion
which follows, about Abraham in his uncircumcised state, we are
also forewarned that circumcision, the principal, and controversial
distinguishing mark between Jews and Christians, will be an important theme for Justin. This passage anticipates the extended discussion of the patriarch's circumcision at chapters 19 and 46, as well
as further comment elsewhere (92; 113, on Joshua). That Adam,
Abel, Enoch and Abraham himself could please God while still uncir-
cumcized is an argument which Justin relishes: 'to you therefore
alone was this circumcision necessary' (19.5).

The doctrine of supersession makes further appearances in the
earlier part of the work, figuring also as passing remark, and even
as taunt: 'Do you know these things, Trypho? They are contained
in your scriptures; or rather, not yours but ours' (29). These claims
to the scriptures prepare the way for a more elaborate and even
more assertive demonstration that, since the prophecies of the later
prophets apply to Jesus, it is only the Christians who could possibly
be identified with 'Israel, his inheritance'. This climactic point, when
it is reached, is evolved out of an elaborate mesh of citations punctuated by exegetical comment and intermingled with dreadful warn-
ings. We might compare the strong language deployed in that
distinctive form of contemporizing interpretation known as *pesher*,
which is characteristic of Qumran literature:

> 'Therefore, behold, I will again remove this people, saith the Lord'
> (Isaiah 29:14) . . . Deservedly, too, for you are neither wise nor under-
> standing, but crafty and unscrupulous; wise only to do evil, but utterly
> unable to know the hidden plan of God, or the faithful covenant of
> the Lord, or to find out the everlasting paths. (123)

Trypho, it should be noted, has only once been angered—showing
the displeasure on his face, as Justin tells us [34] (79). But now Trypho's

---

[34] This is the opening of a chapter which some have thought misplaced. See
Williams, *ad loc.*

response is merely a plea for clarification. Justin reminds Trypho, *de haut en bas*, that he has already assented to all the proofs, but since Trypho's friends may need help, he offers a ringing declaration from the lips of third Isaiah, a declaration which carries all the solemnity of the great promissory passages of the Hebrew Bible: 'Jacob is my servant, I will help him; Israel is my chosen, I will set my spirit upon him, and he shall bring forth judgement to the Gentiles. He shall not strive nor cry; neither shall any hear his voice in the broad places . . .' (123; Isaiah 42:1). Those magnificent assurances were indeed worth fighting over.

Towards the end of the dialogue, it emerges that not one of Trypho's group of friends, directly addressed by Justin, is able, or at any rate willing, to answer his question as to what the name 'Israel' signifies (125). There could be no more graphic demonstration that they lack any claim to the title.

Sadly there is no quarter for the defeated. This is a contest for the very essence of the opponent's being, its object to strip him of his identity and his future:

> Some of the children of your race will be found to be children of Abraham, and found in the portion of Christ; but . . . there are others who are indeed children of Abraham, but who are like the sand on the sea-shore, which is barren and fruitless, copious and without number, bearing no fruit whatsoever, and only drinking the water of the sea. And a large number within your race are convicted of being of this kind, imbibing doctrines of bitterness and atheism, and spurning the word of God. (120)

The contest, as depicted, is almost entirely one-sided. It is true that Trypho excludes the Christians from salvation, and dismisses Jesus' status, when he first meets Justin and learns of his conversion from Platonism, but with an impact wholly different from Justin's. There, we are still within reach of the civilized, Platonizing reaches of the dialogue, and Trypho's utterance is cast in terms which are matter-of-fact and moderate in tone; there are no slights on character or conduct. The case in his view is one of plain error:

> For while you remained in that mode of philosophy and lived a blameless life, a hope was left to you of a better fate. But having forsaken God, and placed your hope on a man, what kind of salvation remains for you? . . . You people, by accepting a worthless rumour, shape a kind of Messiah for yourselves, and for his sake are obliviously perishing. (8)

Within the overarching demonstration that Israel is the church and the Jewish prophecies are of Christ, specific battle areas are staked out and revisited. These are areas of head-on collision, and two of them are particularly important. The first is the claim to possession of the correct (Greek) biblical text (137), and to the correct understanding of it (e.g. 131). Occasional points of agreement in interpretation are acknowledged. A striking case is that of the millennium, where both parties agree about the expectation of a future rebuilding of Jerusalem (80): but in this case, one is tempted to suggest that agreement with the Jew is facilitated by this matter being a point of controversy with Christian heretics, whom Justin forthwith turns to attack.

Secondly, the Jews are charged with twisting (84) the text, with tampering with it and with cutting out passages. Thus Justin claims that from the words in Psalm 95 (96), 'the Lord reigned from the tree' the 'leaders of the people' had cut out 'from the tree' (73); the words are not in the Septuagint Greek. This is no light offence:

> It seems incredible. For it is more awful than the making of the golden calf, which they made in the wilderness when they were filled with manna on the earth, or than sacrificing children to demons, or than slaying the prophets themselves.[35]

All this is rather far from a disagreement between scholars as to the correct reading of a text. It is interesting that Justin's versions, which diverge for the most part from known Septuagint readings, have been taken by some scholars as representing a consistent pattern of serious textual variants. The reality is that even the use of divergent authoritative translations of any length by the two groups cannot be safely inferred from the disparities noted in this dialogue, which seem rather to reveal a startling freedom with the words on the part of *ad hoc* interpreters of selected key passages.[36]

Another battleground is the repeated allegation that Jews are dedicated to persecuting Christians and their faith: that they have long been sending out delegations to vilify them (17), that they spread

---

[35] On Jews sacrificing their children to demons, cf. 131.

[36] Upon these divergent readings rests what is still a basic tenet of scholarship, the belief that the Jews abandoned the Septuagint (and any other Old Greek) versions, and withdrew into extreme literalism, accepting only their own new translation by Aquila. This is followed e.g. by Wilson 1996: 271 and n. 44. But see Rajak, Grinfield Lectures 1994–96, forthcoming.

shameful stories about them (108), that they abuse them, and curse them in the synagogue (16, 47, cf. 38, on non-communication with Christians). In fact, consistent Jewish attacks on Christians are alluded to, and Justin ascribes great importance to them. What Horbury has called 'the corporate Jewish rejection of Christianity' is a central support of Justin's denunciation of Judaism.[37] The supposed cursing and exclusion from the synagogue of *minim*, heretics, 'after the prayer' has already figured at chapter 38. These allegations are particularly hard to assess, since some of them are unspecific, while for the appearance of a curse in the *Amidah* prayer at this period Justin constitutes our only direct evidence.[38] Again, many scholars simply take the statements *au pied de la lettre*.[39]

Audience and purpose

For Justin's *Apologies*, a pagan audience was indicated in the body of the text, even if a Christian one is also to be envisaged.[40] In the case of the *Trypho*, nothing is said. A variety of possibilities has been entertained, but nearly all carry with them serious difficulties.

1. Certain commentators have held that Justin was writing to win over pagan Gentiles. Various arguments support this view, but there are also strong counter-arguments.
   a) Since Justin's *Apologies* are ostensibly directed at pagan recipients, and their author appears concerned to set out various Christian principles and to explain them, we might expect Justin's other writings to follow suit. However, even in the case of the *Apologies*, the imperial and senatorial audience is not to be taken wholly seriously.[41]

---

[37] Horbury 1992: 343. The author accepts as essentially accurate the dossier of such attacks presented here and elsewhere. But see Taylor 1995: 91–97, on the paucity of references to specific contemporary activity by Jews in early patristic literature.

[38] Kimelman 1980; Horbury 1982; van der Horst 1994. On the allegations in general, Goodman 1994: 142.

[39] But see the excellent discussion of the various uncertainties and doubts in Lieu 1996: 132–136; 143.

[40] Further on the audience of these and other Christian texts, see Young 1999.

[41] See Millar 1977: 562–563 on the problem of assessing whether the *First Apology* was genuinely intended for Antoninus Pius; cf. the remarks of Edwards 1995: 279–280.

b) Here some of the content is quite beyond the grasp of those with no knowledge of Judaism or Christianity. It is hard to believe that the discussions of proof texts which make up the bulk of the book could be other than profoundly bewildering, if not wholly unintelligible, to those with an exclusively Greek, or Greco-Roman education. We should take into consideration too the patchy and harsh quality of the Greek style in which the arguments are couched.

c) Greeks, in any sense, are by no means at the centre of the stage in the *Trypho*, even if the introduction, with the detailed account of Justin's conversion from paganism, are rendered of interest to them.

d) The repentance and conversion of the Gentiles is envisaged and welcomed (28; 131). By contrast, Justin asserts that, for the hard-hearted Jews, persistent traducers of Christ, only prayer is possible. None the less, there is no immediate message for pagan readers, since even the Gentile conversion is a long-term prospect: we are told that it is something foreordained, and the prophecy in Micah 4, 'And many nations shall go and say, come let us go up to the mountain of the Lord, and to the house of the God of Jacob' is also taken to refer to this event (119).

e) Greek religion is criticized in chapters 69 and 70. But even here there is no direct address to pagans since the criticism is here embedded in a specific context, that of distinguishing absurd pagan stories in which human beings such as Bacchus and Hercules can become gods, from the Christian story, and, again, the so-called mysteries of Mithras in their cave, from the prophecies of Daniel about cutting a stone without hands out of a great mountain. There is not enough here to rattle let alone to disillusion pagans.

f) A dedicatee, Marcus Pompeius, is once named (141.5) and once addressed without name (8.3), if the MSS are to be relied upon. The assumption that, whoever he was, he is unlikely to have been a Jew, is a reasonable one.[42] It is not clear, however, why the possibility of his being a Christian has been excluded.

---

[42] Goodenough 1923: 97–99, together with a discussion of the possibility of a lost prologue.

g) There seems little advantage in envisaging an audience of
pagans who were Jewish sympathizers, or God-fearers, and
there is nothing in the dialogue to support this position. The
proposal of god-fearers involves questionable presuppositions
about the religious and cultural distinctiveness implied by the
term, as well as about the centrality of god-fearers in the spread
of Christianity. However we chose to understand the label, it
is hard to justify making it the name of a definable constituency,
its membership defined by its integration of Greco-Roman cultural values with monotheistic religious instincts.[43]

2. A more common idea is that the dialogue was directed at Jews.
Here there is a somewhat stronger case. Some aspects of the book
do indeed point in this direction. But there are still some difficulties.

   a) Jews, or some of them, would know the biblical texts, and
   might relish quotation and discussion of them. To outsiders,
   these texts were barbarous.

   b) The methodology of the discourse may be regarded as deriving from Jewish exegetical tradition, of which Justin seems to
   have some knowledge. Its procedure of progressing by extracting significance from a loosely-related series of texts has been
   described as essentially Midrashic.[44]

   c) The Jewish view of Israel's history is incorporated. Notably,
   in chapter 131, Justin evokes at length the redemption from
   Egypt, a saga Jews will have recalled at each and every Passover,
   one of the cornerstones, of their continuation as a people.

   d) No New Testament citations are deployed as proof-texts by
   Justin, even though he speaks of a Gospel. He seems to have
   known Matthew, Luke and Corinthians, though not the Acts,
   and it has been argued that he incorporated sayings of Jesus
   from extra-canonical texts into his own prose.[45] The focus on
   the Old Testament would satisfy Jews. But it is hard to make
   much of this, for such a focus in any case arises naturally out
   of the subject matter.

---

[43] Cf. the similar argument of Lieu 1996: 107.
[44] On Jewish exegesis generally in the *Trypho*, Lieu 1996: 108–109 and the literature, covering over a century, cited in n. 18. On Midrashic pattterns, Horbury
1988.
[45] Skarsaune 1987, on Justin's knowledge. For sayings of Jesus, Bellinzoni 1967.

e) Justin is engaged at times in a violent counter-offensive, as we have seen, against Jewish attacks on Christians. We might wish to see this as having a practical purpose, to hit back. On the other hand, such allegations can be adequately explained as serving a useful internal function in sharpening Christian hostility to Judaism.

f) The work may have been designed as an instrument for the conversion of the Jews, even if, as we have seen, Justin goes out of his way to declare Gentiles better potential Christians. There are explicit references to such a possibility, and the call is at moments quite urgent: 'so short a time is left to you in which to become proselytes.' (28) It also figures in a more muffled form (30; 137). One can, however, scarcely speak of tempting invitations; in the last occurrence, the call is entangled with the repetition of the hostile allegations about institutionalized synagogal execration of Christ, which we are now given to understand as a practice dictated by the synagogue chiefs, described as ἀρχισυνάγωγοι.[46] When, finally, the sun is setting on the second day, and the discussion has to end, nothing firm has been accomplished. There is still, we learn, a long way to go. Thus the whole thrust has been to expose the obstinacy and hard-heartedness, σκληροκαρδία, less of Trypho and his little band than of the Jewish people as a whole, whose presence lurks behind the individuals. We witness how the prospect of shifting them depends on being able and willing tirelessly to go over the texts again and again, repeatedly to extract their message. In the course of the dialogue, the Jews are given a chance, they are shown the right way. But the point is that they listen and they do not learn. Conversion, then, can be spoken of as the ultimate aim only on the theological level. Justin's accomplishment is supposedly to have left the door open, to have persuaded Trypho and his friends to search the scriptures. But these are the very same Jews whose reading of the Bible he had earlier compared to the swarming of flies. If any serious expectation of a conversion

---

[46] See above, n. 29. On Christian distortions of the role of these officials, see Rajak & Noy 1993: 78–81 = Ch. 20: 398–404.

of the Jews could survive this, then, it could only be a millennial one—even more millennial, if that be possible, than
the anticipated conversion of the Gentiles.

g) Whatever the case, for some readers all the positive arguments
above fall away in the face of one simple question. Is it conceivable that Jews would choose to read this repeatedly offensive
tract?[47] As subtle as the appeal to a philosophically-minded
Greek at the opening is, so unsubtle is the treatment of the
Jews. Nothing is changed by the device whereby, at the end
of it all, the puppets of the dialogue declare themselves keen
to be Justin's friends, and readily pray for his welfare, as he
does for their eventual conversion.[48] The author might, it is
true, be viewed as insensitive, unaware and ineffectual. But
such an attempt to save the hypothesis of a Jewish readership
accords ill with the understanding of Judaism generally ascribed
to the author by the exponents of the hypothesis.

3. That a work of this kind would arouse interest among the faithful and the converted is to be expected, and scarcely needs discussion. But there are considerations which justify our going
further, to suppose that a Christian readership of this kind was
Justin's principal conscious target.

a) A Christian, or at least, Jewish-Christian audience must be
expected for the attacks on false Christians and various heresies which crop up, for example in chapter 35, Marcians,
Valentinians, Basilidians, Saturnilians, as a response to an inter-
jection of Trypho's, that many so-called Christians are said to
eat meat offered to idols, without harm coming to them.

b) It is evident that the struggle to define Christianity through
the opposition with Judaism is of benefit primarily to Christians
themselves. They were, as we know, asking urgent questions
about their relationship to the Old Testament and especially
about the application of its promises.

c) It has been considered appropriate to invoke in this context
such outside evidence as exists to show that it was felt necessary to wean new Christians from Judaism and to inoculate
them against its continuing attractions. However, it should be
noted that the most explicit evidence comes from considerably

---

[47] Asked by Goodenough 1923: 99, but by few others. Cf. Stylianopoulos 1975.
[48] I do not find this as satisfactory as does Stanton 1985: 389.

later, principally the sermons of John Chrysostom which belong
to the second half of the fourth century.[49]

Although conclusive demonstration is impossible, it emerges that the
case for a principally Christian readership is the most acceptable, or
at any rate the least difficult to sustain. The arguments in support
of the other possibilities come up against serious objections. In general, the *Dialogue with Trypho*, though looking outwards in two directions, is aptly described as a contribution to Christian thought, as
apologetic often is. Considerable theological exertion has gone into
this text. It is not just the adaptation of an extant collection of proof
texts. It is a work written from within a religious system, in spite of
the apparent openness of its early chapters. It engages immensely
seriously, on its own terms, with the prophetic texts. In its homiletic
endeavours there was probably substantial innovation. It represents
a conscious contribution to a new Christian literature, serving to
educate, to offer intellectual fodder, to consolidate, both for new and
old members, the experience of belonging—as in some sense all literature does, and apologetic literature in an even stronger sense.
That is why the old literary frameworks were inadequate. It is perhaps not wholly far-fetched to suggest that the *Dialogue with Trypho*,
though presented as an apologetic dialogue, is less a discussion than
a Christian *pesher* on Isaiah and the other prophets.

As was the case with the Qumran sectaries, the group solidarity of
the Christians depended upon establishing that there was only one
true way[50] and thus on the evocation of a host of adversaries and
besetting dangers. Sharing the heritage of the Jews with its owners
was not an option which fitted the bill for the majority in the evolving church. John's Gospel took one route, boldly identifying Judaism
with the works of the Devil. Justin's apologetic technique was equally
exclusionary, and equally damning. He brought a relentless sense of
the presence of the enemy into the heart of an ostensibly friendly
dialogue and into the exegetical process itself. Dialogue, in such
hands, acquired a new meaning. Apologetic became a battle of the
books and also a battle for souls.

---

[49] Much is made of these attractions by Marcel Simon 1986: see especially chapter 11. For a vigorous challenge, see Taylor 1995: 26–40.
[50] Justin, on consideration, does allow that Christians who still adhered to some
Jewish practices might just be admitted (47–48).

BIBLIOGRAPHY

1. *Primary sources*

Dods, Marcus, Reith, George, & Pratten, B.P. 1879. *The Writings of Justin Martyr and Athenagoras*, vol. 2. Anti-Nicene Christian Library. Edinburgh (transl. Reith).
Goodspeed, E.J. 1914. *Die ältesten Apologeten. Texte mit kurzen Einleitungen.* Göttingen.
Migne, J.-P. 1857. *Patrologia Graeca.* Vol. 6. Paris.
Riedweg, C. 1994. *Ps-Justin (Markel von Ankyra?) 'ad Graecos de vera religione' ('Cohortatio ad Graecos'). Einleitung und Kommentar*, 2 vols. Basel.
Wartelle, A. 1987. *Saint Justin, Apologies. Introduction, texte critique, traduction, commentaire et index.* Paris.
Williams, A. Lukyn. 1930. *The Dialogue with Trypho.* Transl., intro. and notes. London.

2. *Secondary sources*

Barnard, L.W. 1966. *Justin Martyr. His Life and Thought.* Cambridge.
Bellinzoni, A.J. 1967. *The Sayings of Jesus in the Writings of Justin Martyr.* Leiden.
Chadwick, H. 1965. 'Justin Martyr's Defence of Christianity', *Bulletin of the John Rylands Library* 47: 275–297.
Edwards, M.J. 1991. 'On the Platonic Schooling of Justin Martyr', *JTS* 42: 17–34.
——— 1995. 'Justin's Logos and the Word of God', *Journal of Early Christian Studies* 3.3: 261–280.
Goodenough, E.R. 1923. *The Theology of Justin Martyr. An Investigation into the Conception of Early Christian Literature and its Hellenistic and Judaistic Influences.* Jena. repr. Amsterdam 1960.
Goodman, M. 1994. *Mission and Conversion. Proselytizing in the Religious History of the Roman Empire.* Oxford.
——— 1999. 'Josephus' Treatise *Against Apion*', in M. Edwards, M. Goodman & S. Price, with C. Rowland (eds), *Apologetics in the Roman Empire: Pagans, Jews and Christians.* Oxford, 45–58.
Goppelt, L. 1954. *Christentum und Judentum im ersten und zweiten Jahrhundert.* Gütersloh.
Harnack, A. 1913. *Judentum und Judenchristentum in Justins Dialog mit Trypho.* Texte und Untersuchungen 39. Leipzig.
Hoffmann, M. 1966. *Der Dialog bei der Christlichen Schriftstellern der erster vier Jahrhundert.* Berlin.
Horbury, W. 1982. 'The Benediction of the *Minim* and Jewish-Christian Controversy', *JTS* n.s. 23: 19–61.
——— 1988. 'Old Testament Interpretation in the Writings of the Church Fathers', in M.J. Mulder and H. Sysling (eds). *Mikra*, 727–787. Assen/Philadelphia.
——— 1992. 'Jewish-Christian Relations in Barnabas and Justin Martyr', in Dunn, J.D.G. (ed.), *Jews and Christians. The Parting of the Ways A.D. 70–135.* Wissenschaftliche Untersuchungen zum Neuen Testament 66. Tübingen, 315–345.
Horst, P.W. van der. 1994. 'The Birkat ha-Minim in Recent Research', *Expository Times* 105: 363–368.
Hyldahl, N. 1956. 'Tryphon and Tarpho', *Studia Theologica* 10: 77–88.
——— 1966. *Philosophie und Christentum. Eine Intepretation der Einleitung zum Dialog Justins.* Acta Theologica Danica 9. Copenhagen.
Joly, R. 1973. *Christianisme et philosophie. Etudes sur Justin et les apologistes grecs du deuxième siècle.* Brussels.
Kimelman, R. 1981. '*Birkat ha-Minim* and the Lack of Evidence for an Anti-Christian Jewish Prayer in Late Antiquity', in E.P. Sanders *et al.* (eds), *Jewish and Christian Self-Definition.* Vol. 2, 226–244.

Krauss, S. 1996. *The Jewish Christian Controversy. From the Earliest Times to 1789*. Ed. and revised by William Horbury. Vol. 1. *History*. Tübingen.

Lieu, J. 1994 'The Parting of the Ways': Theological Construct or Historical Reality?', *JSNT* 56: 101–119.

—— 1996. *Image and Reality. The Jews in the World of the Christians in the Second Century*. Edinburgh.

Millar, F. 1977. *The Emperor in the Roman World (31 B.C. to A.D. 337)*. London.

Nilson, J. 1977. 'To Whom is Justin's *Dialogue with Trypho* Addressed?' *Theological Studies* 38: 538–546.

Osborn, E.F. 1973. *Justin Martyr*. Beiträge zur historischen Theologie 47. Tübingen.

Rajak, T. & Noy, D. 1993. '*Archisynagogoi*: Office, Title and Social Status in the Greco-Jewish Synagogue', *JRS* 83, 75–93 = Ch. 20 in this volume.

Remus, H. 1986. 'Justin Martyr's Argument with Judaism', in S.G. Wilson (ed.), *Anti-Judaism in Early Christianity*, 2 vols. Waterloo. (ed.). 59–80.

Rives, J. 1995. 'Human Sacrifice among Pagans and Christians', *JRS* 85: 65–85.

Rokeah, David. 1982. *Jews, Pagans and Christians in Conflict*. Jerusalem/Leiden.

Sanders, J.T. 1973. *Schismatics, Sectarians, Dissidents, Deviants*. London.

Shotwell, W.A. 1965. *The Biblical Exegesis of Justin Martyr*. London.

Sigal, P. 1978–79. 'An Enquiry into Aspects of Judaism in *Justin Martyr's Dialogue with Trypho*', *Abr-Nahrain* 18: 74–100.

Simon, M. 1986 (in French 1964). *Verus Israel. A Study of the Relations between Christians and Jews in the Roman Empire (A.D. 135–425)*. Oxford.

Skarsaune, Oskar. 1976. 'The Conversion of Justin Martyr', *Studia Theologica* 30: 53–73.

—— 1987. *The Proof from Prophecy*. Supplements to *Novum Testamentum* 56. Leiden.

Stanton, G.N. 1985. 'Aspects of Early Christian-Jewish Polemic and Apologetic', *NTS* 31: 377–391.

Stylianopoulos, T. 1975. *Justin Martyr and the Mosaic Law*. Society of Biblical Literature, Dissertation Series 20. Missoula, Montana.

Taylor, M.S. 1995. *Anti-Judaism and Early Christian Identity. A Critique of the Scholarly Consensus*. Leiden.

Trakatellis, D. 1986. 'Justin Martyr's Trypho' in G.W. Nickelsburg with G.W. MacRae (eds), *Christians among Jews and Gentiles*, 287–297. Philadelphia.

Vogel, C.J. de. 1978. 'Problems concerning Justin Martyr', *Mnemosyne* 31: 360–388.

Voss, B.R. 1970. *Der Dialog in der Früchristlichen Literatur*. Munich.

Wilde, R. 1949. *Treatment of the Jews in the Early Christian Writers of the First Three Centuries*. Washington.

Wilson, S.G. 1996. *Related Strangers. Jews and Christians 70–170 A.D.* Minneapolis.

Winden, J.C.M. van. 1979. *An Early Christian Philosopher. Justin Martyr's Dialogue with Trypho, Chapters One to Nine*. Philosophia Patrum 1. Leiden.

Young, F. 1999. 'Greek Apologists of the Second Century', in M. Edwards, M. Goodman & S. Price, with C. Rowland (eds), *Apologetics in the Roman Empire: Pagans, Jews and Christians*. Oxford, 81–104.

CHAPTER TWENTY-SEVEN

JEWS AND GREEKS: THE INVENTION AND EXPLOITATION OF POLARITIES IN THE NINETEENTH CENTURY

The idea of the twin roots of European civilization, the one Hellenic and the other Hebraic, has served, from the second half of the eighteenth century on, both as a sophisticated theoretical and scholarly tool and as a widespread commonplace. Moreover, in the guise of the once widely-accepted dichotomy between Aryan and Semite, the conception fused with notions of race to fuel various political doctrines. Groups create and sharpen their sense of identity in relation to 'the other', to those whom they perceive as opposing them or differing from them, and theories of culture are often built around polarities. The construction of ethnic definition in terms of binary models, operating both as comparison and contrast, is now widely understood.[1] Moreover, binary schemes continue to be invoked by scholars. Bernal's much-discussed *Black Athena* opposes an 'Oriental Model' of cultural origins to an 'Aryan Model', claiming that the former was the model accepted in antiquity but that it was suppressed by the European Enlightenment.[2] For Bernal, the choice remains polarized: either the Greeks invented civilization or else it came from Egypt and Black Africa.[3] So familiar have the oppositions Greek/Oriental or Greek/Hebrew become that they may seem to be perfectly obvious, almost natural. But, they are, of course, as much a creation of their interpreters as any other polarity, and they have their own history. It is to this history that we need to look to understand the long-lived argument between Hellenes and Hebrews.

The post-Enlightenment idealization of classical Greece was not without its problems. Since Philhellenism involved the creation of models for the present age as much as the invention of fictionalized cultural origins, any exalted valuation of the Greek inheritance produced tension over values. The classical Greeks held a longstanding

---

[1] See the comments of Shavit 1997: 16–20. Cf. Hall 1989.
[2] Bernal 1987.
[3] See also Bernal 1991. On Bernal's binary model, see Coleman 1996.

position of honour to which they had been assigned by antiquity itself. They were accepted as supreme. But their rampant polytheism was a fly in the ointment. There were pinnacles which, in some eyes, Classical culture could never have surmounted. Those eyes were Christian eyes. It was the standing of the Bible as society's basic code which was perceived to be threatened. Thus the Irish classicist J.P. Mahaffy, writing in 1897, defined the subject-matter of his *Survey of Greek Civilization* as follows: 'what was possible for the human intellect apart from revelation and what flaws and faults adhered to the highest manifestations of the intellect'.[4]

We shall discover various strategies for resolution. In principle, one might seek to determine which side ought to dominate, or one might strive for fusion. Both approaches produced results which can appear to us quite laughable. A seemingly eccentric, but far from obscure case, is Gladstone's idea that Homeric religion shared in God's covenant with Abraham.[5] In 1888, the leading statesman of his day could write (to Mrs Humphrey Ward): 'there are still two things left for me to do. One is to carry Home Rule—the other is to prove the intimate connection between the Hebrew and Olympian revelations.'[6] So it can be seen that these were pressing questions.

The Bible now comprised the New Testament as well as the Old, and Christianity was deemed the new and the true Israel; thus, unless they were wrenched apart, the Bible's claims coincided with the claims of the Christian faith, now very much on the defensive. Hebrew, in fact, might simply mean Christian. This was taken further when Matthew Arnold drew upon the Hebrew-Greek distinction in order to address his attention to that major Victorian preoccupation, internal differences within the church. The Hebrew legacy stood in for Puritanism and Hellenism could readily denote Roman Catholicism, with all its esteem of visual imagery. Where such shifts are consistent, the terms 'Hebrew' and 'Hellene' serve merely as badges.

There was yet another twist. The New Testament in the form in which we have it is, after all, a text written in Greek. The Hebrew tradition arrived, in the books of the New Testament, conveniently laundered, with the elements already in place of a synthesis with Hellenism. This way could lie a happy resolution of the tension. It

[4] Mahaffy 1897: Preface, p. vii. See Gustav Billeter's useful collection, 1911: 233.
[5] 1858: *passim*. On Gladstone's numerous Homeric writings, see Jenkyns 1980: 199–204; Turner 1981: 159–170.
[6] Quoted in Jenkyns 1980: 200.

was exceptionally lucky that Paul had preached on the Areopagus. The Jewish inheritance could thus, if necessary, be regarded as altogether by-passed. Here belongs the image of Jesus as 'pale Galilean', who is marked as a figure only liminally Jewish, hovering somewhere between two worlds and tinged with the aesthetic of Greek marbles.[7]

There were major issues at stake. The claims of the Old Testament were insistent, even to the superficially sceptical. This text was the great repository of moral law and prophetic justice. And herein lay a complication: the exponents of the Hebrew system, that is to say, the Jews, were still around, and, in the Europe of the late eighteenth and nineteenth centuries, they were becoming uncomfortably visible (in social terms it did not necessarily help, although it may have done theologically, if, like Heine, they converted to Christianity). Contemporary Jews were not infrequently perceived as embodiments of the Hebraic religion of the Old Testament.[8] Theories of culture tended to operate, especially in Germany, on the world-historical plane, embracing the future and the present as well as the past. So the question of the Jewish people, their character, their religion, and their individual and national prospects came to be bound up with the dichotomy. The writers we shall be considering were by no means overtly antisemitic, and they were sometimes even pro-Jewish. None the less there is no doubt that the relentless story of European literary and philosophical antisemitism, both Christian and—as part of the Enlightenment opposition to religion—secular, plays a significant role in the development of the polarity.

It is paradoxical then, but perhaps not surprising, that the Jews made their own contribution to the evolution of the schema and were ready to internalize it. In particular, thinkers of the German and East European Jewish Enlightenment movement (*Haskalah*), when they defended emancipation and grappled with its ideological and practical problems, had to construct a Judaism which was part of civil society. They defined relations with the outside world in largely cultural terms, and for them the interaction between Hellenism and Judaism was a central metaphor and almost an obsession.[9] It was not for nothing that Moses Mendelssohn, their founding father and

---

[7] See Prickett 1989: 148–149. More specifically, scholars like Renan could detach the Galilee from Judaea, claiming a non-Jewish population in the former.

[8] On visible Jews in relation to the Old Testament, see Manuel 1983: chapter 5, 'Israel and the Christian Enlightenment'.

[9] Shavit 1997: especially chapters V, XII and XIII.

symbol, who remained an orthodox Jew, was dubbed 'the German Socrates'.[10] That the confrontation between Judaea and Greece was one of the world's large historical processes became a basic principle for a burgeoning tradition of modern Jewish historical thought. Writers identified a continuous line of development, with its starting point in the Maccabees' celebrated struggle against a Hellenistic monarchy in the mid-second century B.C. It was not forgotten that there had been a longer conflict with Roman power, but the Greek experience, seductive as well as threatening, dominated cultural history. Historians were well aware that the very word 'Hellenism', *hellenismos*, was itself an invention of Greek-Jewish literature, appearing first in the second book of Maccabees (chapter 4), where it represents a way of life alien to ancestral practices and where it is connected with the enthusiasm of a sector of the high priesthood for displays of the naked human body in a Jerusalem gymnasium.[11]

Thus idealization (of classical culture) generated polarization. And the polarization was multi-dimensional: historical (in explaining the origins and development of culture on a world scale), ethical (in debating values), sociological (in analysing the make-up of contemporary society), theological, and psychological (in interpreting different types of individual temperament). German aesthetic Hellenism, the idealizing conviction descended from Winckelmann, by which Greek art was understood as the embodiment of perfect beauty, was rarely far from the picture; nor was that notion, of which Goethe had been the most eloquent exponent, that the Greeks were the closest to nature and most quintessentially human of all peoples.

But the contrasts were manifold. The Greek/Hebrew opposition could take surprising forms: beauty versus truth; or else beauty and truth versus indifference to the physical; harmony with nature versus disharmony;[12] art and science versus morality; pleasure versus guilt; cheerfulness versus solemnity; optimism versus pessimism; man versus God; an immanent versus a transcendent God; universality versus

---

[10] On the title, and on Mendelssohn's Socratic dialogue, *Phaedon*, see Altmann 1973: 140–179.

[11] The so-called Hellenizing faction built a gymnasium in Jerusalem in the 170's B.C. The terms used of their activities, 'a climax of Hellenism', 'Hellenic character' and 'Hellenic beliefs' represent a developed vocabulary of cultural stereotyping in *koine* Greek. See Rajak 1990 = Ch. 4 in this volume.

[12] See Lloyd-Jones 1982: Chapter II, and the bibliography cited there.

exclusivity; adaptability versus tenacity; flexibility versus rigidity; reason versus dogma; patriotism versus political helplessness; liberty versus authority; even liberalism versus socialism.

The essential feature of such patterns of thought is that, even where there is deep engagement with the ancient world, broad stereotypes may be plucked out with cavalier disregard of any specific context. The stereotypes fluctuate; and their mutations, it is fair to say, are driven primarily by contemporary interests. Moreover, while the nineteenth century in Germany saw the emergence of modern classical scholarship and the creation of many of its greatest monuments, we should not assume that these were untouched by the process of cultural stereotyping. The point has been forcefully put by Grafton:[13]

> But when [German] scholars argued for the pre-eminence of Greek in secondary and university education, they rested their case less on the method they applied—which could, after all, be applied as well to Rome or Israel—than on the object to which they applied it. They argued that Greek culture was more coherent, more original, more orderly, or more free than any other—choosing the epithet that qualified it as their prejudices and the needs of the moment dictated. From Wolf at the beginning of the century to Wilamowitz at the end, influential scholars set out research programmes that called for a rigorous historicism, but insisted on their personal allegiance to the unique superiority of Hellenism. No *Greek History* was more severely technical and critical, more insistent on the need for philological rigour and more devoid of romance, than that of K.J. Beloch. Yet Beloch, captivated both by his idealized vision of the Greeks and by the anthropology and linguistics of his day, which seemed to him to provide scientific support for his prejudices, began by arguing that only 'we Aryans' could have brought forth . . . 'a culture in the full sense'.

My concern is with how stereotypes are influenced by the sense of a radical opposition. The Greeks are understood as being what the Hebrews are understood as not being. Similarities and points of affinity are, by contrast, less readily commented on—although, as hardly needs saying, if we want to look for them, they are just as much there in the texts. More particularly, I want to ask about the shaping of the two constructs in opposition to one another. I would like to be able to suggest that a sense of the other substantially influenced the moulding of each construct at key moments, and in

---

[13] Grafton 1992: 239.

particular that the well-known idealizations of ancient Greece are indebted to this antithesis. In the following discussion of four major authors, I have stressed, where possible, the connections between ideas and social issues, highlighting what is perhaps a less discussed aspect, the role played in the working out of the polarity by attitudes to Jewish history and the Jewish people (however conceptualized).

Constructions of Hebrews and Greeks:
Johann Gottfried von Herder (1744–1803)

In Herder's writings originate many currents of thought important in the nineteenth century. Seen as a precursor both of Romanticism and of modern nationalism, he was a historian of culture and religion, a friend of the philosopher Kant, and an Enlightenment thinker of whom many widely differing interpretations have been offered. Herder prized the natural creative spirit in peoples. His major contribution for our purposes was to bring the contrast between Jews and Greeks into the sphere of definitions of national character. He singled out the climate of Greece as responsible for the Greeks' many advantages: 'From their dress, the fine proportion and the outline of their thoughts, the natural vivacity of their sentiments and lastly from the melodious rhythm of their language, which never yet found its equal, we have much to learn. In all the arts of life . . . the Greeks attained almost the highest point.'[14] These arts, which they owed to their environment, included the art of politics, while the homeland of the Hebrews, by contrast, emerged as a puny, insignificant place (Herodotus had said much the same about Greece!), which produced a people who 'never established a mature political culture in their own land, and so never attained a true feeling of honour and freedom . . . and they were already from time immemorial deprived of the virtues of a patriot.'[15]

Many of the most enduring of our stereotypes are crystallized in Herder, even though he himself, valuing differences between nations,

[14] Ideen zur Philosophie der Geschichte der Menschheit (1784–1791), IV.3. Translated in: Reflections on the Philosophy of the History of Mankind (1968). For a summary of Herder's view of the Greeks, see Rawson 1969: 311–312.
[15] See XII.3, on the 'Hebrews'. Judgements of Herder's critique differ widely. Some read in these and similar remarks a sympathetic appreciation of the Jews' need for a land of their own. See Barnard 1959: 533–546; Low 1979: 55–66.

scorned the imitation of one culture by another.[16] In Herder, a long-lived contrast between pre-exilic and post-exilic Judaism is developed. Moses, a great lawgiver, made this people's religion noble: they were also in his day patriotic and warlike. Afterwards they became pharisaic, text-obsessed. Even their natural advantages were not exploited:

> In the arts . . . the Jews were always inexpert, though their country was situated between Egypt and Phoenicia; for even Solomon was obliged to employ foreign workmen . . . Though they possessed the Red Sea ports for some time and lived so close to the shores of the Mediterranean, they never became a seafaring people . . . In science, their most eminent men have displayed more servile punctuality and order than productive freedom of mind.[17]

Among the arts and sciences which remained stultified in the hands of the Jews was that of sculpture, which had been promoted in Greece by the nature of Greek religion. Here, Herder echoes Winckelmann's brief but rather more complicated discussion of the absence of art among the Hebrews.[18]

The prophets' criticisms of an obstinate and inflexible people appear as lastingly applicable; and this in spite of the fact that Herder (unlike Kant) admired the Hebrew Bible.[19] The implicit contrast with the Greeks is made explicit in a passage from the *Letters on the Study of Theology* (1790).[20] Here Herder extols the uniqueness of the Jewish people and commends their survival 'as the most convincing proof of the miracles and Scripture which indeed we have from them . . . you see, my friends, how holy and sublime these books are to me, and how very much a Jew I am, as in Voltaire's jest, when I read them . . . For must we not be Greeks and Romans when we read their books too?' The society of the patriarchs was for Herder the childhood of man; Greece represented adolescence (and Rome, maturity). Or, alternatively, Jerusalem was the cradle, Alexandria the school.

---

[16] On Herder's pluralism, see Berlin 1976: 145–216.

[17] Translation adapted from Manuel 1968. Cf. Wells 1959: 82.

[18] The comments occur between the excursuses on Phoenician and on Persian art: see Winckelmann 1764: Part II, Chapter II. Winckelmann invokes the prohibition of images in the Mosaic law, but argues, interestingly, that the Jews must have managed some of the visual arts since 2 Kings has Nebuchadnezzar taking thousands of craftsmen into exile. I owe this reference to Alex Potts.

[19] For bibliography on Herder and the Jews, see Rose 1990: 97, n. 13.

[20] Quoted in Rose 1990: 101.

Nazarenes, Jews, and Hellenes in Heinrich Heine (1797–1856)

Among Heine's many passions was an obsession with 'the so-called Greek perfection which has haunted the minds of German poets from that day to this'.[21] In this, at least, he was not unusual; nor even in his ability to read Homer in the original. Butler is able to claim that 'Winckelmann's Greece was the essential factor in the development of German poetry throughout the latter half of the eighteenth and the whole of the nineteenth century.' At the same time, Heine's Romanticism, is reflected in his conception of a great and irreconcilable struggle between opposing forces. And he was also influenced by Hegel's view of world history, like many German radicals of his generation. He had heard Hegel's lectures as a student in Berlin and was in contact with him later. In Heine's writings, classical allusions, which are abundant, frequently appear in some comparison, contrast or juxtaposition with Jewish, Christian or, occasionally, eastern mythology. In some cases there is more weight behind the parallellisms than in others.

Heine's own Jewish heritage, which he formally discarded but, near the end of his life, claimed never to have left, together with his tortured temperament, condemned him to inner conflict. Converted German-Jewish intellectuals at this period defined their new identity variously. For Heine, the opposites remained ever-present. A sentence written near the end of his life, as he lay on his 'mattress-grave', has become famous: 'a great change has come over me . . . I am . . . no longer a joyful Hellene . . . I am only a poor Jew sick unto death.'[22]

The polarity was a tool of analysis, which Heine employed in correspondence, in his often satirical prose-writing, and in poetry. Sometimes, the non-Hellenic side were given the striking name 'Nazarenes' in order, it would seem, to incorporate the religion of Jesus the Jew in the category (though a hazy recollection by the poet of the Hebrew *nezir*, a monk or Nazirite has been suggested).[23] Often Heine envisaged a conflict of a desperate kind between the two sides. The Nazarene side of the equation represents, among other things, a negation of pleasure and of sensuality:

---

[21] Butler 1935: 250–251.
[22] For the full text, see Hugo Bieber 1946: 18. On this persona of Heine's, see Rose 1940: 166–170; Prawer 1983: 531.
[23] See Shavit 1997: 41, n. 2.

Then suddenly a pale Jew, dripping with blood, with a crown of thorns on his head and a great wooden cross on his shoulder came panting up; and he threw the cross on the high table of the gods, so that the golden cups shivered and the gods fell silent and grew livid, and they became ever more pale until they finally dissolved in mist. Now came a sad time, and the world became gray and dark. There were no more happy gods, Olympus became an infirmary where flayed, roasted and skewered gods skulked about in boredom, bound their wounds and sang sad songs. Religion no longer gave joy . . .[24]

It is clear, too that the Nazarene category might include both Christians and Jews. At the same time, the polarity might equally be a straightforward one between 'Jews and Greeks', 'Juden und Hellenen', which are taken as mutually exclusive categories with contemporary applicability. In his critique of Ludwig Börne, a journalist and, like himself, a baptized Jew in exile in Paris, Heine delivered himself of the often-quoted judgement that 'all people are either Jews or Hellenes' ('alle Menschen sind entweder Juden oder Hellenen'), and he went on to explain that there are 'people with natures ('Wesen') that are ascetic, image-hating ('bildfeindlichen') and ravenous for spiritualization ('vergeistigungsüchtigen'), and there are 'people of a nature that rejoices in life, is proud of display, and is realistic'. These concepts amount to personality-types: similar to those in our contemporary division between ectomorphs and endomorphs. Heine's types, too, had distinct physical characteristics, so that Hellenes are sometimes said to be plump, Nazarenes thin. At this stage, Heine (though acknowledging his roots), liked to see himself as a German Hellene, and Börne, in spite of his conversion, was mercilessly satirized as a Nazarene.[25] In an analysis notable as much for its viciousness as for its Eurocentricity, Heine writes: 'A quarrel, which is as old as the world, declares itself in all histories of the human race and stood out most glaringly in the quarrel that Judaic spiritualism carried on against the Hellenic splendour of life, a duel that has not yet been decided and that will perhaps never be fought to a finish: the little Nazarene hated the great Greek, who was, moreover, a Greek god.'[26]

---

[24] *The Town of Lucca*, chapter 6 (1829). In English in Robertson 1993: 160. For discussion, see Sammons 1979: 148, from whom this rendering is taken. On the motif of the disappearance of the gods, cf. Shavit 1997: 42–43.

[25] *Ludwig Börne: Eine Denkschrift* (1840), in Heinrich Heine, *Sämtliche Werke*, vol. 11: 18–19. See Prawer 1983: 343, 373, 377–379; Gilman 1986: 169–172.

[26] The allusion is to Börne's hostility to Goethe. Translation from Butler 1931: 282.

That the issue of artistic creation was in Heine's mind is shown by a reported conversation concerning the painter Heinrich Lehmann for whom the poet did not much care: 'Heine was inclined to pardon Judaism's failure to cultivate the fine arts. The Jews, he said, had been idolators, and it was therefore necessary to prevent them from making images—otherwise there would have been even more backsliding into their bad old ways. Besides, Moses was a prophet: this meant that he foresaw that Lehmann would become a painter, and he did what he could to prevent that.'[27]

Hellenic and biblical merge and perish together, in cataclysmic fashion, in Heine's strange last unpublished poem, known as *Für die Mouche*: La Mouche was the name he gave to Elise Krinitz, alias Camille Selden, his last mistress. This poem represents a tragic dream, dreamt on a summer's night,—in which the poet describes the carvings on a sarcophagus, eaten away by time, 'the worst syphilis'. A passion flower symbolizes his love. But what are the mythological figures? The choices are bizarre and unexpected images. Sammons rightly point out that 'the figures are grouped by incongruities'.[28] Those discordant scenes include, in a jumble, Adam and Eve in fig-leaves, the fall of Troy, Moses and Aaron, Judith and Holofernes, Esther and Haman, Bacchus with Priapus and Silenus, Lot drunk with his daughters, a lecherous Jove seducing Leda and Danae in his different guises, the chaste Diana hunting, Hercules spinning in women's clothes, Abraham's binding of Isaac; but we should also note, as Sammons does not, that Christian images are included: Herodias dancing with the Baptist's head, Jesus teaching in the temple 'among the orthodox', Peter with the keys to heaven. Then the poet realizes that the sarcophagus is his own and that he is looking down on himself lying in it. The figures begin to fight, creating havoc. The uproar is drowned out only by the hee-hawing of Balaam's ass. The passion flower growing at the poet's head is often read as hinting at a self-identification with Christ: Heine had for many years been haunted by dreams of the crucifixion.[29] Ultimately, none the less, there is a struggle to the death between two protagonists, this time described as Greeks and Barbarians, with perhaps a degree of irony:

---

[27] For the reported anecdote see Prawer 1983: 748.
[28] Sammons 1979: 334.
[29] Butler 1931: 283–284.

Does ancient superstition haunt the stone?
Do marbled phantoms brawl in sculptured poses?
The wood god Pan's wild cry of fear is thrown
Against the wild anathemas of Moses.[30]

This strife can never end nor yet remit.
Truth always fights with Beauty in these scenes.
The hosts of mankind always will be split
Into two camps, Barbarians and Hellenes.[31]

Jews and Greeks in the History of Christianity: Ernest Renan (1823–92)

In France the polarity is closely associated with a figure who was
not only one of the leading intellectuals of the nineteenth century
but also the holder of high academic posts. Ernest Renan was originally destined for the priesthood but later viewed as a heretic. He
became Professor of Hebrew at the Collège de France and eventually its head, and he was also well-known in the literary Paris of his
day, one of the circle of illustrious regulars at Magny's restaurant.
Renan's learned and extensive writings, even those on Christianity,
evince a quite remarkable preoccupation with the Greek ideal.[32]
Indeed, such was the admiration that even St Paul came in for severe
criticism for his indifference to Greek art. In this perspective, Renan
struggles time and again with the issue of the Jewishness of Jesus
and his followers. As an historian, he found the matter problematic.
At the same time, in composing the *Vie de Jésus*, the massive *Origines
du Christianisme* (1863–1882) of which the Jesus biography was a part,
and, later, the uncompleted *Histoire du peuple d'Israël* (1887–93), he
was also responding, as a somewhat idiosyncratic liberal, to social
and political issues of the day. These works had massive circulation,
and were translated into English in their entirety. They are still
immensely readable.

Volume 4 of the *Origines* is concerned with the emperor Nero (the
'Antichrist'), but it also contains a detailed analysis of the Jewish revolutionary sects in the revolt of 66–73/4 against Rome. In one passage, which covers all the sects, those descendants of the biblical

---

[30] Note here the use of a jarring Greek word in connection with an archetypal
Jewish figure.

[31] Translated by Draper 1982.

[32] See Seznec 1979: 349–362.

prophets are set up as embodiments of fundamentalism, the eternal 'other' to the rationalism of classical civilization. The contemporary meaning is made explicit in Renan's revealing analogy, Islam versus France:

> The Jews had their faith, founded upon quite other bases than the Roman law, and at bottom quite irreconcilable with that law. Before having been cruelly harassed, they could not content themselves with a simple tolerance, those who believed they had the words of eternity, the secret of a constitution of a righteous city. They were like the Mussulmans of Algeria. Our society, though infinitely superior, inspires in these only repugnance; their revealed law, at once civil and religious, fills them with pride and renders them incapable of giving themselves to a philosophical legislation [i.e. French Law], founded upon the simple idea of the relations of men to each other. Add to that a profound ignorance which hinders fanatic sects from taking account of the forces of the civilized world.[33]

This could suggest a wholly negative view of the Hebrews on the author's part. For Renan, however, 'the movement of the world is the outcome of the parallelogram of two forces, liberalism upon the one hand and socialism upon the other . . . liberalism impelling its adepts to the highest degree of human development; socialism, accounting above all else justice most strictly interpreted.' Obviously, liberalism was of Greek origin and socialism of Hebraic.[34] Renan maintained that both the Greek immortalization of the individual and the Hebrew vision of God were necessary for the establishment and the continuation of civilization. He criticized the Greeks for their disregard of the downtrodden.[35]

Renan, even more than Heine, thought in terms of a Hegelian dialectical process, and the temporary Semitic advantage had therefore necessarily been overtaken:

> The Semites could then rightly pity them [the Aryans] as senseless, worshipping passing shadows; and for all that the privilege of which the former were proud did not amount to real superiority. The character trait which preserved them from the fables and superstitions of paganism would forbid them one day any rich and varied civilization.

---

[33] *L'Antéchrist*, in *Oeuvres complètes de Ernest Renan*, ed. Henriette Psichari, Volume IV (Paris: Calmann Lévy, 1949), pp. 1264–1265.
[34] *Histoire du peuple d'Israël* II.4, in *Oeuvres complètes*, ed. Psichari, Volume VI, 649.
[35] *Histoire du peuple d'Israël*, ibid., p. 11.

Thus they became a stumbling block in the march of humanity after having been the cause of its great progress.[36]

Renan's position on the connection between Judaism and Christianity changed substantially in the course of his life, as did his relationship with the Church, but his preoccupation with the Hebrew/Hellene polarity survived. In *Origines du Christianisme*, Renan is found claiming that Jesus definitively left the Jewish fold, and, in the *Vie de Jésus*, he insisted that it was Galilee as distinct from Jerusalem that had conquered the world.[37] The third volume of *Origines*, on St Paul, contrasts the scale of Hellenic achievement with Semitic mental narrowness. Lee detects at this stage a softer attitude on Renan's part consequent on France's defeat of 1870, as well as an increasing interest in the contradictory duality at the heart of Christianity. In Volume 5, on the Gospels, Luke is described as 'simultaneously Hebraic and Hellenic, combining the emotions of the drama with the serenity of the idyll. All is laughter, all tears, all song; everywhere weeping and canticles'.[38]

As a linguist, Renan shared the interest of the age in the discovery of the distinct Indo-European and the Semitic groups. Humboldt's theories of the connection between national character and language had wide currency and, in this vein, Renan wrote extensively on the contrasting characteristics of Hebrew and Greek. In Hebrew, with its deficient syntax, everything is black and white and lacking in variety; Greek is flexible and seductive. Hebrew lacks the capacity for abstraction and for detail.[39] Remarkably, these anxieties were widely internalized and we find them voiced by the two most important Jewish advocates of the modern Hebrew revival.[40] The notion that there is a special affinity between Greek and German, as Aryan languages, is another extraordinary dimension of such theories.[41]

---

[36] Quoted from *Nouvelles considérations sur le caractère général des peuples sémitiques*. Paris, 1859, in Almog 1988: 260.

[37] *Vie de Jésus*, in *Oeuvres complètes de Ernest Renan*, ed. Psichari, vol. 6, 125. Cf. Hadas-Lebel 1993.

[38] See Lee 1996: 222.

[39] See Almog 1988: 257 and 265; Lee 1996: 227; Shavit 1997: 234–237.

[40] See Shavit 1997: 236–237 on acceptance by Ahad Ha-Am and Bialik.

[41] On Renan's linguistics and racist ideology, see Davies 1994: 164. For one instance of the survival of such ideas (in Martin Heidegger), see Norton 1996: 406.

The ambivalences in Renan's view of the Hebrews correlate not only with his complex attitude to his Christian faith but also with his mixed response to the Jewish presence in French society; this was the man who could report that he had looked around him in the National Library and had noticed that Jews were not all of one physical type.[42] The Hebrew-Greek polarity gave suitable expression to these ambivalences. There is a certain irony in the fact that it was precisely their negative aspect that drew Jewish intellectuals to make much of them. Emotionally involved as they were with the polarity, they took Renan particularly seriously and produced indignant rejoinders, including one at book–length by A. Sulzbach in 1867.[43] Among others to respond were the socialist Moses Hess, the Zionist M.L. Lilienblum, and later, from Jerusalem, the scholar Joseph Klausner.[44]

In the last stages of his life, Renan maintained that not only Judaism but also Christianity would come to an end. Hellenism would be the victor: 'Judaism and Christianity will both disappear. The work of the Jew will have its end; the work of the Greek—in other words, science, and civilization, rational, experimental, without charlatanism, without revelation, a civilization founded upon reason and liberty—will last forever . . . The trace of Israel, however, will be eternal.'[45] One biographer sees this last concession as an expression of some degree of rapprochement with religion.[46] More interesting to us is the conjuring up of a contest reminiscent of that of Heine's imaginings, destined to go on to the end of time.

Hebrews and Hellenes in English Society: Matthew Arnold (1822–1888)

In 1869 Matthew Arnold enshrined the Hebrew/Hellene polarity in the collection of essays which he published as *Culture and Anarchy*. As an inspector of schools and as the son of England's most famous public school headmaster, Matthew Arnold could claim a special understanding in matters of education. He was to become an influential figure as essayist, literary critic, polemicist, public speaker, poet, and

[42] Almog 1988: 267.
[43] Shavit 1997: 223, n. 9.
[44] Shavit 1997: 197, 395, 248–250.
[45] *Histoire du peuple d'Israël*, ed. Psichari, vol. 6, 1517.
[46] Wardman 1964: 196–202.

professor (of poetry at Oxford). Thus, 'Hellenism' and 'Hebraism' became terms of common literary and cultural usage.

Arnold's book imported into the English language the term 'Philistine' in a broad application;[47] and, in fact, its main purpose was to be a head–on assault on British 'Philistinism'. In the fourth, and probably most famous, essay, which is entitled 'Hebraism and Hellenism', and also elsewhere, Arnold expounded his interpretation of the constituent forces in British culture and his prescriptions for a fresh balance. Britain had become parochial, respectable, and narrow in outlook, to the neglect of matters of the mind and of the spread of education. His criticisms are often seen as a response to the consequences of industrialization.[48]

Culture and Anarchy is still regarded as one of the most influential English texts of social theory and criticism, though it is very hard to gauge its precise influence. Arnold was often attacked, but he was certainly noticed.[49] Perhaps the author himself created something of the climate for the attention to his own theories, writing to his mother in the year of the volume's publication that, on the subject of Hebraism and Hellenism, these ideas were 'so true that they will form a kind of centre for English thought and speculation'.[50] We hear that, by the time a second edition was produced, in 1875, chapter headings 'were supplied', as Arnold put it, 'by the phrases in the book which have become famous', among them 'Hebraism' and 'Hellenism'.[51] These are the chapter headings to be found in Dover Wilson's edition, itself something of a classic.[52] For this editor, *Culture and Anarchy* is 'the finest apology for education in the English language.'[53] Whatever our judgment, Turner aptly points out that the frequent inclusion of Arnold's discussion of Hellenism in later anthologies of English literature marks out the book's status as 'part of the standard literary canon'.[54]

---

[47] An earlier, less general use by Carlyle is recorded in ApRoberts 1983: 115. Cf. Prickett 1989: 138–139.
[48] Discussion in Collini 1988: 78.
[49] For some of the criticisms, see Coulling 1974: 181–216.
[50] Arnold 1895. *Letters, 1848–88*, II, 11. See deLaura 1969: 173.
[51] See Matthew Arnold, *Culture and Anarchy* in Super 1960–77: vol. 5, 413.
[52] This edition (see n. 51 above) combines features of Arnold's 1869 and 1875 versions.
[53] Matthew Arnold, *Culture and Anarchy* (ed. Wilson), xii.
[54] Turner 1981: 18.

The distinction of the essays does not lie in the quality of their detailed argumentation. Jenkyns[55] criticizes Arnold's analysis for being 'flat and partial' and he tracks down a number of 'great mistakes' in it. But the impact of *Culture and Anarchy* was perhaps increased by its inconsistencies. Arnold's proposals of 1869 were presented, as we might expect, in terms of synthesis, rather than of any violent confrontation between the two forces. The Hellenic tradition represented life's graces and refinements. These graces, however, were more than just that, for civilization had a moral claim almost matching that of morality itself and a relevance to the whole of society. Hellenism was 'sweetness and light', a phrase Arnold took from the fable of the bees and the spider in Jonathan Swift's *Battle of the Books*. It was his revered Homer; it was the simplicity of Greek art; it was Sophocles' capacity to 'see life steady and see it whole'; it was the clarity and rationalism of Plato and Aristotle; all of them ideals which could be attained in his own world.[56] Hebraism, the other vital ingredient of civilized life, entailed the complexity of the old law and that sense of sin without which, equally, human beings could not flourish:

> Both Hellenism and Hebraism arise out of the wants of human nature and address themselves to satisfying those wants. But their methods are so different ... To get rid of one's ignorance, to see things as they are, and by seeing them as they are to see them in their beauty, is the simple and attractive ideal which Hellenism holds out before human nature ... and, human life in the hands of Hellenism, is invested with a kind of aërial ease, clearness and radiancy; they are full of what we call sweetness and light ... Hebraism,—and here is the source of its wonderful strength,—has always been preoccupied with an awful sense of the impossibility of being at ease in Zion ... The space which sin fills in Hebraism as compared with Hellenism is indeed prodigious.[57]

England therefore needed to redress the balance in favour of Hellenism. In European history, according to Arnold, the two forces had held sway alternately. Now, modern England required a new dose of Hellenism.[58]

Concluding *Literature and Dogma* (1873), which sold more than any of his other writings during his lifetime, Arnold is able to offer his

---

[55] Jenkyns 1980: 270–274.
[56] For Arnold's understanding of Greek literature, see Anderson 1965: Chapter 10; Ebel 1965.
[57] Super 1960–77: vol. 5, 167–168.
[58] For a helpful exposition, see Carroll 1982: 90–94.

readers a recipe which quantifies the correct proportions of Hebraism and Hellenism: 'Greece was the lifter-up to the nations of the banner of art and science, as Israel was the lifter-up of the banner of righteousness . . . But conduct, plain matter as it is, is six-eighths of life, while art and science are only two eighths.' This, as Arnold pointed out, amounted to a reversal of the judgment he had previously expressed (evidently in *Culture and Anarchy*) in praising culture and criticizing too much Hebraism.[59]

Commentators have pointed out that some of the time Arnold's 'Hebraism', which could extend to cover Christianity too, was a label applicable within the Church. Hebraic legalism describes the dissenters and Arnold has points to make about their coming closer to the established Church. The value of a broad Church and the challenge of non–conformism were acute problems in mid-Victorian public life, and in *Dissent and Dogma*, as well as in other essays, Arnold attacked Christian sectarianism head-on. On the other hand, the position of the Jews in society does not seem to have been a practical issue which concerned him, even if his father had opposed their admission to Parliament and had expostulated when he was not allowed to call Jesus 'the Christ' in the examination of a Jewish history student at London University.[60]

None the less, the view that Arnold's Hebrews were always non-conformists, never Jews cannot be sustained.[61] For one thing, the argument goes well beyond the affairs of the Church. A broader purpose emerges in *Culture and Anarchy* than any critique of narrow Protestantism: the purpose of saving religion *tout court* while building British education along classical lines. The clash between Hebraism and Hellenism is thus in no sense ephemeral. Hebraism cannot always mean Protestantism, and at points it means specifically the inescapable legacy of the Jews, with all its strengths and defects.

There is evidence that Arnold was responsive to the Jewish heritage in the abstract: he was able to write eloquently about its meaning for Heine; and, in the opening of his essay on 'Spinoza and the Bible', he conjured up the atheist philosopher's excommunication by the Spanish-Portugese synagogue of Amsterdam.[62] We find revealing

---

[59] In Super 1960–77: vol. 6, 407.
[60] Trilling 1949: 60.
[61] Turner 1981: 21.
[62] See *Heinrich Heine* and *Spinoza and the Bible* in Super 1960–77: vol. 8.

reports of rumours circulating after the publication of *Literature and Dogma* to the effect that the Rothschilds had employed him for a fee of a million francs to cast aspersions on Christ and the Trinity. Oddly, the same rumours are associated with Renan.[63]

At the same time, that real Jews, so to speak, were not wholly outside Arnold's mind emerges from a number of highly ambivalent statements in his work, of a rather familiar type.[64] Thus, in *Literature and Dogma*, we find an assertion in which in which the Hebrew-Hellene contrast, in its traditional terms, is implicit; and in which, also, the Jews of history and the despised Jewish stereotype of the European present mingle indissolubly, and with the utmost vagueness:

> In spite of all which in them and in their character is unattractive, nay, repellent,—in spite of their shortcomings even in righteousness itself and their insignificance in everything else,—this petty, unsuccessful, unamiable people, without politics, without science, without art, without charm, deserve their great place in the world's regard, and are likely to have it more, as the world goes on, rather than less.[65]

Arnold's highly charged responses to actual Jews whom he met over this period are also relevant, in particular the three Rachel sonnets about the French-Jewish actress whom he much admired, the meeting with Emanuel Deutsch, author of an article on the Talmud in the *Quarterly Review* of 1867 which excited literary London, and his friendship with Lady Louisa de Rothschild. I have pursued these elsewhere.[66]

There is one angle on the Jews which Arnold shares with Renan: the racist Semite-Aryan divide is occasionally deployed in *Culture and Anarchy*, with statements such as: 'Hebraism is of Semitic growth; and we English, a nation of Indo-European stock, seem to belong naturally to the movement of Hellenism.'[67] It is not unreasonable to suspect direct influence. For not only did Arnold have close contacts with France, but we know that he thought well of the French scholar, and that, moreover, there had been direct contact between them over the Celtic heritage to which both laid claim.[68]

---

[63] For Arnold, see Faverty 1951: 185; for Renan, Almog 1088: 257.
[64] Cheyette 1993: 14–22, analyses the ambivalence. See also Faverty 1951: 191.
[65] Super 1960–77: vol. 5, 164.
[66] Rajak 1977.
[67] Super 1960–77: vol. 5, 173–174.
[68] Wardman 1964: 69.

Between Arnold and Heine the connections are strong. Arnold's evaluation in *Essays in Criticism* (1865) and his discussion in *Pagan and Mediaeval Religious Sentiment* were concerned to promote the German poet's reputation in England.[69] Much in his appreciation is still valuable and the essay on Heine continues to be noticed. Arnold comments thus on a passage from *Doktor Faustus*:

> He [Heine] has excellently pointed out how in the sixteenth century there was a double renascence—a Hellenic renascence and a Hebrew renascence—and how both have been great powers ever since. He himself had in him both the spirit of Greece and the spirit of Judaea. Both these spirits reach the infinite, which is the true goal of all poetry and all art—the Greek spirit by beauty, the Hebrew by sublimity. By his perfection of literary form, by his love of clearness, by his love of beauty, Heine was Greek; by his intensity, by his untameableness, by his longing which cannot be uttered, he is Hebrew. . . .[70]

Arnold's application of the dichotomy to Heine personally is revealing, even if there is little to recommend the commonly-held view that he derived it entirely from the German poet.[71] Arnold knew and admired Herder's writings too.[72] And the points of contact between Arnold and Heine lie not in exact borrowings, but in a general approach, especially in Arnold's reading of the two elements as embodied in psychological types, and perhaps in the inclusion of an unstable Christian component on the Hebrew side of the equation.

Conclusion

Tracking the genealogy down to its origins is generally an unprofitable activity. The Greek-Jewish polarity made its appearance in numerous shapes and guises and in a surprising range of contexts. I have given here no more than an impression of some of these. For adoration of Hellenism regularly brings the polarity in its wake. In

---

[69] See Wormley 1943: 113.

[70] Super 1960–77: vol. 5, 127–128. On Arnold's use of the term 'renascence', see Bullen 1994: 246.

[71] An unsatisfactory attempt to prove dependence is to be found in Tesdorpf 1971. She is, however, followed by Carroll 1982: 241; and by Jenkyns 1980: 270. Turner 1981: 24, is more tentative, while deLaura 1969: 191, speaks of a 'springboard'. On the other hand, Prickett 1989: 148, in listing German influences on Arnold's thought, omits Heine altogether.

[72] deLaura 1969: 184.

Bernal's view indeed, idealization of Hellenism was nothing other than an assertion of cultural and racial superiority on the part of its European exponents;[73] a one-sided polarity with the oriental was therefore built into this idealization. It is not necessary to accept this extreme position to acknowledge that idealized descriptions of Greece were often propelled and shaped by distinction and contrast rather than by close observation. In the material we have considered, the 'other' was a complex entity, comprising three main components— the Bible, the Christian religion, and the Jews. Not always clearly distinguished, these were able to push the equation in several different directions. The 'other' was, moreover, paradoxical: both close to home—in Christianity—and deeply alien, in the shape of the Jews. Here racism entered. But that the 'other' would constantly take second place, as necessarily inferior, was far from a foregone conclusion. It is a great mistake to suppose that the position of the Greeks on their pedestal was uncontested. Their opponents' pull was powerful. What is more, the built-in ambiguity as to the nature of those opponents was to some extent transferred to the Greek side too. For all the clarity ascribed to the Greek mind, it was often far from transparent who or what the Greeks were when comparisons were being made—and perhaps also when they were not. Even in its heyday, the European reception of Greece was not a straightforward act of adoption but a tense and problematic experience.

BIBLIOGRAPHY

1. *Primary sources*

Arnold, M. 1869. *Culture and Anarchy*, R.H. Super (ed.). 1965. Michigan; J. Dover Wilson (ed.). 1932. Cambridge; pbk. 1960; esp. ch. 1, 'Sweetness and Light' and ch. 4, 'Hebraism and Hellenism'.
—— 1895. *Letters, 1848–88*, collected and arranged by G.E. Russell. London.
—— *Lectures and Essays in Criticism*, R.H. Super (ed.). 1962. Michigan (for *Heinrich Heine* and *Spinoza and the Bible*).
—— *Dissent and Dogma*, R.H. Super (ed.). 1968. Michigan. (for *St Paul and Protestantism* and *Literature and Dogma*).
Hegel, G.W.F. *Vorlesungen über die Philosophie der Geschichte* (2nd posthumous ed. 1840) = *The Philosophy of History*.
Heine, Heinrich. *Sämtliche Werke*, K. Briegleb *et al.* (eds). 1968–76. Munich.
Translations in: *The Poetry and Prose*, Frederick Ewen (ed.), transl. Louis Untemeyer *et al.* 1948. New York.

[73] Norton 1996: 405.

Bieber, H. 1946. *Heinrich Heine: jüdisches Manifest*, 2nd ed. New York (key texts in German) = in translation, Hadas, M. (ed.). 1956. *Heine: A Biographical Anthology*. Philadelphia.

Draper, H. 1982. *The Complete Poems of Heinrich Heine: A Modern English Version*. Boston.

Robertson, R. 1993. *Selected Prose, Heinrich Heine*, translated and edited with introduction and notes. London.

Herder, J.G. *Ideen zur Philosophie der Geschichte der Menschheit* (1787–1971) = Johann Gottfried von Herder, *Reflections on the Philosophy of the History of Mankind*, abridged and with an introduction by Frank E. Manuel. Chicago/London (1968).

Renan, E. *Histoire du Peuple Israël*, 5 vols. Paris.

Translations of relevant vols.: I—London, 1989; III—Boston, 1905; V—Boston, 1907.

Winckelmann, J.J. 1764. *Geschichte der Kunst des Altertums* = *History of Ancient Art*, translated from the German. London, 1881.

2. *Secondary sources*

Adler, E. 1990. 'Johann Gottfried Herder und das Judentum', in *Herder Today*. Contributions from the International Herder Conference, Nov. 5–8 1987. Berlin, 382–401.

Almog, S. 1988. 'The Racial Motive in Renan's Attitude to Jews and Judaism', in S. Almog (ed.), *Antisemitism through the Ages*. Studies in Antisemitism. Published for the Vidal Sassoon International Center for the Study of Judaism, the Hebrew University, Jerusalem; Hebrew edn. 1980, 255–278.

Altmann, A. 1973. *Moses Mendelssohn. A Biographical Study*. Littman Library of Jewish Civilization. London.

Anderson, W.D. 1965. *Matthew Arnold and the Classical Tradition*. Ann Arbor, Michigan.

ApRoberts, R. 1983. *Arnold and God*. Berkeley.

Barnard, F.M. 1959. 'The Hebrews and Herder's Political Creed', *Modern Language Review* 54: 533–546.

Bernal, M. 1987. *Black Athena: The Afro-Asian Roots of Classical Civilization*, vol. 1. *The Fabrication of Ancient Greece 1785–1985*. London/New Brunswick, New Jersey.

—— 1991. *Black Athena: The Afroasiatic Roots of Classical Civilization*. Volume II, *The Archaeological and Documentary Evidence*. London/New Brunswick, New Jersey.

Berlin, I. 1977. *Vico and Herder: Two Studies in the History of Ideas*. New York.

Billeter, G. 1911. *Die Anschauungen vom Wesen des Griechentums*. Leipzig.

Bullen, J.B. 1994. *The Myth of the Renaissance in Nineteenth Century Writing*. Oxford.

Butler, E.M. 1931. *The Tyranny of Greece over Germany: A Study of the Influences Exercized by Greek Art and Poetry over the Great German Writers of the Eighteenth, Nineteenth and Twentieth Centuries*. Cambridge.

Carroll, J. 1982. *The Cultural Theory of Matthew Arnold*. Berkeley/Los Angeles/London.

Cheyette, B. 1993. *Constructions of 'the Jew' in English Literature and Society: Racial Representations, 1875–1945*. Cambridge.

Clarke, M.L, 1959. *Classical Education in Victorian Britain 1500–1900*. Cambridge.

Coleman, J.E. 1996. 'Did Egypt Shape the Glory that was Greece?', in M.R. Lefkowitz & G.M. Rogers (eds), *Black Athena Revisited*. Chapel Hill/London.

Collini, S. 1988. *Arnold*. Past Masters. Oxford.

Coulling, S.M.B. 1974. *Matthew Arnold and his Critics: A Study of Arnold's Controversy*. Athens, Ohio.

Davies, A.M. 1994. 'La linguistica del ottocento' in G.C. Lepschy (ed.), *Storia della Linguistica*, vol. 3. Bologna.

deLaura, D.J. 1969. *Hebrew and Hellene in Victorian England: Newman, Arnold and Pater*. Austin.

Ebel, H. 1965. 'Matthew Arnold and Classical Culture', *Arion* 4, 188–220.

Faverty, F.E. 1951. *Matthew Arnold, the Ethnologist*. Illinois.

Geiger, L. 1910. *Die deutsche Literatur und die Juden*. Berlin.

Gilman, S.L. 1986. *Jewish Self-Hatred: Anti-Semitism and the Hidden Language of the Jews*.Baltimore/London.

Gladstone, W. 1858. *Studies on Homer and the Homeric Age*, vol. 2. Oxford.

Grafton, A. 1992 'Germany and the West 1830–1900', in K.J. Dover (ed.), *Perceptions of Ancient Greece*. Oxford, 225–245.

Hadas-Lebel, M. 1993. 'Renan et le judaïsme', *Commentaire* 62: 369–379.

Hall, E. 1989. *Inventing the Barbarian: Greek Self-Definition through Tragedy*. Oxford.

Harris, H.A. 1976. *Greek Athletics and the Jews*. Cardiff.

Janicaud, D. 1975. *Hegel et le destin de la Grèce*. Paris.

Jenkyns, R. 1980. *The Victorians and Ancient Greece*. Cambridge.

Knox, B. 1989. 'The Greek Conquest of Britain', in *Essays, Ancient and Modern*. Baltimore and London, 149–161 (review of Turner and Jenkyns, originally in *NYRB* June 11, 1981).

Lee, D.C.J. 1996. *Ernest Renan. In the Shadow of Faith*. London.

Lefkowitz, M.R. & Rogers, G. MacLean. 1996. *Black Athena Revisited*. Chapel Hill/London.

Liebeschütz, H. 1967. *Die Judentum im deutchen Geschichtsbild von Hegel bis Max Weber*. Tübingen.

Lloyd-Jones, H. 1982. *Blood for the Ghosts. Classical Influences in the Nineteenth and Twentieth Centuries*. London.

Low, A.D. 1979. *Jews in the Eyes of the Germans: from the Enlightenment to Imperial Germany*. Philadelphia.

Mahaffy, J.P. 1897. *A Survey of Greek Civilization*. London.

Manuel, F.E. 1983. *The Changing of the Gods*. Hanover/London.

Meyer, M. 1959. *The Origins of the Modern Jew: European Culture and Jewish Identity in Germany 1794–1824*. Detroit.

Momigliano, A.D. 1992 'Prologue in Germany', in *Nono contributo alla storia degli studi classici e del mondo antico*. Rome, 544–562.

Murray, N. 1996. *A Life of Matthew Arnold*. London.

Norton, R.E. 1996. 'The Tyranny of Germany over Greece?: Bernal, Herder and the German Appropriation of Greece', in M.R. Lefkowitz & G.M. Rogers (eds), *Black Athena Revisited*. Chapel Hill/London.

Poliakov, L. 1975. *The History of Antisemitism*, vol. III. From Voltaire to Wagner, English transl. London.

Prawer, S.S. 1983. *Heine's Jewish Comedy*. Oxford.

Prickett, S. 1989. '"Hebrew" versus "Hellene" as a Principle of Literary Criticism' in G.W. Clarke (ed.), *Rediscovering Hellenism. The Hellenic Inheritance and the English Imagination*. Cambridge, 137–160.

Quillien, J. 1983. *G.D. Humboldt et la Grèce*. Lille.

Rajak, T. 1977. 'Defining the Hebrews in Matthew Arnold's Hebraism and Hellenism', *SCI* XVI (Studies in Memory of Abraham Wasserstein II), 239–251.

—— 1990. 'The Hasmoneans and the Uses of Hellenism', in P.R. Davies & R.T. White (eds), *A Tribute to Geza Vermes. Essays on Jewish and Christian History*. Sheffield, 261–281 = Ch. 4 in this volume.

Rawson, E. 1969. *The Spartan Tradition in European Thought*. Oxford.

Reeves, N. 1974. *Heinrich Heine. Poetry and Politics*. Oxford.

Rose, P.L. 1990. *Revolutionary Antisemitism in Germany from Kant to Wagner*. Princeton, New Jersey.

Rotenstreich, N. 1984. *Jews and German Philosophy*. New York.

Said, E. 1978. *Orientalism*. New York.

Sammons, J.L. 1979. *Heinrich Heine. A Modern Biography*. Princeton.

Seznec, J. 1979. 'Renan et la philologie classique', in R.R. Bolgar (ed.), *Classical Influences on Western Thought A.D. 1650–1870*. Cambridge/London/New York/Melbourne, 349–362.

Shavit, J. 1997. *Athens in Jerusalem. Classical Antiquity and Hellenism in the Making of the Modern Secular Jew.* Littman Library. London.
Super, R.H. 1960–77. (ed.), *Matthew Arnold, Lectures and Essays in Criticism. The Complete Prose Works of Matthew Arnold,* 11 vols. Ann Arbor.
Taylor, C. 1975. *Hegel.* Cambridge.
Tesdorpf, Ilse-Maria. 1971. *Die Auseinandersetzung Matthew Arnolds mit Heinrich Heine. Ein besonderer Fall von konstruktiven Missverständnis und eigenwilliger Entlehung.* Neue Beiträge zur Anglistik und Amerikanistik 6. Frankfurt.
Trilling, L. 1949. *Matthew Arnold.* London.
Turner, F.M. 1981. *The Greek Heritage in Victorian Britain.* New Haven/London.
Wardman, H.W. 1964. *Ernest Renan: a Critical Biography.* London.
Wells, G.A. 1959. *Herder and After: A Study in the Development of Sociology.* 'S-Gravenhage.
Williams, R. 1958. *Culture and Society 1780–1950.* London.
Wormley, S.L. 1943. *Heine in England.* Chapel Hill.

INDEX OF NAMES AND SUBJECTS

Compiled by J.K. Aitken

Well-known individuals are where possible listed by their commonly used names. Famous Greek names and those current in the Roman period are as a rule Romanized.

INDEX OF AUTHORS